MUSIC
FROM THE
HEART

by

ROD KENNEDY

Edited by HUGH C. SPARKS

EAKIN PRESS ★ Austin, Texas

Many photographers provided the visuals which appear on almost every page of this book. We consci-
entiously tried in every instance to be accurate in crediting the source of each photo. If there are credit errors
which slighted any photographer whose work appears between these covers, please notify the publisher, at
the earliest date possible, and we will make the correction in the second edition.

For additional information about the Kerrville Music Festivals
or Silverwolf recordings of the Kerrville Folk Festival, please contact the author at:

Kerrville Festivals, Inc.
P.O. Box 1466
Kerrville, TX 78029-1466
(830)-257-3600

CONTENTS

FOREWORD

Seated on a high, cushioned stool at the edge of the Kerrville Folk Festival stage, Rod Kennedy is beaming. His joy is visibly rapturous as he listens to the music of a new artist that he picked from literally hundreds who apply each year to play the festival. Now, she joins the legions of those who have built the remarkable reputation of what is arguably the most effective platform in the country for recognizing, encouraging, and discovering new talent.

On the stage, mid-set, the artist is floating on the relaxed wave of energy her first songs have created. She rides the audience's embrace. Rod's smiles are now accompanied by his tears. The beauty of the music, the expressiveness of her voice, the authority of her delivery; none of this escapes Rod's legendary antennae. He is so proud of the artist, so in awe of her talent, so grateful to see her rise to the occasion. He knows, with absolute certainty, that the performance will help her achieve the next level of attention and recognition, sparking her career. She has gained new confidence in herself and validated her belief in her own talent.

The above vignette image personifies the Rod Kennedy who utterly deserves the distinction of the characterization "a life well lived." It is a snapshot, one that I've witnessed literally hundreds of times, that is part and parcel of the ultimate product of his demon-like devotion, unshakable conviction, and interminable hard work. Like the classic ballet company managers who think, eat, and sleep "only the art, only the work," Rod has driven himself mercilessly, throughout the twenty-seven years I've known him, to shepherd his Kerrville dream.

The man, himself, is one of the most complex, obstinate, fun-loving, hyper-serious, imperious, humble, self-contradictory people on this planet. He is also one of my closest friends. One minute you observe his humanity, his sensitive, unabashed state-of-grace love of the music and the artists, and the next minute you watch a steel-trap Marine judgmental mask come down over his face, his jaw set and his eyes darting and blazing because of his perception of an injury that someone has visited upon his festival. Someone has interfered with his sense of the way the music must be presented, his sense of the lore of what Kerrville has been and must always be.

Rod and I met in the first year of what Peter Paul and Mary lovingly call our "seven-year hiatus." We had split up to rediscover our separate identities and enjoy more private, personal lives for a while. George Wein, whom I knew from my days on the Newport Folk Festival Board of Directors, and a former partner of Peter Paul and Mary's genius manager, Albert Grossman, had introduced me to his long-time friend and colleague, Rod Kennedy. Rod was invited to produce a series of concerts for me, as a solo performer, in the Southwest.

In the many hours that we traveled across Texas in Rod's gigantic, beat-up Cadillac, we became friends. Oceans of disparate backgrounds separated us, but a similar sense of passion, adventurousness, and vulnerability connected us. We argued and laughed and commiserated over the disappointing attendance at the concerts. (We've done that for almost three decades now in a variety of venues, including Kerrville, when the rains came and washed away the Texas dirt, the audience, and the festival's solvency.)

In time, Rod and I worked together in the organizing and planning of the New Folks concert at Kerrville. That story is well told in this book. In it, Rod will tell you how Kerrville was conceived, reveal his own remarkable story, and possibly give you an insight into how and why such an institution as the Kerrville Folk Festival came to be all that it has become. In addition, this book could give you a blueprint if you were to attempt to replicate some of the Kerrville Folk Festival's gifts elsewhere. But from my perspective, what Rod can't describe, and I can, is the critical energy and true genius that he possesses, without which Kerrville never would have begun—or been sustained.

Taste and an absolute, bottom-line respect for the art and the heart of the music are not easily replicable. Others may extrapolate the spirit and the construction of Kerrville to create another festival that will resonate with the Kerrville model, the paradigm of Rod's extraordinary achievement. But such attempts will ultimately have to stand or fail based on the passion, taste, and determination of the creators of any new effort.

Take this book, learn from it, and enjoy a fascinating story. Know that no one who is at the vortex of such a complex and exhausting hurricane, who has been whipped and impoverished, tested and lauded, vilified and admired, will come through to clear skies without detractors, hangers-on, and a bit of hubris, side by side with humility and some degree of amazement. All of the above is understandable. Much of what Rod has gotten, he has deserved or created by virtue of his own iron will. And to make sense of it all, to gain any perspective, he, and we, must face ourselves in the mirror, brush our teeth, and watch as time gives us wisdom and wrinkles.

Ultimately, Rod is just a remarkable, insatiably curious, brilliant, and talented person whose life has managed to give the world an incomparable gift. He is the first to say it could not have been done without others—his list of acknowledgments goes on for pages.

For me, the music can set us free and help us remember that we love each other. Without Rod, there would be so many, many artists whose words and music might never have been given the chance—who might never have tried—might never have believed in themselves.

For this, we love and admire Rod and crown him with a wreath of well-deserved adulation. We can also give him the respect that he deserves by recognizing that in his strengths and weaknesses, success and failure, he, too, has feet of clay and can be, and should be, our dear, loved, and sometimes faulted friend.

After all these years, I'll take "the package" and hold dear all those gestures of concern, all those acts of generosity, all those brave, self-revealing moments of brother-to-brother closeness that have so immeasurably enriched my life.

You're in for a remarkable journey when you read this book. Enjoy the ride.

PETER YARROW
October 15, 1997

PREFACE

This book is the story of my life in music from 1935, when, at age five, I first remember hearing music. I began to accumulate my love for many different kinds of music, and became a professional in music as a vocalist with a regional band when I was sixteen.

I have tried in these chapters to provide a yearly, monthly, and sometimes daily, chronicle of what it was like for me to be involved in the music business, as a fan, as a hobbyist, and then as a full-time producer.

There were some sidetracks, and I have included those which held the most fascination for me.

Somewhere along the way I developed a penchant for loving, supporting, producing, and promoting music that was outside the mainstream of commercial popular taste. In fact, I feel a driving need to supplement the massive pop culture of America with music that gives me both emotional and intellectual nutrition.

For the past thirty years or so (twenty-five of those as producer of the music festivals at Kerrville), I have focused my attention on building audiences for original artists who write and perform their own music that says what they want to say, rather than what the industry thinks they should say.

My life has been fun, and it still is. The mistakes I've made were, in some cases, costly, so I didn't get to do everything I wanted to do. But I've been blessed for most of my life by people around me who supplied dedicated support for what I wanted to do. I wish I could let all of them know how really important their being in my corner has been.

I've left hundreds of these loving supporters out of this book, and I feel uncomfortable about it.

Last of all, I hope that this view of America's music business as I've seen it will give those who love original songs some additional perspective, and that my story might build another bridge for the artists in the book and those yet to come so that they can continue to contribute to our culture their music, music that is sorely needed to remind us of our humanity . . . music from the heart.

ACKNOWLEDGMENTS

Special thanks to my editor, Hugh C. Sparks, a friend for over thirty years, who worked with me for many months, sometimes until the wee hours of the morning, and never lost his sense of humor.

Much credit goes to my publisher Ed Eakin and his staff, especially editor Bill Paulk and associate publisher Virginia Gholson Messer. Their enthusiasm and constant belief in this project kept me going when I needed it.

Also my heartfelt thanks to these folks who were each, in some way, helpful in getting all of this together in time for the publication deadline.

Dalis Allen
David Amram
Alan Arnapole
Austin American-Statesman
Austin History Center, Austin Public Library
Craig Barker
Bobby Bridger
John Briggs
David Broza
John Bustin
David Card
Barbara Carlson
Dallas Morning News
Allen Damron
Bill Dozier
Mary Jane Farmer
Kinky Friedman
Ft. Worth Star-Telegraph
Dick Goodwin
Lee Green
Bill and Bonnie Hearne
Herring Printing Co.
Carolyn Hester
Sara Hickman
Hill Country Camera
Jim Hornfischer
Bob Jones
Robert Earl Keene, Jr.
Nancylee Kennedy

Kerrville Daily Times
Murray Krugman
Andrea LeBlanc
Los Angeles Times
Reeve Love
Linda Lowe
Karen Musick
Joe Nick Patoski
Bobby Rector
San Antonio Express News
Saturday Evening Post
Ken Schmidt
Pete Seeger
Becky Smyth
Roger Sovine
Kay Sparks
Pat Streetman
Texas Monthly
Texas Music Collection, Center for American History, The University of Texas at Austin
Theatre Arts Collection, Harry Ransom Humanities Research Center, The University of Texas at Austin
Faith Thompson
Susan Werner
John Wheat
Peter Yarrow
Brian Young

Peter Yarrow and I at the twenty-fifth birthday of the Kerrville Folk Festival in Texas. 1996.

— Courtesy Alan Pogue.

A Texas sort of thing — my car license plate supporting folk music and the Texas Commission on the Arts. 1996.

— Courtesy Alan Pogue.

HEAD OVER HEELS IN LOVE

(1935–1951)

The constant heavy rains continued. The concert was over and the performers, crew, and sparse crowd had all left the outdoor theater as I stood depressed and alone on the Kerrville Folk Festival stage.

It had been raining continuously for the first eleven days of the eighteen-day festival, and as its producer, I didn't know how we'd make it through the final week.

We had been hit by rains many times in past years and were trying to continue under a severe deficit that had just increased by another $100,000. And it was still raining.

I began to have serious doubts about my future and wondered how I ever got into the music business. As I thought about it, I realized I knew exactly when and how it all started—and it was a long, long time ago.

Even though it's been more than sixty years, I can remember it as if it were yesterday. I was one of a couple of dozen five-year-olds in little black and white clown suits our mothers had made. We somersaulted en masse around the Park School gymnasium floor to the first music I ever remember hearing. The intriguing melody, I learned later, was "Golliwog's Cake Walk" from Debussy's *Children's Corner,* played on the piano by our teacher while we obediently somersaulted around the hardwood floor. Our parents proudly watched what must have been quite a sight.

I've been head over heels in love with music ever since.

I was born in Buffalo, New York, on January 22, 1930, to Dorne and Leo Kennedy, growing up with my older brother Jim and younger brother Colin.

We lived on a farm in Amherst when I began my formal education. During those times, when my parents could afford it, they sent me to the Park School, a rather expensive country day school outside Buffalo. The rest of the time I attended public schools with exciting names like School No. 30, No. 56, and No. 66. Meanwhile, we moved from Amherst to Williamsville and then to Buffalo.

I don't recall much about music in those schools, but, while growing up in Buffalo, music was all around me. I sang in the choir in church on Sundays, my mother played ukulele, and my dad sang a lot. I remember parties at our various houses in Buffalo where people always gathered around the Steinway to play and sing. During these nighttime gatherings, I would sneak out of bed and sit quietly, unnoticed, at the top of the stairs, listening to the wonderful sounds.

One particular couple, the Browses, not only played the piano but had a pair of matching German shepherds that sat on the piano bench, making quite a racket while "playing" duets. We really looked forward to their annual Christmas cards featuring their dogs at the piano.

One Sunday, when I was eleven years old, I was sitting alone in my favorite overstuffed chair in the living room of our Lancaster Avenue house in Buffalo. I was listening to the New York Philharmonic broadcast when, suddenly, it was interrupted by an announcement: "This morning the Japanese bombed and strafed Hickam Field near Manila!" It was December 7, 1941, and we were about to find ourselves profoundly propelled into World War II.

The songs of the war years were either very sentimental or very patriotic, and I loved what was happening with the big bands and with the weekly celebrity radio shows like Bing Crosby's "Kraft Music Hall" and "Your Hit Parade."

During those years, we kids could go to the neighborhood movie theater for eleven cents to see a feature and a chapter of a serial starring Tom Mix, Buck Rogers, or the Green Hornet.

For thirty cents we could go downtown to the Shea's Hippodrome and see a major movie release preceded by theater organ music which shook the whole building. The organ interlude was followed by an hour-long "live" show by one of the big bands of the day: the Dorsey Brothers, Vaughan Monroe, Kay Keyser, or Spike Jones and His City Slickers. As the theme song played, the entire band sank out of sight into the orchestra pit and the movie began. I was privileged to see all the great ones, including Glenn Miller and Harry James.

All of these big bands were really impressive and featured from seventeen to twenty-one players, dressed in matching dinner jackets and black bow ties, arranged with five or six saxes in the front row, trombones behind them, and trumpets on the top riser. The trumpets often stood as a section and played like crazy, sometimes waving matching mutes shaped like derby hats to send out the sound in changing waves. The grand piano was usually to one side, and the rhythm section at the back of the highest riser often featuring a showy drummer. At the back of Spike Jones' City Slickers, one of the biggest bands, were all sorts of percussionists and a tall, statuesque blond playing the harp with a big black cigar in her mouth.

Bands like Les Brown and Kay Keyser always had one band member, often a sax player in the front row, who did some sort of comedy act and then stepped back into the section, an entertainment device left over from Burlesque. All of the players in the ensembles were top professionals and many of them were featured on virtuosic solos.

All the bands had a female singer, a male singer, and often a vocal group like the "Moon Maids" (Vaughan Monroe), the "Satisfiers" (Tommy Dorsey), and the "Modernaires" (Glenn Miller). Combined with exhilarating and eye-popping lighting effects, these movie theater big band shows offered a lot of excitement for the money.

At home at night I tuned the radio next to my bed to shows broadcast from the famous ballrooms and clubs across the U.S. The ballrooms were located in Manhattan, on the Loop in Chicago, and along the Jersey Turnpike, and they broadcast in fifteen-minute segments late into the night, featuring music by Randy Brooks, Charlie Spivak, Benny Goodman, Artie Shaw, and others. The radio network could take you all across the country from coast-to-coast, and the announcers would make it sound very romantic. You could hear the crowds enjoying themselves in these famous places that "overlooked beautiful downtown" somewhere.

During those growing-up years in Buffalo, my father took me to Buffalo's Erlanger Theater to see a professional production of Sigmund Romberg's *The Student Prince.* I came away highly impressed and inspired by its rousing student choruses, drinking songs, romantic solos and duets, and bright, regal costumes. He also took me to see Disney's spectacular new fantasy film, *Fantasia,* with its colorful cartoon impressions played out on the big screen to classical music. The soundtrack, one of the first stereo recordings ever produced and directed by Leopold Stokowski, seemed to come from everywhere!

Later, in junior high school, I participated in the school's mixed chorus, where I was introduced to the delightful and entertaining arrangements by Fred Waring. My class in school also attended concerts by the Buffalo Philharmonic, with William Steinberg conducting on at least one occasion, at the brand new Kleinhan's Music Hall.

Music was a major interest for my whole family as well. My older brother, Jim, played the piano by ear and was in great demand at parties. He played tunes of the day like "White Cliffs of Dover," "Boogie Woogie," and many of the popular wartime songs about waiting for sons and husbands to come home from overseas.

My mother was a fan of Rudy Vallee and Bing Crosby, and the whole family listened to the "Eddy Cantor Show" every Sunday night along with the comedy shows "Jack Benny" and "Fred Allen."

In some of the school productions and regularly in church, I became a soloist in spite of the fact that I was scared to death. But then, as time went on and I gained more experience, I became more comfortable doing it and enjoyed the extra attention I received.

My high school years were a time of discovery for me, going to five different high schools in four different states. With family finances undermined by the stock market crash years before, and with the increased needs of three boys growing up, my mother had gone to work to supplement my dad's income and to provide herself some discretionary income. Operating out of our home, she became a distributor for the Klad-E-Z line of children's clothing that included shorts and playsuits with drop rear ends.

She did really quite well and, before long, she earned an executive position buying girls' and children's clothes for Buffalo's leading specialty store, Flint and Kent. While Mother's earning power increased and her stature grew as a buyer, my brothers and I became aware of a growing resentment on the part of my dad.

When she was offered and accepted the buyer's job at McManus & Reiley in Wheeling, West Virginia, my younger brother Colin and I went with her. My freshman year of high school, then, was spent at the Linsly Military Institute in Wheeling, where I also became a Golden Gloves featherweight boxer. It was mostly out of self-defense: I had to fight coal miners' kids to keep from being branded a sissy for singing in public. I was fourteen.

With Mother's increased income, she could afford to send me to Pennsylvania to Mercersburg Academy, a boarding prep school for Princeton, where I sang in the chapel choir and waited on tables to help pay my tuition. A far cry from military day school in Wheeling, at Mercersburg we wore coats and ties, belonged to debating societies, and dated young women from Penn Hall, while battling Andover and Exeter on the soccer field. A remarkable history and geopolitics professor there inspired me to explore becoming a serious student and to begin feeling good about academic accomplishment.

While I was away at Mercersburg, Mother accepted a better position as buyer at Godchaux's on Canal Street in New Orleans. It was the city's leading specialty store, and Mother was buying for larger departments at a considerably larger salary. So, in 1945, I joined her there and attended The Newman School as a sophomore. While at Newman, I sang in the glee club and mixed chorus and got to sing a minor lead part in the school production of Gilbert and Sullivan's *The Gondoliers.* I made friends with a classmate, Jan Trish, and he and I together discovered the French Quarter and The Old French Opera House Bar, where a long-legged beauty named Stormy danced on the bar and stripped to jazz music.

Because of my extracurricular activities, I failed three out of four courses that year. I did, however, make an "A" in my Louisiana State Civics with its fascinating gangster stories of Huey P. Long's

regime. Capping off my non-academic endeavors, I celebrated along with hundreds of thousands of other New Orleaneans V-E Day (end of the war in Europe), V-J Day (end of the war with Japan), and the first post-war Mardi Gras festivities, which lasted several weeks!

With good weather almost all year around, Jan and I did a lot of cruising around the Crescent City on his Cushman motor scooter, joy riding out to Lake Pontchartrain and to the Audubon Park swimming pool. It was a good life with a lot of partying for a fifteen-year-old, especially when Mother was in New York on buying trips for Godchaux's.

Late in the summer of 1945, my mother again advanced up the ladder in the merchandising business by becoming a buyer at Houston's Palais Royal department store. I followed her to Houston, where I repeated my junior year at the new Lamar High School out near River Oaks.

At Lamar, as a teenager, I fell in love for the first time with a beautiful girl named Ann Playter, whose suntanned Texas beauty hit me right between the eyes. Besides that, she was bright and affectionate and liked me! The affection was genuine, and I knew this new heart-pounding experience was true love incarnate. Our song was "I'll See You in My Dreams," recorded by Tony Martin. In addition to what I felt for Ann, it was reassuring to be warmly welcomed into a happy, loving, and completely functional family who treated me like one of their own.

While at Lamar, I played football as a reserve, continued singing both in the Lamar High chorus and in a modern popular music trio with schoolmates. Among my classmates were Ross Sterling, who later became a judge, and "Rampaging Robert" Smith and Juany Champion, who both went on to great college football careers. Another friend was Ann's older brother, Dick.

My big discovery in Houston, aside from finding out that cowboy boots really could be comfortable, was the stunning sound of Tex Ritter's "Rye Whiskey" and "Boll Weevil," which utilized an echo chamber effect. I had never heard Texas honky tonk music before!

Right away I became a fan of the lively and different sounds of Bob Wills Western Swing music. It seemed like the big band charts played on country music instruments. The hollering by Bob and his great fiddle tunes, interspersed with steel guitar solos and cowboy vocals, was a completely mind-boggling experience for me, one I'd never forget.

Mom's Palais Royal job fell short of its promise and, at the end of my first semester at Lamar, I had to return to my dad's home in Buffalo. Leaving Ann, her family, and my other Texas friends behind was hard to take!

Back in Buffalo, I enrolled at Lafayette High School to finish my junior year. My older brother, Jim, who had come home from the air force, was all excited about cars and Dixieland jazz, two loves that rubbed off on me.

I didn't get to hang out with Jim much, as he was running with his college friends and I was still in high school. However, one of the things we did get to do together with our dad was attend the midget auto races at Civic Stadium. It was a quarter-mile asphalt flat track and the Fords, Chevys, outboards, and Offys really created excitement running wheel to wheel. Each of the four different kinds of engines had distinctive sounds, and soon we could identify them before we even climbed up the long ramps to our stadium seats. Some of the machines were professionally prepared Curtis Kraft cars with hand-rubbed paint jobs, lots of chrome, and great looking racing numbers on them. We knew many of the drivers by name after attending regularly for a few weeks, names like Rex Mays, the Hurtubise Brothers, and one-legged Bill Shindler. The smell of the Castrol racing oil was also a reminder of our enthusiasm for well-engineered cars driven with great skill by drivers with lots of nerve. If your car became entangled with the car next to yours, the momentum could flip the cars high in the air and roll them end-over-end several times.

Something else we did with each other frequently was to sing barbershop harmony together. My dad was an active member of the SPEBSQSA (Society for the Preservation and Encouragement of Barbershop Quartet Singing in America) and Jim and I both considered ourselves grown up when we went to the weekly meetings to "bust a chord" with the businessmen who belonged.

Four of these men eventually became the Buffalo Bills Barbershop Quartet (long before the Buffalo Bills football team) who sang on Broadway in Meredith Wilson's show *The Music Man*. They made hits out of songs from the score like "Lida Rose." As the quartet's attorney, my dad helped to negotiate the contract with their producer. Eventually, I think they all moved to New York and divorced their wives.

On my sixteenth birthday, in 1946, Mother took me to New York to see my first real Broadway

show. It was an awe-inspiring original cast production of the new Broadway hit *Brigadoon*, with all sorts of sets and scenery, pit orchestra, fabulous costumes, a large cast of great voices, a remarkable lighting scheme, and dancers who seemed to move in and out of great transparent screens. Special effects included fog and entire stage settings that changed before your eyes. The music, with its Celtic influences, was another new experience for me, and I became excited about what Broadway producers and writers had to offer.

Later that year, back in Buffalo, I became the boy singer for the Bill Creighton Orchestra, playing cotillions, debutante balls, and large private parties. The band varied from twelve to seventeen players, depending on the sponsor's budget, and I sang the romantic ballads of those post-World War II years

Singing with the Bill Creighton Orchestra, February 14, 1947.
— Courtesy Kennedy Family Photo Album.

including "I'll Be Around," "The Old Lamplighter," and "Moonlight Becomes You."

During that stint with the band, I also became the music librarian, handling all the big chart books for each instrumentalist, and eventually making up the early evening sets to get us started: a couple of fast instrumentals, a slow vocal, and a medium instrumental. Then Bill Creighton asked me to take care of the band stands and stand lights. Next, I was to see that the piano was in tune and in the right spot on the stage before the band arrived to play. I finally added the publicity and then the booking to my chore list, and so, received my first experience at sixteen of working with the complicated logistics of getting a performance on stage. It was a good experience, and I enjoyed the women who came to the bandstand to request their favorite songs. I was in heaven.

When I completed my semester at Lafayette

and my stint with the Bill Creighton Orchestra, I found myself really missing Ann down in Texas, so I hurried back to Houston for summer vacation.

During one two-week period, Ann and I, her brother Dick and his girlfriend, and Ann's folks all went to Bandera for a vacation at Prade Ranch. It was my first experience with the Texas Hill Country, and riding through it on horseback, I thought how great it would be to own a ranch in the Texas hills.

In the meantime, my mother had accepted the buyer's job at McManus & Reiley in Albany, NY, and asked me to join her there to finish my high school year as a senior at The Milne School.

Once again, I found myself in a new town, with a new school, new opportunities, and the chance to sing in school productions again. I also took the challenge to work on the school paper as a writer. Then word came down that a radio show producer was looking for young performers for a "live" radio show to be broadcast from the stage of the largest movie theater in downtown Albany.

I passed the audition and became co-host of a weekly Saturday morning children's radio show, where I got to read what seemed like a pretty bad script and sing solos and a weekly duet with my teen-aged co-host, a pretty dark-haired girl named Dodo. She was cute and lively and talented and fun to work with, and the show actually won a national award. We had guest stars every week, the best of whom was Cab Calloway, whose hit song, "Minnie the Moocher," had swept the country, first in theaters, then on the radio, and finally on 78 rpm records. Cab was an enthusiastic, dynamic performer and treated me like an equal. I remained a fan of his into the 1990s.

That following summer, I again headed for Texas to spend sunny and happy weeks in Houston with Ann and her family.

With Ann Playter in Houston before heading north to enroll at Emerson College, September 3, 1948.
— Courtesy Kennedy Family Photo Album.

Premiere broadcast on WABY Radio from the stage of the Strand Theater, Albany, NY, with Cab Calloway (center) and my co-host Dodo Einstein (right), January 10, 1948.
— Courtesy Kennedy Family Photo Album.

In the fall of 1949, I returned north. My dad offered to pay my college tuition, so I left for Boston and radio school at Emerson College. I discovered Boston's dynamic jazz scene and soon founded a fan club for the Bob Wilber Jazz Band, one of the hottest traditional jazz groups in town.

Bob Wilber was a young soprano sax protégé of the famed New Orleans veteran Sidney Bechet, and Bob's ragtime piano player, Dick Wellstood, had been a classmate of Bob's and a fellow member of

The Bob Wilber Dixieland Jazz Band at the Savoy Cafe in Boston. From left: Dick Wellstood (piano), Bob Wilber (clarinet), Pops Foster (bass), Henry Goodwin (trumpet), Jimmy Archy (trombone), Tommy Benford (drums). 1949.
— Courtesy Robert Parent.

the regionally popular Scarsdale (NY) High School Jazz Band. These two young white guys were tearing up the two-beat music with some great older black musicians. Jimmy Archy on trombone, Tommy Binford on drums, and trumpet player Henry Goodwin had all been with Jelly Roll Morton's Red Hot Peppers. Bassist George "Pops" Foster had played with everyone up and down the Mississippi. He claimed to have originated plucking the bass when he left his bow behind on a riverboat gig, and most people believed him.

I spent too many nights at Steve Connally's Savoy Cafe listening to Bob Wilber and to a slightly more contemporary New Orleans-flavored quartet led by clarinetist Edmond Hall. Hall was one of the greats of jazz and played with Louis Armstrong and

Postcard from the Savoy Cafe promoting Bob Wilber and Edmond Hall, 1949.

other nationally known jazz giants like trombonist Jack Teagarden and cornet player Bobby Hackett. But more than that, Ed Hall was a gentleman, extremely polite and soft spoken. We developed a warm relationship. His piano player was a young Boston University pre-med student named George Wein who played swinging piano with style. George and I became fast friends and spent a lot of time together. He always had big plans to promote jazz.

I put together a weekly traditional jazz radio show on WVOM, Brookline, and got to know Nat Hentoff real well, as he had his own jazz show on WMEX and also hung out at the Savoy. Nat urged me to step outside the limits of old-time New Orleans jazz and also embrace some of the newer jazz music. He even gave me tickets to hear the big Stan Kenton Orchestra with vocal sensation June Christy performing at Symphony Hall.

I was so impressed with the complexity, colorful contrasts, huge ensemble work, unbelievable arrangements, Kenton's piano, and the exciting percussion work of Pete Rugolo, that I immediately changed the name of our jazz society from the "Bob Wilber Dixieland Jazz Club of Boston" to the "Jazz Club of Boston."

We still spent the majority of our efforts promoting traditional jazz and undertook to welcome Bob Wilber's band back to Boston from Nice,

At Back Bay Station, welcoming the Bob Wilber Band back to Boston from Nice, France, January 3, 1949.
— Courtesy Robert Parent.

France, with a parade led by the band playing in a horse-drawn wagon with Jimmy Archy playing real tailgate trombone out of the rear. A huge crowd turned out for the parade, and we got a lot of good press. Thus encouraged, we began producing concerts in some of Boston's larger halls. We brought in Wild Bill Davidson, Pee Wee Russell, Georg Brunis, J. C. "Higgy" Higginbotham, Vic Dickenson, Willie

Jimmy Archy (right) playing real "tailgate" trombone with Bob Wilber (soprano sax) and Henry Goodwin (trumpet) at the homecoming parade, January 3, 1949.
— Courtesy Robert Parent.

The Savoy Cafe on Mass Avenue, Boston, 1949.
— Courtesy Kennedy Family Photo Album.

"The Lion" Smith, and all kinds of Dixielanders from throughout New England and New York City.

Another Savoy Cafe acquaintance, an MCA executive named Dick Mascot who promoted "danceable jazz" in the Boston area, urged me to go to New York's Piano Bar and hear a young English piano player named George Shearing. A month or two later, I helped him bring Shearing on a train to Boston to play an event for us at the Fensgate Hotel on Beacon Street.

I'll never forget Shearing or that event. Shearing, who was blind, played a unique style of contemporary jazz piano while being a really nice person with a good sense of humor.

While we were trying with this event to intro-

duce him to Boston's jazz community at our little session, a wedding going on down the hall overflowed into our lounge. Some of the happily intoxicated wedding guests kept requesting a really commercial pop tune that was at the top of "Your Hit Parade" at the time. I was embarrassed for George and quite concerned about how he might react to repeated requests for "Cruising Down The River" from intrusive and noisy revelers. Finally, he smiled and then launched into the greatest version of the tune I've ever heard! And, as I turned and looked out the lounge window, a Harvard crew rowed by on the St. Charles River. I thought, "Man, I can't believe this!"

Shearing's appearance in Boston was another great success, one we hoped would contribute to the growth of his popularity which was just then beginning to gain momentum. We put him back on the train, and I didn't think about him for many years.

The hotel apparently thought it was quite a success, and the management was encouraged enough to let George Wein and me open the Frankie Newton Room with the giant, gentle, black muted-trumpet player as the central figure. Frankie had made some historic recordings, including the classic "Strange Fruit" with Billie Holiday, but he had fallen on hard times, and George thought he deserved a hearing. So I jumped in to help convert this hotel room into a unique kind of music room.

George played the piano in the Frankie Newton Trio, and I did the publicity and got the Jazz Club behind it. The club room was truly extraordinary! We designed it so that all of the guests sat on the carpeted floor at twelve-inch-high tables and reclined on pillows stacked around the room. It was quite a scene, the ambiance was great, the music was incredible, and the room and Frankie caught on.

While going to Emerson and running the Jazz Club with my MIT roommate Ward Kiddoo, I also got a job working two shows a night as a spotlight operator at the Oval Room of the Copley Plaza Hotel. I had never been a spotlight operator before, but I figured it out and literally jumped into it, operating two spotlights eight feet apart by leaping back and forth between two platforms with carpeted stairs leading up to the lights! In reality, there were supposed to be two spotlight operators. So, while I fooled them into thinking I was a spotlight operator, they fooled me into thinking that it was normal for one man to operate two lights! Not knowing any better, I thought it was a great deal, and between shows, I'd run off to the Savoy Cafe for a set or two of jazz.

The Oval Room hosted some pretty lavish shows, including the Ted Straiter Orchestra and, later, the Carmen Miranda Show. She was a Latin singer and dancer famous for her energy, heavy lipstick, fruit-laden headdress, and wildly swaying body.

One night after the second show at the Oval Room, Carmen and all her dancers and musicians joined me at the Frankie Newton Room to celebrate her birthday. The ambiance of the room slowly changed into a wild Latin scene. I watched in amazement as she danced seven partners to the floor. She was dynamic and dazzling, and, without her stage makeup and headdress, she was a sexy and really exotic five-foot-four, olive-skinned beauty.

Driving Texas Tubing's "hot shot" Ford pickup, Victoria, Texas, 1950.
— Courtesy Kennedy Family Photo Album.

Obviously, my school work suffered, and I wasn't really into the curriculum at Emerson. While being a radio school, it was also a drama school and I found it a little too dramatic for my taste. I decided to sell everything I couldn't carry and hitch-hike back to Texas where I could work off my dissipation in the oil fields and be with Ann again. Her father connected me with Texas Tubing & Supply Company, and they hired me to run the warehouse at their new operation in Victoria, Texas, and drive a brand new hot-shot Ford pickup on emergency runs. The biggest reason for Texas Tubing to be there was the huge construction site for a new DuPont plant. I enjoyed working hard at physical labor, loading pipe and fittings and heavy tools for industrial construction. I was tan, healthy, and hard as a rock with an appreciative boss who spent most of his time on the road selling. One of the things that I thought was neat was that Texas Tubing had phone number "1" in Victoria. I had never heard of that before.

Later that year I received a call from Ann's father, who moved me to a C. F. Braun construction site at a Phillips 66 refinery closer to Houston as the person in charge of all the industrial parts, supplies, and fittings coming into the site. I devised inventory control systems and checked all materials into the site and out to the foremen on the job using purchase orders, blueprints, and shipping slips.

I was doing very well with Braun and enjoyed working for the company that Ann's father had been an executive with for years. The only problem was I hadn't foreseen, when I left college, that I would lose my draft deferment by being out of school. I had been in submarines in the Navy Reserve in Boston, but now I was about to be drafted into the army. I thought about the army, remembered the submarines, and decided that if I had to fight in Korea I'd rather get the best training there was, so I volunteered for the marines. I joined along with about fifty other members of a Houston platoon. It was 1951, and we were going to make it rough on the Chinese and the North Koreans.

THE MARINE CORPS YEARS

(1951–1954)

Marine Corps boot camp at San Diego was not at all what I had expected. Indeed, I was shocked and shaken by the extremes of the discipline and the treatment of the recruits by the drill instructors. The idea seemed to be to destroy every possible tie with home and family life through ridicule and depersonalization, and then rebuild each man by intimidation, rigorous exercise, drills, marches, and indoctrination. This scheme worked pretty well, and each of us lost our "mama's boy" attitude, replacing it with a gung-ho teamwork attitude in which only the team mattered.

My personal indoctrination was tinged with painful humor when my drill instructor discovered my music background and immediately dubbed me "Choir Boy." While no recruit was permitted to laugh, there were many silent smirks as "Choir Boy" hopped around the marching platoon while carrying a heavy pack. The result was that I was in great shape at the end of the thirteen weeks at the Marine Corps Recruit Depot.

In addition to learning a whole new vocabulary, how to kill a man with a rifle butt or bayonet, and how to field-strip and fire a number of weapons, I was down to 165 pounds of muscle at five-foot-ten with a forty-four-inch chest and a twenty-eight-inch waist.

The proudest moment of the whole indoctrinary ordeal was the final passing in review, looking "eyes right," down a long row of precise former recruits who were now a well-oiled machine as the Marine Corps Band played "Semper Fideles."

Our final passes off the depot into San Diego found a lot of now unbeatable Marines getting into fights, especially with sailors, and returning to the base bruised and battered.

My twenty-one-day leave following boot camp

Home on leave in Houston with my mother and father, January 1952.
— Courtesy Kennedy Family Photo Album.

saw my return to Houston where my mom and dad were together for the moment to meet me. I was a Private First Class in great shape and looking forward to my assignment to the supply depot at Barstow in the Mojave Desert in California. My previous work with Texas Tubing and C. F. Braun qualified me with a supply primary MOS (military occupational specialty) and an infantry secondary MOS. Most of the new marines with infantry MOSs went to combat training at Camp Pendleton, California, and then straight into the trenches of Korea.

I was surprised at how the Marine Corps used my extensive inventory control experience on arrival at Barstow. For many months, five days a week, my assignment was to walk up and down long, seemingly endless warehouses slamming pallets of military supplies into alignment behind white aisle lines on the cool concrete floors. I did this swinging a huge long-handled thirty-five-pound wooden mallet. Anytime a forklift would slightly misalign any cartons, I'd swing my mallet against the bottom pallet until the stack lined up perfectly. Then I'd move on to the next one. At least I was in long, breezy, and comparatively cool warehouses in the heat of the day, and I stayed in good physical condition.

Not accustomed to being on the bottom of the chain of command and used to taking full responsibility for the supplies in my charge, the boredom began to sink in. I lived for weekend liberty in Hollywood, Los Angeles, Big Bear Lake, and Las Vegas.

As I swung that big mallet day after day, I thought about my beginning days in radio in Albany and Boston, and I thought I'd try to take some typing instruction after hours so I'd be equipped to write my own radio scripts when I got out of service.

The typing lessons went as well as could be expected for a slightly hammer-handed twenty-one-year-old, and I became friends with a number of the non-commissioned officers in Special Services.

Near the end of the first month of working on my typing, the sergeant asked if I'd like to get out of the warehouses and become a writer for *The Prospector,* the weekly base newspaper. That sounded like a good idea to me, and I switched.

Aside from covering the normal base news of visiting dignitaries, transfers, promotions, special recognitions, and news the brass wanted the troops to know, I also wrote two columns: "Liberty Call," on where to go, what to do, and how much it cost, and "Rick's Ramblings," a more detailed editorial commentary on really special places I'd been.

"Rick," incidentally, became my name in the marines, instead of Rod, as a result of troops hearing my name at mail call two or three times a week. When the corporal would call out, "Kennedy, Roderick," with emphasis on the last syllable of Roderick, Rick was the name that really stuck in everyone's mind. To this day, when traveling, I know that anyone who calls me Rick knew me in the Marine Corps.

With this new newspaper duty assignment, I was almost on "official business" when I went on liberty to the casinos of Las Vegas or the film studios and night clubs of Hollywood. Soon I was promoted to corporal.

My presence in the club and studio surroundings opened many doors for me. As a regular at The Royal Room jazz club, I came to know jazz stars such as Pete Daily and His Chicagoans, legendary Texas trombonist Jack Teagarden, and Red Nichols and His Five Pennies.

With the depot situated way out there in the Mojave Desert, the troops' morale was not very good and there was a dearth of decent entertainment. Few complained, however, since supply depot duty was certainly preferable to a combat assignment in Korea. Nonetheless, as I had become friends with Gene Norman of "Gene Norman Presents," I soon was able to work out presenting some jazz concerts for the troops out at Barstow.

I arranged for a series of stage shows, concerts, and local radio broadcasts called "Parade Rest." Stars playing these shows included Pete Daily and his band, Shorty Rogers and the Giants, and songstress April Stevens. I also produced base talent shows, USO variety shows, and, finally, the big one: "The Bob Hope Show" with Claudette Colbert, Les Brown's Band of Renown, and vocalist Joanne Woodward.

Bob Hope and Claudette Colbert arrive at Barstow by private plane for "The Bob Hope Show," January 29, 1952.
— Courtesy USMC.

Les Brown and his Band of Renown at Barstow, California, January 31, 1952.
— Courtesy USMC.

Pete Daily and the Chicagoans at Nebo Gymnasium, Marine Corps Supply Depot, Barstow. From left: Out of photo on left Skippy Anderson (piano), Bert Johnson (trombone), Hugh Allison (drums), Pete Daily (cornet), out of sight behind clarinetist, Bud Hatch (tuba), Hots O'Casey (clarinet), Pud Brown (saxophone).
— Courtesy USMC

From left: Cpl. Rod Kennedy, popular bop and boogie harmonica player Les Thompson, disc jockey and jazz producer Gene Norman, and twenty-one-year-old April Stevens, whose RCA hit recording "I'm in Love Again" had sold 600,000 copies, shown at Barstow's Marine Corps Supply Depot, February 16, 1952.
— Courtesy USMC.

My frequent weekends in Hollywood allowed me to become associated with many of the people in the film industry. Before long I was escorting starlets to movie premieres in my dress blues and attending various galas, receptions, and parties.

I actually saw polo matches in Santa Monica with Fernando Lama and Lana Turner, danced with Marilyn Monroe at the Golden Globe Awards, was Gene Kelly's guest for the MGM Studio screening of

An American in Paris before its world premiere, and met Leslie Caron, Doris Day, Dan Daley, Arthur Kennedy, Corrine Calvet, and countless other stars, directors, and foreign press people. I got to know Julie Mitchum quite well and her brother Robert Mitchum, who was going through a big frame-up for smoking dope. For a young marine who worked on a remote supply depot in the middle of the desert all week, the weekends were unbelievable!

Soon my time came to join a combat group in Korea, and I sailed with 2,000 other seasick marines to Japan on our way to Korea. We were to join the Second Battalion of the First Marine Division that was settled into a somewhat static position adjacent to the Panmunjon peace corridor.

It was more like World War I than World War II: trench warfare with the peace corridor on our left flank. The Chinese would set up mortar positions just outside the corridor and lob rounds into our trenches and patrols. If we fired back and into the corridor, we created an "international incident," in violation of the no-fire zone, and the peace talks were postponed again.

The division was assigned a long ridge line with extensive trenches and bunkers to defend. Two battalions operated forward with one in reserve. The forward battalions kept two companies up and one in reserve, backed up by H&S Company with supply, motor pool, ammo dump, and the hospital unit.

Combat consisted of artillery and mortar fire, machine gun, and sniper fire. Our highly mobile rocket units fired over our heads at the Chinese and

"Bug Out Cave" in the Panmunjon sector, Western Front, Korea, December 1952.

— Courtesy Kennedy Family Photo Album.

Near the Panmunjon Peace Corridor, February 1953.

— Courtesy Kennedy Family Photo Album.

Holy communion on the hood of a Jeep at Easy Company, Second Battalion, Seventh Marines, Korea, November 12, 1952.

— Courtesy Kennedy Family Photo Album.

North Koreans, and then scooted for another site from which to fire to avoid the incoming response of the enemy.

In addition to this "static position" kind of combat, there were frequent patrols and probes by reinforced infantry on both sides and sometimes tanks and air support. There were some days that blended into night with constant firing, heavy explosions, and aggressive attacks by thousands of Chinese and North Koreans. While most of the enemy troops were short in stature, we occasionally fought giant Mongolian troops. We were fighting alongside Canadians, Aussies, South Africans, and the Hellenic forces from Greece.

War was the loudest, most disorienting experience I've ever known. The noise, death and destruction, pain and tragedy were close to unbelievable. And, when it was over, no ground had been taken or given.

In between the larger confrontations, there were still surprise deaths of marines getting their throats slit while on the john or dying from a tiny piece of shrapnel through the ear or forehead. Land mines were a constant threat.

In addition, the weather was miserable, ranging from 140 degrees and rainy in the summer down to 40 below in the winter with snow, ice, and cutting winds.

Yet, through it all, some music emerged. The most familiar and intriguing music out of all those months in Korea was a plaintive melody called "China Night." Everyone hummed it, and whenever we caught a broadcast by Hanoi Sally, that song was on the radio.

The drafts of marines rotating home, with replacements arriving regularly, went on constantly, so it was hard to know who was killed in action and who was sent home. We heard on our way home, after a year had passed, that out of our original battalion of 1,050, only 200 came home, but I was never able to confirm it. We did have heavy casualties.

I know that combat, the killing and maiming, and the loss of buddies, created deep within me a heartfelt gratefulness to be alive followed by a silent pledge to devote the rest of my life to something that would benefit a lot of people. My earlier prewar life seemed selfish and self-centered in perspective, and I vowed to do something about it when I got out of the Marine Corps.

"You mean, you know who Shearing is?" I asked.

"Of course. He sold out the Cow Palace earlier this week," came the reply.

In the months I had been in boot camp, Barstow, combat training, and Korea, I hadn't even thought about the Englishman whom we had brought to the Fensgate Hotel in Boston. In those past twenty-two months, Shearing had become a major force in American popular music, and I missed it somehow, along with a lot of other civilized happenings.

The remaining months stateside, spent teaching map reading along with the compass and firing matches as a member of the Marine Corps Rifle Team, seemed frustrating, especially as a cease fire

The sight of the Golden Gate bridge was thrilling coming home from Korea on the USS General Walker, *May 1953.*
— Courtesy Kennedy Family Photo Album.

Checking with the score keepers at the Camp Pendleton Fall Rifle Matches, November 1953.
— Courtesy Kennedy Family Photo Album.

The sight of the Golden Gate Bridge was thrilling! The rush of what it really meant to be alive and back in the States began to overwhelm me.

Once cleared and on liberty, I rushed to have a real hamburger, then a Scotch and water, and then a hot fudge sundae. Consuming these three luxuries at my own pace even preceded a call home.

Somewhere in the background of a San Francisco cafe I heard a familiar sound and I turned to someone near me and said, "That sounds like Shearing." They replied, "Sure it does, it's George Shearing."

and truce was declared in Korea shortly after we rotated home.

When I was finally ready for discharge following my final months at Camp Pendleton, bracketed with weekends in Hollywood, Laguna Beach, Big Bear Lake, and other favorite California haunts, I headed straight for Austin, Texas, and The University of Texas. I drove almost non-stop for thirty-six hours from Camp Pendleton, through Death Valley, and on to Central Texas in a used Jeepster loaded down with marine buddies and sea bags.

I dropped them off at or near hometowns

In the used Jeepster that would take me home to The University of Texas in February 1954. Camp Pendleton, July 1953.
— Courtesy Kennedy Family Photo Album.

along the way after having blown all four overloaded tires on the roller coaster desert highways of California, Arizona, and New Mexico.

By the time I got to Austin, I was already over a week late for the start of the 1954 spring semester at UT. I hurried to register for classes as a twenty-four-year-old second semester freshman who had been out of school for so long that my dear Ann had gone on with her life without me. Without my first love, I focused on getting into the swing of civilian life and campus life as a veteran on the G.I. Bill with not a familiar friend in sight.

THE UNIVERSITY YEARS

(1954–1956)

The "Forty Acres" of The University of Texas campus at Austin were much larger and more confusing to find my way around than I ever imagined they could be. I kept thinking that many small-town freshmen new to The University must really be having an orientation problem on a campus possibly larger than their hometowns.

My housing was in some World War II temporary prefabricated shacks where the floor was so slanted that when you dropped your pencil it kept rolling until it hit the wall. Nonetheless, it was cheap and right on the campus.

Many of the veterans at UT seemed to keep to themselves and were making obvious political statements and forming their own student party. They were anti-fraternity and bragged about being GDIs ("God-damned independents").

I elected instead to become part of the student body at large since that's where the girls were. First, however, I had to catch up on my studies. Having arrived on campus in February of 1954, several weeks after classes started, not only did I have to deal with having been out of college for four years, but I was already behind in assignments when I hit the campus.

The G.I. Bill was paying $110 a month for my tuition and living expenses, and I took out a student loan to buy my books. I began to look for some kind of work to provide for some extra cash. Then, to make things tighter, the Marine Corps decided I'd been overpaid for combat pay while in Korea and demanded that I repay it. I paid $5 a month for twenty-seven months as my affection for the Marine Corps diminished.

As a result, the early semesters at UT were on a really tight budget, and I only drove my Jeepster

My Jeepster (right) finds two new friends at The University of Texas, April 1954.
— Courtesy Kennedy Family Photo Album.

when absolutely necessary. I worked at odd jobs, studied hard and enthusiastically, and determined to make a success as a twenty-four-year-old second-semester freshman working toward a radio-TV degree.

I did well academically, earning eight A's and three B's during the first four semesters of English, history, economics, journalism, drama (TV rehearsal and production), speech, music appreciation, and radio, earning Magna Cum Laude in Fine Arts.

My academic success was in spite of my having become a fraternity member, president of the Fraternity Presidents Council, a Fine Arts Assemblyman alongside Neal Spelce (who later became a newsman with KTBC-TV), and a member of the Silver Spurs honorary service organization.

During my years as a member of Lambda Chi Alpha, I came through pledgeship with the eighteen-year-olds and moved into the fraternity house, leaving the shacks behind forever. I soon became social chairman, dating 108 girls and getting them dates with my fraternity brothers. I did well enough, I guess, as I was elected president of the fraternity the next year. My campus activities included emceeing for both the *Round Up Review* and *Sing Song.*

I was lucky that my fraternity "big brother," Allen Heard, was a good student and a good influence on me. As roommates, we studied a lot, but he also could get excited about going out on a "mid-

With Nancylee Davis, Ginny Jenuell, and Allen Heard at the Silver Spurs Formal, February 1956.
— Courtesy Jack's Party Pictures.

night requisition" mission for building supplies or a late-night snack. His girlfriend, Ginny, became our fraternity sweetheart, and she and Allen and I double-dated often. When I found out that I couldn't get a job in radio because I had not yet learned how to cue a record, I approached the head of the radio school about applying for a construction permit to build a university radio station.

I had been to see Cactus Pryor at KTBC, Austin, and Robert Reed at WOAI, San Antonio, about working for the summer or part-time during the school year, and both of them told me to get some experience and then come back. So, I thought, if we built a university station, I could get some experience to become a disc jockey. My earlier work at WABY, Albany, as a singing host of a kid's show, at WVOM, Brookline, as a host of a jazz show, and as the writer-producer host of the Marine Corps series "Parade Rest," had not provided me with the kind of background I needed to work at the radio "power stations" in Texas.

Having received the go-ahead from the radio-

TV department to start raising money for my radio station project, I approached the Panhellenic and Interfraternity Councils about donating the proceeds of the forthcoming 1955 *Varsity Carnival* to fund the construction of a radio station for UT. They went for it.

Varsity Carnival was a couple of acres of original shows, musicals, skits, and concessions put on by dozens of fraternities and sororities, and it had a huge attendance. Invariably, it was a roaring party, and many of the shows proved pretty raucous, each organization seeing what they could get past the censors.

Singing to Tri-Delt Gloria Hoffmann in the Lambda Chi Alpha show at the 1955 Varsity Carnival *to raise money to build KUT-FM.*
— Courtesy Jack's Party Pictures.

The Lambda Chi show was pretty tame and included a mock Glenn Miller Band, a scene where I sang a love duet with a pretty sorority girl in a little convertible on top of Mt. Bonnell, and a harem dance by a beautiful Kappa named Nancylee Davis. I had music class with her, and we were dating regularly at the time. The 108 girls of the previous years were forgotten, and by the end of my university years, we were pinned and then engaged.

Dating on a limited budget proved not to be the obstacle one might imagine. The University Blanket Tax allowed us to attend football games in Austin, Houston, Dallas, Waco, and College Station, as well as take in great music events at Gregory Gymnasium. The shows were top flight and as diverse as Broadway highlights with stars like Mary Martin, concerts by artists like Harry Belafonte, and even the Houston Symphony conducted by Sir Thomas Beecham. Nancylee and I fell in love with the Franck D minor Symphony at that concert.

We also sang in the various university choruses of Morris Beachy, including opera choruses by Verdi and Puccini performed downtown with the Austin Symphony Orchestra. These, and other university activities, combined with fraternity functions ranging from house parties, dinners at the house, and even a weekend at Prade Ranch in Bandera, Texas, allowed Nancylee and me to spend a lot of time together for not much money.

Other social activities included picnics and swimming at Barton Springs and at the lake and

Nancylee and I at a Lambda Chi Alpha buffet following the Rice Institute football game, October 22, 1955.
— Courtesy Jack's Party Pictures.

quick weekend trips to either Nancylee's home in Waco or my mother's new home in Houston.

During the spring of my last university year, on March 25, 1956, a classical music station signed on in Austin at 98.3 and I began to listen to it pretty regularly. In fact, I thought it might provide me with a chance to work in radio. I had a good background in classical music as well as many other kinds, and I had some radio experience, so I went over to the station at 3004 Guadalupe Street and applied.

The station was small, tucked into two back rooms of High Fidelity, Inc., an upscale hi-fi components store owned by Jimmy Moore. The station operated off an eighty-foot tower at about 780 watts and reached most of Austin with its signal.

Going to work for KHFI-FM in October of 1956 and getting to know Jimmy Moore would change my life forever.

THE RADIO YEARS

(1957–1964)

I was excited about being an announcer and in charge of sales and promotion for the station. The new job in radio meant that I could give up my yard work job, but I continued to wait tables at the Lambda Chi fraternity house to pay for my room rent and meals. And, by now, my mother was a successful buyer and fashion coordinator at Sakowitz in Houston, and she bought me a brand new 1957 Ford convertible, so things were looking up!

The station was on the air from 3:00 P.M. to midnight, seven days a week when I joined the staff. By the time I was appointed station manager on April 1, 1957, we had expanded to signing on at 7:00 A.M. Monday through Saturday and added a popular 11:00 P.M. to 2:00 A.M. "Dance Party" show on Saturday night.

In addition to expanding my popular music awareness, I became knowledgeable about classical music of all kinds under the tutelage of program director Leonard Masters. My on-the-air schedule included more than twenty-five hours of weekly classical programming, three hours of jazz, and two hours of special interest shows (Broadway, big bands, celebrity artists like Harry Belafonte, Julie Andrews, and Carlos Montoya). The Sunday "Folk Music of the World" show began to feature less and less worldly traditional music and instead was more and more oriented toward the contemporary singer/songwriter under my care-taking.

After six months of on-the-air management and sales work, I began to find that it was really difficult keeping up with my scholastic pursuits. Solving theoretical problems constantly gave way to solving real problems every day at the station, like meeting weekly payroll and keeping everything else going.

Nancylee graduated in May 1957, and by then she and I were engaged to be married the following September. When she left for Europe on a graduation trip financed by her uncle, I was station manager. By the time she returned, Jimmy Moore had offered to sell us the station, and she rushed home to find out what was going on.

We decided to take him up on the offer, since he said he would co-sign a loan for us. On July 1, 1957, J. Moore Enterprises sold us KHFI-FM for $21,000 so that they could put another FM station on the air with a jazz format. KHFI-FM and the new KAZZ-FM soon moved into new studios and offices encompassing 3006 Guadalupe Street as High Fidelity, Inc., expanded into Audioland. The two-station concept and new facilities were conceived by Jimmy Moore and his partners to sell more FM tuners and their hi-fi components to a wider audience.

So, by the time we were married in Waco on September 7, we had owned the station for a couple of months, and after our short honeymoon at Lake Austin, Nancylee came to work as continuity director for the station.

KHFI-FM began to enjoy greater acceptance as the months passed. Leonard Masters, whose brilliant programming, erudite commentary, and overly precise announcing all belied his Pampa, Texas, origins, cut quite a figure in classical music circles. His tremendous 300-pound bulk destroyed more than one lifetime-warranted armchair in the radio studio.

His patience with my foreign language shortcomings and taste for various forms of popular, folk, and jazz music seemed unending. His serious music skills and my ability to sell it to sponsors and the public made us a good team. The more he saw I was producing income to support his uncompromising classical efforts, the closer we became, and we had a warm and respectful business and personal relationship.

His announcing style was a controversial topic of conversation all over town. One unforgettable phone call I still recall with a laugh was when a listener called for him, asking to speak with our "pronouncer."

On the other end of the staff spectrum was Nancylee, who toiled daily for four years writing commercials for the growing assortment of sponsors I was bringing in. She worked hard and did a good job. Her natural intelligence and her University of Texas liberal arts background made her a knowledgeable writer whose commercials were well-crafted and in good taste. When you consider that we ran the station for years on a peanut butter sandwich budget, the on-the-air results were all the more remarkable.

As we progressed, it became obvious that we needed a survey of our audience that would offer some kind of acceptable documentation that people were actually listening to us. I hired Bill Moyers' research company to do a telephone survey of 1,200 homes using professional survey practices, and the survey came back with impressive statistics that helped me sell more advertising. We believed at the time that those same results found their way to Lady Bird Johnson's people, who were then jump started into applying to the FCC for a license to build KTBC-FM.

KHFI-FM was the first commercially successful FM station in the state of Texas. Most FM channels simply were being used by their AM radio affiliates to duplicate AM programming, while a few tried programming separately part of the day. A small number struggled to establish themselves as independents. We eventually called a dozen of them together and organized the Texas FM Broadcasters Association.

Our loyal pioneering sponsors included Bill Gammon of William Gammon Insurance, Hiram Brown of Cabaniss-Brown Furniture, John Kavanaugh of J. R. Reed Music Company, Harry Aikin of Nighthawk Restaurants, and Bob Ross, general manager of the Driskill Hotel. Bob invited me in for lunch, signed a year's program sponsorship contract, later renewed, and brought our FM signal and specially imprinted copies of our monthly program guide into every hotel room. This was at a time when many prospective advertisers were refusing to even talk with us about contracting with our station.

At twenty-seven years old, beginning to feel at home on the air. At the KHFI-FM console 1957.

— Courtesy *Austin American-Statesman.*

Another major encouragement was the signing of what was probably the longest radio contract in history, a five-year commitment by Charlie Goodnight, owner of the twenty-four-hour "sizzling steak" Hills Cafe on South Congress Avenue, for three hours of dance music every Saturday night on our new 11:00 P.M. to 2:00 A.M. "Dance Party."

These early key Austin businesses gave us the income we needed to survive and grow and an increasing commercial legitimacy that allowed us to raise Leonard Masters' salary to near a living wage.

The miracle makers, though, were our chief engineers: Dale Jones, who built and maintained KHFI-FM the two years it was in the back of High Fidelity, Inc., and Knocky Willett, who became our engineer in 1958 when Jones moved to KAZZ-FM and we occupied our new studios in Audioland. Knocky was also part of the team that put my long-dreamed-of University of Texas station, KUT-FM, on the air on November 10, 1958.

In that KHFI-FM had been built with used equipment, we often found it necessary to employ innovative technical solutions to periodic problems. Among the unique techniques devised by our engineers were punching the transmitter where they scratched an X on the front (to bring the dials and meters into alignment and eliminate on-the-air distortion), and, if that didn't work, putting on a long-play record and running into the bathroom for glasses of water to fill buckets which were then poured down a hole at the base of our antenna tower. Theoretically, this would re-establish the necessary ground plane to stabilize the station's signal. The bathroom sink was too small to get a bucket under the faucets, so the frustration of having to use a small glass to fill the bucket repeatedly made the task even more inconceivable and frustrating.

In 1958, when Jimmy Moore had built the KAZZ-FM studio right next to the new KHFI-FM studio as part of his new Audioland, Dale and Knocky and City Planner Hoyle Osborne, an avid hi-fi music fan and investor in Audioland, drilled a hole through the wall between the studios and ran wires from an Ampex601-2 stereo tape recorder/playback machine to both studio consoles so we could broadcast for thirty minutes a week the first FM stereo in Texas history!

These shows were put together dubbing my recorded announcing and cuts on two-track tape from a limited number of available RCA stereo releases of both classical and popular music plus an occasional cut from a laboratory demonstration stereo disc of sounds like a thunder storm or a ping-pong game.

The way people listened to these stereocasts, which soon expanded to an hour in length, was to tune one radio to KHFI-FM 98.3 on the right and a second set to KAZZ-FM 95.5 on the left and then sit back at the apex of an imaginary triangle and listen. We sold thousands of $39 Granco table model FM radios to listeners who wanted a second channel to hear Cabaniss-Brown's stereocast.

Eventually, we increased the number of special stereo programs and included some of up to five hours in length as more recorded material in stereo became available. We even went out and recorded local music events in stereo, which we then would broadcast as part of our community service effort. However, in spite of increased sales of stereo rigs by the owners of KAZZ-FM, who also owned Audioland, these intrusions on the jazz programming of KAZZ-FM grew to be a problem that had to be negotiated carefully and programmed sparingly.

Later, the industry developed the Multiplex broadcasting system, whereby a single FM station could split its own signal for reception on a special stereo tuner designed to decipher and separate the two channels for home listening. Two speakers and a stereo amplifier completed this revolutionary new system.

After we acquired the station, we realized that we were the only commercial station in town with-

out a station vehicle, so I bought a little 1951 British MG-TD roadster, put on a new top and tires, painted it white, put a station logo on the doors, and installed a Blaupunkt AM-FM radio. It attracted considerable attention and was living proof to the motoring public that an FM station actually existed in town. That car, formerly owned and raced by Texas racing legend Carroll Shelby, became the first sports car in what would later become a major collection of ARKAY Vintage Racing machines.

Our MG-TD was classic proof that our FM station existed.
— Courtesy KHFI-FM Publicity Photo.

KHFI-FM was a very community-active station, taping Austin Symphony Orchestra concerts complete with intermission interviews with soloists like Lisa Della Casa, Leonard Pennario, Isaac Stern, or conductor Ezra Rachlin. The broadcasts of these concerts greatly increased the visibility of the symphony and proved to be an excellent means of publicity for the Austin Symphony Orchestra.

We publicized University fine arts events, the emerging Austin theater and ballet scene, and fund-raising efforts of all the arts organizations. We even held taped auditions for the Philadelphia Academy of Music, recording in the parlor of the Texas Federation of Women's Clubs, and earned scholarships for at least two of Willa Stewart's UT opera students.

I enjoyed my relationships with dozens of classical artists, including piano master Dalies Franz, who coached such notables as Pennario and John Browning as well as others, and was a prime teacher for James Dick. I also enjoyed the acquaintance of visiting artists such as Benno Moiseivich, Blanche Thebom, Robert Rouseville, and our own orchestra's concertmaster Leopold LaFosse.

During these years, I served as an officer or board member of the Austin Symphony Orchestra (1958-1971), Austin Ballet Society (1960-1963), Austin Civic Theater (1959-1963), which later became the Zachary Scott Theater Center, the International Good Neighbor Council, and the Austin Advertising Club. I was also a founding member of the Austin chapter of the SPEBSQSA (Society for the Preservation and Enouragement of Barber Shop Quartet Singing in America) and enjoyed singing four-part harmony on the old songs for the first time since those years with my dad in Buffalo. One of the members was Marlin "Griff" Griffith, whose daughter Nanci would later become an important part of my life.

As a director, and then president, of the Austin Advertising Club (1963), most of my efforts were directed toward lobbying the state legislature to allow, first, the Texas Highway Department (under Tom Taylor's direction) to advertise, and then, second, the state of Texas itself to advertise, resulting in the formation of the Texas Tourist Development Agency under Frank Hildebrand. This agency would later create an event in a small Texas Hill Country community that would precipitate the start of the Kerrville Folk Festival.

Among my Advertising Club cohorts during this period were Austin Chamber of Commerce manager Vic Mathias, Duplex Signs executive Ed St. John, artist Windy Winn, advertising account executive Bonner McLane, who eventually became head of the Texas Association of Broadcasters, *Austin American-Statesman* publisher Dick Brown, and some of the people who helped start *Texas Monthly* magazine.

The station received one of its greatest boosts through the constant and continuing publicity over many years generated by *Austin American-Statesman* amusements editor John Bustin. We paid tribute to him on KHFI-FM's fifth anniversary 1961 at a banquet at South Austin's popular Green Pastures Restaurant run by Mary Kooch. Attending were the presidents of the symphony, the ballet, theater, and the Austin Fine Arts Society, whose interest was the visual arts. We presented him with a collection of sixty Glenn Miller Orchestra recordings and then entertained everyone with a "live" folk concert performed by Segle Fry, Roger Abrahams, and others.

The station broadcast a wide selection of British Broadcasting Corporation programs throughout the first three years, and for our fourth anniversary, March 25, 1960, Leonard Masters and I put together a full day of BBC programming beginning at 10:00 A.M. and continuing until midnight.

Through special arrangement with the transcription service of the BBC in London, twenty-six different programs were heard, including concerts of light music, jazz, drama, documentaries, radio games, comedy, and short stories. We also published our own version of the BBC's *London Calling* newspaper and brought in from Houston's Red Lion Pub a London taxi on loan from George and Marjorie Crowder.

The BBC programming included music from the Aldeburgh Festival, a concert by the London Philharmonic, *The Goon Show* with Peter Sellers, and a stereocast of Mahler's "Symphony of a Thousand" from Royal Albert Hall. At 9:00 P.M. we also had a broadcast of the Big Ben chimes and the "latest" BBC News on tape flown in from London that same day. We also hired three Austin-based Englishmen to help enhance the "Britishness" of the program by employing their accents when announcing station breaks, commercials, and other transitional material between programs from the BBC.

The celebration featured unique programming of the highest quality and created a good deal of publicity and good will for the station both locally and nationally via the Associated Press newswire.

Nineteen-sixty-one was not only a busy broadcast and civic work year, but I was also active in the Travis County Republican Party as a member of the county executive committee. I was the only broadcaster in Austin to publicly support and assist a Wichita Falls college professor named John Tower to run against Lyndon Johnson for the U.S. Senate.

Beryl Milburn, an attractive and well-spoken Austin-area party worker, asked me to help Tower announce his candidacy. When I met John, I liked him immediately. He was a former board member of the Wichita Falls Civic Theater, supported his local symphony society, was a graduate of the London School of Economics, and a spokesman for most of the conservative ideals that I had personally held for years. In spite of his short stature, John Tower appeared larger than life with a great voice and an impressive way of presenting his ideas. He and his wife Lou became good personal friends to Nancylee and me, and we worked hard to get him elected.

I made the first arrangements with the Sergeant-At-Arms of the Texas Legislature to set up Tower's first press conference for the Capitol press corps and also planned and produced his first

KHFI-FM, AUSTIN, TEXAS

London Calling

AUSTIN EDITION

BBC OVERSEAS PROGRAMMES: MARCH 21-25, 1960

BBC COMES TO AUSTIN

KHFI-FM Marks Fourth Anniversary with BBC Schedule

Austin's Classical Music Station, KHFI-FM, will observe the fourth anniversary of its first broadcast on Friday, March 25, 1960, with a full day of programs from the British Broadcasting Corporation. The British programs begin at 10:00 A.M. on Friday morning and continue until after midnight. During the fourteen and one-half hour schedule, twenty-six different programs will be heard including concerts, light music, jazz, drama, documentaries, radio games and short stories.

KHFI-FM arranged for the special day of programs through extended correspondence with the Transcription Service of the BBC in London. In the London office Peter Stewart furnished from the BBC publicity departments all of the photographs appearing in this paper. William Ash, Assistant Head of Transcription Service, completed all of the arangements for the programs, some of them which were shipped here from England by air. Three of the program segments were actually scheduled by the BBC upon request of KHFI-FM's program department.

It is believed that this is the first time that a radio station anywhere in the world has tried to duplicate a day of BBC programs. The local schedule is a composite of three separate program services of the BBC: the famous "Third Programme", the "Light Programme" and the "Home Service" (here the "Overseas Service") A complete schedule of the day's programs is given in Col. 1, Page 2 of this publication. Detailed stories concerning each program will be found throughout the paper together with photographs of some of the principal personalities involved.

DEDICATION

On this March 25, 1960, the Fourth Anniversary of KHFI-FM's first FM Broadcast, this station dedicates a full day of BBC programs to the thousands of loyal Austin FM listeners who have given continued support and encouragement and to the spirit of international understanding of our fellow man in Britain and elsewhere during a time when man is striving for peace in the world. We further rededicate ourselves to the policies of continued honesty and integrity in advertising, and to "the furthering of those cultural facets of our community life which are the heritage of hundreds of years of artistic endeavor by the creative minds of humanity."

The Staff, KHFI-FM, Austin

THE FAMOUS TOWER HOUSING BIG BEN together with its unique sound represents Britain to the rest of the world, just as the Statue of Liberty is the symbol of the United States. During World War II, it was found that the chimes of the quarters and nine strokes of Big Ben lasted exactly sixty seconds. As the broadcast of the striking of Nine o'clock chimes by the BBC was always followed by the Nine-o-clock News to which most people in Britain and overseas listened, it was decided to dedicate the sixty seconds to silent prayer for those away from home. So meaningful did this gesture become that today the 'Big Ben Minute' is a permanent feature of BBC programs. The feature will be presented at 9:00 P.M. on KHFI-FM on Friday, March 25th, followed by a report from the News.

PETER PEARS, tenor, appears with the English Opera Group Ensemble in an unusual 'Purcell Cabaret' at Aldeburgh.

From Aldeburgh:
A Purcell Cabaret

An unusual musical entertainment called 'A Purcell Cabaret' was devised for the Aldeburgh Festival last year by Raymond Leppard and Colin Graham with music by Henry Purcell. It was an amusing and informal concert of songs, catches and airs by Purcell in honor of the tricentenary year of his birth in 1659. Most of these songs were difficult to place in an ordinary program, but too good to miss. Purcell wrote many delightfully gay drinking-songs, love songs and catches for the merry London of Charles II, and in this program an attempt was made to recapture something of the liveliness of his period.

Dennis Stevens will introduce and narrate the entertainment which is enjoyably created by April Cantelo (soprano), Peter Pears (tenor), Marjorie Thomas (alto), Joseph Ward (baritone) and Trevor Anthony (bass) with The English Opera Group Ensemble, conducted from the harpsichord by Raymond Leppard.

The Cabaret will be heard Friday afternoon at 3:00.

ALDEBURGH FESTIVAL OPENS BBC PROGRAMMING MONDAY

Five half-hour programs from the 1959 Aldeburgh Festival of Music and the Arts will act as an introductory series to KHFI-FM's full day of BBC programs. Scheduled as additional programming Monday through Friday mornings, March 21-25 at 10 o'clock, the broadcasts will present church music of the 16th and 17th Centuries recorded in the little town of Aldeburgh at the annual festival which has been held every summer since 1948. The festival, founded by Benjamin Britten, has become the center of the musical life of Britain for a week each June, and last year included, in addition to the early church music, recitals of chamber music, song cycles, a concert by the Cambridge University Madrigal Society, and a performance of Rossini's mass, Petite Messe Solennelle.

The five concerts from the Aldeburgh Parish Church are to be broadcast as follows:

Monday, March 21-Motets by William Byrd performed by the Deller Consort with soloists Honor Sheppard (soprano), Wilfred Brown (tenor), Alfred Deller (counter tenor), Gerald English (tenor), and Maurice Bevan (baritone). William Byrd was described by a contemporary of his as 'a great Master of Music', while a modern musical scholar, E. H. Fellowes has written, 'He excelled in every branch of composition known in his day and led the way into fields not previously explored.' Byrd's motets are still sung in many churches and cathedrals in England.

Tuesday, March 22-Music for Viols and Voices in performances by soprano soloists April Cantelo and Patricia Clark with the Elizabethan Players conducted by Dennis Nesbitt. The viols were the most important family of instruments in

See ALDEBURGH (P. 2, Col. 3)

COMPLETE BBC SCHEDULE (Col. 1, Page 2)

London Taxi On Display at KHFI-FM, March 24 & 25

Pictured here are (left to right) an unidentified salesman, Marjory Crowder and George Crowder in England picking up their London Taxi which was shipped to Houston to be used by the Red Lion pub, a little bit of London in the shadow of Houston's Shamrock Hotel. The Crowders are the landlords at the Red Lion (a KHFI-FM sponsor) and will be visiting Austin with their famous Morris taxi during KHFI-FM's BBC Day. The taxi will be on display in front of KHFI-FM's studios at 3006 Guadalupe all day Thursday and Friday, March 24th and 25th.

Austin public rally at Wooldridge Park. I recorded his speech at the rally, edited out the professorial pauses, and bought time on the Johnson family's KTBC radio station to broadcast the speech on Sunday night. From that time on, the campaign was off and running.

Through a whole series of elections, including primaries, general elections, and run-offs, we worked with John and Lou and their growing campaign staff. Among the chores was to be certain that we had an empty wooden Coca-Cola box for John to stand on so he could be seen over the podium.

One night John and Lou were to be our guests for the Austin Symphony Ball, and John's luggage had been lost by Braniff Airlines, owned by his opponent William Blakely. Since the ball was formal, we scrambled around town late on a Saturday to try to find John a tuxedo. Finally, some friends of ours who owned Longhorn Cleaners and rented tuxedos were called at home and persuaded to come down to the shop to try to outfit John in a tux. The jacket was no problem, but we had trouble finding pants that were short enough. Having no alterations people on hand, we took Tower campaign buttons and pinned up the legs to the right length and went on our way. He looked great and the Towers had a fine time meeting everyone in that elegant social setting. The only problem was that by the end of the evening both of John's legs were all scratched up from the protruding pins on the campaign buttons! We had a good laugh about it and applied the iodine.

Finally, in 1961, John Tower was elected to the Senate and thereby launched the modern conservative movement in Texas. He was re-elected many times and was a major force in Texas, national, and international public service for the next twenty-five years until his death in a plane crash.

In 1962, as our FM station continued to gain in popularity, we decided again to make the anniversary of the first broadcast a major production, and on March 25, we again devoted a full broadcast day to anniversary programming of a special nature. This time it was twelve hours of music we called "Saludos a Mexico," consisting of a few selected commercial recordings from Mexico for bridges and interludes but mostly featuring recordings I made on a week-long trip to Mexico City. While in that amazing metropolis, using a portable Ampex tape recorder and an introduction from the Mexican Tourist Office, I proceeded to record reels and reels of special musical performances by outstanding Mexican ensembles.

I received permission to record the Mexican National Symphony Orchestra and interviewed its conductor, Luis Herrera de la Fuente. I also recorded the National Police Band and its conductor Jenaro Nunez, composer of such famous band marches as "Zacatecas." Maestro Nunez honored us by playing the most exciting and passionate version of the American national anthem I've ever heard! We stood proud and smiling and applauded enthusiastically, and then sat down when the band launched into a very beautiful but unfamiliar melody, which, with elbow prodding from my interpreter, I suddenly realized was the Mexican national anthem!

We also recorded the mariachi and marimba bands of the city and even an organ grinder on the street corner.

One of the most exciting evenings was spent high up in the rafters of the ceiling of the magnificent Palace of Fine Arts, looking down below as we recorded a performance of the Ballet Folklorico de Mexico. After the spectacular three-hour show came to an end and the famed glass curtain closed, we were ushered, with much fanfare, into the dressing room of Folklorico founder-director Amalia Hernandez, who graciously answered our interview questions on tape. All of these special features were blended into a ten-hour broadcast special.

The complete air check of this special was submitted to Columbia University, whose officials awarded us, in their first national competition, the first Armstrong Foundation Award for FM Broadcasting Excellence. The late Major Armstrong had invented FM radio, and his widow presented us with a handsome bronze plaque and $500 at an elaborate black tie dinner at which our station was the honoree and I was the keynote speaker. It was at this dinner that we learned from a very proud New York lady that New York was the center of culture in the U.S. I'm not certain she was charmed by the idea of a provincial station from Texas winning this first prestigious award.

All of this activity attracted attention to our station, and at least one listener had high expectations from me personally.

I was on the air hosting "Folk Music of the World" one Sunday afternoon early in April when an Austin woman called me to tell me about her daughter who was a folk singer in New York.

The woman said her name was Ruth Hester and that her daughter Carolyn had become quite popular in the Northeast and especially in New York, where she was about to release her first album with a national record label. "But," Ruth Hester said, "Carolyn has never had a concert in Austin, and I'd like you to present her."

"I don't know," I said in as friendly a manner as I could muster. "I'd need quite a bit of information, recordings, photos, reviews, and biographical stuff to make a decision."

"You mean you'd consider it?" she asked.

Gulping, I said, "Well, it sounds interesting, and I guess I just need to get more information."

She was really excited about the possibility and promised to get me the materials I'd asked for. In less than a week, the Carolyn Hester packet arrived, including some photos, notices about her singing at the Black Angus in Austin in 1959, and reviews from *The New York Times* describing her voice as "airy and delicate."

Also included was her 1961 album on the Tradition label with songs like "The House of the Rising Sun," "The Water Is Wide," an original called "Jaime," and the most incredible version of "Summertime" I had ever heard. It revealed a multi-octave range for Carolyn's voice and a folk-like character that I had never heard in this Gershwin classic before.

She had already appeared at The Showboat in Washington, D.C., both the Caucus Room and Baker's Keyboard in Detroit, at Chicago's Gate of Horn, The Village Gate in Greenwich Village, The Golden Vanity in Boston, and the Club 47 in Cambridge. In New York she had also appeared at The Left Bank, Gerdes Folk City, One Sheridan Square, The Blue Angel and at Carnegie Hall! In addition, she had played campus concerts at Yale, Harvard, Fairfield College, Cornell, and Wagner College.

I was impressed with her recordings and her press materials and jumped right in to setting two dates for Carolyn at the Austin Civic Theater Playhouse at Fifth and Lavaca on a Tuesday and Wednesday night in May when the theater would be dark.

She had already appeared in almost every folk club in Britain, performed a concert at London's Cecil Sharp House and made BBC television appearances at both their London and South Hampton studios. She also had a concert at Oxford University that spring and several important performances in Scotland, which led to her appearance as the only American singer to appear at the Edinburgh Folk Festival.

We set dates for May 8 and 9, hoping to pull

Carolyn Hester, 1961.
— Courtesy Agency for the Performing Arts Publicity Photo.

the concerts off as a record release party for her new Columbia album, but learned about ten days before the concert that it wouldn't be released until May 20. We forged ahead anyway, using the new album's cover photo as the front cover of the concert program. We also arranged for Carolyn's twenty-year-old brother, Dean, to be the opening act. He was a folk and blues singer with a following around The University of Texas campus. It would be fun to have a brother and sister on the same concert.

To complete the celebration, we added a popular young Austin duo named Tommy and Sandy. Following their guest appearance on the Arthur Godfrey CBS show, this pair had recently been taken on by the William Morris Agency and signed a United Artists contract.

Cactus Pryor, KTBC's most popular personality, helped us by talking about Carolyn on his radio and television shows and having her make guest appearances before the concert. The mayor proclaimed "Carolyn Hester Day," and radio stations KASE, KNOW, KTBC-AM-FM, KAZZ-FM, and our own KHFI-FM promoted the homecoming along with John Bustin at the *American-Statesman.*

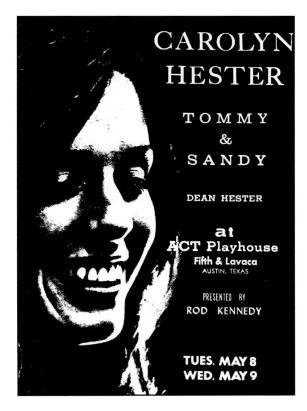

The ACT Concert program cover, May 8–9, 1962.

Meeting with Carolyn about her concert at the ACT, 1962.
— Courtesy Neal Douglas.

The Daily Texan at The University of Texas joined in as well.

A number of copies of Carolyn's Tradition LP were being played by the stations, and Clarence Saegert's Texas Mailing and Printing Company donated the printed program.

The first meeting with Carolyn when she came home in advance of the concert was really a treat. She was an enthusiastic and very genuine person with a gentle way about her. Her lovely long amber hair shined and crowned a classically beautiful face with the warmest smile I'd ever seen. I loved her immediately and looked forward eagerly to the concerts.

The concerts were packed almost to capacity, with 450 attending over the two nights. It was a surprisingly good turnout for weeknights. Just Carolyn's family and relatives alone filled several rows! The concert lived up to its advance promotion, and everyone had a great time. We all agreed the concerts were a terrific experience, although Carolyn wept in the car outside the theater afterward when she learned I had lost $35! I wept with her, not because of the loss, but because I was so moved by her compassion. We bonded right there. Little did I know that this was the beginning of a

long road of artistic successes that could lose money!

When the album came out several weeks after the concert, there was considerable excitement over it in Austin and around the world. A little-known friend of hers named Bob Dylan played harmonica on three cuts, and the album was sparingly produced by John Hammond. Needless to say, the Carolyn Hester album, with her incredibly expressive, bell-like voice and refreshing songs, was heard frequently on KHFI-FM after that, and the Hesters and Kennedys became life-long friends.

In the meantime, at the Texas Capitol complex, the legislative funding and approval moved quickly forward for the Texas Tourist Development Agency to promote the Lone Star State as a tourist destination. Up to this point, the only state funding for tourism had been to the Texas Highway Department's highway maps and beginning construction of tourist information centers at gateway highways into the state. The new TTDA would also begin work, under the direction of Frank Hildebrand, with privately owned Texas attractions and events to coordinate promotion so as to maximize an appealing image of Texas as *the* place to visit.

Also in 1962, the Austin Aqua Festival started as a ten-day civic event sponsored by the Austin Chamber of Commerce to publicize Austin's water resources, including Town Lake in the middle of town and the string of beautiful Highland Lakes. Surveys had shown that most people outside of Texas considered the Lone Star State to be little more than a desert full of sand and cactus.

Among the festival organizers were many of my friends from the Austin Advertising Club, including Ed St. John, Chamber executive Vic

Mathias, dairy executive John Simpson, former UT football star Hub Bechtol, and City Recreation Department director Beverly Sheffield, along with a host of others.

So, of course, I joined my friends in a small way in helping to put the festival together and by organizing the bathing-beauty contest that would select "Miss Austin Aqua Beauty" to represent the festival at special events.

The first festival got off to a good start, and I was especially pleased with our first Miss Austin Aqua Beauty, a sweet and personable young woman from Lockhart, Texas, named Toni Fox. As the 1962 Aqua Beauty, she became an outstanding public relations representative for the new festival, traveling and speaking on behalf of the festival all over the state.

By 1963, I was appointed a vice commodore. This level of "command" in the festival was the leader of a division of events. The Aqua Beauty contest would be my area, and I would have the help of a team of about twenty-five volunteers chosen from my friends and associates. For the 1963 Miss Austin Aqua Beauty, we put together an elaborate showcase called the Dixieland Jubilee, emceed by former KHFI-FM and KAZZ-FM announcer and good friend, Mike Pengra. By that time, he had three or four job titles at the educational channel KLRN-TV9.

We presented tenor banjo player Joe Latting, whom we'd found at a pizza parlor, Chuck Reiley's

Alamo City Jazz Band from San Antonio, which arrived on stage in an antique car, the Austin Chord Rangers barbershop harmony chorus from the SPEBSQSA, and Leon Prima's New Orleans All-Stars, including famed veteran trombonist Emil Christian, who had been a member of the legendary 1918 "Original Dixieland Jass Band" (back before the spelling changed to "Jazz.") Kal Kalladay, an alumnus of the bands of Charlie Spivak, Charlie Barnett, and Stan Kenton, put two local jazz bands together for the finale while he played his "Pocket Cornet," a sawed-off tiny horn which was louder than all the other musicians put together!

A long-legged blond beauty named Cheryl Lyn Scott of Columbus, Texas, won the Miss Austin Aqua Beauty contest, with Toni Fox handing over her title. Cheryl Lyn became another good public relations person for the young festival, and we all learned a lot about her hometown of Columbus.

I had assembled a list of some sixty business sponsors to fund the jubilee and receive VIP seats. The event was paid for, and the sponsors had a fantastic evening. I began to think about what other events I might put together using this kind of sponsorship approach.

In Washington, D.C., in August of 1963, the political leaders continued to feel the increasing pressure of those who were opposed to racial discrimination in American society. One of the most passionate appeals for equality came from Dr. Martin Luther King, Jr., at an August 8 Freedom March involving some 200,000 people. It was here that "I have a dream" became so eloquent an appeal that most people remember the speech and the event as a turning point in American public opinion on the matter of racial equality.

Nineteen-sixty-three was a turning point for me, too, in many ways. I had, by then, brought my fraternity brother Allen Heard into the business and moved KHFI-FM from a failing Audioland into a new expanded space occupying the second floor of Bill Gaston Boats and Motors at 29th and North Lamar. Bill and Dusty Gaston had been good friends for years, and the move would do us all some good. We would not only be in a compatible environment with Bill as our landlord, but his boat dealership, serving the entire Highland Lakes region, would gain extensive publicity with a radio station on board.

When we moved, we upped the power with a new four-bay Andrews antenna mounted on a taller tower, increasing our power considerably. We now also had two studios, one for production and one for on the air. Our larger offices were attractive and provided space for accounting and traffic, which Allen Heard ran, a larger record library for Leonard Masters, and a beautiful continuity and reception area where Nancylee worked, and was later joined by Mrs. C. B. Eleanor Smith.

Also by late 1963, when I was in the advance stages of planning a new week-long music festival for Austin's Zilker Park for 1964, I was approached by a group of businessmen to join them in an effort to put together KHFI-AM-FM-TV, with a UHF television station targeted for completion in 1965.

This association of investors, fifteen in all, came from all strata of business: a concrete block manufacturer, a wholesale marketer of frozen turkey, an insurance agency owner, a newspaper publisher, an international highway contractor, and others. All had three things in common: they were Republicans, they had considerable incomes, and they did not know a lot about the broadcasting business. What they did know was that the combined AM-FM-TV station would be a much more powerful media package than a lone classical music FM station, and that, perhaps, they could balance the public impact of what they perceived was an unfair monopoly held by LBJ's KTBC-TV, Austin's only television station with its triple network affiliations of CBS, ABC, and NBC.

As paperwork, planning, and financial arrangements for the new TV station continued, the group also purchased KASE radio station and moved it from its downtown location to our new building, where it was converted to KHFI-AM 970 as part of the new package.

Allen Heard and I became more and more involved in directing the group toward FCC procedures, recruiting fellow TV and radio people around the city whom we felt would make a good team, and hiring Knocky Willett as one of the team of engineers on the project.

While downtown investors celebrated the ground breaking for the new Crest Hotel at the Congress Avenue bridge over Town Lake, NASA sent Ranger 7 to the moon to send back the first close-up views of the moon's surface. More Ranger missions were to follow as the space administration's plans to send American astronauts to the moon matured. Within a very few years, they would need a much better idea of what the lunar surface was like.

At Southwest Republic Corporation, KHFI-FM's transfer was approved by the FCC, and I was named KHFI-AM-FM-TV vice-president in charge

of sales and promotion, while Allen Heard was named general manager. Leonard Masters was to continue as FM program director.

In the meantime, I continued full time with my FM management chores, sales, promotion and program assignments, as well as extensive on-the-air shifts. I also began to finalize plans for what would become the first KHFI-FM Summer Music Festival at Zilker Park in July of 1964, while becoming more active in the planning and running of the fast growing but still in debt Austin Aqua Festival. It was a busy and exciting time.

Nationally, the popular music scene was dominated by Joan Baez, the Kingston Trio, The Limeliters with their string of RCA albums, and by Peter Paul and Mary who won a Grammy for "If I

Peter Paul and Mary won a Grammy in 1964 for "If I Had a Hammer."

— Courtesy Robert Corwin.

Had a Hammer." They were emerging as the most influential popular music group in the history of American politics.

During this same time, I also continued as an active volunteer in Republican politics, working on local and regional campaigns for the state legislature and the U.S. Congress. I was also a key member of the team working with the Secret Service on the downtown parade route for the Austin appearance of vice-presidential candidate Congressman Bill Miller.

Senator Barry Goldwater, our presidential candidate, and Senator John Tower had already been through Austin several times, and Goldwater had given our TV station plans additional impetus by commenting publicly that it was easy to find Austin from the air as it was the only city of its size in America with only one TV tower.

The invocation of similar humor by Tower in his campaign (he had said, in response to LBJ's running for both president and re-election to his own Senate seat, that "Lyndon was greasing the tracks of the political railroad with Johnson & Johnson oil") was a great relief from the difficulty of trying to establish a two-party state in Texas, where the Democrats had dominated historically.

President John F. Kennedy was coming to Texas escorted by Vice-President Johnson, Governor John Connally, Senator Ralph Yarbrough, and all of the other leaders in Texas Democratic politics. They were to be in Dallas on November 22 and then hit Austin for a big dinner and rally that evening at Municipal Auditorium (later renamed Palmer Auditorium in honor of Mayor Lester Palmer). Because of the scheduled presidential visit, I had canceled an appearance of the Glenn Miller Orchestra in the building for the same date.

On November 22 I was having lunch with Hiram Brown of Cabaniss-Brown Furniture, my stereocast sponsors, when the word reached us that Kennedy had been shot in Dallas. We were shocked and upset, then angry and deeply saddened.

An hour after I returned to KHFI-FM from lunch, I received a call from the Secret Service to come downtown to their outpost at the Stephen F. Austin Hotel. I was suddenly struck with fear because there was wide-spread public reaction to the assassination, and I had been an outspoken critic of Kennedy.

Not knowing what to expect, I went quickly back downtown to the hotel room the Secret Service was using for their outpost and was met at the door by a large shirtsleeved agent wearing a shoulder holster. He told me that he had mistakenly picked up my Stetson at lunch and wanted to return it to me in exchange for his. He had found my business card in my hat band and called me. Of course, I was tremendously relieved and hurried back to the station to retrieve the agent's hat hanging in my office and returned it to him. Before Kennedy arrived in Dallas, Johnson had all of the Secret Service Agents out to the LBJ Ranch for barbecue and presented them all with Stetsons. The agent wanted his treasured hat, and I was glad to oblige.

The tragedies, in-fighting, fear, and fatigue that seemed to accompany all of this took the fun out of politics for me and for many others around me. In fact, the entire nation became a little more cynical and sad during this time.

Things didn't quite return to normal for Texans in politics, and I reimmersed myself in running my FM station, preparing for the AM and TV stations to come, and completing plans for the first Summer Music Festival coming up in eight months.

I had also worked out with our program director, Leonard Masters, a series of twenty-six two-hour 9:00 P.M. Wednesday night "Special Event" programs drawn from our record library. These thematic programs included everything from a United Nations documentary to specials entitled "Benny Goodman—Golden Age of Swing," "Jerome Kern Showcase," "American Composers Hall of Fame—Popular," "Glenn Miller Revisited," "The Best of Gilbert and Sullivan," "Honoring Julie Andrews," "A Musical Tour of Germany," and sixteen others. Sponsored by the Nighthawk Restaurants, they ran from September 20, 1963, to March 14, 1964, and drew good comments from our audience, while giving the newspapers something they could understand to write about.

Our normal program week was devoted to eighty-five percent classical music, and, while five of the twenty-six shows were classical ("The Symphonic Poem," "The Sea Set to Music," "An Evening With Morton Gould," and others), the bulk of these thematic programs contrasted with the customary classical fare and broadened our listenership.

On May 30, 1964, *The Saturday Evening Post*, one of the nation's biggest and most read national magazines, published a feature story on the American folk singers who were becoming popular favorites through their recordings, concerts, and appearances on national television. My friend Carolyn Hester was among those cited, and her picture was on the front cover! In spite of folk songs and folk stars on the hit lists and on TV shows like ABC's "Hullabaloo," the magazine described, perhaps rightly, the current national interest across the country as a "folk music fad."

By February 1964, the pop music audience was excited about the anticipated appearance on the 7th by the English quartet The Beatles, who appeared

—Courtesy of *The Saturday Evening Post.*

Austin Symphony Orchestra conductor Ezra Rachlin and I look over the Zilker Hillside Theater setting for the 1964 KHFI-FM Summer Music Festival.
— Courtesy F. W. Schmidt.

first on the "Ed Sullivan Show" and then started their national tour at Carnegie Hall on February 12. In spite of the fact that Peter Paul and Mary won another Grammy in 1964 as the Best Group for "Blowin' In The Wind," The Beatles' arrival signaled that a major change in pop music was also blowing in the wind and that, perhaps, folk music had run its commercial course, at least for now.

The year 1964 finally saw the debut of my KHFI-FM Summer Music Festival, which played at the city's Zilker Hillside Theater for six nights of free concerts, July 13-18.

The outdoor theater had been built in 1937 and had been operated by the City Recreation Department for twenty-seven years. Our festival, under the sponsorship of local businesses, was the first effort in all those years to provide professional concerts free of charge to the community. Most of the entertainment at the park had been civic or amateur variety shows, band concerts, nature films, and ambitious productions of musicals starring local talent.

My approach, instead, was to organize six concerts of different kinds of music performed by over 130 professional musicians and singers from all over Texas and the U.S. I sold packages of radio spots on

KHFI-FM to fifty advertisers who were listed in the pre-festival brochures, and who had complimentary tickets to distribute to the public, which brought traffic into their stores. Even though the concerts were free, the tickets acted as an invitation to attend and a reminder of the concert times and formats.

I had Austin artist Ed Triggs design a neo-classical figure, nicknamed "Arky," holding a harp, as our festival logo. A variation of that original design is still used in the nineties as the Kerrville Music Foundation logo.

Monday night was folk music, headlined by Carolyn Hester, Mance Lipscomb, and Sam "Lightnin'" Hopkins, along with John Lomax, Jr., Segle Fry, and

Maestro Rachlin and I with our festival logo "Arky," 1964.
— Courtesy F. W. Schmidt.

29

Navasota bluesman Mance Lipscomb at the Summer Music Festival, 1964.
— Courtesy F. W. Schmidt.

Austin Mayor Lester Palmer welcomes the crowd at the Summer Music Festival, 1964.
— Courtesy F. W. Schmidt.

The crowd at Zilker Hillside Theater, 1964.
— Courtesy F. W. Schmidt.

a duo called Mickey and Marty. The 8:00 P.M. concert drew over 5,000 well-behaved fans, breaking the all-time attendance record at the Zilker Hillside Theater.

Mance Lipscomb and Lightnin' Hopkins, while both being Texas country bluesmen, had totally different personalities. Mance was a gentleman, a life-long sharecropper from Navasota who, at the age of sixty-five, made more money in that year playing his music for college kids and folk music fans than he had earned in all of his years as a cotton field worker. He was still unspoiled and gentle and spent most of the money putting his kids, nephews, nieces, and grandkids through school. He was an innovative bottle-neck blues player who used, instead, a pocket knife, to fret his strings. Mance never had a bad thing to say about anyone. The worst thing I ever heard him say was, "That Lightnin' Hopkins, he only plays in one key, I plays in four."

Lightnin', on the other hand, was a hard-drinking performer who, most of the time, played blitzed. Dressed in a black suit, he ate dinner with John Lomax and me at the hotel, where we could keep an eye on him before the performance so he could appear sober. Lightnin' got up from the table to get some cigarettes from the drugstore in the hotel and neither Lomax nor I remembered that the drugstore had a small liquor department. But when Lightnin' got into the van and breathed on us, it was obvious that he had imbibed quickly on a pint in his coat pocket. So much for careful supervision. Lomax should have known, as he was the man who got Lightnin' out of prison in Sugarland and helped start his performing career. Lightnin's show, while interspersed with long stories about long black cars

Summer Music Festival brochure art by editorial cartoonist Hartley.

The Ed Gerlach Orchestra from Houston at Zilker Park, 1964.
— Courtesy F. W. Schmidt.

with big white-wall tires, was filled with great music and the crowd loved it. In fact, the whole night was a fulfilling success.

The next night we presented traditional jazz by Chuck Reiley's Alamo City Jazz Band, with special guest, noted baritone sax star Ernie Caceras, whom I'd heard so many times on Eddie Condon's Commodore Records. In the second half of the evening, we featured modern jazz by Ed Gerlach's Orchestra, "The Big Band From Texas," with soloists formerly of the Gulf Coast Giants of Jazz. Another huge crowd and standing ovations greeted this concert.

Choral music was on the menu for Wednesday night, with The University of Texas Men's Glee Club under the direction of Jim Woodle. A portion of the evening was devoted to American-born concert

Chuck Reiley (trombone) and his Alamo City Jazz Band, 1964.
— Courtesy F. W. Schmidt.

pianist Lucien Lemieux playing Bach, Scarlatti, Mozart, Chopin, and Gershwin. The crowd loved it.

Thursday night presented a fourteen-piece "Festival Stage Band" led by Kal Kalladay, with vocal and instrumental soloists in an evening of music by Cole Porter, Leonard Bernstein, Jerome Kern, and others. It was an evening of good listening well per-

Kal Kalloday leads the Festival Stage Band in music by Cole Porter, 1964.

— Courtesy F. W. Schmidt.

formed by local musicians especially rehearsed for the occasion.

The Friday night program offered an evening of chamber music played by the "Festival String Quartet" made up of Austin and Houston Symphony concert masters and other first chair players. For the finale, Austin Symphony conductor Ezra Rachlin was the pianist in the Schubert "Trout" Quintet with bassist Keith Robinson. Considering the limited appeal of chamber music in the general scheme of things, it was a big turnout, and High Fidelity Inc.'s subtle sound reinforcement allowed the entire crowd to enjoy every nuance of the intimate music played.

The finale for the entire festival was Saturday night's "Festival Orchestra" concert. The twenty-member ensemble was recruited, rehearsed, and conducted by Ezra Rachlin with eleven-year-old Mary Davis as soloist in the Haydn D major Piano Concerto. It was another totally successful concert evening, with warm and appreciative applause and encores called for from the large audience.

According to the City of Austin Parks and

John Lomax, Jr., at the festival, 1964. Note his log and ax in the background.

— Courtesy F. W. Schmidt.

Recreation Department, the official estimated total attendance for the six nights was 15,518!

Mayor Lester Palmer, who officially opened the festival, joined many other city officials in commending the event. Reviewer John Bustin of the *Austin American-Statesman* gave the festival rave reviews, and it earned tremendous publicity for KHFI-FM in the Houston, San Antonio, and

The finale by the Festival Orchestra, conducted by Ezra Rachlin, 1964.

— Courtesy F. W. Schmidt.

Corpus Christi dailies, as well as *The Denver Post* and New York's nationally circulated magazine, *Musical America.*

We couldn't have been happier, and not only did we begin to talk about a 1965 event, but I thought I'd call George Wein in New York to see if he could bring his Newport Jazz Festival All-Stars to Austin as part of the festival in 1965.

Right after the Zilker Park success, I was drawn busily into the third annual Austin Aqua Festival as a vice-commodore in charge of the Miss Austin Aqua Beauty pageant, which was becoming an important part of the festival as it grew in reputation and public acceptance.

The festival took place in early August with character actor Ken Curtis, the sidekick "Festus" on television's "Gunsmoke," as honorary commodore and visiting host of the pageant at Festival Beach, east of the Interstate-35 bridge on the north shore of Town Lake.

City Recreation director Beverly Sheffield put the show together under festival president Ed St. John and his Commodore, Colonel Vance Murphy, who had been the Bergstrom Air Force Base Commander from 1954-1958. Reigning Aqua Beauty Cheryl Lyn Scott of Columbus presented the 1964 title to San Marcos entrant Carol Lou Holt.

Competing with the pageant across town was the Festival Grand Ole Opry Show, starring Roger Miller, Ernest Tubb, Slim Whitman, Sonny James, Dave Dudley, and Claude King. Admission tickets were $1.75!

KHFI-FM kept a high profile during the festival by providing "live" broadcast coverage of the Aqua Festival Texas Spokes Sports Car Club Gymkhana, a medium-high-speed event with all types and sizes of sports cars running in classes against the clock for best time through a challenging course. I drove the KHFI-FM MG roadster, getting it up on two wheels several times. We decided to install a roll bar for the next event.

Following the Aqua Festival, I plowed right back into my full-time FM radio schedule and the growing effort to launch Austin's second TV station early in 1965. My job was to begin intensive efforts to interest radio and television wholesale

Three-wheeling the MG-TD after installing the roll bar, 1964.

— Courtesy Virgil Johnson.

houses and their dealers to promote the sales of thousands of inexpensive UHF converters, which, attached to a TV, would allow one to tune into the new station.

"Watch for Channel 42 in 1965 with a $29.95 converter," and "Coming soon on Austin's new 42, the Jimmy Dean Show!" "Don't Miss It!" "Get UHF-TV now!"

While there was no picture on the TV screen yet, our new building on 19th Street was well under construction and was the first tangible evidence for the public that this miracle station was actually going to happen. The first of our operations to move into the building was the former KASE Radio, which moved from the Perry Brooks Building downtown. It became KHFI-AM-970, with popular former KTBC personality Dan Love and our new staff on the air promoting daily the forthcoming TV channel, with a few plugs on the side for the existing FM station.

By now, KTBC-FM, owned by Lady Bird Johnson, had joined KHFI-FM and KAZZ-FM on the air, so we were looking forward to moving our FM station into the new building, where we already had FCC approval to triple its power. Nineteen-sixty-five would mean that we could finally launch our triple package of KHFI-AM-FM-TV. I had some fun and exciting promotional plans for the kick off and couldn't wait to spring them on the public and our competition.

THE TELEVISION YEARS

(1965–1967)

By January 2, 1965, the final touches were being made in the new TV studios, new color cameras were unpacked, nearly 100 light fixtures had arrived to be hung overhead on the grid, and the news, sports, and weather sets were under construction.

We assembled a great broadcast staff team by joining FM programmer Leonard Masters, with KASE-AM manager John Krieger and Bill Simpson as sales manager. Many of the TV personalities, including sports anchor Mel Pennington, doubled on the AM station. Charles Stewart headed up the news department.

Dan Love had come from Houston's KPRC-TV, following his long stint at KTBC, and he brought TV program director Ridge Radney with him. Former Broadway scenic-designer Lyle Hendricks came over from The University of Texas to design and build the sets, rear screen units, and trade show booths. Outside artist Ed Triggs assisted us in realizing billboards, logos, signs, promotional slides, and other art work.

Our chief engineer, Al Beck, who built the TV station from the ground up in five and a half months, joined us from a six-year run as chief engineer at KGBT and had previously built three other TV stations and a weather radar installation. Women's "Coffee Time" hostess Maimie St. George joined us from Arizona, and an attractive young blond became children's personality "Miss Pinafore."

While KTAL-TV, Shreveport, was the former home of TV sales manager Joe Foster, our on-the-air weatherman, Bill Richardson, came to us from KLBK-TV in Lubbock.

We were a quickly melded and enthusiastic team!

Then, right in the middle of our dash to success, my former partner, fraternity brother, and best man, Allen Heard, resigned from the station and went on active duty in the army from his reserve status in the ROTC. He was having some serious personal problems and left Ginny and the kids behind, eventually serving in Vietnam. No explanation was ever given, and I sure missed having him to talk with about our exciting future.

While the physical facilities were coming together, I continued to deal daily with the national press who followed the impending debut of our new TV station in the market historically dominated by Lyndon Johnson's lone channel with its primary CBS affiliation and its first choice of ABC and NBC programs.

Most media representatives were looking for a political bomb to throw, and I threaded my way carefully through the barrage of questions, feigning normal procedural progress, on a daily basis.

Behind the scenes, our Washington lawyers were complaining of restraint of trade before the Federal Trade Commission and the Federal Communications Commission.

At the same time, our corporate officers and TV general manager, Dan Love, continued constant negotiations with the networks for programming, while also buying film rights to fill the inevitable gaps left by our not having a primary network affiliation.

While keeping a flow of stories going to the press about the TV station under construction, I hired twenty-five-year-old Tracy Barnes, a Minneapolis-based balloonist holding five world altitude records, to bring his hot air balloon to Austin for a press luncheon and tethered flights at Municipal

Auditorium during the January 22-24 Boat and Travel Show. His balloon had a huge KHFI-TV42 logo on it, and inside the show we had a booth to promote the sale of UHF converters. Barnes was a good public relations man for us, and the promotion attracted massive press and public attention.

Gradually the networks confirmed shows that were not being carried by KTBC-TV and, in spite of the news being dominated by LBJ's struggle to deal with the Vietnam War, we earned prominent local and national coverage almost daily. The Texas media were on it constantly, and we also earned coverage from *The New York Times*, *The Philadelphia Inquirer*, *The Chicago Tribune*, *The Long Island News Day*, and many other major metropolitan dailies. Radio and television interviews were a regular part of my daily life.

By February 1, I stepped up the local publicity campaign to announce the acquisition of four ABC shows. On February 5, Dan Love announced four more ABC shows, and on the 6th we announced a target sign-on date of February 12.

On February 7, I had a full-page advertisement in the *Austin American-Statesman* announcing "The Bing Crosby Show" (ABC), children's personality "Captain Kangaroo" (CBS), "The Virginian" (NBC), and our own "Dan Love News 42" and "Saturday Racing Special" (sports car films).

Key programs to establishing Channel 42 included Walter Cronkite's five day a week "CBS Evening News," the NBC "Tonight Show" with Johnny Carson, and the newly established Houston Astros Baseball Network from the new Astrodome in Houston. The locally produced "Carolyn Hester Show" would air in March.

Dealers began running more advertising and stories to promote converting to UHF. Some converters were available now at only $15.95, and we would soon see if public discontent with one channel was real or not.

We believed that there were fewer than 3,000 homes capable of receiving our UHF signal prior to the beginning of our promotion, so we had a long way to go to provide a large enough audience to justify spending advertising dollars with us. However, by the time we signed on, we had converted an estimated 20,000 homes to UHF.

We also began a teaser campaign of newspaper and billboard advertising utilizing our cute platinum-colored registered Cocker Spaniel puppy. I figured we needed to reach the women and children to get conversions and that Punch, our station mas-

Showing television distributors and dealers a model of our forty-eight-foot spectacular billboard, 1964.

— Courtesy F. W. Schmidt.

cot, would certainly do that. Our slogans were "Dog-gone Good Television," "A Nose for News," and "Your Constant Companion." One spectacular forty-eight-foot billboard had a huge eighteen-foot-high cutout of Punch with a nodding head. We first put on the board "Dog," then "Dog-gone," then "Dog-gone Good," and finally "Dog-gone Good Television." People were fascinated as every three or four days another word was added. Then, of course, the board became a big Channel 42 advertisement with a changeable marquee panel showing the week's featured promotion.

On February 12, 1965, Bob Wills and his Texas Playboys played at the Skyline Club, but none of us got to see them. It was a busy and historic day for Austin, as KHFI-TV42 signed on with much fanfare. An expanded *Austin American-Statesman* had literally a dozen pages of stories and congratulatory advertisements.

Signing on at 7:30 P.M. with all sorts of celebrities, civic leaders, and government officials, including an FCC commissioner, in attendance, Dan Love introduced all of our TV personalities and staff.

At 8:00 P.M., the Warner Brothers musical *Pajama Game*, with Doris Day and John Raitt, was our first Saturday Night Movie, followed by our first 10:00 P.M. "News Final 42." The debut evening concluded with the ninety-minute colorcast of NBC's "Tonight Show" with Johnny Carson.

We were off and running, and we all celebrated as our signal blanketed 11,000 square miles of Central

Texas from our 1,199-foot tall tower—Texas' tallest. Austin now had two television stations!

In the days that followed, in spite of all the television excitement, our FM station continued its unique community service to the arts by staging its fourth annual Philadelphia Academy of Vocal Arts auditions at the Texas Federation of Women's Clubs at 24th and San Gabriel.

In the first three years, we had two national winners and one national finalist. The prizes in the national competition were one-year renewable scholarships to the thirty-one-year-old academy, and the academy provided finalists with an all-expense-paid trip to Philly for the finals. While Frederika Wisehart, a KHFI-FM entry from Austin, was the winner in 1962, Carolyn Hefner was a national finalist in 1963, and Ryan H. Edwards won the scholarship in 1964.

With everything else going on, I was appointed commodore of the Aqua Festival by festival president Vance Murphy. The commodore is the working volunteer leader of all the various vice-commodores and their captain's teams. By now, the ten-day festival had expanded to sixty events and hundreds of volunteers. I named Duplex Advertising's Steve Price to take over the Aqua Beauty event.

I also continued a slow retreat from local political activity as my friend Beryl Milburn resigned after nine years on the State Republican Executive Committee. She was the official who first called me to help on the John Tower campaign years before. I needed to back out of some of my activities and concentrate not only on the Aqua Festival but also on the KHFI-FM Summer Music Festival, which would precede it by a month.

Outside of work, I was adding to my ARKAY Vintage Racing collection of early racing and sports cars. I started with the 1951 MG-TD, which I kept when Allen and I transferred the rest of KHFI-FM's assets to our new Southwest Republic Corporation.

Joining the MG in the fledgling collection was a 1918 Model T Frontenac-Ford dirt-track racing car restored to mint condition and assigned the number 12. It won a second place trophy in its first showing in the 1965 Austin Autocapades at the Auditorium.

The Fronty-Ford was acquired from a man named Bruce Simister, who restored it, but not much was known about the origins of the car. It was believed to have raced throughout the southwest dirt-track circuit during the years 1918-1928.

At the wheel of the old Fronty-Ford dirt-track car.
— Courtesy ARKAY Vintage Team Publicity Photo.

It had been rebuilt several times and had components from most of those post-World War I years, the latest equipment being 1927 Model T wheels. The Frontenac overhead valve conversion was designed and sold by the Chevrolet Brothers and made the old Model T's capable of speeds exceeding 100 miles per hour.

The other car acquired during this period was a 1939 Morgan Supersport three-wheeler, the last of the British-made two-cylinder sports cars. It was the only one of its kind in Texas and one of only six known cars of its type in the U.S.

The Morgan was powered by a large Matchless motorcycle engine, which provided plenty of pep. Other three-wheeled Morgans often had Japanese motorcycle engines. This car was British Racing Green, and we added a bright yellow racing stripe,

Our 1939 Morgan three-wheeler displayed with yellow jackets and green berets at the 1965 Autocapades.
— Courtesy ARKAY Vintage Team Publicity Photo.

the ARKAY Vintage Team decals, and the number 32 on both sides. At the rear, capping off its tubular-shaped body, was the spare wheel and tire. The two wheels in front steered the car and the single rear wheel powered it. It was pretty stable, although I had it up on two wheels more than once running it in gymkhanas. The Morgan appeared in two shows, winning two trophies, and I drove it in two gymkhanas, where it was the curiosity of those events. When the headlight lenses fell out from the vibration of its Matchless engine, I decided to protect it a little by using it a bit more gently. It still wore its British license plate HJO 401.

During 1964 and 1965, we took monthly breaks from our heavy radio and television schedules to take our vintage cars and my 1965 Mustang GT to auto shows, gymkhanas, high-speed autocross events on abandoned military airports, and to sanctioned hill climbs.

All of our team cars were sponsored by Sinclair Oil and ran their decals in return for cash, oil, and other support. The 1965 Aqua Festival Gymkhana drew sixty-five entries and over 1,000 spectators, a fair indication of the popularity of speed events, and a thirty-minute special on it was televised by our new Channel 42 mobile unit.

The second music festival at Zilker Park was set for July 12-17, and the six-night event would again encompass folk music, instrumental jazz, a choral concert, piano and vocal jazz, chamber music, and a final evening featuring our Festival Orchestra.

Even though many of our FM advertisers were also being tapped by our expanded sales staff to advertise on KHFI-AM radio and television, we kept all but a handful of our original Summer Music Festival sponsors, so I could spend most of my time putting the concerts together, contacting the artists, and generating publicity.

The opening night folk concert headlined nationally known Tom Paxton, Southwestern balladeer Brownie McNeil, singer-collector Roger Abrahams, father and son black blues musicians Teodar and T. J. Jackson, and the Dallas County Jug Band. This young aggregation included Mike Murphey, Segle Fry, Steve Fromholz, and others.

Paxton was one of the best known of the new generation of folk songwriter-performers, and the *New York Times* described him as "a superb melodist, using tunes that ring original and familiar." Among those familiar new songs of Paxton's was his "I Can't Help But Wonder Where I'm

Twenty-seven-year-old Tom Paxton at the 1965 Summer Music Festival.

— Courtesy Glass Studio.

Bound," which had already been recorded by the Chad Mitchell Trio, Carolyn Hester, the Au-Go-Go Singers, and by Paxton himself.

Carolyn Hester had recorded other Paxton songs too, including "Mama's Tough Little Soldier," which she introduced to 5,000 Austin fans at the previous year's Zilker Hillside festival. Paxton's "Every Time" was also on a Hester album.

Paxton could write a sharp-tongued topical ballad with the best of them, but he also had a wonderful gift for melody and a flair for writing songs of warm, tender romanticism.

He had been a big hit at the 1963 Newport Folk Festival, where Vanguard had recorded his performance of his best-known song, "Ramblin' Boy," along with his "The Willing Conscript." He also had an album of his songs on the Elektra label.

Two months before coming to Austin, he was among a large group of American folk singers who took England by storm. Through coincidence more than anything else, England was treated, in a single week, to personal appearances by Joan Baez, Theodore Bikel, Carolyn Hester, Bob Dylan, and Tom Paxton. All were in the British Isles plugging their best-selling recordings, doing guest spots on British radio and TV, singing concerts, and filling London club dates.

Paxton was originally from Woody Guthrie's home state of Oklahoma, and where Guthrie was one of the driving forces behind the socially oriented songwriting of the decade 1938-1948, Paxton had been hailed as a leader of the "folk song renaissance" of the 1960s, and a principal originator of the new cycle of folk songwriting.

At twenty-seven, Paxton was living in New York City and told the press, "I think protest songs are very healthy. We all have gripes, and I think it's great to get them out of our system."

He viewed Bob Dylan as the true genius of the age and cited Carolyn Hester as his favorite female folk singer because of her deep personal warmth and earthy sensitivity.

On Tuesday night, true to his word, George Wein brought his Newport Jazz Festival All-Star Quintet to town. Joining pianist Wein were Bud Freeman, *saxophone*, Ruby Braff, *cornet*, Cody Sandifer, *drums*, and Don Jones, *bass*. Opening for them was Maurice Wilson's twenty-piece stage band of local teenagers.

Left to right: Ruby Braff (cornet), Don Jones (bass), and Bud Freeman (sax) of the Newport All-Stars, 1965.
— Courtesy Allen Simmons.

Prior to his arrival in Austin, Wein had already recorded for the Atlantic, Victor, Columbia, Impulse, Smash, and United Artists labels and was internationally recognized as the world's leading jazz impresario. He had produced festivals in Newport, Tokyo, Paris, Berlin, Scandinavia, Pittsburgh, and elsewhere.

Jazz saxophone pioneer Bud Freeman was one of the world's most revered jazz musicians, a true jazz immortal who had been a frequent winner of *Downbeat* and *Metronome* polls as the top U.S. saxophonist. A real gentleman, always immaculately dressed, he had, in forty years, recorded for every major jazz label and played with such important jazz groups as the Tommy Dorsey and Benny Goodman organizations.

Cornetist Ruby Braff, the 1965 *Downbeat* "Critic's Award" winner, had been the critics' choice as best young cornet player in jazz for over ten years. He had appeared at jazz festivals all over the world, including Great Britain, France, Germany, Scandinavia, Italy, and Holland. For his Austin appearance, Braff flew in directly from a European concert date.

The Newport Jazz Festival All-Star Quintet had recently appeared at Newport, Pittsburgh, and Ohio Valley, completed two European tours, and played college concert dates on twenty-two campuses, including Dartmouth, Yale, Harvard, and Syracuse. Their Texas appearance was a renewal celebration of my friendship with Wein from eighteen years before when I was president of the Jazz Club of Boston in college.

The quintet was a big hit, playing to over 5,000 enthusiastic fans, and the press described them as "possibly the outstanding musical talent to be presented in Austin this year."

Before the concert, we had thrown a press party for Wein and the quintet, so the press already felt that they knew each of them on a first-name basis.

The Wednesday evening choral concert was also impressive, with ensembles, solos, and duets by Austin's best professional and amateur voices under the direction of Dr. Morris Beachy. J. Frank Elsass joined them as trumpet soloist in a Dello Joio work, and Barbara Carson directed the *corps de ballet* of the Austin Ballet Society.

Our concert pianist for Wednesday evening was a young contest winner from Equador named Joyce Arce. She had already appeared with the Miami and Dallas Symphony Orchestras and was in Austin studying with Dalies Franz at UT. Response from the audience was warm, and approval was spontaneous as she took several bows for her performance.

The Thursday night jazz concert presented three of the great traditional jazz pianists from across the nation and focused on the differences in style between Chicago's famed White Russian legend Art Hodes, stride piano star Ralph Sutton from San Francisco, and Corpus Christi's swinging Red Camp.

Getting Art Hodes down from Chicago was a real victory for me. I had been an avid fan of his for years and had visited with him several times in Chicago. He had been nationally recognized in the blues piano field since the 1920s and had been described by one critic as "the greatest white piano jazz stylist playing anywhere today."

Hodes played in the 1920s with a band which featured trumpeter Wingy Manone, drummer Gene Krupa, saxophonist Bud Freeman, and the legendary clarinet star Frank Teschemacher. He jammed with Benny Goodman, Louis Armstrong, Jack Teagarden, Sidney Bechet, Eddie Condon, and others. His "Backroom Blues" on Bluenote Records was a personal favorite of mine, and he wrote for *Downbeat*, co-edited a jazz magazine, and was a jazz lecturer and moderator of a radio jazz show.

The three pianists together were sensational in their contrasting styles, and at the end of the concert I rolled out three pianos for them to take turns outdoing each other, backing each other, and trading keyboard licks during an extended and surprisingly musical jam session. The crowd was knocked out and screamed for more.

The Friday night chamber music recital of Haydn and Turina quartets and a Brahms quintet was played by members of the Houston Symphony, including concertmaster Rafael Fliegel, *first violin*; George Bennett, *second violin*; Leonard Gibbs, *viola*; and Carl Fasshauer, *cello*, with Austin's Ezra

Three great traditional jazz pianists in finale. From left: Red Camp, Art Hodes, and Ralph Sutton.
— Courtesy Glass Studio.

Rachlin joining them as pianist in the finale, the Brahms Quintet for Piano and Strings. It was another stirring chamber music experience marked by extraordinary audience response.

Rachlin returned to the podium on Saturday night to conduct the twenty-four-member Festival Orchestra in the music of Mozart, Haydn, Bach, and others to close out the festival.

Rachlin's continued enthusiastic participation in the event was particularly gratifying to me since, in addition to conducting the Austin Symphony concert season, he had accepted that summer the leadership of the Houston Summer Symphony, a new post with the Fort Worth Symphony Orchestra, and the forthcoming KHFI-FM/*Austin American-Statesman* co-sponsored Dollar Pops Concert in August. He also had composed my "Festival Fanfare" on commission from the station and was my constant advisor on the classical evenings.

His concert at Zilker Park included Bach's "Sheep May Safely Graze," which was the popular sign-off theme for KHFI-FM every night. The well-received concert program also included, among other things, a Mozart overture and the Haydn Symphony No. 88.

The Summer Music Festival was again a great success, with crowds breaking attendance records at the theater. It was a pleasure to produce and a real joy to be working with so many talented artists from so many different musical disciplines.

We recorded the entire six nights of the Summer Music Festival with plans to broadcast it as part of the Austin Symphony fund drive on KHFI-FM in October.

The festival was now a major part of KHFI's community relations program, and Newport's George Wein became fired up with the Austin area. Before he left town, we talked seriously about establishing an annual jazz festival in Austin with him as producer, and we vowed to get on it right away.

I jumped from the Summer Music Festival to the fourth annual Austin Aqua Festival, where sixty events were scheduled during the festival's ten-day run. In addition to mandatory appearances as commodore at the kick-off luncheon, the land parade up Congress Avenue, and the water parade on Town Lake, there was a "Fun Frolic" with Chuck Reiley's Alamo City Jazz Band and contrasting country music by Pete Drake and his Western Band. Due to rain, the August 8 Aquacade preliminaries were postponed to the evening of the August 11 finals.

At the Southwest Drag Boat Races, colorful teams such as oil well firefighter Red Adair's drew huge crowds to Festival Beach. He and his team were quite a sight in their red overalls, red Cadillacs, and red racing boats hauled in large luxurious red vans.

On the night of the Aqua Beauty finals, hosted by reigning Aqua Beauty Rocky Tomkins, an interesting problem arose when my favorite contestant, Vicki Hudson, was unable to wear her shoes due to having dropped a scuba tank on her foot. In spite of the specific contest rules calling for high-heeled shoes, and following a long discussion in which all the rest of the competitors offered also to compete without shoes, it was finally decided that only Vicki would compete bare footed, and she won.

Vicki was a lovely young woman with penetrating gray-green eyes and soft, black hair in a feathercut. Long, tanned legs drew attention to a slim and graceful and perfectly proportioned body, and she had an engaging and genuine smile. Working with Vicki during the coming year would be a rewarding experience I anticipated with enthusiasm.

The same night as the Aqua Beauty finals, the Festival Western Show was staged in the Municipal Auditorium starring Eddy Arnold, Willie Nelson, Don Bowman and Wade Ray. Tickets were $2 for adults and $1 for children, and the crowd was so large I was amazed anyone was left to go to the Aqua Beauty event. But by this fourth year, it seemed that there was a large turnout for everything on the festival schedule.

This was certainly true when the KHFI-TV/*Austin American-Statesman*-sponsored Dollar Pops Concert by the Austin Symphony sold out. The concert marked the six-month anniversary of the television station's sign-on. The music, conducted by Ezra Rachlin, was by Von Suppe, Schubert, Strauss, Copland, Barber, and Bernstein.

The final Aqua Festival weekend was filled with sports car racing around the Municipal Auditorium on the city streets during the Carrera de la Capitol III. Volkswagen dealer C. B. Smith, Jr., was the vice-commodore in charge of the event, and retired Col. Joe McCrosky, who loved racing his number zero Formula Vee open-wheeled racing car, was the Sports Car Club of America race chairman.

I had several cars displayed in the infield vintage and collectors car show, including our white MG-TD. Other cars displayed were John Mecom Jr.'s "Hussein I" sports racing car named for his friend King Hussein of Jordan, MGs, Alfa Romeos, Ferraris, a 1937 Cord, a Mustang dragster, a Shelby Mustang GT350, a Rolls Royce, and a JXK Allard with a Cadillac engine.

At the Admiral's Ball, G. G. McCuistion, the 1965 Queen, placed the jeweled tiara on the head of newly named 1966 Queen Chica Grey.

The 1965 Aqua Festival was everything we wanted it to be, drawing literally thousands of visitors to Austin and giving hometown people something to celebrate together. But we needed to do something very soon to get the operation into the black. While the attendance and income were up, and the debt from the previous years was shrinking, we were still confronted with bank loans to pay off and set our sights on that ambitious goal.

The schedule on our television station still had huge gaps in it. Broadcasting eighteen hours a day, seven days a week without a primary network affiliation, there were many open hours to fill. Films and special productions like the automobile racing series took up some of the slack, but we needed to produce large blocks of our own programming. We also felt that if we produced the right programs with intense local appeal, we could speed up the conversion of more homes to UHF.

When everyone on our management and programming teams agreed with this vision, we embarked on what was probably the greatest local television production schedule ever seen. In addition to twelve hours of news, sports, and weather each week, five hours of "live" children's programming featuring some film cartoons, five hours of "Coffee Break" morning programming in the studio featuring live guests, interviews on coming events, cooking and homemaking insights, and limited film features, I started producing a thirteen-week, thirty-minute show starring Carolyn Hester with guest musicians. When that series was in the can and on the air, we worked on developing a mobile television unit, built into a trailer, to take our cameras and crews to every possible local event of interest we could get permission to televise. The arrival of new color videotape machines would make the task easier, and we looked forward to getting it into operation.

Soon I went to work putting the team together for staging the Fifth Anniversary 1966 Austin Aqua Festival. As its new president, I thought I had a chance to refocus the philosophical approach of the festival leadership and also, perhaps, create some feature or attraction which could pull the event out of debt and put it, finally, in the profit column.

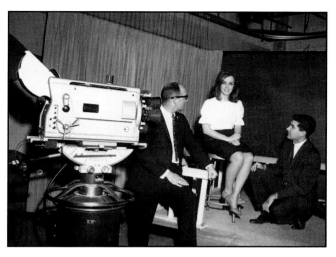

Carolyn Hester on the Channel 42 set. 1966.
— Courtesy KHFI-TV Publicity Photo.

The original motivation for developing a city-wide festival was to create a massive schedule of activities that would attract attention to Austin and celebrate its water resources. It was a chamber of commerce approach to sell the public, near and far, on a new and more enticing image of Austin. In place of the stereotypical view of Central Texas as a sand and cactus movie backdrop, we hoped to project the reality of rolling green hills and attractive lakes that ran right through the middle of town and into the surrounding Hill Country. It had even been reinforced by the renaming of the dammed-up portion of the Colorado River running through Austin as Town Lake.

With the water ski championships, the drag boat races, and the water parade all amplifying the image of plenty of water, the original goals of the civic leaders were being realized, and hundreds of thousands of tourists arrived each August to celebrate Austin and her lakes.

But for me, the real value of the festival was the breaking down of barriers between the many social, economic, political, and ethnic segments of the community. The stratification of city life had always bothered me, and I saw in the festival a golden opportunity for commerce and community to come together at many levels.

Somehow, I always had friends and warm relationships with many people from widely divergent walks of life. The potential of dissolving all those invisible boundaries made me believe in the possibilities for great cross-cultural involvement with people who were not a part of my normal daily life.

I thought that it could be important and re-warding for business owners and employees to work on the same projects and for East Austin and West Austin to sit down at the same table to plan and execute successful events together. It was really satisfying to see the learning experiences enjoyed by executives who were being shown the practical ways to accomplish the thousands of tasks at ground level that needed to succeed in order for an entire event to reach realization.

The warmth and excitement generated by working with people of differing social backgrounds, income, and educational levels was most rewarding and indicative of a growing tolerance and regard for people different from ourselves. This began, through the Aqua Festival, to be a growing sense of community. It was fun, and everyone was helping everyone else.

There was considerable excitement and positive energy within the East Austin black and Mexican-American civic organizations when I first invited them to submit Aqua Beauty contestants for the festival. While that move was not immediately greeted with unanimous approval by my West Austin compatriots, Chamber Manager Vic Mathias supported me, and eventually the inclusion of all Austin citizens, regardless of ethnic or social background, became the norm.

I named Ken Brown of the Brown Schools as our commodore with the full support of Col. Vance Murphy. Ken was an educated, fair-thinking, and broad-minded individual who always seemed to grasp the ideals I had for having the festival serve to bring the whole city together by breaking down the walls of prejudice.

In the midst of all the logistical planning for the 1966 festival, work had to proceed for promoting Channel 42. Suddenly, *"POW! BAP!"* I had a flash of inspiration for creating a festival event that had the potential for being that keystone event I was looking for.

A new twice-weekly television series drawn from the *Batman* comics was creating all kinds of excitement as producer William Dozier convinced major stars to appear on the show in the roles of the various villains. These were remarkable characters, and the stars were standing in line to play them.

Before too many installments had aired, former Miss America Lee Ann Meriwether had played Catwoman, Latin lover Cesar Romero played The Joker, television's comic impressionist Frank Gorshin played The Riddler, and Burgess Meredith, a well-respected character actor from films and

41

Broadway, played The Penguin. With Adam West as Batman and Burt Ward as Robin, and the special effects team reproducing the comic book "balloons" with exclamations like *"Pow!," "Wham!," and "Boom!,"* the melodramatic scripts and campy directing made *Batman* the national joke that had America laughing.

Taken at the Hollywood Studios, this staged publicity shot with Adam West subtly focuses on the coming Austin Aqua Festival. 1966.

— Courtesy 20th Century Fox Publicity.

From left: Burgess Meredith (The Penguin), Frank Gorshin (The Riddler), Lee Meriwether (Cat Woman), and Cesar Romero (The Joker) as the villains in the film Batman. *1966.*

— Courtesy 20th Century Fox Publicity.

At the same time Batman was hitting television, William Dozier was working on a full-length film. I wanted the world premiere of that movie as the center piece for the 1966 Fifth Anniversary Aqua Festival.

I began with a call to producer Dozier who thought it was a great idea! Shortly, with the approval of the Aqua Festival board, I made a full proposal to 20th Century Fox Studios. With an enthusiastic affirmative from the studio, I made a quick trip to Hollywood, where I met the cast, worked out details with William Dozier for the premiere, and had some publicity photos taken. I returned to Austin all fired up to get the ball rolling and to integrate the Batman publicity into the Aqua Festival brochures, press kits, and promotional campaign.

In the meantime, plans with George Wein for a 1966 jazz festival moved ahead as twenty-five of my friends and associates, including Nancylee and Carolyn Hester, joined me in a partnership, with each of the partners throwing $1,000 into the pot. Each "investor" knew they could lose the money but agreed that it was a great way to do it, and there

Batman *supporting character actors Stafford Reff (left) and Neil Hamilton (right) pose for Aqua Festival promotion. 1966.*

— Courtesy 20th Century Fox Publicity.

was actually a chance that the festival might be financially successful the first year.

With the partnership completed, I gave George Wein the go-ahead, had a logo designed for the first Longhorn Jazz Festival, and George flew down so we could lease Disch Field from the Austin Braves organization for April 2 and 3. While George was in town, we went over artists rosters and picked a whole slate of national stars who would fit our proposed format and budget. With George's approval, I added a handful of outstanding local artists to supplement the lineup.

During this time I added another vintage car to my ARKAY team when I had the opportunity to acquire a rare 1936 Miller 91 two-seater roadster originally built by Eugene Frary in Los Angeles from Harry Miller specifications. Miller became famous for his racing engines, and this machine retained the original hand-built four cylinder double overhead cam "Miller" engine which was the immediate predecessor of the Offenhauser 110. Fred Offenhauser was Miller's chief mechanic and expertly carried on the racing engine business.

This little car won its greatest victories at Gilmore Stadium and Culver City Motor Speedway in California in its original midget racer configuration. Millers were so competitive in their day that they were often banned from the tracks to assure the crowd of closer races.

We called it a "1936 Miller Special," although it should have been more accurately described as a "1945 Allen Special," as the original single-seat Miller 91 (ninety-one cubic inches of displacement) midget was rebodied by C. L. Allen of Dallas in 1945 for post-World War II sports car racing. Top speed in its present sports car form was near 95. I assigned it number 42 and had "Miller Special" painted on the hood.

Work also proceeded on the Third Annual Summer Music Festival planned for Zilker Park for July 11-16. The six-night format would again open with a folk music night and close with the Festival Orchestra, but because of conflicts in Ezra Rachlin's busy schedule, I asked Houston Symphony Associate Conductor A. Clyde Roller to rehearse and conduct the final concert. Arrangements were also begun to get New Orleans clarinetist Edmond Hall to headline the Tuesday traditional jazz night.

The music scene around Austin was pretty diverse during the 1960s, and while I didn't have a lot of time to hang out, I did enjoy going out to Threadgill's gas station on North Lamar. It was a small, smoke-filled and cluttered beer joint, but on Wednesday nights an assortment of musicians would show up and share an informal evening of music. Someone would play guitar for Kenneth Threadgill while he yodeled, and various other guitar players, harmonica players, fiddlers, and singers would join in. It was all very laid back and fun. Some

of the classical music students from The University of Texas would come out and try to improvise in contrast to their daily schedule of playing precise classical scores all week. It was a diverse and friendly get-together and soon became the place to be on Wednesday nights. In fact, several times the fire marshal showed up to complain about the number of people jammed into the little rooms.

I first saw Mary Egan, later of Greazy Wheels, there. One of the other young women to show up there periodically was a kid from Port Arthur named Janis Joplin. In spite of her being generally unkempt, ungroomed, and wearing dirty clothes, when she sang "Going Down To Brownsville" and some of her other songs, she really got people's attention.

Another place I did get time to drop in on, one night after a business reception downtown, was a club at 11th and Red River called the 11th Door. It

Allen Damron at the 11th Door. 1966.
— Courtesy Merri Lu Park.

was a dark, one-room club, simply furnished, and owned and operated by a young man named Bill Simonson. On stage was a really rousing singer who threw his head back and sang Pete Seeger songs like they were his own. He was tall and extremely slim, and one couldn't miss the contagious energy and joy of performing that emanated from this animated artist. He had the crowd going every time he hit the stage, and when I met him I discovered that he was as enthusiastic about sports cars as I was.

Allen Damron was from Raymondville, Texas, down in the Rio Grande Valley. In addition to being an entertainer, he had been a hunting guide on the ranches of South Texas, like his guitar-playing father, and he had a lot of stories to tell. I went to see him as often as I could after that, and, occasionally, I'd have him over to the house to talk about music and sports cars.

Prior to my meeting Allen, he had earned an associate of arts degree in drama at Lon Morris College in Jacksonville, Texas, where he gave his first professional performance in 1957. By 1962, he was in Washington, D.C., where he sang at the Unicorn. His first record album, "Two for the Show," with Carol Hedin, was released on Franc Records there and sold thousands of copies to his fans.

He seemed to me to be a natural choice to accompany Carolyn Hester on a planned state-wide press tour to publicize the new Longhorn Jazz Festival.

On March 27, loaded down with press kits and enthusiasm, the pair set out for Temple, Waco, Fort Worth, Dallas, Houston, Bryan, San Antonio, and San Marcos, arriving back in Austin a week later in time to attend the kick-off party for the festival at our home at 2508 Jarratt Avenue.

Allen had quickly become a fully participating member of our growing musical family, and, upon his return from the tour with Carolyn, I added him to the lineup for the opening night of the Summer Music Festival coming up in July.

Attending the jazz party, in addition to George Wein, his CPA Arnold London, other members of his staff, and a number of the early arriving jazz stars, were our twenty-five jazz festival backers, including Peal's Potato Chips president Jim Peal; Bernard Snyder of Snyder-Chenards clothing stores; Volkswagen dealer C. B. Smith, Jr.; theatrical supply executive Bill Leet; *American-Statesman* publisher Dick Brown (who also owned a vintage Jaguar); Dick Reynolds (a partner in Reynolds Penland men's store downtown); Ken Brown, president of The Brown Schools and commodore of the 1966 Aqua Festival; UT constitutional law professor, author, and arts patron Charles Alan Wright; Nancylee's uncle Dr. Joe Thorne Gilbert, Dillard's department store president Huber Hughes; attorney Tom Gee; Carolyn Hester; Ralph Moreland (owner of the Holiday House Restaurants); Jim Alford of Alford Outdoor Advertising; advertising executive Ellen Pendergraft;

attorney Will Davis; Trans Texas Theaters owner Earl Podolnik; insurance man Bill Gammon; realtor Frank Montgomery; State Senator Charles Herring; Gage Furniture owner Leslie Gage; and Bradford's Gallery owner Roland Persons. It was a splendid, compatible group of underwriters who enjoyed their involvement immensely. For their $1,000, each backer received six box seats and got to rub shoulders with a whole house full of living legends.

Jazz stars joining in on the party along with Mayor Lester Palmer, newspaper columnist John Bustin, jazz critic Leonard Feather, and James Drury (star of NBC-TV show "The Virginian,") included Ruby Braff, Bud Freeman, Jack Lesberg, and Maury Feld from the Newport All-Stars, and two Austin-born jazz luminaries, pianist Teddy Wilson and horn player Kenny Dorham. The party was a roaring success and a monumental kickoff for the festival, which would open the next evening at 7:00 with a warm up set by Chuck Reiley's Alamo City Jazz Band.

The Jazz Festival kick-off luncheon head table (from left) Carolyn Hester, Rod Kennedy, James "The Virginian" Drury, Aqua Festival Queen Chica Grey, George Wein, and Leonard Feather.

— Courtesy Longhorn Jazz Festival.

The pre-festival luncheon also included invited guests James Drury, the mayor, Carolyn Hester, my brother Jim and his wife Susan, and the Aqua Festival royalty, among others. We all shared the meal, special presentations, and some well thought out comments by George Wein. Playing at the luncheon in their first public appearance was the new experimental University of Texas Jazz Lab Band founded by trombonist John Leisenring and led by Dick Goodwin.

One of the festival billboards prior to the 1966 event.
— Courtesy Longhorn Jazz Festival.

Gerry Mulligan, Bud Freeman, and Ruby Braff providing an exciting front line for the Newport All-Stars at the Longhorn Jazz Festival. 1966.
— Courtesy Longhorn Jazz Festival.

The band, drawn primarily from classical music students, had no saxophones as there were no sax students in the UT Music Department at this time! The band consisted of a brass section of three French horns, four trombones, tuba, and four trumpets, along with piano, bass, and drums. Also playing the luncheon, and attending the festival as our guests, were the twenty-three teenage members of Robbin's Hoods stage band lead by Maurice Wilson.

The festival itself was a truly memorable event outdoors under the stars at the baseball stadium. Gerry Mulligan, esteemed baritone sax star, was a special guest during the Newport All-Stars set. Local quartet, The Blue Crew, showcased Austin's popular jazz musicians Jerry Storm on drums, Fred Smith on sax, James Polk at the piano, and Bob Bruno on drums. The first half of the opening night's concert ended with Teddy Wilson at the piano backed by All-Stars bassist Jack Lesberg and drummer Maury Feld.

Trumpet player Howard McGhee at the 1966 Longhorn Jazz Festival.
— Courtesy Longhorn Jazz Festival.

Carolyn Hester, family, and friends in their box seats at the 1966 Longhorn Jazz Festival.
— Courtesy Longhorn Jazz Festival.

Teddy Wilson, who was born in Austin in 1912, was given a warm homecoming as he returned to Austin as one of the most influential instrumentalists of the swing era. He was a member of the Benny Goodman Trio and Quartet from 1935 to 1939, led his own big band in 1939 and 1940. During the next twenty years, he played clubs around the world with his own sextet, was a staff pianist at radio and television stations in New York, and played a number of reunions with Benny Goodman. In addition to national television appearances on "The Mike Douglas Show," "The Tonight Show," "The Today Show," and "The Telephone Hour," Teddy Wilson played jazz festivals in Australia, toured Russia with Benny Goodman, and played European tours between 1960 and 1965. He had recordings on Columbia, RCA, and Cameo, including a 1960s RCA-recorded reunion of the original Benny Goodman Quartet with Lionel Hampton on vibes and Gene Krupa on drums. The Benny Goodman Quartet was the first nationally popular integrated jazz group.

Following Wilson's gently swinging trio set and the intermission, Lightnin' Hopkins provided a rural Texas accent to the evening, followed by the Dave Brubeck Quartet featuring Paul Desmond.

The finale for the opening night was provided by the Longhorn Jazz Festival All-Stars with

"Voice of America's" Willis Conover with pianist Toshiko Mariano. 1966.

— Courtesy Longhorn Jazz Festival.

Leon Breeden leads the award-winning NTSU One O'clock Lab Band. 1966.

— Courtesy Longhorn Jazz Festival.

Toshiko Mariano at the piano and front line trumpets Howard McGhee and Kenny Dorham, with the bass of Don Jones and drums of Elvin Jones. It was an exciting freestyle jam of the first order.

At noon on Saturday the crowd was filing into Disch Field for the 1:00 P.M. opening of the Longhorn Jazz Festival's second day with Austin's Bob Sardo Trio playing the warm up set. Following at 2:00 P.M. was a "Jazz From North Texas" workshop featuring the award-winning One O'clock North Texas State University Lab Band, the Bill Farmer Quartet, and vocalist Janet Wildman. Director Leon Breeden put them through their paces, and it was immediately evident why North Texas State was internationally recognized for their undergraduate jazz program.

Following a brief intermission, jazz authority Leonard Feather conducted an amazing "History of the Jazz Piano" workshop with Teddy Wilson at the keyboard.

When the audience reassembled following the dinner break, the Austin-based Obie Jones Trio provided the jazz prelude at 5:00 P.M., with the contrasting quartets of Pete Fountain and Stan Getz following. Popular cornet star Bobby Hackett was there to sit in with Fountain's New Orleans aggregation, and Getz quartet consisted of young vibraphonist Gary Burton, bassist Steve Swallow, and percussionist Roy Haynes.

Following intermission, Maynard Ferguson, who had earned so much fame with his "Jazz at the Philharmonic" recordings, headed an ensemble to back vocalist Chris Connor. The scheduled John Coltrane Sextet had canceled as Coltrane was recovering from having a pot of hot coffee dumped down his boot in New York.

As the festival's final riffs at the park faded into

Cornetist Bobby Hackett sat in with the Pete Fountain Quartet. 1966.

— Courtesy Longhorn Jazz Festival.

the night, the players dispersed all over town and jazz once again was alive and well in Austin, Texas. We would do it again in 1967!

Back at KHFI-AM-FM-TV, I acted as executive producer of twenty-two weeks of "The Younger Set" on television, with Tim Lively and the Profits as the house band and Allen Damron as host. Guest stars on this TV rock series were Lavender Hill Express, Vicki Hudson, Jerry Jeff Walker, and a dozen others. All of the artists were based in Austin, and the show had a good viewership. It was one of the shows our new mobile unit allowed us to videotape, and we did it from a skating rink with simple but imaginative sets by Lyle Hendricks.

We gained significant slices of new audience by also taping and airing dog shows, fashion shows, Little League games, sports car events, and the Aqua Festival parades and water events. Everyone who had a friend or a family member participating in any of these projects ran out to get a converter or a new all-channel TV set so they could see them on TV. While filling many empty spots in our schedule, we continued to convert homes to UHF at a rapid rate.

Having started the Wednesday night two-hour

"Special Event" shows on FM in 1964 with a twenty-six-week series, the show had continued in 1965 in a new thirty-nine-week series that spilled over into 1966. The spring section of that series included such "Special Events" as "Carolyn Hester: Hometown Girl Makes Good," "Dave Brubeck at Carnegie Hall," "An Evening With The Limeliters," and "American Folk Singers: Part I and Part II." The program was now sponsored by the Texas State Bank located on Guadalupe, near the UT campus.

Coming up in a hurry was the third annual KHFI-FM Summer Music Festival and, since I had invited Jimmy Driftwood and Allen Damron both to play the opening night folk music concert on July 11, I thought it might be a good idea to run up to Timbo, Arkansas, to see Jimmy and introduce him to Allen so they could swap a few songs. Our timing proved most fortuitous since it was festival time in the Ozarks.

Allen and I jumped into my 1965 Ford Mustang GT "factory car." I had acquired it while test driving similar models at Ford's Dearborn Proving Grounds months earlier. I had showed it off, at Ford's request, drag racing it, driving in parades, using it as the pace car at the Speed-O-Rama stock car races (where I almost got run off the track by Waldo Harper), and competed with it in A-automatic classes in gymkhanas and autocross high-speed events. But I had never had it on the road in the mountains. Needless to day, we really enjoyed the trip up and back to the Fourth Annual Rackensack Folk Festival and Jimmy Driftwood's farm near Timbo.

Driftwood had produced three successful rural festivals at Mountainview, Arkansas, and hoped to build a major folk arts center. He had also appeared at the Festival of American Folklore at the Smithsonian in Washington, D.C.

His art was pure Ozark music, handed down from generation to generation by the plain people of the hills—timber cutters, farmers, housewives, merchants, and others. This local warmth was projected into the national spotlight when Driftwood was advised to take to Nashville a song he'd composed for his history class in 1958. The song, conceived to create interest in the study of history of the War of 1812, became a national hit on RCA as "The Battle of New Orleans."

Then Driftwood's "Tennessee Stud" was recorded by Eddy Arnold and became a big hit of the 1960-61 season. Jimmy also composed "He Had

A Long Chain On," which was recorded by Peter Paul and Mary and later by himself on RCA.

Driftwood was a popular star to the buyers of more than three million recordings of his songs in the previous seven years, but to his neighbors he was just a friend and a good teacher who could pick.

Allen and I left Austin and drove to Little Rock through Dallas, then north to Leslie, and right to Jimmy's farm near Timbo Creek. Our welcome by Jimmy and his wife Cleda was warm and sincere, and we felt immediately at home. After dinner, Allen and Jimmy swapped songs for a while until Jimmy suddenly said, "You know, tomorrow's festival at Mountainview is mostly by my neighbors from the hills around here. Each of them will be singing one song. Would you like to join the bunch and do one?"

It didn't take Allen long to say "Yes," and he had the good sense not to ask to do two songs, although I hoped he would get that chance the next day. The night, which was spent nestled under down comforters, was short but filled with good solid sleep in the mountain air.

At dawn as we all washed and dressed for early breakfast, Jimmy asked me if I wanted to help get it on the table. I said, "Sure," and he handed me a pan full of good-sized brown eggs to scramble. As I looked out the kitchen window across the hills, the mist was just rising from the grassy meadows and the cows were just beginning to move around.

After hitting the first egg on the side of the pan four or five times without having any effect, I noticed a strange silence in the room behind me until I turned around to look and everyone burst out laughing. It seems the eggs were turkey eggs with a very thick membrane inside the shell, and they all were waiting to see how long it would take me to catch on, and what kind of a sport I would be about it.

After a good laugh and a short course in getting a turkey egg open, we had a huge family breakfast with pan-browned ham, scrambled eggs, piping hot biscuits, homemade bread and preserves, steaming hot coffee, and lots of heart-warming conversation.

Then we piled into our vehicles and headed east twelve miles to Mountainview for the festival. Allen and I didn't know what to expect, but weren't really prepared for what we saw. The gymnasium was already packed. In the area outside the temporary stage, it looked like more than a hundred folks with all kinds of guitars, fiddles, dulcimers, and autoharps were more or less lined up waiting to go on. Allen was inserted into this line of folks with

numerous "Howdies," and I settled down to await Allen's one-song set.

It was a folk festival in the truest sense, with very rural folks playing old-time mountain tunes, singing simple songs in raspy, rural voices, or doing jigs by themselves or with family members. It was obvious that these were not professionals but, rather, homespun people from the hills sharing their own family music with their neighbors.

It was no surprise, therefore, that Allen's song brought down the house, and they broke their one-song rule and asked for an encore once the gym quieted down and everyone was through making some sort of a comment to his neighbor.

We relished the long day of home-grown music and the hundreds of crafts arrayed around the outside of the gym on hay bales, under trees, and in the backs and on the running boards of pickup trucks. We especially admired the hand-crafted dulcimers. But we also ate many servings of homemade cakes, cookies, smoked meats, and fresh bread and jelly.

We stayed with Jimmy and Cleda again that night in a tired but pleasantly subdued atmosphere. With some regret at having to leave, we said our goodbyes and enjoyed the sportscar handling of the Mustang all the way home. Allen asked, "Do you want me to drive?" and then promptly dropped off to sleep.

Shortly after we returned from Arkansas, I flew to Washington, D.C., to represent our corporation at the National Association of Broadcasters convention. I was there a week, participating especially in those sessions having to do with FM. Our company was well-known nationally among broadcasters, not only because of our independently successful FM station, but because of our television competition with the President of the United States. We were warmly greeted in the Capitol and treated with respect.

When I returned from D.C., I was shocked to find that Leonard Masters had been fired, the classical library packed away in storage boxes, and the format of KHFI-FM transformed into a pop station without there having been any discussion between me and my "partners." They had to have had the change planned for months without telling me, as permission to drastically change the format and community service commitments of the station had to come from the FCC. I began to see the real character of my corporate partners and did not like what I saw. I would make a major change soon.

The shocked and hurt response from the public over the loss of the classical music programming on KHFI-FM was overwhelming!

Immediately, I joined with attorney Tom Gee's wife, Jackie, State Republican Party executive director Jim Leonard's wife, Jane, and law professor Charles Alan Wright to form a Classical Music For Austin Association to raise immediate funds to put another FM station on the air as soon as possible with Leonard Masters as the program director.

While Jackie Gee and Jane Leonard did most of the day-to-day, door-to-door money raising, many other former KHFI-FM fans joined them to get the funds together. Our old friend, broadcast engineer Knocky Willett, put the engineering package together, donated some of his own equipment, and helped file the application with the FCC for a station to be called KMFA (Klassical Music for Austin). And now we all waited for the approval.

Changing directions, I renewed my efforts to complete the final details of my own Summer Music Festival and the Fifth Anniversary Austin Aqua Festival, which would follow it a month later.

At the music festival, Damron was to join Jimmy Driftwood on the opening night, along with the Beers Family of New Year, Montana, twelve-string guitarist/songwriter Mark Spoelstra from California, and the Red River Ramblers from The University.

At 8:00 P.M. on Monday, 5,000 fans were packed into the Zilker Hillside Theater, and Damron did a great opening set, his unpretentious showmanship and polished performance earning the crowd's devoted favor.

They were also impressed with Mark Spoelstra, who was known for his contemporary protest songs. However, as John Bustin wrote in his review of the evening, "Those expecting him to rail against Vietnam and social injustice were probably agreeably surprised to find him a gentle, almost wistful performer whose original songs, especially a uniquely conceived 'Children's Blues' and a provocative 'Drawings in the Sand,' had a poignant, touching poetry about them."

The airline strike had stranded Jimmy Driftwood in Little Rock, but, as Bustin noted:

Big Bill Moss stepped in on short notice and proved to be more than adequate compensation for Driftwood's absence. . . . A prodigious performer on the twelve-string guitar, Moss can put an uncommon amount of drive and vitality into his numbers (a

pulsing blues and a tricky variation on 'Frankie and Johnny' were among the most vibrant of his offerings), and he supports his facile musicianship with a show-wise stage presence and a quick wit which made him, even in this company Monday night, probably the most entertaining single performer of the evening.

Quietly closing the evening was the Beers Family, father, mother and daughter, Bob, Evelyn, and Martha, whose early traditional folk songs, dating from the American Revolution, were performed on the psaltery which dates from Biblical times as well as on dulcimer, Tennessee bow, and the British zither banjo.

The Beers Family had been recorded on the Prestige, Folkways, and Columbia Masterworks labels and had appeared on "The Tonight Show," and many other network TV programs.

It was a contrasting and fully entertaining evening, going until midnight but holding the crowd.

Big Bill Moss at the 1966 Summer Music Festival.
— Courtesy Summer Music Festival.

Tuesday night, continuing for the third year the format of traditional jazz on the festival's second night, starred New Orleans clarinetist Edmond Hall with a group of outstanding regional musicians, including blind pianist Forrest Goodenough with San Antonio's Don Albert on trumpet, Chuck Reiley on trombone, Dave Sloan on bass, and John Iacobelli on drums.

Ed Hall, with whose quartet George Wein was pianist at Boston's Savoy Cafe back in 1948, had toured with New Orleans bands in the 1920s, going to New York City in 1928. During the 1930s, he played with Claude Hopkins and other big bands. In the 1940s, Hall played with Henry "Red" Allen and Teddy Wilson combos and with his own groups. Hall played Eddie Condon's in the Village from 1950-55 and with Louis Armstrong for the next three years before freelancing around New York.

In 1962 Hall toured England and Scandinavia, and in 1964 he was a featured soloist with the Dukes of Dixieland on a tour of Japan. He played many jazz festivals across the U.S. before returning to Eddie Condon's in 1962. He also appeared on numerous national TV shows and recorded with Harry Belafonte.

Edmond Hall was always neatly dressed and soft-spoken. His clarinet playing had an unusually personal sound, and he was widely respected around the world, especially by other musicians.

Opening at Zilker for Hall was a Dallas band called the Garner Clark Bearcats with trombonist Emil Orth, clarinetist Dub Gable, drummer Bob McClendon, and bassist Horace Rollins joining cornetist Clark.

Wednesday night saw the return of Dr. Morris Beachy's widely respected professional forty-voice Austin Chorale, performing music by Bach, Gabrielli, and Brahms as well as some lighter fare by Meredith Wilson and others. Special guest for the evening was Puerto Rican dramatic tenor Benjamino Ocasio from the Metropolitan Opera Workshop in New York. He passionately sang arias by Puccini, Verdi, Leoncavallo, and Donizetti as well as some melodic Neapolitan songs. He was accompanied by pianist Lita Guerra, and it was an exceptional evening, warmly received by the hillside audience.

The Thursday night modern jazz concert headlined Japanese jazz pianist Toshiko Mariano, who flew in from New York to appear in both solo and ensemble performances of her own compositions and those of other contemporary composers.

The concert began with a thirty-minute set by Dick Goodwin's University of Texas Jazz Lab Band. Then the Blue Crew Jazz Quartet, lead by drummer Jerry Storm, played a set featuring Fred Smith on tenor and soprano saxes, James Polk at the piano, and Luiz Natalicio on bass and guitar. San Antonio's Ike Ramirez was a guest performer on trumpet. When Toshiko sat in with the Blue Crew for her ensemble tunes, James Polk moved from piano to sax. The group and Toshiko meshed beautifully and some rewarding things happened musically.

On Friday, the 1966 version of the Festival String Quartet, made up of the same Houston Symphony artists as the previous year, performed with Moreland Kortkamp Roller as pianist in the Dvorak "Quintet for Piano and String Quartet," Opus 81. She had recently appeared as soloist with the Houston Symphony Orchestra conducted by Andre Kostelanetz.

The evening opened with the Haydn String Quartet No. 4, known as "The Sunrise," then Turina's "La Oracion del Torero" and the "Quartet Satz" of Franz Schubert.

Over the years, these evenings of classical music probably provided the largest crowds ever to hear chamber music in Austin, as the audience frequently surpassed 3,000 in number.

The climax of the festival on Saturday night found our Festival Orchestra on stage with A. Clyde Roller conducting an evening of music by Wolf-Ferrari, Gluck, Schubert, Grieg, and including the return of pianist Joyce Arce in the Chopin "Concerto in F minor" for piano and orchestra.

Ms. Arce, who was the 1965-66 recipient of the Ima Hogg Scholarship Award, had appeared with both the Dallas and Amarillo Symphony Orchestras and had appeared briefly on the choral evening of the 1965 KHFI-FM Summer Music Festival. She had won four major awards since 1963 and was selected to play twice in 1967 with the Miami Philharmonic Orchestra after winning their competition just prior to our festival.

While Gordon Kelso did a good job of stage managing, and we enjoyed another successful festival, described by *Billboard* as "a big league event," we found that crowd control by the city was deteriorating. The too frequent popping of fireworks in the crowd and the sound of motorcycles permitted to roar past the rear of the stage made me think twice about coming back in 1967.

I was pleased to receive confirmation from George Wein that both Carolyn Hester and Allen Damron would appear at the Newport Folk Festival coming up. George Wein was impressed by these Texas artists.

The Austin Aqua Festival was only a few weeks away, and while the schedule was complete, and more than 1,000 volunteers were working on preparations, there remained considerable fine-tuning to do on what would become a double world premiere of "Batman" as a major pre-festival event.

We scheduled a 4:00 P.M. children's premiere in costumes and makeup and an 8:30 evening adult premier in formal wear with spotlights and live TV coverage by the Channel 42 mobile unit. There would be two processions up Congress Avenue from the Wilbur Clark Crest Hotel to the Paramount Theater with a VIP reception and dinner for top ticket buyers and the press at the hotel in between the two showings.

To understand the national impact of the Batmania that was sweeping the country, you should know that Adam West was receiving an average of 30,000 fan letters a week, and the projected sales for "Batgadgetry" and "Battoys" for 1966 was $75-80 million. The shows were being broadcast in England, Europe, Japan, Canada, and Latin America.

In Austin, retailers were advertising Batman t-shirts, boots, helmets and capes, wrist radios and bicycle ornaments, walkie-talkies, beach towels, hand puppets, TV nightlights, rugs, masks, jigsaw puzzles, socks, caps, pendants, games, scopes, colorforms, 45-rpm records of Neal Hefti's Batman theme, the Nelson Riddle instrumental soundtrack LP, and Batman ice cream products.

Bill Gaston's Glastron Boat Company had created the Batboat, which was unveiled at the premiere and then run wide open up and down Town Lake. Gaston gave away free Batboat photos at his dealership. The film also featured a modified Bell Batcopter and a Batmobile designed by George Burris.

At the time of the 1966 TV series and movie, Batman had been a part of American life for twenty-seven years, evolving from the original 1939 comic strip to a 1943 movie series to the ABC-TV series, and now the 20th Century Fox Deluxe Color feature.

William Dozier was a thirty-year veteran of visual media when he partnered with 20th Century Fox to make the TV series and the film. He had been with Paramount for six years and then executive assistant to Charles Kenner at RKO, producing box office hits like *Notorious*, *The Spiral Staircase*, *The Enchanted Cottage*, *The Farmer's Daughter*, *Murder My Sweet*, and *Crossfire*.

Later, as television swept the country, Dozier moved to CBS, where he was in charge of Hollywood programming, resulting in "Studio One," "Danger," "Perry Mason," "Gunsmoke," "Rawhide," "Suspense," "You Are There," "Playhouse 90," "Climax," "Twilight Zone," and "Have Gun, Will Travel."

He then went to Screen Gems, where he produced "The Donna Reed Show," "The Farmer's Daughter," and "Hazel." Then one day, out of the blue, he had an idea for a new television series based on the comic book character "Batman."

His exaggerated seriousness and use of cliché made the "Batman" productions so bad they were good. But behind it all Dozier maintained that he was trying to say something: there should be a much greater respect for law and order, an adherence to the time-worn cliché that crime does not pay, and a much broader determination on the part of the public to cooperate with law enforcement officers. All through "Batman," some very basic moralities were expressed. In all of this, the "high camp" quality of the production attracted fans from six to sixty as the Batman mystique swept the country.

Dozier's choice of Adam West to play Bruce Wayne and Batman was based on West's work in previous TV series and his chiseled good looks, which would still be obvious behind a mask. The choice of twenty-year-old Burt Ward to play Robin, the Boy Wonder, was the result of Ward's athletic ability and his being able to carry off the role of Bruce Wayne's fifteen-year-old friend Dick Grayson. Ward looked young enough and was able to scale steep walls, leap over automobiles, and engage in hand-to-hand combat with the villains as a result of his lettering in track, wrestling, and tennis in school, plus winning a brown belt in karate. He was also a skilled skater and won the Beverly Hills decathlon. Ward came to the role from the Theater Arts Department at UCLA, where he was a student.

Dozier's genius was further reflected in his choice of major stars to play the villains and his production crew's ability to come up with every kind of prop imaginable from the Batgun to an anti-shark repellent.

Former Miss California, Lee Ann Meriwether, had used her $5,000 Miss America scholarship money to go to New York to study with famed Lee Strasberg, founder of Actors Studio. First, she earned the daily assignment as women's editor on NBC-TV's "The Today Show," and from there she went to Hollywood, where she played roles in theater productions and eventually in several TV series. She appeared on "F.B.I." and "Twelve O'Clock High," "The Man From U.N.C.L.E.," and became a regular cast member of the "Perry Mason" series. Then, of course, she gained instant international fame as the svelte Catwoman in the Batman production.

Cesar Romero, one of Hollywood's most dashing Latin lovers for close to forty years, originally created the Joker role for the TV series and went over to do the movie. It was a complete change for Romero, who most generally had been cast as a suave man of the world for most of his thirty-nine years on the stage and screen. He had played on Broadway in the 1920s and began his film career in the 1930s in the featured role in *The Thin Man.* Except for time out as a World War II Coast Guard gunner in the South Pacific, he had remained in Hollywood ever since. He starred for a number of years as the Cisco Kid, then was prominent in a number of Betty Grable musicals. His more adventurous roles included *Vera Cruz, The Racers,* and the television series "Diplomatic Courier."

Joining Romero in the Batman production was one of America's most respected character actors, Burgess Meredith, who said the Penguin role was "the most fun I've ever had."

Meredith had played in *The Barretts of Wimpole Street* with Katherine Cornell on Broadway and gained full stardom in 1936 in *Winterset,* written especially for him by Maxwell Anderson.

Hollywood imported him for the film version of *Winterset,* and he remained in the film capital to make John Steinbeck's *Of Mice and Men* with Lon Chaney, Jr.

After a stint in the Army Air Corps during World War II, Meredith returned to play the popular war correspondent Ernie Pyle in *The Story of G.I. Joe,* and he had alternated freely between the stage and screen ever since. At the time of his appearance in Austin and the *Batman* premiere, he was preparing to go to New York to participate with his partner Zero Mostel in a new repertory theater.

So, at 1:30 P.M. on Saturday, July 30, 1966, Adam "Batman" West, Lee "Catwoman" Meriwether, and executive producer William Dozier and his 20th Century Fox entourage flew into Austin's Municipal Airport. Five minutes later, Burgess Meredith arrived in his own private plane, piloted by his wife.

The arrival time was supposed to be secret, but the airport was "nevertheless alive with wide-eyed youngsters and not a few adults who had somehow gotten wind of the schedule and had come out for an advance look at the stars," according to John Bustin's front page description in the Austin paper.

Burt Ward, who was supposed to accompany the other stars, had remained behind to tend to the imminent arrival of his first baby.

The ensuing city-wide wave of excitement outdid anything else of its kind that the city had ever witnessed.

We had the young people's premiere parade near 4:00 P.M., and even before we could get started, Congress Avenue was jammed. A sizable throng mobbed the Crest Hotel parking lot as the stars, now colorfully decked out in their fanciful film make-up and costumes, tried to find their way to their convertibles.

In addition to the movie stars, the parade included convertibles for the mayor, the festival president and commodore, the royalty and Aqua Beauty, and the children's personalities from Austin's two television stations, including Uncle Jay, Packer Jack, Mary Melody, and Miss Pinafore.

The crowd was so immense, estimated at between 20,000 and 30,000, that the parade had to creep along the avenue to the Paramount Theater, wending its way slowly between the throngs of spectators who packed Congress Avenue from store fronts to the automobile procession itself.

Thousands of children wanted to touch the stars and shake hands with them and shouted welcoming greetings. The police did their friendly best to allow the procession to keep moving, and everyone, including William Dozier, was in complete disbelief. We could hear the live rock band playing the Batman theme as we neared the Paramount. The cheer that went up sounded like a football crowd.

The stars were interviewed on live TV out front and, inside, I orchestrated the on-stage introductions of the TV personalities and the unveiling of the Batboat until the stars could make their way in and greet the sell-out crowd. It was joyous mayhem.

The tumultuous response continued all the way through the movie. The audience cheered everything, especially the filmed appearance of the Austin-built Batboat.

The movie plot? The Dynamic Duo versus the most infamous of all criminal emporiums, United Underworld, an amalgamation of the most evil anti-heroes known to man, who, of course, get their comeuppance in the end. Adam West as Batman and

The crowd mobbed Adam West's official convertible as he arrived at the Paramount Theater. 1966.
— Courtesy *Austin American-Statesman.*

KHFI-TV's Bill Richardson talks with Lee Meriwether as Cat Woman. KTBC-TV's Uncle Jay and Packer Jack can be seen getting out of their car in the background.
— Courtesy *Austin American-Statesman.*

Burgess Meredith as the Penguin, being interviewed by KHFI-TV's Bill Richardson. 1966.
— Courtesy *Austin American-Statesman.*

Burt Ward as Robin unashamedly knocked the stuffing out of evil.

Meanwhile, the stars were smuggled out of the Paramount and back to the hotel to prepare for the evening's formal reception, dinner, and adult premiere.

Following the reception and sold-out dinner with all its ceremonial presentations and congenial remarks, we did it all over again, this time in tuxedos and beautiful gowns and searchlights. It was a repeat of the wall-to-wall people experience of the afternoon, with another rousingly successful screening before a cheering, applauding audience, capping off the long day's phenomenal schedule.

In the comparative quiet of the late evening, a small group of us joined the festival royalty and the stars, now decked out in sweatshirts and jeans, to sit around singing and playing guitars in the afterglow of the day's high-energy activities. William Dozier leaned back in his chair, beaming, and said that it had been the best premiere he'd seen in years. "That's the way we used to do it," he exclaimed.

The day after the premiere, the rest of the pre-festival events cascaded on us like a landslide. Water-ski kite flying, a golf tournament, sailing regatta, Boy Scout hike, a sports car gymkhana at

Kingsland, and the kick-off barbecue for the Highland Lakes canoe race were all under way.

The next day, August 1, a tragedy struck Austin when a deranged man with a rifle started shooting people in the streets from the tower on The University of Texas campus. Charles Whitman shot and killed thirteen and wounded thirty-one before police could kill him.

I was on my way to a meeting at the Villa Capri Hotel east of the campus when I heard the familiar sound of bullets whizzing overhead. I desperately shouted at people to take cover, and they, not knowing what was going on, looked at me like I was crazy or ignored me completely. A few more bullets ricocheted off the buildings near me and then Whitman turned his attention to closer targets. I immediately got to a phone and called the KHFI news department. The Texas tower massacre was a frustrating, frightening, and sickening experience with lingering anger and disbelief persisting well after it was over.

The massacre news stories locally and nationally continued, and it was difficult to restart the festival publicity or to look ahead to a city-wide celebration. Thank heaven the Batman momentum carried us into the festival week. We all voted to go ahead. We felt it was just what the city needed right then, so we went to work with double commitment, and the festival continued.

As expected, the preparatory activities snowballed on us as we moved into the actual August 4-14th schedule. The official kick-off luncheon was Friday the 5th, with young blond television actress Melody Patterson as special guest. She was also the parade marshal the next day. Melody was the female interest in ABC-TV's "F Troop," a popular comedy carried on KHFI-TV.

Saturday the spectacular land parade presented more than 100 units with fifty floats, bands, and a variety of marching organizations, including military from all four branches of service. The president, commodore, and Melody Patterson rode in convertibles, while the queen and her court and Miss Austin Aqua Beauty, Vicki Hudson, rode on huge colorfully decorated floats. Many thousands of people turned out to watch the parade, and it was seen on our Channel 42 as well.

While the automobile show remained downtown in the auditorium, the sports car races moved out to a new racetrack. The revised and upgraded

pre-festival Autorama displayed vintage cars, many custom cars, hot rods, dragsters, motorcycles, go-carts, and other showcars. The final day of its two-day run was highlighted by the Aqua Festival Gymkhana outside and the preliminaries of the "Battle of the Bands" inside.

The races, meanwhile, moved from the city streets around the auditorium, where they'd created such public interest in the past, to the new banked 1.75 mile Austin Raceway Park, located nine miles north of Austin, just west of Interstate-35.

I was sorry to see these Carrera de la Capital IV sports car races moved off the streets, where they were a truly newsworthy and unique event. But it was at Austin Raceway Park where I spotted the next addition to my car collection. It was a beautiful five-year-old Italian racing red Ferrari roadster. And, it was for sale!

When I finally found the owner and learned that it was, in fact, available, the anticipation of actually owning a Ferrari began to well up in me. My desire to acquire that incredible machine was constantly on my mind, but the owner lived in San Antonio, and I had a full ten days of festival events to preside over: the Texas Water-ski Championship, the Aqua Beauty competition's three nights, where Vicki Hudson would hand over her title, the "Battle of the Bands" finals, two days of the 250-Mile Enduro speed boat races, the nighttime lighted water parade and dazzling Jax fireworks display, the Governor's Cup Sailing Regatta on Lake Travis, Southwest Championship Drag Boat Races, swimming championships, and many smaller events.

Nancylee and I also attended the final Saturday night Admiral's Ball, where Queen Chica Grey and her court retired from their ceremonial year of duty, and two days later we learned from the festival treasurer that the Aqua Festival was in the black. It was what I wanted to hear! Ken Brown, as 1967 president, could start the festival with $8,000 in the bank and no debts.

Now, I could head to San Antonio and pick up my Ferrari.

It was a 1961 Scaglietti "California" type 250 V12 GT Roadster, one of three built, and was beautifully styled. In fact, it was more beautiful five years old than all of the newer American cars. It had been originally raced at the Sebring International Twelve Hours of Endurance by Allen Newman in 1961 and was raced at Nassau and elsewhere by Charlie Hayes and Bob Grossman in 1961 and 1962. It was originally priced in the $13,000 range, and I acquired it for less than half that amount. I really loved the car and enjoyed every moment at the wheel.

When the fall television season began, nearly the entire schedule of shows was in color. Television was growing up rapidly and more than half the sets being sold across the country were color sets.

In early September, I received a call from the city of Houston asking me to put together a jazz event for the opening week of Houston's new Jones Hall for the Performing Arts. I answered in the affirmative and called George Wein in New York.

My 1961 Ferrari Type 250 Short Wheel Base "California" roadster by Scaglietti.

— Courtesy Tom Lankes.

He confirmed that he could bring his Newport Jazz Festival All-Star Quintet for the October 2 opening week, and he added Errol Garner as the headliner. The concert was standing room only and showed Houston that Jones Hall was not just a facility for symphony, opera, and ballet. We had a great time, and I had a good visit with George and the members of the quintet.

Among the things we visited about were the successful appearances of Carolyn Hester and Allen Damron at Newport, and Wein asked if I knew of any other artists from Texas that I thought should play. I told him about Kenneth Threadgill, and he asked me to send an audition tape to the Newport board of directors. I brought Kenneth into the KHFI-TV studios to tape three Jimmie Rodgers songs backed by Bill Neeley, Chuck Joyce, Awald Ziegler, and Tary Owens on various guitars, with Powell St. John on harmonica. I sent the tape off, and we waited to see if Kenneth would make the trip.

During the months since Aqua Festival, administrators at the Radio/Television/Film Department at The University of Texas approached me about helping them raise funds to finance KLRN-TV9 Public Television. Channel 9's programming originated from studios in both San Antonio and Austin and was split about 50-50 between black-and-white and color programming. The administrators were projecting a one hundred percent color schedule from new color studios in both San Antonio and Austin within two or three years, and it would take a huge increase in cash to make this happen.

I recognized the value of well-programmed public television and considered the challenge of identifying region-wide funding for KLRN an intriguing idea. Further, it would begin to put a little distance between me and a group of people with whom I was beginning to become more than just a little disenchanted.

I spoke as carefully as I could with my corporate partners about the possibility of a leave of absence. They looked favorably upon the idea, since by now, we had accomplished ninety percent of our UHF conversion campaign aided by the FCC mandate that all new TV sets sold must include both VHF and UHF capability. Our three-station package successfully had been launched, the press coverage had been massive, and by now, a large working advertising sales team had taken over all my FM accounts and was providing tangible operating revenue for the stations.

I requested a two-year leave of absence and told my former KUT-FM associates that I was, indeed, available to become development director for KLRN.

I left my paneled vice-president's office behind at KHFI-AM-FM-TV to begin to tackle the funding of the tremendous costs of educational television in transition. With no commercials on ETV, programming, staffing, and general ledger expenses were supported primarily by contributions from corporations, foundations, and individuals.

We planned to establish an on-the-air television auction with thousands of dollars worth of donated items sold to viewers during an annual telethon spectacular. Attractive personalities from academic, sports, entertainment, and political fields would be recruited to participate as auctioneers.

In other parts of the country, auctions of this nature were becoming popular and quite successful at raising substantial sums of money. I planned to visit one or more successful stations to see how they put their auctions together.

My two years at the top of the Aqua Festival were the two richest years of my public life, seeing the open generosity and willingness of people to give financial, physical, and organizational support to projects once they understood their goals.

The real rewards for volunteers, in addition to the satisfaction of successfully supporting their favorite cause, were the personal relationships that developed. The Aqua Festival transcended all economic, social, and political levels. The parking lot attendant worked with the bank president to make the festival a success. I was certain the same spirit would engender enough momentum to make the KLRN campaign work.

The press quoted me as saying:

> We all realize that there are lots of good things in the world, like good jazz, educational TV, symphony orchestras, libraries, and other cultural influences, which are limited in the rewards they can bring a community by the amount of support they get from that community.
>
> In this country, where private support of the arts and broadcasting is crucial to the effectiveness of its influence, the private citizen has to respond. I have found that responding personally and obtaining responses from other people is a very rewarding way to invest one's life.

The other thing about a massive fundraising effort of any kind is that, regardless of how much or how little money you raise, in the course of the campaign you have to explain the organization's goals, background, needs, and personality, so you are also accomplishing an equally important educational effort.

Among my first assignments on arrival, after getting to know key members of the staff like Chub Benjamin and producer Bill Arhos, with whom I'd be working the on-camera auction, was to pick an especially experienced and successful public television station whose auction really worked. My task, then, was to study the format and to adapt it to KLRN's two-city, two-studio situation.

I chose WGBH in Boston and spent four days with their auction manager learning what to do and what not to do. In addition to getting a good running start from them, I enjoyed the seafood and the Boston baked beans and weenies. I was disappointed to find that the Boston jazz scene was not near as active as it had been years before. But jazz and folk music on the radio was very much in evidence, especially on the college and university stations. By now,

Emerson College had their own FM station, and it was one of the most listened to stations in the Boston area. They were playing plenty of Tom Paxton, Odetta, Carolyn Hester, and Joan Baez.

Upon returning to Austin, planning began on the auction — how it would work and how it would look on the air. Moveable tables with blackboards attached listing the auction items, donors, and retail values, would be loaded up with six or eight items for a staffer and a celebrity auctioneer to sell. The bids would come in on a phone bank manned by volunteers, and would be written on the boards in the last column. When that table was sold out, its paperwork and the table would roll away and the next one rolled on in its place.

Other items, including such intangibles as vacations, dinners, theater tickets, etc., would be listed on other boards where the cameras would focus while the new tables were rolled in. It looked like the format would work by switching back and forth between studios in the two cities every few tables or in fifteen to twenty minute blocks of time.

The other major job was to recruit 1,000 "go-getters" who would call on pre-selected lists of donor prospects in each city and obtain their donations. The perks for donating included visibility on the air for their business or product and a tax deduction for making the gift.

The newly acquired Ferrari was great for racing back and forth the seventy-five miles between my two offices several times a week. I couldn't understand why I never received a speeding ticket. Recruiting and training more than 900 women and a handful of men was done by group leaders whom I coached. The leaders were selected by the stations from various society, military, educational, and business groups in each city. I had the opportunity, during the two auctions I managed, to work with Alice Reynolds (Mrs. Dick Reynolds) and Ann Butler (Mrs. Roy Butler) as city chairpersons, and they were outstanding and a pleasure to work with.

We also had to find centrally located storage buildings in each city for "Pick Up and Pay," where successful bidders could go get their purchases.

The KLRN auctions of 1967 and 1968 were fun and successful. Not only did they raise the profile of educational television in both cities, but they raised something in excess of $480,000.

One of the best parts of working for KLRN was that it was, for the most part, only a forty-hour week, which left time from my former sixty-hour schedule to continue civic work, including assuming the presidency of the International Good Neighbor Council. The council was a non-governmental civic organization in support of the Governor's International Good Neighbor Commission.

Since the popular success of our KHFI-FM ten-hour "Saludos a Mexico" anniversary broadcast and its ensuing publicity, I had been thrust willingly into a group of people focusing on international relations, especially with Mexico, but also with the Sister Cities program worldwide. Monthly we had some sort of dinner program, reception, or other special event, but I had trouble reconciling the VIP treatment given visitors from Mexico when we continued to treat Mexican Americans so poorly. I served my year's term and did what I could, and then retired from the organization.

Late in January of 1967, the news reached us of the deaths of three astronauts as the result of a launch pad fire at Cape Kennedy during the Apollo tests. The space program was expensive in both lives and dollars, but for the most part it was widely supported by the public and was moving forward one step at a time with the long-term goals of exploring space and protecting our American interests from space somewhere down the line.

In spite of the work schedule at KLRN, I still had time to work on the 1967 Longhorn Jazz Festival and the Fourth KHFI-FM Summer Music Festival. I also began to consider the possibility of buying the 11th Door club with the idea of putting Allen Damron in a singing host/management situation.

While Bill Simonson didn't want a large amount of money for the 11th Door, after meeting with him about the purchase, I thought we might do better starting from scratch and building our own club somewhere else. We began looking for a suitable building.

About this time, I was able to acquire another car for my collection. It was a sleek twelve-year-old front-engine "Formula Junior" Stanguellini racing car which the late German champion, Count Von Trips, campaigned in Germany in 1958, including at the famed Nurburgring race course.

It was built by Vittorio Stanguellini in Modena, Italy, in 1958, and was the 128th car he built using modified Fiat components. The Stanguellinis were the first cars to go into production under the new European rules. Its 1100cc four-cylinder engine with dual Weber double-choke carburetors in its light tubular frame was capable of speeds up to 125 mph. While Von Trips drove for Ferrari in Formula 1, he

The 1958 Stanguellini in an early outing at a sports car club gymkhana against the clock through a complicated parking lot course. 1966.

— Courtesy Photo Graphics.

also successfully campaigned the Stang in Formula Junior. Front-engined cars of this type were competitive up until 1960 when Formula Junior became international, but by 1961, lighter rear-engined cars took over.

I had the car taken to The Pit Stop shop on 6th Street for a complete check up, some minor repairs and tune-up, and then took it to Doug Scales Body Shop to be spiffed up with body repairs and twenty coats of shiny black hand-rubbed lacquer. It was beautiful when it came out of the shop, and with new Goodyear Blue Streak racing tires mounted, I planned to have fun with it in gymkhanas and hill climbs.

The 1967 Longhorn Jazz Festival was going to be expanded to three days, Friday, Saturday and Sunday, April 28-30, which would allow us to present five different programs at the Disch Field baseball park.

Partly as a result of my Houston Astros television relationship with the local and regional Schlitz Beer people, especially national brands manager Ben Barkin in Milwaukee, I was able to get good strong support for our non-profit group to establish scholarships supporting jazz lab band programs at various colleges and universities throughout Texas. Once this relationship had been cleared, following meetings with Coke Stevenson at the Texas Liquor Control Board, the 1967 festival played under the banner of the Schlitz "Salute to Jazz."

Just prior to the festival, I presented a $250 Schlitz Scholarship to the UT Jazz Ensemble in Austin, and George Wein presented a $250 scholarship at an affair in Houston to the Sam Houston State Teachers College Stage Band.

Both Mayor Lester Palmer and Texas Governor John Connally helped welcome out-of-town guests to the festival by writing letters and making their offices available to us for support. We hired

Graphic Designs to handle an extensive public relations and advertising campaign in twelve Texas cities. In addition, Sears stores throughout the state would sell advance tickets, and we set up a publicity schedule with more than 300 newspapers and fifty radio and television stations in Texas. We were trying to double last year's attendance of 12,000.

The U.S. Information Service, "Voice of America," which had broadcast highlights of the previous year's festival to countries as far away as Turkey, would be back to record the expanded schedule of two workshops and three major evening concerts.

Our home on Jarrett Avenue became the site of another big pre-festival house party celebrating the return of the jazz community. The city's top officials extended an official welcome to Wein and his jazz stars at a kick-off luncheon which was broadcast and featured the growing and exciting nineteen-piece University of Texas Experimental Jazz Ensemble with Dick Goodwin at the helm.

Wein and I had scheduled more than seventy-five performers to provide the greatest lineup of jazz personalities ever to be assembled in Texas in one place at one time.

Carolyn Hester and George Wein visit at the 1967 Jazz Festival kick-off luncheon.
— Courtesy Bert Bollinger.

Top drawing attractions like Nina Simone, who was the singing sensation of the 1966 Newport Jazz Festival, would appear on the same concert with jazz greats like Dizzy Gillespie and his Quintet, the Thelonius Monk Quartet, and trumpeter Kenny Dorham and drummer Elvin Jones appearing as guest stars with the Sam Houston State Teachers College Stage Band led by Harley Rex.

Dick Goodwin and I at the 1967 Longhorn Jazz Festival.
— Courtesy Center for American History,
The University of Texas at Austin.

When the festival opened on Friday night, the Alamo City Jazz Band returned to play while people were finding their seats for the 8:00 P.M. concert. But because of a long-range forecast for rain, they played their welcoming set in the air-conditioned 6,000-seat Austin Municipal Auditorium, where the entire festival was moved for the weekend.

Friday night was a special treat for me because Father Norman O'Connor, the "Jazz Priest" who had success in communicating with the youth of New York and Boston, would be hosting the concert. Father O'Connor had been at the first Newport Jazz Festival fourteen years before and had taken part in many major festivals in both the U.S. and Europe ever since.

Additionally, Father O'Connor co-hosted a series of fifty-two educational TV shows for National Educational Television, which had been seen in Austin and San Antonio on KLRN, Channel 9.

Dizzy Gillespie was to open the festival at 8:00 P.M. The long-famed trumpeter was universally regarded as one of the prime attractions in jazz.

Along with the late Charlie "Yardbird" Parker and Thelonius Monk, Gillespie was credited with creating Bebop in the 1940s and, as a result, helping give jazz of the 1960s much of its present form.

His under-the-lip goatee, horn-rimmed glasses, and beret were all personal innovations that came to be accepted as trademarks of modern jazz. But his personality and sense of showmanship never diminished his stature as a serious musician. Jazz experts generally conceded that he was the most influential trumpeter to come along since Louis Armstrong.

The whole opening concert was exceptional.

*Dizzy Gillespie at the 1967 Longhorn Jazz
Festival.*
— Courtesy Center for American History,
The University of Texas at Austin.

*Thelonius Monk at the 1967 Longhorn
Jazz Festival.*
— Courtesy Center for American History,
The University of Texas at Austin.

The Dizzy Gillespie Quintet included James
Moody, and the Thelonius Monk Quartet included
Charlie Rouse. Following the intermission, Nina
Simone performed an emotional set with her trio,
and capping off the evening was the big
Houstonians stage band with Kenny Dorham, the
famed charter member of Art Blakey's Jazz Mes-
sengers, and Elvin Jones, former drummer with the
John Coltrane Sextet.

The Saturday afternoon workshop began with a
1:00 P.M. warm-up set by old-time cornetist Garner

*Austin-born Kenny Dorham returned home to play the
Longhorn Jazz Festival. 1967.*
— Courtesy Festival Productions, Inc., NY.

Clark and his Bearcats, with baritone sax giant Ernie
Casceras as a featured guest.

At 2:00 P.M. the Woody Herman Orchestra
strode on stage to play a fascinating workshop, "The
History of the Herman Herds," hosted by eminent
jazz critic and author Leonard Feather. Feather's
Encyclopedia of Jazz was one of the most authorita-
tive books on jazz in the world.

Leader of widely popular bands since the 1930s,
Woody Herman had been at the forefront of big
band jazz since 1944, when he introduced his "First
Herd." Since that time, the fifty-three-year-old

Herman had consistently fronted swinging crews which brought prominence to such instrumental stars as Stan Getz, Zoot Sims, Jimmy Giuffre, Shorty Rogers, Neal Hefti, and Urbie Green.

The workshop was informal but fast-paced, informative, and packed with great Herman jazz charts and not a few outstanding soloists. Feather's commentary was stimulating, punctuated with humor, and presented a fulfilling survey of twenty-three years of Herman's music.

The big Saturday night concert saw the Bearcats and Casceras doing the warm-up again, and then, at 8:00 P.M., the Gary Burton Quartet got the main event under way. The twenty-three-year-old Burton, a Boston native and a product of the Berklee School of Music, had been vibist at the 1966 festival with the Stan Getz Quartet, with whom he was featured over the past two years, while also recording with his own group. He had been a child prodigy who made his recording debut while still a teenager, but he had worked with the George Shearing Quintet before joining Getz.

The Gary Burton Quartet included bassist Steve Swallow and drummer Roy Haynes, colleagues from the Getz Quartet, and guitarist Larry Coryell. Their original sound had a great appeal, especially among the younger jazz fans.

Following Burton was the Jimmy Smith Trio with Howard McGhee. Jimmy Smith, unanimously rated jazz' top organ virtuoso, provided effective support for McGhee's impressive trumpet playing. Then, together, they provided back-up for big-voiced Joe Williams, who was recognized all over the world for his vocal work with Count Basie, to close the first half of the concert. Williams had found great favor with the fans at Newport, but his reputation as a blues singer dated back to 1943 when he joined the Lionel Hampton Band in partnership with Dinah Washington.

Herbie Mann's Quintet came on after the intermission with a complete change of texture, color, and pace. Originally a sax player, Mann had switched to flute in 1954 and quickly was renown as America's premier jazz flutist. His fame soared with his Afro-Jazz Septet that toured Africa on a State Department tour in 1960. His ethnic jazz gained a wide audience, probably at its strongest since his Brazilian *bossa nova* period.

The Woody Herman Orchestra put the frosting on the cake in closing the Saturday night concert.

The final day began with a 1:00 P.M. warm-up by the Arnett Cobb Sextet from Houston. Cobb, a

Young vibist Gary Burton, formerly with the Stan Getz Quartet, brought his own quartet to the 1967 festival.
— Courtesy Festival Productions, Inc., NY.

great crowd pleaser, had earned notoriety on tenor sax when he replaced Illinois Jacquet in Lionel Hampton's Band, 1942-1947. He toured with his own band until he was seriously injured in an accident. He returned to Houston, where he had his own big band in 1959 and 1960.

The workshop itself, hosted by George Wein, was an entertaining and quite amazing session with drummers Elvin Jones, Jo Jones, Don Lamond, and UT Jazz Ensemble drummer Emory Whipple, replacing Art Blakey whose plane was late getting in.

Each drummer played portions of the program devoted to their own particular style, with Wein narrating and sitting in on the piano as a foil for their drumming. The surprising thing was that student Whipple more than held his own, with the crowd giving him tremendous support. As a finale, Wein had the drummers put together an improvised suite of drumming in which all of them played as an ensemble, playing off each other, imitating each other, trading licks, and, ultimately, trying to outdo each other. In the end, Whipple, again, received the best response. It was great fun!

The 6:00 P.M. evening concert opened with the Newport Jazz Festival All-Star Sextet that included original All-Stars George Wein, Ruby Braff, and Jack Lesberg. Added were Texas-born saxophone star Buddy Tate, whose most notable years perhaps were his dozen or so with Count Basie; clarinetist Pee Wee Russell, who was a mainstay at Nick's in the Village and at Eddie Condon's following his pioneering years in the twenties and thirties when he was associated with Peck Kelly, Bix Beiderbeck, Frank Trumbauer, and Red Nichols, among others; trombone veteran Lou McGarity, who had played and recorded with a long list of luminaries like Benny Goodman, the Lawson-Haggart Jazz Band, Ben Burnie, Wingy Manone, Wild Bill Davidson, and Max Kaminsky. He played on record sessions for Columbia, Decca, RCA, Epic, Kapp, MGM, and a dozen others. Joining the sextet on drums was former Woody Herman drummer Don Lamond.

Teddy Wilson was back at the festival following his triumphant homecoming of 1966, again teamed with Jack Lesberg on bass and with Don Lamond replacing the late Maury Feld.

The pre-intermission set by the 1967 Longhorn Jazz Festival All-Stars turned into a stirring tenor sax showcase, reuniting Illinois Jacquet, Arnett Cobb, and Buddy Tate, backed by Milt Buckner's organ and Jo Jones' artful drumming. Jones, with his flashing smile, was poetic to watch as the sticks moved so fast you couldn't see them, and all sorts of original rhythmic patterns supported the music.

The intermission passed quickly, and the Charlie Byrd Trio came on with Byrd's unique jazz guitar style reflecting his earlier years of classical study, including a year in Italy with Andres Segovia. Byrd's back-country blues from his native Virginia combined with his classical influences to give him an uncommon "finger-style" technique. Byrd had jumped into international popularity as a *bossa nova* pioneer who introduced "Desafinado" and earned "Hit Parade" status with Stan Getz on his "Jazz Samba" album.

The finale for the entire three days was impressively provided by Art Blakey and the Jazz Messengers. Nat Hentoff had described Blakey as "perhaps the most emotionally unbridled drummer in jazz."

Blakey had been with the Fletcher Henderson Orchestra in 1939, and in ensuing years, played with Mary Lou Williams, Billy Ekstine, Buddy DeFranco, and the Birdland sessions. He formed the Jazz Messengers in 1955 and toured successfully in the U.S. and Europe. A long list of distinguished Messengers alumni included Kenny Dorham, Benny Golson, Wayne Shorter, Freddie Hubbard, Junior Mance, and others.

Blakey had recorded on Blue Note, Columbia, Elektra, Atlantic, MGM, Impulse, United Artists, Pacific Jazz, and countless other labels. Through all of his evolution of the Messengers, he continued to dominate the hard bop world.

While the crowds, the reviewers, and all of the participants gave the festival glowing and tumultuous praise, the tangible results fell $19,800 short of our goal, and we needed to consider an alternate format for 1968. Schlitz picked up the tab for the shortfall.

The next big event on my calendar, between weeks of ardent effort for KLRN, was the 1967 KHFI-FM Summer Music Festival, even though I was on leave from KHFI-FM. Dan Love wanted the festival to continue, and I enjoyed working with him on the sponsorship and publicity side.

The fourth festival would follow the general format of the previous three events at Zilker Park. Made a little nervous by the rain and loss at the jazz festival, I arranged with the city for the use of the City Coliseum and with The University for one of their halls if we needed to move into them.

Festival dates were July 10-15, and I decided to have Allen Damron open the festival again. He and I, incidentally, had found a possible building for our new folk club during all of the other scheduled work, and we were to begin work on it if the terms of the lease and all of the other details could be worked out. However, we put that behind us for the moment and concentrated on the final plans and publicity in earnest for the July 10 Zilker Hillside event.

Along with Allen on the concert would be a friend of Carolyn Hester's named Sandy Rhodes, a popular New York exponent of folk rock. Her writing and playing were influenced by a jazz background. Her records on the Senate label were in distribution by ABC Paramount.

The most enjoyable part of the evening for me was going to be having a chance to introduce two of my favorite acoustic blues singers, both white and very different from each other.

First was twenty-three-year-old Townes Van Zandt, a Fort Worth native now working out of Houston, who had become very well known in that city and was the featured performer at Club Jester. When he was growing up, he traveled with his family to Montana, Colorado, Illinois, and finally to Minnesota, where he became rhythm guitarist and singer in a rhythm and blues band.

That early blues experience was still very much evident in this young singer's writing and performing when he came to Austin to play several extended engagements at the 11th Door. By the time he arrived in Austin, he had nearly four dozen original songs in his impressive collection of material. His songs were both traditional and contemporary in style. He'd written lyric ballads, tragic epics, and humorous tunes. His commentary between songs was tinged with humor and in stark contrast to his singing and playing which were internalized and mostly produced with his eyes closed. While subdued, he was definitely developing a distinctive persona, strengthened by his playing on five-string banjo or six-string guitar.

The other blues artist was considerably older than Townes, and although a local artist, he was much better known in Austin than Townes. In fact, Kenneth Threadgill, born in Hurst County in 1909, was considered nearly legendary by those who attended his Wednesday night musical get-togethers at his place out on North Lamar. Threadgill had operated his converted gas station tavern since 1933, and his establishment had been sought out by many big name country and folk stars when they passed through Austin.

Threadgill's finally became so popular that the fire marshal shut him down, and for the past two years he'd been playing at the Split Rail.

Threadgill had come to be considered a traditional folk artist in the purest sense of the word. He was also regarded as a leading purveyor of the country blues popularized by the late Jimmie Rodgers in the 1920s and 1930s. Threadgill, who first heard Rodgers as a performer with the Barnum & Bailey Circus in Beaumont, got to meet him in 1928 at Loew's State Theater in Houston, where nineteen-year-old Kenneth was working as an usher. Threadgill stopped singing Al Jolson songs and had been carrying on the Rodgers tradition of songs and blue yodels ever since. He began yodeling and singing in earnest after World War II, when he sang on the weekends at Dessau, Skyline, and other Austin clubs with pianist and singer Delores and the Bluebonnet Boys until 1956.

Threadgill had started his Wednesday sing-alongs at his tavern around 1945. He told me he still remembered when a blind boy named Fred Lowry used to stop by his place on the way to the State School for the Blind to sit in and whistle a while. That was in 1931. Lowry later became America's most popular whistler on radio and records. Kenneth also told me about the day in 1931 or 1932 when Will Rogers and Jimmie Rodgers visited his place to get some booze on the way to Rodger's Blue Yodeler's Paradise, Rodgers' home in Kerrville.

At the festival, the fifty-five-year-old Threadgill was backed by a band that had Chuck Joyce on rhythm guitar and doing some harmony singing; Bert McGuire, who played what he described as a "moderately amplified" lead guitar; and Julie Paul, a University of Texas student and the youngest member of the group, on a second rhythm guitar.

The concert took the crowd by storm! They loved every performer, and by the time Threadgill came on stage with his yodeling and his band, everyone was on their feet. It was a good kick-off for the six nights.

The Tuesday night jazz concert saw the return of the Ed Gerlach Orchestra from Houston, who had been so well received on the 1964 festival. This large aggregation, led by the affable saxophone player, was recognized state-wide as Texas' most prominent society orchestra, playing for all the biggest weddings, debutante parties, and country club gatherings. While the band did play a number of these society dates and was constantly in demand for them, the band was always staffed with the best instrumental players in the Southwest. Among the personnel in their ranks on this particular Tuesday night were Joe Mendez, *lead trumpet*, Charlie Ribble, *trombone*, Bob Hill, *tenor sax*, Bob Gieseke, *alto sax*, and Johnny Gonzales, *flute*. With vocalist Janet Smith, the band also included more than a dozen other notable players.

Gerlach's "Salute to the Big Bands" was not only a showcase for the depth of expertise in the band but also a stirring trip down memory lane, echoing with the sounds of thirty years of favorite big band modern jazz arrangements from Tommy Dorsey, Glenn Miller, Artie Shaw, Benny Goodman, Woody Herman, and others. It was a stellar evening for big band fans.

Dr. Morris Beachy's professional Austin Chorale of forty voices filled Wednesday night with a nearly two-hour panorama of American songs from the Old West, the Gay Nineties, motion pictures, medleys from three Broadway musicals, and a dramatic closing with Howard Hanson's heroic "Song of Democracy." Beachy had already become well known nationally as an outstanding choral director for his work with the UT Madrigal Singers, Chamber Singers, and A Cappella Choir. In the past year, his Austin Chorale had appeared with the Atlanta Symphony Orchestra.

As a contrasting feature during the choral concert, we presented flamenco guitarist Fernando Herrera, who had appeared on the "Ed Sullivan Show" on national TV, played for President Kennedy, entertained distinguished guests at President Johnson's ranch, and toured Mexico City, Buenos Aires, Vancouver, San Francisco, and Dallas, and was featured in the Spanish Pavilion at the Seattle World's Fair.

The Thursday night modern jazz concert was an encore appearance for Arnett Cobb, who had made such a hit at the Longhorn Jazz Festival playing his brief one-hour warm-up set. He returned to Austin with his best players: Jimmy Ford, *alto sax*, Charlie Pettiford, *trumpet*, Cedric Haywood, *piano*, Samuel Evans, *bass*, and Ronnie Wynn, *drums*, with vocals by Joy Ann Tobin.

Cobb had recorded for Mercury, Columbia, and other major labels with the Lionel Hampton Band and his own septet. He had toured the country from 1947 until 1956, when a tragic automobile accident nearly cut short his career. He finally won a ten-year battle to recuperate from his injuries.

His Longhorn Jazz Festival appearance brought him an immediate invitation from Wein to play the 1968 Newport Jazz Festival and from me to play the Summer Music Festival. The acclaim he had earned at the Longhorn Jazz Festival was not a fluke. The crowd of 3,000 at Zilker Hillside Theater gave him an impressive welcome and was disappointed when rain interrupted the concert, and then finally shut it down.

I worked with Austin Symphony concert master Leopold LaFosse to put together both the Friday chamber music concert and the Saturday orchestra finale, as Rachlin was on a guest conducting tour of Australia.

Well known in Central Texas as both soloist and concert master with the Austin Symphony Orchestra, LaFosse had also been concert master of the San Antonio Symphony, the Dallas Symphony under both Hendl and Kletzki, the Aspen Festival Orchestra under Izler Solomon, and the National Symphony of Peru under Luis Herrera de la Fuente.

As a soloist, LaFosse had a repertoire of twenty-five concerti, an even greater number of sonatas and other major works, and over 100 works in the

Kreisler, Sarasate, and Heifetz transcription category. His recent Town Hall debut in New York was enthusiastically received by both the press and the numerous musicians in attendance.

He performed on a beautiful instrument from the hands of renowned Italian violin maker, J. B. Guadagnini, made in 1776.

For the Friday chamber music program, LaFosse had former Chicago Symphony concert master Robert Quick, now playing with the San Antonio Symphony, as second violinist; Donald Wright, professor of viola at UT, who had performed as a member of the Eastman Rochester Philharmonic, the Houston Symphony, and the 1963 Marlboro Festival Orchestra under Pablo Casals, played viola with the quartet. Wright had recently been honored by the Corpus Christi Symphony Orchestra which commissioned the Samuel Adler "Song And Dance" especially for him. In 1966 Wright had performed a debut recital in London's Wigmore Hall. The cellist for the quartet was Austin Symphony first chair Louisa Marks, who had played with Robert Craft's Louisville Symphony Orchestra, with the Kentucky Orchestra, the Orlando Symphony, and the Chautauqua, NY, Festival Orchestra of Walter Hendl.

These players provided another stimulating and well-received chamber music evening.

For the final night, in place of the Festival Orchestra heard in former years, LaFosse put together the fourteen-member Festival Baroque Ensemble drawn from string players of the Austin, San Antonio, and University of Texas symphony orchestras, as well as some of the best known members of The University's music faculty.

Principal players, in addition to LaFosse, were violinist Jocylyn Rudeloff, Lita Guerra on cembalo, violist Donald Wright, and cellist Louisa Marks.

The concert featured early Italian classics by Corelli including Suite in Three Movements and his Concerto Grosso, Opus 6, No. 7. The program also presented "Summer" from Vivaldi's *The Seasons*, Bach's Brandenburg Concerto No. 3, and opened with Handel's Concerto Grosso, Opus 6, No. 10.

In case of rain, we reserved UT's Hogg Auditorium, but, thankfully, didn't need it, as it was a beautiful night and an eloquent finale for the festival.

This would be the last of the Summer Music Festivals, as my ties with KHFI were becoming looser with the passing months. But, I'd have to say, the four-year, twenty-four concert experience of providing free open-air concerts for more than

63

60,000 people was stimulating and an extraordinary chapter in my becoming a diverse concert producer.

As Allen and I were working on putting our folk music club together, I thought about how great the Monday night folk concerts had been during the past four years and began to retreat from the idea of not having any Zilker Park festival at all. Maybe we could just have a one-night folk music concert out there in the future. We filed the idea for the future and began the process of trying to work out a lease on a building we liked near 14th and Lavaca, just seven blocks south of the UT campus and on one of the main routes from downtown going north.

In the middle of our leasing negotiations, I learned that the Santa Fe Opera Theater in New Mexico had burned down on July 27. Even though I had never been there, I had read and heard for years about what a beautiful facility it was, and I deeply regretted their misfortune. It seems that they were able to save enough of the costumes to continue producing in a gymnasium. For all the years Nancylee and I had KHFI-FM, we'd been going to the San Antonio Grand Opera performances sixty-five miles down the road and had become avid opera fans with the hope that someday we'd be able to get to Santa Fe.

The thought of fire weighed heavy on my mind since I had my car collection stored in various garages and buildings around town without fire insurance, and we were about to sign a lease on an historic old building at 1411 Lavaca that had housed a militia unit in the late 1880s. One could still see where the old gunpowder room used to be. In fact, we thought we would use it as a tune-up room for the club. It turned out that our site was less than two blocks from the State Capitol, and, therefore, it was considered to be in the city's "Fire Zone One," so the city fire marshal gave us guidelines for minimizing fire hazards. Most of the building was old brick, and where we were going to put the kitchen and a room for talking and eating, we would use highly fire-resistant sheet rock and the best grade electrical wiring we could get.

Our lease began on August 1, 1967, and we went to work day, night, and weekends building our new club and remodeling our south end of this historic structure. I decided to build it around a racing theme, the unlikely theme of "folk songs and fast cars." I also decided to use the French spelling of the club's name, "Chequered Flag."

In the midst of our club preparations, the Aqua

Festival returned. I didn't have to be as involved as before, however, since my presidency was over and I had only ceremonial appearances to make. As a special project, I arranged an Austin premiere of the film *Grand Prix*, starring James Garner, as a fund-raising event. It also served, of course, as a publicity stunt that could help boost attendance at the sports car races.

Since we wouldn't even ask James Garner to come in for a local premiere, we instead scheduled a parade of convertibles, floats, and racing cars on trailers with 1967 Sports Car Club of America Pro Formula Champion Gus Hutchinson as honorary parade marshal.

Gus, at thirty-one, was president of the million-dollar Chemscope Corporation of Dallas, a chemical manufacturing firm specializing in aerosols and chemical specialties, cleaners, lubricants, degreasers, pesticides, anti-corrosives solutions, and pollution control chemicals.

Gus ran his Chemscope Racing Team as a serious hobby like many other SCCA amateurs. But he moved quickly into the professional ranks when he entered his Brabham Formula B open-wheel racing car in the SCCA pro series, winning it dramatically with a number of spectacular victories. His name and photo had been all over the local and regional papers, and he was a genuine and likable guy.

Gus had always worked on his own engines from the time he first started racing an old MG on a shoestring budget in 1958. His early reliability and successes were beginning to create a demand for his fledgling Hutchinson Racing Engines endeavor.

The movie premiere and parade and associated events were really enjoyable and were a moderately successful fund raiser for the festival. The best part of it for those of us active in motorsports was the camaraderie of being together without the pressure of competition.

With the exception of putting some of my ARKAY cars in the auto show and doing support work for the SCCA at the two days of racing, my participation in the Aqua Festival was minimal for the first time in six years.

Immediately following the end of the last race, I refocused on getting the club ready for Allen.

Our plan was for the main club room to seat nearly 100, and at Allen's suggestion, we built the stage with a two-foot-wide counter around it, and seating so that people could sit very close to the stage. Carrying out the racing theme, we built a checker board canopy over the stage. We kept the exposed brick just like it was as an attractive background for the performers. We put a large blackboard for the menu and coming attractions on the wall at stage left between the stage and the doorway to what would become the "bench racing room." There drivers and fans could talk without disturbing the performances in the main club room.

Working on the club together were Allen, Segle Fry, Nancylee, Rudy Landeros from KHFI-TV, and various assorted volunteers who came and went. The main club room would become a soft, darkened atmosphere of old brick, beamed ceilings, and candlelight. The tables for four would have red, green, or yellow table cloths, three of the colors of official racing flags. Photos of the cars from the ARKAY collection, and some other professional racing photos and prints were placed around the walls. We also made a down payment on an electric marquee installed over the front entranceway with the new Chequered Flag logo on the front and changeable panels on each side for listing our nightly stars.

Nancylee, Allen, and I became the board of directors of the Chequered Flag, Inc., and its officers. Attorney Tom Gee filed the incorporation papers with the Secretary of State.

We were jubilant as we approached the target opening date of September 22, 1967.

THE CHEQUERED FLAG YEARS

(1967–1970)

While my main motivation for building the Chequered Flag was to provide Allen Damron with a showcase for his talent and to increase his popularity and his income, I thought the club also might give his career some long-term momentum. Allen, however, was not the only key figure in the creation and opening of the Chequered Flag.

Segle Fry was there from the beginning, providing the manpower, sense of humor, and not a little manual labor. In addition to building and decorating the club, once it was open Segle would be the second "in-house" entertainer, would run the cash register many nights, and would also provide some of the business acumen he had acquired in his family's clothing business in Tyler. Segle's stage presence was a good contrast to Allen's "full speed ahead" approach, as Segle had a soft, gentle voice, a good choice of old time blues and Woody Guthrie favorites, as well as a warm and personable demeanor.

With Allen and Segle to build upon, our various staff members through the years became an affectionate, close-knit, and effective operating team. Waitresses through the years included Sue Poole, Joanie Herbst, Reeve Love, Carol Jackson, Patsy Taylor, and Bonnie Nelson, with Nancylee and me occasionally messing things up by trying to contribute. Bill Head, Rudy Landeros, and Bayard Breeding were among those tending bar, and Allen, Segle, and I would jump in when needed. Finally, when we could afford it, Meredith Nelson became our first official dishwasher. I had become tired of having my hands in the hot water between introducing artists on stage.

FOLK SONGS and fast cars!

AT THE
CHEQUERED FLAG
1411 LAVACA   AUSTIN, TEXAS

Allen Damron poster. 1967.

The first of the three opening nights, September 22, was packed with invited guests, press, suppliers, and some undaunted members of the public who just couldn't wait until the next two nights. Allen and Segle lived up to my expectations and their advanced billing and wowed the standing-room-only audiences every night.

Woody Guthrie died on October 3, in our third week of operation, and the ensuing tribute evening was one of the early memorable moments in the club's history.

We were open six nights a week, closed on Mondays, and decided that, after giving ourselves a few weeks to make certain everything worked, we would schedule Carolyn Hester for a run of five nights, starting Wednesday, October 11, and running through Sunday, the 15th.

Since we weren't certain how successful we'd be in meeting the fee we felt she should have, we also booked her for a one-hour afternoon concert at the Gary Job Corps Training Center thirty-five miles down the road at San Marcos. While this show did provide some cash, the audience there was not the ideal "folk" audience.

Allen welcomes Carolyn Hester to her first appearance at he Flag, October 11-15, 1967.
— Courtesy Neal Douglas Photography.

The club was packed on Carolyn's opening night and every night during her five-night run, and Allen and Carolyn were great together. Allen dressed in a coat and tie every night in Carolyn's honor, and she was in top form. While the engagement was a smashing success, and Carolyn was a major boost to our morale, we all had battle fatigue when it was over from dealing with the huge crowds in our new facility. Still, everything worked, and when our Monday off finally came, we were relieved and pleased as we put the pieces back together at a more leisurely pace.

A week after Carolyn's engagement at the Flag, on October 22, in Washington, D.C., more than 50,000 people staged an anti-war march on the Capitol, and, while there were also local demonstrations on the Texas Capitol grounds just two blocks away, I hoped that the club would not become embroiled and would continue free of politics to remain a retreat from the world's problems and shortcomings. So far, the club atmosphere was a peaceful, family setting.

Once the club was up and running, there was no shortage of young artists wanting to play our stage. Allen and Segle were our regulars, playing two shows a night plus an "after hours coffee set" on Saturday nights at 1:00 A.M. For $1.50 you could get hot chocolate or coffee and a "Formula Junior" roast beef sandwich along with an hour of music until 2:00 A.M.

Our roast beef sandwiches were something really special!

Eighteen years before, I had eaten roast beef sandwiches at Meyer's Tavern in Buffalo, NY, and I wanted to duplicate them at the Flag. The secret lay in well-prepared beef served on a unique German Kummelwick roll, dipped in greaseless but flavorful gravy. Meyer's Tavern sold 100 pounds of beef sandwiches every day.

I called them and had four of the special salty rolls flown down to Austin to be reproduced for us by the Joe Carriage Bakery. Reaction to the sandwiches on first tasting was amazing, and they became a popular and immediately famous part of our club scene.

Also listed on our green "blackboard" menu was a "Caution Flag" sandwich: hot grilled-cheese cooked to order for our hungry patrons.

In addition to the sandwiches, chips, and coffee, we also served a Sprite float with vanilla ice cream and called it a "Damron Cooler."

The racing decor of the air-conditioned club was carried out on one wall by a display of international racing shields, on another by *Road & Track* color prints, while an inscribed Chaparral spoiler-wing from Jim Hall's early prototype racing car was hung over the doorway to the "Other Room."

Information on various sports car events was pinned on a bulletin board across the club, and

Bill Head and Rudy Landeros tending bar at the Chequered Flag, 1967.
— Courtesy Robert Anshutz.

behind the twenty-five-foot bar area hung a four-by-eight-foot sign that had marked the stage at the first two Longhorn Jazz Festivals of 1966 and 1967, prompting fans to ask us when we were going to bring back some of the jazz stars.

The bar served twelve- and twenty-four-ounce frosted glasses of draft beer, five brands of Texas and out-of-state canned beer, set ups, ice, Damron Coolers, coffee, and hot tea for those who liked British racing.

The "Other Room" displayed five of our vintage cars and a 1933 Pan American road racing car valued at $20,000 on loan from San Antonio's Tiny Smith. More than 100 old-time racing photos from Indy and elsewhere were framed in a big four-by-twenty-foot block along one wall. There were also

several long tables and benches available for "bench racing" conversations and refreshments away from the music in the main club room.

Allen's format for auditioning prospective new performers was to have the ones we liked do a couple of weeknight guest sets. Those who turned out to be popular, including a young woman named Kathie Morrison, eventually had a chance to do guest sets with Segle and Allen on the big weekend nights. Soon, Kathie was able to have her own ten-day stand, sharing the stage with Allen, and she also was featured on our special holiday shows.

Also playing at the Flag in the early months were ragtime guitarist and blues singer John Alford, the romantic Mexican trio Los Tres Amigos, rockers Tim Lively and the Profits from "The Younger Set" TV show, and the Exit, who had been playing downtown at the Red Lion on Sixth Street.

Yodeling Kenneth Threadgill had been playing at the Split Rail regularly on weekends and tried the Chequered Flag for his first appearance on Tuesday, November 14, drawing good crowds to three shows with a $1 cover charge.

On November 17, we learned that KOKE, a daytime-only country music station, had filed with the FCC to buy KAZZ-FM and convert it to a twenty-four-hour country music station, so the radio spectrum was slowly changing in Austin.

Segle Fry was getting a real job traveling on the road selling Levi's and so played a series of farewell concerts starting on November 21, accompanied by Travis Holland, and then again on November 25. His final three nights on November 28-30 were all well attended. Segle received a good send-off from everyone.

"The Other Room" at the Flag with (from left) Lester MG, Three-Wheeled Morgan, 1961 Ferrari. 1967. The Chequered Flag, 1967.
— Courtesy Robert Anshutz.

The main club room at the Flag, 1967.
— Courtesy Robert Anshutz.

A week later, a young San Antonio folksinger, who had been doing some successful guest sets at the club, brought his repertoire of 300 Israeli folk songs to the Flag stage for his own week alongside Allen Damron.

Jim Schulman, who also played and taught classical, folk, and *bossa nova* guitar, was a member of a musical family and began singing with his brother and sister at the age of six. Fifteen years later, he was a professional folk singer, and his brother was leading a combo in which his sister was the vocalist. Jim's interest in folk music had grown with the hootenanny movement of 1962, when he started doing folk music shows for private parties and church groups.

A year in Israel, 1965-66, gave him the foundation for his interest in and knowledge of Israeli folk music. He not only knew over 300 folk songs of Israel but knew the origins of most of them and could translate all of them from the original Hebrew. One of his greatest thrills had been appearing at the Club Baccus in Jerusalem.

Coming on like a young Theodore Bikel, Jim's week at the club was wildly received, with the audience rejoicing in singing the robust, melodic Israeli songs in four-part harmony at the top of their lungs.

We added Jim to the special Saturday "Christmas Festival" at the club, where he joined Allen Damron, Kathie Morrison, Los Tres Amigos, and Ricardo Gamez, whose flamenco and *bossa nova* guitar styles were catching on at the Flag.

Five nights before Christmas, we tried a "Barbershop Harmony Night" that was so successful we scheduled another one for January. Folk music? Well, if people loved Luis Balderas and his mariachi band, why not barbershop quartets?

The three ninety-minute festivals of Christmas folk carols were a popular change of pace, and for New Year's Eve we scheduled our old friend Chuck Reiley and his Alamo City Jazz Band.

That night the club was packed, the crowd was cheerfully boisterous, and the atmosphere was filled with colored balloons and streamers. When the band swung into their version of "Auld Lang Syne" at midnight and everyone was hugging and kissing, Meredith peeked out of the kitchen and exclaimed, "Wow! Just like in the movies!"

While the Chequered Flag was moving into 1968 with good crowds, including some beyond capacity who had to be turned away, Bill Simonson's 11th Door continued to operate as a showcase

for Sleepy John Estes, Townes Van Zandt, Mance Lipscomb, Don Sanders, and Big Bill Moss.

Down at the Vulcan Gas Company on lower Congress Avenue, another audience was enjoying Lightnin' Hopkins, Roky Erickson and the 13th Floor Elevators from Kerrville, Shiva's Head Band, and the Conqueroo.

Out on South Congress, Kenneth Threadgill and the Hootenanny Hoots was still a big weekend draw at the Split Rail. On West 6th Street, Cody Hubach held forth at the Red Lion.

Bill Simonson, not satisfied with just operating the 11th Door, opened the old Yank Theater on East 6th as "The Pleasure Dome" for rock 'n' roll, blues, old-time movies (especially James Dean), and light shows.

The Jade Room, a regular stopping place for Rusty Wier's Lavender Hill Express, and the New Orleans Club, also began to make themselves known as music venues on Red River Street, while out at the Villa Capri's Club Caravan an energetic Don Dean scheduled the Royal Tahitians from Disneyland and promised to bring in "Sugar Blues" specialist Clyde McCoy.

I continued to serve during this time as a volunteer development consultant for KMFA-FM, the non-profit radio station that featured Leonard Masters' classical programming broadcast via a 750-foot antenna furnished by KHFI.

A week after New Year's, Allen's old Washington, D.C., recording and singing partner, Carol Hedin, came in to play the club for a week and was held over for a second week. Guitarist Ricardo Gamez, Carolyn Baer, the Balderas mariachis, Jim Schulman, and another Barbershop Harmony Night filled out most of the month of January.

There was at this time much drum beating for the upcoming world's fair at San Antonio, scheduled to begin April 6. Its 622-foot-high Tower of the Americas was the largest construction project of its type since the Eiffel Tower. An economic boom was projected for Austin as a direct result of the predicted 7.2 million visitors expected to show up for the Hemisfair just an hour from us. We all bought it and became enthusiastic supporters of the expected good times for all just down the road.

In March of 1968, I had worked out a contract with the Austin Jaycees for Carolyn Hester to fly back to Austin as the celebrity star of the Jaycees Cavalcade of Commerce at Municipal Auditorium. An immense blowup of J. Nuhn's sketch of Carolyn was featured on Jaycees billboards all over town,

J. Nuhn's sketch of Carolyn Hester appeared on billboards around Austin for the Jaycees Cavalcade, and was later used on the first brochures and programs for the 1972 Kerrville Folk Festival.
— Courtesy *Austin American-Statesman.*

Carolyn Hester singing at the Jaycees' pre-Cavalcade luncheon.
— Courtesy Robert Anshutz.

A nice looking model: the 1954 Monza Ferrari Type 750.
— Courtesy Robert Anshutz.

and she was the special guest at the Jaycees luncheon prior to the March 26-28 event, where she made six appearances.

Also at the Cavalcade was an exhibit of three of my Italian racing cars, including a recently acquired Ferrari which first appeared at the renowned Monza circuit in 1954 with Hawthorne/Magioli driving. They won that grueling race, thus earning for the car the nickname "Monza Ferrari," and my car was the second place Gonzales/Trintignant team car at that outing. It was a Type 750, four-cylinder, three-liter car with two spark plugs per cylinder, and was brought to the U.S. and driven by the Marque de Portago in the Mexican Road Race of 1954. It was a beast of a machine: the large pistons would shake the entire chassis with the engine at idle, and it wouldn't smooth out until it hit about 3000 rpm. The body was designed by Ferrari's son Dino, built by Scaglietti, and was the forerunner of the first

Testa Rossa 500s of 1956. I was showing it for the first time at the Cavalcade since buying it from Hale B. Ingram who had completely restored it to pristine condition.

The Chequered Flag operated during its first nine months with varying degrees of success. One of the people who became a popular regular was Big Bill Moss, who had been so well received when he replaced Jimmy Driftwood on the Summer Music Festival.

Moss, who had been appearing at the 11th Door, tipped the scales at well over 200 pounds, played a big twelve-string guitar, and, depending upon his diet that month, called himself an American Indian Negro of Spanish descent. The fact that he was born in Canada, grew up in an Italian neighborhood in Cleveland, Ohio, and thought that he was Italian until he was twelve years old, made Moss an interesting cosmology that was, all at once, a study in ethnic and musical contrasts.

Most obvious about Moss on first impression was his huge bulk, his toothy grin, and his fantastic guitar technique. His mother had been a teacher of music and art during Bill's elementary and junior high school years in Ohio, so it was natural that he should go on to the Cleveland Conservatory of Music and to the Oberlin School of Music, where he received a good foundation in orchestral theory and composition.

Following a six-year stint in the navy, both stateside and in Korea, he worked in New York as a photo lab assistant for an advertising agency.

His musical background haunted him, and he began to visit the folk clubs in the New York area, where he met and studied with the great Josh White. When Moss discovered that he could understand and express himself through folk music and blues, he began to perform professionally in and around New York, including bookings at such well-known clubs as the Gaslight and the Bitter End.

Reassured and encouraged by his success, Moss started on what was to be a three-year tour of clubs in ten states from coast to coast, with his most notable successes at the Vanguard and Castaway Clubs in Kansas City.

Moss became grounded in Texas in the same week the club he was playing went broke and his guitar was stolen. He went to work as a full-time photographer while still playing the Chequered Flag ten or twelve times a year.

While shooting photos for a living, Moss still practiced his guitar four times a week and took some music courses to keep his hand in.

His favorite photographic subjects were children and racing cars, and when he sang and told stories from the stage, his repertoire ranged from the ridiculous to the sublime. He poked fun at everything with all stops out. His material ran ninety-nine percent adult.

While realizing that there were serious problems in a society concerned with integration and civil rights, Moss's musical approach was one of looking at the humorous side of the conflict.

"I can make people think about the injustices of the old standards and enjoy their reappraisal by making them laugh at themselves," Moss pointed out. "I myself have never been bitter because I always figured there was some way around the problem."

One of Moss's favorite bits was to stop in the middle of a great throbbing blues and begin to plink out a slow, pedantic waltz, while commenting, "This is the white part."

Other performers who became regulars at the Flag were singer-songwriter Richard Dean, who was also an outstanding guitarist, the duo of Bob and Cindy, and, of course, Jim Schulman, with his rich

The Chequered Flag at 1411 Lavaca.
— Courtesy *Austin American-Statesman*

collection of Israeli singalongs. On occasion, Travis Holland would appear on bass with Schulman.

There were also memorable nights with Ramblin' Jack Elliott, Mike Murphey, Jerry Jeff Walker, and the duo of Steve Fromholz and Dan McCrimmon as "Frummox." Both Rusty Wier, formerly of the Lavender Hill Express, and songwriter Willis Alan Ramsey made their solo debuts at the Flag.

Following their popular receptions at various Longhorn Jazz Festivals, pianists Teddy Wilson and Toshiko Akiyoshi (formerly married to Charlie Mariano) played to good houses at the club, and drummer Jo Jones appeared with a local jazz trio.

As we moved into 1968, following the traditional jazz welcome of the New Year, we realized that when the club was sold out, we couldn't capitalize on the most popular artists because our seating capacity was so limited and we had to turn people away. Many other nights the club would play to half-a-house or less and we were not breaking even.

We started looking into getting more space from the unoccupied north end of the building so that we could move the bar out of the club room and put in more seating.

Two other forces were in motion to encourage me to enlarge the club. First, there was that great outpouring from San Antonio about the 1968 Hemisfair and the huge amount of tourist dollars that would pour into Austin and every other town on the Interstate-35 corridor leading to the Alamo City. The other thing happening was that my racing car collection was growing to the point where I was considering putting together a museum to put them in.

I had already acquired and restored a 1951 Lester MG, built in England by Harry Lester, which

Our restored 1951 Lester MG endurance car.
— Courtesy Robert Anshutz.

Allen Damron hosted "Folk Sound of the City" five nights a week on KHFI-FM.
— Courtesy Ray Chambers.

was one of the team cars winning the 1952 British Empire (Isle of Man) Trophy Race, the 1952 Jersey Road Race, the 1952 Borham 100, and placed one-two-three at the 1952 Goodwood Nine-Hours Endurance Race. This car was the last one we could tuck into the "Other Room" without taking out the 1961 Ferrari and putting it back on the street, thus destroying the meaning of our slogan "the folk club with the built-in Ferrari."

In addition, I had already bought the ex-Jud Larson midget racing car that had given this late Austin dirt track ace his first competitive ride in 1947-48. Larson had gone on to win five USAC championships before his untimely death at Reading, Pennsylvania, in 1966. The car was powered by one of Tiny Smith's legendary "Jiggler" V-60 engines built in San Antonio. The car was being restored by Doug Scales Body Shop, and I was negotiating for two more cars.

With Allen hosting "Folk Sound of the City" five nights a week on KHFI-FM, and with all the other publicity in the local newspapers, magazines, and tourist-oriented publications, we were getting

The ex-Jud Larson Dreyer midget racer. 1967.
— Courtesy Robert Anshutz.

an excellent response at the club. We began to believe that if we added a museum as an attraction we could probably fill up the club even on weeknights with the Hemisfair travelers who couldn't stay in overbooked San Antonio.

So we went for it.

We would target the 4th of July for our grand opening, four months after the opening of Hemisfair, and we'd buy a big billboard on Interstate-35 to advertise it.

I began to talk with our landlord about leasing the rest of the building.

Our club frontage at 1411 Lavaca was fifty-two-feet and there was another seventy-six-feet of frontage on our long building encompassing 1415, 1417, and 1419 Lavaca. The rent would only be another $200 a month for 6,000 additional square feet for seventeen months starting April 1 and then would only go up $25 a month for each two-year renewal period in the future. Leasing it April 1 would give us time to do a first-class job of remodeling, painting, and building displays for our proposed Texas Speed Museum. We signed the lease and began to clean out the old building.

Early April was filled with emotionally loaded days. We happily signed the lease on April 1 and were looking forward to the opening of Hemisfair on the 6th. Then, on the 4th, Dr. Martin Luther King, Jr., was shot and killed by a sniper in Memphis.

Like the ripples across the water after a stone is thrown, the impact of this tragic slaying swept across the country in ever-widening circles. Besides the loss of a great man whose cause was just, there was a sense of appalling disbelief and agonizing melancholy that came over the whole country. The idea of killing a man who simply but eloquently advocated equality was in violation of all I had been taught growing up as an American.

We really needed a bright spot and so were more than ready for the scheduled return of Carolyn Hester for six nights, two shows nightly at 8:30 and 10:30, with after-hours sets scheduled for Friday and Saturday nights. She would open on Tuesday night, April 17.

Her previous appearances in Austin were all sell-outs, including the big 1966 Cultural Entertainment Committee Concert at Municipal Auditorium. She had just returned to the U.S. from a two-week tour of England with appearances on "The Rolf Harris Show" and "The Late Night Line Up" show on England's commercial network ATV. She also performed before a capacity crowd at the 1968 Art Festival at Exeter University in Devon.

Just prior to her overseas tour, she had appeared at Williams College and Dartmouth College and recorded twelve cuts for a new LP album with her folk-rock band, the Carolyn Hester Coalition. The LP was to feature nine new songs and new arrangements of "Half the World," "Get Together," and "East Virginia."

Appearing with her at the Flag would be thirty-six-year-old Boston composer-arranger-performer Dave Blume, who was best known for his song "Turn Down Day." He would appear with Carolyn as her accompanist on bass and as a jazz piano soloist.

The music, while taking on a slightly different hue with Blume's presence, was refreshingly Carolyn Hester, and, again, she did well for the club and herself, with the week feeling like a family reunion. All the artists who had played the Flag were there just to hang out and enjoy, and, once again, Carolyn attracted large numbers of press people with resulting good coverage of her engagement.

During this time, in the months that ensued before the opening of the Speed Museum, I acquired two more important cars for my collection. I was pleased that I was able to add a 1959 German RSK Porsche and an Italian 1935 "monoposto" Maserati in time to restore them and have them ready for the museum opening.

The 1959 Porsche Spyder RSK RS60 1600 was

1959 RSK Porsche Spyder from Germany. 1967.
— Courtesy Robert Anshutz.

one of about twenty-five sold to private owners. The car was developed by the factory to compete in the two-liter class. With a five-speed transmission in a 1,200-pound space-framed car with a titanium body, it attained speeds of 156 mph.

To balance my collection, it was important to me to have a German car, especially a Porsche. Porsche had won one-two-three at the 1968 Sebring 12 Hours and had previously won the U.S. National Championships in SCCA every year from 1957-1964 and again in 1966 by drivers like Bob Holbert, Roger Penske, and Joe Buzetta.

We knew that this particular Porsche was formerly owned by Andy Steele of Norwalk, Connecticut, but we could never verify that it also had been owned and campaigned by Carroll Shelby's design engineer and racing driver, Ken Miles, who contributed to the design of the Shelby Cobras.

Before World War II, Dr. Ferdinand Porsche was an Austrian consulting engineer who was the leader of the Auto Union design team. He also designed the VW, which his son Perry Porsche developed into a sports car in 1952. Our 1959 machine was a direct descendant of that 1952 innovation.

The other car, an old 1935 Type 4C Maserati, had been found in a garage in the mountains of Ethiopia in the city of Asmara by C. B. Smith's son, David, who was serving there in the military.

The car's owner, Christopher Bigi, reputedly had won the 1934 Mille Miglia and had acquired the 4C Maserati the following year to compete in "voiturette" racing, a smaller class car affectionately described as a "Baby Grand Prix" car, its engine

Driving my 1935 4C Maserati "Baby Grand Prix" car.
— Courtesy Frank Armstrong.

being half the size of those cars on the European Grand Prix circuit.

With Alfa Romeo so dominating Grand Prix racing in Italy and all over Europe for three or four years, Maserati, Bugatti, and other manufacturers turned their attention to smaller "voiturette" racing cars of 1100 to 1500 cc where they enjoyed some success while Alfa won the Grand Prix events. The GP cars were eight-cylinder cars while the voiturette cars were four-cylinder.

At any rate, David wrote that the car was in reasonably good condition and could be bought for $2,500 Ethiopian. We continued writing back and forth from 1966 to 1968 and finally, arrangements were made to buy the car, crate it, and ship it, when David had a motorcycle accident and everything was delayed while he healed.

Expenses of crating the car, transporting it from Asmara to Masawa, getting it aboard a ship, the freight for shipping it, a broker's commission, plus insurance, totaled only $845 American. Then the shipping cost suddenly increased twenty-five percent from the original amount because the Suez Canal was closed due to the war between Israel and Egypt, and the car had to be shipped around the Cape. The crate with the Maserati in it sat on the dock at Masawa for a month, waiting for a Houston-bound ship with extra cargo space.

Finally, the car was shipped to Texas aboard the *Alcoa Mariner*, and we were notified that it was at the Port of Houston.

I gave Col. Joe McCrosky power of attorney to go pick it up at the dock. He signed for one Maserati, Type 4C, broke it out of its crate, and trailered it back to Austin. The transaction involv-

ing all of the various steps on David's end in Ethiopia, and all of the letter writing, negotiations, questions and instructions, funding, and all of the other details, took over two years to complete!

But the car arrived in Austin and it looked pretty solid. The paint was a faded red but the "boiler plate" steel body was perfect, with not a dent anywhere. The spoked wheels were perfect and the huge drum brakes were unscored. David had fixed the bent front spindle before the car was crated. It looked great.

When we pulled off the hood, which was louvered for cooling and held down by a pair of spring-loaded clamps and a leather strap on each side, we discovered a beautiful supercharged V-4 double overhead cam engine. While the engine was spotless on the exterior, I didn't know what condition it was in on the inside, so we trailered it up to my Ferrari mechanic, Burney Hillan, in Fort Worth, and asked him to go through it before starting it.

Within a matter of days, Burney called all excited with the news that the engine was perfect and sounded like a crisp Offy 110. He said clearances were good, compression balanced, everything worked beautifully, including the supercharger and the starter (with a new battery and cable added). He told me to come and get it.

When I got to Fort Worth and Burney fired it up, I was like a kid with a new toy. The Maserati fairly purred, and I was pleased and excited as I trailered it back to Austin to have the exterior sanded and painted by Doug Scales Body Shop. While it was there, I ordered new tires and had the driver's seat reupholstered in black naugahyde.

The Maser came out of the shop painted Italian racing red with white spoked wheels with newly chromed lug bolts, a white grill and newly chromed exhaust pipe running the length of the left side. New nickel-plated clamps and new leather straps on each side of the hood made the little car look as if it had just rolled out of the factory.

It was a beauty, and I couldn't wait to get it out on a track to see how it handled at top speed.

In late May George Wein and I collaborated on a jazz concert at the Municipal Auditorium. Wein was on his way to play Mexico with Dave Brubeck, Gerry Mulligan, and Woody Herman, and by side-tracking a few miles to Austin on the way, we were able to produce a successful concert on May 21. We used the event to announce the coming July 4 opening of the Speed Museum and a special folk concert at Zilker Park to celebrate it. We also announced the revised three-city format for the Longhorn Jazz Festival eight days later on July 12 (Dallas), July 13 (Austin), and July 14 (Houston). After the jazz concert and a quick visit with Wein, I again turned my attention to getting the cars together for the Speed Museum.

While I was in Fort Worth picking up the 1935 Maserati, Burney Russell told me that I could have the 1960 Type 61 Maserati that had been sitting under cover in his garage for several years. The price was $1,000, complete with trailer!

I jumped at the chance to acquire this car even though the original engine had long since been removed. The car was now obsolete for racing, even though it had won the SCCA Southwest Division Championship three years before, powered by a Ferrari Testa Rossa V-12 and driven by Doc McGuire. Burney told me that the car had been owned by Alan Connell and formerly had a four-cylinder in-line double overhead cam two-liter Maserati engine with two spark plugs per cylinder and twin Weber carburetors.

The frame and body were unique, designed by an engineer named Alfieri. His "birdcage" chassis design, built upon an infinite number of tubes of varying size and thickness, gave the car great strength with extreme lightness. He used the same Maserati suspension components as the Grand Prix car of 1959-60 with disc brakes fitted.

Enough victories were chalked up by the first five or six cars built to leave the racing world highly impressed. The fog-shrouded victory at the 1960 Nurburgring 1000 km by Sterling Moss and Dan Gurney was one of Maserati's historic victories.

This particular long-tailed birdcage, chassis number 2,461, was one of three Camoradi Team cars entered by the late Lucky Cassner in the 1960 Sebring 12 Hours Endurance Race. One of those cars turned in a lap record at Sebring, and Texas' Carroll Shelby drove one to victory at *The Examiner* Grand Prix at Riverside the following month in a field that included Lance Reventlow's Scarab, Dan Gurney's Buick-powered "Old Yaller II," Krause's Chevy-powered D-Jag, Ken Miles' Porsche RS60, a three-liter Ferrari driven by Lovely, and Jack Brabham's Cooper Monaco.

We retrieved the Birdcage Maserati and trailer from Burney on the next trip to Fort Worth and turned it over to Doug Scales Body Shop to have its aluminum body, Borani spoked wheels, and exhaust

Twenty-five years of Italian racing design evolution: (top) 1960 Long-Tailed Birdcage Maserati; (bottom) 1934 4C "monoposto" Maserati at The Texas Speed Museum. 1968.
— Courtesy Merri Lu Park.

system prettied up for its new life in the Speed Museum.

We built a display where the 1960 Maserati would set above and behind the 1935 Maserati on the floor, a stark contrast in Italian design evolution over twenty-five years.

As the work progressed on the museum, we cranked up the publicity on the forthcoming opening and displayed some of our cars in Houston and San Antonio and ran some of them in gymkhanas and autocross events. Two days before I was supposed to load up the 1935 Maserati and the Monza Ferrari for the June 7-9 "Race Cars '68" show in Dallas, the media was saturated with the news that Robert F. Kennedy had been shot in Los Angeles, and again we were jarred back into the stark reality of how vulnerable we all were to the whims of armed extremists. This chain of assassinations was tearing away at America's confidence and comfort. Would American life ever be the same? Or, were we in for even more devastating violence in the coming years?

We hardly had returned from the Dallas show, when we realized our target date for the museum opening was less than three weeks away. Construction and painting well into the night every night, continuing operations six nights a week at the Chequered Flag club, and the logistics of creating displays, hanging photographs, and getting the history together on each car in the collection for display plaques took more time every day than we ever dreamed it would.

At the same time, I had made the final payment on a mint-conditioned 1956 British D-Jaguar with under 1,500 miles on its odometer. I acquired it from Charles E. Brown in Monroe, Louisiana, who had successfully competed in Southwestern SCCA racing in Texas, Oklahoma, and Louisiana in the late 1950s before putting it up on blocks for storage. The sleek midnight blue machine had a few tiny gravel dings on the nose, which still displayed the original Jaguar decal, and the Dunlop decals were still on the wheels. It was, essentially, a brand new twelve-year-old car. What a find!

The D-Type was the most powerful Jaguar ever built at the time of its introduction at the LeMans 24-Hour Race in May of 1954. It was "the car" on the international racing calendar of 1954-1957, winning LeMans the last three consecutive years of this period. The early D-Type was timed on the LeMans straight with Sterling Moss at the wheel at 172.8

1956 British D-Jaguar racing car, which was the forerunner of the XKE street versions.

— Courtesy Robert Anshutz.

mph, and its final 1957-58 version's maximum speed was said to be around 190!

In the U.S., D-Type Jags driven by the late Walt Hansgen won the SCCA national class championships in 1956 and 1957.

So, this was a gem of a collector's marque to obtain, and it was probably the best existing D-Jaguar in the world. It even smelled like a new car.

While we didn't have to restore it, we took it up to Fort Worth to be checked out after its lengthy storage, and with a little tune-up and oil change

Burney Russell had it sounding like the new twelve-year-old it was.

We decided to close the Chequered Flag for the first four days of July while we put everything in shape for both the opening of the Speed Museum on July 5-7, and the club's simultaneous second grand opening in nine months.

The night of July 4 we staged a free three-hour "American Folk Festival" at the Hillside Theater at Zilker Park designed to replace the now defunct KHFI-FM Summer Music Festival and to herald the opening of the Speed Museum.

On stage, I introduced the near-capacity crowd to young Dallas folk singer Richard Dean, Kenneth Threadgill and his band, the Exit Folk Trio, *sitar* player John Steele, Chequered Flag manager Allen Damron, and then capped off the evening with the romantic voice of Luis Balderas with the trumpets and guitars of *Mariachi Eco de Mexico*. The crowd saluted the concert boisterously with cheers, applause, and standing ovations.

Our racing Texans wall in the museum included (top, from left): A. J. Foyt, Jim Hall, and Carroll Shelby with Lloyd Ruby, Jim McElreath, and Johnny Rutherford (lower left).

— Courtesy Robert Anshutz.

At the concert we freely distributed $1 passes to the museum's grand opening that admitted two-for-the-price-of-one during the ceremonial three days, July 5-7. For 50¢ a head, they could see the permanent display of vintage and post-war sports and racing cars from England, Germany, Italy, and the U.S., representing fifty years of automotive competition.

Bill Head, one-time Flag bartender, became manager of the museum, working with Chequered Flag manager Allen Damron. Bill had been working on getting the museum open for months and eagerly supervised the registration for a free pedal-powered Lotus Ford racing car for three- to eight-year-olds to be given away on July 8. Bill also distributed free Vintage Race posters for the coming Aqua Festival event, where we planned to roll out as many museum cars as we could for an exhibition race on the city streets with the Carrera de la Capital Sports Car Races.

The largest gallery of The Texas Speed Museum included (from left) Monza Ferrari, Lester MG, RSK Porsche, D-Jaguar, and the two Maseratis.

— Courtesy Robert Anshutz.

Hours for the museum were 1:00 to 8:00 P.M. daily with admission for adults at $1. After 8:00 P.M., patrons of the Chequered Flag were admitted free to view the cars, racing paintings by noted American artist Peter Helck, and racing memorabilia.

In one small section of the building, at 1415 Lavaca, our friend Bettie Biggs opened her "unique boutique" called PIZZAZZ, with its fashions for "young outdoors people going places."

The opening was a great success, and with the bar moved out of the Chequered Flag main club room, the seating increased to 150. As the summer season wore on, we opened a Paddock Shop in the museum, where competition drivers could purchase fire-resistant Nomex driving suits, Bell helmets, goggles, driving gloves, racing shoes, Champion

Spark Plugs, Castrol Motor Oil, Classic Car Wax, and many other automotive items and accessories like racing mirrors and tire gauges.

In the meantime, Kenneth Threadgill headed up to the 1968 Newport Folk Festival in response to George Wein's invitation and, while Threadgill was well received there, he was most thrilled by his reunion with Janis Joplin, who by now had become a major pop star.

Kenneth Threadgill's biggest thrill playing the Newport Folk Festival was getting to spend some time with Janis Joplin.

— Courtesy David Gahr.

While they were together at Newport, Janis promised Threadgill that she would get him an audition for a recording date. While Janis died before she could fulfill her promise, she did tell Kris Kristofferson about Threadgill, and Kris finally had a chance several years later to hear Threadgill at Darrell Royal's home during the 1972 Dripping Springs Reunion. That meeting immediately resulted in a Nashville session for Threadgill produced by Kristofferson's people. That recording has never been released.

There were two other cars added to the ARKAY collection prior to the opening of the museum.

The first of these was a beautiful British racing green 1938 MG-TA roadster purchased from Air Force Lt. David Stripling. The MG-TA was the first of the T-Type Midgets made by MG. It first appeared in 1936 and became popular enough for 3400 Types TA and TB to be built and sold prior to the September 1939 outbreak of World War II when production ceased. Six years later, in 1945, the first TCs were built and exported to the U.S., where they

In the British area of the museum our 1951 MG-TD (left) and 1938 MG-TA were displayed along with some of our gymkhana, hillclimb, auto cross, and racing trophies and plaques.

— Courtesy Robert Anshutz.

John Hancock driving our 1958 Type 250 Testa Rossa Ferrari, which was the spare factory team car for the 1958 LeMans 24-Hour Race. 1968.

— Courtesy Robert Anshutz.

were an immediate sensation and established "sports cars" in America. Ten thousand TCs were built before giving way to the newer MG-TD in 1949. Between 1949 and 1953, 30,000 MG-TDs were built and nearly 20,000 of them were sold in the U.S. Nine-thousand-six-hundred MG-TF and MG-TF1500s were built during 1953-1955 to end the T-Type reign of twenty years that closed with the introduction of the first "envelope bodied" MGA1500s in September of 1955.

The other car, a 1958 Type 250 "pontoon fendered" Testa Rossa Ferrari, was finally acquired from Carl Kleiner of Cisco, Texas, after many months of consideration and hesitance on Kleiner's part to release the car to us. He ultimately decided to sell the car, and it became the most important of our collection and our final acquisition.

The Testa Rossa Ferraris dominated Ferrari sports car racing activity for five years, from 1956-1961, and ran in four-cylinder form (Types 500 and 625) and in twelve-cylinder form (Type 250). Our car was the three-liter Type 250 V-12 DOHC with six dual Weber carburetors, the same power plant that Scaglietti adapted for his California roadster in 1961.

The Type 250s were the most successful and were introduced in prototype form at the 1957 Mille Miglia. The first major win for the car was at the 1958 Sebring 12-Hour Endurance Race, in which Collins and Hill co-drove to first place. Testa Rossa also won the 1958 Targa Florio, took second behind Aston Martin at the Nurburgring, and then the Hill/Gendbien Testa Rossa won the 1958 LeMans 24 Hours.

Other Testa Rossa international victories included the 1959 Sebring 12 Hours (1-2-4-6); 1959 Nurburgring (2-3); 1960 Buenos Aries (1-2); 1960 Sebring (3); 1960 Targa Florio (2); 1960 Nurburgring (3); and the 1960 LeMans 24 Hours (1-2).

This special "pontoon fendered" left-hand drive with its aerodynamic cut-away fenders was a spare car for the 1958 LeMans Race, where its mate won first place. The car was then sold to Fort Worth oil man Gary Laughlin, who drove it to three second places at Oklahoma City, Hammond, and San Marcos at races that included drivers like Jim Hall, Jack Hinkle, and Hap Sharp. It was then owned in succession by Jim Hall, John Mecom, Jr., and Leroy Melcher.

Five days after the Speed Museum opening, I joined George Wein in Dallas for the opening concert of the newly revised Longhorn Jazz Festival that would play the Dallas State Fair Coliseum on July 12, the Municipal Auditorium in Austin on July 13, and the Houston Coliseum on July 14 as the "Schlitz Salute to Jazz."

From the Austin beginnings, the relationship with Schlitz grew to sponsorship of "the largest jazz festival ever to embark on a nationwide tour." The artists appearing in Texas included Dionne Warwick, the Wes Montgomery Quintet, the Cannonball Adderly Quintet, the Herbie Mann Quintet, and the Gary Burton Quartet.

Wein explained, "Texas jazz fans had to travel so far to come to Austin these past two years, we thought it would be best to take the festival to them, so we have built a big one-night show which will play Dallas and Houston, as well as Austin."

The tour, which played twenty other major cities coast-to-coast, did so well in Texas that Schlitz was repaid their previous year's underwriting. Although I emceed the concerts, handled the publicity and concert hall and hotel logistics, assisted by Sue Poole and Dino Santangelo of Cincinnati's Ohio Valley Jazz Festival, this was in-

Longhorn Jazz Festival logo.

The second lap of the 1968 Vintage Sports Car Race (from left) Sanderson's MG-TD, Bob Sieberg in the Stanguellini, my 4C Maserati, Joe McCrosky in the RSK Porsche, to his right rear Haines' Elva Formula Junior, and Bob Samm in the D-Jaguar.

— Courtesy Austin American-Statesman.

creasingly George's show. Following the festival and a brief meeting to wrap things up, George and the musicians headed for Omaha, Denver, and Oklahoma City to continue the tour. At the 1968 Newport Jazz Festival, Schlitz also sponsored a big "Schlitz Salute to the Big Bands."

In addition to this twenty-four city tour in 1968, George also produced festivals in Boston, Charlotte, Atlanta, Hampton Institute, and, of course, Newport. Overseas, he produced events in London, Paris, Berlin, Helsinki, Stockholm, Copenhagen, Rotterdam, Brussels, Venice, Lecco, Tel Aviv, Dublin, Barcelona, Belfast, Frankfurt, and Japan.

Returning to Austin, I attended two driver's schools to get my SCCA competition license. My early success in winning both drivers' school races in my Stanguellini only fired my enthusiasm for racing, and I went on to win five more races, a sanctioned hill climb, and two auto-crosses during the remainder of the season. We raced about every other weekend at road courses like Hammond, Green Valley, Galveston, San Marcos, Hondo, and Aloe Field, winning a regional championship in Formula C.

During the racing season we bought a Ford F-100 van, and to support our racing and fulfill sponsorship commitments to Castrol, Champion, and Classic, we sold accessories, oil, plugs, and equipment to drivers in the pits at trackside. To publicize the museum, the Texas Speed Museum logo was painted on the sides of the Stang, alongside our sponsorship decals from Castrol, Champion Spark Plugs, and Goodyear Tires.

In August, during the Aqua Festival, my involvement was totally Speed Museum related, one of the bonuses of retirement. We staged and publicized the first Vintage Sports Car Race, co-sponsored by Peal's Potato Chip Company and the

Piloting the supercharged 1935 Maserati was a great experience. 1968.

— Courtesy Austin American-Statesman.

Speed Museum. The event would feature sports cars of fifteen years or older and front-engined formula cars of the pre-1960 period and would run as a special event of the Aqua Festival SCCA National Championship Sports Car Races that had returned to the streets of Austin around the Municipal Auditorium.

The new Austin Raceway Park north of town turned its attention increasingly to drag racing.

The museum committed nine cars from the collection, and it took all day Friday to drive them one or two at a time from the 14th and Lavaca location to the course in South Austin, where they were stored overnight in the Municipal Auditorium.

Drivers for my cars were chosen from the best

79

Newspaper publisher Dick Brown's XK120 Jaguar leads the Maserati through the esses. 1968.

— Courtesy *Austin American-Statesman.*

A lap ahead of everyone else, the RSK Porsche driven by Joe McCrosky wins by a nose over the D-Jaguar piloted by Bob Samm. 1968.

— Courtesy *Austin American-Statesman.*

in our region, plus museum mechanic Jerome Fields, who drove our second Stanguellini. My SCCA car, the black number 2 ex-Von Trips Stanguellini, was driven by Bob Sieberg, while Allen Damron (who had already been to one SCCA drivers' school) drove our ex-Carroll Shelby MG-TD number 22. Race chairman Russell Fish drove the 1958 Testa Rossa Ferrari, and I piloted my 1935 4C Maserati. Rod Allen took the wheel of the MG-TA and my old friend, Citroen and Volvo dealer Earlton Smith, drove the Lester MG Team Car number 52. Col. Joe McCrosky drove the black RSK Porsche number 122 and Houston's Bob Samm, a former Sebring driver, piloted the midnight blue D-Jaguar number 6.

Other entries included newspaper publisher Dick Brown's XK120 Jaguar, Bill Brauder's J2X Allard motorcycle-fendered machine, a yellow Elva Formula Junior driven by Mike Haines from Beaumont, a 1963 Cunningham Coupe, and others. Burney Russell came down from Fort Worth to fine tune and maintain my cars and to help anyone else who needed assistance.

The race was even more fun than I anticipated and, for me, driving the 1935 Maserati at top speed was a great thrill. I got to open it up on the straightaways and loved it when my head snapped back from the supercharger kicking in. It handled surprisingly well through the tight turns and the esses, its big mechanical brakes working smoothly. However, the hard rubber tires didn't provide all of the traction I expected, nor the stability I was accustomed to with racing compound tires. As a result, I spun out on one turn halfway through the race and had to fight my way back up to finish sixth out of the field of fifteen cars.

On the last four laps of the race, the D-Jag and the RSK staged quite a battle for first place, with Col. McCrosky pulling the Porsche ahead at the last moment to nose out Samm's Jaguar. Bob Sieberg finished third in the Von Trips Stang. The first three cars had lapped the field in the ten-lap event on the 1.2-mile course. The cars received a standing ovation from the crowd, and all of us had animated descriptions to share of our rides in the old cars.

When the race was over, all the cars finally returned to the museum and cleaned up for display, we celebrated at the Chequered Flag, where Big Bill Moss and Richard Dean were entertaining. We all agreed that we should hold another vintage race next year, and I also began to solidify plans to take

We commissioned this original painting by Peter Helck of Taruffi winning the 1954 Targa Floio in a Lancia. The painting was later destroyed in a house fire in Kerrville. 1968.

— Courtesy Robert Anshutz.

Another of our collection of Peter Helck originals is this one of Nuvolari's Alfa winning the 1935 Targa Florio. This painting was later shipped back to Helck. 1968.
                                    — Courtesy Robert Anshutz.

the 1935 Maserati to Bridgehampton, where a big vintage race would be held the next month in conjunction with a Can-Am race.

Among the acquisitions at our Texas Speed Museum were several original paintings by famed automotive artist Peter Helck. Helck's illustrations were featured in national advertising for new cars and trucks for many years, but he distinguished himself internationally with his renderings of classic racing scenes.

We owned Helck's original of the number 16 Locomobile at the 1908 Vanderbilt Cup Race as well as the painting of Nuvolari's Alfa number 2 at the 1935 Targa Florio. Further, we later commissioned Helck to create for us a large painting of Taruffi winning the 1954 Targa Florgio in a Lancia, which we unveiled at the 1970 fall reunion of the American Lancia Club at Princeton, New Jersey. We also had a number of Helck's notable prints matted and framed and on display. These prints and the Helck originals added a special dimension to our museum gallery and attracted much attention and comment from museum visitors.

Bob Holland, the SCCA's chief starter for our region, agreed to accompany me to Bridgehampton and share the long drive up and back. Practice for the Can-Am on Long Island was set for Friday, September 13, and Bob and I targeted our arrival for the 12th, taking a fairly leisurely three days towing the 1935 Maserati on a trailer behind our museum pickup and sleeping each night with one eye open, concerned that someone would mess with our thirty-three-year-old Italian machine.

We arrived in plenty of time and in good shape, and the weather for the weekend was expected to be clear and sunny. We were accorded a warm welcome as one of the twenty-eight vintage racers entered in the exhibition race. We had almost unlimited access to the pits, the people, and the cars. It was difficult to be casual and cool about being there, but we did our best to overcome the excitement of getting to know Sterling Moss. The former World Champion Grand Prix driver was friendly, personable, amusing, and articulate. He wrote his London address on the back of my pit pass in the event I wanted to get together with him at some future date.

Among the Can-Am competitors, I visited with Mexico's Pedro Rodriguez, Dan Gurney, who was sponsored by Castrol, and the Penske crew, including Mark Donahue. These were among the world's fastest drivers in whatever they drove. They were all well-educated, congenial, friendly, and expressed considerable interest in my Maserati and the Texas Speed Museum in Austin.

The vintage car owners and drivers were an equally affable bunch and included some of the most respected names in automotive circles. Among them was Austin Clark, who entered five cars in the vintage race, including a 1911 Simplex, a 1911 Mercer, a 1926 Bugatti, a 1919 Stutz, and a 1939 MG-TC. Karl Ludvigson, author of the Ferrari book, was also on hand and entered a 1948 Connaught.

After the Friday time trials for the Can-Am, nearly all the vintage car people went to Austin Clark's Long Island Automotive Museum for cocktails and then out for dinner. During the course of these social get-togethers, I had a chance to meet and chat with many of the Vintage Sports Car Club of America leaders, including John Willock, R. Willis Leith, Fred Herdeen (whose 1950 Type 166 Ferrari won the Ferrari Club silver trophy presented by Luigi Chinetti), and Stanley Nowack. These were among the nation's top vintage car enthusiasts whose interest in cars had taken them to the pinnacle of the 1960s automotive circles.

On Saturday the dawn was bright and clear, and the Can-Am cars practiced from 10:30 until noon, turning incredible lap times on the 2.85-mile winding Bridgehampton Race Circuit. Following the practice, nearly thirty vintage cars assembled on the starting grid, including Ferraris, Bentleys, a couple of Siatas, a 1954 HRG, and Jim McAllister in his 1954 Maserati 2000.

My heart was pounding in my throat as I waited

The starting grid at Bridgehampton, NY, 1968 Vintage Race, with my 1935 Maserati in the middle of the pack. 1968.

— Courtesy Bob Holland.

on the grid in my old Maserati, waiting for the pace car to lead us around the course for the pace lap. The Maserati fired right up, sounding crisp and eager, the smell of Castrol castor bean oil wafting up from the exhaust along my left side. Glancing to my left, I was suddenly aware of thousands of racing fans in the stands at the start-finish line. Then the pack of vintage machines, spanning more than fifty years of automotive history, began to move off and circled the more than two-mile course with its often photographed Chevron Bridge and Lowenbrau Bridge, its tight hairpin turn numbers 10 and 11, with Arents Turn, before hitting the long front straight. At every turn crowds of fans were settled in for the day with field glasses, picnic lunches, sun hats and glasses, and their colorful race programs in hand.

At the end of the pace lap, the green starting flag dropped, and although we had been advised in the pre-race drivers meeting that this was strictly an exhibition, in seconds, most of the pack was charging hard toward turn one, Hansgen Turn, just past the Chevron Bridge, and gray exhaust smoke suddenly filled the air above the field of fast-moving cars. Jim McAllister spun his Maserati at the second turn, Millstone Turn, and, as I began to get the feel of the 4C Maserati, I increased my speeds. In fact, I was clocked at 109 mph on the main straight as I passed everything except the 1954 LeMans Fraser-Nash and the 1950s Ferraris and Maseratis.

The run lasted nearly an hour, and the 4C flew as it rapidly took each ensuing turn in a sliding four-wheel drift, the signs and banners and crowds blurring by. Remembering the spinout at Austin, I exercised some caution at the tight turn number 3 and going through the hairpin, but for the most part I kept the accelerator down, enjoying the thrill of how this thirty-three-year-old car was performing. I felt right at home in the cockpit, gripping the sturdy steering wheel, shifting gears up and down through the turns, and feeling the supercharger kicking in on the straights.

It was one of the most fun excursions I'd ever had, and it only occurred to me after the checkered flag that I had only now learned the limitations of the huge mechanical drum brakes, which worked remarkably well without grabbing or pulling to one side or the other. I was also relieved that the large twenty-seven-inch wheels held up even at harsh G-forces through the turns at high speed. After all, the car had no roll bar and was made out of heavy boiler plate that would have flattened me like a mashed potato in the event of a roll over.

The car, the crowd, the event, and the people we met were all part of an exceptional experience, and the trip was outstanding from beginning to end. We did have trouble with our tow truck transmission coming home through Buffalo, NY, to see my dad, but his Ford dealer took care of everything, and we were on our way after a pleasant visit and a one-day delay.

Back in Austin, our September calendar at the Chequered Flag was highlighted by our first anniversary weekend, Friday through Sunday, September 20-22, with Allen Damron teamed with a different club favorite every night—Richard Dean on Friday, Big Bill Moss on Saturday, and Jim Schulman on Sunday. The audiences celebrated each night with the first round of drinks free.

During the rest of the month, the same four performers played in various combinations, with San Antonio's Shane and Kitty Appling joining

The LeMans-winning Ford Mark IV GT of A. J. Foyt and Dan Gurney. 1968.

— Courtesy Robert Anshutz.

Damron on October 4. One of the shows at the auditorium during that week starred Ray Price and Marty Robbins, and Bob Wills played the Broken Spoke a few days later.

I had been talking with the racing division of Ford Motor Company about lending us their LeMans-winning Mark IV GT for display at the

The 1967 Chaparral 2F loaned to us by Jim Hall of Midland, Texas, was the lap record-holder at both Sebring and Daytona, co-driven by Phil Hill and Mike Spencer. 1969.

— Courtesy Robert Anshutz.

museum, and the car showed up to be displayed by the 17th of the month. Houstonian A. J. Foyt had co-driven it to the twenty-four-hour victory with Dan Gurney, and when its display time at the museum was over, Ford gave A. J. the car as a gesture of appreciation.

On the 18th of the month, a young blind girl named Bonnie Cross made her first billed appearance at the Flag, teamed with Damron and Dean. She had an incredibly beautiful voice and quickly gained self-confidence, winning for herself a return engagement on the 25th. Just prior to her return, Willie Nelson and the Record Men played the Broken Spoke.

Allen Damron and Richard Dean filled out the rest of the October calendar with Him, He and Me, from San Antonio's Kelly's Pub, doing three shows on the 26th. Having been heavily promoted on stage by Allen for several weeks, we had a good advance reservation list, and they did well for a first-time appearance. The contemporary trio had good energy and warm harmonies and created a big sound. We climaxed the month on the 31st with a Halloween party starring Damron, Richard Dean, Bonnie

Cross, and Big Bill Moss, plus a free beer promotion for the funniest face with or without a mask.

While we were doing our folk thing, UT drama professor B. Iden Payne was honored for his seventy years in theater. He had staged many spectacularly successful productions and was widely recognized as a leading Shakespearean authority. He was a very intense but very approachable man, quick to smile.

November at the Flag kicked off with a two-night return appearance by Segle Fry, and the month finished out with Damron, Richard Dean, Bonnie Cross, the Radiant Set, Big Bill Moss, Jim Schulman, and San Antonio's Him, He and Me all making appearances. We had heavy traffic on the second weekend when the Starving Artists accepted our invitation to come in out of the unexpectedly wet and chilly weather and hold their two-day show indoors at The Flag. Our staff jumped in and did all of the extra setting up and tearing down both days, as though it were part of our regular routine.

Even with the 11th Door now closed, there was plenty of activity in town. The University of Texas Student Union opened their coffeehouse on campus with a concert by the Exit (Bob Watkins, Gayle Epperson, and Doug Beaty), followed a few days later by Keith Sykes, Richard Dean, and Becky Stevens. Meanwhile, across town on the 11th, KOKE presented a country music show at the auditorium with Jeanie C. Riley, Charlie Pride, LeRoy Van Dyke, Conway Twitty, and Stonewall Jackson, while Jose Feliciano played on campus on the 18th at a packed Gregory Gym. Near the end of the month in Houston, Nina Vance was opening her new Alley Theatre.

December continued with Damron and Dean playing most of the nights, with a couple of dates played by Segle Fry. On one evening Segle was joined by Travis Holland, Gloria Holland, and Drake Bryant. We also staged a three-night "Christmas Festival of Folk Carols," with Allen Damron being joined by Moss, Dean, Bonnie Cross, and Scott Stripling for the weekend before Christmas. Closed for the 24th and 25th, Moss and Damron played the week between Christmas and New Year's, with Him, He and Me playing New Year's Eve to a full house at $15 a couple, including champagne (the real stuff?), hats, noisemakers, beer, and an after-hours set by Damron with complimentary roast beef sandwiches. Earlier in the month, Ernest Tubb and the Texas Troubadors played at the Broken Spoke.

As 1969 opened, the Flag featured Damron and Dean, with Moss, Allen Case, Segle, Wayne Holtzman, and Diane Larkin each doing a few evenings. The 19th was Inauguration Day, with Preston Smith and Ben Barnes taking oaths for governor and lieutenant governor in Austin, and in Washington, D.C., Nixon and Agnew were sworn in as the thirty-seventh president and vice-president. Allen and I reflected on the night we put on a huge campaign party for Senator John Tower in Dallas, where we first saw Agnew in person. We were not too impressed with him but enjoyed the giant fund raiser with John Wayne, Zsa Zsa Gabor, Buzz Aldrin, Mel Blanc, Tex Ritter, and Holly Bond and the Bluegrass Texans. Wayne knocked me down when he leaped from a stagecoach, breaking his leap by putting his huge hand on my shoulder. With Inauguration Day behind us, we looked forward to Willie Nelson and Waylon Jennings playing the grand opening night of the "beautiful new" Dessau Hall out north of Austin.

One of the things we learned early in the new year was that the Newport Folk Festival would not happen in 1969. Apparently, the directors decided to take a year off and to revise it in some manner. The event had focused national attention on many regional artists during the years past and helped both traditional and contemporary artists at all levels to earn recognition and a bigger following, resulting in careers that worked and better living income. We wondered if Newport would return in 1970.

At the club in Austin, the major performers continued to be Damron and Moss, along with pairings with Dave Houston and Karen Burk, plus a few nights with Segle or Wayne Holtzman.

This was the time when the Beatles new album *Yellow Submarine* was being introduced, Steve McQueen was starring in the film *Bullet,* Harry Aikin of the Night Hawk Restaurants was mayor, and Travis LaRue was mayor pro tem. The Beach Boys, Van Cliburn, Spanish Flamenco guitarist Carlos Montoya, and country star Eddy Arnold all made Austin appearances, while Kenneth Threadgill was a mainstay at the Broken Spoke. Our guitar-playing friend, Bob Landis Armstrong, was in the state legislature, and, in Washington, Nixon was talking troop withdrawals from Vietnam. In sports, the Green Bay Packers were saying farewell to Vince Lombardi, following a legendary decade of professional football.

On the auto sports scene, *Austin American-Statesman* readers were getting good coverage of all kinds of auto racing activities in weekly columns by T. Q. Jones and Mary Ann Chapman. The regional coverage of all racing was outstanding: Sports Car Club of America (SCCA), National Association of Stock Car Racing (NASCAR), United States Auto Club (USAC), motorcycles, and local and regional stock car racing were all getting space on the sports pages.

For our part, we took two cars to the Polar Prix races at Green Valley up near Fort Worth, and I won my first 1969 outing in the Stanguellini, while Mexican driver Rodolfo Junco de la Vega placed well in our RSK Porsche. Rodolfo's family owned the *El Norte* newspaper in Monterrey. Our new Winkelmann Racing Division was represented by Austin owner-driver John Hancock in his new Winkelmann Formula Ford as the SCCA national season kicked off.

Champion driver and designer Roy Winkelmann and our Austin mechanic Jerome Shields had established a dealership for Formula Ford and Formula B cars, marketing them under the Speed Museum umbrella and using our limited garage space that opened out onto 14th Street at the north end of the Chequered Flag building. Museum visitors could now see a modern racing car operation right along side the vintage displays. While the space was small, quite a few of the sleek fiberglass-bodied open wheel cars were sold out of it, and Shields managed to do limited repair work and race preparation there.

In the meantime, I had negotiated a deal for Holiday House Restaurants owner Ralph Moreland to sponsor an Offenhauser midget entrant in the $50,000 Astro Grand Prix in the coming month of March. It was a big deal, widely publicized internationally and seemingly drawing entries from everywhere. Well-known five-time Indy veteran Johnny Rutherford would drive the car under the banner of the "Austin Aqua Festival Special."

During this period, I bought a DeTomaso Formula C car from Michigan, which, while it was still a front-engined car, was newer and supposedly faster than our Von Trips Stanguellini. I only won one race in it because it was unreliable and planned to sell it. If I was going to competitively race nationally in the under 1100 cc Formula C class, I obviously needed a newer rear-engined car capable of much higher speeds and acceleration along with faster cornering.

During March, our regulars continued to play the Flag with Three Faces West (made up of Rick Fowler, Wayne Kidd, and Ray Hubbard) scheduled to play March 7 and 8, while I was at the Astro Grand Prix with Rutherford. Two days before the big Houston race, we had a Speed Museum open house so the public could meet Johnny, and see the spiffy number 6 Offy owned by Scott Hunter. Joining Hunter and Rutherford at the open house and at a special dinner at the Villa Capri were international drivers Jochin Rindt and Paul Nigel Bates, England's Bob Winkelmann, who was sponsor of brother Roy's Formula 2 Winkelmann Racing Team, plus Ralph Moreland, who held a drawing for six pairs of tickets to the races at the Astrodome.

The big Astrodome Grand Prix scheduled two 100-lap feature races both nights and drew such stellar drivers as Mario Andretti and top Texas drivers, including A. J. Foyt, Lloyd Ruby, and Jim MacElreath, but midget racing proved again its total unpredictability, and the big prize money was won by Lee Kunzman.

Five days before the races, on March 3, NASA's most ambitious undertaking, a ten-day mission to the moon, known as Apollo 9, was successful, splashing down in the Atlantic on March 13. At the same time rumors reached us of the impending breakup of America's most famous bluegrass partnership: Lester Flatt and Earl Scruggs were going their separate ways.

While Jerome Shields was busying himself with the Winkelmann Racing effort, I was negotiating for a dealership with Italian automaker Lancia. Their automobiles had a long heritage in competition, including the factory team winning in the under-two-liter category at the Sebring 12 Hours of Florida in 1968. Sterling Moss and Innes Ireland were among the famous drivers piloting Lancia's in 1969, and among other wins across Europe, Lancia won one-two-three in the 1,000-mile Italian Rallye of San Remo. Perhaps Lancia would be my chance to compete in the Sebring 12 Hours with the possibility of finishing and even winning my class!

At any rate, my negotiations with the Lancia importer-distributor, Algar Enterprises in Pennsylvania, moved quickly ahead, and as I waited for the first shipment of new Lancia cars, I was invited to Sebring as a guest of the Lancia factory team on the weekend of March 20-23. All kinds of things were going on in Texas as Peter Paul and Mary were scheduled for a sold-out concert at Municipal Auditorium, and, over at Bryan/College Station, the ground was being broken for a giant new Texas International Speedway with all of our

SCCA Lone Star Region officials invited. I winced at all the choices but went on to the Sebring 12 Hours with the team.

It was exciting being on hand at close quarters with the team and to watch their professional effort to repeat the Lancia win of 1968. During practice, the social times around the swank hotel swimming pool, and during the race itself, I struck up a friendship with Innes Ireland's co-driver Mike Tillson from Philadelphia. He was young and slight of form, smiled easily, but had a focused intensity about him that reflected his commitment to winning.

The Lancia entry led the under-two-liter touring class for a good portion of the race, but just when the race looked as if it would go to Lancia again, the car ran out of gas and coasted to a stop short of the finish line. This loss and the increasing expenses of fielding factory teams solidified the factory's decision not to enter a factory team in 1970. While I keenly felt the sting of defeat along with the rest of the Lancia team members, the glimmer of hope that I could mount a better managed effort with a private entry at the 1970 Sebring Classic began to define itself. I returned to Texas with renewed resolve, and a plan to compete began to take shape in my mind. I found it hard to think of anything else, but there were a lot of things going on as I pulled into Austin on the 25th.

We had to get some cars ready for an auto show on the coming weekend, and the night I came home, Buffy St. Marie played a sold-out concert at Gregory Gym on the UT campus. Her "Universal Soldier," with its view of all wars, had swept across the country. Campus protests against the war in Vietnam were so severe and numerous that President Nixon spoke about it often, and the Texas legislature passed a law allowing police to go on campuses across the state to maintain the peace and protect property.

The same week, President "Ike" Eisenhower died, and the promoter of the March 28 Eddy Arnold concert was so relieved to see a large crowd in the face of national mourning that he finally decided to go ahead with it.

Over the weekend, we displayed our RSK Porsche and one of the new Winkelmann cars at a Capital Plaza Auto Show. The shopping center event was a mixture of new cars, antiques, dune buggies, and racing cars. In addition to working the auto show, we all kept up on the news of the Eisenhower funeral train to Abilene, Kansas, as the nation mourned Ike's passing. On the 30th, almost unnoticed, radio station KASE signed on as the FM side of KVET without much fanfare. Eisenhower's passing was a personal loss for many of us who served in Korea, and I didn't feel like going to see Roy Acuff when he played at the Broken Spoke on April l. It was more comfortable to just drop by the Flag and catch a set by Allen Damron and Dave Houston.

That weekend, Damron was joined on stage by Richard Dean, and we were all talking about the cancellation of the Smothers Brothers Comedy Hour by CBS-TV. The controversy would remain a topic of conversation for all of us concerned about program content censorship.

Entertainment at the club included multiple dates by Bill Hearne, a three-day weekend appearance by Three Faces West, and a rare appearance by Houston's John Lomax, Jr. Folklorist Lomax shared an illustrious folk music heritage with his late father and his brother Alan Lomax. Together the three men had built a reputation of such status that their name was synonymous with folk collecting and recording.

In contrast to commercial trends of the day, Lomax sang, without accompaniment, the authentic old songs of the past. As Lomax explained it, "Workers hollerin' and bellerin' their work songs while swinging an ax had no hands free to pluck a guitar." We all remembered Lomax knocking wood chips into the front rows of the Zilker Park Hillside Theater audience as he picked up an ax and attacked a log on stage to provide the proper cadence to one of his work songs at the 1964 KHFI-FM Summer Music Festival.

His frontier, prison, and work songs recreated earlier times for a good enthusiastic audience at the Flag.

We closed the club to host an SCCA party one Sunday following a drivers' school and regional race at the renamed Austin Dragway Park. In spite of the wind, rain, and hail over the weekend, we were able to celebrate John Hancock's win at the regionals in his Winkelmann Formula Ford.

Throughout the month, the CBS-Smothers Brothers controversy continued as CBS charged that the show had breached an agreement, and Tommy Smothers countered that CBS had canceled the show because of content when they said, "No!" to a David Steinberg monologue.

While hopes for the Smothers Brothers chances on the air faded, in Houston hopes rose

momentarily for heart patients as Dr. Denton Cooley performed the first artificial heart transplant. Although the patient died four days later, it was evident that heart surgery techniques were rapidly gaining in technical sophistication and that the hoped-for success was just around the corner.

Our Winkelmann Formula Cars showed very well in customers' hands during the first weekend of May while Segle Fry and Bill Hearne held down the fort at the Chequered Flag. The "Carrera del Alamo" sports car races were on the road course at Austin Dragway Park, and in the Formula Ford class Winkelmanns placed second and third on Saturday and first and third on Sunday.

During the coming week Dave Houston and Bill Hearne played the Flag, with Big Bill Moss and Three Faces West starring on the weekend. Meanwhile, a demolition crew started tearing down Disch Field, which had been the home of the Austin Braves since 1947 and home to the first Longhorn Jazz Festival in 1966. Since the Braves' departure from Austin, the city had been looking longingly at the abandoned ball park for additional parking for the coliseum.

On the next Monday, Governor Preston Smith hosted the first Tourist Development Conference at the Terrace Motor Hotel, sparked by delegates like San Antonio's H. B. Zachary and Brackettville's Happy Shahan, who had attracted major Hollywood film studios to his Texas ranch. That evening at the Austin Municipal Auditorium, Jerry Lee Lewis headlined a concert with Marty Robbins, Willie Nelson, Lynn Anderson, and Bobby Bare—a good buy at $2.50 and $3.50 a ticket!

During the week, while Houston's Don Sanders shared the Flag stage with Bonnie Cross, American Raceways announced the November 9 target date for the first big race at the new eight-million-dollar Texas International Speedway now under construction 100 miles from Austin at College Station. Leo Margolian would be general manager and vice-president under president Lawrence LoPatin. The track would be designed in multiple layouts for stock car, championship, sports car, and grand prix racing, as well as for international driver training and for industry test facilities. The first event would be the eleventh and final race of the million-dollar 1969 Canadian-American Challenge Cup Series of International Road Races.

For ourselves, we were in contact with Margolian about including our vintage racing cars as a special

Castrol exhibition race during the debut of this 800-acre, four-tracks-in-one: two-mile banked oval, three-mile road course, an interior road course for testing and driver's school, and a two-mile road course incorporating a portion of the three-mile circuit.

At the Flag, Bill Hearne replaced Bonnie Cross on Saturday night, but her beautiful bell-like voice could be heard singing harmony from the audience! It was truly a magical moment for all of us! The next day, Nancylee and I headed out to Laguna Gloria Gallery for the nineteenth annual Fiesta of Arts and Crafts to listen to the big Nash Hernandez Orchestra. For many years, since becoming a KHFI-FM supporter of the Texas Fine Arts Association's gallery and grounds on the lake at the foot of 35th Street, I looked forward to going each year, visiting the booths spread out under the trees, and dining on the terrace and in the formal garden. In the early years, prior to his death in 1964, we enjoyed visiting with such stimulating folks as white-suited J. Frank Dobie and later with my friend the former national broadcaster and humorist John Henry Faulk.

Simultaneously, it was announced in New York that Leonard Bernstein, at age fifty, would retire from his directorship of the New York Philharmonic, a post he had held since age twenty-four. That seemed to be a huge change as Bernstein had been there and on television and in the news as the orchestra's leader for more than two decades.

The next Thursday, we announced to the public and the racing world across the Southwest that we were adding a new racing division under the Speed Museum umbrella, as we unveiled two of the wedge-shaped Lotus 61 Formula Fords to be sold, along with Dunlop Racing Tires, under the new Lone Star Lotus dealership.

With Damron and Moss on stage at the Flag over the weekend, and news that Houston's A. J. Foyt, a three-time winner at the Indy 500, had captured the pole for this year's race, I headed to Indianapolis with the Castrol crew to support Dan Gurney's effort. It was a dazzling experience being on the inside of all the activity at the world's greatest professional championship car race. While our job was to merchandise for Castrol, seeing that the banners were up, product was on hand for the teams sponsored by Castrol, and that someone saw to it that Dan Gurney was wearing a Castrol cap in the winners circle if he made it there, I also had a good

chance to visit with Rutherford, Gurney, MacElreath, and many of the other racing pros I had met at other events.

In the race itself, A. J. was on the pole next to Mario Andretti, Gurney's All-American Racers Castrol entry was in the fourth row, Rutherford was two rows back on the sixth row, and Lloyd Ruby from Wichita Falls was on the seventh row. Andretti won the race, followed by Dan Gurney in second! Castrol was pleased with its effort and with Gurney's overall showing. They had received their money's worth, and Gurney was truly an all-American boy, good looking, friendly, congenial, and everyone's idea of how a hero should look. For me, it was a really rewarding experience all the way around.

While I was away at the Indy 500, Governor Smith and the Texas legislature paid tribute to Texas Hall of Famers Ernest Tubb, Bob Wills, and Tex Ritter at the State Capitol. While he was in town, Tex Ritter played a night at the Broken Spoke.

I flew straight back from Indy to drive my Stanguellini in a pair of successful wins at the Lake Charles, Louisiana, SCCA championship races. Even though we won, I couldn't help compare the color and excitement of the massive Indianapolis event with the large but scattered crowd around the long airport course.

Also during May, NASA announced that Apollo 10 would scout a future moon landing site, and last-ditch efforts were made to save the Driskill Hotel, which closed as slated on June 1.

Damron and Houston played the Flag the first week in June, with Moss replacing Houston over the weekend, and Bill Hearne teaming with Damron on the next weekend.

At the next weekend's SCCA championship races, I took the DeTomaso out instead of the Stanguellini and maintained my division championship point lead by placing second. At the same event, Winkelmann scored its first Formula B win in Texas at the hands of new owner Joe Duran.

When I returned to Austin, I announced the 1969 Austin Aqua Festival Vintage Races for Sunday, August 3, on the 1.2-mile city streets course around the Municipal Auditorium. I expected to be driving my 1935 Maserati during the Vintage Race, the Stanguellini or DeTomaso in Formula C, and to have my Facetti-prepared Lancia HF Coupe ready for its debut in C Sedan. The two SCCA races were for championship points, and I was also seeking to accrue as much experience in the 1.3 Lancia as I could if I was really going to compete in the 1970 Sebring 12 Hours next March.

Richard Dean returned to the club for a couple of dates alongside Damron, and Dave Houston did five nights. In Washington the White House announced that 8,000 American troops would be withdrawn from Vietnam as the first of 23,000 to be withdrawn by August.

As the month of June passed the halfway point with Damron, Fry, and Houston sharing nights from the 17th to the 22nd, we announced that Damron would headline the second annual July 4 American Folk Festival at Zilker Park, along with the duo called Frummox and Segle Fry. On the 23rd, we received the news of Judy Garland's death in London, the same week I announced that Blood Sweat and Tears would play the forthcoming Longhorn Jazz Festival's three-city tour of Texas. With Pepsi in the sponsoring role, thanks in great part to the efforts of Austin Pepsi distributor Charles Sandahl, the festival would play Austin on July 19, the middle date of the tour. It was a busy week, working simultaneously on the American Folk Festival, the Longhorn Jazz Festival, and the Vintage Race.

On the 24th, Frummox returned for a six-night engagement at the Chequered Flag. Frummox had been gaining in popularity, touring folk clubs across the U.S., including dates in San Francisco, Denver, Kansas City, and New York. Our fans already recognized songs like "Texas Trilogy," "Man With the Big Hat," and "White China Canyon," all written by Steve Fromholz, who, along with Dan McCrimmen, made up the folk duo. Many of Fromholz' more than 100 songs were about small Texas towns. The guitar and harmonica work by McCrimmen combined with the original songs of Fromholz to provide the refreshing Frummox mood and setting for the songs. McCrimmen had sung with a group called Triade and as a single before joining forces with Fromholz.

Back in Texas after cutting a new LP album, Frummox could provide a spellbinding evening of contemporary material, humor, and story songs of the early Texas frontier.

They were booked for the American Folk Festival and then would be held over at the club for six more nights, so it was especially unpleasant for me to have to call them down for making derogatory remarks about Vice-President Agnew in an angry tone while not deleting their expletives on our stage.

The club was intended as a family place, so the language was unacceptable. And, in spite of the fact that I was well-known as a Republican, I never used my stage, the stage at Zilker Park, or my position as an Aqua Festival leader to make political statements.

I didn't expect to pay performers on my payroll to use abrasive political attacks as part of their show. If they had the artistic capability of Tom Paxton to make entertainment of their viewpoints, it would have been different. We had a heated discussion outside in front of the club following the show, and I hoped it was settled.

Like the experienced troopers they were, they came through for me from then on, but I felt our friendship had suffered more than a minor setback. I had always felt we were working together, sharing the same standards, and now I had the feeling that they felt they were working *for* me rather than *with* me.

Around Austin in those years, Lavender Hill Express continued to play the Jade Room and the New Orleans Club, and one of the favorite places for Nancylee and me to eat was at Victor's Italian Village that had moved from East Austin to Guadalupe Street north of the UT campus. We became close friends with Mr. and Mrs. Victor Nardeccia and enjoyed our frequent evenings with them.

While Frummox closed out June with near capacity crowds every night at the Flag, Willie Nelson made a one-night appearance at Dessau Hall on the 27th. We still had standing-room-only shows that Friday night and Saturday night and looked forward to Jerry Jeff Walker's return to the club for July 1-3, an after-hours show following the Zilker Park Festival on the 4th, and then Saturday and Sunday nights of the July 4 weekend.

The 1968 recording of Jerry Jeff's "Mr. Bo Jangles" had skyrocketed him to fame. A New Yorker who called the USA his "rambling ground," Jerry Jeff had been a frequent Austin visitor and had spent some time at my home on previous trips and traded songs and stories with Allen Damron.

Walker had left Austin and spent some time in a New Orleans jail when the local law enforcement people doubted that "writing folk songs" was gainful employment. While in the cell, he met a character who inspired the song that brought him acclaim.

After a brief but successful stint as head of his own recording rock band, "Circus Maximus," Walker returned to the folk material that he had known in Texas when he and Damron played the same clubs. Many of Walker's songs mentioned Austin, which had become as much a home as any town had been to this itinerant folk artist and raconteur.

With guest shots on the "Today Show," Johnny Carson, and Merv Griffin shows, a much heralded appearance at the Newport Folk Festival, and a new recording on Vanguard, Walker was now considered one of the nation's leading writers of contemporary material. He came to the Flag following dates at the Hungry I, Cellar Door, and the Bitter End, and his shows at the Flag were near sell-outs every night.

At Zilker Park on the night of July 4, our American Folk Festival showcased Bonnie Cross, Frummox, Segle Fry and Drake Brent, Big Bill Moss, Mary Hoekstra, and Allen Damron for a crowd of 4,500 Hillside Theater fans. Then, at the club from 11:00 P.M. to 2:00 A.M., Jerry Jeff was joined by Segle, Frummox, and Bill and Bonnie for a packed after-hours show.

While Jerry Jeff closed out the weekend, I towed my Stanguellini to Galveston to take second in Formula C, maintaining my national championship point lead but getting frustrated again because the old front-engined Stanguellini scrubbed off efficiency broadsliding through the turns and then took too long to recover its top speed coming out of the turns. I decided then and there to go ahead and acquire a used lighter-weight Lotus Ford rear-engined Formula C car that had higher torque, wider tires to push it more quickly through the turns and to a higher speed on the straights.

I felt a little better about the weekend when we celebrated Winkelmann's biggest package of victories: first and second in Formula Ford, and first and second in Formula B with Gordon Beavers debuting his new machine.

It had been a long and busy week, so busy we hardly noticed that KASE-FM debuted their Big Band Stereo at 100.7. We needed Monday and Tuesday off, and when all the racing cars were back in the Speed Museum and the Flag reopened on Wednesday, it was for another successful five-night run by Frummox. At their final Sunday night show on July 13, we received a call from David Smith at Warbonnet Raceway in Tulsa letting us know he had finished second in the Formula ford championship race in his new Winkelmann.

During this time, I was in my twelfth year as a director of the Austin Symphony Society, which, under the leadership and influence of fellow board member and attorney Frank Erwin, voted to shut down the symphony for the 1969-70 season because

of an unpaid deficit. Anger and frustration welled up in me, and I undertook with some of the other more optimistic board members to quickly put together a short season of three special events to get the symphony back on track. I began to work on this project as I added it to my work schedule.

Apollo 11 was launched on August 17 with Neil Armstrong, Buzz Aldrin, and Michael Collins on board, headed for the moon.

At the club, Dave Houston and Big Bill Moss were set for the weekend, and I took off for Dallas to meet George Wein for the first of three nights on the road with the Longhorn Jazz Festival.

The three-city lineup added the rock of Blood Sweat and Tears to a roster headlined by Miles Davis, South African trumpeter Hugh Masekela, bluesman B. B. King, vocalist Nina Simone, and Young-Holt Unlimited (led by bassist Eldee Young and drummer Red Holt, who constituted two-thirds of the Ramsey Lewis Trio).

The shows in Dallas on Friday and Austin on Saturday were big crowd pleasers with BS&T drawing additional crowds of younger fans, just as Wein had hoped. And, in Austin on Saturday afternoon, workshops featured the now fully matured UT Experimental Jazz Ensemble, the Sam Houston State University Jazz Octet, and some of the instrumental stars of the North Texas State University One O'clock Lab Band with several members of BS&T sitting in. It was young and exciting and raucous and fun, and after the evening concert at Austin Municipal Auditorium, there was a swinging jam at Rueben Kogut's New Orleans Club on Red River Street featuring festival performers sitting in with soloists from Dick Goodwin's UT jazz groups.

Following the late night, it was a tough 156-mile drive to Houston on Sunday morning for everyone except Miles Davis, who had hired a funeral home limo for his three-city tour. But even Miles was upset when we got to the Houston Music Hall to find that the only rental concert grand piano available had been destroyed by a rock band the night before. Miles was upset enough to refuse to play after I introduced him to the audience until, following a short discussion with him, he condescended to play into the baby grand piano with his back to the audience for his entire set. The audience, not knowing what was going on, thought it was cool.

But that was not the most distracting thing about the Houston Festival date. This was the date chosen by NASA to land on the moon, and as I stood on the stage looking out at 9,000 jazz fans in the darkened hall, I could see hundreds of spots of soft, reflected light, dimly lit faces peering at portable TV screens watching as the "Eagle" landed with Neil Armstrong saying, "One small step for man, one giant leap for mankind."

In spite of massive daily press on the Apollo moon landing, we still had a good crowd. Miles' Quintet of Chick Corea, *keyboards*, Wayne Shorter, *tenor sax*, Dave Hamilton, *bass*, and Jack Dejanet, *percussion*, provided an appropriate and stellar finale to the final Longhorn Jazz Festival concert of the tour.

George and I met on Monday morning to talk briefly about the festival and quick preliminary plans for the 1970 festival. Then he was back on the road and I headed to Austin. As I drove, I was reminded that while we were in Dallas, there was a lot of optimistic talk about the Dallas Cowboys rookie quarterback, Roger Staubach, but by the time I reached Austin three hours later after five days out of town, thoughts of the Cowboys were left far behind, and I was immediately reimmersed in the saga of the Austin Symphony's future. John DeFord had been retained as the new manager and was looking favorably at my short season proposal. Damron was at the Flag, partnering variously with Segle Fry, Bill Hearne, and Strange Alliance as the July calendar ran out.

There were major motorcycle races all summer at Manor Downs, and, as August began, the Austin Aqua Festival Sports Car Races and our vintage race were fast upon us, plus the Alamo Region of the SCCA in San Antonio had scheduled national races at the end of the month.

Prior to the August 3 Aqua Festival races, I took the newly acquired rear-engined Lotus-Ford out to Austin Dragway Park to become accustomed to the high rpm's required to maintain the power needed to take advantage of its faster cornering capabilities. We also personalized the car by making adjustments in the cockpit, and I tried to familiarize myself with both the car's shifting peculiarities and its quicker handling. Everything was happening much faster, and the gear box would only shift quickly if everything was in sync. After more than ninety laps of practice and many adjustments to the carburetor and the suspension, I felt comfortable enough to compete in traffic a few days later.

We also set up the Lancia HF coupe that was brand new from Facetti's shop in Italy and my first

front-wheel drive racing car. Keeping the power on going into and all the way through the turns while the front end pulled me through was a totally different experience from dirt-tracking the old MG-TD or the Stanguellini. We experimented with tire pressures and marveled at the stability of the little car and the amount of horsepower delivered to the wide Goodyear racing tires. Italian tuning ace Facetti lived up to his reputation. I quickly gained comfort and confidence at the wheel of the Lancia as it just sat down and went flying through the turns with zero slippage. It was going to be fun racing it in front of my hometown fans for the first time. Neither the Austin Dragway Park nor the downtown street course was going to allow me to get it into fifth gear, but the DOHC engine felt comfortable at well over 7000 rpm's in fourth with still plenty of power and no valve float evident.

Lining up on the grid for the 1969 Vintage Race. John Hancock is in the Ferrari in the foreground, and Damron can be seen grinning at the wheel of the MG-TA behind the D-Jag. 1969.

— Courtesy Frank Armstrong.

It took all day Friday making final checks on each vintage car and moving eight of them from the museum to the auditorium. We again took the three MGs, the Testa Rossa Ferrari, the D-Jag, the RSK Porsche, the Stanguellini, and the 1935 Maserati. We would load and trailer the Lotus-Ford and the Lancia HF coupe early the next morning to get in line for tech inspection. Both nights that weekend, Allen and Segle were singing at the Flag, and the club was filled with racing teams and fans and SCCA officials from all over the U.S.

Large fields of cars were on hand for almost every class as the Austin street races were drawing

Damron signals to come into the pits in the 1935 MG-TA. 1969.

— Courtesy Frank Armstrong.

The 1935 Maserati making the best out of a tight turn in the 1969 Aqua Festival Vintage Race. 1969.

— Courtesy Frank Armstrong.

entries from near and far. The uniqueness of the course, the attraction of outstanding facilities, big crowds, and heavy press coverage all contributed to the popularity of these races.

We had Saturday practice, and I felt great in both the Lancia and the old Maserati. The Lotus-Ford was another matter, and my mechanic, Jerome Shields, was not only having trouble getting the carburetor to stabilize, but he was also distracted by trying to service more than a half-dozen of our customers whose Formula Fords and Formula B cars each needed minor adjustments or, at least, Jerome's technical advice. I didn't get in very many satisfactory practice laps in the Lotus-Ford, and the car stalled once and had to be pushed in, losing valuable practice time.

Bob Samm in the Jaguar looks back over his shoulder at the menacing Ferrari with John Hancock at the wheel. 1969.

— Courtesy Frank Armstrong.

Preliminary races went well on Saturday, and Sunday's vintage race came off beautifully, with large crowds cheering us on and the 1935 Maserati purring like a new car and winding up near the front of the pack, though a lap down, when the twenty-minute event ended.

The Lancia was a dream, setting a lap record for C sedans, but only coming in fifth place in the championship race behind the Mini Coopers. The Mini's were the rage at the time and often came in ahead of a number of the larger and faster cars because of their finesse in getting through the turns. I would have to learn that finesse better.

The Lotus-Ford was another matter. Carburetor problems persisted, and I had to pit halfway through the race for more tinkering. When I pulled back on the course, the carburetor jammed wide open, and I couldn't get the rpm's to drop, and, struggling with the shifter, I inadvertently jerked the car to the right while struggling with the gear shift lever, and into the path of the rapidly moving second place Merlyn. As the two cars collided and careened off course, pieces of both cars scattered everywhere. After jumping the curb from the impact, the Lotus-Ford came to rest on the grass while the faster-moving Merlyn bounced after hitting me from behind at three times my speed and kept on going until it hit the base of a street light that had been hidden beneath a protective pile of hay bales. The Merlyn was badly damaged and the driver slightly injured when his heels were hit by the street lamp mounting bolts sticking up out of the concrete that tore the bottom out of his car. While I was out of the Lotus-Ford, shaken but without a scratch, my rear-engined formula car racing came to an end! The other driver, a Merlyn dealer, was more understanding about the mishap than I expected, and we went on about our business.

We all know when we enter a race that accidents can and will happen, but I had never so inexcusably created a situation on a race track where another car and driver was knocked out of competition because of my driving. It took much of the joy out of an otherwise great day at the races. And it didn't help when it appeared after the crash that we had left the stone guard off the carburetor during that first tinkering. Little was I to know that there would be another crash later that season that would almost jeopardize my planned trip to Sebring.

At the Chequered Flag, all of the regular entertainers were in and out of the club in the coming weeks, alongside Damron with appearances in various combinations by Dave Houston, Bonnie Cross, Big Bill Moss, Segle Fry, Strange Alliance, Mary Hoekstra, and others. At the Vulcan Gas Company, Shiva's Headband continued to be a major draw.

In my new Lancia HF at Green Valley Raceway. October 16, 1969.

— Courtesy Tom Bayne.

While the widely talked about Woodstock Music and Art Fair played to hundreds of thousands at Max Yusgur's dairy farm August 15-17, losing $1.2 million, they said, I took the Lancia HF to the Green Valley Raceway regional races up near Dallas and won my class in both races, finishing first overall in one and second overall in the other, ahead of three other classes of production cars. The Lancia was fast, efficient, and responsive, a well designed, engineered, and prepared machine, and I was quickly establishing a stimulating and fulfilling relationship with this marvel of Italian ingenuity. Later in the month, I took a first and a second in the championship races at the airport road course at Camp Gary near San Marcos, earning the lead in C sedan in the Southwest.

At this time, I was also honored to be selected as the first regional vice-president of the Vintage Sports Car Club of America by my new friends in New England. It was a singular compliment from a group of automotive celebrities I much admired.

While Louisiana and Mississippi, especially Gulfport, cleaned up from Hurricane Camille, we announced the opening in Austin of my new Driver Profile Service from my new public relations office at 6615 North Lamar. The service was conceived to provide publicity and marketing for both amateur and professional racing teams, and, in exceptional cases, commercial sponsorships for those teams. I had established excellent contacts throughout motorsports, and I felt that I could provide professional publicity and marketing to a dozen teams whose efforts made them attractive to the racing press, the fans, and in some cases, to sponsors. I was able to link up many of these teams with my own sponsors: Castrol Oil, Champion Spark Plugs, Goodyear Racing Tires, and Classic Car Wax, as well as Exide Batteries and Fram Filters.

Over the Labor Day weekend, Dallas hosted the "first annual" Texas International Pop Festival with Janis Joplin, Johnny Winter, Canned Heat, Chicago Transit Authority, Led Zeppelin, B.B. King, and Freddy King. We did not participate, but the event came off well enough for the promoters to consider it again for the next year.

September was a busy month at the Flag, with The University back in session and many of the lobbyists and legislators back in town. Frummox's four-day engagement at mid-month was capped off by the September 18 second anniversary celebration of the club's opening. On that date, they were joined by Damron, Jim Schulman, Richard Dean, and Big Bill Moss, while Freddy King appeared the next night at the Vulcan Gas Company.

Frummox was held over five more nights while, at the Gas Company, Mother Earth shared the stage with Mance Lipscomb. The month at the Flag closed with a Sunday night "family night" played by Peter Jacobson and Dave Houston.

During this time, I worked to generate publicity and advertising for our first major folk concert at Austin Municipal Auditorium. Joining with Pepsi-Cola, I put together an October 15 evening headlined by Canadian Gordon Lightfoot, whose singles "Spin, Spin" and "Black Day in July" were getting considerable air play all across the U.S.

Lightfoot was Canada's number-one entertainer with four United Artists' LP's of his original, melodic, free-flow songs. His songs had also been recorded by Peter Paul and Mary ("For Lovin' Me"),

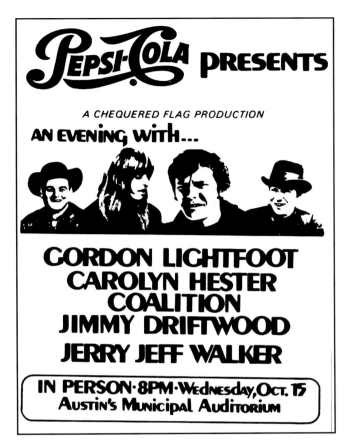

Program cover for the October 15, 1969, concert by Gordon Lightfoot.

Marty Robbins ("River of Darkness"), George Hamilton IV ("Steel Rail Blues"), plus himself — gems like "Early Mornin' Rain," "I'm Not Sayin'," "Canadian River Trilogy," "Did He Mention My Name." But his popularity in the U.S. was just starting to build, and our Austin concert would be his first Texas appearance.

Before we could get to the concert, however, we had a heavy schedule at the Flag — a five-night engagement with Jerry Jeff Walker, and bookings by Big Bill Moss, Richard Dean, and Three Faces West.

Jerry Jeff's "Mr. Bo Jangles" and "Little Bird" were getting a lot of air play, and on the 15th, Jerry Jeff joined Lightfoot at the auditorium along with Carolyn Hester and Jimmy Driftwood. The concert was a fine musical evening, but we didn't break even. We were grateful to Lightfoot for reducing his fee by half when he saw only half a house in spite of our extra promotional effort.

Carolyn Hester stayed over after the Lightfoot concert to play the Flag for four nights, drawing a good crowd even opposite a sold-out Janis Joplin

show at UT's Gregory Gym sponsored by the UT Student Union.

I neglected to mention that early in October, Poco played the Vulcan Gas Company and Jerry Lee Lewis was in town at Mr. Gee's. For our part, at the club, our search for new revenue sources led us to open it up for lunch five days a week.

Right on the heels of Carolyn's booking, Arlo Guthrie played a capacity house on October 22 at Municipal Auditorium produced by Jam Productions of San Antonio. And at the Flag, Fred Argir, Beverly Bernard, Segle, Dave Houston, and Strange Alliance played out the month, with Three Faces West joining in for a Halloween celebration on the 31st.

Earlier in the month, the Austin Symphony announced the abbreviated three-event season I had put together with the special board committee. Jazz flutist Herbie Mann and his Quintet would appear in concert on December 6 with a pops orchestra of local musicians. On December 23 the symphony would receive proceeds from the Austin premiere of the film *Paint Your Wagon*, while the quickie season would climax on April 16 with the San Antonio Grand Opera's production of Puccini's opera *Madame Butterfly*. The campaign, called "Face the Music," was designed to retire the symphony's $25,000 deficit and keep the orchestra's dilemma in the public eye while keeping the ticket holder's list active under the direction of new manager John DeFord. We also built in several services for the orchestra's out-of-work members.

Two other events that got my attention also took place in October. One of these events was my crash at Mid-America Raceway at St. Louis, when an MG spun out in front of me on a tight turn and the Lancia dove for the ditch when I took my foot off the accelerator to avoid hitting the spinning MG. What I learned from this accident, in addition to how long it takes to heal your insides after your chest suddenly bows out between the shoulder harness and the impact bends double the tempered steel steering wheel in your hands so that it wraps around the steering post, was not to commit full blast to a turn with front-wheel-drive unless you plan to keep your foot in it all the way through. When you are half way through a turn with the wheels in a right turn mode and then cut the power, the car will abruptly follow the direction of the wheels.

While I hurt all over as I towed my damaged Lancia home, I was more concerned about determining how serious the under-frame and front-wheel-drive damage was from the wreck. I knew the windshield had popped out on impact and that the ditch stopped the car instantly when it was traveling at sixty mph. It was a serious situation with Sebring only five months away. I had won three out of five races and placed second once to place the Lancia fifth in the national point standings, but now that didn't seem to be important. My question was: could we rebuild in time for a winning effort at Sebring in March?

The other October event was a quick four-day trip to Mexico City for the Eighth Mexican Grand Prix with a small group from our racing family. The race at the Autodromo de Mexico gave me a chance to revisit Jochin Rindt, Chris Amon, Joe Siffert, Bruce McLaren, and Pedro Rodriguez.

When we returned from the October 19 Grand Prix, I was still nursing my chest injuries, which hurt, especially when I laughed or hugged someone. There was not time, however, to take a break, as we had committed seven of our vintage cars to a Castrol-sponsored appearance at the November 9 grand opening of Texas International Speedway just three weeks away. When I talked to Johnny Rutherford on the phone about my injuries, he said that it was just what he and his fellow championship car drivers called a "USAC chest." "Anyone who has ever flipped a championship car or hit the wall going fast knows what one is," he said. "You'll survive. Just try to avoid being with people who make you laugh!"

On November 1, the Speed Museum hosted a dinner for SCCA members, with Ferrari's Chris Amon as the guest speaker talking about racing safety. At this dinner we announced our co-sponsorship of Amon's Ferrari at the Texas Can-Am race.

Bringing my 1935 Maserati to the staging area in the pits at Texas International Speedway. 1969.

— Courtesy Ludvigsen.

In spite of everything on his agenda, Margolian was quick to work out for us passes for our Glastron Motorhome and five Speed Museum tow vehicles, pit passes for crews and drivers, garage area for the racing machines, and the staging arrangements and approval of my script for the exhibition race. Logistically, it went without a hitch.

SCCA dinner honoring New Zealander Chris Amon, whose Ferrari we were to sponsor at the grand opening Texas International Speedway Can-Am. From left: John and Gayle Hancock, Chris Amon, Nancylee and myself, Vivian and David Bland. 1969.

— Courtesy Tom Bayne.

On the grid at TIS (left) Frank McBee's 200SI Maserati driven by Bill Moyer while Switzerland's Joe "Seppi" Siffert drove our number 12 RSK Porsche. 1969.

— Courtesy Tom Bayne.

Moyer and Siffert on the banked track at TIS. 1969.
— Courtesy Tom Bayne.

Looking pretty serious in my vintage Maserati at speed at Texas' newest raceway. 1969.
— Courtesy Tom Bayne.

The six-mile exhibition race was sponsored by Castrol Oil. As the Speed Museum was co-sponsoring Chris Amon's Ferrari in the Can-Am, Chris agreed to drive our Testa Rossa Ferrari in the vintage race. Porsche team driver Joe Siffert was running our RSK Porsche, while Bob Samm piloted our D-Jaguar. I drove my 1935 Maserati, race chairman Bob Sieberg handled the MG-TA, John Hancock took the wheel of the long-bodied, yellow Lester MG endurance car, while Jerome Shields raced in the Stanguellini. Damron fielded his recently acquired ex-Mecom Team Bandini.

Guest drivers and cars included *American-Statesman* publisher Dick Brown in his XK120 Jaguar, Larry Fiske in an XK150 Jaguar, Tracor president Frank McBee's 200SI Maserati driven by Bill Moyer, Sandy Sanderson in his MG-TD, and

architect Bill Bauder in his Ford 289-powered J2X Allard.

We all hit the staging area at 11:15 A.M., were on the starting grid at 12:20, and seven minutes later, after the scripted introduction to the thousands of Can-Am race fans, we were off and running on the three-mile road course that included a large portion of the banked D-shaped oval.

The two laps went quickly and without incident with Amon and Siffert playing tag in the Ferrari and Porsche with Samm's D-Jag right behind,

A smiling Chris Amon, just out of our Testa Rossa Ferrari and about to begin the Can-Am. Twenty-six-year-old Amon co-drove the 1966 LeMans-winning Ford with Bruce McLaren, and, driving for Ferrari in 1967, won the Daytona 24 Hours and the Monza 1,000, co-driving with Lorenzo Bandini. Amon was a Ferrari Team driver for Grand Prix, Tasman Series (Australia), sports prototype endurance events and the Can-Am, as well as test driver for Ferrari's development program. 1969.
— Courtesy Tom Bayne.

and all of us were enjoying not only the speed and fun of driving, but also the spectacular view of the colorful infield and the stands from the high-banked turns. A five-minute cool-off lap, and it was all over.

The Can-Am race itself was fast and furious with a field of twenty-four cars entered, represent-

Chris Amon and his teammates with his Texas Speed Museum-sponsored Ferrari before the TIS Can-Am. 1969.
— Courtesy Tom Bayne.

ing the interests of Ford, Porsche, Ferrari, Chevrolet-powered McLarens, Chaparral, Lolas, and a number of specials. Tim Dutton drove the Chaparral as Jim Hall was recovering from his 1968 accident at Stardust Raceway in the Las Vegas Can-Am. The roster of drivers also included Mario Andretti, Jack Brabham, Bruce McLaren and teammate Dennis Hulme, Chuck Parsons, Jackie Oliver, Chris Amon, Joe Siffert, Peter Revson, and Lothar Motschenbacher, among others.

McLaren took home the championship with Chris Amon finishing third in the series standings in spite of the fact that his Ferrari overheated and did not finish at TIS. It was announced that Amon would drive a Ferrari-powered Indy car at the 1970 Indy 500.

It was an auspicious debut for the new track and an extraordinary weekend. Our sponsor, Castrol, was impressed and pleased with our participation. I, in turn, enjoyed another lengthy visit with Sterling Moss, who was there both as a consultant to the Canadian-American Cup Series and as racing director for the Johnson Wax organization, promoting their new JWax.

By the time we finally returned to Austin, got the motorhome back to Bill Gaston, unloaded, drained, cleaned up, and waxed all the cars before putting them back on display, most of the week was gone. Damron, Dean, Schulman, and Fry had all been on the club calendar during that time, and all kinds of historic events were going on around us. First, astronauts Conrad, Gordon, and Bean made the second moon expedition on Apollo 12, planting

an American flag on the moon and bringing boxes of rocks back for study; second, on the 15th, 250,000 anti-war protesters joined in a great Peace Walk in Washington, D.C. Nixon had already announced additional troop withdrawals on the third. In Austin we were glad to have Mike Murphey back at the Flag with Damron for the weekend.

Then on the 20th, the Fifth Dimension was at Municipal Auditorium, drawing 5,000 fans, and, as Damron and Fry hosted the weekend of the 21st and 22nd at the Flag, 100 Native Americans took over Alcatraz to call attention to their need for increased aid for 100,000 California Indians and help rebuilding their burned Indian Center.

That week, on the 14th, the Speed Museum displayed for the first time a fuel-burning dragster, looking like a nightmarish monster of the future among the collection of vintage cars.

On display for ninety days, the dragster had scored over two dozen wins since January 1967 from a standing start down quarter-mile drag strips in Austin, Amarillo, Odessa, and Greenville, Mississippi, where the car held track records. It was Fred Rowsey's $10,000 "Banzai" with a supercharged Chrysler competition engine, driven by George Cox to second in the nation in 1967 and third in 1968. Top time was 6.85 seconds elapsed time to chalk up a speed of 236 mph.

Dividing my time among three racing cars and wrecking two of them during the season, I still won the Formula C Southwest Division Championship. So we decided to take the old Stanguellini to Daytona in response to an invitation to compete in the SCCA's American Road Race of Champions. Along with John Hancock and other Winkelmann drivers who had qualified for the championship races in Formula Ford, we would take the trusty old front-engined Stanguellini to represent the Speed Museum and see where we could place. We set about preparing the car as if we were going to win.

I don't know what I thought I was doing driving the old Stanguellini against the thirty-two fastest Formula C cars in the nation on the banked track at Daytona International Speedway, but I finished 15th overall and had a great time while learning the ARRC ropes for 1971, when I hoped to return as a serious contender in the Lancia. Back home, Jim Schulman and Big Bill Moss played the Flag.

Shortly after we returned, on December 3 at Austin Municipal Auditorium, a good crowd turned out for the first "Face the Music" special event for the

Austin Symphony. With guest conductor William Fisher, Herbie Mann played the Fisher-Mann "Concerto Grosso in D Blues" and some other special arrangements with the Austin Symphony Pops Orchestra. After intermission, Mann closed the concert with some of his best known quintet hits. A good number of those attending had bought season tickets, so there would be a good starting crowd for the next two events as well.

The following weekend, as a new $12 million Highland Mall was announced to open in August of 1971, Frummox returned to the Flag to sing their songs about small Texas towns, and young David Smith and I took off for the SCCA regional races at Green Valley Raceway. Since this wasn't for points, and my Lancia was still being rebuilt for Sebring, I hooked up the RSK Porsche and David followed with his Speed Museum-sponsored Vee. We had a great no-pressure weekend of racing. David won Formula Vee, and I won B-Sports Racing. We also sold accessories, spark plugs, and oil from our trackside van while enjoying the chance to visit with everyone in the pits. By now, we were dealers for mini-bikes, and it was easy for me to get from one end to the other of the huge pit area and talk to hundreds of racers and other friends.

With all of our efforts to promote it, our Winkelmann Racing Division never made a profit. Prior to my Green Valley trip, I terminated my business relationship with Jerome Shields, worked out a settlement for the in-stock Winkelmann cars and parts, and turned everything over to Jerome and his new partner Mike Lowe. Jerome now operated his racing dealership under the name of Vector Systems Research. While their new business lasted, they got into dune buggies and other related automotive competition products.

Our annual Christmas Festival of Folk Carols was upon us the next weekend at the Flag. This weekend was one I looked forward to every year with the club decorated in pine bows and the soft flickering light of candles creating a warm glow. The folk singers didn't always sing Christmas songs and carols or even gospel songs, but they all thought carefully about their song list, and the resulting selections enhanced the warmth and joy of the season. It was a non-commercial respite from the commercialization of the modern Christmas (shopping) season.

Allen Damron hosted the "festival" and for two nights shared the stage with Mary Hoekstra, Dave Houston, Big Bill Moss, and Jim Schulman. We did

two sets each night, one at 8:30 and one at 10:30, with many of the Flag customers opting to stay for both candlelight performances, and not a few of them bringing youngsters with them. Many were home from school for the holidays and joined their folks in laughing at some of Bill Moss's very un-Christmas-like songs and stories. It was a seasonal homecoming for all of us and one of the most special times of the year. The non-alcoholic eggnog was one of the most popular drinks, even surpassing Texas beer and Damron coolers. The evening's gentle glow lasted well into the Saturday night after-hours set.

The Tuesday after the festival weekend, December 23, was the second of the "Face the Music" benefits for the symphony, and I had spent almost every free moment for weeks cranking out publicity. So it was quite rewarding when I arrived at the Americana Theater to see a large festive crowd in the lobby and in line to get tickets for the Austin premiere of the film version of Lerner and Lowe's musical *Paint Your Wagon*, which had additional music by Andre Previn and scoring and conducting by Nelson Riddle.

While the cast, led by Lee Marvin, Clint Eastwood, and Jean Seberg, didn't sound like a typical cast for a Broadway musical, they did a creditable job with the help of the Nitty Gritty Dirt Band. It was a happy evening with the well-dressed holiday crowd paying up to $37.50 for a "Gold Card Angel" seat. Most of the 750 season tickets had been sold in advance, so this was an enjoyable and successful benefit, with Trans-Texas Theater owners Earl and Lena Podolnik turning the proceeds over to the Symphony Society. The third and final "Face the Music" benefit would be in late April when the San Antonio Grand Opera would bring *Madame Butterfly* to town.

The weekend before New Year's, Damron and Moss played the Flag and then were joined on New Year's Eve by Mike Murphey, whose growing popularity made him a good draw at $15 a couple. In addition to a rewarding evening of varied songs from these favorite artists, our fans also enjoyed a bottle of champagne and cheered the New Year in with noise makers, streamers, and foil hats. A pleasantly quiet set was the scene for complimentary coffee and roast beef sandwiches after-hours until 2:00 A.M.

New Year's Day 1970 saw snow flurries in Austin as well as the pandemonium resulting from the UT defeat of Notre Dame in the Cotton Bowl at Dallas to take the national title in college football for the year. The tower on The University campus glowed orange for several days.

While we and a few thousand others were primarily occupied with sports car racing as our sport, most Texans were (and still are) dedicated football fans. It starts with Little League and continues through junior high, high school, and college, where the Southwest Conference was one of the most unpredictable conferences in the nation. UT football coach Darrell Royal was a "national" hero to most Texans, and the rivalries of Texas-Texas A&M and Texas-Oklahoma were like major battles of the century, every year. The next step up was pro ball, and the Dallas Cowboys under Tom Landry's coaching were becoming a more and more important part of every Texan's life with each ensuing game quarterbacked by young Roger Staubach.

Up to this point in my sport I had won the Southwest Division Championship in Formula C, most of my races in the Lancia in C Sedan, and a B-Sports Racing title in the Porsche, in addition to running three vintage races, managing the sponsorship of Johnny Rutherford's Astrodome midget race effort, and co-sponsoring Chris Amon at TIS. I had also attended the Bridgehampton Can-Am, the Sebring 12 Hours, the Grand Prix of Mexico, and the TIS Can-Am. I felt ready to combine my racing background with my fourteen years of public relations experience, and when I launched my Driver Profile Service from my new offices on North Lamar, I received a good send-off from the press throughout the automotive world.

The service provided mass photos of cars and drivers taken by appointment at southwestern racing circuits, complete biographical sketches of drivers and their team efforts, and racing team logo designs coordinated so that car color, stationery, helmets, team jackets, tow vehicles, etc., all reflected the team image. SCCA race chairmen were always looking for professional publicity material to use in local papers before their region's annual racing events. The publicity materials would also help drivers seeking recognition, sponsorship, and a boost into the ranks of the professionals.

As we continued preparations for our own participation in the Sebring 12 Hours, all of this promotional activity was also under way for our own team. I had selected Bob Samm of Houston as one co-driver, and Mike Tillson of Philadelphia as the other. Both had Sebring experience, and Mike, who co-drove a factory Lancia at Sebring in 1969 with Ireland, would bring his own Lancia HF as a practice car and his mechanic would become our team mechanic. During

the next thirty days I needed to confirm and make specific the terms of our many sponsorship deals with a half-dozen national corporations.

The day after New Year's Day was a Friday, and the club reopened with Mike Murphey and Allen Damron doing an encore show with Segle and Allen playing on Saturday night. Kenneth Threadgill was still playing regularly on weekends at the Split Rail.

Bill Moss played alongside Damron during the next week, and then Murphey and Fry played the four-day weekend starting with Thursday night, while Pattie Ricker and Segle shared the following weekend. Damron and Moss closed out January on the final weekend, while I kept a keen eye on the Daytona 24 Hours, where I got the first look at some of our potential Sebring competition. It appeared as though our toughest opponent in the under-two-liter touring class would be from Alfa Romeo.

The Lancia HF was finally back in my hands following extensive repairs, rebuilding, and alignment by Doug Scales' crew, and all of the final running-gear checks and engine re-installation and tuning was performed by Burney Russell in Fort Worth. During the ordering and shipping of all the Lancia parts from Algar Enterprises in Pennsylvania, I struck a deal with Algar to furnish us with all of the backup parts we might need to complete the grueling twelve hours at Sebring. They would give everything to Mike Tillson to bring down to Florida, and we would pay only for what we actually used, sending the rest of the parts back. This arrangement would put us on a par with the other professional racing teams without having to lay out more cash in advance of the race.

At the head of the overall standing at Daytona were two factory Porsches placing one-two, with Rodriguez and Wyer in the winning car and Joe Siffert teamed with Brian Redman in second.

The first week in February saw a $10,000 gift to the Austin Symphony from the Women's Symphony League to keep the hopes high for a 1970-71 season. Designated to support the cost of three student concerts, the gift nonetheless brought the possibility of the orchestra's return to a regular season closer to reality.

Back at the Flag, Jim Schulman and Segle Fry played the first weekend, Three Faces West and Big Bill Moss the second, Bill Hearne and Bob and Cindy the third, with Richard Dean and Peter Jacobson closing out the month.

We received word from Dallas that Bob Wills was critically ill early in February, and Washington announced that fatalities in Vietnam had passed the 40,000 mark. Segle Fry started teaching guitar at the Flag with free admission to the entertainment at the club each evening the class was held. I liked the idea of the club serving a broader base. The middle weekend in February was an interesting one from a promotional standpoint with Friday the 13th and Valentine's Day on the same weekend. Incidentally, Ernest Tubb and the Texas Troubadors were at the Broken Spoke the next night.

The Lancia HF at the Polar Prix at Green Valley Raceway. 1970.

— Courtesy Tom Bayne.

On the third weekend, I took the rebuilt Lancia HF to the Polar Prix Race at Green Valley Raceway for its first test in actual competition since the crash at St. Louis. I placed second in C-Sedan after a classic twelve-lap battle with Gerald Brown's Mini-Cooper, in which the lead changed many times. We were constantly running bumper to bumper and fender to fender, passing inside and outside, even in tight turns. Gerald was a great sportsman and a good driver in his well-prepared Mini-Cooper. It should be pointed out that a Mini-Cooper won the C-Sedan National Championship in 1966, 1967, and 1968, with Richard McDaniel driving for Overseas Motors. Anyway, Gerald and I both felt exhilarated after that battle and heartily congratulated each other in the pits afterward.

The rewarding thing to me was that the car was totally back to its old competitive self, and I felt comfortable in spite of my injuries. I was confident and at home behind the wheel as the Lancia responded quickly to every command. While it was highly competitive on a short course like Green Valley, Lancia had earned an international reputa-

tion for its endurance in long races. I looked forward eagerly to Sebring as I read T. Q. Jones' story about our win at Green Valley.

Three nights later, back in Austin, Nancylee and I took an evening away from the club to enjoy Van Cliburn's performance as part of the UT Cultural Entertainment season. Here in the concert hall was another remarkable Texan who continued to claim the hearts of classical music lovers everywhere with his winning piano artistry and charming stage presence.

On March 1 our friend Toby Hooper announced that he had completed his Peter Paul and Mary film. Jim Schulman had been working on it with him, and the screening was a joyful, sharing experience. The other news was that LBJ was being hospitalized with chest pains and would be under observation for a week or more. Meanwhile, Chuck Berry played the Austin Coliseum, and the next day our news release broke in the local press announcing my co-drivers for Sebring. The race was two weeks away, and we had a great deal to accomplish in a very short amount of time.

At the club, the weekend introduced to our fans the trio of Argir, Bernard & Hoberd (Fred Argir, Betsy Bernard, and Gloria Hoberd) and, while the crowd was not particularly large, it was most enthusiastic.

It was getting to be more and more difficult to fill the enlarged club unless the artists had a really hot reputation locally. Damron and Moss even drew just a modest crowd on Sunday night. It had been many months since the club had put together a string of financially successful dates, and we had cut our newspaper advertising from seven days a week to running just on the weekends. We felt that if our reputation and word of mouth hadn't let enough people know the validity of what we were doing at the Flag, we weren't going to draw people regularly by simply pouring more money into entertainment page advertising seven days a week.

On Monday it was announced that Austin Dragway (Raceway) Park had been sold and would be closed to make room for development. On the same day the news was filled with reports of LBJ's improvement. Johnny Winter was at the Vulcan Gas Company as we prepared our Lancia HF for display at the San Antonio Auto Show, where we would announce our team sponsorship by Castrol Oil, Classic Car Wax, and Exide Batteries. We were awaiting confirmation of our Goodyear Racing Tire sponsorship, worked out in essence with our good friend Bob Schroeder's Goodyear Service, but the confirmation had not come through. We also had two or three other deals in the mill that would have to be announced later. As we worked on the display at the car show on Friday the 13th, we received the news of LBJ's return to his ranch at Johnson City.

While I was in San Antonio at the car show, we also displayed the MG-TA in Austin at the Jaycees Cavalcade of Commerce, where Damron and Moss appeared on Friday night, Fry and Hearne on Saturday, and Dave Houston and Whistler on Sunday.

We were glad the club was closed on Monday so we could get the cars back in the museum, get ourselves reorganized and ready for our big St. Patrick's Day Special featuring those three popular Irish entertainers: Bill Moss, Peter Jacobson, and Segle Fry. While Judy Collins sang for a sold-out CEC show with Theodore Bikel that I had helped put together, the Flag drew a fair crowd too. After the concert, Judy and Theo, Charlie Seeger, and a few others came by the house to visit and talk over a few drinks. I was really impressed with Bikel as an especially warm and congenial person and a heck of an entertainer. His Israeli songs provided a crowd of 3,000 with a joyous excuse to sing their lungs out. Godfrey Cambridge was also at the house that night and tried to wake up the neighbors at 2:00 A.M. singing "Way Down Upon the Swanee River" while strumming an imaginary banjo and leaning up against the pillar of our somewhat colonial house.

We left for Sebring the next day with Nancylee, Allen Damron, his girlfriend Judy James, and me in the Speed Museum van trailering the Lancia HF. Bob Samm was coming on his own from Houston. We drove by way of New Orleans, and, with four phone calls from the French Quarter, finalized additional sponsorships from Goodyear, Gulf Gasoline (who would provide us with a gravity quick-flow fueling tank, hose, and nozzle), Champion Spark Plugs, and STP Radiator Treatment. Both the Gulf Gasoline and STP Radiator Treatment deals had to be cleared with Castrol.

We arrived at Sebring late in the day on Wednesday the 18th and met Mike Tillson and our team mechanic, Eric Van Valkenburg, who had worked with Mike on the Lancia factory team for two years.

The Harder Hall Golf Resort was filled with racing teams, and it was like old home week in the dining room and around the swimming pool. We saw Joe Siffert, Pedro Rodriguez, Ferrari importer Luigi Chinetti, Jr., Dan Gurney, Revlon heir Peter Revson, and from England Brian Redman, Vic Elford, and Mike Parks, along with many familiar faces we couldn't match up with names.

While we visited, Mike and Eric ran us through a long check-list to make certain we hadn't left any detail unattended. It was reassuring to work with experienced team members who took the initiative, and we looked forward to the next few days together.

Of the top-ranked officials at Sebring, we were impressed by Alec Ullman and Reggie Smith whose effective and hospitable administration of the event made it a fulfilling experience for all of us.

Tech inspection, medical check-up, and qualifying took all day Thursday with some after-dark practice on the course until 9 P.M. There were more qualifying trials on Friday, and the twentieth anniversary 12 Hours Grand Prix of Endurance was to run Saturday March 21, from 11:00 A.M. to 11:00 P.M. It was announced at the drivers' meeting that the "LeMans Start," where drivers sprinted to their waiting machines, lined up with the fastest qualifiers at the head, was canceled in favor of a rolling start with the cars assembled on the grid in rows of two with the fastest car on the pole. At 10:45 A.M. an official pace car would lead the pack of seventy cars around the 5.2-mile course, pulling off into the pit lane after passing the timing booth. At the Jaguar Tower the starter would drop the green flag.

Five classes of cars were competing, including prototype sports cars up to 3000 cc, production sports cars up to 5000 cc, special grand touring cars with no limit, production grand touring cars with no limit, and touring cars of up to 5000 cc. Our Lancia HF was one of eight under-two-liter touring cars qualifying, including the Daytona-winning Alfa Romeo GTV. Our car qualified for sixtieth grid spot in the field of seventy entries, and way up at the front of the pack were the Ferraris of Rodriguez, Andretti, and Ickx, the Matras of Gurney and Pescarolo, the Porsches of Ahrens, Siffert, and McQueen, and the Alfas of Stommelman and Masten Gregory. Hot GT Corvettes, Camaros, and Mustangs filled out the early grid, while just up ahead of us were the MGBs, Fiat Abarth, Alfas, and the number 33 Austin Healy Sprite Prototype of Rosemary Smith and Janet Guthrie.

When the green flag dropped, pylons and debris scattered everywhere as many cars suddenly tried to widen the course into the first turn. One of

Mike Tillson shouts to our team mechanic to tape down the hood while Bob Samm and Allen Damron refuel the Lancia. 1970.

— Courtesy Don Bok, Daytona.

Looking good with Bob Samm at the wheel. The lap times varied only five seconds between all three drivers as the Lancia HF gradually passed the leaders in our class and many others. 1970.

— Courtesy Don Bok, Daytona.

As I wind through the esses, I'm aware of the faster Ickx Ferrari 512 and the DeLorenzo Corvette GT on my tail lights, waiting for a chance to pass. 1970.

— Courtesy Hal Crocker.

the large rubber pylon course markers hit the front of our car so hard it wiped out one of our driving lights and bent our hood so badly that Eric had to tape it down with silver tape when Mike Tillson came in with the car on the sixteenth lap to hand it over to Bob Samm. By the end of the second hour we were in the fiftieth position. Co-drivers were driving in about sixty-minute shifts, and by the end of the third hour we had moved up to forty-first. By the fifth hour we were thirty-ninth.

Near the end of my second shift of driving, Sam Posey's number 24 Ferrari 312P slammed into my right hand door in the hairpin turn, his car's fiberglass body disintegrating in the process. I held my line through the hairpin and maintained rpm's near 6800 all the way around and into the pits so the crew could determine the damage. Aside from a huge dent in the door, the car appeared raceworthy, and, after a quick servicing, Mike Tillson took over. While there was controversy concerning the accident in the hairpin, the corner crew cleared me of any blame while an ensuing accident behind us resulted in the black-flagging of one of the other under-two-liter cars involved with a Porsche.

At the end of Mike's hour, we discovered extreme front tire wear and had to replace both of them due to an alignment problem resulting from the shunt with the Ferrari. We were in second place in class by then, and Bob Samm took over. We were running thirty-ninth overall at the end of seven hours, when the car failed to come past our pit

where Nancylee and Judy James were keeping the lap charts. Team manager Bob Samm was verifying the lap charts when Mike Tillson came running into our pit from the infield behind us out of breath and shouting that the car had quit on the backstretch and instructing me to grab the standby Exide battery and follow him to the car where it was stalled. I was already fully dressed in Nomex driving suit, gloves, scarf, and helmet, ready to take over on the next pit stop. I picked up the heavy battery and tried to keep up with him as he ran sideways, talking excitedly all the way as we ran through parking lots, picnics, and across a wide stretch of meadow to the edge of the airport course where the Lancia sat, abandoned.

The team of Bob Samm and Allen Damron safely refuel the Lancia. We refueled, changed drivers and front tires about every hour and ten minutes as the twelve-hour race wore on following the hairpin collision. 1970.

— Courtesy Don Bok, Daytona.

Showing the right side damage from the fourth hour, I take the Lancia back out on course following our mechanical breakdown. 1970.

— Courtesy Don Bok, Daytona.

He had shouted that he couldn't touch the car by the rules as he had been relieved and it would be my job to get the hood open, install the battery, strap myself in, get the car started and get back on the course. It seemed as if it took forever but at least we knew the third place car in our class was fourteen laps behind us and beginning to develop problems of its own. In front of us by half a lap was another independently entered Lancia 1600 from Miami co-driven by Robert Clark and Wayne Marsula.

Our car seemed to fly along smoothly once back on the course, but I could hardly see from the sweat pouring into my eyes from the running and carrying and installing and the pressure of getting going again. I made the two right-hand turns and just passed under the Martini & Rossi bridge when the car stalled again and I coasted toward our pit hoping against hope that I'd make it. The Lancia rolled to a stop three car lengths short after almost running over Hollywood photographers hanging around Steve McQueen, who was two pits down from us.

My crew ran toward me telling me that they could not touch the car until it was fully into our pit area, and by then one of the pit stewards came running to observe what was going on. I tugged the steering wheel to the right, against the resistance of the wide racing tires, and then started pushing the car toward the pit, slipping and falling down more than once. Our crew and the Hollywood types and a gathering crowd of mechanics, press people, and drivers from other teams urged me on until, with one

final push, I slipped to the ground, exhausted as the car rolled the final inches to a stop in our pit, and instantly Eric was under the hood. He found that the starter had grounded out, pulling the battery down.

Eric pulled out the starter, dismantled it by removing the grounded shaft, and replaced it with a shaft from one of the new Algar Enterprises starters. After putting the old starter with the new shaft installed into the car, he then pulled the starter out again, pulled the new shaft out of it and into the new starter, and then installed the new starter with the new shaft in the car, thus "repairing" the starter that was in the car rather than "replacing" it. While all this rapid switching was going on to comply with IF rules about repairing but not replacing major components, the rest of the team changed front tires again, topped up the fuel and washed the windshield, and the car roared to life seventeen minutes after the breakdown. I took it back out on the course and it continued to purr.

By the ninth hour, at 8:00 P.M., we were back up to thirty-ninth place overall and first in class, and even though I lost the course in the dark once and ran around for a minute looking for the wiped out hay bales and pylons, by the tenth hour we were thirty-fifth overall. We were black-flagged for our dragging tailpipe that was showering the track with sparks, but Eric tied it back up and we were back on course in thirty-sixth overall in the eleventh hour. The darkness and long race took its toll in the final hour and, by the time the checkered flag dropped, we were twenty-eighth overall and winners in the under-two-liter class. As the Lancia headed to the winner's circle, the whole crew piled on the car, caving in the only previously undamaged aluminum surface.

We were weary but exhilarated! I had realized a fourteen-year dream with the help of one of the best racing teams I could imagine. Everyone had done an outstanding job getting us through the twelve hours.

We finished 270 miles ahead of the second place BMW, completing 157 laps to cover 816.4 miles, winning under-two-liter touring, and finishing eighth overall in touring behind the Camaros and Mustangs. We averaged an on-course speed of 75.58 mph for ten hours, forty minutes, and thirty-five seconds, while eating up eight Goodyear racing tires.

Andretti's Ferrari won the 12 Hours with McQueen's Porsche taking second. The women's team Austin Healy Sprite Prototype finished about ten places ahead of us, and we were excited for them.

I've included another version of the race as it was reported by T. Q. Jones (next page) when we returned to Austin to a surprise party thrown by the Lone Star Region SCCA members. I announced my racing retirement after the party so I could administer an amateur racing program for Castrol. Or, so I thought.

It was good to be back in Austin as a Sebring winner, and Nancylee and I were joined by Damron and Judy as we acted like customers at the Chequered Flag on Friday and Saturday night after unloading and cleaning up the damaged and weary but victorious Lancia HF for display in the museum. On stage both nights were Jim Schulman, Segle Fry, and Peter Jacobson, and they never sounded better.

Early in April, President Nixon was urging the American public to support an increase in first-class postage to ten cents an ounce, and we wondered when it would ever end! But we were busy with a private party at the Flag for the Young Americans Club, and our entertainment for that whole weekend included Three Faces West, Bill Moss, and Segle Fry.

Three Faces West played the second weekend as well, with Segle and Dallas-based Lu Mitchell singing her tongue-in-cheek songs on Sunday night. Clark Terry was a guest soloist with the UT Jazz Ensemble, but I missed it all as I took our trackside van to the grand opening of the Dallas International Speedway. Dallas International was an elaborate new road course with an attractive starting/timing tower, spec-

tator stands, and infield pit area. It had been selected as a possible site for the 1970 American Road Race of Champions, so even though no championship points were awarded for the restricted regional opening SCCA race, there was a large field in all classes with drivers looking to become familiar with the course. We had an enjoyable time watching the drivers sort out the track and at the scheduled parties afterward. We also received a good response at our trackside accessories van.

Perhaps more memorable that weekend was the announcement that Paul McCartney was leaving The Beatles for a solo career.

On Monday, April 13, astronauts Swigert, Lovell, and Halse were launched on Apollo 13, beginning the most dramatic struggle in the history of the space program. A violent eruption of a pressurized oxygen tank 200,000 miles out in space crippled the spacecraft and put the astronauts in severe peril. The world watched as they struggled to bring the craft back to Earth while their oxygen and power supply diminished. There was little concern at that moment for the canceled third planned moon landing, as there was a good chance of the crew being stranded in space. Somehow, though, the trio managed to correct enough of the problems to bring Apollo 13 in for a splashdown in the Pacific near Samoa on the 17th. The world sighed with relief as history's most perilous space adventure came to a close.

While all of this was going on in space, in Austin the symphony was back on track with the appointment of Evelyn and Clarence Saegert to head up the 1970-71 fund drive. The Saegerts owned and operated Texas Mailing and Printing Company and had years of marketing and fund-raising experience. They had worked with me on many projects dating back to my university days as Clarence was an alumnus of my fraternity Lambda Chi Alpha. At the same time as the Saegerts' appointment, an accord was reached with The University of Texas Department of Music that provided a whole series of mutually beneficial programs that would help the financial and artistic goals of both organizations.

In Austin motorsports, the Texas Sports Car Club annual hill climb at Mansfield Dam was a good get-together for everyone, and a few days after that I was able to confirm a Castrol sponsorship for John Hancock and his Winkelmann Formula Ford effort.

At the Flag, Allen Damron, Jim Schulman, Electric Frog, and Patti Ricker entertained along with Peter Jacobson. Frummox returned to play the

Racing

by T. Q. JONES

Psychedelic Trip?

What's it like to drive at Sebring at night?

"Psychedelic," says Austin driver Rod Kennedy, who with Bob Samm of Houston and Mike Tilllson of Philadelphia drove the Texas Speed Museum's Lancia Fulvia to the Under-two liter Touring class win last weekend.

"Approaching the MG Bridge you can't see the rest of the track and have to set up for the corner blind. As you go under the bridge you may see a couple kissing, standing on the bridge; and as you come out in the clear you can see a brightly-lit Ferris wheel turning in the amusement park off to the left.

"On the right, in the paddock area, campfires reflect off the sides of house trailers and the smoke from the fires drifts across the track in front of you, blinding you with the reflection of your own lights. This is the beginning of the Esses, which lead to the hairpin, so you can see the lights of other cars in front of you going in twenty different directions.

"Then one of the Ferraris or Porsches comes up behind you and sits four inches off your tail waiting for a chance to pass and you begin to wonder what you are doing here . . ."

Then, of course, they had problems. I am well known for my contention that if you try to run a race car for 12 hours it'll probably break; Mario broke. So did Kennedy's Lancia.

Don't Break

But the trick is to break fewer times than your competition, which is what happened; though for awhile it didn't look as tough they would make it.

First, there were cars with bigger engines that should have been faster, but only one was: another Lancia with a larger engine and a five-speed transmission. This car qualified one second faster than the Texas Speed Museum entry: on a 5.2 mile course that isn't much margin.

But the third qualifier was only one second behind Kennedy-Samm-Tillson and the fourth place qualifier one more second back. Things looked a bit tight. Mike Tillson has had the most experience driving at Sebring, so he was elected to deal with the traffic at the start.

A good idea, but on the second lap a leading car threw a pylon into the front of the Lancia and buckled the hood. Tillson drove 17 laps with the hood flapping and then made the first of many pit stops. The damage to the hood wasn't serious, but after every stop it had to be taped down with the racer's friend, refrigerator tape.

Nearing the halfway mark the TSM Lancia was in second place but seven laps down, and Kennedy had survived a fourth-hour shunt with Sam Posey's Ferrari that bashed in the right-side door of the Lancia and bent the frame. Then the leading Lancia broke, and shortly the TSM car was in first place.

T. Q. Jones' reprint. 1970.
— Courtesy Austin American-Statesman —
used by permission

Breakdown on the Track

Then the car stopped. Seventeen minutes went by before the battery could be replaced: since the driver can't have any help while the car is stopped on the track, the 40-year-old Kennedy had to run from the pits to the car lugging a fresh battery with 25-year-old Mike Tillson running along sideways saying "Come on, Rod!"

Electrical problems which were eventually traced to the starter caused this stop and two pit stops, one of 23 minutes and another of 30 minutes; the average pit stop for tires and fuel ran behind about three minutes.

But behind them the BMW in second place was having worse problems and at the end was nearly 40 laps down. And battered and tired, having worn out eleven tires and three drivers, the TSM Lancia flashed across the line in 28th place out of 70 starters: First in class.

So there it was: one team at Sebring. I'd like to have seen Bob Samm, in full driver's regalia, crashing the exclusive Auto Racing Club of Florida clubroom in the middle of the race to find the owner of the only Lancia in the paddock so the TSM crew could rob some parts off the car's alternator; or watched Allen Damron, folk singer and sometime race driver, handling the 10-gallon refueling cans all day into the night in the glare of the pits . . . Oh, well.

The Kennedy Lancia will be on display this weekend at the Texas Speed Museum, just as it came from Sebring; bent and triumphant.

final weekend of the month, and just a couple of days after that, on the 26th, the final "Face the Music" benefit for the symphony provided a successful finale to our mini-season. The San Antonio Grand Opera's production of Puccini's melodic *Madame Butterfly* was conducted by Victor Allesandro before a full house at the 3,000-seat Municipal Auditorium. The symphony was now assured of continuing with a full season in the fall!

The election primaries were held all across Texas the first Saturday in May with Bob Landis Armstrong getting the Democratic nod for Texas land commissioner and Lloyd Bentsen for Democratic candidate for the U.S. Senate opposite Republican nominee George Bush.

Frummox and Alan Ramsey provided contrasting energies at the Flag on May 2 and 3, while overseas Joe Siffert and Brian Redman co-drove a Porsche to victory in Italy's Targa Florio. Also, over the weekend at Kent State University in Ohio, an anti-war rally got out of hand when an alleged roof-top sniper fired on National Guardsmen. In the resulting riot, tear gas and bullets flew and, when it was all over, four students were dead.

During the week all hell broke loose when Austin became involved in scheduled national protests against the war. On Wednesday, the 6th, several thousand protesters started out from the UT campus headed for the Capitol at the head of Congress

Avenue downtown. Hundreds of anti-war marchers became unruly, throwing rocks and bottles, and ultimately breaking the antique windows in the Capitol doors. The police responded with tear gas and someone phoned in a bomb threat. The attempt to march down Congress Avenue was thwarted, and traffic finally returned to normal. Similar protests were staged in Kentucky, Illinois, Michigan, and Delaware.

The recriminations and criticisms following this unfortunate scene brought into focus the more reasonable leadership of the anti-war movement in Austin. The next day they staged a peaceful and effective march of 10,000 with many shaking hands of the police officers along the way. Organizers had hundreds of volunteer parade marshals on sidewalks along the route keeping things channeled. The march came off without incident, leaving a little better taste in everyone's mouth. The ensuing protest in Washington, D.C., saw 60,000 demonstrating in front of a barricaded White House.

At the Flag, Frummox and Segle Fry presided over a considerably better-natured environment. Sunday night we received word that Jochin Rindt had won the Monaco Grand Prix. Monday's headlines refocused on the protests when Killeen, Texas, vetoed an anti-war parade after Jane Fonda was apprehended by military police near Ft. Hood.

As things settled down, life went on. Schulman and Shane & Kitty were at the Flag, Little Richard played Gregory Gym at UT, and Charlie Pride headlined a country music show at the Municipal Auditorium with Faron Young and Johnny Duncan.

At the symphony office, John DeFord handed the press a news release announcing Maurice Peress as new conductor for the 1970-71 Austin Symphony season. He had been conducting the Corpus Christi Symphony and had been closely associated with Leonard Bernstein. He was musical director for the Bernstein *Mass*, an immense theater piece for singers, players, and dancers created for the opening of the John F. Kennedy Center for the Performing Arts. The *Mass* had become a widely heralded but controversial work released on Columbia Masterworks in 1971. So, with Maestro Peress on board, Austin looked forward to the resumption of the symphony season with its associated children's concerts and other special programs.

While Colorado's Pike's Peak fans cheered the Indy 500 win by Al Unser, those of us who knew Bruce McLaren joined thousands of racing fans

around the world in mourning his death. McLaren was killed at Goodwood, England, when part of the body shell of his new McLaren Can-Am prototype flew off at 170 mph, abruptly terminating the testing of the advanced machine. McLaren had become one of the sport's winningest and most respected drivers and builders. I wondered how many others, besides myself, had begun to reconsider our own vulnerability as competitors.

I had served the Austin Civic Theater as a board member and vice-president from 1959 to 1963, so I was very pleased to see that now, seven years later, one of the dreams we had was about to become reality. With permission from his mother, the ACT had been renamed the Zachary Scott Theater, and now radio and television personality Cactus Pryor was being named to head up the drive to finally build the new center on South Lamar Boulevard near Town Lake. It had been a long road to this point, and the effort would take a while longer, even under the enthusiastic leadership of Cactus Pryor.

The Flag continued to be the summer place for folk music fans and racing drivers and enthusiasts to gather, and one night there was a warm toast to UT's Dick Goodwin, who had recently traveled to Monterrey, Mexico, to play two concerts with his jazz ensemble. During this time, another toast was raised to our Speed Museum Formula Vee Team that found itself leading the SCCA national points competition with Gaylon Lyons and teammate David Smith running first and second.

On June 7, Pedro Rodriguez won the Belgian Grand Prix with Chris Amon finishing second. Four days later we were notified by the national office of SCCA that they would no longer sanction the Austin street course for the Aqua Festival event and there would be no race in 1970. This came on top of the closing of Austin Dragway Park just a short time earlier, so Austin's nearest race course would be the abandoned air strip at San Marcos thirty-five miles south on Interstate-35.

Ten days later, I hosted a press luncheon to announce the July 17-19, 1970, Longhorn Jazz Festival with poll-winning saxophonist Cannonball Adderly as a headliner. That night Nancylee and I attended a University of Texas Student Union barbecue on campus to listen to the Jimmie Rodgers blue-yodeling of Kenneth Threadgill, backed by his Hootenanny Hoots. The next weekend we went to Zilker Park Hillside Theater to hear Alfonso Ramos and three other Latin bands. It was a treat just to go to the theater to enjoy and not have to be concerned about scheduling, logistics, sound, and lights. It was refreshing to hear this music out of East Austin.

The symphony organization moved closer to their season on June 21 by hiring Nita Killen as personnel manager to start signing orchestra members as Peress auditioned and cleared them for specific chairs in the ensemble.

We were shocked by another racing death when we learned that Piers Courage had met his death in the Dutch Grand Prix. He was one of the drivers we had met earlier at Sebring. I again thought that my decision to retire from racing was a good one, but there was no denying that I missed the exhilaration of active competition. Attending races and servicing other teams while signing up drivers for Castrol was not like running wheel-to-wheel on the course. The Lancia had been repaired from the damaging race at Sebring, and I still had second thoughts about sitting it out. Again, I was pulled the other way by the deaths of some of the world's top automotive engineers who knew much more about their machines than I did about mine. "Accidents will happen" was a truism that pulled me back to reality.

The final June weekend at the Flag was fun. In addition to Alan Ramsey, Rusty Wier was scheduled to make his solo debut following the breakup of Lavender Hill Express. Damron played, making the two nights a real celebration. In addition to Rusty's debut, it was a farewell party for Bettie Biggs, who had notified us that she was moving her PIZZAZZ Boutique to another larger location.

As part of our own financial planning, we had elected not to produce our American Folk Festival at Zilker Park on July 4. The crew from the Red Lion took over the event, freeing me to leave Damron, Hoekstra, and Rusty Wier behind at the Flag while I took the museum's accessory trackside van up to the L&M Continental Formula Car Championship Races at Dallas International Speedway. The Continental series was a new pro series for Formula A and B cars in which owner-driver-engine builder Gus Hutchinson was fully involved, so I had an opportunity to visit with him and his team and to watch him compete. A number of the cars in the series were running Gus' HRE racing engines and his own company, Chemscope in Dallas, was one of his team sponsors.

While Damron and Bill Hearne were playing a four-night run at the Flag, thousands of Central Texans gathered to honor Kenneth Threadgill at the KT Jubilee organized by land commissioner candi-

Kenneth Threadgill told me once that, "The longhairs and I get along just fine. I like what they do and they like what I do." Thousands of fans, including longhairs, showed up at the KT Jubilee.

— Courtesy Brian Kanof.

date Bob Armstrong and a number of other state officials at the BRW Party Barn.

As described by Wayne Oaks, writing in *The Texas Observer*, the event was attended by an estimated 3,000 to 5,000 people! One of the surprises was Janis Joplin, who flew in from Honolulu especially to honor Threadgill.

As part of this celebration, Congressman J. J. "Jake" Pickle read into the Congressional Record, "I cannot explain his [Threadgill's] magic; neither can his followers. All we know is that listening to this man is a pleasure that blots out the wrongs of our time and emphasizes the good."

A couple of days later, George Jones and Tammy Wynett played a Municipal Auditorium concert, and that weekend Damron, Hoekstra, and Alan Ramsey played the Flag while I took off to join George Wein in Dallas to go on the road with the fifth annual Longhorn Jazz Festival.

The 1970 festival, under the sponsorship of Pepsi-Cola, was the most solidly jazz-built festival since George Wein had added more commercial names like Blood Sweat and Tears and Dionne Warwick. The festival was a series of three talent-packed one-nighters in Dallas (17th), Austin (18th), and Houston (19th).

Headlining was the Cannonball Adderly Quintet with brother Nat on cornet and the electric piano of Josef Zawinal. The trio of electronic saxophonist Eddie Harris was a crowd pleaser, as was the trio of jazz organist Jimmy Smith that was driven by the drumming of former Dizzy Gillespie percussionist Candy Finch. Songstress-pianist Roberta Flack was just coming into her own nationally but found many converts among the three city audiences. Her version of "The First Time Ever I Saw Your Face" was worth the price of admission alone! She was a lovely person and a great performer. Her excitement at being on the tour was tempered by her nervousness about playing as a black artist in Texas.

The fifth ace in this jazz deck was pianist Les McCann, who took his Texas appearance more in stride. He and I were swimming in the Holiday Inn swimming pool before the Houston concert, and I asked him if he, as a black musician, was as uncomfortable as Roberta was, and he said, "No, I think these people are really polite. When I dive into the pool, they all get out and let me have it all to myself!" His big grin disappeared beneath the water as he blithely swam away.

As in previous years, when the Longhorn Jazz Festival came to Austin, its origin city, Saturday afternoon master classes and workshops were scheduled. By now, the UT Jazz Ensemble, under the leadership of Dick Goodwin, had reached full flower. John Bustin, writing in the *American-Statesman,* said, "There wasn't anything on the Saturday night program that was better or more exhilarating than the University Jazz Ensemble, a crisp but steadily punching aggregation that brings big band jazz up to date in some fine arrangements (many of them originals from band members or director Dick Goodwin). The band, which boasts some excellent soloists, was thrilling to hear!"

With Houston's Ed Gerlach emceeing, and throwing in a tenor sax rendition of "Blue and Sentimental," described by Bustin as "certainly one of the highlights of the festival," the afternoon featured as special guest ex-Brubeck Quartet drummer Joe Morello, plus a superb quintet of college all-stars drawn from the lab bands around Texas. That group included LJF scholarship winner Ronnie Laws from Stephen F. Austin State University on tenor, alto, soprano, and flute, and Joe Zawinal sitting in on piano.

When the final concert of this festival was over in Houston, George and I took our Texas agendas our separate ways. George wanted to get out from under the non-profit status of the Longhorn Jazz Festival partnership to make things work better financially in his overall scheme. I chose, instead, to continue the non-profit effort by scheduling the first College Jazz Festival at Austin in the spring of 1971. George would, over the next several years, produce in Texas a Kool (cigarettes) Jazz Festival and an annual Astro Jazz Festival at Houston's Astrodome. We parted good friends and took our separate roads.

On the way back to Austin from the final concert, I heard on the car radio that Jochin Rindt had won the British Grand Prix, and that in New York what was being described as a "tribal rock musical" called *Hair* had opened to raves and controversy about its frontal nudity and "peace and flowers" approach to the war in Vietnam. I hurried back to Austin to prepare a news release to announce the first College Jazz Festival for March 13 with the Texas Southern University Jazz Ensemble as the first drawing card. I wanted to strike while the publicity momentum of the previous Saturday was still hot. Damron and Moss were a relaxing treat to come home to at the Flag.

All of these years of independent work since leaving KHFI-AM-FM-TV were supported and boosted by friends who, in many cases, owned businesses that provided professional services to me. Certainly, William Gammon Insurance was one of the most constant, along with the smiling and enthusiastic support of Johnny Jones at The Whitley Company. This man and this company grew with my efforts and became one of those suppliers whom I could always count on from day to day. Through Jones' special efforts, extraordinary support, and credit leniency in slow times, I was able to have first professional printing of the highest for every project, special event, and for my racing clients.

The month of July ended with Damron and Bob and Cindy on stage at The Flag for the final weekend.

By August, the Vulcan Gas Company had closed, but right across the river in South Austin preparations were under way to open a huge new venue in a former National Guard Armory. A block away, at the auditorium parking lot, seventy-five sports cars entered a pre-Aqua Festival gymkhana, the only automotive event left in the festival since SCCA voted down the street races. This outdoor event was run just in time to avoid heavy rains spinning off from Hurricane Celia that had struck the Gulf Coast.

The annual invasion of severe storms and heavy rains was something that Gulf Coast residents had become accustomed to, but this one was especially devastating as it hit Corpus Christi, Port Aransas, Port O'Connor, and other coastline communities, killing twelve and causing property losses for 65,000 families.

In the Corpus Christi area alone, losses exceeded $200 million with another $150 million in crop losses inland and along the coast. Austinites had vivid reminders of Celia's impact when hundreds of refugees began arriving at Austin Red Cross shelters.

There was some good news for us on Sunday night when we received word that Jochin Rindt had won the Belgian Grand Prix at Hockenheim with Jacky Ickx second.

The following week's press noted "monumental reforms" with the creation of a new independent national postal service, and, although it wasn't universally greeted by all of Washington as good news, most people hoped that the service would improve and that escalating costs could be better controlled under the revised organization.

As the Aqua Festival officially opened that weekend with a huge parade for 25,000 spectators on Congress Avenue, the former armory across the river to the south opened with the unlikely name of the Armadillo World Headquarters. Shiva's Head Band, which had been a mainstay at the old Vulcan Gas Company, was on hand for the opening, along with the Hub City Movers and Whistler. This laid-back opening would be followed by a big open house to officially kick the Armadillo off several weeks later.

The next day we learned some of the particulars about the new Austin Symphony/University of Texas relationship as both conductor Maurice Peress and soon-to-be concert master Leopold LaFosse joined the Music Department faculty. Peress would lecture and conduct The University of Texas Symphony while LaFosse would teach violin, providing both musicians with a higher guaranteed

income and The University with two first-rate and highly visible additions to their music staff.

Incidentally, by now the Smothers Brothers were back on the air for the summer on ABC, and we were all waiting to see if their contract would be renewed for the long season after Labor Day weekend. Dick Smothers was still racing, and I had visited with him at several races and automobile shows. Tommy, the supposedly "dumb one," was busy making a movie for Warner Brothers.

This same week, Dick and Alice Reynolds gave $10,000 to the Zachary Scott Theater Center, bringing it closer to its goal. Alice had been one of my KLRN Auction chairpersons, and Dick, who ran Reynolds-Penland men's clothing store downtown, were among my favorite people to be with as they were stimulating and seemed to enjoy participating in all facets of community life. They, like Bill Gammon's wife Eleanor, and J. Chrys Dougherty's wife, Miggy, always went the extra mile to help build support for the arts and for public television. As often as not, they were joined on many civic and cultural projects by downtown's two major jewelry store owners, Bill Koen and Aaron and Edith Kruger.

At the Flag, with Steve Fromholz out of town for a wedding in Wisconsin, Damron booked Fromholz' Frummox partner, Dan McCrimmon, into the club for a rare five-night solo run. At the Armadillo, Denton's Ebner and Ed Doggett teamed up with Dallas-based Heaven and Earth, with Shiva's Head Band returning on Sunday. Other clubs continuing around town with live music included the New Orleans Club and the Jade Room with more country-oriented artists playing the Split Rail.

Meanwhile, up in New York state's Hudson River Valley, Pete Seeger was tirelessly pursuing his efforts to clean up the polluted waterway. He operated from his sloop *Clearwater*. He was sailing up and down the Hudson raising money, beginning new cleanup projects, and doing concerts to publicize the problem. Years later, Pete would tell me, "At one time, I tried to save the world. Now, I'm just trying to save the Hudson. But, you know, if everyone saved their part of the world, the world would be saved!"

A few days later, the Warren Commission report came out on the Kent State fiasco, and it stated, "clearly there was no sniper on a rooftop," and that "only Guardsmen fired their weapons."

On the fourth weekend in August, while Damron and Alan Ramsey played the Flag, the Armadillo World Headquarters presented Ramon

Ramon and The 4 Daddy-O's plus T. Thelonius Troll. Then, on Sunday, the Armadillo held a big open house so people could come to see their monstrous undertaking and listen to music and enjoy arts and crafts. While initially the majority of the music was staged indoors, they were beginning a long-term project of building a rock garden and patio area for outdoor events. It would be surrounded by a six-foot privacy fence.

The next weekend, while I was on my way out to the little town of Elgin where Republican candidates were having an old-fashioned political rally featuring Senator John Tower, I noted that the Armadillo had Mance Lipscomb booked along with what was fast becoming the club's house band, Shiva's Head Band. Mel Tillis was at the Circle 8, and at the Flag, Moss, Mary Hoekstra, Damron, and Segle Fry held forth. On Sunday, near Stonewall, Texas, between Austin and Fredericksburg on 290, LBJ and Lady Bird Johnson were on hand as the Alabama-Coushatta Indians danced at the dedication of LBJ State Park.

With August behind us, the first day of September started with a gathering at Scholz's Beer Garden, where John Henry Faulk emceed a "Capitol Eye" anniversary party with UT Law School's Dean Page Keeton as the guest speaker. This gathering of press, politicos, and public figures was to support the non-profit radio-TV press panel program that gave area listeners and viewers firsthand insights into the workings of state government. There was, as one can well imagine, an air of camaraderie with much table-hopping, hand-shaking, and back-slapping going on.

During the final weekend, we received the tragic news that our friend Jochin Rindt had been killed practicing for the Italian Grand Prix at Monza!

It seemed that no matter how well engineered the cars were, how strong the roll bars, how efficient the automatic fire systems or how diligent the crash crews, we were still losing some of the world's brightest and most gifted drivers. It was an overwhelming loss that left a sick feeling in the pit of my stomach as I recalled many warm and friendly conversations with Jochin at the Speed Museum, over dinner, and in the pits at major race courses all over the U.S. and Mexico.

I had been working on my Lancia HF with thoughts that if I could win one more national race in it, I could place second in the Southwest Division and qualify for the ARRC championship races at Road Atlanta in November. I suppose every race

driver thinks fatal accidents only happen to someone else, but Jochin's death gave me more than I wanted to think about.

Some other things weren't exactly working out either. The sluggishness of the Zachary Scott $125,000 fund drive forced postponement of the targeted October opening of the theater center until the summer of 1971. Then, over at Texas International Speedway, Carroll Shelby took over direction of the massive racing complex as all of the racing events were "postponed." The number of dollars optimistically projected to make the huge track pay off had not materialized, even with a number of major sanctioned events featuring world-class drivers.

The local music scene in mid-September included Kenneth Threadgill at the Split Rail, while Damron, Rusty Wier, Moss, and Segle Fry held forth at the Flag. The Armadillo scheduled Heaven and Earth, Wildfire, and Cross Country, and The University of Texas Cultural Entertainment Committee staged a one-day "rock festival" starring the Allman Brothers, Leon Russell, It's A Beautiful Day, and Pacific Gas & Electric Company. Our audiences were becoming increasingly fractured, and the racing scene was becoming increasingly invisible as far as the area media were concerned.

In spite of careful club bookings, thousands of dollars spent on newspaper advertising, and all kinds of special promotions, the Chequered Flag continued to fall well short of the break-even point, and attendance at the Speed Museum never approached the projections we envisioned prior to the opening of San Antonio's Hemisfair.

After extensive consultations with my bankers E. R. L. Eddie Wroe and his brother Bill at American Bank, and with my CPA, Marvin Henry, I reached the conclusion that the club had lost an average of $50 a day for every day it was open for three years. That, combined with the racing car company losses and slower than anticipated growth of the Chequered Flag Chemical Division, my radio-television stock sale nest egg was fast being depleted. I had also accumulated a huge debt balance from the mishandling of the Winkelmann floor-planning at the bank. In addition, Nancylee had put some of her money into two of the museum cars as well as underwriting some other ventures.

The only choice for me at this point was to shut things down, cut our overhead, and sell some or all of the Speed Museum collection of cars.

After a visit with my landlord, I learned that he

had a good prospect for the entire north end of the building and could confirm letting me out of the Museum lease in a day or two. It only took one day to confirm an agreeable termination, and I started to look for a place to store twenty-three cars and all the exhibits, including the valuable Peter Helck paintings.

When I sat down with Allen Damron and Segle Fry to discuss closing down the whole operation, they thought they might be able to put together a deal to save the club. I wished them well, but proceeded to prepare a press announcement that the club and museum would close "due to tight money, high interest rates, and the requirement for investment capital in other enterprises."

Closing date was set for September 19, about a week away. I would continue my public relations business and automotive products marketing division, put the Lancia back on the track to qualify for the ARRC, and select some major productions to stage under the banner of "Rod Kennedy Presents."

Emerging from the intense meetings of the weekend, it was good to read in Sunday's paper the confirming announcement of the appointment of Leopold LaFosse as concertmaster of the Austin Symphony Orchestra. The unveiling of the 1970-71 symphony season was featured as well. At least that deal was coming to fruition!

Damron and Fry were joined by Alan Ramsey and Cross Country for the weekend at the Flag. It rained two inches on Friday, the day the world would learn that Jimi Hendrix had died. We were saddened by the loss but had our hands full with our own problems, which had been given a brief stay with the confirmation from Allen and Segle that they had an investor who would help them keep the club open. So, what was to have been the final night turned into a celebration of sorts as we projected that it would take a month or two to sort things out. I agreed to keep the Flag open for sixty more days so that it would not lose any momentum in the change-over.

As the word spread around town that the Flag's days were numbered, and we boarded off the museum while the cars and other property were sold off or moved to storage, the fans turned out in larger numbers to hear Damron, Fry, Moss, and Jim Richey play the final weekend in September.

On October 1, I entered and won an SCCA national race in my Lancia HF coupe, thereby locking up second place in the 1970 Southwest standings to guarantee an invitation to the American Road Race of Champions in Atlanta over Thanksgiving

weekend. I was already committed to go to administer the Castrol Amateur Racing Support Program. Now I had the choice of taking the Lancia and competing for the national championship.

The club continued open into October on a five-night basis, closing on Sunday and Monday nights, but our celebration was short-lived with the stunning news that on Sunday, October 4, Janis Joplin had been found dead in her Hollywood hotel room at age twenty-seven. She had become close to a number of people in Austin while she was here, and many of them took her loss personally as did many of her fans who had never met her.

As the week continued, Dolly Parton and Porter Wagoner were at the Municipal Auditorium on Thursday, Bill Hearne, Bonnie Cross, and Jim Travis returned to the Broken Spoke as "Crosswind" for the weekend, while Moss, Richey, and Damron continued at the Flag.

The long-awaited, much-hoped-for season of the Austin Symphony Orchestra finally opened on Sunday with a large, responsive audience turning out in a forty-nine-degree wintry chill for the resurrection. This first concert of the reorganized symphony season began with four fanfares by composers associated with conductor Maurice Peress, who had solicited them for scores. Responding were John Corigliano, David Amram, John Lewis, and Duke Ellington, and their contrasting fanfares preceded Stravinsky's "Star Spangled Banner." That unique opening was followed by Mahler's "Resurrection" Symphony No. 2 with UT Fine Arts Dean William Doty at the organ. It was an impressive evening according to the reviewers, but one that I had to miss.

I had received a call from my clients at the Autodromo de Monterrey in Mexico that they needed a champion from the U.S. to spark up a pair of modified touring races they were staging for the October 7 and 8 for the new track's grand opening. All of the champions they could contact were entered in a major race at Riverside, California. They asked if I thought I could bring my Lancia HF down as the Sebring winner so they could rev up their pre-race publicity and give the race an international dimension.

I liked the drive, energy, and enthusiasm of the Auto Club Monterrey leadership, so I gave them an affirmative and quickly began preparing the car. I loaded up and headed for Mexico.

At the big new track, I was impressed with the

Mexican racing fans gather around my Lancia HF at Autodromo Monterrey. 1970.
— Courtesy *El Norte*, Monterrey.

flowing design of the wide asphalt circuit, the spectator tunnel to the infield, and the immense grandstands coming out of the turn into the front straight.

Practice and qualifying were a little disorganized, but what surprised me the most was that most of the drivers were drinking beer in the pits between practice sessions, and it appeared that more than a few of them were also smoking marijuana! I knew there was no clean drinking water on the site so could justify somewhat the beer, but smoking grass?

Anyway, it felt good back on the track, and I wound up with several record lap times and two third-place finishes in front of 15,000 cheering Mexican racing fans. We did a good job for Castrol at this Prix Oil-sponsored pair of races. I felt I was ready for Atlanta in November.

Back home, Ford Motor Company announced that price increases for 1971 would raise the cost of a new Mustang to $2,800. The price of everything was inching up month by month, but $2,800 for a Mustang still seemed like a good deal to me.

The Zachary Scott Theater Center fund drive turned the corner on October 11, when the Moody Foundation committed a $50,000 construction grant to the theater's project. Manager Jerry Harris, expressing gratitude for the support, said that construction could start within thirty days.

The non-profit groups we were working with seemed to be hitting the jackpot. I had been working on the importation of the New York production of the Broadway show *George M.* It had received raves on its tour all across the U.S., and this week-

end we started accepting mail orders for the show. The ensuing funds would be required for the theater's utilities, lighting, furniture, and fixtures, so the cash flow was definitely needed.

In addition to the folk music at the Flag by Moss, Damron, Richey, and Fry, there was also folk music on campus as the Texas Union Potpourri Coffee House was in full swing promoting Keith Sykes at $1. On Saturday afternoon, Governor Smith and Lt. Governor Ben Barnes honored Apollo 11 astronauts Neil Armstrong, Buzz Aldrin, and Michael Collins in the chamber of the Texas House of Representatives, presenting them with Texas Medals of Valor.

By Monday, the newscasts told us that a special Ohio Grand Jury exonerated the Kent State National Guard troops who fired on students, killing four, but said that M-1's and other high-powered rifles were not suited for campus duty. They recommended that non-lethal weapons be made available to the Guard in the future. Parents of some of the deceased students were extremely upset with the grand jury findings, and the whole tragedy would be discussed and argued for years.

Marty Javors, formerly of the duo Mickey and Marty, who had played the Zilker Hillside Theater Summer Music Festival, joined Rusty Wier on stage at the Flag that week, and Keith Sykes moved over to the St. Edward's coffeehouse for two nights. On the weekend, Willie Nelson was at the Broken Spoke, while Crosswind was playing nightly on a regular basis at the Split Rail. We were no longer the only show in town for our kind of music.

As noted earlier, Nancylee and I enjoyed going to Victor's Italian Village for dinner, and by now there was, in addition to the Driskill dining room, another impressive place to eat in town. With the decline of the Barn Steakhouse out near Highway 183, Norman Eaton's Polonaise Restaurant on the twenty-third floor of the Westgate became extremely popular. It overlooked the State Capitol grounds and attracted many lobbyists and legislators, in addition to the financial community and countless others who enjoyed continental cuisine, a fine wine list, and personal service.

While Moss and Fry played the Flag and Jim Franklin presided over the Halloween Pumpkin Stomp at the Armadillo, early evening diners at Norman Eaton's looked down on the wind-up of the University Mobilization Committee's peaceful parade of 5,000 anti-war marchers.

On November 1 the Austin Symphony played

a special all-Beethoven concert with pianist Leonard Shure at Hogg Auditorium on the UT campus as part of The University's Beethoven Festival. That not only gave our orchestra members an additional service, but, again, drew the city's orchestra and The University closer together under the enthusiastic guidance of Maurice Peress.

Tuesday, November 3, was Election Day. At the Flag, Frummox and Damron played to a half-full club while 9,000 UT Blanket Tax holders and local citizens attended two UT Cultural Entertainment Committee concerts by the Temptations at the Municipal Auditorium. At the ballot box, Bentsen defeated Bush for U.S. Senator, even though Austin and Travis County went for Bush by a 3,000-vote margin. Preston Smith and Ben Barnes were re-elected to the state's two top jobs, and Bob Landis Armstrong became Texas Land Commissioner.

Frummox and Damron continued at the Flag, and on Friday night, in thirty-six-degree weather, the Austin Symphony concert included Mozart's "Symphony Concertante" for Violin, Viola and Orchestra, with UT faculty members Leonard Posner and Donald Wright as soloists. Out at the Split Rail, Kenneth Threadgill showed off his blue yodeling while Willie Nelson and the Record Men played at Circle 8.

Three Faces West opened a five-night engagement at the Flag on Tuesday night, and on Wednesday, November 11, the UT CEC presented John Hartford and The New Christy Minstrels to a full house at Municipal Auditorium. On the 15th, Sunday afternoon, the benefit road show for the ZSTC building fund played to a full house at the same building. The George M. Cohan songs in the production were jubilant, and the sparkling show lived up to its advance reviews. Tony Tanner played Cohan, the musical director was Julian Stein, one-time arranger and musical director for *The Fantastics*. It was a good fund raiser and created many pages of positive publicity for the new theater center.

The next night, Hank Williams, Jr., Waylon Jennings, and Sammi Smith played the auditorium, and on Tuesday, Mike Williams opened a five-night run with Bill Moss at the Flag. Mike drew well as his song "Is There A Heaven for Balloons" had become a mainstay of Damron's shows, and everyone who had heard it wanted to meet the writer. They were surprised to meet a six-foot-plus giant with wild, flaming-red hair down past his shoulders and a full and expressive voice that ranged from a booming bass to a soaring and quite beautiful tenor. His

songs of love and adventure ranged from the humorous to those threaded with pathos.

Opposite Williams and Moss that weekend at the Armadillo World Headquarters were England's Incredible String Band and Shiva's Head Band.

As I made preparations to spend the forthcoming Thanksgiving weekend at Road Atlanta, outside my garage out on North Lamar, where I was preparing the Lancia and packing the van, the temperature slid through the mid-thirties as the north wind picked up to forty mph. The night before I left, temperatures dropped to a low of twenty-seven degrees.

Along with race preparations and getting ready to service and sign up Castrol drivers at Atlanta, I was also able to complete the transfer of the Flag to Allen Damron and Segle Fry and their partner Art Eatman. They were eager to get going with their ideas of how to make the club pay and to institute a happy hour. They also wanted to convert the former bench racing room into a game room with foosball machines, a football pool, and a large color TV for watching Southwest Conference and professional football games. I wished them luck and headed for Atlanta trailering the Lancia. It would be a long and busy five-day weekend, and I was looking forward to it. As I drove, I felt the lingering disappointment of letting the Chequered Flag go and all of the dreams that went with it.

At Gainesville, Georgia, home of the Road Atlanta track, hundreds of competitors were arriving from all over the U.S. to participate in sixteen races to determine national championships in twenty-two classes of sports, sports racing, formula cars, and sedans, most of them production machines.

Among the 462 entries were many defending title-holders hoping to repeat their successes of the year before. All of the drivers had qualified to participate by ranking in the top three in their class in their home divisions across the country. Sponsored by Atlanta-based Coca-Cola Company, the races were held on a winding and hilly 2.85-mile course that displayed many Coca-Cola banners.

In addition to qualifying my Lancia for starting grid position in C-Sedan on Friday, I spent many hours explaining the Castrol Amateur Racing Support Program and signing up new drivers as well as distributing new Castrol decals to many of our regular Castrol teams.

While the races are for national amateur standings, there were a number of top drivers from the professional ranks, including Bob Tullius, Peter

Gregg, Jerry Hanson, Chuck Dietrich, and Oscar Kobeleski. And, while the championships were run for trophies, there was at least $120,000 in prize, accessory, and contingency money as well as products to be won from programs like Castrol's that were administered by tire companies, spark plug manufacturers, helmet makers, and other oil companies. There was also an amazing presence of car makers, especially Triumph and Porsche, and various Formula Vee and Formula Ford builders.

When I was finally able to focus on my driving, the Lancia responded beautifully, turning in good qualifying times on the wide, smooth, and undulating track. I was a little uncomfortable with the occasional blind corners where you couldn't see very far in front of you until you topped a hill or came flying around a bend full bore, but otherwise I thought the course was exceptional.

I qualified well near the front of a field of several dozen sedans, but in the championship race, after leading a pack of NSU Prinz and MiniCoopers around the course at breakneck speeds for many laps, I missed a shift coming out of a turn and blew my engine. As the car suddenly slowed, a whole slew of cars sped by me and the Lancia limped to the pits.

I had bent several valves in the Facetti-tuned engine. It was an expensive lesson. If I was going to drive, I needed to concentrate more and fully focus on racing without trying to combine it with the massive job of administering a national support program.

In spite of the DNF (did not finish) on the timers' charts, it was still a memorable weekend with lots of good fellowship, spectacular racing, and a large number of Castrol drivers coming in with top honors.

Towing my Lancia back to Texas, hundreds of vivid memories filled my mind as the miles flew by. I would return to my new offices at 6615 North Lamar, where I had installed the new Rod Kennedy Presents sign on the brick building just before leaving for Georgia. Now, on the road, I looked back with mixed emotions and then looked forward with optimism. I knew I faced a new lifestyle. The Texas Speed Museum was closed, the club was sold, and the Chequered Flag years were over.

Leading a pack of NSU Prinz and Mini-Coopers at Road Atlanta before blowing the Lancia's engine at the November 29, 1970, American Road Race of Champions.
— Courtesy *Motor Racing Graphics*, Atlanta.

113

ROD KENNEDY PRESENTS

(1971–1972)

I pretty well considered that my racing days were behind me, at least those days when I actually drove in competition.

In early December of 1970 I flew down to Monterrey, Mexico, to meet with officials of the Auto Club Monterrey, clients with whom I would spend a large portion of my time in 1971. Simon Abramsky, who spoke fluent English, was my main contact and was race chairman for a big race scheduled for February 7 at Monterrey Autodromo.

They wanted me to recruit American drivers and to help them organize their races to be attractive to American teams. We talked about entry fees, safety, competition classes of cars, registration arrangements, the headquarters' hotel, border crossing arrangements, publicity, gridding procedures, prize award schedules, and many other topics. Helpful in answering many of my questions was the club president, thirty-three-year-old Filiberto Jiménez, businessman and furniture manufacturer who founded the club in 1964.

His original idea was to get drag racing off the city streets and get them organized and run under supervision. With eighteen private investors and an architect who visited and studied major American raceways from Daytona to Riverside, he broke ground for the new track in 1970 and attracted 125 entries for the first drag races attended by 7,500 paying fans. He had been running monthly local drag races while the road course was under construction.

Then, the next event on October 4 drew 105 entries and 30,000 spectators. Frequent rains delayed the completion of the road course for three months. The standing joke at the autodromo was

that when the track finally opened, the pace car would be a bulldozer.

Simon Abramsky, also thirty-three, was a business administration graduate of Monterrey Tech with a major in advertising and marketing. He was a primary organizer of Auto Club Monterrey, public relations director for the autodromo, and conducted relations with me and other U.S. advisors because of his fluency in English. He had a ready smile and a quick sense of humor that made it fun to work with him.

Abramsky had become associated with Jiménez, handling the advertising for Jiménez Auto Clinica, one of Jiménez' various businesses. The club held weekly business meetings and a monthly social, and now they were getting ready to fully explore the potential for the road course.

I agreed to start putting out entry blanks and recruiting drivers as soon as I returned to Austin. With the exception of fulfilling my continuing role of advisor to the Austin Arts Council and handling my other Driver Profile Service customers, I could clear my slate to work on the February 7 race. The first College Jazz Festival wasn't scheduled until March 13, and I worked on it a part of each day.

As the weeks passed, I began American publicity and driver recruiting, registering sixteen American racing teams to participate within the Mexican competition categories. Getting them across the border with spares and equipment was the most difficult part.

When, at last, we had all arrived at the track on the afternoon of February 5 for the optional 2:00 P.M. extra practice, no one was there from the ACM. We asked each team to provide a volunteer corner worker and a fire extinguisher and began limited speed familiarization runs around the course.

Two hours later, Simon arrived with about twenty volunteers from the ACM. They were excited to see us and to see the cars on the track. It hadn't occurred to them that the big pre-race TV show downtown was at the same time as the optional practice. Even using English, communications were not always perfect.

The race was a big success, however, and the twenty-five-lap Formula B race proved especially exciting. Rodolfo Junco finished half a car length ahead of Sandy Shepherd from Denton, with Brabhams, driven by Nick Craw and Fred Opert, finishing third and fourth, and Jerardo Martinez fifth in a Winkelmann. In the Formula Vee race, Bob Samm finished third. The 1.9-mile course was described as "fun to drive" and it received high marks from the American and Mexican competitors on its initial outing. Twenty thousand Mexicans celebrated Junco's victory over the visiting Americans.

With the success of this race, the ACM immediately asked me to help them with the Five Hours of Monterrey scheduled for March 21, just six weeks away.

Between the February 7 race and the Five Hours of Monterrey, however, I had scheduled the first College Jazz Festival in Austin on March 13, so I mixed my office days doing festival publicity and logistics with accommodations arrangements and registering recruited American teams for the Five Hours. Eager to come from Philadelphia was my former Sebring teammate, Mike Tillson, with his 1.6 Lancia HF. He would co-drive with German Dieter Oest who had driven Lancias, Porsches, and a Ford GT40 over a three-season period (1968 to 1970) at endurance events held at Sebring, Daytona, and Watkins Glen.

I also recruited the Camaro and Corvette team of Jim Lockhart, and the Elva Courier of Willie McKemie and Bill Moyer. Joining me as co-driver of my silver Lancia Zagato would be last year's Southwest Region SCCA National Champion point leader in C Sedan, Alan Acree. We had competed against each other for two seasons and now would drive as a team.

After forwarding the entry forms and fees, publicity information, and photos, I turned to preparing my street Lancia for the trip south and finalizing plans and arrangements for the College Jazz Festival.

While Simon and Garfunkle's "Bridge Over Troubled Waters" was winning a Grammy for Best Record, my staff and I were deeply involved in the complicated arrangements for the College Jazz Festival. Helping me were my office staff Carol Porterfield, Mamie Keeton, and Kathy Richardson. While it was a college event, we staged it at the Municipal Auditorium so it would be more accessible to our city-wide jazz audience.

College jazz bands had been an important part of every Longhorn Jazz Festival since the festival's inception in 1966. That year, the North Texas State University's award-winning and internationally feted One-O'clock Lab Band appeared, and, in the ensuing years, the Sam Houston State University Houstonians, the UT Jazz Ensemble, the Texas Southern University Jazz Ensemble, and several groups of college and university all-star ensembles and soloists had also made appearances.

Lanny Steele leads his Texas Southern University Jazz Ensemble at the first College Jazz Festival. 1972.
— Courtesy *Austin American-Statesman.*

After consultation with Dick Goodwin, I invited vibist Gary Burton, trumpet star Dizzy Gillespie, sax star Cannonball Adderly, and baritone sax veteran Gerry Mulligan as guest headliners along with jazz critic and author Leonard Feather.

A large roster of college jazz groups participated from The University of Texas, Stephen F. Austin State University, Texas Southern University, Southern Methodist University, Loyola University (New Orleans), Sam Houston State, and North Texas State University.

Mike Mordecai and Walker Smith smoothly stage-managed what could have been a nightmare. Ed Gerlach and Phil Manning also were on hand to assist with the judging of bands.

Other VIPs adding dimension to the festival

included composer Alec Wilder, who had written a quintet honoring Gerry Mulligan and featuring French horn soloist James Barrington. "Voice of America's" Willis Conover was also there to assist Leonard Feather with the individual and group awards. We also recorded the festival for broadcast by "Voice of America" and for a limited edition LP record.

For those unfamiliar with Alec Wilder, he had written several hundred compositions for almost every instrument in the orchestra, five film scores, ballets, eight musical comedies, symphonic music, operas, incidental music for plays, and more than 300 popular songs. Among his best known popular songs were "I'll Be Around," "It's So Peaceful In The Country," "Who Can I Turn To?," and "Love Among the Young."

After the Saturday night concert, the Dick Goodwin Trio was the center of a great late-night jam session at the New Orleans Club that really put the frosting on a most rewarding weekend! I guess the big surprise of the weekend had to be Dizzy's talk to the festival banquet at the Downtowner, in which he told the students about the importance of the pause in music and its value in solos. Dick and I were already looking forward to the 1972 festival with great anticipation.

There were only nine days between the festival and the Mexican endurance race, so we had to rush, packing up one project and getting on the road to Monterrey for press appearances, receptions, registration, and practice before the race. Although Alan Acree had never driven my Lancia, and I had never driven it on a race track at full speed, it was a beau-

Our Lancia Zagato got off to a good LeMans start as I sprinted to the car and took first turn at the wheel, alternating with Alan Acree. The Lancia of Tillson-Oest can be seen coming off the start line just over the back of our Lancia. 1972.

— Courtesy *El Norte*, Monterrey.

tifully engineered car, and we were optimistic about its performance.

The entry list for the five-hour event included four American teams (including the two Lancias) and eleven Mexican entries. The field listed a BMW from Guatemala, an "unlimited" Camaro, a Porsche, a Mustang, a Datsun, a Valiant, an MG, a GTS, and a Mini-Cooper.

The long race was relatively accident-free, though we did lose the BMW when it blew a tire coming off the banked sweeper and rolled. Tillman and Oest hit the wall when they blew a tire in the fourth hour, but managed to limp back to the pits, change wheels, and finish third overall. Rodolfo Junco co-drove the Porsche with Fred Opert and finished second behind the father and son Quintanilla team Camaro. The Quintanillas drove a good race at an average speed of 85.99 mph and returned to Nuevo Laredo with the big cash and the big trophy. The Datsun finished fourth and Alan Acree and I drove a steady conservative race in the street Lancia to finish fifth overall at an average speed of 72.58 mph, covering 362.9 miles.

We had a successful weekend all around. The auto club was pleased with the race and so was the crowd of 15,000 who cheered their native winner with great exuberance. They respectfully greeted me with the title of "Champion" even though our team was fifth.

Now ACM and I looked to our next project in June, a major SCCA-sanctioned pair of Formula B Continental Championship races in Monterrey and Mexico City. Much of my public relations and coordinating effort, therefore, was on behalf of my client ACM, but, while traveling and working in Mexico, I also established a relationship with the National Dance Company of Mexico, Folklorico. I might also mention at this time that "hot pants" had become the rage internationally and were nowhere more in evidence than in Mexico!

While in Mexico, we became interested in the famed Mexico 24-Hour Rally scheduled for July, and, as a result, I put together a serious effort to acquire a 1.8 Lancia rally car from Ferrari importer Luigi Chinetti, Jr.

One of the headline events in Austin in May was the opening and dedication of the LBJ Library on the 22nd. A couple of weeks later, in early June, the Native American occupation of Alcatraz finally ended after nineteen months.

In July riots shut down the Newport Jazz Festival. It all started, strangely enough, with Dionne

Warwick on stage singing "What The World Needs Now Is Love Sweet Love." The Newport Folk Festival was put out of business, too, when the city denied their license.

On June 20 at Monterrey, the ACM staged the first of the SCCA-sanctioned Continental Championship Races for Formula B cars. Working many months with SCCA director of professional racing, Hank Loudenback, I had tried to put together a series of three pro races for Formula B cars at Monterrey, Guadalajara, and Mexico City, but the Guadalajara date did not work out.

My multifaceted assignment was to handle all of the arrangements on both sides of the border, including getting fifty percent of the $12,000 guaranteed prize money deposited in my bank in the States. I ultimately arranged for one hundred percent of it to be deposited in Austin before the races. I was also to assist SCCA officials in communicating and defining for the Mexican officials all of the rules and regulations, schedules, and safety requirements. One of the biggest jobs was getting all of the visiting teams to fill out the papers correctly, so I could get the cars, trailers, tools, spares, and drivers across the border and back.

These two races, set for June 20 in Monterrey and June 27 in Mexico City, were the first professional SCCA points races to go south of the border in a history-making and unprecedented premiere of Formula B racing in Mexico.

The SCCA races were co-sponsored by a newly consolidated *Associasion Deportiva Automovilistia Mexicana* (ADAM) and sponsored by Mexico's *PRIX Additivos,* who put up a sizable amount of cash and a beautiful engraved silver cup (the Prix Cup or *Copa Prix,* after which the races were named by the Mexicans). The giant cup would go to the winner of the most championship points earned by running both races.

We further complicated the already complex logistics of the weekend by adding preliminary Formula Vee races with $1,600 prize money in both cities, where crowds would see the debut of new Mexican Vees patterned after the American Zink cars.

The Monterrey races would be held at the much-improved autodromo. In Mexico City, a week later, the races would be held at the Ricardo Rodriguez Autodromo, formerly called Magdelena Mayuca, now named in memory of Pedro Rodriguez' late brother Ricardo who had been a popular driver and a national hero prior to his death.

The 3.1-mile Mexico City course had hosted nine Mexican Grand Prix events since 1962 in the beautiful 7,200-foot-high public park in the heart of the world's sixth largest city. With crowd control problems solved, several dozen Formula B teams looked forward to racing on the two circuits.

The Continental Series was established by the SCCA to further Formula B racing for the development of professional road racers on the way to the top. A forty-five-lap championship race was run June 20 at the 1.9-mile road course at Monterrey, and a thirty-lap race at the 3.1-mile Ricardo Rodriguez Autodromo in Mexico City on June 27.

Rodolfo Junco, a twenty-two-year-old, well-sponsored amateur, was the Mexican driver to watch, and he and his *El Norte* newspaper were a strong force in getting the two races scheduled. Fred Opert and I did most of the liaison work with SCCA and coordinated the special arrangements for border crossing and customs clearance for the teams and their cars. As complicated as it was, we received substantial support from Mexican government staffers at the border, getting everyone and their equipment across.

The races in both cities were very successful, with teams entered from the U.S., Canada, Japan, Switzerland, and Mexico. As far as I know, eventually everyone was able to get their equipment out of Mexico and return home. Gus Hutchinson's HRE engines had some problems because he flew some spare engines into Mexico City that did not clear the border on the original manifest when he entered. But even the Swiss driver with the expired passport made it home again.

While we were in Mexico, our 1.8 Lancia rally car had arrived in Austin and was undergoing a rebuild and conversion from a Canadian cold weather rally car with steel-studded snow tires and a huge heater to a hot weather mountain road machine with new high speed Pirelli tires.

New battery, belts, hoses, brakes, radiator clean-out, serious tune-up, new paint job in our team colors of black and white, and extensive installation of rallying gear, computers, etc., were all under the supervision of our navigator, Dan Amato. I considered being the pilot for a while but deferred to Jerardo Martinez of Monterrey who was much more familiar with the roads and Mexican regulations and instructions. He was also bilingual, often interpreting for Dan Amato and dealing with rally officials, police, and fans.

The rally took place July 9 to 11, and we were among those favored to win. In fact, the Lancia led

Our 1.8 Lancia rally car in Mexico City prior to the Mexico 24-Hours. 1972.

— Courtesy Jean Calvin.

the rally for the first eight hours and three checkpoints, but the rough terrain of Central Mexico proved too much for the water pump. More than half of the seventy-six entries were out by the halfway point. Using radio communications provided by the rally organizers, we located the car, loaded it up on the trailer, and spent a couple of days at Gerardo's avocado ranch near Monterrey to rest up before the trip home.

We repaired and cleaned up the rally car, and Dan Amato drove it in the Austin Aqua Festival land parade to give our sponsors exposure. It was a great-looking car, and, except for the oversight of not replacing water and fuel pump diaphragms, we made a valiant effort.

In August, as a special event of the Aqua Festival, I presented the North American debut and exclusive Texas engagement of the Vienna State Opera Ballet's company of fifty with Heinz Lambrecht conducting selected members of the Austin Symphony Orchestra in the pit.

Among the excellent ballets on the two-day programs were the colorful and dramatic "Miraculous Mandarin," "Blue Danube," "Nachtmusik," "Paquita," and a popular "Vienna Divertissement." Both our production company and the Aqua Festival officials were impressed with the company and the audiences that turned out for the performances. The international event also generated many column-inches of extra publicity for the festival. I had flown in critics from four major metropolitan dailies and their reviews were most complimentary.

About this time, I was approached by the Travis County Republican executive committee to stage some sort of a special event to help cover campaign expenses of a number of defeated candidates. The timing was perfect, because the Willard Alexander office in Chicago had just called to offer me a date with the Duke Ellington Orchestra.

I set up the benefit dance in the basement of the Austin Municipal Auditorium. Over 400 Republican supporters and Ellington fans turned out for a fulfilling evening of music by Duke and his legendary orchestra. Classics like "Take The A Train" and "Mood Indigo" filled the cabaret-like setting with sensational solos by many of Duke's all-time great players.

When Duke discovered that it was a Republican fund raiser, he took me aside and protested, "If this ever gets out that I raised money for the Republicans, my name won't be Duke, it'll be mud!"

I replied that Lionel Hampton had raised money for the GOP with no problem, and Duke exclaimed, "Hamp can do anything he wants, I don't want to be known as Mud Ellington!"

In spite of Duke's trepidation, at the end of the evening, he told the audience that he "loved them madly" and played three encores. The dance raised a large amount of money, and we were all better for having spent an intimate evening with one of America's music legends.

Right after this, I received a call from the office of Michael Butler, whose Broadway show *Hair* had become the biggest hit in the history of the "great white way." It was a smash with a record-breaking run continuing in New York and a large road show company beginning a coast-to-coast tour of the U.S., and I was asked if I wanted to present the show in Austin. It sounded like a great match-up—this show and Austin audiences—and I immediately cleared three early December dates for the company.

Through the contacts made in Mexico, my name was in the mill for the tour of the National Dance Company of Mexico, Folklorico, operating out of the Palace of Fine Arts. A smaller but similar version of Amalia Hernandez' spectacular Ballet Folklorico de Mexico, the Silvia Lozano company of fifty was funded by Mexico's Social Security office. They wanted an early October date in Austin and I jumped at the chance to present this beautifully costumed company of singers, dancers, and musicians. An October 11 date was set at Municipal Auditorium.

In Mexico the company was known as *Ballet Aztlan de Mexico*, but toured the world under the more familiar Folklorico name. Silvia Lozano had founded the company in 1960 after many years of research into the history of regional dances in cooperation with leading Mexican anthropologists and archaeologists. By the time I met the company in 1971, it had become one of only two Mexican groups to be endorsed by the Mexican government as a "national company." The company was dedicated to the interpretation and preservation of authentic folk cultures, and the simple and engaging appeal of the dances and costumes, combined with the melodic and moving accompaniment, made the show a highly salable and entertaining evening.

Opening with the gaiety of a Tarascan wedding and closing with an exuberant "Fiesta in Vera Cruz," the two-part, three-hour spectacular also showcased the dramatic "Dance of the Deer" from Sonora, the mariachi music of Jalisco, the lively *jarana* dance of the Yucatan, a festive Nuhautl scene from the ancient pre-Aztec culture, plus music and dances of Oaxaca in northern Mexico and other regional traditional dances. The enchanting music of a Tex-Mex trio, a seven-member mariachi band, and the scintillating music of the *jarochos*, with intricate and virtuosic harp playing, especially on the popular "La Bamba," kept American audiences on the edge of their seats.

My show date was a total sell-out, and the tour directors asked if I would consider some other dates for the company. I felt good about the offer and began to work on future dates, not realizing how much a part of my life this company would become.

I had Zachary Scott Theater Center volunteers ushering at the Folklorico event, as I did at many of my auditorium shows, and announced the advanced sale of tickets for the three performances of *Hair* on December 1-3.

Just prior to the Folklorico, I received confirmation from Kolmar-Luth in New York that a Carlos Montoya date had become available, and that my requested date of November 11 had been approved. That gave me just four weeks to shuffle the concert into my already full deck and get up and running.

Montoya was known the world over as the foremost solo flamenco guitarist. He had stepped out on his own in 1948, breaking the tradition that the guitar would only be heard as accompaniment for dancing or singing. He was the first to capture the exquisite improvisation, creativity, and sensitive musicianship of the flamenco art and render it into a complete musical whole that could be understood by the public at large.

Montoya's last Austin concert was a sell-out appearance for The University of Texas Cultural Entertainment Committee, and because so many UT Blanket Tax holders snapped up the tickets, the off-campus audience never had a chance to see him.

So, I accepted the date eagerly and mounted an immense publicity campaign with the full cooperation of John Bustin and many others in the media.

The three-part concert of seventeen Spanish Gypsy songs was a high-energy and emotion-packed evening played to a sell-out audience with many fans being turned away at the box office. There was no question that Montoya was one of the great creative players of our time.

Leaning heavily on the traditional themes and tempos of each song, Montoya added new variations to his pieces at every performance. While Montoya could not read music, the essence of flamenco is the improvisation that comes from the heart (some say soul) of the Spanish Gypsy tradition.

Carlos, himself, was a gentle and genuine gentleman who always looked you directly in the eye as he talked, or while listening to you. This focused attention was also very evident in his imposing stage presence.

On the first visit and collaboration, we became fast friends, not only with Carlos, but also with his American wife Sally, a former school teacher who, of course, spoke perfect English and helped Carlos understand some of the subtleties of our conversations.

As we talked over dinner after the concert, I came to realize that 1972 would mark the silver anniversary of his stepping out on his own as a solo artist, and a plan for his 1972 return began to generate itself. The concert, and the new relationship with Carlos and Sally, was extremely rewarding for Nancylee and me as Rod Kennedy Presents began to earn a place of honor in the public eye.

The first of the three *Hair* performances was only nineteen days away, and I had become embroiled in a struggle with the Municipal Auditorium manager over the propriety of the show, which he did not want playing on his stage. To me, this was censorship, and I hired the AFL-CIO attorney Sam Houston Clinton to advise me and to take the battle to the city council chambers if necessary. He advised me to call the mayor and each of the council members individually at home and to speak with them about the possible consequences of censorship of this sort. It would brand the capital of Texas as a provincial town with narrow-minded leadership when the cancellation of the show hit the press across the United States. I reminded them that the disturbing protests on the steps of City Hall by Joan Baez and her followers would look like a mini-circus compared to the backlash if they imposed the censorship being recommended by the auditorium manager.

Led by Mayor Roy Butler, the city council, in private session, refused the auditorium manager's request to toss the show out and strongly recommended that he give me full cooperation in presenting the show.

The December 1-3 dates sold out completely in advance, and we scheduled a bonus matinee on December 4.

The show was presented by a cast of thirty-eight with a seven-piece rock band. With music by Tim Rice and lyrics by Andrew Lloyd Webber, the score was filled with gems like "Aquarius," "Good Morning Starshine," and "Let The Sunshine In." Thirty-two songs were packed into two acts.

Hair had been seen by twelve million people when it celebrated its third anniversary six months before coming to Austin. The Austin company turned out to be one of three touring companies playing fifty cities in the past fourteen months. It had played twenty-five countries and been performed in fourteen languages.

It would have been the perfect presentation financially if, simultaneously, the Auto Club Monterrey check for $12,000 hadn't bounced, and if Texas State Bank hadn't drafted on the *Hair* account to cover it. We were paying seventy-two percent to the *Hair* producers and had little or nothing left after the protective action taken by the bank.

A quick call to the Mexican attorney general in Nuevo Leon told us that if we forwarded the details to him, and it was as we said, he would get us paid or see all of the club members in jail.

We never found out why the check bounced, because we terminated our relationship with our client and let the law take its course. True to his word, though, the attorney general forwarded us a $100 check weekly through Frost Bank's international department for the next 120 weeks, until it was repaid in full. The payments seemed interminable and suggested very strongly to us not to do further business with Mexico.

At this time, I received another life-changing phone call. This time the call was from the governor's office.

Maury Coats, who was the executive director of the new Texas Commission on the Arts and Humanities, called me to say that the Texas Tourist Development Agency was to stage a new Texas State Arts and Crafts Fair the following June in the Hill Country resort community of Kerrville. He told me that since the state-funded Texas Folklife Festival would be starting at San Antonio the following year, the Kerrville arts and crafts event would not have music and the Folklife event would not have any arts and crafts. The rationale was that legislators would not be voting on funding for two separate events that would duplicate each other. Then he asked if I would consider, as part of the private sector, doing some kind of Texas music in the evenings to complement the fair. I told him I would take a look and call him back.

I discovered that Kerrville had a 1,200-seat auditorium and that it was available for the arts and crafts weekend, June 1-3, 1972. I put a hold on it until I could drive the 100 miles to Kerrville and look it over.

Shortly after that, we eased out of our financial slump from the *Hair*/Monterrey incident when, on December 23, I finally sold the 1935 Maserati for $10,000 and the Bandini and DeTomaso for $3,000 to Tiny Gould's museum in Pennsylvania. We at least ended the year with some cash on hand. Russell Fish, who had been SCCA regional executive before I had the assignment, had already loaned me $1,000 to keep us going, so we greeted 1972 optimistically.

Activities under the banner Rod Kennedy Presents spread like wildfire in 1972. In addition to being hired as consultants and producers for the January 15 opening of the new Waco Convention Center, I had also scheduled the New York road show of *Butterflies Are Free*, starring Jan Sterling, for the auditorium on January 31.

On January 15 I received information on the Kerrville auditorium from city clerk, Mrs. Gene Blount, and a sample contract. At this point I sent Allen Damron a memo outlining my tentative plans for a festival in Kerrville and asked him if he would open each of the three concerts. He agreed with enthusiasm, and I started to compile a list of other possible performers for the June event. I wanted Mike

Murphey, John Lomax, Jr., Carolyn Hester, and Mance Lipscomb, and I wanted a good Texas fiddler.

The Waco Civic Center opening included a whole week of activities such as barbershop harmony by the Austin Chord Rangers chorus and the River City Four, two-beat music by Dick Goodwin's "Civic Center Six" Dixieland Band, bluegrass gospel music by the Lewis Family and the Happy Goodmans, a celebrity concert by popular pianist Peter Nero, a concert by the Earl Scruggs Revue, and a January 22 grand opening ball with Ray McKinley's Orchestra. I even helped write the mayor's ribbon-cutting speech. We were so busy that we couldn't even watch the Dallas Cowboys defeat the Miami Dolphins 24-3 in Superbowl VI.

Publicity and advertising were rolling on *Butterflies Are Free* in my absence, and advance ticket orders were fairly decent. The comedy was in its second season in New York at the Booth Theatre, and tour manager Tom Mallow's publicity people sent great press materials and advertising layouts. The production came off very successfully, providing us with a charming evening of comedy and a modest profit.

Two days later, we staged a big benefit concert at the auditorium to celebrate KMFA-FM's fifth anniversary. I had Earl Scruggs follow us from Waco to Austin to be a soloist with a KMFA Stage Orchestra of thirty-two players conducted by Hollywood's Frank DeVol. He and I had met on vacation in Acapulco when we ended up in the same taxi coming in from the airport and enjoyed each other's company enough to want to do something together down the road. This was it.

DeVol, in addition to being an entertaining character actor, also had received Academy Award nominations for his film scores for *Cat Ballou, Pillow Talk, Guess Who's Coming To Dinner,* and *Hush, Hush Sweet Charlotte.* He was also known for his hit arrangements of "Nature Boy" for Nat King Cole and "*Que Sera Sera*" for Doris Day. Currently, his TV series scores were providing settings for "My Three Sons," "Family Affair," and "The Brady Bunch."

With Frank DeVol to conduct and Dick Goodwin to write an overture for the stage orchestra, I brought in Bobby Hackett and his sweet cornet, along with Claude Thornhill's former star-vocalist Fran Warren as soloists. Hackett, whom I'd known for a number of years, had gained national promi-

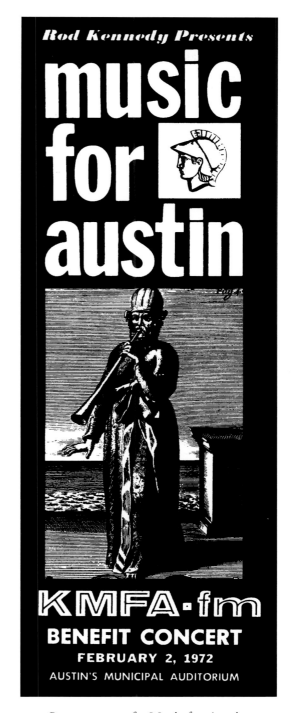

Program cover for Music for Austin.

nence as soloist on the Jackie Gleason albums, and Fran Warren had sold a million copies of "Sunday Kind of Love" with the Thornhill Orchestra.

Violinist Leopold LaFosse opened the evening with four Bach favorites on which he conducted the "LaFosse Bach Ensemble" and played solo violin. He also arranged the song "Shadow of Your Smile" for Bobby Hackett's mellow cornet with the stage orchestra for later in the evening. Hackett also played the Glen Gray arrangement of "String of Pearls."

The final section of the concert featured Frank DeVol as composer-conductor with the stage orchestra doing great old radio themes and "My Foolish Heart." Then Les Elgart came out to do "Stella By Starlight" and several other songs. Elgart had twelve LP albums with Columbia Records, including four "Sophisticated Swing" records. After being a trumpet star with Bunny Berigan, Harry James, and Charlie Spivak, he led his own orchestra, starting in 1948.

Next, Dallas society orchestra leader Frank Bettancourt sat down at the piano to play a very lush version of "Love Story," arranged and conducted by Frank DeVol. That was followed by the contrasting music of Earl Scruggs and his five-string banjo, accompanied by his sons and the full orchestra. I don't know who was the most surprised, Frank DeVol or Earl Scruggs. DeVol had never heard Scruggs' amazing banjo playing and couldn't help but repeatedly glance over his shoulder to watch Earl's flying fingers. Earl, who had never, in his long career, ever played with a "live" orchestra of this size, was amazed by the whole experience and grinned from ear to ear, making frequent eye contact with Frank DeVol conducting from the podium behind him.

DeVol followed with his theme from *The Happening* and then conducted the LaFosse arrangement of "Autumn Leaves" for Hackett's lyric cornet. Hackett followed with a Dixieland encore with a sextet out of the stage orchestra, and finally, everyone followed Hackett's lead on the finale, "Way Down Yonder In New Orleans."

Everyone, audience and performers alike, had a new experience, and we raised some money for KMFA. I don't know who enjoyed whom more. I just know the local musicians had a blast, and I loved the whole evening. It was much more fun being a producer and presenter than just being a presenter.

Fran Warren was our house guest, and Nancylee and I enjoyed swapping stories with her until late that night.

A week later (February 8) we produced a concert by the bright and brassy Harry James swinging band for the Austin Jaycees at the auditorium. We noticed that James' trumpet sound was still round and full but that he tended to let the younger players hit the high notes. The band was a disciplined

Harry James.
— Courtesy Willard Alexander, Inc.

and spirited ensemble of fifteen players who did a creditable job of recreating James' standards like "You Made Me Love You," "Cherry," "I'll Get By," "Ciribiribin," and "I Can't Begin To Tell You," which was originally recorded with his wife Betty Grable. There was a fair audience turnout and the Jaycees seemed pleased with the results.

We had one more major project in February, and I had been publicizing it for several months. We had arranged to bring in the Vienna Opera Company productions of *Gypsy Baron* and *Fledermaus*. Since there was little opera available in Austin, and the San Antonio Grand Opera production had done so well on our Austin Symphony miniseason, I thought I'd undertake this outstanding project to offer the only Texas appearance of this 120-member company direct from Vienna on their first North American tour.

Soloists Teresa Stich-Randall, Karl Terkal, Otto Edelmann, Jose Maria Perez, and others from the Vienna State Opera and Vienna Volksoper were headliners. The company was made up of a choral ensemble, a corps de ballet, an opera orchestra of thirty, and they managed two lavish productions in one day.

A meeting was set in Kerrville for March 1 for me to see the auditorium and to meet with Chamber of Commerce executive director Ed Phelps and Gene Ball of the Hill Country Arts Foundation.

Before I left for Kerrville, I reserved a block of rooms for the June weekend at the Purple Sage Motel and had confirmed seven of the artists I wanted. I also had in hand a confirmed agreement that Sears stores would sell our tickets state-wide.

In addition to having a good meeting with Phelps and Ball, I also met with Bill Dozier, publisher of the *Kerrville Daily Times,* Tom Joyner, manager of KERV radio station, and Naomi Ingram, owner of the Del Norte Restaurant and leader of Kerrville's newly organized "Company's a-Comin'" committee. She was planning information seminars and tourism briefings for Kerrville's hospitality industries such as hotels, motels, restaurants, service stations, and convenience stores.

I liked everyone I met and thought that their hearts were in the right place. Once they met me and learned of my goals and intentions, they were considerably less edgy about my bringing "sex, drugs, and rock 'n roll" to Kerrville.

A big meeting at the Kerrville Municipal Auditorium was set for March 14 as a Kerr County tourist-industry area-wide briefing, and they hastened to include me on their agenda to announce the festival. I said that I'd do better than that, I'd bring one of the entertainers. I thought that if Allen Damron couldn't disarm some of the less confident committee members, no one could.

On the 14th, Allen and I arrived at the auditorium for the meeting, and when it came my turn to speak, I announced that the opening night would be "dedicated to the people of Kerrville and would be co-sponsored by the *Kerrville Daily Times* and radio station KERV."

Damron entertained briefly and was a major hit with everyone. I also told of our state-wide promotional plans for the festival and that twenty Sears stores would be selling tickets in San Antonio, Austin, Waco, Houston, Dallas, and Fort Worth.

I also told them, "On opening night, the legendary Kenneth Threadgill will be here to sing again the songs of the great Jimmie Rodgers, whose last years were spent right here and whose home is still standing in this city."

I also said, "Texas' best known girl folk singer, Carolyn Hester, will be flying in from New York to appear at the festival on opening night." We then announced that tickets would go on sale in Kerrville at $2.50 per person per concert.

We were warmly welcomed into the family of folks who were going to boost Kerrville into becoming a major tourist town, and the forces were formidable.

The Texas Tourist Development Agency had assigned Phil Davis to organize the fair with help from agency board member Gene Lehman and his real estate partner Gordon Monroe, with the co-operation of the city of Kerrville and the town's only college, Schreiner Institute, on whose campus the fair would be set. Also involved were the Hill Country Arts Foundation, Texas Commission on the Arts and Humanities, and the Texas Agricultural Department, along with the ever-cooperative Chamber of Commerce and their volunteers. It was going to be a big deal for everyone, and we began to feel the excitement building two-and-a-half months ahead of time.

Allen and I headed back to Austin, knowing that there was plenty to do to get our part off the ground. Kerrville city officials were extremely helpful, including city manager Ancil Douthit, and while we were involved in a number of other projects a hundred miles away from Kerrville, Phil Davis and others kept regularly in touch to assist us.

By the first week in March, we had confirmed Michael Murphey, Texas old-time-fiddler and national champion Dick Barrett from Pottsboro, Segle Fry, Navasota bluesman Mance Lipscomb, John Lomax, Jr., barrel house blues legend pianist Robert Shaw, along with Carolyn Hester, Kenneth Threadgill, and, of course, Allen Damron.

The only artists we tried to add but couldn't were Sam "Lightnin'" Hopkins and Tex Ritter. The lineup, however, was more than filled out with Ray Hubbard and his Texas Fever (formerly Three Faces West), Bill and Bonnie Hearne, who were now married, and Steve Fromholz.

Our bank account for the festival was opened at Charles Schreiner Bank, and bank president Raymond Barker agreed that the bank would underwrite a documentary LP recording of the festival concerts at the Municipal Auditorium. Our publicity mailings began to hit 100 Texas newspapers and several dozen radio and TV stations.

On March 21, as part of my Rod Kennedy Presents 1971-72 season, I sponsored the New York road show-production of Rodgers and Hammer-stein's *Carousel* at the Austin auditorium. John Raitt had won the New York Drama Critics Award for his 1945 debut performance in the show, and he was in Austin to headline the 1972 show, co-starring with Linda Michelle.

The show was stunningly produced with a full production—sets, scenery, costumes, lighting, New York pit orchestra, and a cast of forty. The tunes seemed as fresh and pleasing to the near-capacity audience as they had been twenty-seven years earlier. Included were such golden gems as "You'll Never Walk Alone," "June Is Bustin' Out All Over," "Soliloquy," and "Carousel Waltz."

The show was tuneful and colorful with its large cast and fantastic dancing. The cast of headliners, in addition to Raitt and Michelle, included Penny Carroll, Ruth Harcourt, Brooks Martin, John Kimball, W. P. Dremak, and Maurine Corbett, with Milton Setzer conducting the *Carousel* Orchestra. One of the most beloved songs in the show was "If I Loved You," a song I had sung with the Bill Creighton Orchestra twenty-five years before.

It was another impressive production from Tom Mallow's American Theater Productions, but this entire production was under the supervision of and directed by John Raitt. It was a most rewarding and extraordinary working relationship to be involved with this dynamic artist as his presenter.

Along with getting ready for the folk festival 100 miles away in Kerrville, I had four other projects on the boards for April, including a concert by popular pianist Peter Nero, who had played for us in Waco. He was riding high on his recent hits "Theme from *Summer of '42*" and "Theme from *Love Story*."

Nero had recorded twenty-three albums for RCA and signed with Columbia Records in 1969. By 1972, he had three best-selling albums on Columbia, had done five specials for London's BBC, and toured the world. His latest audience-pleasing idea was appearing with symphony orchestras as conductor, soloist, and with his trio.

His Austin concert with his trio offered his hit themes, of course, but also music by Carole King, Simon and Garfunkle, a suite from *Porgy and Bess*, and selections from *Jesus Christ Superstar*.

On April 15, I helped the Austin chapter of the SPEBSQSA with their "Make Mine Barbershop" show and then had two back-to-back sellouts of Ottmar Hermann's Royal Lippizan Stallions at the Austin City Coliseum. These shows filled the parking lot where the old Austin Braves Stadium had

once stood. Further, the shows were a stirring and amazing insight into the history of these remarkable horses and their "airs above the ground," taught centuries ago as combat maneuvers.

We had also been working on Peter Yarrow's first solo tour since the breakup of Peter Paul and Mary in 1970. George Wein called me from New York to ask if I would go on the road with Peter and handle some of the logistics, promotion, and business of the four-city tour set for May 5-9, and I gladly accepted the assignment.

However, before the tour with Peter Yarrow, I had the second College Jazz Festival at Austin Municipal Auditorium with concerts at 2:00 and 8:00 P.M.

We again had a great turn-out of college jazz bands — ten of them, including North Texas State University's One O'clock Lab Band under Leon Breeden, winners of our festival competition in 1971. As the previous year's winner, the NTSU band showcased in 1972 as part of the finale. The other nine bands, combos, and vocalists were all in competition.

Schools performing at the festival were Sam Houston State University's Houstonians, led by Harley Rex; Lamar University of Beaumont's Jazz Band A, directed by James Simmons; Lubbock's Texas Tech Jazz-Rock Ensemble under Paul Mazzacano's leadership; Baylor University's Jazz Ensemble from Waco, directed by Gene Smith; the Tarleton State College Jazz Ensemble from Stephenville, under the direction of Dennis Guillaume; Paul Guerrero's SMU Stage Band from Dallas; East Texas State University's Jazz Ensemble from Converse, directed by Gail R. Hall; Lanny Steele's Texas Southern University Jazz Ensemble from Houston; and, of course, Dick Goodwin's University of Texas Experimental Jazz Ensemble.

In addition, we presented the UT Jazz Quintet, Lamar University vocalist Greg Isaacs, the SMU combo "Joint Effort," 1971 winning TSU combo with New York pianist Billy Taylor as guest soloist, TSU vocalist Anita Moore, and UT vocalist Shirley Tennyson with "Merging Traffic."

When we added a special guitar session with Hollywood's Laurindo Almeida and our final judges' jam session with Billy Taylor's piano, Almeida's guitar, Roy Haynes on drums, the sax of Cannonball Adderly, Joe Newman on trumpet, Dick Goodwin's bass, and assorted other musicians sitting in, the festival was as diverse and entertaining a one-day, two-concert festival as we'd ever seen.

We also had a number of special guests involved, including Jimmy Lyons, producer of California's Monterey Jazz Festival. With the support of J. R. Reed Music Company, Strait Music Company, American Bank, Ed Jungbluth's Shakey's Pizza Parlor, and others, the festival was not only a musical success but a financial success as well. We also were thrilled to announce that the 1972 winning jazz ensemble would be going to the American College Jazz Festival at the Kennedy Center in Washington, D. C., to represent the best of Texas college jazz!

Next up was the Peter Yarrow tour just two weeks away, plus additional preparations for the Kerrville event three weeks after that.

I was really up for touring with Peter Yarrow, but didn't really know what to expect. He was touring as a single for the first time, along with a young group called Lazarus, and we'd be playing Texas Hall at Arlington in the Dallas-Fort Worth area, the Caldwell Auditorium in Tyler, the Theater for the Performing Arts in San Antonio, and Austin's Municipal Auditorium. It was a series of four one-nighters, Friday, May 5, through Tuesday, May 9. Lazarus, the sound crew, and other support people, traveled separately, and Peter and I drove in my car.

Prior to meeting Peter Yarrow face-to-face and touring together for five days, I envisioned that he was a bomb-throwing, left-wing liberal with little regard for our court system and the law. This prejudiced view was typical of that held by many of my conservative friends.

It was, therefore, an eye-opening revelation to discover a remarkably patriotic and passionate defender of human rights. Peter was a man of fervent passion for the causes of people who were receiving what he perceived to be unequal treatment under the law. He was an ardent advocate for equal rights at every level. Instead of a bomb-thrower, I found a sensitive, eloquent, dedicated, and well-informed activist who believed in using the American political system to communicate his viewpoint.

Regarding his music, which I found to be very personal and moving, his thing seemed to be getting to know people to share in true togetherness.

We talked for hours together on the road and afterward over late dinners each night. When he found out I was producing a folk festival at Kerrville, he asked to be included. I was excited about his interest, but told him about the low artist fees. Peter

replied that he didn't care about the money and that he would like to come for all three days.

At the stage doors many nights after the concerts, there were young songwriters waiting for us to listen to their songs, and Peter always took time to listen.

Following the third night of these impromptu listening sessions, Peter asked me if we had any system built into the Kerrville event for unknown songwriters. I responded that over half of the booked songwriters at Kerrville were only regional artists. Honing in more clearly, he said, "No, I mean unknown writers who have no advocates, who have no one to connect them to a larger audience."

I told him we didn't.

He immediately described the New Folks concerts at the Newport Folk Festival, where unknowns were given a spot to sing and play their songs in front of an audience, and pointed out that Buffy St. Marie was one of the artists to receive encouragement through those introductory showcases.

I said that I was willing to consider a daytime "New Folk" event and asked him how we would notify writers that we had such an event with the festival just three weeks away. He assured me, "Just set up some rules and send a story out to the press soliciting entries." I asked, "Do we charge them to get in, or what?" He replied, "That's up to you. How do you want to run it?" I quickly responded, "I don't think we ought to charge them."

So, by the time the five touring days were over, we had come to many human and musical understandings, and the New Folk concerts were ready to become a reality at Kerrville. And one thing I did learn, as a right-wing conservative moving toward the middle, was that liberals seemed to have more fun!

We were becoming good friends, and I returned to my office with a new performer to close Saturday night and a New Folk concert to get approved for the daytime schedule at the Texas State Arts and Crafts Fair, a double-barreled press release to get out to our 100 newspapers, plus some additional hotel arrangements and passes to work out.

It was one of those chance situations and associations, thanks to George Wein, that I have never stopped celebrating. Little did I know that this acquaintanceship would evolve into a bond that would have significant spiritual, musical, and financial impact on the little festival that was to begin in June 1972, with three indoor concerts priced at $2.50 in the small Hill Country town of Kerrville, Texas.

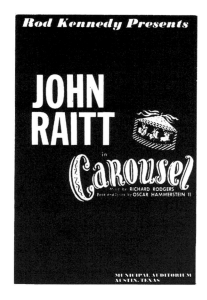

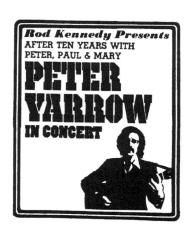

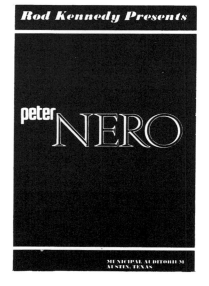

KERRVILLE FOLK FESTIVAL: INDOORS

(1972-1973)

There is something about driving into the Texas Hill Country from Austin that suddenly takes the weight off your shoulders.

The green rolling hills, the vistas, the small towns, and the myriad springtime Texas bluebonnets along the two-hour drive to Kerrville changed my outlook. It was like a massage or a vacation or a breath of fresh air — revitalizing, relaxing.

I had made this trip numerous times in recent weeks, and each time I had the same feeling, so I knew it was real. The Hill Country would be the perfect place for the folk festival, and the combination of the setting and teaming up with the arts and crafts fair had me going into the long weekend with a jubilant and optimistic outlook. In addition to being together with more than a dozen performers I admired, there was the excitement of the unexpected.

Regardless of what happened, it would be a stimulating new experience in a new location, and it looked to me as though this could be the beginning of a significant ongoing event.

The Texas State Arts and Crafts Fair, organized and directed by the Texas Tourist Development Agency's Phil Davis, was in a perfect spot on the Schreiner Institute campus. The institute president, Sam Junkin, had a great attitude and managed to balance a hospitable welcome for the invasion of his campus with maintaining the Schreiner Institute's long-established policies of propriety.

The result was a universally hospitable and congenial atmosphere with hundreds of local volunteers welcoming hundreds of artists, concessionaires, and other participants to the weekend fair that actually started on Wednesday. The multistriped tents, the exhibits, and the holiday mindset of everyone provided a festive and relaxed environment. Even the Kerrville police officers lounged comfortably in golf carts and chatted amiably with passing spectators.

Unlike most of the locals, many of the visitors were long-haired artisans whose attitudes and lifestyles were not immediately appreciated. The festive air persisted, however, and the fairgrounds provided a welcoming stage for our New Folk entrants and Texas old-time fiddlers, among other entertainers.

The Folk Festival poster printed before Peter Yarrow signed on and before we learned to spell "Fromholz."

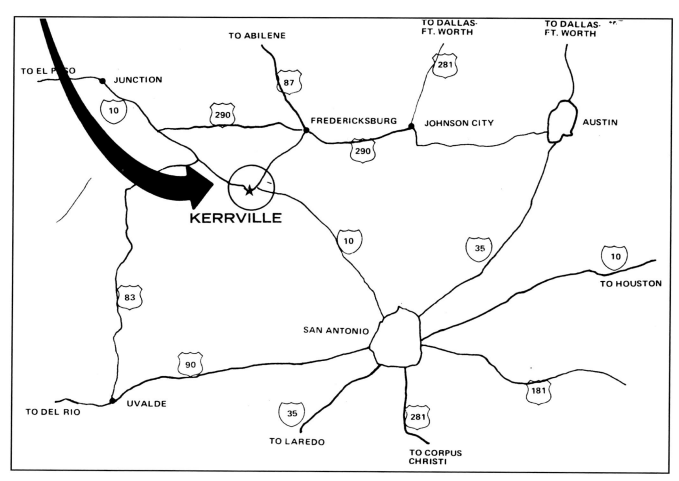

City firemen Fikes and Golden (left and center) and Lt. Bill Lynn install the festival banner at Kerrville Municipal Auditorium. 1972.

— Courtesy *Kerrville Daily Times.*

The fair was a five-day, daytime event, Wednesday, May 31, Memorial Day, through Sunday, June 4, and our folk festival provided evening concerts a few blocks from the campus on Thursday, Friday, and Saturday nights, June 1-3. Our New Folk concerts were scheduled on the fairgrounds Friday afternoon, with a festival blues concert Saturday afternoon, and our Folk Mass Sunday morning.

The fair had 177 separate exhibits from sixty-three Texas communities, and included pottery, jewelry, leather, wood-working, stained glass, instrument-making, sculpture, water colors and oils, old-time printing, and numerous other arts and crafts. Funded by a $10,000 grant from the Kerrville-based Peterson Foundation and a $5,000 grant from the Texas Commission on the Arts and Humanities, the fair provided a genuine welcome to arts and crafts people who displayed their wares under brightly colored tents and beautiful shade trees. A cool creek wound its way through the campus, and the fair attracted over 25,000 paid attendance, many of them children who found wading in the creek a refreshing experience.

Nancylee and I came to Kerrville on Wednesday and checked into our rooms at the Del Norte Motel. I had met the owners, Jimmy and Jewel Childs, a number of times during the preceding weeks at meetings, where we worked on publicity arrangements and had wide-ranging discussions about the coming event. Among the things we did together was to raise enough money to obtain a camera crew to make a film of the fair and festival this first year. We had hopes that it could be used to publicize future events. At any rate, we had a number of rooms at the Del Norte, in addition to those reserved earlier at the Purple Sage.

My business manager, Joe Bermea, and his box office helper, Doug Crossland, arrived the next day. They brought with them our recording engineer, Pedro Gutierrez, a Cuban refugee who had built his own Austin studio using his own wits, ingenuity, and limited financial resources. Having done other recordings for me, he fit right in and worked hard with the equipment we had to get the best documentation he could of the three evening concerts at the auditorium.

Dick Goodwin from UT volunteered to run sound for the evening concerts, utilizing a double Shure Brothers Vocal Master sound system, and Dean Rayburn's San Angelo-based Spirit Sound volunteered to do sound reinforcement for the daytime outdoor events at the fair. Rayburn's company had done the sound for the Bangladesh Benefit at Madison Square Garden, the Atlanta Pop Festival, and the Mary del Sol Festival in Puerto Rico.

Almost everyone was a volunteer; none of us drew paychecks for the long weekend's work, and the musicians were paid something like a hundred dollars for their appearances. We all knew, however, that money was not what it was all about, and all of us loved the endeavor.

Texas Fever with Ray Hubbard (center). 1972.
— Courtesy Athena Enterprises.

Allen Damron and Peter Yarrow also arrived on Thursday, along with our opening night line-up for that night: Kenneth Threadgill and his band (including fiddler Cotton Collins), Carolyn Hester from New York, John Lomax, Jr., from Houston, and Texas Fever from Red River, New Mexico. They were the same trio known earlier as Three Faces West, who had been so popular at the Chequered Flag. We also added a quintet from Lubbock called the Flatlanders, whom we had met at the fair on Thursday afternoon.

The 1,200-seat Kerrville Municipal Auditorium held nearly 800 expectant fans, and no one was disappointed. There began to grow, right then, a joyous feeling that was almost too much to contain.

The evening took on even greater import with the arrival of former President and Mrs. Lyndon Johnson, UT coach Darrell Royal and his wife Edith, and other members of their party (including the ubiquitous Secret Service contingent.) They arrived quietly during Carolyn Hester's set, smiling and nodding to everyone while enjoying, especially, a song dedicated by Carolyn to LBJ. During Kenneth Threadgill's set of old-time Jimmie Rodgers blue yodels, the Johnson party tapped their feet, clapped their hands, and jumped to their feet at

Folklorist-performer John Lomax, Jr. 1972.
— Courtesy Lomax Family.

UT football coach Darrell Royal with Lady Bird and Lyndon Baines Johnson enjoying the folk festival. 1972.
— Courtesy *Kerrville Daily Times.*

the end of the set, then left quietly about halfway through John Lomax's set. LBJ was making his first public appearance since his April heart attack, and the news of his attendance hit the Associated News trunk line all across the U.S.

Another surprise treat for everyone, following the Flatlanders' rewarding guest set, was the brief two-song appearance by Peter Yarrow, who led the singing, swaying audience in "When Day Is Done" and "This Land Is Your Land" to close the enchanted evening near midnight.

On Friday afternoon we staged our first event on the grounds of the arts and crafts fair. Peter Yarrow hosted nearly two-dozen unknown writer-performers who had arrived on the scene in response to our well-publicized invitation to play the New Folk concerts.

Among the more memorable entries were Bill Priest from Dallas, who had shown up at several of Peter's tour concerts just weeks before; Bobby Bridger from Louisiana, who we later learned had a new LP on RCA; blues enthusiast Kurt Van Sickle, who quickly became a protégé of Mance Lipscomb over the weekend; Jim Schulman's sister Sunny; Austin's Bob and Eve Long, who also ushered at the

evening concerts along with Paige Allen and Cindy Lowe; a trio called Mack Truck Amateur Night, made up of Bill Oliver, Glenn Myers, and J. L. Quelch; Carlton S. White, a very funny Kerrville-based writer who wore a ten-gallon western hat; and the Flatlanders from Lubbock, who had done the guest set on the previous night's concert. Performing in this acoustic country group were Jimmie Dale Gilmore, Butch Hancock, and Joe Ely, among others, showcasing such originals as "Dallas From a DC-9 at Night."

With Peter hosting and adjusting mikes for the "new" artists, and with Allen Damron, Carolyn Hester, and me helping them on and off the miniature stage in some order, nearly two-dozen performers entertained until near 7:00 P.M. to a large audience. The fair was slated to last "until dark," and we received an enthusiastic welcome from hundreds of fans stretched out on the grass, leaning against shade trees, and perched on hay bales. It was a great beginning, and we were already celebrating how good it was to be in Kerrville.

Back at the box office for the 8:00 P.M. Friday night concert, the crowd outside the auditorium almost overwhelmed the building's entryway.

We already had a packed house when Damron played his rousing opening set. Peter Yarrow hosted the concert that continued with the earthy rural blues of Navasota bluesman Mance Lipscomb, and then fiddling champion Dick Barrett, who, like Damron, were both greeted by standing ovations and calls for encores as their sets ended.

Dick Barrett had captured the National Old-time Fiddling title at Weiser, Idaho, in 1971 at the

Kenneth Threadgill dances a jig to Cotton Collins' fiddle in this famous photo with LBJ in the audience. 1972.
— Courtesy *Kerrville Daily Times.*

"Olympics of fiddling" and eliminated all of his competitors in four days of competition. He had previously won the Texas State Championship and had earned himself the title of Tennessee Valley Old-Time Fiddle King.

Carolyn Hester at the Kerrville Folk Festival. 1972
— Courtesy *Kerrville Daily Times*.

Allen Damron at the 1972 folk festival. 1972.
— Courtesy *Kerrville Daily Times*.

Now traveling 25,000 miles a year to contests and concerts, Barrett performed with his fourteen-year-old son Brett on bass plus his sixteen-year-old daughter Christie and Chris Hazelwood of Mineral Wells on guitars. Barrett's earlier experience came from touring with T. Texas Tyler, Tex Ritter, and the Sons of the Pioneers. His renditions of "Black and White Rag" and "Orange Blossom Special" brought the house to its feet, cheering and clapping before the break.

Following the brief intermission, Carolyn Hester made her second festival appearance and was greeted with great delight. Her shining countenance, beautiful voice, articulate guitar playing, and gentleness earned the crowd's affection.

Then Peter Yarrow introduced Michael Murphey and his band, who immediately received a rousing welcome from the audience with everyone joining in on "Geronimo's Cadillac." His songs were already known to many in the audience and

Michael Murphey. 1972.
— Courtesy Ron Burnham.

Peter Yarrow (left) with arts and crafts fair director Phil Davis. 1972.

would soon become known nation-wide and identifiable as part of the "Austin Sound."

The evening finale featured Peter Yarrow, reinforcing the togetherness he had helped to build from the beginning of the festival. With Dick Goodwin backing him on bass, Peter set the whole mood and spirit of the festival, where sharing replaced competition, and simple heart-felt melodies with gentle lyrics put everyone at ease. The audience joined in singing with damp eyes and clapping hands, almost not believing that this feeling of belonging together could move them so much. The concert was a joyful celebration.

Back at the fair Saturday afternoon, Carolyn Hester joined Mance Lipscomb, Robert Shaw, and others in a 2:00 P.M. blues workshop. It was a quiet and relaxing afternoon with the older black bluesmen playing the blues as they had for more than forty years, and the younger white performers singing and playing the blues they had come to know through their urban experience.

At 8:00 P.M. Saturday night, the auditorium was mobbed again for the final evening concert. In fact, as the crowd rushed in for seats when the doors

opened, I became a little uneasy. But the gentle joyfulness of the weekend settled on the crowd as Damron regaled them with his songs and stories, punctuated with humorous anecdotes and a rich sampling of Mexican songs so popular in Damron's native South Texas.

It was a complete change of pace when I brought on recently rediscovered Austin "barrel house" piano player Robert Shaw, who, though in his sixties, remained a strong exponent of this old traditional style. Shaw, one of the performers selected to represent the U.S. at the American Pavilion at the Montreal World's Fair, rocked the audience with his earthy piano and wailing blues songs. Interjecting his own simple, straight-forward folksy comments between songs further endeared him to the audience. Shaw had a big smile and often applauded the audience when they applauded him. They loved his songs "Mess Around," "Alley Cat Blues," and "Walked From Dallas To Wichita Falls." Like many other artists on the concerts, Shaw wrote many of the songs he played, and these songs reflected another time in our history and Shaw's unique and sometimes quirky view of those times.

Segle Fry closed the first half of the concert, accompanied by Travis Holland, who lent an air of levity to a set consisting of classics by Ernest Tubb, Wayne Raney, W. C. Handy, and T. Texas Tyler, among others, sung in Segle's soft, quiet style. In fact, Tubb's "Walkin' The Floor Over You" had no twang at all, and the crowd loved it!

The final appearance by seventy-three-year-old Mance Lipscomb opened the second half of the evening with the audience fascinated by Mance's pocketknife slide-guitar technique, his honest simplicity, and songs like his popular "Night Time Is The Right Time."

Bill and Bonnie Hearne picked up the tempo after Mance with Bonnie's gospel-sounding piano and Bill's rapid, accurate flat-picking providing the accompaniment for color songs like "Tennessee Green," "Red Wine," "Blue Morning," and "White Line Fever." The entire audience was moving in time to their up-tempo tunes and extremely quiet during Bonnie's sweet-voiced lyric ballads. Their set was greeted with repeated and almost continuous cheering and applause.

Steve Fromholz, former partner in Frummox, offered some of the festival's most hilarious moments while showcasing his remarkable knack for combining accessible and emotionally loaded words and music. Backed by the fine guitar picking

The finale to the last concert of the Kerrville Folk Festival. From left: Damron, Threadgill, Collins, Yarrow, Kennedy.
1972.

— Courtesy *Kerrville Daily Times.*

and wry humor of Travis Holland, Fromholz' funniest song was "Birds and Wolverines" and the most poignant was "Texas Trilogy." He came back to encore "I'd Have to be Crazy, Half Out of my Mind, to Fall Out of Love with You."

Following Steve's tumultuous reception, the audience was treated to an unannounced encore performance by Kenneth Threadgill and his band. Threadgill had so much fun on opening night, he decided to come back to help close the festival with more yodeling Jimmie Rodgers songs.

Joining all of the other evening's performers on stage, and closing the festival with "This Land Is Your Land," was Peter Yarrow. The entire audience locked arms and swayed and sang, overjoyed by what they had witnessed and saddened by its ending. I finally made it to the mike to say "Goodnight" and to promise that we would be back.

We had one more event on Sunday at 12:15 P.M. as Rev. Charles Sumners, Jr., led our folk song service based upon the "Rejoice" Folk Mass of the Episcopal Church. Reverend Charlie was assisted by three other ministers, including Dr. Sam Junkin. We all joined in the non-denominational service and

were further supported by ten musicians from Austin who had led these services in churches before. It was a fitting and moving completion to an amazing and emotional four days for all of us. Press reviewers wrote of the beauty, impact, and splendor of the soul-stirring experienced.

As I looked back on the whole festival, I was impressed with how warmly the audience received *every* performer. The older, traditional artists were each exceptional, and only the enthusiasm for the contemporary songs topped their welcome. Each of the contemporary performers displayed such respect and appreciation for their older counterparts that there was a vibrant, almost overwhelming sense of unity all weekend long. In fact, Mance Lipscomb attracted life-long allegiance from both Kurt Van Sickle and Glenn Myers, two of the New Folk. We were all regretful that it had to come to an end, but grateful to have been a part of so many magic moments.

One of the outcomes of all this was that Kerrville, Phil Davis and the arts and crafts fair, and Schreiner Institute all looked forward to a second pairing of the festival and the fair in 1973. To top it all off, Jason Wakefield reported that he had sold out of festival t-shirts!

Through the intense associations of the festival days, we became good friends with Bill Salter, photographer and writer from the *Kerrville Daily Times*, whose photos, along with those of Lafayette Reed, are seen throughout the pages of this chapter. We also found a loyal supporter in Becky Dozier, daughter of *Times* publisher Bill Dozier.

Other long-term friendships begun during this time period were with Ford dealer Ken Stoepel and realtor Gene Lehman, who served a pivotal role on the board of the Texas Tourist Development Agency in bringing the fair to Kerrville. Then, too, numerous city of Kerrville officials, both staff and elected, became part of our circle of friends along with the almost inseparable trio of tireless civic leaders Naomi Ingram, who operated the Del Norte Restaurant, and Jimmy and Jewel Childs, who owned and operated our home away from home, the Del Norte Motel.

We had much to think about as we turned for home with the echo of songs and applause in our heads and the warmth of the whole experience still filling our hearts.

Following Kerrville, the summer rushed by us as my staff and I scheduled a dozen events for my 1972-73 season of entertainment and some contrasting shows which would stand on their own as single events.

In August I had the chance to present Silvia Lozano's Folklorico company from Mexico City as my first bonus event for Kerrville. When we were playing the folk festival concerts in the Kerrville Municipal Auditorium, I had noticed what a fine floor the large stage had, and with the city of Kerrville agreeing to update the stage lighting, I booked the troupe August 7 and 8 in Austin, as part of the Aqua Festival, and then brought the company to Kerrville on August 9. It was well received at all three performances with near-capacity crowds of 2,700 and 2,800 in Austin and near 1,000 in Kerrville, where I had again received good support from KERV's Tom Joyner and Bill Dozier at the *Times*.

I knew that Carlos Montoya would be back in Texas in September, and I proposed to Bill Dozier a Montoya concert for Kerrville in conjunction with my Austin Montoya Silver Anniversary celebration. Bill thought it was a good idea, and we confirmed a Kerrville date in about a month.

Back in Austin, I spent several hundred hours

putting together the 1972 Kerrville Folk Festival highlights LP and the first of two *Allen Damron "Live" at the Kerrville Folk Festival* LPs. Both albums were edited and mixed at PSG Studios by Pedro Gutierrez. I also produced an edition of 1,000 large Allen Damron black-and-white posters based upon the color photo on the front of Damron's LP record jacket. Then we created a Threadgill poster using the *Kerrville Daily Times* photo of Kenneth dancing for LBJ with Cotton Collins fiddling in the background. As our schedules cleared, we were even looking ahead to the end of the year when we would help premiere in Kerrville the film of the festival and fair produced for the Chamber of Commerce.

September arrived in a hurry, and with it a letter from LBJ thanking us for his copy of our festival LP! I also received a letter from Ginny Heard with the news that my former partner, best man, and fraternity brother Allen Heard had died on September 4 of heart failure in Washington, D.C., a Vietnam Agent Orange victim. I hadn't heard from either of them in quite some time, so this news was unexpected and I was deeply saddened by it.

But I was swamped with the launching of my 1972-73 season of ten events and had to focus immediately on the preparation of the season kick-off on September 18, the day after the Montoya concert in Kerrville.

The Kerrville concert was modestly successful, and Carlos and Sally, Nancylee, and I drove back to Austin for the black tie banquet I had planned the next evening at the Villa España Restaurant to cele-

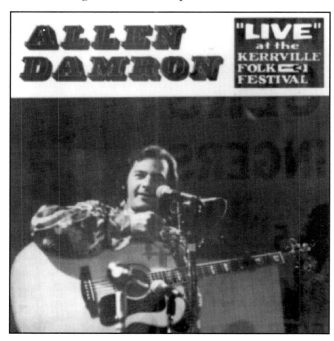

brate Montoya's Silver Anniversary of becoming a solo flamenco guitarist.

I had flown Carlos' good friend Jose Greco in from Madrid as a surprise, and had also arranged with the governor's office for Preston Smith to be a guest of honor at the banquet to make Carlos an honorary Texan. And, after secretly getting Carlos' hat size from Sally weeks before, the governor presented Carlos with a beautiful custom-made and personalized western hat from Texas Hatters. Montoya put the hat on and grinned from ear to ear like a little kid.

It was appropriate that we did all this at the Villa España at 12th and Lamar with its Spanish courtyard decor. A young flamenco guitarist from San Antonio entertained briefly following a delicious steak dinner and many toasts of champagne. There were also speeches, a bouquet for Sally, words of admiration and affection from Jose Greco, and, finally, a smiling Carlos Montoya expressing his gratitude and joy at being remembered this way. By late evening, I had learned that the next night's anniversary concert was completely sold out, and I announced it to the more than 100 admirers as the dinner ended with cheering and hugs and congratulations all around.

After the three-day fiesta-like celebration with Carlos and Sally, we saw them to their flight and turned our attention to our second event of the season. Since we had sold several hundred season tickets through Scarbrough's Department Store and by mail

AUSTIN, TEXAS

Dear Mr. Kennedy:

We had a wonderful time at the Kerrville Folk Festival. And it will be nice to be able to enjoy it all again many times over through the fine recording you sent us.

We appreciate your thoughtfulness and your talent and thank you for adding to our pleasure this way.

Sincerely,

Mr. Rod Kennedy
6615 North Lamar
Austin, Texas 78752

September 8, 1972

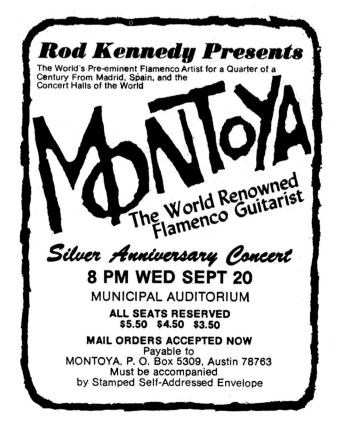

Special Banquet To Honor Flamenco Genius Montoya

The great Spanish Flamenco guitarist Carlos Montoya arrives in Austin Tuesday the day before his silver anniversary concert at Municipal Auditorium, to be honored at a special banquet in recognition of his 25 years as the world's leading solo Flamenco performer.

Honoring the 66-year-old Flamenco genius will be some of the Southwest's best known figures in th...

Spanish Flamenco tradition, William Champion of San Antonio, known as "El Curro". Montoya will receive a nickel-silver plaque, inscribed to him, will receive honorary Texas citizenship complete with a silverwhite Stetson, and Mrs. Montoya will receive a finely carved silver guitar pendant hand-made for her by Te... best known ———

Humanities Commission executive director Maurice Coats, concert pianist James Dick, the new Austin Symphony Orchestra conductor Lawrence Smith and his concert-pianist wife Joy Smith Pettis, former Ballet Russe de Monte Carlo dancers the Eugene Slavin... have recent...

Silver Anniversary Event
Montoya Concert Tonight

When flamenco guitarist Carlos Montoya sits down to play his concert at Municipal Auditorium Wednesday at 8 p.m., he begins his 25th season as the world's leading solo flamenco guitarist, and a number of VIP's will join the audience in celebrating this silver anniversary event.

Tuesday night Montoya became an "Honorary Texan," complete with an official certificate presented personally by Gov. Preston Smith who also placed a custom-made, personalized silver-gray Texas Stetson on the head of the veteran performer who was born in Madrid, Spain, some 66 years ago.

The ceremonies, attended by a black tie crowd of more than 100 at the Villa Espana, included Montoya's old friend, world famous flamenco dancer Jose Greco who presented Montoya with a silver plaque commemorating his concert anniversary.

Other guests included Austin Symphony conductor Lawrence Smith, Austin Civic Ballet director Eugene Slavin, University of Texas music department chairman Robert Bays, flamenco guitarist El Curro, the Threadgills and other music and arts personalities, including Austin entertainment producer Rod Kennedy.

All of these banquet VIPS, including Greco and the Governor will be attending Wednesday's concert along with such other Texas music personalities as concert pianist James Dick.

The concert program will include many of the old Spanish gypsy melodies for which Montoya has gained performance fame during the past 25-years including his own arrangements of fandangos, jotas, zambras and the often requested "Saeta" which depicts the Holy Week procession in Sevilla.

A good selection of tickets in all price brackets ($3.50, $4.50, $5.50) remains on sale

Wed. from 10 a.m. to 8 p.m. concert time at the Municipal Auditorium box office. Both BankAmericard and Master Charge cards are accepted at the box office as well as cash purchases but card holders are requested to purchase tickets before 7:30 p.m. to eliminate delays.

...nes whose early career was associated with Montoya's ...nd that this confirmation ...ould come no later than ...onday. He said that the ...cial guest would also be ...nding Montoya's concert ...g with other well-known ...onalities.

...kets for Montoya's ...esday night, September 20, anniversary concert are ...through Tuesday at both ...oughs, Sears Hancock ...e University co-op, and ...et office at 6615 N. All tickets will be ...o the box office on ...y with sales beginning ...a.m. The Montoya ...by invitation only ...guest list includes ...ket holders and ...Kennedy's 10-event

Carlos Montoya. 1972.
— Courtesy Kolmar-Luth
Entertainment.

order, we concentrated on selling the rest of the seats during the remaining three weeks before the arrival of Columbia Artists road show production of the Tony Award musical *Applause*, starring Patrice Munsel. The show had done well on Broadway, where it played for over two years, and now this company was playing 114 cities across the U.S.

Applause was based upon the 1950 movie *All About Eve* that was turned into a Broadway show by Betty Comden and Adolf Green. Patrice Munsel had been a Metropolitan Opera star who had successfully made the transition to Broadway playing in *Kiss Me Kate, South Pacific, Can-Can, The King and I, Song of Norway, Hello, Dolly!, Sound of Music,* and *My Fair Lady.* Her star power provided us with an excellent advance sale two weeks ahead of time. And the cast included other major artists like Pia Zadora, so, while not totally a sell-out, it did very well, earning an excellent review from John Bustin. Also, we found the entire company easy to work with, which made it doubly pleasurable for us.

While all of this was going on, we were also promoting our next event five days later on the

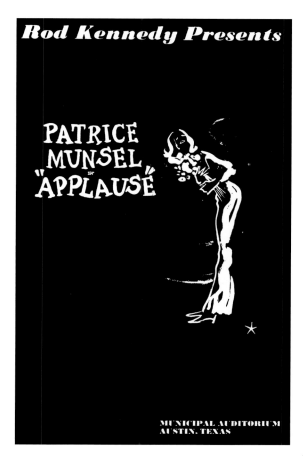

19th, when we were to unveil "Tzigane," a large company of forty Gypsy dancers, singers, and musicians on their first tour of the U.S. Formed by the Violin Primas of Hungary, including the leading Hungarian Gypsy orchestra, Gypsy Redzepova, the spectacular dancers and passionate singers were accompanied by the thrilling sounds of violins, pan pipes, and cembalo. The performers were from Hungary, Russia, Romania, Spain, Greece, Turkey, Bulgaria, and Yugoslavia. In spite of a number of threatening phone calls for bringing "the bad magic of Gypsy bands" into town, we had a good audience turnout. The brilliant show was greeted with wild applause and cheering, earning the company several encores and repeated curtain calls.

Three weeks later, on November 8, ragtime pianist Max Morath flew in for his first personal appearance in Austin to star in our Ragtime Concert with the Jim Cullum Happy Jazz Band, which had a ten-year following from playing at the Landing in San Antonio.

Morath, now a Vanguard Records artist, had two award-winning national TV series, a sixteen-week run in New York in 1969 in his show "At The Turn of the Century," and had been a guest on a half-dozen major network TV shows. He had introduced millions of fans to the music of Scott Joplin, Jelly Roll Morton, James Scott, and Joseph Lamb. The Baldwin grand piano had never sounded better!

Cullum's band played good-time music that complemented and contrasted perfectly with Morath's piano, and in the end, they all joined forces to close the show. The Cullum aggregation at this time featured Jim's dad on clarinet, Gene McKinney on trombone, Cliff Gillette's piano, Wilson Davis' Sousaphone, Curley Williams' banjo, and Harvey Kindervater's drums. It was a fun evening attended by about 1,500 fans who enjoyed music from the Gay Nineties to the Roaring Twenties.

We had been trying to find a format that would attract and entertain the older people of Kerrville, since our folk festival crowd was predominately younger than the average age in Kerrville, where sixty percent of the population was over fifty-five. Watching the older audience at this ragtime concert started me thinking about a ragtime event for Kerrville for 1973, perhaps around the 4th of July.

Our next event in Austin's Municipal Auditorium showed me that not everyone shared

my taste in music. I had scheduled award-winning guitarist Charlie Byrd and his trio for my fifth season event, along with singing star and former Miss America Anita Bryant. Her twelve-piece orchestra was conducted, believe it or not, by Charlie Byrd!

Both parts of the concert were outstanding as far as I could see, but the Charlie Byrd fans disliked Anita Bryant and the Anita Bryant fans hated Charlie Byrd!

One of the fans who did enjoy the whole concert was former president Lyndon Johnson, an avid Anita Bryant fan. Charlie Byrd had long been a Washington, D. C., favorite, extremely popular in both political and social circles in the Capitol. At the end of the concert, LBJ asked me to accompany him backstage to see Anita. We both shared our appreciation for Anita as an artist, and, by now, a warm bond had developed between us. When LBJ put his arm around my shoulders, it was easy to understand the power and charisma he had exerted on wavering members of Congress when he wanted something done. This "affectionate" gesture by LBJ was known in Washington circles as a "half Lyndon," in reference to the familiar wrestling hold called a "half Nelson."

In the end, however, the general turnout for the evening proved insufficient to carry the bill. Even with season ticket holders, we lost a little money on this one.

Rod Kennedy Presents

anita bryant

charlie byrd

MUNICIPAL AUDITORIUM
AUSTIN, TEXAS

Meeting Anita Bryant at the Austin airport. 1972.
— Courtesy Nolen E. Williamson.

About this time we also were greeted with a cancellation by the Franz Lehar Orchestra of Vienna, originally scheduled for December 4, so I promised our season ticket holders a replacement

show in the spring. I ended up presenting three different shows in three different venues that night!

At the auditorium, which I had already contracted, I presented William Windom in *Thurber*. Windom was best known at the time for his Emmy Award-winning lead role in TV's "My World And Welcome To It," which was based on the writings of James Thurber. His stage show consisted of 14 Thurber vignettes in the form of stories, reports, and fables, and was very well done.

At the same time, 200 yards away at the City Coliseum, I presented the Roller Derby, featuring some of the nation's fastest and toughest skaters, many of them women! It was not unlike a low-flying, fast-moving wrestling match on skates with all the rules thrown out and a few good punches thrown in. The large and noisy crowd loved it and yelled throughout the evening.

Also at 8:00 P.M. that night at Gregory Gymnasium out on the UT campus, the UT Student Government and I produced a powerful concert featuring Hot Tuna with Papa John Creech, Commander Cody and The Lost Planet Airmen, and an opening act featuring Austin's own The Storm, with Jimmy Vaughn, Paul Ray, Lewis Condrey, Freddie Warden, and Mike Kindred.

These were three unique, contrasting shows, appealing to three quite different audiences, and the outcome was that I took the huge profit from the Roller Derby and paid off the losses on the other two shows. But, oh, what a night!

My staff and I heaved a collective sigh of relief when it was over and blissfully looked forward to a few weeks of recovery time with only the Christmas holidays and the Kerrville movie premiere between us and 1973. We were also at work on marketing our first show of the New Year, the 1970-71 Tony Award-winning mystery thriller *Sleuth*, set for January 21 at the city auditorium.

For personal recreation during these paperwork breaks, we mostly listened to music. In addition to symphony and ballet evenings, we also went to the

Saxon Pub out on the Interstate at 38th Street to enjoy Steve Fromholz, the trio of Rusty (Wier), Layton (DePenning), and John (Inmon), Pat Garvey, and Kenneth Threadgill and his Hootenanny Hoots, including Chuck and Julie Joyce, Bill Campbell, and fiddling Cotton Collins.

Another activity that occurred during the off time involved Silvia Lozano's National Dance Company of Mexico. They liked what I did for them on publicity — so much so that we negotiated an arrangement whereby I became their North American touring press officer, writing feature stories, reproducing photos and slides for press kits, and doing various sizes of advertising layouts, as well as furnishing cassettes of music from the shows to provide background for radio commercials. These packages of promotional materials were sent out to hundreds of presenters who were offering the Folklorico company to their audiences all across the U.S.

Just as 1972 was winding down, the premiere showing of the twenty-eight-minute film *Hill Country Happening*, produced by Bob Elkins and Toby Hooper and featuring fair and festival highlights, was scheduled for December 27 at 7:30 P.M. at the Kerrville Municipal Auditorium. For the premiere, I arranged for entertainment by the Threadgills, a musical family of nine young singers and instrumentalists ranging in age from six to twenty-two years. They had moved to Austin from Corpus Christi during the summer, had already appeared at a dozen local events, and I knew their youth and charm would really appeal to the premiere crowd.

By the time we got there, the Threadgills were set up, and the film was ready to go. A large crowd was on hand, thanks to advance sales by the local banks, savings and loans, and restaurants, and we visited with event chairman Si Ragsdale, KERV's Tom Joyner, fair chairman Phil Davis, Arts and Humanities executive Maury Coats, Sam Junkin, Bill Dozier, the Childs, Naomi Ingram, and others. The $2 admission for the premiere helped reduce the $4,000 balance due on the production costs.

The film, designed to promote the fair and festival on television stations across the country, was people — people at the fair, looking, talking, walking, wading, eating, buying, and enjoying. It moved quickly but smoothly across the festive arts and crafts fair but also featured picturesque views of the beautiful Hill Country and glimpses of streams, wildflowers, and waving fields.

Rod Kennedy Presents

HOT TUNA

COMMANDER CODY & his *Lost Planet Airmen*

Sponsored By Student Government At The University of Texas

8 PM MON. DEC. 4 GREGORY GYMNASIUM

STUDENTS $3.50 ADVANCE $4.50 AT THE DOOR (STUDENT I.D. REQUIRED) NON-STUDENT $4.50 ADVANCE $5.50 AT THE DOOR
ADVANCE TICKET SALE NOW THRU DECEMBER 2 HOG AUD. BOX OFC. — UNIVERSITY CO-OP — RECORD TOWN
TICKET OFFICE 6615 N. LAMAR (9-6 MON.-FRI.)

AT THE DOOR PRICES IN EFFECT DAY OF PERFORMANCE
GREGORY GYMNASIUM BOX OFFICE OPENS NOON DEC. 4

There was no narration or dialogue on the soundtrack, but music flowed throughout — music by such folk festival performers as the Flatlanders, bluesman Mance Lipscomb, national fiddling champion Dick Barrett, and Peter Yarrow singing "This will be what a festival should be . . ."

Seeing the film, rekindling the memories, and visiting with friends was a great way to send off the old year as we went into a long New Year's weekend in Austin. On New Year's Day, Austin's KOKE-FM debuted its "progressive country" format, wherein program director Rusty Bell intermixed such artists as Jerry Jeff Walker, Uncle Walt's Band, Michael Murphey, Greazy Wheels, Frieda and the Firedogs, the Sir Douglas Quintet, Willie Nelson, Kinky Friedman, and Billy Joe Shaver. It was meant to be a broadcast reflection of what was going on in the Austin club scene, and we felt sure we were witness to the dawning of a new musical era in Texas.

Our first 1973 event, *Sleuth*, opened on January 21 and was the seventh of our announced season. Involving the love triangle ploy of a thrilling mystery, it had caught everyone's imagination and was earning incredible publicity and ticket response, selling over 1,000 seats in addition to the season ticket holders.

It had been a major success in New York and featured popular British actors George Rose and David Haviland, and its great appeal lay in its engrossing plot, wherein a mystery writer becomes entangled in games of reality and fantasy with his wife at great peril. The production's absorbing combination of super-ingenious plot, urbane conversation, laughter, wit, and puzzlement also contributed to the production's great popularity.

The playwright, Anthony Shaffer, had also written the screenplay for the recent Hitchcock film, *Frenzy*, and the audience was kept on the edge of their seats from the first curtain. The suspense was chilling, but mostly the play entertained at a sustained high level because of its cleverness and scintillating dialogue delivered so effectively by the two British actors — all in all a baffling and wildly funny way to begin our 1973 season.

The next day, January 22, my forty-third birthday, the nation learned of the death of Lyndon Johnson, and I wept for his passing. On television, the flashbacks showed LBJ in a Kerrville Folk Festival t-shirt, the one that Allen Damron had given him, cooking barbecue for German dignitaries. And at the funeral, Anita Bryant sang for her late admirer.

In contrast to *Sleuth*, our first February event, on the fourth, sold out completely, well in advance even though it was not part of our "season."

I finally had been given the opportunity to present the Glenn Miller Orchestra in their first Austin appearance as a benefit for the UT Jazz Ensemble's travel and scholarship fund. I had originally scheduled the band the day President Kennedy was assassinated in Dallas, but the Democratic National Committee needed the Austin auditorium cleared well before the President's arrival the next day for a huge dinner, and I was asked to reschedule.

Now, years later, I had my chance, and I

thought I'd try something different. I had all the theater seats removed from the immense main floor of the auditorium and set up 160 tables for ten people each, all the way from a large dance floor in front of the stage back to the sixty-foot, ceiling-high windows that framed the Austin skyline as a backdrop.

With an extensive publicity campaign supported by John Bustin at the *Austin American-Statesman*, along with several radio stations and a direct mail campaign, we told the whole romantic/tragic story of Glenn Miller, resulting in tremendous response from the audience.

The concert-dance ensemble was the famed sixteen-piece traveling road band led by Buddy DeFranco and owned by the Miller estate, playing

Buddy DeFrano led the Glenn Miller Orchestra, 1966-1974.

— Courtesy James J. Friegan-
Willard Alexander, Inc.

the original Glenn Miller arrangements. It was probably the most imitated band in the world and continued to be the band that sold the most records of dance music in the history of RCA Victor.

Miller's unique style emphasized the reed section with DeFranco's clarinet carrying the melody in unison with a single tenor saxophone, the instruments playing the tune an octave apart, while the sax section played the divided harmonies. This golden sound was worth a million dollars a year before the famous bandleader disappeared over the English Channel during World War II.

Ten years after the war, the orchestra was reorganized under the direction of Ray McKinley, Miller's Army Air Force Band drummer, who had been tapped to lead the band when Miller disappeared.

When McKinley retired in 1966 after ten years on the road, award-winning clarinetist Buddy DeFranco assumed the leadership role and toured the world for the next seven years. The band under DeFranco's direction was not a pickup band but rather a full-time, sixteen-piece professional ensemble especially auditioned and trained in the Miller style for touring. The band was tight and disciplined.

I was amazed to see the affection and hero worship accorded the band and its music thirty years after Miller's disappearance. The sell-out crowd of more than 1,600 loved dancing again to the sounds of "String of Pearls," first recorded with Bobby Hackett's trumpet solo in 1941, "In The Mood" (1939), "Tuxedo Junction" (1940), and his famous theme "Moonlight Serenade" (1939).

On February 20, in co-sponsorship with UNICEF, I presented the next event on my season, the American premiere of "Radost," a youth company of sixty performers including the Abrasevic Ensemble. The ensemble was made up of a teenage dance group, an all-girl sextet, a children's ensemble, and the Abrasevic Orchestra, directed by Miodrag Stevanovic.

The concert of lusty, high, wide, and handsome Slavic folk songs, dances from Serbia, Slovania, Rumania, Hungary, Yugoslavia, Bulgaria, and Sicily included the famed *czardas* and *tarantella* dances.

The beautifully costumed troupe of performers, aged eleven to eighteen, won first prize in the 1970-71 competition in Europe, and then again at

Belgrade, where Radost was the first prize winner at the UNICEF World Folk Festival.

While the company had presented hundreds of performances of their visually resplendent singing and dancing pyrotechnics throughout Europe and the Orient, they only drew 500 people in Austin, including nearly 300 season ticket holders. However, when that 500 stood and cheered for encores, they sounded like thousands. Somehow, though, this one got away from us.

Five days later, on February 25, we offered as a replacement for one of our season cancellations an evening with Fred Waring and his Pennsylvanians, who were celebrating their fifty-sixth season.

Waring, whose group had set the standard for American popular choral singing over the past half century, had started in 1918 when he was seventeen and his group was a quartet called "Banjazzatra." It grew from a foursome to eight and then to sixteen. That's when he put down his banjo and picked up the leader's baton.

Changing the name to Waring's Collegians,

and then to Fred Waring's Pennsylvanians, he made radio history in early broadcasts and played the nation's top vaudeville houses and universities, becoming a national sensation.

He and his Pennsylvanians had starring roles in motion pictures as soon as sound techniques were developed enough to produce big musicals. He presented TV audiences with their first musical spectaculars, and then deserted television for the concert stage, touring the nation for twenty-four years. He soon became America's number one concert box office draw.

In addition, in 1923, he began a recording career and became one of the nation's biggest selling recording artists on the Victor, Decca, Capital, Reprise, and Mega labels.

His 1973 edition of the Pennsylvanians included twenty-four singers, among them Poley McClintock, a member of the original quartet. The Waring concert was a magnificent demonstration of show business at its best — music, color, routines, lighting, and sound. It was a complete top-flight package, and the radiant evening of stirring entertainment was greeted by

143

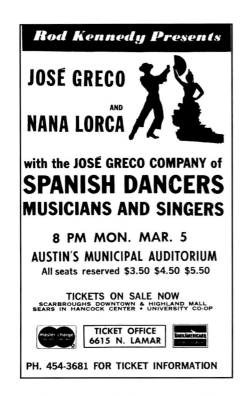

standing ovations and calls for encores. It was a treat for me to watch how Waring worked and to get to be his presenter.

As we prepared for our March 5 Jose Greco show, we heard that Roberta Flack had finally won a Grammy for her "First Time Ever I Saw Your Face." It had taken years for this recording to catch on across the U.S.

Jose Greco brought his dance partner, Nana Lorca, and his famous company of Spanish dancers, singers, and musicians to our stage for thirteen rousing scenes that included the beautiful "Intermezzo" from Granados' *Goyescas*. Greco was internationally recognized as the world's most famous flamenco dancer, and those who had not seen him in person had seen his high-energy dancing in the film *Around The World In 80 Days*. The evening closed with the entire company presenting the uninhibited and emotional "Andalucia Flamenca."

On Monday, March 26, we again cleared out the auditorium for a special concert-dance of Warren Covington playing the music made famous by Tommy Dorsey. Covington, an arranger, leader, singer, and trombonist who had sold over eight million records on his own, was our house guest and drew his band from Dick Goodwin's best UT Jazz

Ensemble players. These kids did a creditable and convincing job of recreating Dorsey's theme "Getting Sentimental Over You," featuring Covington's mellow trombone, plus such Dorsey standards as "Song of India," "Marie," "I'll Never Smile Again," "Sunny Side of the Street," and "Opus No. 1."

Playing opposite the fifteen-piece big band for intermissions was Chuck Reiley's Alamo City Jazz Band. The dancers were on the floor constantly, and we filled hundreds of table reservations for dancers as well as balcony seats for listeners.

As we began to finalize preparations for our second Kerrville Folk Festival and stepped up the state-wide publicity campaign for that May 24-28 event, we still had two late April events to present: the opening of Jack Ray's Feed Lot Restaurant out Highway 2222, northwest of Austin on Friday, April 27, followed by the College Jazz Festival the next day.

For the Feed Lot steak house, I asked Dick Goodwin to put together a five-piece jazz group to be fronted by Max Kaminsky as well as a twelve-man ensemble to be fronted by trombonist Buddy Morrow, a nationally known big band leader since 1951, best remembered for his recordings of "Night Train" and "One Mint Julep." Kaminsky and Morrow flew in from New York for the date.

Goodwin also arranged for four strolling violinists, and I hired a Mexican trio called Los Amigos to play *musica romantica.* Strait Music Company furnished the pianos and sound reinforcement system.

The opening, though hampered by cold weather that made the large patio area unusable, was jammed with members of the Texas Congressional Delegation and the Texas Legislature, as well as local dignitaries and other long-time customers of Jack Ray's old restaurant, The Barn, on Balcones Drive. We managed to put the whole evening together for right at $3,000!

Getting up the next day was a little difficult, and we were relieved that the first jazz festival event wasn't until 2:00 P.M. We were back at Municipal Auditorium with an opening concert featuring The University of Texas Combo, Aubrey Tucker's University of Houston Monday Lab Band, the Southwestern State College Jazz Ensemble from Oklahoma, led by Terry Segress, and a memorial tribute to Austin's late, great trumpet star, Kenny Dorham, who had died in 1972. Sonny Stitt led this jam, assisted by Jimmy Owens, Richard Davis, Bubba Thomas, and others.

Following the intermission, the festival featured performances by the Sam Houston State Houstonians Quintet, the Tarleton State College Jazz Ensemble (Dennis Guillaume directing), the Texas Southern University Combo (from Houston), and the Southern Methodist University Stage Band under Paul Guerrero. Vibist Gary Burton presented one of the most fulfilling solo sets I've heard right before the SMU segment, and I was glad that the "Voice of America" recorded that one!

Following our festival banquet, Dick Goodwin's University of Texas Jazz Ensemble opened the 8:00 P.M. evening concert that continued with SMU's "Joint Effort" with guest Barry Miles (the 1972 College Jazz Festival Winning Combo.) Sam Houston State University vocalist Gary Powell did a short set followed by that school's Houstonians, directed by Harley Rex, to close the first segment.

Part two opened with Max Kaminsky, Teddy Wilson, Dick Goodwin, and Paul Guerrero in an effective quartet set that explored everything from Dixieland to swing. Next came Wayne Harrison directing the Henderson State University Contemporary Jazz Band, followed by Lamar University vocalist Suzanne Blackshear and Lamar's Jazz Quintet (James Simmons directing.)

Part three of the concert offered the Texas Southern University Jazz Ensemble (the 1972 College Jazz Festival Winning Big Band) with vocal award-winner Anita Moore and guest Arnett Cobb. Lanny Steele directed this hot session.

Following the presentation of individual awards, the judges' jam session was a rousing set by Gary Burton, Jimmy Owens, Richard Davis, Barry Miles, Arnett Cobb, Teddy Wilson, and others.

Again, it was an uncommon and fulfilling day and evening of jazz by some of Texas' and the nation's most highly regarded student and professional artists. I enjoyed trying to keep it together and rolling as the emcee.

With the College Jazz Festival behind us, we could jump full-time into getting the folk festival off the ground. This second year's event had been expanded to five evening concerts in four nights at the auditorium, and four free daytime events on the fairgrounds. All of the evening concerts were scheduled for 8:30, except Saturday night's double-dip, when we did the same lineup at both 6:00 and 10:00 P.M.

We sold tickets by mail order and out of our

MUSIC FROM

KERRVILLE FOLK 🎸 FESTIVAL MAY 24-28

KERRVILLE MUNICIPAL AUDITORIUM
DURING THE TEXAS STATE ARTS & CRAFTS FAIR
KERRVILLE, TEXAS

**DICK BARRETT • BLUEGRASS RAMBLERS
ALLEN DAMRON • EWING STREET TIMES
STEVE FROMHOLZ • BILL & BONNIE HEARNE
CAROLYN HESTER • MANCE LIPSCOMB
BIG BILL MOSS • MICHAEL MURPHEY
WILLIE NELSON • ROYAL LIGHT SINGERS
SUNNY SCHULMAN • ROBERT SHAW
B. W. STEVENSON • KENNETH THREADGILL
THE THREADGILLS • TIMBERLINE ROSE
TOWNES VAN ZANT • JERRY JEFF WALKER
PETER YARROW**

TICKETS FOR EACH EVENING CONCERT ARE $3.50 AND MAY BE MAIL ORDERED IN ADVANCE.

Mail orders should be payable to: FOLK FEST, Box 5309, Austin, Texas 78763

Enclose stamped, self-addressed envelope & if ordering tickets for Saturday night
indicate first preference of the early or late concert.

EXCLUSIVE ADVANCE TICKET LOCATIONS
AUSTIN
Festival Ticket Office · 6615 N. Lamar (512) 454-3681
Sears in Hancock Center · University Co-op
KERRVILLE
Del Norte Restaurant · Chas. Schreiner Bank

Remaining tickets go on sale beginning May 24 at Kerrville Municipal Auditorium Box Office
and beginning May 25 also at the Folk Festival Ticket & Information booth at the fair.

demonstrating seventy-five different arts and crafts, representing an increase of 114 exhibitors and twenty-one new crafts over 1972's event.

I also facilitated the addition of more music to the fair. Working with Dick Barrett, we had arranged for a new event, an officially sanctioned Texas Old-Time Fiddlers' Contest on the last day.

As before, the fair setting at Schreiner was ideal, and the colorfully striped canvas of the tents and the bright banners and other decorations lent a truly festive air to the campus.

The opening festival event was the 8:30 P.M. concert on Thursday, sponsored once again by the *Kerrville Daily Times*. In order to eliminate any chance of repeating last year's crush, we opened the doors a full hour before concert time. The result was that the crowd simply assembled an hour earlier, so we still had a jam and a rush for seats, but everyone seemed to be happy once settled and set for an extraordinary evening's entertainment.

The young Threadgills, all nine of them, opened the concert, followed by a return visit from Fromholz, again capitalizing on his rich baritone

office at 6615 North Lamar, plus in Kerrville at the Del Norte Restaurant and Schreiner Bank. During the festival, we had the auditorium box office open daily while also selling tickets at the information booth of the Texas State Arts and Crafts Fair.

With the four-day expanded schedule, we were able to present twenty-one performers instead of the previous year's thirteen. Ten were repeat artists from 1972: Dick Barrett, Allen Damron, Steve Fromholz, Bill and Bonnie Hearne, Carolyn Hester, Mance Lipscomb, Michael Murphey, Robert Shaw, Kenneth Threadgill, and Peter Yarrow.

Added newcomers really expanded the songwriter side of the festival with Willie Nelson, Jerry Jeff Walker, Townes Van Zandt, B. W. Stevenson, Ewing Street Times from Houston, Sunny Schulman (one of last year's New Folk,) her brother Jim Schulman with Richard Dean in a duo called Timberline Rose, and the young singing family called the Threadgills.

The second fair was set for May 25-28, with the festival playing on May 24-28. Phil Davis had been doing his homework, and the fair grew to 289 artists

Steve Fromholz at Kerrville. 1973.
— Courtesy *Kerrville Daily Times.*

Bobby Bridger's opening night appearance. 1973.
— Courtesy *Kerrville Daily Times.*

Asking Willie to do one more song for an emotional audience who didn't want to go home. 1973.
— Courtesy *Kerrville Daily Times.*

and his outlandish sense of humor. The following set by Ewing Street Times added a glowing four-part dimension to the concert. The soft, quiet voice of Shake Russell and romantic lyrics and melodies like his "Deep In The West," the bluesy bounce of original and collected songs energized by John Vandiver, and the expressive harmony vocals, electric bass, and sometimes steel guitar of Michael Mashkes, supported by Billy Bucher's tasteful drumming, filled the hall and propelled people out of their seats at the end of what seemed to be too short a set.

For the second half, as a substitute for the originally scheduled but now ill Mance Lipscomb, we presented a deserving 1972 New Folk artist named Bobby Bridger. Bridger's full tenor voice, familiar sounding original songs, and great accompaniment immediately earned for him a long-term place in my plans for the future.

Next up, and to close the concert, was a beaming Willie Nelson, who had already escaped from Nashville country music by playing Austin's Armadillo World Headquarters and then joining us at the folk festival. Backed by his band, including his sister Bobby on piano and Mickey Raphael on harmonica, Willie revealed himself to be a remarkable songwriter with an appealing genuineness and a friendly attitude toward everyone. Relaxed and smiling, Willie sang a whole string of his classics, closing the concert with "The Party's Over." He was, of course, greeted by rousing standing ovations

and calls for more from a pleased and emotional audience who didn't want to break the spell.

The next day at 2:00 P.M. over at the fair, Peter Yarrow again hosted the opening New Folk concert that included, among others, Courtney Campbell of Denver, Austin's Bill Oliver, and "Plum Nelly," a duo of young Jerry Jo Jones and Bill Stoner. This was the first of two New Folk concerts, the other being

Jim Shulman (left) and Richard Dean (center) with bassist Robert McEntree (right) as Timberline Rose.
— Courtesy Lafayette Reed.

147

scheduled for the next afternoon, and included seventeen writers, twelve of whom were from Austin.

Friday night's indoor concert started with Timberline Rose, a pairing of two of the most popular Chequered Flag performers. Richard Dean and Jim Schulman were an upbeat, up-tempo, tight-harmony duo. Schulman had laid aside his Israeli sing-a-longs for very contemporary and insightful original songs that gained immediate acceptance from the

Johnny Martin on guitar leads his Bluegrass Ramblers from LaPorte. 1973.

audience. After this warmly received set, Richard and Jim joined Jim's sister, Sunny, a 1972 New Folk performer, in a bluesy, modern presentation of some of her original songs.

Kenneth Threadgill then yodeled his way back into the hearts of his Kerrville audience, proving that last year's wild response was not a fluke. The way the audience switched from the contemporary impact of the first part of the concert to the old-time sentiments and melodies of Jimmie Rodgers was quite remarkable. Threadgill received the expected standing ovation for his set as the concert broke for a brief intermission to prepare for a set by the Bluegrass Ramblers.

The Ramblers' hard-driving set of traditional bluegrass standards built on the solidarity of the quintet's ten years together under the lovingly disciplined leadership of Johnny Martin. As expected, the crowd responded enthusiastically, especially to a hilarious version of "Cripple Creek," and adapted to yet another change of pace with cheers and cries for more.

The much-anticipated appearance of Peter Yarrow on our stage was greeted with emotional affection from the whole audience, standing as one, welcoming him back. Rev. Charlie Sumners had set up Peter's return, appearing briefly before Peter's

Peter Yarrow closed the second night's concert with a gang of folks on stage including Rev. Charlie Sumners, the Bluegrass Ramblers, Dick Goodwin, Tony Ullrich, New Folk singer Bill Priest, and (right) the singing Threadgills. 1973.

— Courtesy *Kerrville Daily Times.*

set to sing an original tribute Charlie called "Peter's Song." Peter responded with his "River of Jordan" and a nearly full-hour of gems including "Puff, The Magic Dragon" and "Weave Me The Sunshine" with ardent harmonic accompaniment provided by the whole audience singing along with him. It was a beautiful climax to a beautiful night.

Since each performer was restricted to a thirty minute set, and each was itching to play more, I had leased Alta Loma Lodges, Naomi Ingram's small, camp-like motel in Ingram, just outside Kerrville, where everyone could get together and enjoy food and refreshments and share the fun of getting to know each other while jamming together after the show. Fatigue finally brought the session to an end in the wee hours of the morning.

Surprisingly, everyone was bright and cheerful as Allen Damron hosted the second day of our New Folk concerts at the fair with two hours of songs by a dozen more artists who had passed our screening. Among the artists who enjoyed the best reception from the big crowd were four young women. From Austin, singer-songwriter Lynn Langham contrasted with classically trained but country-inclined fiddler Mary Egan, backed by Bill Neeley and Larry Kirbo. The other two women were Carol Collins-Baer from Houston and Michele Murphy, whose songs and singing showed that they were both confidently headed for careers as professional musicians. In addition, the concert revealed a talented writer-performer in Austin's Jim Richey. We then enjoyed the contrasting colors and sounds of bluegrass by the San Antonio-based Backwoods Volunteers.

We cleared out of the fairgrounds on time as the evening concert, a double-header beginning at 6:00 P.M., was bound to bring out a rowdy Saturday night crowd. We were right. With such nationally known acts as Jerry Jeff Walker and Michael Murphey joining last year's festival favorites Allen Damron, Bill and Bonnie Hearne, and congenial barrel house piano player Robert Shaw, both concerts were close to sold-out in advance. Since we opened the doors an hour before the concert, the crowd picked out their seats in a fairly leisurely manner, moving over to fill empty seats as additional fans moved into their rows.

The Saturday night concerts were the real hot ticket items, and, as the first concert neared its 9:00 P.M. conclusion, more than 1,000 people gathered to wait patiently until they could get in for the 10:00 P.M. concert. I was either backstage or on stage and not immediately concerned about the end of the

Crowd waiting to get into the sold-out second concert on Saturday night. 1973.

— Courtesy *Kerrville Daily Times.*

Robert Shaw at the piano. Note the Deaf Cowboy Band poster. 1973.

— Courtesy *Kerrville Daily Times.*

first concert. Rather, I was more concerned with Robert Shaw's having to wait three or four hours before playing again on the second show since he was scheduled fourth on the five-artist line-up. My concern was because Robert had a history of heart trouble and his stamina at his age worried me. So I

149

A happy, young audience registers its approval! 1973.
— Courtesy *Kerrville Daily Times.*

waited until the end of his set, and while Michael was playing, asked Robert if he'd like to move up closer to the beginning of the concert so he could return to Ingram and get some rest instead of waiting until sometime after midnight. He said that would be all right, so I moved him into the second slot between Jerry Jeff and Bill and Bonnie.

When the applause and cheering finally ended the first concert and we had cleared the hall, we weren't fully prepared for what happened next. Apparently no one had anticipated what might happen as the doors were opened for round two, but we suddenly found people charging in, pushing and shoving frantically as they scrambled for seats. This frightening pace of the crowd didn't taper off until the auditorium was nearly half-full and those still arriving were assured that they would get in and get their pick of the few remaining seats. Finally, we seated the last arrivals on the benches at the back of the hall and things settled down. Windburned and sunburned faces were relaxing and smiling and everyone was chatting amiably awaiting the beginning of the concert.

Remembering the termination of the Newport Festivals because of the lack of crowd control, I knew that if we continued in 1974 we'd have to go outside somewhere and get away from the limited confines of the small auditorium.

The concerts came off well. There were no incidents and no vandalism, just high-energy enthusi-

Jerry Jeff Walker is joined by his surprise guest Guy Clark (left). 1973.
— Courtesy Rod McKeown-*Dallas Times Herald.*

asm and a shining reverence for what was happening in this small hall in this small Texas town.

Saturday night's highlights included Bill and Bonnie's performance of Ray Hubbard's "Muddy Boggy Banjo Man"; Damron's rousing sing-a-long on the traditional drinking song "Nancy Whiskey," now a mainstay in his repertoire; and Jerry Jeff's surprise guest, Guy Clark, and Jerry's song of respect for master bootmaker Charlie Dunn. Walker was backed up by his Lost Gonzo Band of Gary Nunn, *piano*, Craig Hillis, *guitar*, Herb Steiner, *steel guitar*, Bob Livingston, *bass*, and

Michael Murphey in a quiet moment. 1973.
— Courtesy *Kerrville Daily Times.*

Michael McGreary, *percussion*. Also outstanding were Robert Shaw's rollicking piano and singing on "Piggly Wiggly" and "Here I Come With My Dirty Duckins On," and finally a dozen nationally recorded songs by Michael Murphey like "Calico Silver," "Boy From the Country," and the rousing and humorous "Ft. Worth, I Love You."

Robert Shaw played early on the second concert as I had suggested and left the hall for our retreat at Alta Loma Lodges in Ingram. I didn't get back there myself until close to 2:00 A.M. after paying everyone, visiting with Dick Goodwin, shutting down the stage, and spending a few minutes with business manager Joe Bermea to find out what he was doing with the box office cash since the bank was closed for the weekend.

With those bases covered, I headed for the lodges, and, as I drove up, I thought I heard the unmistakable sound of Robert Shaw's piano! "No," I thought, "Robert must have been in bed for at least a couple of hours."

When I exited our van and started to look around the grounds, I was sure I heard Robert's piano playing. It became louder and louder as I

approached the small stone lodge where I knew the piano was stored.

Quietly forcing the lodge door open, I discovered it full of young music fans sitting all over the floor and on the few pieces of furniture stored there, while at the back of the room, smiling and playing away at his own boogie woogie music, was Robert Shaw!

When he finished the tune, I greeted everyone as I made my way over to the piano. Robert was genuinely glad to see me and greeted me warmly.

Quietly, hoping that no one else in the cabin could hear me, I asked, "What about your heart? I thought you were going to bed early!" Robert replied "I'm just playin' the piano with my hands, and they end here," he said, pointing to his wrists. "My heart is way up here!" he said, indicating his left chest. I gave up trying to preserve Robert's health with my regimen.

Nancylee Kennedy at the Folk Mass. 1973.
— Courtesy *Kerrville Daily Times.*

On Sunday at 12:30, festival participants, our followers, and curious fair-goers gathered around Rev. Charlie Sumners, Jr., for the celebration of our second annual Folk Mass. It emphasized the joy of worship and participation by everyone gathered for the songs, readings, and responses. There was a large turnout, and it was apparent that the stirring

Carolyn Hester and Allen Damron (back to camera) celebrate the finale of the Folk Mass. Rev. Charlie Sumners is to the right with Nancylee and me in the background. Daily Times *photographer Bill Salter is in the straw hat far upper left. 1973.*

— Courtesy Ron McKeown-*Dallas Times Herald.*

The first Texas Old-Time Fiddling Contest at the arts and crafts fair. 1973.
— Courtesy Charles W. Reiley.

Townes Van Zandt sings "Caroline" on the final night. 1973.
— Courtesy *Kerrville Daily Times*.

success of last year's service had earned us many converts and not a few curious onlookers.

That afternoon, as soon as things settled down at the end of the service, a large number of Texas Old-Time Fiddlers joined in a competition for prizes, playing in many different age groups from youngsters to senior players well over seventy-five years old! The grand prize winner was invited to join Dick Barrett on stage at the final folk festival concert that night and receive a $100 bonus. Texas-style breakdowns, waltzes, and rags drew a large crowd to the music glen area.

Our final 8:30 evening concert was also a mixed bag of contrasting treats as Townes Van Zandt opened with favorites like "Caroline" and "Tecumseh Valley," and three hours later B. W. Stevenson closed with his hit "Shambala." In between was the humor, audience howling, twelve-string guitar, and impressive voice of Big Bill Moss and his final "Amen!" chorus. Dick Barrett and his family of musicians and guest fiddling champion fiddled up a storm with Bob Wills favorites and classics like "Kansas City Kitty."

What happened next was one of the most emotionally stirring sets of the whole weekend. I had been introduced to the Royal Light Singers by Reverend Charlie, and after hearing them, I thought it would be great for them to come and do the festival — good for them and good for us. An eight-member veteran black Gospel group from Austin, the Royal Lights started out competently but nervously and wound up with show-stopping, high-energy songs that built slowly but certainly to an emotional pitch. Ardent and enthusiastic clapping, singing, stomping, and cheering was continuous

Big Bill Moss sitting down on the job. 1973.
— Courtesy *Kerrville Daily Times*.

National Fiddling Champion Dick Barrett of Pottsboro, Texas. 1973.
— Courtesy *Kerrville Daily Times.*

from the audience. They were on their feet, crowding down in front of the stage and reaching up to take the hands of many of the singers as they leaned over the footlights. The Royal Lights closed with a joyous six-minute version of "Jesus, My Rock!"

It could have been bad planning, or it could have

Four of the eight Royal Light Singers. 1973.
— Courtesy *Kerrville Daily Times.*

just been that I believed that Carolyn could do it. Regardless, Carolyn Hester followed the exciting, audience-involved performance of the Royal Lights, and she was a study in quiet, commanding grace. The mood, the ambiance, and pace of the evening suddenly became one of gentle introspect and quiet beauty, ranging from the poignancy of her song "My Little Sister Donna" to the multioctave soaring beauty of Carolyn's version of Gershwin's "Summertime." It was a magical set, leaving the audience in grateful awe.

When B. W. Stevenson came on stage to close, he did so with a contrasting palette of songs, painted vividly by his soaring tenor voice and supportive guitar playing, backed by Herb Steiner's steel guitar, Rodney Garrison's bass, and Donny Dolon's drums. Songs like "On My Own" and "Save A Little

Carolyn Hester, B. W. Stevenson, and Allen Damron in the closing finale to the festival. 1973.
— Courtesy *Kerrville Daily Times.*

Time for Love," from his RCA albums, had the audience joining in as part of a huge chorus. It was a glowing closing set with many tender moments contrasted with the soft-rock beat of his more rousing tunes. At the end of this splendid set, B. W. was joined by the rest of the evening's performers, plus Allen Damron, Carolyn Hester, and Peter Yarrow, as the festival came to a jubilant close with Woody Guthrie's anthem "This Land Is Your Land" resounding from 1,000 voices!

I thought, "What a fantastic four days," and marveled at the lack of problems, considering we moved twenty-one performers on and off the stage in fifteen hours of music for 5,600 fans and did it all with a volunteer staff of a dozen. My Austin staff included Bob Long in the box office and business manager Joe Bermea. The rest were volunteers, including performers Carol Collins-Baer, Glenn Myers, Bill Oliver, and Tony Ullrich, plus Becky Dozier, John Hargis, Paige Allen, and Carolyn Cochran with Damron's housemate, Mack Partain, stage managing. Kerrville's T. Sandlin assisted us with the lighting while Dick Goodwin engineered the evening's sound with Dean Rayburn and Spirit Sound, who once again handled the sound reinforcement at the fair. Pedro was back as our one-man recording crew, and a double-album of twenty-two performances would result from his efforts.

We had done it again, and the songwriters really captured the audience. These talented songwriters, who usually had such a tough job to find an audience, had found one at Kerrville, and I intended to put more emphasis on the original songs and get us outside in a bigger space before something serious happened.

While the crowds were good, they were mostly from out of town and a much younger average age than the town's citizens. I had been working on an event for the July 4 weekend that hopefully would appeal to the older folks. I loved the music anyway, so I launched eagerly into the final preparations and publicity for the first Kerrville Ragtime Festival. The festival was to include not only ragtime piano music, which was enjoying a recording revival, but also good old Dixieland music.

Two obvious choices of Dixieland bands were Chuck Reiley's Alamo City Jazz Band and Jim Cullum's Happy Jazz Band. While Willie Nelson was putting his first 4th of July Picnic together at Dripping Springs, I reconfirmed my arrangements with the St. Louis Ragtimers, Chuck Reiley's ensemble, a Texas Ragtime Orchestra assembled at my request by Dick Goodwin, and Jim Cullum's Happy Jazz Band. Since his last appearance at my Austin Ragtime Concert, clarinet player and Happy Jazz Band founder, Jim Cullum, Sr., had died, and we set about dedicating the festival to his memory.

I assembled a vast array of ragtime pianists from all over the U.S., including Trebor Tichener of St. Louis, Texas' own Knocky Parker, Dick Wellstood from the old Bob Wilber Jazz Band, Corpus Christi's Red Camp, and Cliff Gillette of the Happy Jazz Band, plus Cullum's piano-playing valve trombonist Mark Hess, and then added Robert Shaw's barrel house piano to the mix.

I also added a number of celebrity performers with long résumés in traditional jazz: vocalist Olive Brown, former Bob Crosby drummer Ray Bauduc, noted baritone saxman Ernie Caceras, and Scandinavian clarinetist Orange Kellin, now from New Orleans.

With my small office staff plus the usual gang of volunteers, we ran three 3-hour concerts at Kerrville's Municipal Auditorium. Each night ended

with a swinging jam session featuring all of the players involved, and each night's concert was really fun!

While some estimates placed Willie's crowd over at Dripping Springs at from 50,000 to 100,000, the count obviously the result of an inexact effort, we drew about 1,500 to the local Jaycees 4th of July barbecue at Louise Hays Park that we supplemented with our festival's free-to-the-public Texas Ragtime Piano Championship Contest. Those assembled were treated to a rousing two-hour competition with two fine players, Terry Waldo and Mark Hess, sharing the championship.

While the paid attendance at the evening concerts did not cover all of the costs of the event, we were encouraged by the beginning turnout and by the repeated congratulations and thanks from many of the enthusiastic elderly fans. If it wasn't profitable from a financial standpoint, we at least became known to many of the townspeople, and I could chalk it up to a good time and good community relations.

Back in Austin a month later, we resurfaced in the traditional jazz business when Rod Kennedy

Presents offered an August 7 Preservation Hall Jazz Band concert at Municipal Auditorium with the New Orleans old-timers being joined by Robert Shaw as a special guest performer. The crowd response was terrific, the financial rewards were marginal, but again, it was a fun time for everyone.

As we readied for our September 22 Austin concert called "An Evening From the Kerrville Folk Festival," Nancylee and I continued our lengthy discussions about what we were going to do about Kerrville next year. We both loved the Hill Country and our new friends there, and we discussed with increasing frequency the possibility of acquiring a piece of property in rural Kerr County large enough to live on and to allow us to move the Kerrville Folk Festival outside. If we did that, it would mean selling our beautiful two-story colonial home on Jarrett Avenue and assuming a major change of lifestyle!

We were strongly supported and reassured that this might be a viable option by the strong and often full-page reviews and photo coverage from the *Austin American-Statesman*, the *San Antonio Express News*, the *Dallas Morning News* and the *Dallas Times Herald,* where Susan Barton wrote, "The festival was a spiritual, though not religious, event. But it had something transcendent, something quite out of the ordinary — a rare kind of communication."

She continued, "The overriding atmosphere was joyous and vital, with an unmistakable sense of something happening musically right here and now in Kerrville."

The *Morning News* described the festival as "a fantastic success" and published two- and three-column photos of many of the performers in a full-page Section B story. Then, of course, there was the continuing front-page coverage by Bill Salter and others at the *Kerrville Daily Times* and the support of Schreiner Bank and so many others.

It was a scary step to sell our home, shut down my public relations and production business, and leave behind a twenty-three-year life in Austin!

But once having made the decision, we quickly put our house on the market. Over the next several months Nancylee and I would travel regularly to Kerrville in response to calls from our realtor to look at land we hoped would turn out to be ideal for building our outdoor theater complex. It had to be affordable, on a main road so we wouldn't be dragging heavy traffic past someone else's place, and we wanted it to be capable of handling parking, camping, and our own home site.

In order to support the expense of such an

investment, I figured I'd have to schedule more than one festival each season. With the folk festival firmly established on Memorial Day weekend, and the ragtime festival centered around July 4, my inclination was to try to establish Texas' best and biggest bluegrass festival on Labor Day weekend. That certainly would give us three festivals, about six weeks apart, on the three major holiday weekends, but first we had to find and acquire the right piece of land.

We planned our Austin auditorium concert around five of the festival's performers whom we thought would have the best draw, would provide a good show, and would offer a good cross-section of the festival. Peter Yarrow would come in from New York to close. Nationally known and locally loved Carolyn Hester would fly in from California, and

Rod Kennedy Presents
IN AUSTIN IN CONCERT !
AN EVENING FROM THE
KERRVILLE  PETER YARROW
BLUEGRASS RAMBLERS
FOLK ALLEN DAMRON
CAROLYN HESTER
FESTIVAL ROYAL LIGHT SINGERS

Recreating for a few memorable hours the pure joy and gladness of the musical warmth of the KERRVILLE FOLK FESTIVAL, five of the most popular performers including special guest PETER YARROW in a happy, songfilled concert at Austin's Municipal Auditorium. A family treat! Have a nice day!

8PM SATURDAY SEPT. 22
AUSTIN'S MUNICIPAL AUDITORIUM

the popular Bluegrass Ramblers would drive in from LaPorte, Texas, down on the Gulf Coast. Austin performers Allen Damron and the seven-member Royal Light Singers would anchor the event. We would try, in an urban setting, to recreate the "pure joy and gladness and the musical warmth" of the festival. At $5, $4 and $3, it was presented on Saturday night, September 22, as a family treat, a special event.

A few days before the concert, Peter called to cancel in the face of a conflict at home in New York, and Willie Nelson and the band offered to come over and close the concert after they finished their sale appearance at an Austin Ford dealership. That promotion should be over at 9:00 and they'd have plenty of time to get to our concert.

Willie came, a crowd of about 1,100 came, and all were enthralled with the performance! We even recreated the essence of the Kerrville feeling while not losing any money! Up in North Texas, the giant new Dallas-Ft. Worth Airport was being dedicated, and in a few months Moe Bandy would record a song called "The Biggest Airport in the World."

Between that Kerrville evening on September 22 and our new season opener on October 10, we handled the promotion, box office, and house management for a Ray Price concert that provided ample proof that Price was still a great country vocalist. His arrangements, with a large string section, provided a lush bed for his rich baritone, and he proved that he could still draw a crowd. Among the musicians who had worked for Price, as members of his band not so long ago, were Johnny Bush and Willie Nelson.

On October 10 we kicked off our 1973-74 season of six events. Our kick-off was a traditional jazz event put together by Jim Cullum. He had staged it in San Antonio with great success, and given that we were looking for a concert to maintain our ragtime and traditional jazz momentum, we went for it.

Called "The World Series of Jazz," the event pitted The World's Greatest Jazz Band of Yank Lawson and Bob Haggart against Jim Cullum's Happy Jazz Band. In this competition, the audience would be the winner! The Lawson-Haggart aggregation included Bud Freeman's sax, Bob Wilber's soprano sax, and Ralph Sutton's piano, among others. It was a roaring good concert of real traditional jazz with enthusiastic customers enjoying the whole affair from cabaret seating. Out in the real world, others were celebrating Agnew's resignation that night, followed two days later by Nixon's nomination of Gerald Ford for vice-president.

On October 19 I made a quick trip to Kerrville to join with Schreiner Bank president Raymond Barker, arts and crafts fair director Phil Davis, and the mayor of Kerrville, Zelma Hardy, for a release party at the bank of our double LP "live" album of 1973 Kerrville Folk Festival highlights. The albums, which included twenty-one performers and ninety minutes of the festival in stereo, were sold as a package for $9 and included considerable audience participation, as in Allen Damron's six-minute version of "Nancy Whiskey." Many Kerrville-area people came by the bank to pick up their own copy, and I had already had requests from twenty-three radio stations in five states for copies to broadcast. We

Rod Kennedy Presents

THE WORLD SERIES OF JAZZ

The World's Greatest Jazzband
of Yank Lawson & Bob Haggart

vs.

Jim Cullum's Happy Jazz

MUNICIPAL AUDITORIUM
AUSTIN, TEXAS

Rod Kennedy Presents

The

EARL SCRUGGS REVUE

IN CONCERT • IN PERSON • IN AUSTIN

TRIBUTE TO KENNETH THREADGILL

WITH SPECIAL GUESTS
KENNETH THREADGILL & FRIENDS

WED. OCT. 24 8 P.M.

AUSTIN'S MUNICIPAL AUDITORIUM
$4.50 $3.50 $2.50

TICKETS ON SALE NOW AT UNIVERSITY CO-OP,
SEARS (HANCOCK), TICKET OFFICE 6615 N. LAMAR

Schreiner Bank president Raymond Barker, Mayor Zelma
Hardy, and (right) arts and crafts fair director Phil Davis
at the introduction of our 1973 limited edition LPs. 1973.
— Courtesy *Kerrville Daily Times.*

Kenneth Threadgill and Earl Scruggs together in the Green
Room at Austin Municipal Auditorium. 1973.
— Courtesy *Austin American-Statesman.*

felt pretty good about Pedro's extensive efforts on
the project.

Our next 1973-74 season event would be an
encore appearance by the Glenn Miller Orchestra,
but first we staged a "Tribute to Kenneth
Threadgill" at the auditorium on Wednesday,
October 24, by the Earl Scruggs Revue with
Kenneth and his band as special guests. We had
about half a house, around 1,500, so the event was
successful, but the sound mix requested by the performers was so loud that only occasionally could
you even discern the sound of either Earl's banjo or
the guitar of his son, Randy. I had listener fatigue
when it was over. Kenneth, on the other hand,
thought it was great.

Tuesday night, November 6, saw us at the
Saxon Pub with Ewing Street Times for an Austin
release party for our two-LP 1973 album. Fans buying the album also received a free pitcher of beer and
a free Kenneth Threadgill poster. The albums went
on sale over the next few days at Inner Sanctum
Records, Discount Records, the UT Co-op Record
Shop, and at Discovery Records in San Marcos.
KOKE-FM broadcast cuts for two days. It was a
good kick-off for a limited edition of only 1,000
albums!

The second event of our regular season was the
return on Sunday, November 11, of the Glenn
Miller Orchestra directed again by Buddy
DeFranco. We offered the same dance-concert format with table reservations, and again it was a smash

success with a good turnout. By now I had come to
know DeFranco, having exchanged letters with him
and his wife. He was an amazingly relaxed man, easy
to get along with, and, of course, a superb musician.
On this trip, I had the feeling that he was finally
going to retire from the Miller project and return
home soon to Florida. He wanted to spend some
time off the road with his wife and be able to play
some other varieties of music.

Rod Kennedy Presents

NATIONAL DANCE COMPANY OF MEXICO
in "Fiesta Folklorico"
(BALLET AZTLAN DE MEXICO DIRECTED BY SILVIA LOZANO)

MUNICIPAL AUDITORIUM
KERRVILLE, TEXAS

In the meantime, Silvia Lozano's Fiesta Folklorico was in its fourth annual tour of the U.S., and I picked up a December 3 date in Austin, my third consecutive year to present the company there, and a December 9 date for Kerrville, a return engagement for the Kerrville auditorium following the August appearance that had been so well received by 800 fans.

Since my first date with the Folklorico three years before, the company had made successful tours in Australia, Spain, Hawaii, Germany, France, Greece, Scandinavia, and Canada, as well as four Central and South American countries. Still fresh and engaging, both the Austin and Kerrville performances were well attended and well received as always.

Within a week of the Kerrville Folklorico event, we were able to close on sixty-three acres of land located nine miles south of Kerrville on Texas Highway 16. We had previously met many dead ends in locating a suitable site, and a couple of properties had been pulled off the market when the sellers learned that we wanted to produce outdoor music festivals.

Ultimately, the land we bought was the most ideal, and Nancylee and I bought it with a Schreiner Bank loan until the sale closed on our house. She and I decided to spend the Christmas holidays mapping out and cleaning up the property while staying at the Del Norte Motel. In fact, after walking the property and looking at a topographical map of it, we thought it would be perfect for our purposes. It was right on a paved highway with only one house anywhere near it, and that was an old stone house on the other half of the property across the highway and set back more than 1,000 feet from the road. That old ranch house was vacant, as all of the property was for sale.

The acreage, which we decided to call Quiet Valley Ranch, was sold to us by the Lamb family (for whom Lamb Creek had been named), who had owned it more than a century. We were, essentially, the second owners of record since the infancy of this country. Somehow, it made the land even more precious to us.

We learned that Highway 16 was originally part of the Old Spanish Trail loop, and Mrs. Milton Lamb had sold us the west portion of the old Lamb Ranch.

In 1866 Isaac Lamb, a native of Canada, and his wife, three sons, and three daughters, came to Texas from Michigan and built a farmhouse of huge cypress logs, which was considered a fine house for the era. Two years later, another son, George,

decided to join the family. In 1886-87, after his marriage, George built for himself and his family the native stone home that still stands across the highway from our main gate. George's son, Milton, and his grandson, George A., modernized the home and improved the fencing around it.

Our part of the ranch ran for three-quarters of a mile along the west side of Texas Highway 16, and we discovered it was laid out in such a way that the north twenty acres would make a perfect campground once the brush and dead trees were cleared away. The slight draw in the middle of the property near our west property line made for a perfect natural amphitheater, and the nearly 500-foot hill toward the south at the back of the property would be perfect for a water well and storage tank. We later named it Hawk Mountain after watching the red tail hawks riding the thermals off its sides. Then, along the highway frontage of the southern portion of the property, there was a huge meadow that, once cleared of hundreds of cedar stumps, made for a parking meadow for nearly 1,000 cars. Just to the west of the south end of that meadow was plenty of room for our cabin home, storage buildings, and a small orchard.

With the help of a skilled neighbor named Ace Hindman, whom we hired full-time for five months, we were able to put together the beginnings of a facility for our first outdoor festival. Whenever we envisioned a need or mentioned something we wanted, Ace always knew "this old boy" who had the answer to our problem. Ace and his sons and several "good-old-boys" laid out our facility following a topographical scale-model made by Nancylee that gave us a chance to adapt the rugged terrain to our plan as seen from above. Roads were planned for good traffic flow along with fences for security and to divide the ranch up into sections for various uses. We separated our private property, including Hawk Mountain with its well, from the theater, the parking meadow, and the mix-master in mid-property where all incoming traffic could easily be routed to campgrounds, theater and service areas, staff and backstage areas, or to the long parking meadow.

The name Quiet Valley Ranch seemed appropriate, partly because it was located midway up a lovely green valley and partly to create a welcoming vision for our fans as well as a non-threatening home site for our outdoor festivals, which had some of the locals worried. Between images of Woodstock and Willie's Picnic, folks had no reason to believe that any good could come from our being there.

The undeveloped campgrounds on the north end of Quiet Valley Ranch. 1974.

— Courtesy Oscar of Kerrville.

Ace Hindman's crew has the festival stage well under construction by April. Our 1951 Jeep was an important workhorse during this time. 1974.

— Courtesy Kerrville Daily Times.

Nineteen seventy-three slipped into 1974 as we cut brush, laid out roads, fence lines, and underground wiring, bulldozed cedar stumps, leveled out berms dozed up some years ago to deter a serious fire on the property, and buried and burned cedar stumps for weeks. From December through January, I spent almost every weekend, and many other days, alongside Nancylee and Ace and his crew as the festival facilities began to take shape. By February we had only sixteen weeks to get ready.

Bandera Electric Coop followed our plan and brought in power lines and transformers. Ace built over a mile of deer-proof (and crowd-proof) fencing, having to blast some of the holes in the rock with blasting powder. He laid out and scraped and built up 4,000 feet of roads while burying 4,000 feet of underground water and electrical service. Tucker Pump Company created the licensed public water system with a 635-foot well and a 10,000-gallon storage tank providing over sixty pounds of water pressure at the base of Hawk Mountain.

In the meantime, Ed Wallace, one of the area's most effective lawyers, helped us negotiate with the Kerr County Commissioners Court for the required permits, the laws having been complicated following Willie's Picnic. Ed was the perfect choice for this ongoing negotiation, for he could see our vision and communicate it well to the local officials who were headed by the county's well-loved Judge Julius Neunhoffer.

Meanwhile, back at the ranch, the outdoor theater with its sixty crafts booths and portable concessions buildings took shape, and we obtained some vintage World War II outdoor movie theater benches, formerly used by ROTC students for watching training films at The University of Texas.

We bought a number of them and trailered the fourteen-foot-long units twelve at a time behind our van from Austin to the ranch, where they received minor repairs and their first two coats of soft green paint.

We also acquired or built a dozen portable buildings for ticket office, business office, staff showers and toilets, two staff cabins, beer, drink and food stands, and built one shelter for first aid and another for sanitation supplies. The sixty 8 x 8-foot crafts booths outlined the south, west, and part of the north sides of the theater area.

Beyond the theater and ticket office to the north was an essentially uncleared future campground that we hoped to get to after the first outdoor festival was over. We would also have to rent port-a-potties until we could build some wooden ones of our own that would better blend with our scheme. The brown, almost dark-olive color we painted everything was designed to make structures blend in with the scenery. The color became known at the paint stores in town as "Quiet Valley Brown."

We finally bought a small real estate sales office with a front porch, trucked it to the south end of the ranch, put it on blocks, dug a septic system, and added a sleeping-porch, full bathroom, and a fairly large walk-in closet, so we could eventually have a small house in which to live. In fact, Nancylee stayed there right away while I drove back and forth to Austin, where I had a bunk and shower at the back of my office on North Lamar. Additional storage buildings accommodated many of her favorite pieces of furniture from the big house on Jarrett Avenue that had been sold to LBJ's sister. Most of the furniture from Jarratt Avenue would not fit into the five-hundred-square-foot house with its pot-belly stove for heat, a ceiling fan for cooling, and a half-kitchen for cooking.

While Nancylee worked at the ranch, I continued with my 1973-74 season in Austin, staging two magnificent fairy tale ballets by the seventy-five-member company of the National Ballet of Washington, D.C., in its first appearance in Austin. In its twelfth year since its 1963 debut under Frederick Franklin, we presented *Coppelia* for the matinee and *Sleeping Beauty* for the evening performance. With the richly romantic music of Tchaikovsky played by the National Ballet Orchestra conducted by Ottavia DeRosa, Ben Stevenson's staging provided a fairy tale setting for the most dazzling ballets with fantastic costumes and great characters. Scotland's Carmen Mathe danced the role of Princess Aurora alongside princi-

1960s.) During this time, I enjoyed the friendship of renowned dancers like Igor Youskevich, formerly of Ballet Russe de Monte Carlo, who was teaching ballet at The University of Texas and at his New York studio. We also knew Nathalie Krassovska of Dallas, who had toured with Youskevich in 1961. I met her when she came to Austin to audition potential dancers for the Austin Civic Ballet Company at the invitation of artistic directors Eugene and Alexandra Slavin, formerly of the Winnipeg Royal Ballet. We later became acquainted with Edward Villella, Miguel Terechov, and other key figures in dance as they visited and danced in Austin.

I assisted the Civic Ballet in staging spring productions, Christmas time *Nutcracker* productions, *Cinderella* and other various ballet gala performances from 1971-1975 while also attending Stanley Hall's Austin Ballet Theater and a number of professional performances by the Joeffrey Ballet

pal dancers Frederic Strobel and Dennis Poole, a dancer whose home was in Texas.

It was a stunning Sunday, February 3, and large audiences turned out for the event. I had been active in the Austin Civic Ballet as a director and officer for many years and had helped them produce a dozen local events (including the first Southwestern Ballet Festival during my KHFI-FM years in the

and others, so we were very much at home with the National Ballet's visit and pleased to be able to bring it to Austin.

As a bonus event three days later, on Thursday night, February 7, we presented the Big Band Cavalcade at the auditorium, starring George Shearing, Bob Crosby, Freddie Martin, and Margaret Whiting. The show was an attractively presented and well-played evening of memories, spotlighting hits like Martin's "Tonight We Love," Crosby's "Big Noise from Winnetka," Whiting's "Moonlight in Vermont," and Shearing originals like "Conception" and "Nothing But D. Best" by his drummer Denzil Best. The fifteen-piece stage band, drawn from alumnae of the three bandleader's former groups, was well-rehearsed and played a solid two-hour show of these hits and many more by other stars of the big band era. It was a genuinely nostalgic time machine.

A week later, after dashing madly to Kerrville and back with updated and hurried instructions for our ranch crew, we brought back Fred Waring and his Pennsylvanians as our fourth event. While the show was stirring and well attended, we noted that the promotional materials, conceding to the cult of youth, called his group the "young, exciting now" Pennsylvanians, recalling more than fifty years of hits by Mr. Waring. Again, it was an astonishing evening revalidating Waring's abilities as a master showman.

Between the Fred Waring concert and our last season event, we were contracted to market the premiere appearance in Austin of the new Circus Vargas at Highland Mall. Mr. Vargas championed the return to the big top at a time when many other circus producers had moved into coliseums and indoor arenas. The huge orange and white striped tent, larger than a football field, was a sight to see! This grand, new circus with its three rings, cast of 125, plus 150 performing animals, included three elephant herds under Col. Wallace Ross, wild animal trainer Pat Anthony and his jungle-bred lions and tigers, plus brainy bears, chimps, horses, dogs, a giant petting zoo, international clowns, high-wire performers, and Cuba's flying trapeze family, the Farias.

In spite of severe weather, which tore down a section of the big top at the end of one performance, the run was successful with near capacity attendance, including thousands of children. Texas Attorney General Mark White helped me welcome the troupe to town for five performances over March 18-20.

As I continued to work on the facilities at Kerrville, and back in my Austin office on the three-event season at our new ranch, I also promoted our final season event set for March 23. It was, in effect, a recapitulation of the 1973 Kerrville Ragtime Festival and a preview of the 1974 ragtime event, featuring a concert by Texas Ragtime Piano champions Mark Hess and Terry Waldo with Chuck

Reiley's Alamo City Jazz Band, plus Max Collie's Rhythm Aces from London. Terry Waldo's wry humor and remarkable classical ragtime playing really captured the crowd's fancy, and the whole show was well received by about 1,000 fans to close our season at Austin Municipal Auditorium.

Our third annual folk festival would not be easy to take in stride. This would be the first big event at our new festival site and the event upon which we would hang our future. We had sold our home and all our racing cars except the Lancia. Even though there were some major Austin events in our future, my office building and warehouse were being sold soon, completing our move to Kerrville. We had exchanged racing cars for a 1951 Jeep with a Chevy V-8 engine and a pickup truck.

Every resource we could pull together we put into Quiet Valley Ranch, and as I learned that Americans were spending $400 million a year on antacids, I hoped we could settle a few stomachs with our efforts to provide a permanent facility for audiences who wanted to escape the pressures, stratification, clutter, and pop culture of urban living.

To introduce our neighbors to the outdoor festivals, I recorded twenty-five weekly thirty-minute radio shows to air on KERV between April 17 and August 28. The shows featured both "live" festival recordings and commercially released recordings of our folk performers until June, then ragtime and jazz recordings by ragtime festival performers until the 4th of July, and then bluegrass records until the Labor Day weekend bluegrass festival. We had four sponsors including Schreiner Bank and the *Kerrville Daily Times*, Joe's Western Wear, and Swiss chef Hans Schlunegger's Alpine Lodge Restaurant that was actually called Annamarie's Alpine Lodge and Tick Tock Club. Schlunegger had come to Houston to chef for John Mecom, Jr., at the Warwick Hotel and then was brought to Kerrville by Gene Lehman to chef at the Inn of the Hills. Later, Hans built his own Alpine Lodge Restaurant next to the Sunday House Inn.

On Sunday, May 5, the *Kerrville Daily Times* published a front-page story for us announcing a free bluegrass concert preview of the new outdoor theater and festival facilities to the public to be held from 3:00 to 5:00 P.M. on May 11. "Free to the general public" was "free" to any person who would pick up six cans or bottles along Texas Highway 16 to deposit in the "Pitch In" fifty-five-gallon barrels at the gate.

Since many of our neighbors were worried about the litter they expected to increase along Highway 16 when our festivals started, we wanted

Advertising sketch of our proposed new stage at Quiet Valley Ranch. 1974.

them to know right from the start that we acknowledged that concern and were doing something about it.

We told the public, "If each person coming out to be our guest will pick up six items of litter from along the highway, it will be a lot prettier when the press people and out-of-town guests attend the press reception from 7:00 P.M. to 9:00 P.M. the same night."

There was a good turnout for both openings. With music by the Backwoods Volunteers and the Texas Bluegrass Boys, we had more than 300 guests in the afternoon, and that night, at the by-invitation-only gathering, we had another several hundred, including a dozen or more radio, TV, and newspaper people from the major papers and from most of the surrounding communities. We also had city, county, and state officials, festival program advertisers, chamber of commerce people, and others who had supported the growth of the festival from the beginning.

The visitors seemed to like the layout and the complimentary beverages, and the stage and theater worked great with the music sounding good. The buzz began in town with the festival only twenty days away.

The format of the May 23-26 outdoor folk festival would be essentially the same as in 1973, with four evening concerts starting at 8:00 P.M., each featuring six or seven performers. Our New Folk concerts would be at the arts and crafts fair at 2:00 P.M. on Friday, Saturday, and Sunday afternoons with eighteen finalists each day for a total of fifty-four. The competition would again be held on the small stage near Quinlan Creek. The Folk Mass would also continue at the fair on Sunday at 12:30, followed by the Texas Old Time Fiddlers Contest. The night-time concerts at the ranch would present

twenty-five performers, over half of them having bands or backup musicians. The gates at the ranch would open daily at 6:00 P.M., two hours early to allow folks easy access and time to eat and get settled down for the evening.

Advance publicity was really outstanding, catching on all over Texas. The major metropolitan dailies were providing us with good pre-festival coverage in Austin, San Antonio, Dallas, and Houston, plus both Kerrville papers as well as advance features in *Southern Living*, *Texas Flyer*, and *Central Texas Go Magazine*.

At the new outdoor theater, Spirit Sound would be doing the big evening concerts. Business manager Joe Bermea from my Austin office would bring Bob Long to handle the box office, and Pedro Gutierrez would be back to record for the third year. Mack Partain and Damron would handle the stage while John Hargis was assigned the new job of parking cars. Our young motorcycle-riding friend, Alan Tillman, headed up security.

We also had the help of Rowan Zachary, Nancy

The new stage with roof cut-a-ways for Spirit Sound's big speaker cabinets. The repaired and repainted University of Texas ROTC theater benches are all in place awaiting opening night crowd expected on May 23, 1974.
— Courtesy Oscar of Kerrville.

Ford, Tony Ullrich, Ray Partain, Dave Houston, and Tim York, plus a newly recruited communications team of Austin CB radio folks. Also added to the staff on ticket, crafts, concessions, and other assignments were Dalis Allen, Carol Battersby, Ann Scarbrough, and a dozen more volunteers, including a group calling themselves the "Super Friends of Kerrville."

I packed up a week early to head for Kerrville, leaving Joe Bermea to pick up the festival program books from The Whitley Company and close out the Austin advance ticket locations at our office and the University Co-op.

In its first two years, the festival had become an eye-opening and humanizing experience for me, and with Charles John Quarto's admonition on my mind, "It's not the way you look, it's the way you see," I piled into our Dodge van and headed for Kerrville, looking forward to embracing my new and growing family.

KERRVILLE FOLK FESTIVAL:
THE EARLY YEARS OUTDOORS

(1974–1981)

Although we initially planned to have camping on the ranch during the festival, the extensive preparation requirements mandated that this would have to wait until the fall. We had yet really to reconnoiter extensively the north end of the ranch and thus had not begun the task of clearing the brush, downed trees, and the thousands of cedar stumps left behind when a hurried crew some years earlier had cut cedar, leaving behind one- to two-foot-high stumps. Much of the area looked like something left over from World War I. We managed to clear about a hundred feet back from the theater fencing so we could park a few staff vehicles there. In addition, we were not prepared to provide either hospitality or security for the public twenty-four hours a day.

Among the last things to come together for our first outdoor concerts at the ranch were the security fencing for the staff camping area and completing last-minute modifications on the building that Lester Inman's smoked turkey sausage crew from Llano would use for their concession stand. The building next to that would contain several new, large, galvanized cattle troughs for icing down beer kegs and soft drinks.

There was also considerable effort and time expended by our attorney, Ed Wallace, to see that we had the blessings of the Kerr County Commissioners Court. As it turned out, one of the ways that these blessings came about was that Texas Alcohol Beverages Commission regional officer Austin Vaughn had promised the court he would round up a large, experienced group of his law officer friends from around the state to come in and keep the peace and protect citizens and their property. I don't know what they expected, but they were ready for whatever it was.

TABC officer Austin Vaughn, 1997.
— Courtesy Dalis Allen.

We were all excited as opening night approached, and everything seemed to be falling into place. The new electrical system was working perfectly, and the stage lighting and sound were what we had hoped they would be.

Opening day at the festival was to be Thursday, May 23, with a four-day run through Sunday, May 26, while the fair would open at noon on Friday and run through Monday, Memorial Day.

We breathed a sigh of relief as more than 1,200 people came on opening night with Inman selling out of his turkey sausage by 9:00 P.M.

Mr. Shaw opened the concert and Willis Alan Ramsey and Tex-Mex accordionist Flaco Jimenez followed, with all three contrasting artists getting

165

Willis Alan Ramsey, writer of "Muskrat Love." 1974.
— Courtesy *Kerrville Daily Times.*

Plum Nelly on stage at the new Outdoor Theater. From left: Bill Stoner, Jerry Jo Jones, Benny Thurman, and Ernie Gammage. 1974.
— Courtesy *Kerrville Daily Times.*

Tex-Mex accordian star Flaco Jiminez (left) with his bajo sexto player. 1974.
— Courtesy *Kerrville Daily Times.*

exceptional welcomes from the crowd. Shaw's barrel house blues and folksy intros set an amiable ambiance for the evening followed by Ramsey's urban hits like "Spider John" striking familiar notes with his following. Then the polkas and waltzes of Jimenez' *conjunto* music put an unmistakable Southwestern brand on the evening. The previous year's favorites, Bill and Bonnie Hearne and Townes Van Zandt, were rousingly received by the audience, as was Plum Nelly (the now expanded Plum Nelly,

which was earning a reputation as one of Austin's hot new groups.) Original members Jerry Jo Jones and Bill Stoner were now joined by 13th Floor Elevator's fiddler Benny Thurman and bassist Ernie Gammage. Jerry Jo had further developed her talents as a tunesmith since her 1972 New Folk appearance, and her emotional vocals and the rousing soft-rock backup musicians were able to bring the crowd to their feet repeatedly.

Over the next three nights, the festival attracted another 4,800 fans with first-time performers earning the same vociferous response from the appreciative audiences as the regulars. Former New

Asleep at the Wheel with vocalist Chris O'Connell, Leroy Preston (drums), and Ray Benson at the mike. Floyd Domino (piano) is seen in the lower left corner with bassist Tony Garnier and Richard Casanova (fiddle). 1974.

— Courtesy Bill Salter.

Folk Bill Priest and Jimmy Johnson, pianist-singer-songwriter Riley Osbourn, and Harold Weeks' Southern Strangers from Muscle Shoals, Alabama, all reached the hearts of the audience as did "Orange Blossom Special" composer-fiddler Chubby Wise. Uncle Walt's Band, a popular trio from Austin, was a last-minute cancellation. Making their first outdoor appearance to a rousing reception was a seven-member western swing band, led by Ray Benson, calling itself Asleep at the Wheel. The Wheel, newly arrived in Austin from California, played Bob Wills songs and their own originals with an infectious style that made sitting still a physical impossibility. The names of its individual members would become legendary in Austin music over the next decade: drummer Leroy Preston shared vocals with Chris O'Connell, while Richard Casanova's fiddle, Floyd Domino's piano, Lucky Oceans' steel guitar, and Tony Garnier's bass gave the band a solid sound as they played tunes ranging from Basie to the Texas Playboys. Benson, a giant of a man who had to duck through some of our doorways, played lead guitar

and towered over the band as they cranked out standards and originals that were capturing the loyalty of western swing fans all across the country.

With Ray Wylie Hubbard having his own band, the Cowboy Twinkies (Terry Joe Ware, *guitar*; Clovis Robbins, *mellotron*; and Jim Herbst, *drums*), Hubbard's former trio, Three Faces West, was now made up of Rick Fowler and Wayne Kidd with Steve Howell replacing Hubbard. As one might have expected, Threadgill, Ewing Street Times (featuring Shake Russell, John Vandiver, and Michael Mashkes), and Peter Yarrow were again among the regulars inspiring the crowd. Other highlights had to include the reunion of Austin's sensational gospel group, the Royal Light Singers, and Old-Time Fiddler's Contest winner, the young Terry Morris, twin-fiddling with Chubby Wise and backed by the Bluegrass Ramblers. Steve Fromholz' set debuted his short-lived "gospel choir" of Segle Fry, Jim Ritchie, Rick Stein, Lynn Langham, Travis Holland, Carol Collins-Baer, and Emily McKenzie.

As promised by TABC's Austin Vaughn, there

Peter Yarrow at Kerrville. 1974.
— Courtesy Willis & Wakefield.

Ewing Street Times. From left: Michael Mashkes, Shake Russell, John Vandiver. 1974.

— Courtesy Jim Willis.

was a veritable platoon of white-shirted Texas lawmen at the festival, their Stetsons and "on duty" demeanor making them stick out in the crowd like bird lime on a bench. By the last night, however, they could be seen lounging and visiting informally in small groups, relaxed, smiling, and cheering, especially for Chubby Wise' fiddle tunes. Several of them came up to me and apologized for having to leave early to get back home to their families. They now, almost to a man, were part of our family of fans and enjoyed the festival immensely. There were no incidents, and the festival's reputation as a family event was becoming solidly established.

We couldn't wait to hear what PSG's new mobile eight-track recording equipment had captured on tape, and we all wanted to know how the new stage affected the sound.

What now had become clear to us was that this "singer-songwriter" music, as sung and played by the songwriters themselves, sounded fantastic on the big sound system under the Texas skies. Aesthetically and logistically, our choices had been vindicated, and we were amazed with the responsibilities assumed by

our volunteer staff and most pleased with the professional job done by our sound crew.

The daytime events at the fair were most successful with outstanding New Folk representing an ever-increasing area. From Austin we had Lynn Langham, Jim Ritchie, Frank Muse, Joe Mike Taylor, Rick Stein, and Denim; from Houston, it was George Ensle, Bill Haymes, and Vince Bell; San Antonio was represented well by Shane and Kitty Appling, while Lubbock's David Ruthstrom and New Orleans' Lucinda Williams each proved that songwriting was alive and well outside the confines of Central Texas. Again, Peter Yarrow was the ever-encouraging, admiring, and affectionate host. At Reverend Charlie's Sunday Folk Mass, Peter, Damron, Carolyn, and many of the New Folk celebrated what once again proved to be the truly joyful highlight of the weekend for many. The Texas Old-Time Fiddlers Contest had good participation from all over the U. S. and a large audience to cheer them on.

In retrospect, though, there was nothing like the concerts out at the ranch under the stars. Much of the festival was taped by KUT-FM in Austin for national broadcast on National Public Radio. In addition, the Texas press people turned out in droves and loved what they heard and saw at our new facility. We truly were on our way and making history, even though the gate receipts (6,000 people who paid $3.50 in advance and $4.50 at the gate) just barely allowed us to break even. While we knew we would have to raise the price in 1975, we still had a great deal to celebrate, and now had less than six weeks before reopening the ranch for our second annual Ragtime Festival, the first one to be staged outdoors.

Without coming up for air, we jumped straight into the publicity and marketing tasks for the ragtime festival while Ace Hindman's crew moved north through the campgrounds to clear the area for our first Labor Day weekend bluegrass festival. Nancylee and I were attending every bluegrass festival within driving distance, distributing our festival brochures, and personally inviting one and all to join us at the ranch. Chubby Wise, Kenneth Threadgill, Allen Damron, Uncle Walt's Band, and the Bluegrass Ramblers all had been to the folk festival and would be back for the bluegrass weekend. They didn't all fit the bluegrass format, but bluegrass was not yet that widely known in Texas, so we were hedging our bets. Additional artists outside the strict mold of bluegrass scheduled for Labor Day weekend were honky tonk legend Lefty Frizzell and folk notable Ramblin' Jack Elliott. Holding up the bluegrass end of things would be national bluegrass favorites Mac Wiseman, the Country Gentlemen, the more contemporary Country Gazette, and fiddling favorites Byron Berline and Howdy Forrester joining Chubby Wise. We knew Texans liked fiddle players and knew we could count on these three to draw a crowd.

The July 4-6 Kerrville Ragtime Festival, in memory of Jim Cullum, Sr., had a dozen famous stars, including New Orleans legendary trombonist Georg Brunis, who wrote "Tin Roof Blues," first recorded in 1924. He was one of the last originators of Dixieland music and a former member of the original New Orleans Rhythm Kings. Our aces in the hole, of course, were Jim Cullum's Happy Jazz Band and Chuck Reiley's Alamo City Jazz Band.

On the ragtime side of the ledger were our 1973 Texas Ragtime Piano co-champions, San Antonio's Mark Hess and the outstanding Eubie Blake protégé Terry Waldo, as well as Dick Wellstood (former Bob Wilber pianist and now major New York attraction) and the all-time-great swing pianist, Austin-born Teddy Wilson, a member of the original Benny Goodman Trio and who later made most of Billie Holiday's recording sessions.

With daytime events including the free opening day Texas Ragtime Piano Championship Contest at the Jaycee's 4th of July Barbecue in Louise Hays Park, plus dollar concerts at the ranch, pairing pianists Teddy Wilson and Mark Hess on July 5 and

Dick Wellstood and Terry Waldo on the 6th, we felt confident that we had the greatest ragtime and traditional jazz event ever to be staged in the Southwest.

The music, ranging from Scott Joplin to Jelly Roll Morton, was cheered wildly by the fans, but again, as in the first year, not enough of them came at $4.50 a ticket to make it work out financially. We knew we would have to do something else in 1975 over the 4th of July weekend.

Mark Hess, Gene McKinney, Harvey Kindervater, Buddy Apfel, Max Kaminsky, (hidden at piano Teddy Wilson), Dick Wellstood, Bobby Gordon, Georg Brunis, and Ray Bauduc at the second Kerrville Ragtime Festival. 1974.
— Courtesy *Kerrville Daily Times.*

After a few days of cleanup, sorting out, and recharging, we were back on track, promoting the bluegrass festival and preparing the campgrounds in time for Labor Day weekend. Though there would be no hookups for camping trailers and motor homes, the more land we cleared, the more we became impressed with what we had. Ace's crew installed underground waterlines and wiring so there would be plenty of available water and just enough mercury-vapor lighting to cast a moonlight glow over the most heavily traveled camping areas.

As the bluegrass festival weekend approached, we were getting good response to the headlining of Lester Flatt and the Nashville Grass in place of an ailing Mac Wiseman. Our visits to the many small bluegrass festivals around a three-state area, plus the big one, Bill Grant's giant event at Hugo, Oklahoma, began to generate an impressive mail order response well in advance of our August 30-September 1 dates. We also announced a Texas Bluegrass Band Championship Contest and a whole string of the better Texas semi-professional bluegrass bands joining the national stars on stage. Among the Texas bands were Johnny Martin's Bluegrass Ramblers, Holly Bond and the Bluegrass Texans, the Backwoods Volunteers from San Antonio, the Watkins Family's bluegrass gospel band, and Kerrville's Poverty Playboys. From Arkansas we brought in Kenny Cantrell, Arnold Johnston and the Green Valley Boys, Elliott Hancock, and the McSpaddens.

With a three-day ticket, including free camping for the first 900 three-day ticket buyers, we expected a big turnout.

We were prepared to provide water, security, chemical toilets, and a camper dumping-station in the campgrounds and our outdoor theater crafts booths and concessions, and all of these massive preparations were in place upon the arrival at the ticket booth of the first cars towing trailers on Friday of Labor Day weekend. As a backup, we advertised $1 unlimited camping per car nine miles away at Kerrville State Park.

The only problem was that rain began late the first afternoon with such intensity that we had to move the opening night concert to the Kerrville Municipal Auditorium in town. Amazingly, everything fell into place with only a few late-comers missing part of the concert when they drove all the way to the ranch and then had to drive back into town. Spirit Sound did a good job of moving equipment around and getting a smaller system up and running. The concert was successful, and by the time it was over, people were heading back out to the ranch to camp.

By noon Saturday, the weather had cleared and the festival went on as scheduled.

We were disappointed that Lefty Frizzell had to cancel his appearance at the last minute due to illness, but we were able to book E. Z. Adams, composer of the popular "Bandera Waltz," as his

From left: Byron Berline, Chubby Wise, and Howdy Forrester plaing Cotton Collins' "Westfalia Waltz" at the bluegrass festival. 1974.

— Courtesy Rick Gardner.

replacement. We also planned a tribute to Kenneth Threadgill's great fiddle player, Cotton Collins, who also was too ill to come to the festival. The triple-fiddling tribute on his "Westfalia Waltz" by Byron Berline, Howdy Forrester, and Chubby Wise, however, was one of the really lovely and emotion-packed moments of the weekend. The afternoon "Newgrass Jam" between the Country Gentlemen and the Country Gazette was another great moment!

Probably the happiest participants that week-

From left: Members of Country Gazette and Country Gentlemen at the 1974 newgrass jam: Ricky Skaggs, Byron Berline, Alan Mundy, Doyle Lawson, Roger Bush, Bill Emerson, Roland White, Charlie Waller, and Jerry Douglas. 1974.

— Courtesy Rick Gardner.

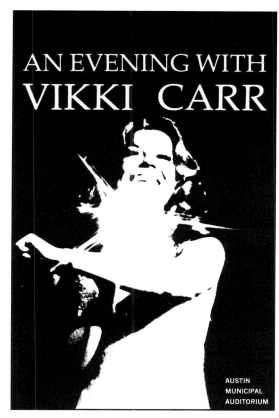

end were the members of the young band, Roanoke, from Denton, Texas, who won our bluegrass band championship and an invitation to play the main stage in 1975.

In spite of the opening night deluge, we broke even over the weekend and were generally pleased with our first season turnout.

There wasn't much time to think about it as I had already approached the Kerrville Chamber of Commerce about my staging a Glenn Miller Orchestra concert at the ranch to raise money to help pay off the new chamber building. The chamber directors thought it was a good idea, and for the next four weeks I worked with Ford dealer Ken Stoepel, who had been assigned to chair the event.

In the meantime, between the bluegrass festival and the Glenn Miller benefit concert, I had a September 11 concert at the Austin Municipal Auditorium for the North Austin Exchange Club. It was an evening with Vikki Carr, who had become the first Mexican-American artist to cross over, attracting thousands of Anglo fans as well as the Hispanic population. She had become an international singing star, performing with her own twenty-seven-piece orchestra, and had played concerts and clubs from Las Vegas to Mexico City and New York to London. With her recordings on Columbia selling in a dozen countries, she was also a favorite on television, and, of course, the El Paso native was especially popular in Texas.

A polished, charismatic performer with an appealing voice, a broad repertoire of popular songs, show tunes, and Latin melodies, Vikki Carr drew a large, loyal, and dedicated audience. All in all it was a rewarding event with which to be involved, and it helped the Exchange Club to raise funds and earn major publicity for their community service projects.

Back in Kerrville, Ken Stoepel and I sold blocks of tickets, program advertising, and business sponsorships, so that by the time September 29 rolled around, we would have a large crowd of enthusiastic Miller fans out to the ranch.

By that time, Buddy DeFranco had retired as leader, being replaced in January 1974, by Peanuts Hucko, former featured soloist on the Lawrence Welk television series as "King of the Clarinet" and guest artist with the Big Band Cavalcade. Of even greater significance, however, was his having been a member of the famous Glenn Miller Air Force Band of World War II. In fact, Miller had been responsible for switching Hucko from tenor saxophone to clarinet at a time when he was looking for a strong clarinetist to complete his reed section and reproduce the Glenn Miller sound.

In the pre-war years, Hucko had played with the Will Bradley, Ray McKinley, and Charlie Spivak bands. When the war was over, Hucko went on to play with Benny Goodman, Jack Teagarden, Eddie Condon, Artie Shaw, Tommy Dorsey, Jimmy Dorsey, Woody Herman, and Louis Armstrong. He

Rod Kennedy Presents
WORLD FAMOUS

GLENN MILLER ORCHESTRA

Playing in the
GLENN MILLER
TRADITION
With the authentic
MILLER arrangements under the direction of

PEANUTS HUCKO

Hear again these great golden hits!
Moonlight Serenade — String of Pearls
In the Mood — Tuxedo Junction — many more!

BENEFIT CONCERT UNDER THE STARS
FOR KERR COUNTRY CHAMBER OF COMMERCE
BUILDING FUND

**OUTDOOR THEATER
QUIET VALLEY RANCH**

Nine miles South of Kerrville
on Texas Highway 16

8 PM SUNDAY, SEPTEMBER 29

Advance tickets $3.50
Groups of 50 or more $3.00
At the gate price $4.50

(ranch gates open at 6 p.m.)

Come early, bring your lawn chair.
Enjoy beer and Inman Barbecue
before the concert.

MAIL ORDERS ACCEPTED NOW . . .
Payable to GLENN MILLER BENEFIT
Box 1466, Kerrville, Texas 78028
(Enclosed stamped, self-addressed envelope)

Peanuts Hucko on the Big Band Cavalcade. 1974.
— Publicity Photo.

had also worked as a staff member of both the ABC and CBS network orchestras and was one of the award-winning soloists at the Newport Jazz Festivals.

So, with Hucko at the helm, the Glenn Miller Orchestra was still in good hands, and together they played to a packed Outdoor Theater at Quiet Valley Ranch. It was a crowd that gave repeated standing ovations and stood close in front of the stage just as thousands of teenagers had done years before when the band was in its original incarnation. We raised more than $2,700 for the Chamber of Commerce and thought we might do it again next year.

We had one more small event at the ranch as we participated in the Kerr County Days celebration with an October 26 concert by Allen Damron, Bill and Bonnie Hearne, Plum Nelly, and a duo called T&M Express. It was a relaxed event and the last one for which Joe Bermea was our business manager. After four years on my team, he wanted to go into business for himself, and I wished him luck.

With our first Kerrville season at our new facility behind us, I looked forward to our November 26 date in Austin with the National Chinese Opera Theatre from Taipei and a December return engagement of Silvia Lozano's National Dance Company of Mexico.

The eighty-member National Chinese Opera appeared by special arrangement with Harold Shaw in New York and presented indescribable and exquisite pageantry, singing, dancing, mime, Kung Fu, and sword fighting.

While it was the company's second U.S. tour, it was its historic first appearance in Austin. Dating back 2,000 years, but embodying 5,000 years of Chinese cultural heritage, ideology, moral principals, and basic themes of righteousness, love, loyalty, and peace, the magnificent company staged a remarkable, fascinating, and lavishly costumed performance. The six operas, excerpts and skits from the Han, Sung, and Ming dynasties, climaxed with "The Immortal Thief." This adventure of the Monkey King was outstanding for its spectacular battle scenes requiring leaps, somersaults, balancing, combat skills, and other stunts requiring years of drill and practice.

Spectacular though it was, the turnout was small, and we had to dip into personal funds from Nancylee's estate to cover the $5,000 shortfall.

172

Rod Kennedy Presents

MUNICIPAL AUDITORIUM
AUSTIN, TEXAS

We ended 1974 with a December 9 performance in the Kerrville Municipal Auditorium by Silvia Lozano's National Dance Company of Mexico with its talented and charming cast of fifty. Again, the show with its contrasting native cultures reflected in regional music, dances, and costumes, was an engaging evening of joyful and sometimes majestic entertainment that was especially well received by a near-full house of patrons from all over the Hill Country. It was a high note to end the year.

Looking back on the year in Kerrville, it was easy to see that our weakest festival financially was the ragtime and traditional jazz event. We had done everything we knew how to do in promoting the music from around the turn of the century using both immensely popular regional Texas artists and a whole roster of legendary national stars. We had also produced a number of thoroughly marketed concerts of the same kind of music over a two-year period and only drawn marginal response. It seemed the ragtime revival was a recording revival, not a live performance revival. Perhaps the older average age of the fans made for a home-listening profile.

Following a number of trips to Nashville on business, to visit the Opry and to attend the Country Music Awards and various fanfares and showcases, we seriously considered replacing the

ragtime festival with one built around the more popular country music heard daily on San Antonio's 50,000-watt KKYX and a hundred other stations across Texas. We could offer country music in a family setting free of cigarette smoke, where even children would be welcome. We decided to give it a two- or three-year try, so we began getting a closer, more focused look at what was popular in Nashville in order to book all the 1975 festivals early and thereby begin building an audience for the folk, country, and bluegrass season.

My new business manager, Shiela Spencer, thought that the three festivals would really work, so we began early in the year to formalize and charter our non-profit Kerrville Music Foundation to create a defined channel through which we could give something back to the industry. Ed Wallace guided us through our organizational meeting, where we elected Nancylee as president, Bill Dozier as vice president, Ed Wallace as secretary, and I served as treasurer. As a foundation logo, I thought it would be great to take the lute out of the hands of our Arky logo from the Summer Music Festival, and replace it with a six-string guitar while the lute with several broken strings languished under one of Arky's feet. This would dramatically demonstrate our turning to folk, country, and bluegrass music in the 1970s.

Then we investigated a variety of ways our new non-profit organization truly could benefit these three fields of music. Since we already had been hosting New Folk concerts (1972-74), we decided for 1975 that we just put them formally under the foundation as a folk festival activity. We had already suspected that later, down the line, we would be inundated with requests from artists who wanted to play, and this would provide a fair system to help us in discovering and assisting really worthwhile but relatively unknown writers. With rules and a screening and reward system in place, we would be able to effectively serve more artists and provide our audience with newcomers selected from the best.

We also thought it would be fun to establish a National Yodeling Championship as our second project. We had already seen how people reacted when Threadgill broke into his "blue yodeling," and we thought we'd delve in the Swiss- and Austrian-based yodeling of more contemporary country music. It seemed to us that the art of yodeling was disappearing and that maybe we could help revitalize the art and encourage those who were trying to be good at it. Perhaps at the same time, an appropriate foundation project for our new C&W Jamboree over the 4th of July would be a country songwriting contest.

Since we had already started a bluegrass band contest at our Labor Day festival, it seemed logical to turn this project over to the foundation to provide it with a more realized and supportive infrastructure for encouraging the young players to strive for quality. When we found it, we would promote it.

We felt good about our immediate plans for the foundation's first year of official activity.

Back to business, we considered that we might draw more attention to our folk festival by working with the hot air balloon enthusiasts. They were looking for a sponsor for the Texas Hot Air Balloon Race and a location to hold the third annual event. At the same time, the Texas State Arts and Crafts Fair decided to try the 4th of July weekend, leaving us with additional local hotel rooms and space in the regional press to promote an extra dimension that just might attract additional people to town and to our events at the ranch. I also looked to expand the appeal of the festival by adding some contrasting bands: mariachis, country-folk, and, perhaps a Cajun band, so I started to look for the best available.

In our Austin schedule of events, I contracted for the Pittsburgh Ballet Theatre production of *Swan Lake* to play the Municipal Auditorium's big stage on Monday night, March 21. Because the program focused on possibly the most popular ballet in history, the young company earned a strong advanced sale. It had undoubtedly also benefited from the public's experience with our National Ballet and Vienna State Opera Ballet performances. For whatever reason, thousands turned out to see the magical love story in a medieval kingdom, set to Tchaikovsky's romantic score and Franklin's choreography.

Prima ballerina Dagmar Kessler danced the role of Odette as a graceful, petite expert heading a company of forty principals, soloists, and corps de ballet. The beautifully lighted and staged four acts were enhanced by impressive sets and costumes, and the company obviously was loaded with talent. Impressive on all counts, *Swan Lake* was a spellbinding, vibrant event that wove its spell on us all.

With the Pittsburgh Ballet behind us, we had nine weeks before our second outdoor season at Kerrville began with the opening of the fourth annual folk festival on May 23.

We restarted our weekly radio show on KERV

on April 30, sponsored by Ken Stoepel Ford and Del Norte Restaurant, with folk music running through May 21, country music through July 2, and then bluegrass up through the last show in the series August 27. We were able to play about a half-dozen cuts each week typical of the festival coming up, talk about special events at each festival, and include two spots for each of our two sponsors.

In the meantime, National Public Radio broadcast two two-hour KUT-FM specials from the 1974 Kerrville Bluegrass and Country Music Festival on more than 100 stations across the U.S. carrying "Folk Music U.S.A." The Radio-Television-Film Department at The University of Texas had recorded much of the festival and was working on two more NPR specials recorded live at the 1974 folk and ragtime festivals.

We also decided to repeat our open house at the ranch a couple of weeks before the festival, and again the public was admitted for $1, or free, if they picked up six cans or bottles off Highway 16 and deposited them in our litter barrel at the gate. We featured bluegrass bands, including Jody Brineger and the Backwoods Volunteers, Grassfire (the former Texas Bluegrass Boys), and Johnny Martin and the Bluegrass Ramblers. Both Allen Damron and Carol Cisneros dropped in to sing some songs, and it was a light-hearted and relaxed day and evening with good attendance. Many of the guests were first-time visitors but the majority were regulars who couldn't wait until the folk festival for a reunion.

The 1975 Kerrville Folk Festival was designed to be a bigger event with four evening concerts beginning at 7:00 P.M., an hour earlier than in previous years in order to accommodate nine performers each night except Friday night, when we started at 6:00 P.M. with the National Yodeling Contest dubbed "The Great American Yodel-Off."

The festival ran from May 22-25 with the finals of the Texas Hot Air Balloon Races scheduled for May 26, Memorial Day.

Additionally, there were special daytime events starting with 11:00 A.M. two-hour Townes Van Zandt Blues Workshops on Friday and Saturday, with Houston bluesman Juke Boy Bonner, barrel house pianist Robert Shaw, and former Ewing Street Times member John Vandiver, who also opened the first evening concert of the festival on Thursday. We opened the fifty crafts booths daily at noon and were pleased to see the return of crafts people like Fleet and Noel Starbuck, Paul and Crow Johnson

Townes Van Zandt at his blues workshop. 1975.
— Courtesy Brian Kanof.

Houston bluesman Juke Boy Bonner. 1975.
— Courtesy Brian Kanof.

with their little ocarina-style flutes, former James Avery designer Jim Morris and his arrowheads, plus the beautiful handcrafted rifles and knives of Davie Boultinghouse.

Peter Yarrow hosted the fourth annual New Folk concerts, now under the foundation's sponsorship. I had selected forty finalists and had twenty per day share their songs with the festival audience. The arts and crafts fair had experimentally moved to the 4th of July weekend, so all of the festival events were at the ranch. Additionally, we decided with this first year to select six New Folk award winners who would receive $50 and the opportunity to sing a twenty-minute set of their songs in a special concert at 2:00 P.M. on Sunday. Judging for these first New Folk award winners was done by Carolyn Hester, Allen Damron, and Mike Seeger.

Among the outstanding New Folk in 1975 were Austinites Jerry Stevens, Paul Colbert, Tom Russell, Shane and Kitty Appling, plus David Ruthstrom of Lubbock, Mark David McKinnon of Nashville, and Bill Haymes of Little Rock.

Our 6:00 P.M. Friday evening yodeling contest was a solid hour of entertainment with the appeal-

Dee Moeller, whose songs had been recorded by Willie Nelson, Waylon Jennings, Faron Young, Dottie West, Gary Stewart, Brenda Lee, and many others. 1975.
— Courtesy Brian Kanof.

175

Mike Seeger with his autoharp at Kerrville. 1974.
— Courtesy Brian Kanof.

The rains of 1975 were reflected on the photo cover of our foundation's limited edition highlights LP.

ing and remarkable Bill Staines of New Hampshire winning the 100 silver dollars and the trophy from judges Kenneth Threadgill, Montana Slim, and Mike Seeger.

The festival main stage concerts were notable for the appearances of many regulars plus Red River Dave (writer of "The Ballad of Amelia Earhart"), writer-songstress-pianist Dee Moeller, Billy Joe Shaver, the Bluegrass Revue from Oklahoma (who did a double Saturday night show when Flaco Jimenez didn't show up, and whose membership included leader and mandolin player Bobby Clark and his guitarist friend Vince Gill), Allen Fontenot's Cajun band, Guy Clark, and Augie Meyers from San Antonio. Ragtime champion Terry Waldo also made his first folk festival appearance as did David Moerbe's Denim from a previous year's New Folk.

The Texas Hot Air Balloon Races were to have had five separate flight schedules along with stunt pilot Lowell Haack and his famed red, white, and blue Pitts Special biplane and a team of skydivers. Much of that schedule was wiped out by bad weath-

er, however. For that matter, the entire state was struck by thunderstorms, hail, high winds, tornadoes, and flooding in a devastating weekend of bad weather.

Most of the evening and afternoon performances made it through the storms and so did about 3,700 fans who gave rain-soaked standing ovations to some of the finest performances in the festival's young history. However, the festival was geared to break even at 6,000 paid attendance budgeted on a daily average of 1,500 for each of the four days. When it was over, no matter how business manager Kirby Lambert counted it, we lost about $15,000!

What kept us going was the spirit of the festivals' supporters, musicians, and staff, good reviews statewide in major metropolitan dailies, plus the blanket press coverage by all media of the first National Yodeling Championships. Many of the staff and performers, and all of the balloonists, asked if we couldn't schedule another event, a special event sometime in the next thirty days to help make up the loss and the national points event for the balloonists. Faced with the severe losses and the enthusiasm of everyone around us, we committed to a benefit event in June.

As soon as we set the dates of June 14-15 for the benefit concerts, camp-out, and balloon races, the commitments began to pour into our office. Ten of the balloonists, the skydivers, and stunt pilot Lowell Haack would all be on hand as would Frank Lamonica's Long Island Sound company.

Then the musicians began to sign up: Bobby Bridger, Kenneth Threadgill, Bill and Bonnie Hearne, Bill Neeley, Plum Nelly, Jimmy Johnson, Rick Stein and the Alley Cat Band, Hubert Fowler (who was runner-up in the yodeling contest), John Vandiver, Richard Dobson, Dave Houston, the Backwoods Volunteers, the Hemmer Ridge Mountain Boys, and others.

We cleaned up the ranch, cranked out three statewide press releases that were picked up by dozens of papers, and I received confirmations from about thirty of the volunteer staff who said they would be back for the two-day event. By the time the event was over, Peter Yarrow, Robert Shaw, Joe Mike Taylor, Rich Minus, and Carol Cisneros had joined us. The two-day ticket was $5 per person, including free camping, and while the gate and concessions covered nearly half of our losses, something else happened as well. The musical dream that had become a rain-drenched disaster also became a turning point in our festival's history, bringing our staff and our performers together as a single family. The audience felt it as well. We were unified in our dedication to the festival, to each other, and what we found together that separated us from the everyday masses. We became special people doing something very special for ourselves and for each other. The spiritual optimism of Kerrville was born in 1975 and would keep us together for decades.

With our losses trimmed by nearly half, and with the morale boost provided by our recent experiences, we headed toward our first C&W Jamboree of country music a little over two weeks away.

Still officing in Kerrville with Kirby Lambert now acting as our business manager and Joe Bermea returning briefly to help with the festival and the benefit, our accounting was in good hands and we knew we had to do well on the 4th of July weekend. Giving us a little breather was a $3,000 loan from Scot Alexander, an Austin volunteer on our ticket crew. We felt rather optimistic about the July 4 weekend.

One of the things that gave us this optimism was a string of fifteen independent country music stations in Austin, San Antonio, Houston, Dallas, Beaumont, Odessa, Arlington, Kerrville, and other communities who were our festival booster network. Also, Kirby McDaniels' crew from KUT-FM at The

University of Texas was returning to record the festival for eighty-five NPR stations across the U.S.

The three-day C&W Jamboree took place Thursday through Saturday, July 3-5, and opening night featured a tribute to Bob Wills by Asleep at the Wheel with special guest fiddler Johnny Gimble, a former Texas Playboy, joining them!

The star-studded weekend saw appearances on our Quiet Valley Ranch stage by Red Steagall, Mickey Gilley, Barbara Fairchild, Red Sovine, Moe Bandy, Crystal Gayle, Freddy Fender, Bobby Bare, Darrell McCall, Johnny Bush, Sherry Bryce, and Hank Thompson, among others. Eleven-year-old World Banjo Champion virtuoso Jimmy Henley of Hobbs, NM, opened each of the evenings at 6:00 P.M.

The festival's $1,000 country song contest was won by the duo of Patricia Hardin and Tom Russell from Austin, who had previously been New Folk finalists.

Young Crystal Gayle at the Kerrville C&W Jamboree. 1975.

— Courtesy Barry Stevens.

The modest crowd had a good time, and, while it was a good beginning, we didn't quite break even, much less earning any needed profit. Scot Alexander again came through, this time with $7,000 to bring his total loan to $10,000!

During July, we were able to release on our own label an LP album for Kenneth Threadgill called *Yesterday and Today* that contained many of the favorites his fans had been asking for: "Waitin' For A Train," "Brakeman's Blues," "Any Old Time," "Peach Pickin' Time in Georgia," and a host of others, with Darrell Royal joining us on the liner notes. The collection of a dozen tracks had been recorded by Threadgill over the previous nine years and included several from Kerrville live recordings and others from the KHFI-TV studio that we'd made to send up to Newport in the 1960s.

After the 4th of July weekend, we had about nine weeks for the final push before our Labor Day weekend bluegrass festival, August 29-31, where the Newgrass Jam, the Southwestern Bluegrass Band Championship Contest, and three giant evening concerts were its pivotal events.

The lineup starred the Lewis Family, Jim and Jesse and the Virginia Boys, Mac Wiseman, Ernest Tubb and the Texas Troubadours, II Generation, Chubby Wise, Red White and Blue(grass), Lonzo and Oscar, Oklahoma's Bill Grant and Delia Bell, and many regional bands including Johnny Martin's Bluegrass Ramblers. Allen Damron and Luckenbach's playful mayor Hondo Crouch pro-

Ernest Tubb and the Texas Troubadours played both the Kerrville C&W Jamboree and the Kerrville Bluegrass and Country Music Festivals in the mid-1970s. 1975.
— Courtesy Peter Ashkenaz

vided a humorous change of pace with song's like Michael Murphey's "Ft. Worth I Love You."

The newly opened campgrounds were working out well with shade tree picking sessions going on day and night. In the festival's second year, we broke even once again.

On September 15, I was invited to be the guest speaker for the Kerrville Music Club to tell them

Allen Damron and Luckenbach's Mayor of Mirth, Hondo Crouch, change the pace of the 1975 bluegrass festival.
— Courtesy Brian Kanof.

about our non-profit Kerrville Music Foundation. While they were most gracious, I sincerely doubt to this day that they had much interest in what we were trying to do.

Back in Austin on the 20th, I presented Tom T. Hall and the Storytellers country music show and had Allen Damron open, backed by fiddling Joe Stuart from Nashville and Kerrville's own Junior Pruneda, former bassist with Ernest Tubb. The show at the 3,000-seat auditorium was a good event, and Damron and Dee Moeller, who also appeared, were warmly received by Tom T.'s audience. It was a rare treat to hear Damron with a band supporting him.

With our second summer season behind us at the ranch, we turned to promoting the return visit of the Glenn Miller Orchestra to our Outdoor Theater on September 28 for the second annual Chamber of Commerce benefit concert. Chamber president Naomi Ingram named Ted Burkhart to chair the event, augmented by Ken Stoepel, Bob Schmerbeck, and chamber executive Ed Phelps.

Jimmy Henderson leads the Glenn Miller Orchestra at the Outdoor Theater, Quiet Valley Ranch. 1975.
— Courtesy *Kerrville Daily Times.*

We had ideal weather, and a huge crowd showed up to hear the band, now directed by Jimmy Henderson who, like Miller, played trombone. Originally from Wichita Falls, Henderson was particularly well known and requested on the West Coast where his orchestra was associated for fifteen years with Hollywood's top entertainment industry functions. He was best known as musical director for the Emmy Awards, Television Academy functions, the Director's Guild of America Annual Awards, and the International Broadcasting Awards, working with such stars as Jack Benny, Lucille Ball, Milton Berle, Johnny Carson, Carole Burnett, Frank Sinatra, and Bob Hope. With Henderson at the helm, the Miller Orchestra sounded great, and over 1,300 attended the evening, generating a sizable sum for the chamber.

Back in Austin for a few days, I assisted the Austin Civic Ballet with their October 7 performance and enjoyed getting to know premiere danseur Edward Villella over the several days we were together. This world-renowned dancer was a gracious professional among the young dancers of

the academy and was an inspiring coach who did everything to encourage the young performing members of the civic ballet. This kind of coaching can have a life-long impact on youngsters.

Our next onstage activity took place on November 23 and 24, when I presented return engagements of Silvia Lozano's Fiesta Folklorico at the Paramount Theater in Austin and at the Municipal Auditorium in Kerrville. It was amazing to rediscover the continuing freshness and panorama of this show of native songs, dances, and costumes from throughout Mexico, accompanied by mariachi, marimba, and Jarocho bands. The spectacle revealed the charm and beauty of the broad tapestry of both past and present Mexican culture. The eighteen handmade white lace Jalisco dresses alone were enough to make the audience catch their breath. The company, just back from Tokyo, Osaka, and Hiroshima, Japan, was returning to Mexico following our dates so the fifty members could be home for the Christmas holidays.

Silvia Lozano, founder-director of the regional Ballet Aztlan, which became the National Dance Company of Mexico, touring the world. 1975.
— Courtesy *Austin American-Statesman.*

I had announced the Folklorico dates at the Glenn Miller concert, and at the Folklorico show, I announced the forthcoming 1976 Kerrville Music Foundation benefit Red Steagall Celebrity Golf Tournament at Kerrville's Riverhill Country Club on the four days preceding our second C&W Jamboree. Even this early, we were able to confirm celebrity players Roy Clark, Mickey Mantle, Darrell Royal, and Hank Thompson for our roster.

The Riverhill Club was owned by Byron Nelson, Chris Schenkle, Sherman and Stuart Hunt, and Selser Pickett and had a national reputation for its excellent golf course. For us, working with club golf pro Jim Shirley was a genuine pleasure. We knew going in that everything on the club side of the event would be well done.

Just before the Christmas holidays, on December 16, I was in Nashville for the Golden Anniversary of the Grand Ole Opry, and took that occasion to distribute press kits to the national press in Music City announcing our 1976 Kerrville season.

Early in January, I received a call from Sol Hurok in New York wanting to know if I could provide a date for his "beloved Vienna Choir Boys" during the fourth week in February.

"We have some time open on their schedule and need a date to provide them with income to cover several days of meals and accommodations," he said. "Based upon your reputation over the years, I would like to entrust this troupe to you in a partnership arrangement. You do everything that you can to present them appropriately, and we will accept fifty percent of the profits." I was not only honored to do this, but enthusiastic about having the opportunity to present this world-famous group.

The Vienna Choir Boys were founded in 1498 by Royal Decree from Maximillian I, who wanted his Chapel "to secure and maintain singers for the purpose of performing at banquets and at the Devine services" as well as at High Mass each day. Centuries later, they were to make their first tour outside Austria in 1926, when they created a sensation on their visit to Switzerland. Since that time, the Vienna Choir Boys had toured Europe, North and South America, Asia, and Australia, and this 1976 tour of the U.S. was their thirty-third since Sol Hurok first brought them to America in 1932.

I chose the Paramount Theater for this distinguished group because of its own history and the appropriateness of the setting it provided. The Paramount first opened as the Gaiety Theatre in 1915, and the 1,278-seat theatre had been returned to its former glory as the home of major stage attractions and movies by a non-profit corporation.

We agreed on February 23 and were pleased to work with Sol Hurok Presents for the first time. Hurok had become a major figure in American entertainment history. His story was legendary through countless articles, books, and documentary films, as well as through Hurok television specials with Isaac Stern, Andre Segovia, Van Cliburn, and the Royal and Bolshoi Ballet companies, among others. I was kidded by the Austin public about being the "local Sol Hurok Presents," but shrugged it off with a grin, knowing that the name of my production company had come out of an article in a San Antonio newspaper writing about my presentation of the Vienna State Opera Ballet at the 1972 Aqua Festival.

America's love of ballet took a major leap forward in 1933 with Hurok's original importation of Ballet Russe de Monte Carlo and the presentation of Anna Pavlova. He later introduced American audiences to the Royal Ballet of England, the Bolshoi, Leningrad-Kirov, and other Russian dance companies, the Stuttgart Ballet, and the Amalia Hernandez' Ballet Folklorico de Mexico. The full list of dance attractions included companies from Denmark, Spain, Japan, Rumania, India, and Israel with such dates as those by Rudolf Nureyev and the National Ballet of Canada included.

By 1976, Sheldon Gold, twenty years with Hurok, was president of the Hurok Concerts organization, which five years before had become part of General Electric.

The Austin date sold out! The twenty-four boys, between the ages of ten and thirteen, presented music from the sixteenth century to the present day, songs by German, Austrian, French, and Italian composers; polkas and waltzes by Johann Strauss, and in full costumes, Haydn's one-act comic opera *The Apothecary*. Our standing-room-only audience was made up of grammar school, high school, and college students, their parents, many of the city's educators, UT faculty and staff, and other classical music followers. It was an incredibly successful and diverse evening.

Our next major event was on March 3, when we introduced to Austin audiences for the first time the magnificent Polish folk company Mazowsze

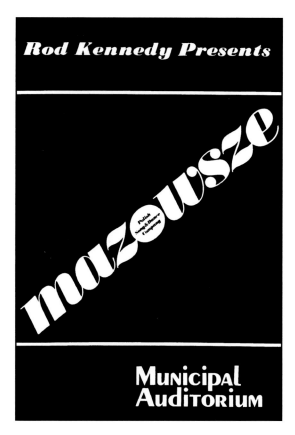

The Mazowsze had played to over three million in Poland and enjoyed great successes in Great Britain, France, Belgian, Switzerland, Austria, Yugoslavia, Japan, China, Berlin, and the Soviet Union. Although this was the company's first Austin appearance, this was its fifth tour of the U.S.

At the March 3 performance of Mazowsze, the outside back cover of the program announced that Nancylee and I were "going to the country" as we notified our patrons of our move to Kerrville. Nancylee had already been there for over a year, and I had been commuting regularly. Our official departure date on March 10 would mark the removal of my offices to the ranch, and the sale and closing of our North Lamar offices.

(pronounced "Mah-zoff-shuh") of 100 dancers, singers, and musicians direct from Warsaw. The company took its name from the central province of Poland, the region where Warsaw is situated.

Also promoted by the Hurok organization, the company was established after World War II by an eminent Polish composer and his wife, a famous Polish actress, and had been the national Polish company since 1950. It owed its popularity around the world to the beauty of Polish folk music, the unusual rhythm of Polish dances, and the colorful costuming, as well as the humor reflected by the songs. In its first decade, it enjoyed many successes at home and had won the Gold Medal at the Brussels World's Fair in 1958.

Ranging in age from eighteen to twenty-five, the members of the company were selected following auditions of more than 5,000 boys and girls from villages all over Central Poland.

Our large audience was thrilled by the performances, the brilliance of its 1,200 costumes, and were attracted to the superb natural beauty of the girls and fine physiques of the men. The mazurkas, waltzes, and polonaises made famous by Chopin actually came alive as dances, providing the audience with a delightful theatrical experience!

However, the success of the two Hurok events would lead to the opportunity for me to present with Hurok the Israel Philharmonic Orchestra in Austin the following fall, and by the time I wrapped things up and packed everything, I wouldn't actually get out of Austin until March 15. With the move to the ranch, Ray Partain would take over the business management for our company.

It was a good feeling to finally be based on the ranch. We had sixty days before our May 15 open house concert at the ranch, and the summer would be a big one with some significant events on our calendar for the fall both in Austin and at the ranch.

Now that I was away from the clutter of city life, I had time to think about what we were trying to do at Kerrville. The press and publicity during the first four years had been abundant and gratifying, but the "nostalgia" aspect of it bothered me. I did not agree with the press descriptions of the festival as a "throw-back to the '60s," as a "gathering of old hippies" or as a "folksy Woodstock." These descriptions only recognized the appeal of the simplicity of the past, while we thought we were rediscovering the human spirit that had a hard time surfacing in a stratified imitative culture. Individualism and real humanity no longer seemed possible in an impersonal world in which stylistic innovation and originality were constantly buried.

The intrusion of popular culture into our spiritual lives was amplified by technology and mass media, resulting in a feeling that technology didn't need people, and that technology, as typified by the proliferation of mindless, clichéd programming on twenty-four channels twenty-four hours a day, was eroding any interest in expressiveness. Everyday consciousness became a reflection of images and messages repeatedly circulated through mass media. Popular culture's restrictions on experience, and the focus on pleasure, were cultivating incoherence and superficiality.

We were also getting more information than we could use coupled with less understanding than we needed. Shaken by the daily contradictions of cultural conformity, we were losing the aesthetic richness and uniqueness of the human spirit that typified simpler times. For me, it was a move from optimistic faith in technology to an awareness that technology, to a great degree, was contributing to the destruction of our world.

At Kerrville, where we could be isolated from the everyday cultural morass, we could contribute an aesthetic richness in opposition to cultural conformity. Rather than a reaction against stifling and confusing modern culture, we could, perhaps, clarify where it does and doesn't fit in our personal scheme of things. We could regenerate the uniqueness of the human spirit and help it to overcome the need to share constantly in the excessiveness and stylistic mannerisms and eccentricities that typify the mimicry of the masses.

We could strive for an inclusive rather than exclusive social structure. We had already done that at the performers' level by doing away with the star system, and, for most performers, it had become a great relief to come to Kerrville to share music rather than compete. Our family of performers was beginning to enjoy a new understanding of themselves and their fellow artists, allowing for an outpouring of human compassion and tolerance, and, ultimately, a "spirit of Kerrville." This was reinforced by new understandings, rich intensities of meaning, and a positive spirituality based upon Peter Yarrow's concept of togetherness and sharing, and my own insistence upon eliminating class divisions.

I had already taken up Charles John Quarto's admonition that, "It's not how you look, it's how you see," and I thought that at Kerrville, away from the fully secular mass culture, we could focus on rediscovering the human dignity in each of us.

We would try to offer Kerrville as a source of support and comfort, where our audiences could join us in finding and sharing physical and emotional self-enhancement. We would provide a protective environment and ambiance for people to put themselves back together with the help of personalized courtesy, respect, and even affection, displayed by a well-informed volunteer staff starting right at the front gate as people drove onto the ranch.

This idea of having original music provide a genuine artistic experience, in combination with an affordable and hospitable site enhanced by a universal feeling of welcome and acceptance from our staff, should provide a rare experience of satisfaction that would overcome the few physical discomforts of being outdoors away from the air-conditioned urban world. We would work to supply what we felt was really important at an affordable price, so everyone who wanted to come could count on some things that would always be here to enrich their lives.

It was a tall order, but it seemed, somehow, that there were few things in everyday life you could count on that didn't come with a long list of discomforts, delays, restrictions, and often a high price that was hidden.

We wanted to provide good value, where people could focus on the present tense, reality, with personal time for themselves away from the other important things in their lives. We wanted to offer a place where everything wasn't perfect, but it worked. Where value, not price, was emphasized, and where the public didn't need to pay more for quality.

Out in the Texas Hill Country scenery and

City children petting Nancylee's horse "Tanche" through the fence separating the Outdoor Theater from our private property. Subtitled "Getting in touch with rural Texas . . . a hands-on expereience." 1975.
— Courtesy Brian Kanof.

wilderness, we could provide a place to meet interesting people, to get some exercise, and where there would be no evidence of motivation to increase spending, outside of an occasional invitation to buy a festival T-shirt or a raffle ticket to support the foundation. We would try hard to make people's time worth more at Kerrville, and through responsiveness, assistance, reliability, and performance, reduce their stress while they relaxed and rediscovered their own common sense.

In addition to 1976 being the fifth anniversary of our folk festival, we had scheduled a celebrity golf tournament (built around the attractive personality and star quality of Red Steagall and his Coleman County Cowboys band) and had geared the C&W Jamboree toward the nationwide Bicentennial celebration with our fans being urged to celebrate the nation's 200th birthday by seeing in person more than thirty country music stars of yesterday and today. We also added a "World Championship Steel Guitar Contest" to the "$1000 Country Western Songwriting Contest."

The Outdoor Theater at Quiet Valley Ranch as seen from Hawk Mountain looking northeast across the campgrounds to the meadows beyond. 1975.

— Courtesy *Kerrville Daily Times.*

In addition, our summer season would end with our third annual Kerrville Bluegrass and Country Music Festival with its bluegrass band championships, new grass jam, and crafts village. A little over a week later, the Glenn Miller Orchestra would return to the ranch for the third annual Chamber of Commerce benefit. So, now that we were settled into our crowded ranch office, we had plenty to keep us busy.

We were fortunate to have our business manager, Ray Partain, move with us to the ranch to handle much of the financial side. In addition, Shiela Spencer, Bob Long, Carol Porterfield, and Nancy Ford from our Austin office would be on board at the folk festival to maintain some staff continuity. They were all experienced, congenial, and totally familiar with both my Austin and Kerrville contacts and production intricacies.

We opened our ranch to the public several weeks before the festival by holding another bluegrass open house on Saturday, May 15. Admission once again was by presenting six cans or bottles picked up off the highway or by donating $1 to our music foundation. The bluegrass music was played by the Country Rogues of Ft. Worth, the Bluegrass Ramblers, Austin's Jim Barr and Grassfire, and Kerrville's Poverty Playboys. Joining them from our folk festival were 1975 New Folk and C&W Jamboree song contest winners Patricia Hardin and Tom Russell, known as Hardin and Russell, Houston's folk veteran Don Sanders (who had done so well at the 1975 folk festival), plus Austin songwriter-performer Rich Minus and blues guitarist Kurt Van Sickle, who had played the first New Folk. As part of the open house, the Kerr County Roadrunners Motorcycle Club ran a rally to the ranch for the music and camping out. We had good attendance and were able to pre-test some of our staffing and traffic control assignments.

Carolyn Hester at our 1976 anniversary festival.
— Courtesy Brian Kanof.

Our fifth anniversary folk festival was dedicated to Peter Yarrow, who was returning for his fifth consecutive year. In fact, several others who were part of the first festival in 1972 (Allen Damron, Carolyn Hester, Kenneth Threadgill, Robert Shaw, and Bill and Bonnie Hearne) were included on the bill as well. All five of these originals had played every year, but Peter's guidance, encouragement, and infusion of the spirit of togetherness, along with his annual guidance and loving energy invested in the New Folk contests, made him a keystone of the festival.

Internationally respected New York classical

Rod Kennedy Presents

5th Anniversary KERRVILLE FOLK FESTIVAL

QUIET VALLEY RANCH
KERRVILLE, TEXAS

Amram left his classical music behind him but loved cele-brating with the folk songwriters at Kerrville. 1976.
— Courtesy of Brian Kanof.

composer-conductor David Amram had been invit-ed to play the festival by Bobby Bridger, and Amram had accepted eagerly. He would fulfill many roles in addition to his Sunday night finale, his his-toric first Amram Jam in memory of John Lomax, Jr. and Mance Lipscomb, and would also judge New Folk at the arts and crafts fair (with poet-songwriter Charles John Quarto of Denver and former Gonzo Band member Gary P. Nunn). The three of them would also conduct a songwriters' workshop, joined by Lee Clayton from Joshua Tree, California.

Bill Staines from New Hampshire, the 1975 yodeling champion, would be back to open the fes-tival and defend his title. Judging the 1976 edition of the yodeling event would be California's legendary Patsy Montana, the first woman to sell a million records back in 1936 with her hit "I Want To Be A Cowboy's Sweetheart," Texas original radio cow-boy and writer of "Amelia Earhart's Last Flight," Red River Dave McHenry, and, of course, Kenneth

Threadgill, whom I had dubbed years before as "Father of Austin's Country Music." The title had stuck.

New Folk winners Mark David McKinnon from Colorado and Bill Haymes from Little Rock would be joining the evening concert lineup. Some of our bluegrass friends would also join the folk lineup, including multi-instrumentalist and former Bill Monroe Bluegrass Boy Joe Stuart, and Grant Boatright's Red White and Blue(grass) from Nashville, who would also host a Saturday work-shop at the arts and crafts fair for us. Chubby Wise and the Bluegrass Ramblers would also return.

On the songwriter side of the ledger, Mike Williams, Milton Carroll, Guy Clark (and his bass player Steve Earle), and Dee Moeller would be focal points along with the contrasting traditional music of Harmonica Frank (who could play the harp with his nose), Terry Waldo from our ragtime festival, and the former Wheatfield, now renamed St. Elmo's Fire. Carolyn Hester and Peter Yarrow hosted the Friday and Saturday New Folk competition at the arts and crafts fair with Gary P. Nunn handling the Sunday award winners concert. Danny Everett of Victoria and Shug Maudlin of Dallas were two of the award winners who would be invited to play the main stage in 1977, and Houston's Kevin Hatcher would also perform as the 1976 Yodeling Champion.

While the return of rain to the festival did little to damage our spirits, it again cut the attendance way down. We were trying not to get accustomed to the bad weather, and moments like Hondo Crouch's spur of the moment recitation of "Luckenbach Daybreak," with Joe Stuart on guitar and photographer Brian Kanof improvising on har-monica behind him, provided one of the many morale-building high spots of the weekend for us. Another highlight that created a hilarious warm-up hour for us at 5:00 P.M. on Friday was the first appearance at the festival of the Star Spangled Washboard Band from Ohio.

The music, the people, and the human experi-ence of our fifth anniversary folk festival were grat-ifying and fulfilling, but again the rain kept us to less than half of our capacity with another resulting financial shortfall.

For our celebration of the American Bicentennial, we planned a country music double-header loaded with star power and events conceived to draw large crowds.

Townes Van Zandt plays for the May 24 crowd at the Quiet Valley Ranch Outdoor Theater. 1976.
— Courtesy Brian Kanof.

Wheatfield, shown here in a Fat Mama Productions publicity photo. From left: Craig Calvert, Connie Mims, Bob Russell, and Cris Idlet, who returned to Kerrville as St. Elmo's Fire in 1976.

First, on June 30 and July 1, with professional help from the golfing world, we put together a fun and attractive Red Steagall Celebrity Golf Tournament at Riverhill club with the popular Texas country music star as host. Red was closer to being a real cowboy than any other country singer we knew. He was a quarterhorse and rodeo enthusiast who also loved Bob Wills western swing music, and his band could play the heck out of it. His current Dot Records hit, "Lone Star Beer and Bob Wills Music," was one of a long string of Red's hits. The tournament would benefit our foundation's projects in folk, bluegrass, and country music, including a hoped-for Texas Music Hall of Fame.

The tournament would give subscribing golfers a chance to play in foursomes with sports celebrities like Frank Broyles, Charley Johnson, Mickey Mantle, Craig Morton, Bum Phillips, Lloyd Ruby, and Darrell Royal, as well as country music stars such as Charlie Pride, Johnny Bush, Willie Nelson, Steve Fromholz, Johnny Gimble, Alex Harvey, Jerry Max Lane, Leon McAuliffe, Ernest Tubb, and

Billy Edd Wheeler, as well as WBAP's Bill Mack, Frank Cody, Tom Kennedy, and more.

The two-day tournament would provide action for the gallery on Wednesday and Thursday during the day with a dollar concert at Kerrville Municipal Auditorium on Wednesday night, hosted by KPFM starring Red Sovine whose hit "Phantom 309" had become a country classic. There was also a big dance at the Water Hole dance hall that night and a big stage show and barbecue at our ranch starring Rex Allen and the tournament celebrities to climax the tournament. The only problem was that two of the key Kerrville businessmen who were responsible respectively for selling regional golfer participation and tournament program advertising did not do their jobs. One pulled out at a crucial point in the preparations and the other just never did anything while talking a good fight. The result of their dropping the ball completely was an event loss in excess of $20,000!

With this behind us, the Bicentennial C&W Jamboree started the next day its three-night run at Quiet Valley. We had tied together the historic reunions of Mother Maybelle and the Carter Family with a reunion of many of Ernest Tubb's Texas Troubadours, including Cal Smith, Billy Byrd, and Junior Pruneda, plus the Light Crust Doughboys from Burris Mills, and a reunion of both the Texas Playboys and the Riders of the Purple Sage.

Other veteran performers joining us included Johnny Bond, Adolph Hofner, Lonzo and Oscar, Hank Snow, Hank Thompson, Red Rector, and the

Duke of Paducah (Whitey Ford) from the Grand Ole Opry, along with WSM's senior announcer Grant Turner, originally from Texas. Contemporary country music performers including young Crystal Gayle, Moe Bandy, Mickey Gilley, Mel Tillis, Melba Montgomery, Sherry Bryce, Johnny Gimble, and more would also be among those on hand, along with KVOO's Bill Parker.

We also scheduled the foundation's $1,000 Songwriting Contest with twenty-four finalists judged by Billy Edd Wheeler, Johnny Bond, and John D. Loudermilk, with KOKE's Joe Gracey helping me co-host. We also staged a new competition, the July 4 World Championship Steel Guitar Contest, as a feature of the 200-year celebration. It was judged by "Take It Away Leon" McAuliffe, originator of the "Steel Guitar Rag," Don Helms of the crying steel of Hank Williams Drifting Cowboys and Ernest Tubb fame, and Jimmy Latham, who was Jim Reeves' first steel player.

Also to be highlighted on the 4th of July were the ceremonial flag-raising and cutting of the 200th birthday cake for 2,000 people made from hundreds of pounds of Burris Mills flour. Max Gardner of KKYX was on hand as was Walter Hailey, the former announcer of the Light Crust Doughboys, and KIKK's Chris Collier.

But what happened on the 4th of July was that it rained hard and kept away all but about 600 hearty fans determined to see the fifteen bands! We could not even meet the payroll as our losses hit $26,000 on top of the $15,000 lost during the 1975 C&W Jamboree. The rains were devastating and flooded the ranch — I can still see Hank Snow wading through a foot of water to get to the stage with his shiny red boots in his hands. We were glad when the two events were over and the six days behind us. We did, however, find out who our friends were and who was in it only for themselves.

One good thing to come out of all this was a proposed Western Swing Festival in Austin on Bob Wills' birthday in March 1977 to help pay off the losses. Also Walter Hailey gathered his friends and many of the golf tournament sponsors around him at the Riverhill Club, and with Nancylee and me each participating on an equal basis, we were able to get the golf tournament losses paid off. Working with Walter was a lesson in focus. ("Will this help us reach our ultimate goal?")

We still had our third annual bluegrass festival ahead of us on Labor Day weekend. Nancylee and I picked ourselves up and traveled to festivals at

187

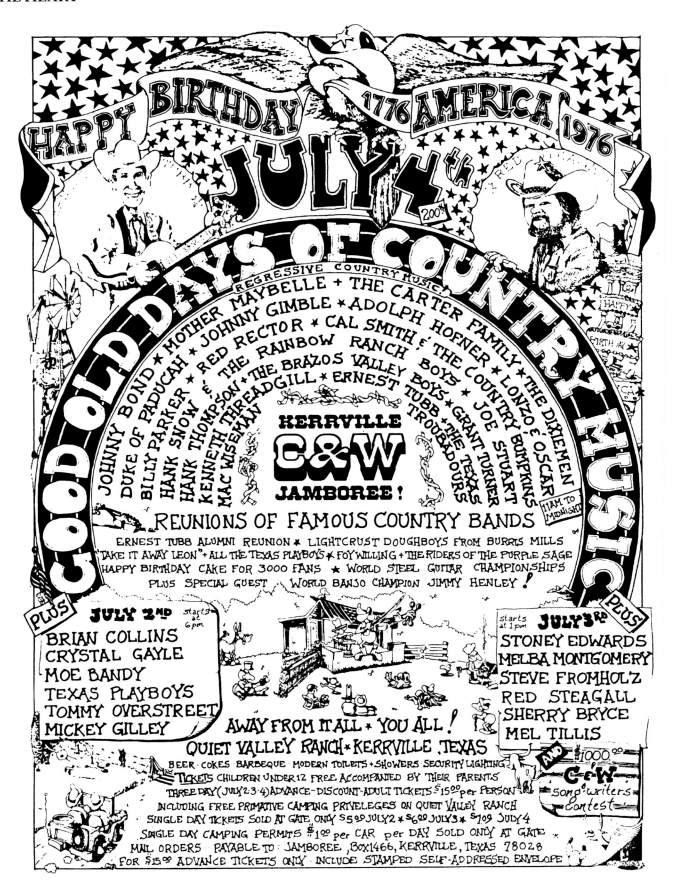

Hugo (Oklahoma), Glen Rose (Texas), and Bossier City (Louisiana), distributing bluegrass brochures and following up on our 7,000-piece mailing. We had also sent out a half-dozen news releases with photos to several hundred press people in four states. We were confident that there would be a good response to all these efforts. Before then, however, I had a huge concert to produce in Austin.

For many months I had been working on a partnership with the Austin Jewish Community Center to host the first and only Texas appearance by the forty-year-old Israel Philharmonic Orchestra

There were more than 32,000 subscribers to the orchestra in Tel Aviv, Jerusalem, and Haifa, with twelve different series of concerts to meet ticket demand. In addition, it played six light classical concerts, five performances for youth, a series for students, plus brought music to *kibbutzim* and small towns throughout Israel, and free concerts for Israel's service men.

Mehta was appointed music advisor in 1969, after having led the orchestra as guest conductor for several years. From Bombay, India, Mehta had led the Vienna, Berlin, and Los Angeles Philharmonics, becoming director of the Los Angeles Orchestra in

The Israel Philharmonic Orchestra on a goodwill tour of the U.S. in celebration of America's Bicentennial. 1976.
— Courtesy Hurok Concerts.

conducted by Zuben Mehta on August 31. Earl and Lena Podolnik were my primary contacts with the community council, but many other friends were involved, including Hyman Samuelson, Mayor Jeff Friedman, Bill Koen, Irving Ravel, the D. J. Sibleys, and Aaron Kruger.

The event would be a major social and cultural happening for the Austin Jewish community, and for several months we encouraged the sale of gold and silver patron sponsorships and program advertising. It was, apparently, an easy sell, but one that required full attention to detail and follow up so everyone would be credited properly.

The orchestra of 106 members was on a national tour as the official representative of the Israeli Government to the U.S. Bicentennial with twenty-six concerts in twenty-one cities. The tour was under the management of our new friends at Hurok Concerts in New York.

Founded in 1936, the orchestra was based in Tel Aviv in the 3,000-seat Frederic R. Mann Hall.

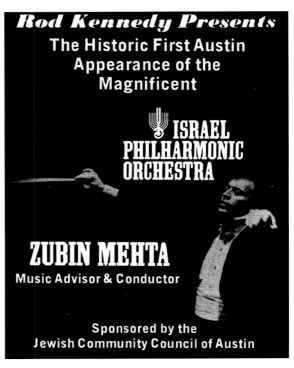

Rod Kennedy Presents
The Historic First Austin Appearance of the Magnificent

ISRAEL PHILHARMONIC ORCHESTRA

ZUBIN MEHTA
Music Advisor & Conductor

Sponsored by the
Jewish Community Council of Austin

1962 at age twenty-six. He was also musical director of the Montreal Symphony Orchestra. Following his U.S. tour, he would succeed Pierre Boulez as director of the New Philharmonic Orchestra as of the 1978-79 season.

The concert of music by Beethoven, Mozart, and Bruckner was first-rate and played to an enthralled capacity audience of 3,000. What few unsold seats remained on the evening of the concert quickly sold out at the box office to lucky late-comers. The whole evening was an unforgettable and enriching experience with the spiritual significance of the event matching the musical impact on all of us.

After the concert, Mehta invited me to join him and some of the orchestra's principals at a late, intimate dinner. He was a charming and outgoing host, and I thoroughly enjoyed the stimulating experience of sharing his table with him.

Two days later I was onstage at Quiet Valley Ranch, introducing Chubby Wise and Grassfire, Mac Wiseman, Lester Flatt, the Kitty Wells Show, the Lewis Family, Charlie Louvin, and the Osborne Brothers, among others. The rain held off, and the Kerrville Bluegrass Festival broke even. That made it three for three at "break even."

September was highlighted by two Glenn Miller Orchestra concerts under the direction of Jimmy Henderson. The band continued to reflect the expected discipline and high regard for the Miller arrangements in their charge. No matter how many times the band played, it was a rewarding experience, no matter who was at the helm. I'm certain that the selectivity of the estate administrators had considerable influence on the quality of the changing leadership.

The Austin concert was an unqualified success, but the indoor concert at Kerrville, moved to the auditorium because of rain, only drew 347 paid admissions for what turned out to be a concert-dance that made it an especially memorable evening for those who did attend. A plus for the band was the addition of young Glenn Harkness, who was reminiscent of vocalists Bob and Ray Eberle who had sung with the Miller and Dorsey orchestras. Among those at the Kerrville performance was Bill Dozier, who gave the band a five-column, front-page headline and an excellent review.

Once the season was over, we started to face the losses of the folk, country, and Glenn Miller

events. We knew we had the right motives for producing our events, and our search for excellence, and the uniquely rewarding events we produced, were the road we wanted to continue to travel. I knew that we had no control over the weather, but I felt that we had to finally hit good weather on our next string of outdoor events.

I thought I should first find out if I was in this by myself, or if I had enough public support to keep it going. My resources were close to depleted, and we were actually flying on unfunded optimism. My friend Ace Hindman, who had built all of my festival facilities and had gone through severe health problems, now had his house burn down and with it, all of our most valuable and irreplaceable possessions stored with him for safety. The stuff that went included Nancylee's sewing machine, my wind-up antique Victrola, a Scottish oil landscape in a rococo gold frame, and the two remaining original Peter Helck paintings from the Speed Museum collection. Ace, however, was philosophical and believed in what we were doing, and, though not an educated judge of musical performances, he encouraged us to find a way to continue. Coming from him, after what he had been through, I felt it was pretty valid advice.

With our friend, neighbor, and building contractor Ace Hindman. 1976.

— Courtesy Tim Crowe.

I talked with Allen Damron, who had already loaned us $3,300, and he could not imagine giving up now. He immediately arranged a $9,700 payment for the thirteen acres of our ranch across the creek at the south end and threw the earlier $3,300 loan into the package, giving us a new lease on life and the ability to pay many of our most needy creditors.

So we had Allen's answer, his check, and his pledge of continuing support.

Next, I headed to Austin to talk with three or four of the folk festival performers. Our telephone had been cut off a couple of times, and I was feeling embarrassed and discouraged to the point where I was losing my confidence. If the performers didn't believe in what we were doing, then I thought I might as well quit now. I think I was looking for an easy way out. Fromholz was there and he said two compelling things to me. First, if we didn't have a festival, he and his friends would lease a flat-bed trailer and throw the festival themselves. Second, when I expressed doubt about the attractiveness of a "folk" festival and suggested we change the name of the event, Steve said, "If you don't keep it the Kerrville Folk Festival, I'll be forced to sing my hit, losing the freedom I now value to sing my less commercial songs." He also told me that having my phone disconnected a couple of times was no big deal and that his had been disconnected several times in years past. A little embarrassed but reinforced by Steve's support, as well as by others in the room, I returned to Kerrville to try to figure out how to get to the next season. It occurred to me that maybe my choice of Kerrville as our location was a mistake, so far way from population centers of Texas. I thought I'd see if the town would express any meaningful support for what we were trying to do.

I devised a $100 sponsorship program similar to the original sponsorship plan of the old KHFI-FM Summer Music Festivals, where the sponsors would receive a pair of tickets for each event of the coming season in addition to being given credit in the programs as a sponsor. I half-heartedly thought if I could sell 100 sponsorships, I would feel validated and would raise the $10,000 I felt I needed to get to the 1977 season.

I went out and called on two of my closest supporters, Bill Dozier and Ken Stoepel, and they both gave me checks on the spot. Then I started on my long list of TV dealers, antique stores, four gas stations, sandwich shops, beer distributors, hamburger stands, J. C. Penney's, gift shops, bars, motels, drugstores, banks, hardware stores, real estate agents, construction companies, two funeral homes, a florist, a lumber company, Mooney Aircraft, insurance agents, and more than seventy other businesses and individuals over the next four months, thinking that I must be able to reach my goal of 100 sponsors.

Thus encouraged, I went back to putting together a 1977 season, with Townsend Miller's daughter, Elaine, known to us all as "Miller," as business manager, replacing Ray Partain following his departure for a more steady-paying job. In the meantime another morale setback was the loss of Hondo Crouch. We'd miss his foolishness, poetry, pranks, and humorous observations and pronouncements. The truth, however, is that being with hundreds of other mourners at the small country church for Hondo's funeral gave us a perspective based on the observation that at least we were all still here to live our lives.

Rod Kennedy Presents
BLUEGRASS BENEFIT
FOLK REUNION

With support from close associates and with new sponsors signing up daily, I began again with reinforced optimism.

The first undertaking of 1977 was to schedule a pair of bluegrass benefit concerts at Kerrville Municipal Auditorium on January 22, my forty-seventh birthday. Playing a matinee and an evening concert to raise money for us were Kerrville's own Poverty Playboys, the Bluegrass Ramblers with a special guest from Nashville, Dobro star Uncle Josh Graves, the Cook Brothers, and Carl Sauceman. Chubby Wise and Grassfire joined the evening concert to provide the finale. A good crowd was on hand, increased by twenty-one business sponsors who bought blocks of tickets and called themselves "Rainmaker Concert Boosters." The farmers in the area had dubbed me "Rod the Rainmaker" and threatened to call on me if a drought occurred.

At this event we announced another pair of

concerts for February 12, drawn this time from the folk festival. These folk festival reunion concerts not only provided proof to the public that we were still alive, but also gave us a chance to publicly acknowledge our new sponsors. Being with the performers again was also a morale boost and created needed cash flow to make things go forward.

So, at 2:00 and 8:00 P.M. on Saturday, February 12, we presented Allen Damron, Robert Shaw, Kenneth Threadgill, Don Sanders, T&M Express, Bill Priest, Jimmy Johnson, Dave Houston, and Mike Williams in concert.

We all had a great time and actually raised a little money, while earning good publicity in the Kerrville papers and entertaining our new sponsors along with ticket buyers who showed up at the box office that day. It was reassuringly successful and much fun, so we thought we'd plan similar concerts in the future.

Two special events of the concerts were the playing for the public, for the first time, portions of the soon-to-be-released 1976 folk festival highlights album, and the first introduction and distribution of a fifth anniversary retrospective forty-four-page booklet of more than eighty photos taken at Kerrville's twelve festivals, 1972-1976. The booklet was entitled "Festival! Texas Music at Kerrville, The First Five Years." In addition, I took this opportunity to thank our new sponsors and to announce the 1977 sixth annual Kerrville Folk Festival with its roster of artists, including a dozen who would appear at Kerrville for the first time.

The big, exciting prospect for the spring, besides preparations for our 1977 season, was the sold-out concert at Austin's Municipal Auditorium by Van Cliburn, who called a few days before the March 3 date to tell me he was too ill to come and play! Sick as he was, though, he told me he would pick up all the expenses of the original date, if I could call him right back with a make-up date. I quickly called the auditorium and canceled the March 3 date and obtained a list of open dates several weeks away after Van would be over his flu and recovered enough to play. When he personally confirmed the new date, we announced to the public a postponement instead of a cancellation and saved all of the 3,000 advance reservations except a handful, which quickly resold.

Nancylee had our car, so I picked Van Cliburn up at the airport in our ranch pickup truck that appalled his manager but reminded Van of his East

Texas upbringing. He promptly threw his luggage in the back, including his set of formal tails, and putting his manager in the middle between us, proceeded to hang out the window all the way to the hotel.

Cliburn had won the Tchaikovsky competition in Moscow on April 13, 1958, six months after the launching of Sputnik and a time when Russia and the U.S. could find no common ground. Following his victory, Premiere Kruschev asked to hear Cliburn and wanted him to play several concerts that were immediately sold out and received with tumultuous acclaim. The victory and the love of the Russian people for this boyish young Texan pianist was front-page news all over the world, and he became the idol of millions.

International cables and telephones buzzed with offers and he returned home to an American concert schedule that was miraculously filled overnight. Now a national hero, President Eisenhower asked to meet him, and New York City welcomed him with the first ticker-tape parade it had ever given to a classical musician.

His tour of the U.S. lived up to the expectations of the public and the critics, and he returned to Europe, where he was universally praised for his

Van Cliburn was an international hero. 1977.
— Courtesy Hurok Concerts.

playing and personal warmth in England, France, Italy, and Belgium. He became an instant goodwill ambassador for America.

Back in America, his concert schedule added up to sixty sold-out performances. RCA gave him an impressive recording contract, and his first recording of the Tchaikovsky First Piano Concerto became an immediate bestseller, as well as the first classical album ever to sell a million copies.

In February 1960, he performed at Madison Square Garden with the Moscow State Symphony under the direction of Kiril Kondrashin with whom he'd performed in Moscow.

By 1977, Cliburn had many bestselling recordings on RCA, and had made triumphant tours world-wide. He had also created the Van Cliburn Foundation in Ft. Worth to recognize excellence in young pianists and to help them on their way in their careers.

Although Cliburn never said anything about it at the dinner at Mary Faulk Koock's Green Pastures restaurant after the Austin concert, I have regularly referred to his 1977 Austin concert as his "farewell Texas concert," since he stopped performing publicly shortly after that March event.

Our capacity audience, including critics from most of the Texas major metropolitan dailies, was

pleased, inspired, and thrilled by Cliburn's performance of works by Schumann, Mozart, Beethoven, Scriabin, and Chopin. He was generous with his encores, and on stage and at dinner afterward we all were charmed by his friendliness, his directness, and his gracious manner. He also introduced me to a young concert pianist named Dickran Atamian, with whom he thought I would be interested in working in some way. Dealing with Cliburn as an artist and as an individual was certainly one of the most enriching and extraordinary experiences of my music career.

In the meantime, while we completed contracting the 1977 artists, our Western Swing Festival benefit concert was being organized for March 6 at Austin's Municipal Auditorium. KOKE-FM signed on as the main sponsor, and a terrific lineup of stellar talent was scheduled.

Joe Gracey from KOKE-FM and I emceed the big four-hour concert starting at 7:00 P.M. on that Sunday night with Alvin Crow and the Pleasant Valley Boys getting things under way. Crow had just signed with Polydor Records for his first national release. Smokey Montgomery and the Light Crust Doughboys from Burris Mills were next. Smokey had been part of the Doughboys since 1935 and had kept the group together for more than forty years. The first half of the concert closed with big Ray Benson leading his popular big band, Asleep at the Wheel. Following the intermission, which in itself looked like a reunion in the audience, we brought out Hank Thompson and the Brazos Valley Boys. By now, it was evident to all of us the subtle variables in each artist's interpretation of western swing. Consistent throughout was the wonderful, free-swinging rhythm of the music that made everyone want to dance. It was a happy, driving, and highly charged music which was really defined when Leon McAuliffe led the reunited Texas Playboys in their set. The bonus in this reunion was getting to hear the vocals of Leon Rausch and the band's original first female vocalist, Laura Lee McBride. This was an historic night, and those present witnessed the living development of the music over four decades with some insight into what the young bands might bring the music in the future. For many of us, including Bob Wills' widow, Betty Wills, it would be the last chance to hear an ailing Jesse Ashlock fiddle with the Playboys.

From left: Former Bob Wills vocalist Leon Rausch with "Take it away, Leon" McAuliffe, composer of "Steel Guitar Rag," and leader of the Texas Playboys reunion bands following Wills' death. 1977.
— Courtesy Charlene Zlotnik.

When the concert was over, Austin's Cooder-Browne Band played for an hour or so of dancing while all of the musicians had a chance to visit and catch up. Everyone felt good about the evening in which all of the bands played for token fees by special arrangement with the Austin Federation of Musicians, so most of the proceeds could go to help cover some of the rain losses of 1975 and 1976.

Darrell and Edith Royal (left) at the Western Swing Festival with Wills vocalist Laura Lee McBride and pianist Al Strickland. 1977.
— Courtesy Charlene Zlotnick.

The 1977 sixth annual Kerrville Folk Festival would be dedicated to the memory of Hondo Crouch and would play May 26-29. Opening the event was 1976 National Yodeling Champion Kevin Hatcher at 6:00 P.M. on Thursday, and Guy Clark would close the festival four days later around midnight on Sunday.

Kerrville Outdoor Theater. 1976.
— Courtesy Kerrville Daily Times.

Seven of the original thirteen performers were back. Newcomers included Tom Paxton, who had last played for us in the 1960s at the KHFI-FM Summer Music Festival. Other first-timers were bluesman Delbert McClinton from Ft. Worth and Austin's blueswoman Marcia Ball. Both artists showed why they were so popular and their bands were hot. Also making her debut was Laura Lee

194

Ft. Worth bluesman Delbert McClinton. 1977.
— Courtesy Brian Kanof.

Steve Young at Kerrville. 1977.
— Courtesy Brian Kanof.

McBride, who had played the western swing benefit and who was daughter of Tex Owens, composer of the famous song "Cattle Call." Laura Lee was Wills' first female vocalist and had appeared with the Playboys on films and on Armed Forces Radio. At Kerrville she would do an evening set of her own and would join Threadgill and Patsy Montana in judging the yodeling contest. Also appearing for the first time on his own was Butch Hancock (who had been a member of the Flatlanders), as well as fiddling Alvin Crow and his band, "Delta Dawn" composer Alex Harvey, and "Seven Bridges Road" writer Steve Young. And, of course, Bill and Bonnie Hearne were back.

Allen Damron and I co-hosted the New Folk concerts with Bobby Bridger, Townes Van Zandt, and Steve Young judging. Townes said afterward, "That was really fun, but I don't ever want to do it again!" It was an exceptional forty writers with Rick Beresford, Jubal Clark, George Ensle, Tim Henderson, Eric Taylor, and Shelley McIntyre winning the awards for the best crafted songs. Other

Bill and Bonnie Hearne. 1977.
— Courtesy Brian Kanof.

195

entries who caught our attention were autoharpist Lindsay Haisley, and Austin's Doak Snead. This was the first year that Peter Yarrow had missed due to an unavoidable family conflict, but his spirit was now so imbedded in the event that we were all hugging the contestants and encouraging them.

Winning the National Yodeling Championship was Ken Brothers from LaGrange, Texas, but winning the heart of the festival crowd was the 4:00 P.M Saturday afternoon "One-Hour Special" reunion of The Flatlanders from Lubbock, who had first appeared as spectators and then surprise guest artists and New Folk at the first festival five years before. Now their best-known member was Dobro player Joe Ely, who was just on the verge of bursting onto the national scene. Not far behind him was prolific writer Butch Hancock and plaintive singer Jimmie Dale Gilmore. Back together for the reunion were bassist Sylvester Rice and musical saw-player Steve Wessen. Heard again were gems like Gilmore's "Dallas" and "I Think I'm Gonna Go Downtown" written with John Reed, Hancock's "You've Never Made Me Cry," and Joe Ely's bluesy Dobro playing. Butch Hancock was also a main stage performer backed by Dee White's guitar, Richard Bowden's fiddle, and Leon Grizzard on bass with surprise guest Jimmie Gilmore sitting in. Butch was already singing original classics like "Fools Fall in Love."

For several years, Bobby Bridger had suggested that the New Folk concerts were getting too competitive, and he'd like to see another event that was

Butch Hancock and Jimmie Gilmore with Hancock's band. 1977.

— Courtesy Brian Kanof.

more a sharing event where anyone who had an original song to sing could find a receptive audience. When Tom Paxton was at the festival the year before, he'd suggested the same thing. So, as an experiment, I arranged for Tom to host what we called a Ballad Tree under the big live oak on Chapel Hill at 1:00 P.M. on Friday. A fairly large group of people showed up and enjoyed singing for each other with Tom hosting and Bridger looking on happily. Several dozen folks who shared their songs was proof enough for me, and I told Bobby we'd set a regular weekend time for daily Ballad Tree sessions the next year.

From left: Milton Carroll, Bobby Bridger, Steve Fromholz, and Gary P. Nunn. Who was sitting in with whom? 1977.
— Courtesy *Kerrville Daily Times.*

By 1977 the performers were already sitting in with each other, creating such surprise pairings and groupings as Dan McCrimmen and John Vandiver sitting in with B. W. Stevenson, and Gary P. Nunn showing up to sit in with Milton Carroll, Bobby Bridger, and Steve Fromholz.

Down in the camping meadow one afternoon, the ACES professional Frisbee team from Chicago conducted demonstrations, games, and competitions.

Pedro Gutierrez was on hand to record again, as he had been every year before, but because of the tremendous foundation losses at the golf tournament, we were unable to release an album with no cash reserve on hand.

The press coverage and response from many attendees encouraged us, as did the attendance that was up by 1,000 fans in spite of Hill Country and regional rains. We were still down on attendance compared to the first year outdoors, but we felt we

Recording engineer Pedro Gutierrez taking a break. 1976.
— Courtesy Brian Kanof.

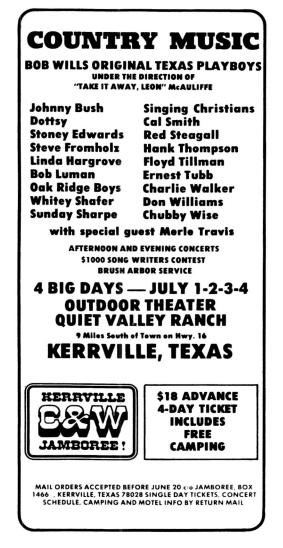

were rebuilding our audience after two years of heavy rains.

We now had the full month of June to complete the final promotion for the third annual July 1-4 C&W Jamboree in an attempt to overcome two years of pouring, blowing rains. In addition to popular artists from previous Jamborees (the Texas Playboys, Ernest Tubb, Hank Thompson, Leon Rausch, Red Steagall, Steve Fromholz, Stoney Edwards, Cal Smith, Johnny Bush, and Chubby Wise), we added Texas' own Dottsy Brodt, Charlie Walker, and Don Williams. Also playing for the first time were the Oak Ridge Boys, who did a gospel show on Chapel Hill on Sunday morning, and reflecting their new direction, a country music show on the main stage Sunday night. Other newcomers included Floyd Tillman, Whitey Shafer, special guest Merle Travis, Bob Luman, young Sunday Sharp, Linda Hargrove, and Austin's rock-a-billy climber Jon Emery. From the folk festival we added Allen Damron, Rick Stein, and the Singing Christians from East Texas. From the bluegrass festival, we added songwriter Tom Uhr and his Shady Grove Ramblers.

Linda Hargrove, Whitey Shafer, and Floyd

Tillman judged the thirty finalists in the $1,000 Songwriting Contest, with Doug Blaser winning top prize followed by San Antonio's Rick Beresford, formerly Rick Casual and the Kitchen Band. Linda Hargrove was so taken by Beresford's writing that she called Pete Drake, who had Rick fly to Nashville where he signed with Drake as a staff writer.

With Hondo Crouch, the late mayor of Luckenbach, still warmly remembered, one of the special events of the jamboree was Allen Damron's one-man show on Saturday afternoon where, in makeup and Hondo getup, he displayed his fondness for Hondo by portraying him with charm, humor, speech, and song in a one-hour tribute before the evening concert.

While the crowd turnout was better than in rain-struck 1976, the third jamboree was only a modest success, and we began to think of how we might spice it up for 1978.

During our events at the ranch, we'd begun to notice the warm response to both the traditional and contemporary gospel songs on both the jamboree and bluegrass festival, and the warm reception to spiritual messages and music on Chapel Hill during the folk festival, so we thought we'd try to stage a Kerrville Gospel Jubilee patterned somewhat after the "all-night singings" of East Texas. For the past year, I had been pursuing the history, traditions, and songs of our gospel music heritage. Among the people whose friendship and insights encouraged us to venture into gospel music were the Lewis Family, Marvin Norcross of Word Records in Waco, Nashville's Don Light, Herman Harper, and Noel Fox. We had also come to know the remarkable Singing Wills Family from North Texas, who were long-time mainstays in recording, publishing, and performing gospel music all over the Southwest. They had one of the longest-running singing ministries in the nation. Our new friends, James Christian and his family, the Singing Christians from East Texas, were also helpful and encouraging.

The showcase of this heritage, with the addition of contemporary Christian music and performers, would be our first Kerrville Gospel Jubilee on the ranch four weeks after the C&W Jamboree. We devoted the inside front cover of the jamboree program to a full-page announcement of the jubilee and talked about the coming gospel event during the concerts where the Oak Ridge Boys and the Singing Christians appeared.

We also traveled to a number of gospel events around the state to establish both an understanding of what was appropriate and a relationship with many of the touring gospel groups.

The major events of the July 29-31 jubilee were, for us, the historic reunion of the beloved Chuck Wagon Gang, including Rose, Anna, Roy, and Eddie Carter, and the appearance of Anna Carter's highly regarded husband, Gov. Jimmy Davis of Louisiana, who, incidentally, composed "You Are My Sunshine."

In addition, we scheduled for the main stage six Southern gospel groups who were charting nationally, including the Downings, the Galileans, the Hemphills, Wendy Bagwell, and the more contemporary Imperials and the Pat Terry Group. Added to these was the bluegrass gospel Sullivan Family from Alabama led by one of America's great ladies,

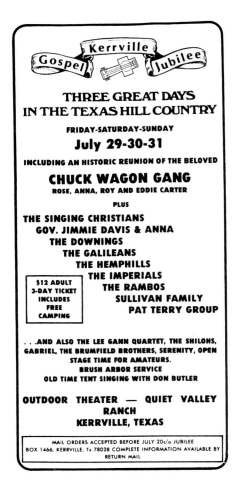

Kerrville Gospel Jubilee

THREE GREAT DAYS
IN THE TEXAS HILL COUNTRY
FRIDAY-SATURDAY-SUNDAY
July 29-30-31
INCLUDING AN HISTORIC REUNION OF THE BELOVED
CHUCK WAGON GANG
ROSE, ANNA, ROY AND EDDIE CARTER
PLUS
THE SINGING CHRISTIANS
GOV. JIMMIE DAVIS & ANNA
THE DOWNINGS
THE GALILEANS
THE HEMPHILLS
THE IMPERIALS
$12 ADULT THE RAMBOS
3-DAY TICKET
INCLUDES SULLIVAN FAMILY
FREE PAT TERRY GROUP
CAMPING

. . .AND ALSO THE LEE GANN QUARTET, THE SHILOHS,
GABRIEL, THE BRUMFIELD BROTHERS, SERENITY, OPEN
STAGE TIME FOR AMATEURS.
BRUSH ARBOR SERVICE
OLD TIME TENT SINGING WITH DON BUTLER

OUTDOOR THEATER — QUIET VALLEY
RANCH
KERRVILLE, TEXAS

MAIL ORDERS ACCEPTED BEFORE JULY 20 c/o JUBILEE
BOX 1466, KERRVILLE, Tx 78028 COMPLETE INFORMATION AVAILABLE BY
RETURN MAIL

Margie Sullivan. Then we added five regional groups from Texas, Oklahoma, and Louisiana, some open stage time for amateurs, a brush arbor service on Chapel Hill, and "tent singing" with the Gospel Music Association's executive director Don Butler leading the singing.

We kicked things off with a free concert on the courthouse square downtown by the entertaining Masters Four from the Grapevine Opry. At $12 for a three-day ticket including free camping out at the ranch, the curious, the faithful, and the skeptical began arriving later that Friday afternoon.

The music was good, the message was clear, and the whole affair was a family-oriented and entertainment-filled three-day weekend. Each of the performers was skilled in their singing and playing and many were extremely charismatic. No alcoholic beverages were permitted, and we put away all of our beer signs for the weekend. I'd have to say that the performers were among the most likable and straightforward people I had ever met in the music business. For us it was a weekend of family entertainment. For the performers and many in the audience it was a ministry. While this approach to religion was new to us, we embraced the idea of doing it again in 1978. We had certainly made many good friends in this dedicated music community and felt close to them and to their audience.

When August 1 dawned, the day after the jubilee, and most of the campers and touring buses were on their way, we began to focus one hundred percent on the forthcoming September 2-4 bluegrass festival.

Miller pointed out to us that we really needed to do more than break even on this year's bluegrass festival, or we'd have to seek some additional cash sources somewhere to get into the 1978 season. Her message was accurate and a good reminder to work hard to generate more cash flow. One thing that would help was the replacement of Lester Inman's limited food service menu and short hours by G&M Catering of Austin. I had met G&M's Jimmy Mosley when he was a youngster at his father's side in the early Mosley Cafeterias when they were advertisers on KHFI-FM in the 1960s. Now Jimmy brought a larger team, a broader menu, and longer hours to our Outdoor Theater food service, and the public ate it up with the profit numbers doubling in this first year.

We covered all the promotional bases for our bluegrass festival, including continuing the local weekly half-hour show on KERV and revisiting regional bluegrass festivals near and far.

The Labor Day weekend festival presented more than thirty hours of music at our Outdoor Theater. Jim and Jesse and the Virginia Boys, the McLain Family Band, and Norman Blake headlined an all-star roster of performers, joining the Lewis Family, Uncle Josh Graves, Red White and Blue(grass), Harold Morrison, Joe Stuart and Carl Sauceman, The Stonemans, Bill Box and the Dixie Drifters, and Oklahoma's Bill Grant and Delia Bell. Texas bands included 1976 champion Cook Brothers and the Bluegrass Kinsmen, Amazing Grass, Grassfire, Johnny Martin's Bluegrass Ramblers, and Kerrville's Poverty Playboys. Bill Grant co-hosted with me, and we had a pretty good turnout including lots of folks we'd met at other smaller bluegrass events.

The crafts booths in the theater were all filled with artisans who appeared to do well, and the campgrounds found picking parties and bluegrass jams under every tree, tent, and canopy. The bottom line, however, was that we still broke even, even

with the new $15, three-day tickets and a thousand or so at-the-gate, single-day ticket and $1 camping permits. It was obvious that the festival was growing but performers' fees were at commercial rates and our budget was up every season.

By the time this bluegrass weekend was over and Miller tallied the year's results to date, it was obvious I needed to do something drastic! Building on growing income and the vast pre-event publicity each season, I put together a package of stock and loans to go out and sell to get us the cash-flow we needed. I had decided I wanted a few $3,000 stockholders whose stock purchase would be accompanied by five-year low-interest loans, renewable for an additional five years. Over the next ninety days I did sell a number of these $3,000 packages. Our friend Ken Stoepel even bought one at a tough cash-flow time for his business when he was selling his new car showroom and service facilities and leasing them back from the buyer to gain cash reserves with which to buy more new model cars! This gesture rekindled my fire.

Then I headed to Ft. Clark and Brackettville, Texas, to see my friend Happy Shahan. While being a Texas Longhorn breeder, discoverer of Johnny Rodriguez and manager-promoter for Dottsy Brodt, Happy also had a knack for creating an attractive facility for film crews from Hollywood including a complete replica of the Alamo mission as it might have looked during the famous battle for Texas independence. The John Wayne *Alamo* film was the major movie made at this location, but there were many others.

I had become close to Happy through our mutual work with the Discover Texas Association (we were both avid promoters of Texas tourism). Also, Nancylee's brother, John Thomas, had given us a beautiful red-and-white Longhorn steer, which we named "Bum," as a mascot for Quiet Valley Ranch. While Happy had a Longhorn herd of 200 to 300 head, we bragged about having Texas' smallest herd, one Bum steer!

I told Happy about what we'd been through with the repeated bad weather, the events that didn't draw, and the expenditure of all our assets to keep going. I was going to ask him how many of the $3,000 stock/loan packages he might want, because together, we were Texas' most active rural promoters.

Happy invited Nancylee and me to take a seat, and he looked me straight in the eyes. Before I could outline my proposal for his participation, he said, "I'm not going to give you any money. I'm not going

Bum Steer, our ranch mascot. 1977.
— Courtesy Dan Thompson.

to lend you any money, and I'm not going to become your partner. But, I have a very young registered Longhorn cow with a calf at her side which needs more attention than I can give her with all of the cattle I have on this place. She was bred accidentally and too young. As a healthy cow-calf pair they will be worth a lot of money growing up. I'd like for you to have them and give them the care they need. You can raise them, you can eat them, you can breed them, you can sell them, but if you have the guts I think you have, you'll take them home and take care of them. I'd like for you to have them."

Nancylee and I were overwhelmed by both his faith in us and in the generosity of his offer. We followed him out to the stockade to meet the cow and calf pair, and they were beautiful, champion-sired examples of the breed!

We immediately agreed to head back to Kerrville and return with our truck and trailer the next day to pick them up. He said, "I'll have the registration papers sent to you," gave us both a big hug, a big knowing smile, and good wishes as we headed back to Kerrville. I was filled with mixed emotions — a little embarrassed by underestimating my ability to survive without a share of what I perceived to be his "wealth," and nearly overwhelmed by his businesslike generosity and the exciting gift of these precious animals. I was suddenly filled with confidence and new resolve and the excitement and pride of ownership that the stewardship of these animals would bring. In a few words, Happy had put me back on track.

Knowing how Happy loved publicity, we prepared a news release about his "tripling our herd." We mentioned Happy's tourist attraction, *Alamo Village,* and his artists Roni Stoneman and Dottsy. It was released with his approval just before Nancylee and I left for San Antonio to attend our first Texas Longhorn Breeders Association of America convention.

Once back on the ranch, we named the cow "Mishap" and the black and white bull calf "Butterfly," after the markings on his broad forehead. Then I got on the phone and put together an all-day, one-day concert at the ranch for Saturday, September 24, called "8 Great Hours at Kerrville," stacking the line up with Marcia Ball, Milton Carroll, Allen Damron, Steve Fromholz, Butch Hancock, Dee Moeller, B. W. Stevenson, John Vandiver, and Rusty Wier. For fun, Manny Gammage at Texas Hatters in Austin threw in a $50 custom-made western hat as the prize for a "Worst Hat Contest" where the winner had to be a real loser! The concert was advertised as a benefit for Kerrville at $6, and the press jumped on it, running most of our three full-length press releases, complimentary display ads, and continuous promotion on many radio stations statewide.

200

When some of our other performers heard about the event, they decided to show up, too, including Texas Jewboy Kinky Friedman and Bobby Bridger, who by now had two RCA albums out. In addition, Marcia Ball was on Capital, Milton Carroll was on Willie's Columbia-Lone Star label, Rusty Wier was on Columbia, Steve Fromholz was on Capital, and B. W. Stevenson was on Warner Bros., so the show was packed with Texans who were on national record labels. The press promoted the "8 Hours" as a "star-studded progressive country rock concert."

The press also explained that we were "still smarting financially from having two to ten inches of rain at six out of our first nine music festivals during 1975-76."

Also in advance of the concert, Paul Pryor Productions of Austin announced they would videotape the "8 Hours" for television. The concert even made it into two editions of *Billboard Magazine*.

People of all ages and musical tastes showed up, as did rock-a-billy performer Jon Emery, who helped judge the forty hats that paraded in the contest with such names as "Willie's Mistake," "Mule Walker," and "Cajun Sun Bucket." Representatives from six radio stations also arrived at the "8 hours" and were knocked out by the music!

It was a fun celebration enjoyed, perhaps, by the performers even more than the audience. It was a real morale booster, as expected, for us and raised clear nearly $9,000!

Then in October I started the sale of the $100 sponsorships and, as mentioned before, sold more than 150 of them over the next thirteen weeks. Most of the townspeople were eager to meet me and happy to support our efforts. All of them thought the package of tickets and sponsor credit was a good deal. An amazing number of them were interested in our trying to revive the old West Texas State Fair in Kerrville that died during World War I. We told them we would consider looking at such a project in the 1980 season on a weekend when The University of Texas was not playing football.

On January 15, 1978, Nancylee and I joined hundreds of people at Luckenbach on a cold and blustery day for the dedication and unveiling of a bronze bust of Luckenbach's late mayor, Hondo Crouch. Luckenbach was packed by people who remembered him with affection. I guess it was at this point that I really began to believe that there

would be a 1978 season for us. Too many performers reminded us that they would see us at Kerrville whether there was a festival or not. By then, we already had over 100 sponsors and that seemed like too many people to disappoint. I decided not to give up without a fight.

In addition to the growing list of sponsors, several times each week we received gifts of cash or a check from fans who said that the festivals were important to them. The seventh festival season at

With Nancylee at Luckenbach, January 15, 1978, for the dedication and unveiling of the bronze bust memorializing Hondo Crouch. 1978.

— Courtesy Gary P. Nunn.

Kerrville, more than any before it, would be the result of the combined efforts, understanding, caring, and cash of lots of people!

After losing $200,000 in personal assets, exhausting $100,000 in bank credit, realizing I was forty-eight years old and had twenty-seven working years invested in knowing the future is no more certain now than it was when I started the whole thing, I had to wonder if it was really worth it.

We had used our savings, the money from our house and racing car collection, our stocks and business holdings, even a significant portion of Nancylee's inheritance from her father. The only thing we had left was the land we had nursed back to health, and finally, we had even sold off some of that, leaving ourselves with an irreducible minimum of fifty acres. That's why it was so important to have the support of performers like Damron, Fromholz, and Peter Yarrow. They shared my dream. With Happy Shahan's reminder of what it takes, I looked for and found the moral and financial support I needed, $100 at a time, from over 150 Kerrville-area businesses and a few fans who heard what we were trying to do.

Little did I know how close and how long the support and friendship would become from Kerrville people like James Avery, Bryant Motors, the Ferris family at the Cowboy Steak House, Naomi Ingram of the Del Norte Restaurant, Walter Hailey, Ben and Kathy Hudson (who eventually bought multiples for their family), Andy Ritch at The Hummingbird, Judge Jackson, Bill Dozier at the *Kerrville Daily Times,* the Cooks at Kerrville Drugs, Junior Fritz at the Mini-Marts, Ray Lehman at Kerrville Color, cartoonist Ace Reid, Bill Fair at the Rose Shop, stockbroker Ed Schleiter, and Bobby Schmerbeck and his family. Also lending major support were Raymond Barker, our Austin realtor friend Bill Smith, Kerrville-area realtors Leslie Sherman, Pat Braden, Burleson Realty, Klein and Company, Lehmann and Monroe Enterprises, Dick Lehman at Leon Long Realty, Bruce McGraw, Schulgen and Associates, plus, of course, Ken Stoepel Ford and Bill Crittenden and his family. It was a tremendous outpouring of support, and the listing only represents a fraction of those participating!

This support, combined with cutting our budget, working smarter to increase crowds, and discovering within ourselves that it was worth it and that we were able to muster what it took, put the drive back into our agenda.

After all, we were in the perfect spot. Kerrville had been a Mecca for sufferers of various lung diseases who came there to enjoy its pure air and fine climate conditions. Some regained their health and some died. Those who recovered often stayed on to form a conservative but cosmopolitan nucleus rare for a community of this size. Some 12,000 to 17,000 citizens were in the Kerrville area, attracted there by the climate and the unspoiled beauty of the hills and streams. They brought with them an appreciation for culture and the arts and triggered another influx, this time of artists, writers, musicians, and other creative people. The area became a perfect haven, away from it all, and I thought it provided the ideal escape from the clutter of telephones, freeways, and traffic, and the commercialism of urban living.

On our small plot of Kerr County during these first three or four years, we had cleared the debris, and Nancylee planted a hundred native trees from one end of the ranch to the other. Day after day she watered them from five-gallon jugs carried in the ranch jeep to bring them through the relentless heat of the Texas summers. Many of these trees were

memorials planted to honor performers who had died, but she gave the same care to every tree, week in and week out, month in and month out.

We had truly invested ourselves in this effort and were not about to give up!

The incongruity of our former city life was dramatically demonstrated by the two events I produced in Austin on February 15 and 16 as we launched our 1978 production schedule following completion of the Kerrville drive for sponsors.

With encouragement from R. W. Blackwood in Nashville, I agreed to produce an evening called "Memories of Elvis," a tribute evening in association with J. D. Sumner of the Stamps Quartet. The Stamps, whose music tradition went back several decades, had appeared with the late Elvis Presley on all of the superstar's concerts, RCA records, and network television shows for the past six years, and, since Presley's passing in August 1977, had been presenting a tribute evening by a cast of sixteen. One of the ideas I liked about the show was that there were none of the usual imitators exploiting the Presley style.

So I agreed to present the concert in association with the Elvis Presley Memorial Foundation. The show opened with R. W. Blackwood and the Blackwood Singers. The second part of the concert starred J. D. Sumner, Ed Enoch, and the Stamps.

The advance publicity for the show told of the "Memories" show playing in Little Rock, Oklahoma City, Kansas City, Chattanooga, and Soldiers Field in Chicago to sell-out crowds.

Our show also included Sandra Steel, Ed Hill, Larry Strickland, Buck Buckles, and the T.C.B Band. In spite of a large cast and good advance publicity, however, the show did not draw any crowd at all. No one, least of all the Elvis Presley Memorial Foundation in Memphis, received any proceeds at all, and we were left with additional debt.

By contrast, the next night our show with the Milwaukee Ballet moved into the same auditorium to present Ravel's *Daphnis and Chloe* with choreography by Jean Paul Comelin, company artistic director since 1974. Daphnis was danced by Nolan T'Sani and Chloe by Leslie McBeth, with six other principals, fourteen featured dancers, and corps de ballet. Scenic design was by Roger LaVoie and the ballet was adapted from Folkine's 1906 libretto. Remarkably, it was accompanied by pianist Melinda Leingruber.

For the Austin audience, the world premiere

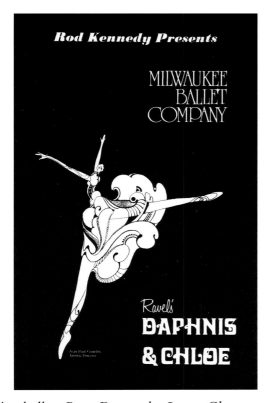

opening ballet, *Rope Dances*, by James Clouser, performed by nine dancers to music by Busoni, was an added treat and an artistic surprise from the choreographer who had previously given us stunning ballets in *Carmina Burana, Caliban,* and *Rasputin,* as well as more than a dozen ballets for the Royal Winnepeg and Alberta ballet companies.

With the great ballet evening in our rearview mirror erasing the "memories" and the loss of the previous evening, we returned to the ranch to complete the wrap-up on our sponsorship drive, and put the rest of the 1978 season together.

Working over an extended period of weeks, the season was quickly finalized. Or at least it seemed so, after being blocked by financial concerns for so long.

Since we had so many local sponsors in our new association, we wanted to have an event they could attend right away as a bonus for their support. I was able to get two of the best groups to come to Kerrville for a special 1978 season opener on Saturday, March 25 at the auditorium downtown — Buck White and the Down Home Folks and the McLain Family Band from Kentucky. There couldn't have been two more family-oriented groups of entertainers in our roster, and the shows they played were really well-received by good crowds, especially the evening show. Between the music and the pure joy of being together again with the Whites

and the McLains, we were starting out the 1978 season with great optimism!

The season would see the seventh folk festival May 25-29, the fourth C&W Jamboree June 30-July 2, and the fifth anniversary bluegrass festival September 1-3. That meant that our three major outdoor festivals were Memorial Day, 4th of July, and Labor Day weekends.

The folk festival would welcome back Peter Yarrow following the historic reunion of Peter Paul and Mary in front of a huge sell-out crowd at the Hollywood Bowl. Paxton would also return, and Bobby Bridger's friend David Amram would come in from New York to host the Ballad Tree on Thursday and stay until Sunday night for his main stage set. Among the others on the evening concerts were our 1976 yodeling champion, Ken Brothers, Dan McCrimmon from Colorado, who would also share a Frummox reunion with Fromholz, Jimmy Driftwood from Arkansas, and Joe Ely in his first main stage set for the festival on opening night.

The next night, Friday, was loaded with Rick Beresford, Robert Shaw, Bill and Bonnie Hearne, Gary P. Nunn, Milton Carroll, Townes Van Zandt, and Guy Clark. What a night!

The 1978 New Folk concerts were the next day at the fair with Steve Fromholz, Gary P. Nunn, and

203

Peter Yarrow at Kerrville Folk Festival number seven.
1978.

— Courtesy *Kerrville Daily Times.*

The Ballad Tree on Chapel Hill. 1978.

— Courtesy Brian Kanof.

Don Sanders judging. Our group of forty finalists
was the best ever, and the crowd surrounding the
little stage was huge. Award winners picked to play
the honor concert on Sunday were Vince Bell,
Jessica Bryan, Lindsay Haisley, Pettigrew and
Blanchard, Steve Sajack, and Kerrville's own Louis
Real, the son of a prominent rancher whose family
went back to the beginning of the settlement of
Kerr County. Other New Folk who got our attention were Jon Ims from Colorado, Nanci Griffith
from Austin, and Steve Earle from Wimberly.

Saturday night's concert featured Austin's
newest Columbia Records artist, Rusty Wier, western swing and bluegrass mandolin-great Buck
White, and Ft. Worth's exciting blues favorite
Delbert McClinton!

The final night was also loaded with Damron,
Amram in his first performance of "Alfred The
Hog," Paxton, Tracy Nelson, John Vandiver, the

Shake Russell Band, and Peter Yarrow closing with
one of those great audience singing celebrations.

The new Ballad Tree sessions, expanded this
second season to two-hours, were a tremendous
success and were hosted by Amram and Bridger the
first day and Gary P. Nunn and Tom Paxton the
next. Also, now firmly an annual part of the festival
at the ranch, was Rev. Charlie Sumners Folk Mass
on Chapel Hill. We had a little problem with the
yodeling contest, in that only two challengers
showed up, but Kenneth Threadgill, backed by Bill
Neeley, came up to do a guest set to kick things off,
so the public didn't really care. Contest winner

Robert Shaw applauds his audience. 1978.
— Courtesy *Kerrville Daily Times.*

Rusty Wier, writer of "Don't It Make You Wanna Dance."
1978.

— Courtesy Barry A. Smith.

Johnny White from Massachusetts won over Robert K. Smith of New York with Threadgill, Damron, and 1976 champion Kevin Hatcher judging. It turned out that White was the performer who inspired and influenced our first champion, Bill Staines, to yodel! One of the highlights of Saturday night was Ken Brothers (1976) and Kevin Hatcher

(1977) sitting in for some spectacular yodeling duets.

There were so many high points during the weekend — Butch Hancock sitting in with Joe Ely, the return and warm reception given Mother of Pearl (formerly Plum Nelly), Guy Clark sitting in with Buck White, New Folk finalist Nanci Griffith sitting in with Eric Taylor, and Amram's huge jam on "Alfred The Hog," aided and abetted by Lindsay Haisley, Bobby Bridger, Gary P. Nunn, and a dozen "Kerrvillaires." Amram had played his "crabgrass" sing-a-long in nine countries and now it was part of the Kerrville tradition.

One major celebration for all of us was the rain — there wasn't any for the first time since 1974. Our attendance was up to 5,000 this year, within 1,000 of our first year outdoors. The patience of our creditors had paid off and now they had a sign that the festival really would be able to continue.

Again, Pedro Gutierrez caught it all on tape, and if we could find funding for the foundation, we'd have another annual album of the festival!

The 4th of July Kerrville C&W Jamboree was on the calendar for Friday through Sunday, June 30-

Buck White, originally from Wichita Falls, seen from backstage at the Outdoor Theater. 1978.
— Courtesy Brian Kanof.

205

July 2, and while we included what we thought was a significant lineup of country music, we also added a Saturday morning parade through downtown Kerrville with Ace Reid and Floyd Tillman as honorary parade marshals, plus Kerr County Sheriff Paul Fields and newspaper country music columnists Wiley Alexander and Townsend Miller as VIP guests. The special attraction in the parade was the horse cavalry platoon from Fort Hood.

On the last day of the jamboree, we added a "Donkey Derby" and Cowboy Horse Races organized by Hazel Calcote and her team of nine local horse people. The event was similar to those at Happy Shahan's big show at Brackettville, and the winner of our races would represent us at Happy's event later in the summer. As a feature between the preliminaries and the finals of the Cowboy Horse Races, with Kent Finlay's High Cotton Express playing in the bandstand at the finish line, was an historic and exciting drill by the First Cavalry soldiers and their mounts.

Our main stage headliners were Linda Hargrove, the western swing of Hoyle Nix with guest fiddler Shoji Tabuchi, Moe Bandy, Fiddling Frenchie Burke, Marcia Ball, and Eddie Rabbitt.

Cowboy Horse Races at the 1978 Kerrville C&W Jamboree.

— Courtesy *Kerrville Daily Times.*

Opening night looked a little like the folk festival with Butch Hancock, Bill and Bonnie Hearne, and Dottsy. Our songwriters' contest judges Red Lane, Glenn Martin, and Sonny Throckmorton also performed a showcase. Others on our roster were Bill Mack of WBAP, Floyd Tillman, Leon Rausch, Leon "Pappy" Selph, Whitey Shafer, Steve Fromholz, the Masters Four, Allen Damron, the

Cooder-Browne Band, Jon Emery, the Tennessee Valley Authority bluegrass band from San Antonio, and twenty-nine song contest finalists, among them Nashville-based contestants Dave Olney, Sonny Hall, and Jim Kent. Dave West of KOKE co-emceed with me, and he and Max Gardner of KKYX helped me to screen the 150 contest entries. As part of the patriotic observance each evening of the holiday weekend, we had a horse-mounted silent flag-raising ceremony just before each evening concert.

There was good press coverage before, during, and after the jamboree with press representatives coming from as far away as West Germany. The attendance was up slightly, and we had cut the budget, but not enough. I had already decided to retire the jamboree and do something else in 1979. Perhaps we'd look at the country fair idea we'd talked about.

Our second Gospel Jubilee was four weeks away as we lowered the flag on what was to be the final C&W Jamboree. In laying out the July 28-30 event for the public, I used the historic forty-year reunion of the original Wills Family as a focal point, and then added the main stage groups headlined by the award-winning Telestials and the Thrasher Brothers of Birmingham, Alabama.

We began as before with a free gospel showcase downtown on the courthouse square, this time with five other quartets joining with the Masters Four.

The concerts out at the ranch were highlighted by appearances by the Singing Christians, the Northam Brothers, Serenity, the Sullivan Family, and Chubby Wise with Grassfire, who really moved the audience playing Bob Wills' "Maiden's Prayer," along with melodies from old hymnals. At Chapel Hill on Sunday, the GMA's Don Butler returned to conduct a Sunrise Service assisted by Kerrville's own Sounds of Praise.

The attendance was up and we had cut the budget slightly and stayed within it, so in addition to the warm welcome accorded the jubilee by its larger audience, we were encouraged by the improved financial side of things to plan a third jubilee for next season.

Between the jubilee and the bluegrass festival on Labor Day weekend, we were pleased to see an eight-page feature on us in the *Dallas Morning News Scene Magazine* supported by a full-color cover and five black and white story photos of us taking care of usual tasks and chores on the ranch. The story gave the public some insight into what we were trying to do and the help we were receiving to overcome the rains. Freelance writers Bill Sloan and Lana Henderson did a thorough and well-written job on including accurate quotes and well thought-out insights. Some of their descriptions and phrasing were included earlier in this chapter, reprinted with the permission of the *Dallas Morning News*.

The fifth anniversary Kerrville Bluegrass and Country Music Festival, September 1-3, offered more than thirty hours of bluegrass music on our stage headlined by Buck White and the Down Home Folks, the Lewis Family, the Bluegrass Alliance, Caffrey Family, McLain Family Band, Pinnacle Boys, flat-picking ace Dan Crary, Peter Rowan, Southern Select, Joe Stuart as a guest fiddler with the Bluegrass Ramblers, and Texas bands Grassfire, Shady Grove Ramblers, and the Poverty Playboys. The darlings of the weekend were TVA from San Antonio, who had won the championship the year before. They could be true to the tradition, but were not afraid to transcribe a Beatles' tune or an original song into their set. Larry Sparks and the Lonesome Ramblers also made an impressive Kerrville debut and were warmly received. By now our Outdoor Theater was being described and advertised as "America's most beautiful bluegrass theater."

In spite of over three inches of rain during the festival, the seven big events of the three days drew sizable and happy crowds of fans, but, again, we simply broke even on the event. While we were increasingly pleased not to lose money, it occurred to us that it might be rewarding to encourage our bankers by really being profitable some time soon.

How did the season do? Folk, bluegrass, and gospel attendance was up. C&W Jamboree attendance was down. As a result, we wound up the season overall without a loss for the first time! Our improved situation was the result of sponsorships and strong attendance growth at the folk festival that was up by more than 2,000 to over 6,800, plus nearly 400 sponsor tickets. We also had an increase in the VIP attendees from record companies, press, management, publishers, television, radio, and magazines. The jamboree, however, had continued its loss pattern and would have to be retired. In its place, we would schedule the Cowboy Horse Races with a few promotional gimmicks, as part of the first Kerr Country Fair at Quiet Valley Ranch in 1979 on June 22-24.

It was strange to us that the events we put together to support the folk festival were either marginal or money losers, and in 1978, it was the folk festival that supported the season. Our decisions over the next few months were to drop the C&W Jamboree, add a fifth evening to the folk festival, and add a day to the bluegrass festival by opening a day earlier as we had been requested to do by so many bluegrass fans. The jubilee would remain a two-day event, and we would add a three-day country fair to the season on a Friday and Saturday and close early on Sunday so people could return home before dark.

We also had long talks with Buck White as we thought it a good idea for his career and for the festival to focus on him and his instrument, the mandolin, which was not being promoted by any of the bluegrass festivals across the U.S. We planned to establish the Buck White International Mandolin Championships in 1979 with the best mandolin players in the nation as judges. We would look for and reward excellence on the mandolin.

By now, we also took notice of the increasing response by the press. The story of our local and statewide support had caught the imagination of magazine, newspaper, and radio people all over the country, and our recognition by the press had brought Kerrville international acclaim as a music center. The local chamber of commerce credited us with bringing in more than 15,000 visitors to Kerrville, who spent more than a quarter-of-a-million dollars while they were here. Attendance, in fact, at all of our festivals over the first four years exceeded 60,000 who shared nearly two million dollars with our merchants. The state's leading magazine, *Texas Monthly*, described the Kerrville festivals as being "for those of us who prefer quality to quantity" and described the atmosphere as "friendly, family oriented and reverent."

Another plus for the Kerrville festivals was the growing interest, support, and endorsement by columnist Townsend Miller of the *Austin American-Statesman* and by the *Houston Post*'s Bob Claypool. They both gave Kerrville priority and plaudits every time the opportunity presented itself.

At the same time, the Austin music scene was thriving and our being a spin-off of that culture gave us a good base of support there. By the late 1970s the Austin clubs included Soap Creek Saloon, Steamboat Springs, Alliance Wagon Yard, the Filling Station, the Back Room, Boondocks, Bull Creek Inn, Rome Inn, and the Armadillo World

Introducing Townsend Miller to the crowd at the folk festival. 1978.

— Courtesy Brian Kanof.

Headquarters, in addition to the Broken Spoke, Split Rail, and country music venues like the Silver Dollar, the Lumberyard, the Skyline Club, and Dessau Hall.

The major downside in Austin was the end of the progressive country program format on KOKE in September of 1977. Music for music's sake gave way to a contemporary country music format.

But the upside locally and nationally was the continued momentum being gained by the "Austin City Limits" TV show on PBS since the airing of its B. W. Stevenson pilot in 1975 and the acceptance and growth from its first official season in 1976. While including commercial country music stars, Terry Likona, who assumed the directorship of the weekly PBS hour, included frequent Austin-styled artists and "folk" writers like Guy Clark and Townes Van Zandt. The show became an invaluable plus to broadening the public interest and favor for original music.

As the 1979 season approached, we were determined to use our best business sense as well as artistic sense to assure the continuance of our efforts, because we also knew it would be a long climb and would need continued loyal support.

With so many new local sponsors in Kerrville, and looking back on the successful special sponsor concert the previous March, we decided to schedule a January-March season of downtown auditorium shows to help us build closer relationships with our sponsors and with the townspeople in general. Since moving the festivals out to the ranch in 1974, we

had felt distanced in more ways than one from Kerrville itself.

All three auditorium shows consisted of a 2:00 P.M. matinee and 8:00 P.M. evening concert on Saturdays. The January 20th show featured the Lewis Family and our 1978 champions Cool Water Bluegrass; on February 24, Allen Damron and Buck White and the Down Home Folks; and on March 17, Nanci Griffith, Don Sanders, Peter Rowan, Southern Select, Lindsay Haisley, and Kerrville's first hometown New Folk winner, Louis Real and Cactus Rose. All three concerts were loaded with good music and good feelings, and it was a treat for us to be among so many of our performers in the "off months."

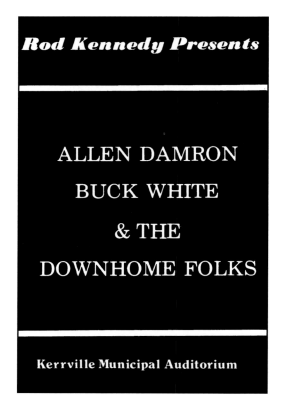

Rod Kennedy Presents

ALLEN DAMRON

BUCK WHITE

& THE

DOWNHOME FOLKS

Kerrville Municipal Auditorium

The 1979 outdoor season at the ranch began with the Eighth Kerrville Folk Festival, May 24-28, our first five-day festival, starting Thursday and running through Monday, Memorial Day. Having run the course of the yodeling contest (only two qualified competitors showed up in 1978), we decided to schedule a "Great Texas Harmonica Blow-Off." While the yodeling event did play out over time, we did gain some national interest for yodeling and met some intriguing performers we might never have met otherwise, including both Patsy Montana and Montana Slim. Bill Staines from

New Hampshire also would be with us for many years to come.

We were very upbeat and optimistic as we approached our eighth season. The *Houston Post* wrote that the festival "created a rich tapestry that entranced us all with scores of memorable moments." Townsend Miller of the *Austin American-Statesman* told his readers, "You simply don't know how much pleasure you're missing" and called the festival "rare out of town entertainment" where audiences are "the most attentive and appreciative fans anywhere." The *Dallas Morning News* said you could go to Kerrville and be "entertained by some of the best 'live' music

Uncle Walt's Band in reunion. From left: David Ball, Walter Hyatt, Champ Hood. 1979.
— Courtesy *Austin American-Statesman.*

Gibson and Camp in reunion at Kerrville. 1979.
— Courtesy *Kerrville Daily Times.*

in America." We also had extensive coverage in Germany and Japan, and we felt good about it all!

The festival had grown from three days in 1972 and 1973 to four days in 1975, and now in 1979, we added a fifth day, allowing us to present another whole evening concert line-up. Newcomers included Hamilton Camp in reunion with Bob Gibson, Louis Real of Kerrville and his band Cactus Rose, Dana Cooper teaming with Shake Russell in the Shake Russell-Dana Cooper Band, Nanci Griffith in her own main stage set for the first time, plus an afternoon reunion of Uncle Walt's Band: Walter Hyatt, David Ball, and Champ Hood. French guitarist and songwriter Pierre Bensusan made his impressive Kerrville debut singing his own lyrics to 400-year-old French folk melodies, and Jimmy Driftwood came to host a workshop as well as play the main stage, teaching us how to play music on a leaf! Gary P. Nunn was there with the Lost Gonzo Band. While Peter Yarrow could not be with us, both Tom Paxton and David Amram did a good job of representing the New York area. The Singing

Christians were back as the Mercy River Boys, and the festival was loaded with great songwriters like Guy Clark, Ray Wylie Hubbard, Willis Alan Ramsey (who wrote "Muskrat Love"), Steve Young, Billy Joe Shaver, Fromholz, Butch Hancock, and Townes Van Zandt.

Backstage on the second night of the festival, while Jimmy Driftwood was on stage, I just hap-

French guitarist Pierre Bensusan. 1979.
— Courtesy *Steven's Stills.*

Bobby Bridger, whose song "Heal in the Wisdom" became the anthem of the Kerrville Folk Festival. 1979.
— Courtesy Brian Kanof.

pened to hear Bobby Bridger singing a new song for John Inmon. He was showing Inmon how it went. I asked Bobby who wrote it because both the melody and the lyrics moved me. He said, "I did." I said, "I think I'd like that song to be our festival anthem." Bobby, who had written the song in memory of two close friends who had died recently, said, "Well, we're going to try it out on the crowd in my set tonight, so let me know if you still want it, and I'd be honored if you do." The song, "Heal in the Wisdom," was greeted with such wild enthusiasm by the crowd that it has been our festival anthem ever since! The date of this inauguration was Friday, May 25, 1979, and the song with its universal themes reflecting exactly how I believed we should feel about each other, became our anthem that night.

Judging New Folk at the Arts and Crafts Fair were Milton Carroll, Peter Rowan, and B. W. Stevenson. The winners were Jon Ims from Denver, Tish Hinojosa from San Antonio, Bill Oliver of Austin, Joseph Brunelle from Midland, and Cordy Lavery and John Paul Walters of Austin and San Antonio, respectively. Roger Crabtree and Butch

Heal In The Wisdom ─────

words and music by Bobby Bridger

MUSIC FROM

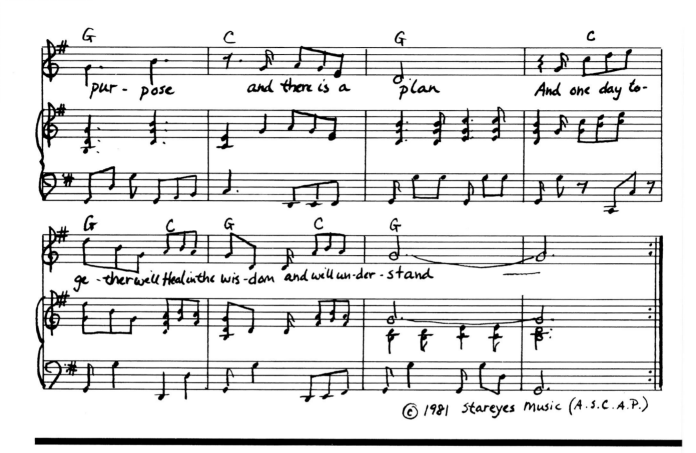

pur - pose and there is a plan And one day to-

ge -ther we'll Heal in the wis-dom and will un-der-stand

© 1981 Stareyes Music (A.S.C.A.P.)

HEAL IN THE WISDOM
By Bobby Bridger © 1981 Stareyes Music (ASCAP) used by permission

I know a man who had it all for a while
He was smart, rich and handsome
With a beautiful smile
Everybody that met him felt nothing to hide
But while still a young man
With so much ahead, he just lay down and he died
He sang

CHORUS
There is a reason, there is a rhyme
There is a season, there is a time
There is a purpose and there is a plan
And one day together we'll heal in the wisdom
And we'll understand.
Yes, one day together we'll heal in the wisdom
And we'll understand

And I knew a woman with nothing at all,
With no one to catch her she had a sad fall.
But while on the bottom she learned how to see.
And today she is flying and teaching her brothers that
they can be free
She sings

CHORUS

And I knew a country with visions that dreamed
all the people were equal or so it all seemed.
But gaining oneness with our fellow man
is so useless not knowing the spirit of oneness
we share with the land.
She sings

CHORUS

And I know a people beginning to learn
it all moves together the wheel always turns.
And we must act swiftly but carefully too.
And if we are honest and learn to believe
we just might continue
To sing

CHORUS

Hancock judged the harmonica contest and gave Austin jeweler Steve Kriechbaum the first prize.

Another special moment at the festival was the Antler Dave Memorial Run in memory of Antler Dave, one of our best-loved volunteer staff who met his death in a tragic automobile accident earlier in the month, and, incidentally, one of the two friends for whom Bridger had written "Heal in the Wisdom." Bridger was joined by Gary P. Nunn in leading the run. A small entry fee for each runner was sent to Dave's family with love from the participants.

Rusty Wier closed the festival to a standing ovation and cheers for encores on Sunday night. It was an eventful festival, our luck was running, and we had only one problem: the campgrounds were getting too full!

Billy Joe Shaver. 1979.
— Courtesy Rod McKeown.

With the C&W Jamboree a thing of the past, we were excited about launching our first Kerr Country Fair four weeks away on June 22-24. We had the kind of entertainment ideal for a family gathering, including favorites from our other festivals such as Allen Damron, who had played all three of my other festivals, five performers from the bluegrass festival including Oklahoma's Bill Grant and Delia Bell, Grassfire, and the Sullivan Family; several performers from the C&W Jamboree including Fiddling Frenchie Burke, and some special artists like Lonnie Glosson and his talking harmonica, and "A Tribute to Hank Williams" by the Original Drifting Cowboys, plus a comedy duo called The Mayor and Buford.

We also had 4H youth exhibits, Kerr County Extension Homemakers adult exhibits with blue ribbon items being auctioned to the highest bidders, a young winners fashion show, a tail-waggin' doggie show, a petting zoo, a "Purtiest Pick-Up Truck Contest," a mini-marathon endurance race for runners called "Kerrville Hills Ten-Miler" and a big trail ride of horses, riders, and wagons which joined up as part of the festival's Country Western Days Parade in downtown Kerrville.

Other special events were the Mr. Pibb Championship Mule Races, Coca-Cola Cowboy Horse Races with a "match race of the century" when I raced my Buckskin mare, Jessie, against a motorcycle that took off and left her in its dust doing a wheelie down the track!

We also had Crouch & Son's Carnival and Midway, the mounted horse platoon from the First Cavalry Division at Fort Hood to ride in the parade and put on their close-order drill, and the spectacular Santa Rosa Palomino Club, two-time national champion mounted team from Vernon, Texas. In addition, there was Joe Bowman, the "Fastest Gun in the West," and young magician Jules Caplan. The crowd was swelled by the Roadrunners Motorcycle Rally, a big camp-out at our fair for family riders.

In addition to the top-flight entertainment, especially the fiddlers, one of the most popular events at the fair was the full schedule of horse-drawn wagon rides in an authentic old wagon from the famous Y.O. Ranch.

We had a real country fair, and it was rewarding

Jessie is outclassed by the motorcycle way out front doing a wheelie. Best two out of three?
— Courtesy Bill Lee.

to see the faces of both the kids and the adults who won ribbons in dozens of categories and then took home cold cash when their prize-winning items were bought by one of the many business leaders who attended the auction.

Everyone involved wanted to get started right away on the 1980 fair!

The only part we didn't enjoy was cleaning up the ranch after the carnival left so we could put our Longhorns back out to pasture!

A month and a couple of days ahead of us was our third annual Gospel Jubilee, three days, July 27-29. We began again at the courthouse square with the Masters Four and five showcase groups playing a free show for all comers. After extending an invitation for those gathered to join us out at the ranch, we headed out there to get the jubilee under way.

Allen Damron and Vikki joined us along with Buck White and the Down Home Folks, the Wills Family, the Galileans, the Kerrville Community Chorus, Mid-South Boys, Mercy River Boys, and Wendy Bagwell and the Sunliners.

As before, the Brush Arbor on Chapel Hill was a popular event on Sunday morning. Even though our roster of Christian artists included some of the best traditional and contemporary gospel groups in the nation, the event wasn't really growing, even after three years. Some of the fans who were disappointed to know that we would not carry on in 1980 suggested that we probably should not have mixed

traditional and contemporary gospel artists on the same event because they thought the two types of music appealed to two entirely different audiences. Now they tell us!

It could have also been that the storms that caused $750 million worth of damage around the state kept a few people from attending.

It was just thirty-one days until our expanded four-day sixth annual bluegrass festival with its new and highly promoted Buck White International Mandolin Championship, that was attracting some fantastic players from all over the U.S.

The main stage artists were Country Gazette, the Down Home Folks, Jethro Burns, Shoji Tabuchi, McLain Family, Jim and Jesse and the Virginia Boys, the Lewis Family, and Peter Rowan.

This was the first time Jim and Jesse had seen our matched buckskin horses, Jim and Jessie, which had been named for them. Nancylee and I had eleven parades on our schedule with the horses during 1979. The two brothers were probably the two most polite, soft-spoken, and undemanding performers in the music business. They were pleased but a little embarrassed to be made such a fuss over. During a break, we had each of them climb into the saddle of their namesake so we could get some publicity photos. We would have had a perfect photo of them on our horses except that Little Roy Lewis slapped Jim's horse on the hindquarters and frightened Jesse's horse into running away with Jim flying in unwilling pursuit. Both the horses and their equally startled riders really took off with the once-proud faux-equestrians holding on for dear life until we could catch them and pry their fingers from the saddlehorns. But, then, we could write a whole book about Little Roy's pranks.

Regional bands on the festival included the Cypress Swamp Stompers, Pickin' Tymes, Poverty Playboys, Cool Water Bluegrass, Shady Grove Ramblers, the House Brothers, and Southern Select.

The bluegrass band contest was joined this year by a Southwestern Banjo Championship. Our new mandolin champion was Dave Harvey from Colorado, competing against entrants from Texas, Oklahoma, North Carolina, California, New York, and Tokyo, Japan. Brad Brashers won the banjo contest and San Antonio's Half Grass walked off with the band championship title.

Everything seemed to be working with lots of good music, jam sessions, and a large, happy audience looking forward to next year. We also received warm response to having added an additional day this year.

At the urging of our folk performers, we had been working on a benefit concert for Saturday, September 29, to raise some cash flow. We were pleased with the idea and called it the "12 Great Hours at Kerrville." The lineup started at 2:00 P.M. with Kenneth Threadgill, Bobby Bridger, Mother of Pearl, B. W. Stevenson, Robert Shaw, Kurt Van Sickle, and Applejack from El Paso.

Following the second annual Worst Hat Contest (I never could figure out how the way you walked, danced, wiggled, moseyed or oozed your way across the stage could possibly change the number of points won or lost by your hat!), it was back to music by Milton Carroll, Don Sanders, Uncle Walt's Band, John Vandiver, Tish Hinojosa, Gary P. Nunn, and Allen Damron. Additionally, Tim Henderson and Lindsay Haisley showed up to play.

Obviously a great day and a profitable one! Many of us would be back together the next month for our first Kerrville on-the-road tour together.

With a road-show roster that listed Bobby Bridger, Milton Carroll, Allen Damron, Steve Fromholz, Bill and Bonnie Hearne, Carolyn Hester, Gary P. Nunn, Don Sanders, Kenneth Threadgill, and John Vandiver, we had a pretty good representation of what the festival was all about. And B. W.

Stevenson would join us on the final concert of the tour.

We boarded our bus in Austin at the Villa Capri Motel at 9:00 A.M. to head for East Texas State University at Commerce and a 3:00 P.M. sound check and an 8:00 P.M. performance. Then we stayed overnight at the University Inn before heading on down to Houston Thursday to play the first two of four shows at Rockefellers, arguably the state's finest showcase club. We played to sold-out houses of over 400 at 7:00 and 10:30 P.M. both nights and all had a great time while earning excellent reviews. On Saturday morning, it was on to Temple to play the Temple Cultural Activities Center at 3:00 P.M outdoors and 7:30 P.M. indoors in their beautiful concert hall.

Kenneth Threadgill and Carolyn Hester visit on the bus during our 1979 Kerrville-on-the-road tour.
— Courtesy Brian Kanof.

It was an unsurpassed and fulfilling experience to be with each other for four full days, sharing news, learning about one another, enjoying informal jam sessions and song-sharing on the bus and, most of all, everyone was impressed and moved by everyone else's fifteen-minute performances. It was a rare and nourishing treat to share the stage with everyone else and rediscover why each performer was so popular. Our new anthem closed every performance and even that ceremony brought us closer together. The enriching celebration happened seven times in four days, and by the time we boarded the bus to leave Temple, we were welded into a highly euphoric state of camaraderie!

We headed for Austin seventy miles away, and the Villa Capri Motel, where our caterer Jimmy Mosley awaited us with omelets and an open bar for

Stopping to eat on the road, Fromholz explains while Carolyn and I listen. 1979.

— Courtesy Brian Kanof.

fifty people, including Townsend Miller, Pat Taggart, John Bustin, Darrell Royal, and a number of guests of the touring performers. It was a great farewell party after seven concerts together, and those who lived in Austin headed for home while the rest of us fell into our beds at the Villa Capri.

We learned that we could all work together on the road and that the diminutive Don Sanders made a great road manager. The bus was definitely the way to go with fifteen performers, road manager, road crew, photographer, and myself as producer-paymaster-emcee. The tour was good public relations and introduced the festival to thousands of people through the press, radio, and television, and played to near-capacity crowds everywhere. It was a good experience for all of us and a memorable way to close out the 1979 season.

Singing the anthem at one of our four sold-out shows at Houston's showcase club Rockefellers on our road tour. From left: Rod Kennedy, Don Sanders, Steven Fromholz, Carolyn Hester, Bobby Bridger, John Vandiver, Gary P. Nunn, Allen Damron, Bill Hearne, Robert Shaw, Milton Carroll. Partially hidden sitting at the piano is Bonnie Hearne. Missing is Kenneth Threadgill. B. W. Stevenson joined us later on the tour at the Temple Cultural Arts Center on the last night. 1979.

— Courtesy Brian Kanof.

Since Van Cliburn introduced me backstage to his young pianist friend, Dickran Atamian, Atamian and I had become good friends, and I had spent some time helping him with his Four Seasons Music Festival in Austin. Many of my friends were also working on the festival, so it was fun and a break from life at the ranch. Dan Strait, of Strait Music Company, was a top officer of Atamian's board of directors.

Nicknamed "Richie," Atamian was of Armenian descent. He had studied at The University of Texas under John Perry, and later under Jorge Bolet. In 1975 Atamian had won the fifth anniversary Naumburg Piano Competition, followed by recitals across the U.S., Mexico, and the Soviet Union. He also played the only solo recital at the Library of Congress in 1977 during the Gala Presidential Inaugural Week Concerts, and later made a triumphant debut at Chicago's Orchestra Hall. His 1978 performance of Prokofiev's Third Piano Concerto with Lorin Maazel and the Cleveland Orchestra was heard on sixty-two radio stations across the U.S., Canada, and Europe. His Russian tour took him to Moscow, Leningrad, and to Yerivan in Armenia.

Now, after months of concentrated study, practice, and rehearsal, Atamian was ready to play the world premiere of Sam Raphling's virtuosic transcription of Stravinsky's "Rite of Spring" at Carnegie Hall, and Richie wanted me to go with him. So, November 12 found me in New York for the premiere and the parties.

As luck would have it, I rode to Carnegie Hall in the same taxi as the national community relations officer of Baldwin Piano Company and on the way I told him about our festivals at Kerrville. I told him of our big new market and our desire to be an official Baldwin festival. He said he could arrange for us to have a new piano at every festival and that he'd like to have us represent Baldwin. We shook hands on it in the taxi and then entered Carnegie Hall for Atamian's recital.

The gloriously beautiful hall was packed, every balcony, to the ceiling. Atamian's performance was brilliant, sensitive, inventive, and fiercely dramatic. His sensational debut was greeted by wild enthusiasm and a rousing standing ovation. We returned to Texas celebrating his dazzling performance and looking forward to the time when Atamian might be signed by a major label to record "The Rite of Spring." Surely, there was no one else in the world who could play like this!

During the holidays, when he returned from his Russian tour, Atamian and I completed arrangements for him to appear in recital playing the Stravinsky at Kerrville's Municipal Auditorium on January 12 for the first performance in America outside Carnegie Hall!

The idea of taping the work for PBS had been on Atamian's agenda for several months, and when we showed the directors the ideal setting provided by the Kerrville auditorium, they quickly gave our proposal serious consideration. The auditorium had hundreds of seats on a slanted floor rising above a smooth flat area that ran all the way from the front of the stage to about the middle of the hall. In other words, the front half of the building was flat for setting up chairs, or tables, or exhibit booths. It was smooth, seamless concrete. We suggested putting Atamian and his Baldwin concert grand in the middle of this flat area where the cameras were free to smoothly dolly all around him. The directors loved it, and with sold-out seating to shoot into and around, the show was superb. Atamian's stalwart performance had listeners and reviewers sitting on the edges of their seats, and spontaneous shouts and thunderous applause from a standing-room-only crowd made Atamian's enormous performance even more dramatic. After the stunning concert, we all adjourned to Fara's Italian Restaurant for a gala dinner party. Even after two premiere performances of the work, I was still stunned by Atamian's virtuosic performing abilities and how well the "Rite" worked for solo piano.

So 1980 began in Kerrville in a pretty spectacular manner, and Atamian and I spoke often in the coming months about what else we might do together.

On Saturday, January 19, one week after Atamian's classical concert, we had a pair of Sponsor Association concerts by quite another piano player at the same auditorium. This time we set up the flat floor area with tables and chairs for cabaret-seating for ragtime champion Terry Waldo, returning to Kerrville following well-received appearances at both the ragtime festival and the folk festival.

Since he had left Kerrville after his last appearance, Waldo had recorded a number of solo, duet, and band albums and had appeared in an extended ragtime piano series for National Public Radio. He had also written a Broadway show about the life and times of Harding, called *Warren G*, had appeared with three symphony orchestras, and had made TV

Tish Hinojosa. 1980.
— Courtesy Brian Kanof.

appearances in New York, New Orleans, St. Louis, and San Francisco.

With eleven albums to his credit, Terry Waldo drew a good crowd and both dazzled and charmed his audiences with classic rags, stride piano, blues, jazz, and novelty tunes from the turn of the century. His wry sense of humor and the cabaret seating were both a big hit.

On Sunday, January 27, we were back in the auditorium for a 3:00 P.M. concert by Kentucky's McLain Family Band as a benefit to help fund the Kerrville Music Foundation sponsored competitions at the 1980 bluegrass festival. This seed money, the entry fees, a few donations, and the raffling of a mandolin during the summer would fund the three competitions for band, banjo, and mandolin. The appearance by the McLains was, as always, cheerful and entertaining.

In February, in the middle of our campaign to renew our sponsorships for 1980, we scheduled a pair of Sponsors Association concerts at the Kerrville Auditorium on Saturday, February 23, starring old-timer Lonnie Glosson and his talking harmonica, Tom Uhr and his Shady Grove Ramblers from Dallas, and the popular Southern Gospel Quartet from the Grapevine Opry, the Masters Four. It was an entertaining mixture of music and the perfect family show. The large audiences went home happy after receiving encores from all three artists, and many fans attended both concerts.

Then on Saturday, March 22, under the format already provided by previous Sponsors Association concerts, we presented a pair of concerts hosting the afternoon preliminaries and the evening finals of our Kerr Country Fair Queen's Contest. We gathered a stellar cast of stars, including the humorous and attractive illusionist, Harry Anderson, one of the nation's finest young magicians who had come up the ranks by performing on the Drag near The University of Texas as a street performer. Harry emceed the Queen's contest and was amusing and tricky, while spectacular Japanese fiddler Shoji Tabuchi performed, backed by Grassfire, and the blind duo of Bill and Bonnie Hearne had the house jumping. The winner of the competition was Queen Nancy Graham who would preside over the Kerr Country Fair at Quiet Valley Ranch on June 20-22.

Since early in December, I had been meeting with a number of area people called together by Charlie Schreiner III to help plan the Y.O. Ranch Centennial on April 12. There were many long planning sessions at the big ranch at Mountain Home about forty miles from Kerrville. And while they were often intensive work sessions, they were also congenial gatherings of people who wanted to help the Schreiners throw the greatest party of the century. We were coordinating and trying to keep up with the commemorative bronzes by Clay Dahlberg, the 200 limited edition Colt Six-Shooters, the Y.O. history book, the wild game menu and beverages for six or seven bars, the huge rental tents, the music and entertainment, the publicity, and the invitations, among the other myriad details for the huge celebration.

The ranch had become known for carrying on the tradition of ranching in Texas since 1880 and for helping to re-establish the heritage of Longhorn cattle. Charlie Schreiner had also devoted himself to putting together one of the largest collections of memorabilia of the Old West, while also being in the forefront of the preservation of wildlife, so it wasn't surprising that there were resolutions honoring the centennial from Kerrville, Kerr County, San Antonio, and the State of Texas.

It was one heck of a party on April 12, in spite of freezing, rainy weather which saw heaters in every tent blazing away in an attempt to overcome the whistling cold. There were sweaters under every tuxedo and long johns slipping down under elegant party gowns. There was also more than one pair of silver slippers or high-heeled shoes lost in the cold, deep mud.

Further than this chilling celebration, the Y.O.

also held a huge three-day Centennial Trail Drive with a gigantic barbecue, costume party, chuck wagon breakfasts, another barbecue, fiddling, dancing, and sleeping out under the stars in bed rolls between two days of driving unwilling Longhorns across vast expanses, up and down ravines, and through streams and gullies for many rugged miles of the Y.O. countryside. For Nancylee, me, and our horses, it was a considerable change from the fifty acres of Quiet Valley Ranch. The Schreiner family had come to earn the reputation of being some of the best hosts in the Southwest, and it took Charlie and all four of his sons, dozens of cowhands and 100 assorted volunteers to pull this one off! It was an incredible experience, and I still keep my Y.O. commemorative bronze on my desk at the office.

Then we had to come back to reality and the continuing preparations for our ninth annual Kerrville Folk Festival, May 22-26, being promoted as "5 Great Days in May." This one turned out to be the largest festival yet, with the attendance climbing to 13,000 for the long weekend.

In addition to the usual audio recording by Pedro Gutierrez, three separate television camera crews showed up. We dedicated the festival to barrel house pianist Robert Shaw, who had played all eight of the previous folk festivals and opened the big Saturday night concert. He also hosted a 1:00 P.M. "Blues for Robert" special event — we thought it might be appropriate to honor him while he was still with us! The Ballad Trees were held the first

four days, and as a special 5:30 warm-up we had Austin's Eaglebone Whistle perform. This quintet of Graham Hall (*banjo, fiddle, vocals*), Jane Gillman (*guitar, harmonica, vocals*), Greg Raskin (*mandolin, hammered dulcimer, vocals*), Stephanie Beardsley (*bass, vocals*), and John Hagen (*cello, vocals*) exuberantly played a mixed bag of music from Ireland, originals by Graham and Jane, bluegrass tunes, and Bob Wills favorites, creating the ambiance I was looking for. The Whistle opened all of the concerts on a "high note," if you'll excuse the expression, getting the audiences all revved up. The band built quite a following over those four days!

Two San Antonio writer-performers with an interest in children had persuaded me to allow them to produce an hour-long "Singing Circus" for kids on the middle three days of the festival, and they and their fellow performers entertained hundreds of kids at their own big tent down near the Council Tree.

Bob Gibson was back again, joined by Guy Clark and ragtime pianist Terry Waldo in judging the New Folk competition that was still held at the Texas State Arts and Crafts Fair. I had narrowed the field to forty finalists out of the 130 entries, and those winning the $50 awards were David Halley of Lubbock, Jan Marra from Minneapolis, Allen Ross from Dallas, San Antonio's Dow Patterson, Iris Harrell of Dallas, and Lizabeth Williams of Georgetown, Texas. Other outstanding finalists

Eaglebone Whistle. From left: Jane Gillman, Greg Raskin, Graham Hall, Stephanie Beardsley, and John Hagen. 1980.

— Courtesy Brenda Ladd.

Steven Fromholz (left) sits in with B. W. Stevenson and his youngster, singing "On My Own" ("Feel like a baby boy just bein' born . . .") 1980.

— Courtesy Brian Kanof.

Bob Gibson, who wrote "Well Well Well" recorded by Peter Paul and Mary. 1980.

— Courtesy Brian Kanof.

included Sid Hausman, Tesuque, NM, Lyle Lovett, College Station, and James Durst, Northland, Illinois. The six top-ranked contestants sang a special Award Winners Concert at the fair on Memorial Day.

Among other special moments were the appearances of Tish Hinojosa, Lucinda Williams, Willis Alan Ramsey, Spider John Koerner (who continued to celebrate in Austin for two weeks), B. W. Stevenson, Guy Clark, Uncle Walt's Band, the second-year appearance by Peter Rowan, and Jon Emery and Leroy Preston's Whiskey Drinkin' Music. Of course, by now priceless performances by our regulars were to be expected and enjoyed. Back home were Butch Hancock, John Vandiver, David Amram, Allen Damron, Gary P. Nunn, Townes Van Zandt, Milton Carroll, Bobby Bridger, Bill and Bonnie Hearne, Kenneth Threadgill, and Carolyn Hester, just to mention a few. Arkansas veteran Jimmy Driftwood and our "poet lariat" Charles John Quarto contributed their own uniqueness to the mix, including a special hour with Quarto at the Ballad Tree on Memorial Day. In addition, the Shake Russell-Dana Cooper Band was back, rekindling the

Nanci Griffith at Kerrville. 1980.
— Courtesy Brian Kanof.

same lyric and melodic excitement as we experienced when they first appeared together at the festival in 1979. This year Nanci Griffith had her own main-stage set accompanied by Eric Taylor and John Hagen of Eaglebone Whistle.

American-Statesman columnist John T. Davis remembered Joe Ely's appearance so vividly that he wrote me this description of it sixteen years after it happened:

> . . . the storm that swept over Quiet Valley Ranch in 1980 was something else — the full panoply of wind, lightning, rain, and thunder that lets you know God is still alive and kicking. And maybe just a little pissed off.
>
> The tempest blew up so suddenly, in the midst of Joe Ely's set. One minute, Ely was singing about West Texas waltzes and high-balling freight trains, and the next it was dead-solid Wizard of Oz howling winds, rain that blew in sideways, and darkness on the face of the earth.
>
> A tremendous bolt of lightning and accompanying cannonade of thunder blew the Kerrville Folk Festival and most of Kerr County off the grid. All that was left functioning on stage was one monitor speaker and Joe's guitar amp.
>
> Ely didn't give an inch. He grabbed the live microphone as sheets of rain blew over him, and in a moment of lunatic Texan bravado, he leaned forward over the lip of the stage and launched into a driving version of Buddy Holly's "Not Fade Away." The storm howled at him, and Ely howled right back. It was one of those moments when everything hung in the balance and anything could happen.
>
> Ely is still among the living, and the

Festival has weathered many storms since. But never again have I seen life and death, and art and magic, dance for a moment on that stage.

Once more, Bobby Bridger covered many bases for us, including a Ballad Tree, heading up the annual Antler Dave Memorial Run, and leading the joyous crowd in our new anthem, his own "Heal in the Wisdom."

The second annual "Great Texas Harmonica Blow-Off!" drew a good crowd with 1979 winner Steve Kriechbaum judging with Lonnie Glosson, and providing a hand-tooled sterling silver-jeweled harmonica for the winner along with the $100 in silver coins.

Lonnie Glosson, it should be said, was born in 1908 (the same year as pianist Robert Shaw), was a star of the WLS National Barndance by 1930 and appeared on all of the radio networks from Renfro Valley and "The Red Foley Show." Teamed with Wayne Rainey, he was heard on over 200 radio stations in the U.S., Canada, and Mexico. His harmonica playing on "I Want My Mama," "Fox Chase," and "Train and Model T Race" are American classics. The 1980 harmonica champion who took home the $100 and the custom harmonica was Paul Orta, very much a blues player!

Even with the expanded five-day format, it looked as though we'd have to add a second weekend if we were going to spread the crowd out and preserve the ambiance of the festival. Next year would be our tenth anniversary and a good time to expand to a two-weekend schedule, since we could reasonably expect even more publicity and more growth due to that anniversary.

Our Country Fair, which became the first official county fair, headed by John Jensen, was four weeks ahead of us as the last car and trailer and motorhome pulled out of the campground. Because of their great popularity with the crowds, we had expanded the number of fiddle players to include Byron Berline and Buddy Spicher in the lineup, which already listed Fiddling Frenchie Burke and Shoji Tabuchi. Leon "Pappy" Self was back, as were the comedy team of The Mayor and Buford. Slight of hand whiz Harry Anderson, who had done such a good job of hosting the queen's preliminaries the previous winter, was scheduled to return, and we added master mime and juggler Turk Pipkin, the popular duo of Bill and Bonnie Hearne, Applejack from El Paso, the Mid-South Boys, and the appealing "Classical Gas" composer, Mason Williams.

The last year's Purtiest Pick-Up Truck Contest was joined by the Ugliest Pick-Up Truck Contest, Country Western Days Parade, the Trail Ride, and the Road Runners Motorcycle Rally. Now that I was an active member of the Texas Longhorn Breeders Association with my herd of three, I added a Texas Longhorn Steer Show of prized animals from ranches all over Texas. Inside the theater area, the arts and crafts booths were active and the special exhibits area was larger.

While the music was great and all of the events were attended by larger numbers of people, somehow our highly promoted Coca-Cola Cowboy Horse Races, Mule Jumping Championships, and Mr. Pibb Mule Races did not draw the size crowds required to make our investment worthwhile. We had talked about moving the fair into town, now that it was up and running, and converting it into a real county fair. The 4H and county agent people were optimistic and thought that, with our help, a move would be good for 1981.

Since there was low cash flow from the country fair, we were eagerly anticipating the third annual 12 Great Hours at Kerrville on the calendar for July 26. We had already advertised Allen Damron, Don Sanders, Robert Shaw, Doak Snead, B. W. Stevenson, Uncle Walt's Band, John Vandiver, and Kurt Van Sickle, and were now able to add Gary P. Nunn, Eaglebone Whistle, Lindsay Haisley, Dan McCrimmen, and the Marcia Ball Band!

The third almost-annual Worst Hat Contest was, again, a humorous interlude in the 2:00 P.M. to 2:00 A.M. schedule of exceptionally appealing music.

The attendance and the number of campfires in the camping area were encouraging. When it was over, there was some money raised to ease the tight budget still suffering from three years of rain and the four C&W Jamborees.

The seventh annual Kerrville Bluegrass Festival would be highlighted by some of America's greatest artists in acoustic music, including mandolin ace David Grissman, who, with Doyle Lawson and Sam Bush, would judge the Buck White International Mandolin Championship, while concert crowds would be entertained by "Gentle On My Mind" writer John Hartford, one of America's leading contemporary bluegrass groups, the incredible New Grass Revival, the fun-loving Larkin Brothers from Church Hill, Tennessee, national autoharp star

Bryan Bowers of Seattle, and the Sullivan Family, moved over from the Gospel Jubilee.

Shoji Tabuchi played opening night to the expected cheers of the crowd, and Peter Rowan proved again his popularity the first two nights. Joining in on the festival were opening act Kerrville's Poverty Playboys, Larry Sparks and the Lonesome Ramblers, the Pinnacle Boys with their twin fiddles, Mac Wiseman, the McLain Family Band, Bill Grant and Delia Bell, with Johnny Martin and the Bluegrass Ramblers. Topping off the list were Buck White and the Down Home Folks with Ricky Skaggs and Jerry Douglas, our 1979 mandolin champion David Harvey with his band from Colorado, and Doyle Lawson and his new band, Quicksilver. Also on the boards were Grassfire, House Brothers, Pickin' Tymes, and the Shady Grove Ramblers, who in addition to performing Tom Uhr's original songs, were becoming known for recreating the harmonic standards of the Sons of the Pioneers.

The music was some of the most rewarding in the history of the festival, and the 1980 mandolin champion was Bobby Clark of Oklahoma, who had led the Bluegrass Revue at our 1975 folk festival, so there were many people pleased with that outcome.

The crowd was big, but the stellar lineup was expensive and, unbelievably, we again came within a few dollars of breaking even. It was becoming easy to say, "We don't produce bluegrass for the money!"

We participated on October 19 in an Austin Street Dance for the non-profit Gaslight Theater which starred Beto y los Fairlanes and Marcia Ball, among others. It was held in the old warehouse district. The night before, Uncle Walt's Band played the first concert at the newly restored Paramount Theater with John Vandiver as special guest.

The club scene was busy that weekend with Joe Ely and Gary P. Nunn at Third Coast, Van Wilks at the Armadillo (Peter Rowan and Flaco had been there Friday night), Alvin Crow with Lou Ann and the Flip Tops at Soap Creek Saloon, Extreme Heat at Steamboat Springs, Stevie Vaughan and Double Trouble at the Bottom Line, and Red Steagall at the Silver Dollar South. In spite of all the apparent competition, the street dance still drew a big crowd. Austin had become known by now for having music everywhere.

While we assisted in producing the street dance, our minds were really on the upcoming Kerrville Music Foundation tour to Hendricks River Ranch for Children north of Abilene, West Texas State University near Amarillo, then back to Austin for Halloween night, followed the next day by two concerts at Armadillo World Headquarters. By this time, we had already committed to expanding next year's tenth anniversary festival to eight days, so I had called a staff meeting at Symphony Square on Sunday to talk about it.

The bus tour to the Texas Panhandle included 1972 original performers Allen Damron, Steven Fromholz, Bill and Bonnie Hearne, Carolyn Hester, Robert Shaw, and Kenneth Threadgill. In addition, the tour starred Bobby Bridger, composer of "Heal in the Wisdom"; Gary P. Nunn, the former leader of the Lost Gonzo Band and composer of "Austin City Limits'" theme song "London Homesick Blues" ("I wanna go home with the Armadillo. . ."); Don Sanders, who by now had earned the title "Dean of Houston folk music"; B. W. Stevenson, now with nine LPs on national labels to his credit; bluesy John Vandiver of Houston; and special guest twelve-string guitarist Bob Gibson of Chicago, who had earned fame at Newport (where he first introduced Joan Baez) and who co-wrote "Abilene"

(though he had never been there) and "Well Well Well" for Peter Paul and Mary.

Again the road trip was great fun, and being able to cap it off with the double benefit concert at the Armadillo put the frosting on the cake. Joining our group for the Armadillo concerts starting at 2:00 and 8:00 P.M. were David Amram, the Shake Russell-Dana Cooper Band, Eaglebone Whistle, Nanci Griffith, Lindsay Haisley, Butch Hancock, mime Turk Pipkin, and Doak Snead.

The three-hour afternoon concert featured Bobby Bridger's "Seekers of the Fleece," Allen Damron's "Tribute to Hondo Crouch," an Amram Jam with Gary P., Haisley, Eaglebone, and the New Austin Cuban Refugee Jazz Band, guided by Pedro Gutierrez!

Even though seating was limited to about 1,500, we raised over $7,500 and had a terrific time performing together in the biggest off-ranch concerts we'd done to date. The anthem was now firmly in place, and if we didn't close a road show concert with it, the audience started singing it to us. We had become a very close family!

KERRVILLE FOLK FESTIVAL

SATURDAY, NOVEMBER 1, 1980
ARMADILLO WORLD HEADQUARTERS
AUSTIN, TEXAS

BENEFIT CONCERT

SHAKE RUSSELL — DANA COOPER BAND

DAVID AMRAM	CAROLYN HESTER
BOBBY BRIDGER	JOHN VANDIVER
ALLEN DAMRON	GARY P. NUNN
EAGLEBONE WHISTLE	TURK PIPKIN
STEVEN FROMHOLZ	DON SANDERS
BOB GIBSON	DOAK SNEAD
NANCI GRIFFITH	ROBERT SHAW
LINDSAY HAISLEY	B. W. STEVENSON
BUTCH HANCOCK	KENNETH THREADGILL
BILL & BONNIE HEARNE	SURPRISE GUESTS!

2 P.M. EVENT $3.50
8 P.M. CONCERT $7.50
ATTEND 2 P.M. EVENT FREE WHEN YOU
MAIL ORDER EVENING
CONCERT TICKETS!
• LIMITED NUMBER OF TICKETS ONLY •

223

While we were already working on the 1981 tenth anniversary season of both classical and folk/bluegrass events, we still had to finish out the season in Kerrville with the third annual pair of performances of *The Nutcracker* at Kerrville Municipal Auditorium by the sixty-member Austin Civic Ballet. It was a lavish production with a number of Kerrville children selected by Nursel Conrad to be pages.

Co-sponsored by the *Kerrville Daily Times* and the Kerrville Music Foundation on December 14 and 15, the performances on Saturday night and Sunday afternoon were again sell-outs, with hun-

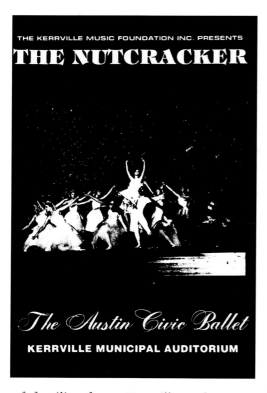

THE KERRVILLE MUSIC FOUNDATION INC. PRESENTS
THE NUTCRACKER

The Austin Civic Ballet

KERRVILLE MUNICIPAL AUDITORIUM

dreds of families from Kerrville and surrounding towns in attendance. The sound system made the stereophonically recorded music seem just like a live orchestra in the pit. Pedro Gutierrez was on hand to supervise the sound reproduction. With the extensive auditorium improvements and additional lighting undertaken by the city of Kerrville, the performances had the advantage of all of the theatrical technology of a major theater.

As many times as I had seen *The Nutcracker* performed by Austin's civic company, I never tired of its flow and beauty.

Our tenth anniversary year was going to be one banner year! We had so many events planned and so

many changes in our regular events, we had to write it all down to keep up with it.

First, our music foundation board of directors joined me in planning some classical music events built around Atamian. The board included Mrs. Ed "Theda" Schleiter, former president of the Kerrville Music Club and soprano singer; Gerald Thomas, manager of Zale's River Hills Mall store; civic and social leader Barbara Lewis Vandervoort; our good friend and business attorney and former county attorney Edward Wallace; Mrs. Ray "Mary Louise" Lehman; *Kerrville Daily Times* publisher Bill Dozier, and Nancylee.

For 1981, on the classical side, we scheduled a January concert downtown in the auditorium and three summer evening concerts at the ranch. There, Atamian would be heard in recital on Friday, as a chamber music player on Saturday, and then as soloist with a festival orchestra on Sunday. It would be a big event.

On the popular music side, we would be in the Kerrville Municipal Auditorium for concerts in January, February, and March, and would produce our eight-day, two-weekend folk festival at the ranch in May, and our four-day Labor Day weekend bluegrass festival, plus a September 13 edition of the "12 Great Hours," dedicated to Kenneth Threadgill. Also in the works were another tour, a street dance, and a tentative event in Bobby Bridger's hometown of Columbus, Louisiana, in October.

At the ranch we needed to review a few things. The original 1974 wooden stage had several problems. For the past six years, we had been replacing large segments of the floor every other year due to dry rot at an annual cost in excess of $1,000. In addition to the maintenance problems, we had come to consider the stage a sort of bass reflex cabinet as far as the acoustics were concerned. It was a "little boomy." And, after cramming the seventeen-member Glenn Miller Orchestra onto the stage two or three times, we began to wish for a larger stage.

The second thing that needed evaluation were the possibilities offered by the new two-weekend format of the folk festival and what we might do with the middle three days. We talked about an anniversary barbecue on Wednesday night for sponsors, press, performers, program advertisers, and volunteers, and whether or not to invite the public. For the anniversary, Fromholz and McCrimmen were talking about a Frummox reunion, and I wanted to do some sort of "Newport Remembered" tribute to recognize Newport's contributions to folk music, since that great festival was still shut down. We asked ourselves if we wanted to do any mini-concerts on Tuesday or Thursday nights of that midweek. There was also the question about whether to consider moving the country fair to town.

During this time, we had begun selling some "Lifetime Tickets" at $300, in addition to our $100 annual sponsorships, and generated a good influx of cash flow just when we needed it.

Our music foundation classical concert for January was set for the tenth featuring Atamian in his first Kerrville appearance since the worldwide release of the premiere recording on RCA Victor of Stravinsky's *Rite of Spring.* The concert would also introduce Kerrville to eighteen-year-old William DeRosa, a spectacular cellist who was emerging from his years as a child prodigy to become an exciting mature performer.

DeRosa, a 1979 first prize winner in the Piatagorsky Competition, had been featured on a CBS television special. Now studying cello with America's leading cellist, Leonard Rose, he had appeared in many solo recitals around the country as well as appearing with major orchestras such as the Los Angeles Philharmonic and the Dallas Chamber Orchestra. He played a Dominicus Montogona ex.-Emperor, 1739 cello with magnificent tone. I had met him at Atamian's Austin festival and wanted him to play the following summer at the Festival Atamian with our orchestra under Amram's baton.

Just as we announced the January concert, which was originally scheduled as a program of sonatas for cello and piano, Atamian canceled all of his dates for early 1981 to rest his painful right arm at the recommendation of his doctor. So DeRosa quickly changed his program to virtuoso cello pieces performed with his own accompanist.

For the second half of the concert, we flew in Amram. I had wanted him to meet DeRosa anyway and Amram was already well known to many in Kerrville. His biography by now was miles long, having first played French horn with Howard Mitchell and the National Symphony Orchestra thirty years before. In the 1970s, now that he was an internationally recognized composer and conductor, Amram began conducting Brooklyn Philharmonic youth concerts, composed his opera *Twelfth Night*, and guest-conducted the National Symphony Orchestra at the Kennedy Center. In 1977 the Philadelphia Orchestra premiered Amram's "Trail of Beauty" with Eugene Ormandy

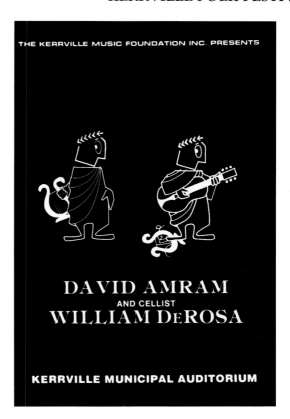

THE KERRVILLE MUSIC FOUNDATION INC. PRESENTS

DAVID AMRAM
AND CELLIST
WILLIAM DeROSA

KERRVILLE MUNICIPAL AUDITORIUM

conducting. He had a concert of his own music at Wolf Trap and received a 1978 International Film Festival Award conducting the Chicago Symphony Orchestra. By now sixteen of his works had been recorded on five record labels, and he'd been a Kerrville Folk Festival performer since 1975.

For his program at the auditorium, which he called "At Home Around The World," Amram demonstrated through instruments and music he'd learned in his travels the sounds of Central America, Brazil, the Sioux Nations, Egypt, Pakistan, penny whistles from Ireland and the Caribbean, and instrumental blues from the U.S. It was quite a trip as he included his audience during the evening, inviting everyone to be part of the "Kerrville Celestial Choir and Percussion Pickers."

The concert was one of contrast and discovery for the sizable audience. They learned that a teenager could thrill them with brilliant playing and that a classical composer could carry them around the world with non-classical music from many cultures and let them have fun doing it. The four- and five-part harmony singing and counter-tempo handclapping created a wild and joyous sound somewhat similar to that of the Holy Rollers. It was a good night for all of us, and DeRosa and Amram hit it off beautifully.

We continued to work on our anniversary folk festival, and I wrote our supporters a five-page summary of where we were financially, how we wanted to maintain our artistic vitality and expand our support even in the face of a shrinking economy. I wrote of how I felt that what we were trying to do had become a public trust and of how important it was to make our festivals and events a tourist's first choice as tourist dollars were in shorter supply. And once tourists got here, how important it was that we deliver quality entertainment at the same bargain prices they had come to expect.

In addition to the millions of dollars Kerrville had enjoyed from our patrons coming to town over the years, Kerrville had also enjoyed a huge increase in exposure in major magazines, metropolitan dailies across the country, on regional and network radio, area TV and national public television as well as European, Scandinavian, and Japanese publications. Just in the past year, thirty-five major dailies and fourteen college newspapers gave significant coverage to our festivals. We also enjoyed five two-hour National Public Radio broadcasts in the past six years and could look forward to the PBS-TV telecast of Atamian's Stravinsky premiere coming up in December.

While still dogged with significant debt and some continuing cash-flow problems, our supporters responded quickly and generously when asked. I had participated in over twenty-five interviews about Kerrville in the past two years and so was feeling that what we were doing had some importance. The other morale booster for us was, of course, the fun of touring Kerrville-on-the-road and all of the positive publicity that touring generated.

In reviewing our mailing lists, ticket orders, and attendance records, we found that patrons were coming from twenty-eight states. We also had been selected to be listed in the 1980 International Guide to Music Festivals published in the U.S., Canada, Great Britain, and Japan. And our foundation had been awarded $7,500 for touring, an award equal to the largest grants awarded to the Houston Symphony and the Dallas Opera! So looking back on 150 concerts we'd produced in Kerrville during the first nine years, and even with our discontinuing of festivals and events which did not give the promise of financial success, we still enjoyed an over sixty-five percent success ratio. The dramatic early loss of over $200,000 and most of our personal reserves over those rainy years had overshadowed the immeasurable success of the majority of our events. By taking inventory, we came to realize that we were part of a growing, living, performing arts effort that had brought both economic and cultural wealth to Kerrville.

For our part, with this perspective clearly in mind, we could enjoy the spiritual wealth and the nourishment that our work provided and go into our tenth anniversary with an optimistic approach. The artistic excellence we had achieved was worth even more to us because of the struggle to achieve it.

A crew under Ace Hindman's direction was tearing down the old sixteen-by-twenty-four-foot stage with its peaked roof, and replacing it with a twenty-four-by-twenty-eight-foot, low-maintenance concrete slab covered by a cantilevered roof which projected six feet over the front with new, more efficient stagelights which would be less expensive to replace. Almost all of the work was done by volunteers, some of whom moved to the ranch to work, and others who drove in for weekends to help.

The new design would allow for a larger number of performers and also meet the requests of television people to raise the roof so they could get a better variety of shots instead of being confined by the old, low-roof profile.

I drew what I wanted on a paper napkin over coffee at the Del Norte Restaurant one morning, then Ace and I designed long, flexible beams with the cantilevered design built in by bolting two two-by-six timbers on each side of quarter-inch steel plate cut to match and welded into our design.

With the stage under construction and our plans for both the foundation classical festival and the tenth anniversary folk festival moving ahead, I appealed to our sponsors for early renewals, multiple year renewals, and solicitation of their friends to join them as sponsors.

Sponsorships were still $100 and sponsors received $300 worth of tickets for their money. We gave up something, but we received income at a time when we were planning our season and when no ticket income was being generated because we hadn't announced our new season yet. By allowing us to be a permanent institution, sponsorships permitted us to concentrate on promotion, quality of the events, and business accountability. Obviously, it also allowed us to continue to meet some of our past-due obligations from the rainy years while planning and publishing extensive direct mail pieces and news releases to generate early response to our anniversary season.

Our new cantilevered stage was almost too good to be true! The new design, originally scratched on a paper napkin, turned out to be an acoustic wonder with its moveable acoustic shell. 1981.
— Courtesy Partain Photographs.

The checks came in with letters of support and thank you notes similar to this one from Midland, Texas: ". . . the best organized and well-run festival of this type I have ever had the pleasure of attending. I would also like you to extend a personal thank you to all those friendly people who make this possible, from the people at the entrance gate to the people at the concession stands as well as the people I did not get to meet behind the stage. I have recommended that all my friends enjoy one or more of the great doings you put on down in Kerrville. I can assure you that all my family will be returning many times."

This was just one of many letters through the years that recognized that other important aspect of our festivals that made them such special events for the visitors. The volunteers were truly a most-important aspect of our hospitality mission and seemed to share our dream of creating a family retreat from what a Houston man described as "the news media, murders, burglaries, and everything else in this mad world, so that I can just sit and listen to the best music."

It wasn't just the volunteers but also my under-paid business manager, Ray Partain, who replaced Miller, and Steve Carruthers, who replaced Partain, and would now see us through our tenth anniversary year. And then there were others still with us like Pedro Gutierrez, recording every concert; photographers Brian Kanof, Merri Lu Park, and Jim Willis, among others; and long-time volunteers like stage manager Mack Partain, staff coordinators and supervisors like Mary Jane Farmer, Jeff Davis, Richard Orton, Tony Wilson, Larry Brooks, Mary Massara, and many more.

Remarkably, every year our new Baldwin piano was showing up on stage because of a handshake in a New York taxi cab. Our new Kerrville-based printer, Herring Printing Company, was giving big city quality and did a good job on our tickets, program books, pre-festival brochures, and press kits.

In addition, they often carried us for several months with a substantial balance due them on our ledger sheet.

So by now, it was evident we had four teams of people pushing us along: our sponsors, our volunteers (like the Austin Radio Club who furnished all the festival communications), our performers, and the professionals from Kerrville who joined us like Herring Printing, G&M Catering, and our sound company called Production Services Group run by Dean Rayburn.

We decided to utilize the three days between the two weekends of the expanded folk festival for a foundation-sponsored songwriters school created by Bob Gibson with a first-year faculty of Gary P. Nunn, B. W. Stevenson, music professor Dick Goodwin, and David Amram. For $100 anyone could attend for three days, camp out free at the ranch for the run of the school, and come to the tenth anniversary party on Wednesday night. When I approached G&M Catering about a barbecue for that night, they suggested that we try, instead, their famous catfish fry, and we agreed to do just that.

In the months of preparing for the summer events, we also had the schedule of sponsor appreciation concerts at the Kerrville auditorium, scaled

down this year for economy to just one 8:00 P.M. concert each month.

The first of these was Allen Damron's "Tribute to Hondo Crouch" on Saturday, January 13. The late mayor of Luckenbach, Texas, loved dogs and children, chili and pickers, and mostly, imagineering. Damron recreated Hondo and his aura, conjuring up unforgettable music and stories. It was an incredible evening reliving some of Texas' tallest tales and tomfoolery.

The second in the series of sponsor events was on Saturday night, February 21. It was a combination tenth anniversary press party and a songwriters concert featuring songwriters from four states. We teamed three former New Folk winners with New Mexico's Eliza Gilkyson to present an evening of contrasting songwriters.

The first part opened with Lindsay Haisley, a Texas-based 1978 winner and autoharp virtuosa, followed by Missouri-based Allen Ross who won in 1980. After intermission, Colorado's Jon Ims, a 1979 winner, began the second half with one of his typically spellbinding performances. The thrill of the evening came with the appearance of tall, lean, angelic-looking, blond singer-songwriter Eliza Gilkyson and her band from New Mexico. Aside from her natural beauty, sometimes powerful, sometimes gentle voice, her songs were entrancing with their spiritual overtones. Behind her, providing haunting harmonies and swaying in tandem with her, was her extraordinarily beautiful brunette back-up singer, Christine Albert. The sight and sound of them together was a shining moment in a luminous evening. A good-sized audience gave them a standing ovation at the conclusion.

The final sponsor event was a big deal, a three-day reunion of many of our bluegrass festival favorites. A Friday-Sunday, March 20-22 reunion, which we called a Bluegrass Winterfest, was headlined by Knoxville's Joe Stuart, the great Japanese fiddle player Shoji Tabuchi, plus Bill Grant and Delia Bell from Oklahoma. Also appearing were nine Texas regional bands, including the Cook Brothers, Swamp Stompers, Hickory Hill from East Texas (who had met in the parking lot at the ranch, won the band contest, and were now a going concern), the House Brothers, Powell Family, Salt Creek Express, the Shady Grove Ramblers, and Kerrville's own Poverty Playboys led by Judge Bob Barton. There were as many or more musicians in the audience as on the stage and so there were many

Rod Kennedy Presents

SONGWRITERS CONCERT
Songwriters from four states!

AND 1981 FOLK FESTIVAL
10TH ANNIVERSARY PRESS PARTY

Municipal Auditorium

THE EARLY YEARS OUTDOORS

jam sessions at every break over the three days. It was actually a three-day *indoor* bluegrass festival. And it worked!

We now had sixty days remaining to complete our stage, finish our pre-festival mailings, poster and brochure distribution, and to make a half-dozen specialized mailings to our regional and national press lists.

Following up on the success of last year's street dance, which drew 3,000 paying guests to the pic-

turesque 4th Street location in downtown Austin, we set up again in April 12 in front of the Gaslight Theater located between Colorado and Lavaca.

Beer, soft drinks, barbecue, and nachos were sold and the music filled the warehouse district from 2 P.M. until almost dark. We had four bands that were playing Kerrville and all of them were based in Austin. Among the four of them, we had every dance tempo you could think of with *salsa* and *cumbia* by Beto y los Fairlanes, Austin "boogie" music by Mother of Pearl, semi-rock and Lubbock blues by the Butch Hancock-Jimmie Gilmore Band, and almost-country by Gary P. Nunn playing two-step, waltzes, and swing music. Area crafts people had tables of stuff to sell, and it was a fiesta atmosphere. The proceeds went to our foundation and the Gaslight, which was also a non-profit group founded in 1974.

While it was work, it was also fun, and the staff and volunteers probably danced as much as any pay-

ing customer. The theater people and music people really got along well and enjoyed working together.

On April 14 the Texas Legislature passed House Concurrent Resolution No. 140 honoring the Kerrville Folk Festival's tenth anniversary. Authored by State Representative Paul Colbert (D-Houston) and Gerald Geistweidt (R-Kerrville), the bill contained the usual number of "whereases" and "resolveds," but with the last one reading, "Resolved, that the Texas Legislature should make an attempt to complete its work before late May, and adjourn *sine die*, thus serving the dual purpose of saving thousands of dollars for the tax-payers and giving legislators the opportunity to attend this outstanding event."

The next morning I gathered a dozen of our folk festival performers at Eddie Wilson's Threadgill's Restaurant on North Lamar for one last cup of coffee before boarding the bus for our anniversary Kerrville on-the-road tour to North Texas State University's Lyceum Theater in Denton, the Richland Community College to play their annual spring picnic, then to Ft Worth to join Ray Wylie Hubbard at Billy Bob's Texas, to KERA-TV for a taping, and to Poor David's Pub on McKinney Avenue in Dallas for two sold-out shows.

Then, on April 18 we made an early departure for Houston, where the Society for the Performing Arts had scheduled us for an 8:30 P.M. free concert at the Miller Outdoor Theatre in Herman Park.

spa

Society for the Performing Arts

in association with the

Kerrville Music Foundation, Inc.

presents the

KERRVILLE FOLK FESTIVAL

on the road

10th Anniversary Tour

April 18, 1981
8:30 PM
Miller Theatre

Performers

(in order of appearance)

Robert Shaw	John Vandiver	Bill and Bonnie Hearne
Bobby Bridger	Don Sanders	Kenneth Threadgill
	INTERMISSION	
Allen Damron	Carolyn Hester	Steve Fromholz
Bob Gibson	B. W. Stevenson	Gary P. Nunn

Tonight's free concert is made possible by generous grants from the
CULTURAL ARTS COUNCIL of Houston and *SHELTON RANCHES* in Kerrville, Texas.

This and other S.P.A. presentations are supported by the Texas Commission on the Arts and the
National Endowment for the Arts, a Federal Agency, with additional funding
by the Combined Arts Corporate Campaign.

In spite of the theater's dire warnings about what to do in case of a riot, we had a rewarding performance before a large well-behaved crowd and then were guests at Houston's oldest folk club, Anderson Fair, where they hospitably fed us breakfast at 2:00 A.M.

While there was a little switching around in the lineup in various locations to permit two or three artists to fulfill other obligations, the three-hour music-packed concerts included John Vandiver, Robert Shaw, Bobby Bridger, Don Sanders, Bill and Bonnie Hearne, Carolyn Hester, Kenneth Threadgill, Allen Damron, Bob Gibson, B. W. Stevenson, and Steven Fromholz, with Shake Russell and Dana Cooper joining Vandiver in Houston on the Miller Theatre Concert.

With each performer doing a three-song set, every night was a full evening of superb music with everyone joining Bridger in the anthem as the finale. Celebrated Austin music reviewer Townsend Miller, our "sound crew" of Pedro Gutierrez and Lee Green, Mary Jane Farmer, and photographer Brian Kanof joined us on this tour along with business manager Steve Carruthers. The tour was partially underwritten by the Texas Commission on the Arts and the National Endowment for the Arts with additional support from Kerrville's Shelton Ranches (for the Houston Miller Theatre date.)

Following nearly a week of traveling together, making music and meeting the public, we arrived back at Threadgill's on Easter Sunday. Having gained additional insight and perspective from this little excursion, I returned to Kerrville to finalize details for the anniversary folk festival.

We decided it was time to move the New Folk concerts from the fair in town out to the ranch so we could get everything under our direct supervision. The tapes were pouring in from everywhere — we received 170 entries that I narrowed down to forty finalists who then were invited to be our guests for the entire five days of the first weekend. We scheduled the two competition concerts for twenty finalists each on the first weekend (Sunday and Monday, Memorial Day), followed the next Sunday by the Award Winners Concert just before the third annual Great Texas Harmonica Blow-Off. Judging were the song writing leader of the Shady Grove Ramblers, Tom Uhr, Bill Hearne, and Butch Hancock.

There was now a Folk Mass celebration conducted by Rev. Charlie Sumners on both Sundays, six Ballad Tree sessions, and the Children's Singing Circus tent (with the Twelve Moon Story Tellers —

David Amram adds his gentle flute to the reading of the Scriptures by Rev. Charlie Sumners at the Folk Mass under the Ballad Tree on Chapel Hill. 1981.
— Courtesy Brian Kanof.

Gayle Ross and Liz Ellis — on the first weekend, and a full-fledged Singing Circus the second weekend led by Sing-A-Long Dave Pipes). We also had the Cypress Swamp Stompers playing the warm-up set at 5:30 daily on the first weekend, and Mariachi Infantile Guadalupano from Austin warming up the second weekend.

Some highlights of the evening concerts included Jimmie Gilmore and Clarence "Gatemouth" Brown debuting on Thursday, Jim Schulman, showing up after an eight-year absence, on Friday, Bill Moss returning on Saturday to open an evening that closed with Bobby Bridger, Riders in the Sky appearing before a wildly approving audience on Sunday, and Nanci Griffith opening the Memorial Day evening show followed by the

Jimmie Gilmore (right) with Butch Hancock sitting in. 1981.
— Courtesy Brian Kanof.

Gatemouth Brown (left) and his band on our new stage. 1981.

— Courtesy *Kerrville Daily Times.*

From left: Odetta, Bob Gibson and Peter Yarrow close the "Newport Remembered" concert. 1981.

— Courtesy Brian Kanof.

Kerrville debut of the Tennessee Gentlemen from Memphis, a reunion of Eaglebone Whistle (who had retired the previous February), and Steven Fromholz to close. As always, almost all of the concert performers sat up with their fans around campfires, picking and making friends until almost dawn.

One of the special events of Memorial Day was a 1:30 P.M. "Newport Remembered" concert by Allen Damron, Carolyn Hester, and Kenneth Threadgill, each of whom had played the old Newport Folk Festival (1959, and 1962-1970). We then presented full sets by Newport giants Jimmy Driftwood, Bob Gibson, Odetta, and Peter Yarrow. Peter had been one of the founders of the Newport Folk Festival, working with George and Joyce Wein, and shared additional Newport insights with his audience. It was an exceptional event and one which the Weins would have enjoyed.

The two Kerrville New Folk concerts were co-hosted by Damron and me, with the six winners being Chuck Pyle, James Durst, Melissa Javors, Lisa Fancher, Judy Price, and Jerry Stevens. But we also were introduced to Jim Ash and his singing family from San Marcos, Texas, and dancing Englishman Rory McLeod, who listed his address as Cancun, Mexico. He would later resurface on the second weekend in a spectacular manner.

The crowds were huge the first weekend, except that Saturday night's rain held the attendance down to 1,600, compared with 6,000 the year before, and those of us who were staying through the second weekend were grateful for the relative quiet of the middle three days. The only activity was

the songwriters school and its thirty-five students and Lee Green's volunteer work crew. Then there was Wednesday night!

We opened our gates at 5:00 P.M. to a large number of invited guests, over 350 actually, plus our volunteers who could come and some of the general public who didn't want to miss anything. Our six-page, two-toned blue invitation invited guests to see our new stage and share in G&M's famous fillets of catfish "Quiet Valley Style," cooked in fifty-five-gallon barrel deep-fryers and served sizzling hot with tartar sauce, red sauce, lemon slices, french fries, tasty Texas hush puppies and butter, coleslaw, tomato wedges, onions, pickles, fresh-baked Hill Country wheat or white bread, iced tea, coffee, beer, lemonade, soft drinks, and mint candy.

The 6:00 P.M. dinner show, hosted by Cactus Pryor, starred the Tennessee Gentlemen and Riders in the Sky. The 8:00 P.M. show opened with my making some remarks, talking about some memories, hosting some awards and tributes, followed at 8:30 by the three-hour memorial concert featuring the original 1972 folk festival performers, hosted by Steve Fromholz.

It was one of those beautiful nights when everything seems right, when everyone is finally thanked and recognized for extraordinary efforts. We were mystified as to why certain things mean so much to us. Here we have the chance to relax and discover original music by some of America's most creative performers, both the unknowns and those internationally recognized. Through our ability to

Riders in the Sky. 1981.
— Courtesy Richard Orton.

relate to these creative people, we are renewed and we rejoice. I am inspired by our own festival! While the financial aspect is still a mountain to be climbed, we have found satisfaction in the ability of our festival to reach out and touch entire families with the authenticity and genuineness of our words and music. Working together for something we believe in is one of the great experiences of being a part of this whole effort. And as producer, now having earned the trust of all of the performers, I feel a bond and responsibility to them. The anniversary and the simple fish fry is part of a ritual that can sustain meaningfulness in our lives. Connection and creativity sustain us, and somehow I begin to realize

creating our event together is more important than the festival product. The going is more important than the getting there, and we need to enjoy the communion, the sharing with one another, the getting there. It's like rediscovering this universal truth: most of us spend a lot of time dreaming of the future, never realizing that a little arrives every day. Somehow peace begins when expectation ends. I have always had a need for both society and solitude, and now, here at this ranch, I have them both, along with the enriching feeling of being able to look at the whole process with understanding and appreciation. I have told others that I often feel in a state of grace being able to do something I believe in and sharing it with others of like mind.

We began the second weekend with a strong Friday night concert, closing with Townes Van Zandt, Rusty Wier, and the Shake Russell-Dana Cooper Band. Saturday started at 11:00 A.M. with a ninety-minute concert by Robin and Linda Williams that gave new life to the traditional songs of the Appalachian Mountains while making an impressive Kerrville debut. Following was another debut show by the nine members of Austin's show band, Beto y los Fairlanes, who had recently toured Mexico and played "Austin City Limits." Trombonist Mike Mordecai and several other members of the band were musicians I had first known when they were UT students in Dick Goodwin's jazz ensemble. It was a homecoming of sorts, and many of the tunes were written by leader Robert "Beto" Skiles, who I learned was the son of San Antonio's famous jazz trumpet player, Dude Skiles. The band was a big hit as it had been everywhere it toured.

The children's mini-festival was in the Singing Circus tent, and David Pipes and his wife Julie were assisted by four other couples and magician Jules Caplan, among others. A large number of children under twelve were vibrating like daddy longlegs spiders in a bunch, singing, playing, imagining, and making things.

The Saturday night concert, limited to about 2,000 fans due to the rain, started with 1980 New Folk winner Allen Ross and continued with Robin and Linda Williams, Uncle Walt's Band, John Vandiver, and Ray Wylie Hubbard.

In a brief intermission on stage, Allen Damron and Gayle Ross made a special anniversary presentation to Nancylee and me with a gift of $946 collected by the staff and performers and given to us for our first vacation in twelve years. They made us promise not to pay bills with it! A short time later, Threadgill

Townes Van Zandt (left) and Mickey White (right) on the new stage. 1981.

— Courtesy James R. Willis.

From left: Nancylee Kennedy, Gayle Ross, and myself with Allen Damron during the presentation of the "vacation money." 1981.

— Courtesy James R. Willis.

Dancing in the theater with Vicki Bell to the music of Beto and the Fairlanes. 1981.

— Courtesy Ed Miller.

presented each of us with a personal check for $1,000 (I did pay bills with mine!), which Kenneth said was "our share" of his royalties earned from two songs on Willie Nelson's *Honeysuckle Rose* soundtrack album. Threadgill had sought my advice prior to the making of the film as to what songs he should perform in the movie. I had suggested he sing two of his own songs, and he had chosen "Comin' Back to Texas" and "Yodeling Blues." Then the album including Threadgill's songs sold more than 100,000 copies.

When the concert resumed, all of the performers joined David Amram on stage with David playing piano, French horn, flute, drums, and various other percussion instruments and leading his Amram Jam. The jam had become a favorite moment at each year's festival since David's first appearance in 1975. The jam continued into the campgrounds and into the night.

While it rained cats and dogs, we at least had rid ourselves of the previous year's "dogs everywhere" problem by banning all pets from the ranch for the first time.

The following day, Sunday, had Rev. Charlie Sumners Folk Mass on Chapel Hill, an impressive New Folk award winners concert, and another in our series of annual harmonica contests. This year's version was judged by 1979 champion Steve Kriechbaum, 1980 champion Paul Orta, and country music columnist Townsend Miller. The other competitors were wiped out by our young English friend Rory McLeod, who had been the hit of the campfires all week long. His uninhibited singing,

233

Rory McLeod from England. 1981.
— Courtesy Brian Kanof.

Peter Yarrow on stage with his daughter Bethany. 1981.
— Courtesy Brian Kanof.

Carolyn Hester and Gary P. Nunn duet at the piano. 1981.
— Courtesy Brian Kanof.

dancing, and high-energy harmonica playing had captured everyone. Now he would be back as our new harmonica champion!

Something else that made the anniversary year special was Peter Yarrow's extended stay at the festival. He was everywhere hugging, encouraging, commiserating, and generally spreading his "togetherness" philosophy amongst the performers, volunteers, and audience. He brought his daughter, Bethany, with him and was in an especially loving and cheerful mode.

The final night's concert by Bill Neeley, 1977 New Folk winner Tim Henderson, Eliza Gilkyson from New Mexico, Peter Rowan, and Gary P. Nunn was an amazing climax to the festival. We had two anthems to close the festival this night: Gary P.'s "London Homesick Blues," which had become a sort of Texas national anthem, and Bobby Bridger's "Heal in the Wisdom," now the official festival anthem. Bridger had a hard time all week trying to leave the festival, was back for the Wednesday night fish fry, and now, here he was back again on stage with Gary and more than fifty other musicians and volunteers leading us all in an anniversary farewell

anthem as tears of joy and fulfillment streamed down our faces.

Some of the weather was fair and beautiful, but there was rain at the festival seven times. Many days sizable crowds came anyway, so despite the rain, which people seemed to be accustomed to seeing at the festival, we had one of the most successful festivals on record. Because of the rains, we did not amortize our historic debt and fell short of covering our festival expenses by about $10,000 plus. Immediately, the performers were suggesting a July benefit concert to keep things going. Even though it fell short of the optimistic mark we had set for it, we felt good about the festival. We knew we had not suffered nearly as much as others when we considered that around the state people were drowned and businesses, homes, and life work were lost due to floods. We only had to shut down or move events three times (out of sixteen), since the rains were heavier in Austin, San Antonio, and surrounding areas than they were at the ranch.

Our new stage had worked beautifully, and all of the new facilities and improvements on the rest of the ranch would provide a perfect setting for the classical music festival coming up at the end of July. There would even be room to spare for the grand piano, Amram's podium, and the festival orchestra on the new stage.

Working with a struggling young Kerr County Fair organization, headed up by John and Betty Jensen, owners of my favorite ice cream parlor in town, Polar Bear Ashburn's, we moved the country fair into Kerrville, where it became a non-profit organization and the official Kerr County Fair in 1981. The Jensens would have lots of help and full support of the county agent of Texas A&M's extension service. By now, after two years, there was a large group of 4H parents and others to help get the catalogue, exhibits, and the fair organized. We were pleased to see a permanent fair organization under way.

Back to our own financial problem solving, two days of special events were scheduled at the Outdoor Theater on Saturday and Sunday, July 11 and 12, to help cover some of the expenses left over from before the anniversary festival.

Under the banner "Kerrville Tears of Joy Reunion," the two-day event drew huge crowds at $10 each from 6:00 P.M. to midnight Saturday and noon to 6:00 P.M. Sunday.

Performing were a dozen Kerrville artists whose names meant something to the public. The list included Butch Hancock, Ray Wylie Hubbard, Dee Moeller, Gary P. Nunn and their bands, the Shake Russell-Dana Cooper Band, who had just released their first album on a major record label, Nanci Griffith, Allen Damron, Don Sanders, Eliza Gilkyson, and 1981 New Folk award winner Melissa Javors of San Antonio. B. W. Stevenson and Rusty Wier both joined the roster at the last minute and put the frosting on the cake for a great Kerrville weekend.

This particular weekend should be counted as one of the finest musical experiences of the decade of the 1980s, and even though we paid all of the performers festival scale to play this benefit event, we still cleared enough unobligated income to pay a significant number of old bills and take the pressure off our business manager, Steve Carruthers. It was a

rewarding weekend all the way around! I can't emphasize enough the morale boost it gave us just to be around these outstanding performers again.

Our next event would be for our music foundation. It was the massive undertaking of the new classical music Festival Atamian over July 31-August 2 with four daytime events downtown at the auditorium and three evening concerts at Quiet Valley Ranch.

Our slogan was "Serious music can be fun!" We assembled an eleven-event festival centered on our young piano virtuoso, but also showcasing Richie's sister Sara, herself an accomplished pianist. We added Austin-based flutist Megan Meisenbach and a whole host of young, talented soloists from all over the U.S. selected from the rosters of the major agencies on both coasts. This remarkable group of prize-winning young artists was made up of violinist Hamao Fujiwara, cellist William DeRosa, clarinetist Stewart Newbold, cellist Mark Volkov, and young blind Kerrville soprano Ruth Ann Harmon.

David Amram would conduct the festival orchestra in two concerts and participate in a daytime children's concert. World-renowned cellist Leonard Rose would play a Sunday afternoon recital, and Houston's Ara Carpetyan would con-

With Gray Hawn at the Festival Atamian reception. 1981.
— Courtesy *Kerrville Daily Times.*

duct the Festival Bach Orchestra and Chorus and soloists. Dick Goodwin was commissioned to write and premiere a "Festival Piece" commemorating the 125th anniversary of the founding of Kerr County in 1856.

On the Wednesday evening before the festival began, we invited a large number of Kerrville-area leaders, ticket holders, sponsors, press, and others to a reception in the lobby of the auditorium to meet the principal performers. They would also view a private opening and preview of our photo exhibit by Austin's highly regarded photographer, Gray Hawn. There was a good turnout of guests sharing the wine and cheese, meeting our honored performers and enjoying Gray's photos, which included some of Amram which had been taken for an album cover. It was a good start for the long weekend.

The Festival Atamian began with five free mini-concerts on Friday. Soprano Ruth Ann Harmon performed at 10 A.M. at the amphitheater of Butt-Holdsworth Library; at 12:30 P.M. guitarist Kevin Taylor played a one-hour recital in Dietert Claim Auditorium, and at 4:00 P.M. another recital at the Hill Country Arts Foundation Gallery in Ingram; while guitarist Christopher Carrington played recitals at 2:00 P.M. at the Hummingbird Gallery and at 6:00 P.M. at Riverhills Mall.

The first auditorium event was at 8:30 that night when Kerrville welcomed Atamian back to play a gala recital of music by Bach, Beethoven, and Chopin. The Chopin Mazurkas, Ballade, Nocturnes, Scherzo, Prelude, and Polonaise were particular favorites with the audience who greeted Atamian's playing with a standing ovation and cheers.

On Saturday morning Brad Hawkins and David Bessinger gave a fascinating but poorly attended percussion concert followed at noon by a well-attended children's concert hosted by David Amram, William DeRosa, and mime Turk Pipkin with some of our best musicians sitting in as surprise guests playing unusual instruments. Then, at 3:00 P.M. our Festival Chamber Trio of Atamian, Fujiwara, and Volkov played a recital of Schubert's Trio No. 1 in B flat major, Opus 99, and Ravel's Trio in A minor for Violin, Cello, and Piano. This was a substantial, brilliant, and rewarding pair of performances.

Out at the ranch's Outdoor Theater that night, with wine service by Fara's Restaurant, Ruth Ann Harmon sang a "Music Lovers Welcome" at 7:30 P.M., including selections by Victor Herbert, Offenbach, and others. Then David Amram led the twenty-five-member festival orchestra in his own "Autobiography for Strings," the Haydn Concerto in D for Piano and Orchestra with Sara Atamian as soloist, and Austin composer Kent Kennan's "Soliloquy for Flute and Strings" with soloist Megan Meisenbach. The evening closed with a marvelous performance by William DeRosa and our orchestra in the Haydn Concerto in C major for Cello and Orchestra. It was an inspired concert of

Amram conducting the Festival Orchestra. 1981.
— Courtesy *Kerrville Daily Times.*

music under the stars and reflected beautifully on the acoustic perfection of our new stage.

Sunday's schedule held two major concerts beginning at 1:00 P.M. downtown in the auditorium with Ara Carpetyan conducting the twenty-one-piece Festival Bach Orchestra and forty-seven-voice chorus. The orchestra members were drawn from the Texas Bach Orchestra of Austin and the chorus members from Morris Beachy's Austin Choral Union. Soloists in the Monteverdi Vespers and the Bach Cantata No. 21 were soprano Jean Howell, mezzo soprano Virginia Dupuy, tenor David Fox, and bass Russell Gregory (the same singer who used to serenade the sorority houses with me at UT!).

The orchestra, chorus, and soloists filled the auditorium stage, and the resulting music soared at a level of excellence seldom heard in a small Texas town.

The recital by Leonard Rose had to be canceled as the cello virtuoso could not get to Texas to perform due to the air controllers' strike.

Our finale that evening at the ranch began with Ruth Ann Harmon's 7:30 P.M. welcome of selections by Lehar, Humperdinck, and others. Then the festival orchestra concert began with the premiere performance of Goodwin's "Festival Piece." The remainder of the evening saw Amram conducting three Mozart concerti with Hamao Fujiwara as soloist in the A major Violin Concerto, K.219, Stewart Newbold as soloist in the A major Clarinet Concerto, K.622, and, following intermission,

Dickran Atamian as soloist in the Concerto No. 13 in E major for Piano and Orchestra, K.499.

It would have been an impressive program on any music festival, and the sound of Mozart's music on that stage in that setting under the stars made for a magical, magnificent evening. I was pleased and impressed with Amram, all of the young soloists, and with our orchestra. For me, the three days and nights provided an awesome experience!

Hamao Fujiwara plays the Mozart Violin Concerto. 1981.
— Courtesy *Kerrville Daily Times.*

With the modest financial success of this first classical festival, we wanted to look at what we might do in the future, but the eighth annual bluegrass festival was just thirty days away, and we went right to work to campaign hard for a big audience through travel, interviews, press mailings, and visits to wherever bluegrass music was being played.

The Labor Day weekend festival, September 3-6, again focused on Buck White and our mandolin championships with Ricky Skaggs, Jesse McReynolds, and 1980 champion Bobby Clark as judges. The main stage was loaded with national stars like Jim and Jesse, Buck White, the McLains, Country Gazette, the Boys From Indiana, fiddling Jana Jae, Lost and Found, Shoji Tabuchi, and Colorado's popular Hot Rize and their alter ego of Red Knuckles and the Trail Blazers, plus the enthusiastic Lost City Mad Dogs from Kobe, Japan.

The regional artists included all the regulars plus our 1980 Southwestern bluegrass band champions, Tennessee Valley Authority (TVA), from San Antonio. The four-day festival on the new stage was an expanded showcase of more than forty hours of scheduled performances plus the band, banjo, and mandolin contests. For the Buck White mandolin championship, Luke Thompson from Louisiana built a handcrafted, one-of-a-kind "Buck White Model" mandolin to accompany the winner's cash prize. The fans were really impressed and pleased with "America's most beautiful bluegrass theater." Paul Glasse from New York state was also pleased as he whisked off with the mandolin, money, and title of mandolin champion, plus a date here for next year. The winning band was Kerrville's String Factory Outlet, providing an appropriate conclusion for the tenth anniversary season!

One week later, we staged our fourth annual "12 Great Hours" with its now expected but amazingly popular Worst Hat Contest. The 2:00 P.M. to 2:00 A.M. concert again provided the extra cash flow that the bluegrass festival failed to provide beyond paying its own bills. But this was also the occasion on which to celebrate Kenneth Threadgill's seventy-second birthday, and the ambiance of the day took on the flavor of a real birthday party. Performers all paying tribute to Kenneth included Bobby Bridger, Allen Damron, Don Sanders, Steven Fromholz, Bill and Bonnie, Gary P. Nunn and his band, and Bill Neeley on hand to accompany Threadgill and grumble a little bit about how much fuss was being made over his friend who couldn't even accompany himself. State Representative Paul Colbert sent a house resolution from the state legislature commemorating the birthday, and there were other gifts and salutations. The music and camaraderie was a real plus for all of us, and we came away from this one-day special event feeling better about our landmark season, which had been tarnished by weather-related set-backs.

Next I began to finalize plans for what Bobby Bridger and I hoped would become the first in a series of annual Louisiana Folk Festivals built on a smaller scale but along the lines of the Kerrville festival with many of Kerrville's performers. The festival was to be a two-day event on the weekend of October 11 and 12 at Bridger's hometown of Columbus on the banks of the Mississippi.

Bridger had left Columbus for Austin and first became associated with me when he appeared at the 1972 New Folk concert at the first Kerrville Folk Festival. He had been an annual festival evening concert performer since 1974, initiated the Ballad Tree in 1977, and as we became friends, I had asked him to serve as a festival director beginning in 1978. Then his song "Heal In The Wisdom" became the official anthem of the festival, so the decision to co-produce

a festival in Columbia seemed like a natural next step in our ten-year professional relationship.

Excited with producing the festival as a part of the twenty-sixth annual Louisiana Art and Folk Festival, we arranged to present dollar concerts by seven Kerrville-related performers.

We announced Allen Damron, Gary P. Nunn, Nanci Griffith, and, of course, Bobby Bridger, and then we added three Louisiana-based artists: the Fuller Family, Julie Jean Reneaux, and the best-known of the three, D. L. Menard and his trio, known nationally as the Louisiana Aces.

We proposed to produce three 3-hour concerts at noon and 4:00 P.M. on Saturday and at 1:00 P.M. on Sunday at the Caldwell Parrish Little League Ball Park adjacent to the art fair.

We thought it was peculiar that there were so few spectators when we started our first performance, but about ten minutes into it, four or five vehicles roared up near the site in a hurry behind the clapboard fence of the ballpark. Within a few minutes, we could see more than a dozen members of a dark blue-uniformed, bulletproof-vested SWAT team creeping along the fence on my right along toward the stage. They stopped about seventy-five feet away, and if we hadn't thought it was so funny, we'd have been really intimidated!

I announced to the small crowd that they now had full protection of a SWAT team, and I urged the team to lay down its arms and join the audience. Within an hour or so the police vanished more quietly than they had arrived with buses and trucks and cars leaving a small cloud of dust where the SWAT team had been.

Thus welcomed, we did our next show at 4:00 P.M. with a slightly larger crowd and no police protection. That night, we asked to be moved into the fairgrounds in the middle of the crowd where we'd at least be able to catch the attention of passersby. The Sunday event was almost a success, and the fair officials paid us as they apologized for the intrusion of the armed force. By then, even Bobby was relieved just to say good-bye to his folks and get out of town back to Texas. His folks were extremely hospitable and friendly, and I'm sure, embarrassed by the whole incident. We did not plan a second Louisiana Folk Festival!

With the taste of real Louisiana hospitality still in our mouths, we returned to Texas, where I called a meeting of our foundation directors, now reinforced by the presence of one of Kerrville's leading arts patrons, actors, singers and musicians, Andy Ritch, who owned the Hummingbird Gallery and whose wife was the director of the Kerrville Community Chorus. We formalized our classical music plans for the end of 1981 and for the spring and summer of 1982. The Kerrville Concerts Association, who had been providing classical community concerts for a number of years, had announced that they would not continue in 1982. I felt, and the board agreed, that we could fill the bill with a season of excellent concerts in the auditorium in the winter and our three-day outdoor festival in the summer. We had already talked with Atamian about changing the July event from Festival Atamian to the Kerrville Summer Music Festival, and we could put our December-through-March season together as the Kerrville Winter Music Festival.

We approved a patron membership drive to sign up fifty couples at $150 as we could set off the 100 best seats in the auditorium as a patron's section and a special area of bench seating as reserved patron seating at the ranch for the summer three-day event. We also had approved, some months before, Jose Greco's offer to play a benefit concert for us on November 1 for just the road expenses of the company, to raise funds for our classical music series.

So, while we planned our 1981-82 season, we also undertook the promotion for the Jose Greco event, adding a $100-per-couple dinner with Greco at Riverhill Country Club after the performance. Theda Schleiter did all the planning. For those who purchased both the $150 patron and the $100 Greco dinner, we offered a premium of an autographed Atamian *Rite of Spring* recording as soon as it was released by RCA, and an invitation-for-two to the patrons reception the night before the Summer Music Festival. Both drives were successful.

Greco arrived in Kerrville with his lovely partner, Nana Lorca, known as the "First Lady of Spanish Dance," and Jorge Tyller, Mexico's premiere dancer, with his Ballet Folklorico Mexicano of fourteen dancers, singers, and musicians including an outstanding mariachi band. Greco had wanted to combine companies of both Mexican and Spanish dance for forty years. This production was arranged by Stephen Rapaport at the National Theatre for Performing Arts in Westport, Connecticut, and this first cross-country tour had begun at the Greek Theatre in Los Angeles.

As a special Kerrville event of the fund raiser, Jane and Ross Rommel of El Buzon of Ingram put on a "Fiesta of Fashions." The Rommels had more than a Southwestern following for their fashion boutique just outside of Kerrville in the small town

At the Greco Riverhill Dinner. Greco is seated next to Nancylee across the table. 1981.

— Courtesy *Kerrville Daily Times.*

of Ingram. They were written up regularly in both fashion and society columns and hosted charity fashion shows at many prominent country clubs around the state. Many of Kerrville's loveliest and most prominent women modeled, including leaders like Nancy Baker, Carolyn Brinkman, Barbara

David Amram.

— Publicity Photo.

Hailey, Sally Ritch, Nancy Wallace, Peggy Monroe, Liz Real, Barbara Vandervoort, and others. It was a gala beginning!

The performance itself was made up of a dozen scenes, four of them featuring Spanish dance, and eight featuring Mexican dance from Aztec tradition, Chiapas, Oaxaca, Veracruz, and Jalisco, with Jorge Tyller recreating his famous "Deer Dance." The entire company was joined by Jose Greco and Nana Lorca to close the colorful, melodic, and elegant show in a frenzied celebration of life, beauty, and romance. The audience exploded into cheers and rousing applause as the performance curtain closed.

KERRVILLE MUSIC FOUNDATION INC. PRESENTS

HANDEL

Messiah!

HIGHLIGHTS

Ruth Ann Harmon (soprano) Elizabeth Real (soprano) Sally Ritch (alto) Maggie Meek (alto) David Dyer (tenor)

KERRVILLE COMMUNITY CHORUS
Sally Ritch, Director

FESTIVAL ORCHESTRA
conducted by
DAVID AMRAM
Also music of Bach, Mendelssohn, Mozart, Tchaikovsky & others

4PM SUN DEC 13

DOORS OPEN 3 PM

KERRVILLE MUNICIPAL AUDITORIUM

ADVANCE ADULT TICKETS $5 ON SALE THRU DEC. 11
AT COMMERCIAL OFFICE SUPPLY & BREHMER'S JEWELERS
$6 AT THE BOX OFFICE •   • YOUTH (under 19) HALF-PRICE

KERRVILLE WINTER MUSIC FESTIVAL

In the printed program, we announced our Winter Music Festival season and the availability of mail orders for our first event, a December 13 performance of highlights from Handel's *Messiah* performed by soloists and Kerrville Community Chorus, Sally Ritch, director, and members of the Festival Orchestra, conducted by David Amram.

My philosophy as a volunteer executive director and producer of all the music foundation events was one of always reaching for excellence. Because of the limitations imposed by a smaller market and limited budget, I needed to utilize the contacts I had made over a thirty-five-year career as a producer. I would continue to seek the cooperation of Atamian, David Amram, Megan Meisenbach, and other outstanding artists who had already earned their credentials in other parts of the nation. Kerrville had already come to know a number of our artists and their performance capacity, and Amram, in particular, had a large following of Kerrville fourth-graders and parents from his work for the foundation in the public schools in Kerrville in early 1981. My hope was that I could both program the level of excellence I envisioned and simultaneously inspire the local patrons to enlarge the family of support following this first full season.

We climaxed our tenth anniversary year with the first event of our new Winter Music Festival. David Amram came back from New York to conduct the Sunday, December 13 concert at the auditorium which was climaxed by the *Messiah* highlights. The outstanding soloists were Ruth Ann Harmon, Elizabeth Real, Sally Ritch, Maggie Meek, and David Dyer. The Kerrville Community Chorus was rich and full, disciplined and inspired. It was a packed house and a monumental artistic accomplishment. I was excited to see our season off to such a rewarding start.

It had been an eventful decade, and now we looked to the next ten years in Kerrville.

KERRVILLE FOLK FESTIVAL: THE MIDDLE YEARS

(1982–1991)

Our second decade of music at Kerrville began on January 22 at the Kerrville Municipal Auditorium with the first appearance in Kerrville of the Texas Opera Theatre.

We began the year with David Miller as our business manager and Mary Jane Farmer continuing as my assistant and as staff coordinator for the outdoor festivals. By now Bob Barton had joined the foundation board of directors, and with everyone else still in place, we eagerly began the 1982 portion of our first classical Kerrville Winter Music Festival.

Beginning with the *Messiah* concert before Christmas, we now were fortunate to have six of the young opera stars of the Texas Opera Theatre, an offshoot of the Houston Grand Opera. This workshop performance called "Is It Broadway or Is It Opera?" featured songs, arias, duets, and quartets from *La Bohême, Carousel, The Italian Girl In Algiers, Annie Get Your Gun, Fidelio, West Side Story, Porgy And Bess, 110 In The Shade,* and *Candide.* The melodic performances were by soprano Michelle McBride, mezzo-soprano Susan-Lee Whalen, tenors Chris Bauman and William Chamberlain, baritone Curt Scheib, and bass-baritone S. Ray Jacobs, accompanied by pianist William Lewis, a truly stellar musician.

Many of the artists had appeared at Santa Fe, Wolf Trap, Central City, and other big summer opera theaters. S. Ray Jacobs had already made his Houston Grand Opera debut in Scott Joplin's *Treemonisha.* William Lewis, who had been music director of more than fifty productions across the country, did an outstanding job of directing what proved to be an entertaining and effective way to approach opera, particularly for audiences who might not already be opera fans. We felt it was a

THE KERRVILLE MUSIC FOUNDATION INC. PRESENTS

KERRVILLE WINTER MUSIC FESTIVAL

Municipal Auditorium

creditable way to begin the year. By now we had sixty-four season patron couples, and attendance exceeded the 700 mark.

Incidentally, one of the big hits of our classical music effort was our offering of t-shirts bearing such slogans as "Bach At The Ranch," "Handel With Care," and "Haydn In The Country."

The third event of the season was the exciting and well-attended return of pianist Dickran Atamian on Sunday, March 7, with his spectacular and spellbinding performance of Mussorgsky's "Pictures At An Exhibition" plus Prokofiev's

Sonata No. 6 in A major, Opus 82 (1940). By now Atamian's 1980 recital videotaped in Kerrville had been awarded "Best of PBS" and was sold to HBO for a seven-year run. Atamian's forceful and brilliant performances had the audience on its feet.

Somehow, three of our five festival events fell in March, and the next one followed Atamian's recital by only six days, when the Texas Opera Theatre workshop returned to Kerrville to sing a children's opera based on a Kate Pogue story in turn based upon Grimm's fairy tale "The Musicians of Bremen." Called *Starbird*, the opera by American composer Henry Mollicone commemorated the previous year's twenty-fifth anniversary of the Houston Grand Opera. The production was on tour following its Kennedy Center premiere in Washington, and by the time it reached Kerrville it had played 135 cities in thirty-one states. Mollicone will be remembered for writing the opera *Face On The Bar Room Floor,* performed annually by the Central City Opera.

Starbird was a young people's science fiction opera in English. It had quickly become a widely heralded work with its melodic score and lavish settings for dog, cat, donkey, starbird, and robots. It was well attended and both the kids and adults thoroughly enjoyed it.

The finale of our Winter Music Festival was the much anticipated appearance of America's leading cellist, Leonard Rose. His performances had earned a worldwide reputation for being superb, thoughtful, and played with a golden tone, impeccable technique, and unerring musicianship. His Kerrville recital, accompanied by Albert Hirsch, included some of the great selections for cello and piano he had recorded for Columbia Masterworks over the past thirty years, including music of Beethoven, Schumann, Bloch, Chopin, and Debussy.

Rose, who had canceled his previously scheduled appearance in Kerrville due to the air traffic controllers' strike, was greeted by a large and appreciative audience that gave him a warm and extended standing ovation. It was an exciting conclusion to our first Kerrville Winter Music Festival.

Rose and I hit it off beautifully and talked at some length about his desire to record with Van Cliburn. He asked if I would be interested in trying to put that together, and I told him that I would certainly consider it. However, Rose died before we could make all the very extensive arrangements to bring his wish to fruition. I have always felt that it would have been a collaboration filled with exciting possibilities.

At the beginning of the new year, we had sent out a newsletter to our national mailing list seeking some underwriting for five Kerrville Folk Festival albums, 1977-1981, recorded but not released because of the cash crunch legacy of the foundation's celebrity golf tournament. The estimated cost per album, using the master tapes we had in the can, would be about $2,500, and we were getting further behind each year, so the newsletter inquiry was a long shot. Where else would we come up with the $12,500 out of the blue?

One afternoon the phone rang, and it was one of our volunteers from Florida named Tim Crowe. He had read the newsletter and remembered our helpful staff who assisted him in getting home in a hurry from the festival when his father became seriously ill. He called to say that his father had died that May and that he would like to establish a memorial for him by underwriting the records. He would make the donation in memory of his father, Dr. Charles W. Crowe. This remarkable gesture of generosity allowed me to proceed with the final production of the first three albums, 1977-1979, in time for the folk festival in May. The 1980 and 1981 albums would follow shortly, and we'd be back on schedule for 1982. It was an incredible gift!

Following last year's success at Houston's Miller Outdoor Theatre, we were invited to return for a pair of concerts on April 16 and 17, 1982, to open the theater's fourteenth season. We were elated and I began our slate with four favorites from the previous year: John Vandiver and Don Sanders from Houston, Kenneth Threadgill (now known universally as "the father of Austin's country music,") and Gary P. Nunn, whose popular "London Homesick Blues" opened and closed every edition of the PBS-TV show "Austin City Limits." Then I added Nanci Griffith, now signed with a national label and also our newest festival director. She had recommended a Houston-based acoustic quartet called the Banded Geckos, known for their harmony singing and instrumental prowess, so I added them and had Nanci introduce them at the concerts. Butch Hancock also accepted. By now he had seven albums to his credit including songs like "West Texas Waltz" and "Big Hotel." Closing out the lineup were Uncle Walt's Band, Bill Neeley, and 1981 New Folk award winner Melissa Javors from San Antonio. We also retained Dean Rayburn from our festival sound company to work with the Miller Theatre sound crew. The two nights were a rewarding mix of what

Kerrville had to offer with each artist singing three songs and then joining with Gary P. Nunn at the close.

After the Friday night concert, we all went to Birra Poretti's Italian Restaurant on West Gray for dinner and wine with Vicki Bell joining our table of sixteen. It was good to have time together off-stage for a change.

We returned to Austin to prepare for another foundation street dance on Sunday afternoon, April 25, following an evening at Emma Joe's club on North Lamar. While undercapitalized, the club had been doing a fine job of providing a place for songwriters to be heard. In March alone, the club hosted Uncle Walt's Band, Nanci Griffith, Townes Van Zandt, Bobby Bridger, Bill Neeley, and an evening with Bob Livingston and Don Sanders. The street dance was another successful party with thousands turning out to dance in front of the Gaslight Theater to B. W. Stevenson and his new band, the Octave Doctors, and Beto y los Fairlanes.

By the time we returned to the ranch on Monday, we were in the advanced stages of publicizing and organizing the logistics for the first Mesquite Folk Festival, May 7–9, at Eastfield College, co-sponsored by the Mesquite Performing Arts Council. The twelve-year-old college had been building a good educational program with both summer and fall schedules, and now their new partnership with the arts council would provide for and promote the performing arts. There was also additional support from the city of Mesquite and the Chamber of Commerce.

While Don Sanders fulfilled a folk residency for the fourth- and fifth-grade children in Mesquite schools, we opened the three-day festival with an 8:00 P.M. Friday concert at the college performance hall called "Old Timers' Night: The Legend Lives," featuring Kenneth Threadgill and Bill Neely, Red River Dave, and Lonnie Glosson with his old radio partner Wayne Rainey.

The next day began with a noon children's concert at City Park played by Don Sanders and Turk Pipkin, the Austin mime whose juggling antics had been seen in major theaters all over Europe. At 3:00 P.M. we hosted a bluegrass band contest at the Mesquite Opry Hall with the Southwestern Bluegrass Association co-hosting. That night the songwriters' concert headlined Nanci Griffith, Bob

Gibson, Don Sanders, and Gary P. Nunn with his Sons of the Bunkhouse Band.

Sunday, the final day, we hosted as a free event a 2:00 P.M. "Rising Stars Competition," based on our New Folk competitions and coordinated by David Card at Poor David's Pub. Our judges were Sanders, Nunn, and Gibson.

At 5:00 P.M. we presented a free gospel concert at the First Methodist Church, starring the Mercy River Boys and the Masters Four.

Our final 8:00 P.M. concert at the performance hall was called "Black and Blue" and starred Odetta, Gatemouth Brown, and Robert Shaw.

It was an entertaining and gratifying three-day event, drawing fans from a dozen surrounding communities. All the participants enjoyed the hospitality provided by our hosts headed by Art Greenhaw.

Meanwhile, back at the ranch, we were just a few weeks away from the May 27–June 6 eleventh Kerrville Folk Festival. We were beginning our second decade, having produced twenty-nine festivals (164 concerts) in the Hill Country since 1972. The folk festival had grown from 2,800 paid attendance the first year to 14,600 during the most recent year's eight-day event. Our latest documented information showed fans coming from 161 communities in forty states plus more than 100 Texas towns and cities. Nancylee and I had already taken our storied vacation in Puerto Vallarta, Mexico, with Bob Gibson, Anne Hills, and a dozen of our friends and volunteers and were now back with renewed energy and inspiration.

We started this series of festivals with a dozen performers and with an enthusiasm for Texas music, and, while enthusiasm was not enough, it had provided an essential element to outlasting the adverse circumstances we faced along the way. Our concerts provided all of us with the possibility of sharing rich and significant experiences with a sense of renewal, relaxation, and recreation. We centered on the unique but often unrecognized talents of original artists who were emerging in Texas. As the years passed and the festivals matured, we saw an air of expectancy grow. We began also to focus on the artistic excellence and charisma of performers from other states, performers like Tom Paxton, Odetta, Bob Gibson, David Amram, and so many others, including out-of-state New Folk finalists and winners.

Music for us, now more than ever before, had become a means for fuller and more effective lives. Within our own family of performers and volunteers, we reduced friction, suspicion, and misunderstanding to a point where we all wondered how long this marvel of sharing could last.

Together, over the first ten years, we developed an ability to recognize and respect excellence and to differentiate that from mediocrity. We knew that some musically trivial and insignificant songs could have a strong and immediate appeal, but little that kept them from being commonplace. While learning to be hospitable to all music, including a broad range and variety of songs from different genres, music conveying defined emotional values with directness, conviction, and originality became the expected standard. While the music should be entertaining, we also expected it to be worthy of dignified treatment. We felt that the way to recognition for our event, while effectively entertaining our audiences, was by settling for nothing less than sheer and uncompromising excellence.

In addition, we now eagerly anticipated the annual return of our faithful volunteer staff. We valued the cumulative Kerrville experience that had become an enriching and far-reaching gift for all of us.

The eleventh festival would include eight 6-hour evening concerts with forty-eight performers and more than twenty daytime events, including a second edition of the songwriting school under Bob Gibson's guidance, and a new guitar school sponsored by the foundation and created by Chicago Old Towne School executive director Ray Tate. He had taught guitar seminars in more than two dozen universities and colleges across the country. Recipient of seven major awards, he also had recorded and performed with more than three dozen stars, including Judy Collins, Arlo Guthrie, Merle Travis, Vassar Clements, Mary Travers, and others. Tate was assisted by Shake Russell-Dana Cooper guitarist Michael Mashkes. More than forty students signed up for each of the two sessions.

We also added an "Earth School" with nutrition, herbology, yoga, traditional Chinese healing, and an herb walk across the ranch. During one afternoon, Lindsay Haisley held a two-hour autoharp workshop, and then we repeated our Wednesday night dinner show to mark another birthday.

David Amram hosted the first day Ballad Tree as the festival opened, and that night's concert was a strong curtain-raiser with Bridger's friend and former producer Fred Carter, Jr., from Nashville on the bill with Vandiver, Carolyn Hester, and Shake Russell closing. New Folk winner Melissa Javors opened the

Introducing Tim Crowe to the Kerrville audience following his gift to the Kerrville Music Foundation. 1982.
— Courtesy Brian Kanof.

Friday night concert joining Bob Zentz from Rambling Conrad's and the Norfolk Folk Festival with headliners being B. W. Stevenson and Riders in the Sky. The Austin Celtic band, Grimalkin, did the 5:00 P.M. warm-up set Friday, Saturday, and Sunday, and the Saturday night concert offered well-received sets by Uncle Walt's Band, Steve Young, Peter Yarrow, and Odetta.

During Saturday night's concert, I invited Tim Crowe on-stage, where I could publicly thank him for his generous contribution to underwrite the albums, thus saving the recorded history of the festival. Tim had always been an especially helpful volunteer on staff and, while being a little reserved in public, he beamed as the crowd showed him their admiration.

On Saturday and Sunday afternoons Allen Damron and I co-hosted the forty finalists in the New Folk with Rick Beresford, Fred Carter, Jr., and Bob Zentz as judges, selecting winners Lizi Line Williams from Austin, Kelly Gazzaway and Norris Mealer of Amarillo, Lubbock Johnson of Houston, Catesby Jones from Kingsville, and Emily Aronson from Dallas. While not award winners, we noted the songs of Emily Kaitz of Austin, Houston's J. W. Weir, and a young man named Larry Williams from Medina as being pretty close to the mark.

The Sunday night concert was a giant event with Southern Manor, Jon Ims, Nanci Griffith, Ray Wylie Hubbard, Gary P. Nunn, and Gatemouth

Jon Ims from Colorado. 1982.
— Courtesy Brian Kanof.

Brown. Monday was the Memorial Day holiday with music starting at 11:00 in the morning with mother-and-son-duo Maggie and Monte Montgomery, a four-hour 1:00 P.M. concert by the 12 Moon Storytellers, Turk Pipkin, and the Louisiana Aces, who had played at Bridger's "homecoming."

Monday evening's concert was also a packed six hours of music by Bob Livingston, Townes Van Zandt, Dottsy, David Amram, Bill and Bonnie, and Beto y los Fairlanes.

The next night and Thursday had the guitar and songwriters' school faculty jam sessions with Bob Gibson on the twelve-string, Dick Goodwin on bass and piano, and with Gary P. Nunn, Peter Rowan, Ray Tate, and Michael Mashkes all participating. Wednesday was a big evening with guests, staff, performers, and press, plus a handful of paying customers, all enjoying complimentary beverage service beginning at 5:00, followed by Turk Pipkin's humorous antics for the first hour of the catfish dinner, and then an hour of Marcia Ball's compelling blues vocals and piano. Then we hosted on-stage a reunion of The University of Texas Jazz Ensemble in a three-hour concert called "The Dick

Goodwin Years, 1965-1973." Many of the alumni of Dick's student bands returned from their professional jobs to play the old charts. It was a rewarding reunion for everyone.

Friday, from noon to 5:00, Bobby Bridger held a workshop on his original epic ballads, *The Mountain Men* and *Lakota* (Sioux), the first two parts of a massive undertaking to be called *Seekers of the Fleece*. Before this, I moderated a two-hour panel discussion of booking, publicity, and promotion for all musicians with the help of Bob Gibson, Mike Williams, and James Durst.

Peter Rowan. 1982.
— Courtesy Steven's Stills.

The final three-day weekend had memorable evening concerts featuring Robert Shaw, Dee Moeller, Damron, Rusty Wier, Threadgill, Dave Van Ronk, a reunion of Frummox, Rosalie Sorrels, Buck White, Peter Rowan, Eliza Gilkyson, and Michael Murphey.

The daytime activity on that final weekend included our first staff concert suggested by Steve Fromholz, who hosted it. More than half our volunteer staff were singer-songwriters, and we established a system by which the staff would pick their own favorite colleagues to perform with other staff

Right foreground to rear: Rev. Charles Sumners, David Amram, Lindsay Haisley, Walter Lee, Dow Patterson, and Bobby Bridger at the Folk Mass on Chapel Hill. 1982.
—Courtesy James R. Willis, Jr.

pickers backing them. It was a high-spirited concert. There was also a jam by past harmonica champions, and, along with our Sunday New Folk award winners concert, we had a 1972 New Folk Reunion on Saturday. Rev. Charlie Sumners' Folk Masses on Chapel Hill were on both Sunday mornings with large crowds attending. Among the best received events of the weekend were the pair of 5:00 P.M. warm-up sets by the Banded Geckos on their first festival appearance. We had a feeling that the Geckos would be part of our family for many years to come.

The eleventh was our most successful festival to date, with attendance up by 5,000 from the previous year!

Changing gears after a break of just a few days, a unique experience for us, we targeted the chores to be done to make ready for the next three events: July 23-25 Summer Music Festival, September 2-5 Bluegrass Festival, and the October 2 "12 Great Hours."

General planning and many of the specifics for these three events had been worked out some months before, but now we tackled the detail work scheduling the various rehearsals for many of the concerts on the classical event and assigning drivers and vehicles for transportation of performers from and to the airport, the hotel, the rehearsals, and the performances. There were also press releases, photo captions, and, in the case of the "12 Great Hours,"

hotel accommodations to be worked out for over a dozen musicians.

We also needed to prepare copy for each event's printed program. When we finally worked up our accounting chart, with its account numbers assigned to various income sources and expenses, we realized how many individual tasks were taking our time and money. There were nearly as many more tasks that did not incur expenses and would not show up in the more than 100 accounting units. As a result of all the preparations going on simultaneously, time flew, and the classical festival arrived almost before we knew it.

Now that the foundation directors had established the Festival Atamian as an annual event, we renamed it the Kerrville Summer Music Festival. Regardless, Atamian would continue to play a central role.

Again in 1982, we scheduled the five free one-hour mini-concerts during the opening day between 10:00 A.M. and 6:00 P.M. at four locations around Kerrville. Playing these sixty-minute recitals were the Waterloo Winds quintet from Austin and duo-pianists Sharon Hudkins Adams and Julie Gage Thomas, whose two recitals at noon and 6:00 P.M. were at the River Hills Mall.

The opening evening concert at the ranch was at 8:30, following the first of three 7:00 P.M. "Music Lovers Welcome" warm-up sessions featuring the spirited Mozart on Fifth trio of New York whose bassoon and two clarinets played music ranging from Mozart to Scott Joplin and provided a relaxing shirt-sleeve kind of informality to set the tone we wanted.

Austin flutist Megan Meisenbach provided the Friday evening concert, bringing with her pianist Erik Hicks, fellow flutist Teresa DeVane, and harpist Kim Gorman to play in various combinations with her the music of Poulenc, Copland, Berlioz, Doppler, Satie, and Ives. Then for the evening climax, Megan was joined by Eliot Chapo, *violin*, Barbara Huster, *viola*, and Mimi Moxley, *cello*, in the charming Mozart Quartet in D major, K285. It was a bright, varied, and intimate concert enjoyed by a good first-night turnout.

There were, again this year, five daytime events over Saturday and Sunday at the Kerrville Municipal Auditorium. In the lobby we exhibited wildlife oils and watercolors by the noted Hill Country artist Travis Keese, a former staff artist for the Houston Museum of Natural Science.

Three daytime events were on Saturday, beginning at 10:00 A.M., with an electronic music concert by the McLean Mix, a husband and wife duo who had toured seven European cities and the northeastern U.S. on their 1981 tour. As unusual as it was, their music had an immediate appeal by virtue of its colorful impressionist textures resulting from combinations of their instrumental and vocal skills with taped and/or live electronics.

The children's concert at 1:00 P.M. was a fast-moving hour of lighthearted moments from original books by pianist-composer Kathryn Mishell and mime Turk Pipkin, already a Kerrville Folk Festival favorite for his magic tricks, juggling feats, and illusions all tinged with his wry humor. He had toured theaters throughout Italy, France, and Belgium as well as major American venues from Chicago to Los Angeles. Their collaboration on excerpts from Saint-Saëns' "Carnival of the Animals" provided the high point that really excited the children.

At 4:00 P.M. we presented the professional debut recital of young mezzo-soprano Paula Patterson, who had previously sung starring roles in college and graduate school productions of ten operas and seven musicals. With piano accompaniment by Robert Thiem, she sang music of Purcell, Mozart, Copland, Massenet, Saint-Saëns, Johann Strauss, and Leonard Bernstein much to the delight of her audience. It was an auspicious debut and a good idea!

The Saturday night Festival Orchestra concert had David Amram conducting an all-Baroque evening featuring a number of brilliant young soloists. Violinist Paul Neubauer, a 1982 Naumburg Special Award Winner, played works by Bach and Telemann. The 1979 Maurice Andre Trumpet Competition (Paris, France) winner Stacey Blair, although blind since birth, had already toured extensively with symphony orchestras. He played unsurpassed performances of Telemann and Tartini trumpet concerti. Megan Meisenbach was joined by violinist Margaret Batjer, harpsichordist Carmen Alvarez, and cellist Delta Hall in the Quantz Trio Sonata in G minor. Megan, Margaret, and Carmen then played principal roles in the Bach Brandenburg Concerto No. 5 to close the concert that had inspired a pre-festival slogan "Go for Baroque to Kerrville."

Amram conducting the Festival Orchestra. 1982.

— Courtesy *Kerrville Daily Times.*

Sunday began with the Concert Chorale of Houston, David Wehr, director, assisted by members of the Festival Orchestra in an extraordinary concert of music by Victoria, Schütz, Byrd, Handel, Bach, Bruckner, and Matheas, climaxing with Cecil Effinger's setting of "America, the Beautiful." Standing ovations were the order of the day.

Our chamber music event at 4:00 P.M. was a program for violin, piano, and viola by Bach, Chausson, and Flackton, and the well-received "Variations on a Russian Folk Song" by Khandoshin for viola and piano. Once more, our young players were Margaret Batjer, Carmen Alvarez, and Paul Neubauer, who each distinguished themselves by providing enthralling performances and a further validation of our "young artists" policy.

The festival ended with a recital at Quiet Valley Ranch by Dickran Atamian who, since his last appearance at the ranch, had recorded a series of recitals for PBS and two LPs, including an all-Chopin album, and performed a series of solo recitals and orchestral appearances.

There was an air of anticipation for this final event as, besides playing works by Mozart, Schumann, and Ravel, Atamian would close his recital with an encore performance of Stravinsky's *Rite of Spring*, the complete ballet arranged for piano.

A sizable and appreciative audience greeted Atamian's return, and he rewarded them with a momentous and compelling evening to close out the first Summer Music Festival with a stirring climax!

The contributions of Amram, Atamian, Baldwin pianos, all the prize-winning young soloists, and the special appearances by other accomplished soloists and the chorale made for a fulfilling weekend of the highest caliber.

While we didn't even have time to travel to Austin to survey the damage, we wished Eddie Wilson a quick rebuild on his Threadgill's Restaurant, severely damaged by fire on August 16. It would be closed for a while.

I was busy working toward the formalization of a new statewide organization of Texas festivals under the sponsorship of the Discover Texas Association, and our ninth annual bluegrass festival was just a couple of weeks away.

Labor Day weekend festival dates were September 2-5, opening on Thursday with a full evening schedule that included Bluegrass 43 from France and a jam session by four of the evening's

Paul Glasse, mandolin champion. 1982.
— Courtesy *Kerrville Daily Times.*

regional bands, coordinated by mandolin champion Bobby Clark. Early arrivals thought it was a great evening and cheered enthusiastically.

By Friday, when Buck White and the Down Home Folks arrived for the mandolin championship preliminaries, the crowd had also begun to arrive in earnest. Then Jana Jae arrived to play fiddle with Grassfire, and Paul Glasse was a special guest, sitting in with Buck White's family to close the evening.

Saturday and Sunday added Frank Wakefield, Hot Rize, David Harvey and the Reasonable Band from Colorado, the Hot Mud Family, Doyle Lawson and Quicksilver, with Mac Wiseman added on Sunday.

The weekend's biggest cheer went up for one of America's winningest young instrumentalists, Mark O'Connor, who showed up with mandolin in hand to win the Buck White Championship judged by former champions David Harvey (1979), Bob Clark (1980), and Paul Glasse (1981).

Tennessee Valley Authority again won the

band contest and became our first two-time Southwestern Bluegrass Band champions by taking on all 1982 contestants.

Despite an unexplained drop in attendance from 8,000 last year to 6,500 the current year, the festival covered its own expenses and pleased the crowd on hand. We thought we'd been really smart to trim the budget to make the festival profitable, but the income shrank with the budget. We were beginning to see a break-even pattern solidifying itself and would probably have rejected the idea of making a profit on anything that was as much fun as bluegrass music.

Right after the bluegrass festival, on September 17, I hastened to San Antonio to meet with a group of festival producers from around the state as we attempted to organize an association to expedite networking by various civic, non-profit, and commercial festivals. I had found that a number of other festival executives wanted to exchange ideas and share experiences. We came to recognize our tourist-oriented activities as having many common problems and opportunities that were significantly different from those of permanent tourist attractions such as resorts, historical sites, theme parks, and other year-round tourist destinations.

So we formalized our organization, set up bylaws, established rules and dues and qualifications for membership, lined out target goals, and elected

officers. I accepted the chairmanship, and we began life as a part of the larger Discover Texas Association, a well-established tourist-trade association with which I'd had a long relationship.

We would deal with our own particular problems and opportunities on one hand, and share goals with DTA on the other hand. DTA executive director Jim Battersby would help me and the festival organization as its executive with DTA picking up the tab until we could develop a budget and some cash flow. The first year of organizing and seeking members would be a difficult job of selling our idea to enough organizations to make it work. In fact, nearly a year later, we would only have thirty members and a small budget of $10,000!

Our one-day annual "12 Great Hours" was just four weeks ahead of us. We mounted our publicity campaigns following up on our summer newsletter sent to all of our Texas followers. We could tell them to come to the ranch "Away From It All" starting at 2:00 P.M. on Saturday, October 2, to hear a dozen hours of music by a dozen Kerrville performers already confirmed, plus surprise guests.

As it turned out, David Amram, Melissa Javors, Butch Hancock, Kinky Friedman, and Ramblin' Jack Elliott all came to play as surprise guests joining the announced lineup of the Dallas Irish string band Tinker's Dam, Nanci Griffith and the Banded Geckos, Lindsay Haisley, Rory McLeod, and Allen Damron. Bobby Bridger also came to get his final taste of Kerrville for a while before leaving for Omaha to take a role in a new musical by Dale Wassermann. Wassermann was known for his *Man of*

Kinky Friedman at the "12 Great Hours." 1982.
— Courtesy Wayne Miller.

At the 1982 "12 Great Hours," the Amram Jam grows as (from left) Brian Wood, Nanci Griffith, Butch Hancock, and Frank Hill join Amram, along with Joe Don Kotrla, Lindsay Haisley, Melissa Javors, and Barbi Springer. 1982.
— Courtesy Wayne Hill.

La Mancha and was trying out his new *Shakespeare and the Indians* at a dinner theater in Omaha.

The fifth annual Worst Hat Contest happened again (good ideas never die!) and provided some humorous moments between the afternoon and evening portions of the celebration. As always, the music was rewarding with everyone sitting in with everyone else. It was a slice of the folk festival itself, and at 2:00 A.M. the singing continued around the campfires. It was a healing final event for our eleventh season. We even had time to visit with Nanci Griffith who was just coming off a tour with Carolyn Hester.

Three days after the "12 Hours," I flew to Chicago to meet Bob Gibson and drive down with him to the Norfolk Festival at the invitation of Bob Zentz. It was a relaxing week well spent, away from the constant schedule in Texas. I returned feeling re-energized and ready for work.

Our 1982-83 classical festival season began, as it had the previous year, with a Christmas concert. This year we scheduled Vivaldi's *Gloria* on December 12 at the auditorium to be performed by soloists, Kerrville Community Chorus, and the festival orchestra. Choral director Sally Ritch and conductor David Amram coordinated selection of scores for the *Gloria* and also scheduled additional music by Corelli, Handel, Copley, Hedges, and others.

Soloists for the concert were sopranos Ruth Ann Harmon, Sally Ritch, and Maggie Meek, with

mezzo-soprano Elizabeth Real. The audience was near capacity and the performance level was superb. Amram and his Festival Orchestra of Austin Symphony members had reached a really compatible and artistically productive relationship that allowed a high level of accomplishment, even with just short rehearsal time, and the participants seemed to enjoy the event as much as the patrons.

We had more than a month, including the Christmas and New Year's holidays, to prepare for the 1983 season and the second event of the Winter Music Festival that would play January 22. There were several days in San Antonio in festival association meetings, and production work in Austin at PSG studios preparing the Kerrville albums. I also presented the Blackwood Brothers in concert at the auditorium, so we managed to stay pretty busy.

I really looked forward to our January 22 concert by Houston Grand Opera soprano Carmen Balthrop and bass-baritone Dorceal Duckins. We had seen them both in the Houston premiere performance of Scott Joplin's melodic ragtime opera *Treemonisha*. She had made her Metropolitan Opera

Soprano Carmen Balthrop. 1982.
— Publicity Photo.

debut in 1977 in *The Magic Flute*. The concert was a gratifying evening of lyric moments from opera and I immediately became a devoted fan of Carmen. When she surprised me by singing "Happy Birthday," I was overwhelmed. It was the most beautiful version of the song I had ever heard and the first time in my life that I really enjoyed it!

On January 29 I made a quick trip to Round Top for one of James Dick's winter concerts with my good friend and travel agent John Miller, and with the exception of the three-day Festivals Association conference at Texas A&M in College Station in the early part of February, every day was devoted to getting out festival newsletters nationally, and getting ready for our February 19 classical concert featuring Carlos Barbosa-Lima, one of the leading guitarists of the world. He had toured Canada, Europe, Mexico, South America, and Israel, as well as all across the U.S., performing his extraordinary transcriptions of music by Scarlatti, Bach, Handel, and other classical masters, intermixed with salty Brazilian compositions and bluesy Gershwin preludes. His most recent ABC album had been selected by a number of leading magazines as one of the best albums of the year. His Kerrville appearance excited and pleased his audience, and he proved to be a warm, direct, and genuine man who also expressed considerable interest in the Kerrville Folk Festival.

Three days promoting our festival at the Houston Travel Show at the end of February and business trips to both Mesquite and Port Arthur were breaks in the constant office work leading up to the March 13 Atamian recital at Kerrville. His concert of Mozart, Ravel, Brahms, and tangos of Luis Jorge Gonzales was capped off with the southwestern premiere of Raphling's transcription of Stravinsky's "Firebird Suite." A big turnout of area fans attended along with patrons from San Antonio and several other cities, and I was pleased to see many of the guests greeting Atamian warmly after the concert by his nickname "Richie." His playing was another unforgettable display of incredibly focused and passionate performing ability. The Ravel "Gaspar de la Nui" alone ran his audience through the full range of emotional and intellectual appreciation.

After seeing Atamian off, I headed for the five-day Dallas Sports and Vacation show, March 16-20, to continue our promotional campaign for the coming outdoor festival season. I was gratified to discover how many people were already familiar with our festivals and to have the opportunity to tell so many others about them.

Six days later our Winter Music Festival offered an evening with Kerrville's own lyric coloratura soprano, Ruth Ann Harmon, in a full recital of songs and arias accompanied by renowned pianist David Garvey, who had most recently toured with Leontyne Price. The highlight of the evening for the large loyal Kerrville audience was Ruth Ann's performance of "Bell Song" from Delibes' *Lakme*.

Our final winter concert was an evening of Gershwin and Cole Porter songs from *Kiss Me Kate, Porgy and Bess*, and other favorites. The five artists were soprano Nancy Elledge, mezzo soprano Kathleen Mesca, tenor Dario Caletta, baritone Francis J. Macca, and bass Nicolas Netos from the stunning new residency company of the Texas Opera Theatre. The turnout was large, probably due to the successful productions of the previous season. This was a bonus event for our season patrons, but there were also many tickets sold at the door. The American celebration of songs was a gratifying close to our second Kerrville Winter Music Festival.

Austin stockbroker Townsend Miller had been writing country music columns for the *American-Statesman* for more than ten years, donating over 4,000 hours researching and writing. The first of his 526 weeks of columns had appeared back when the first Kerrville Folk Festival and the first Willie Nelson Picnic were held. In March 1983, however, he retired from writing the columns, saying the heavy volume of trading on the stock market precluded his continuing. Whatever the reason he stopped his columns, all of us who had received coverage from him were suddenly struck by how important his efforts had become all those years and how we had taken them for granted.

I got together with Ranger Doug (Green) of the Riders in the Sky (to whom I had been introduced by Townsend) and asked if the trio would be willing to play a music foundation benefit at Austin's Paramount Theater to establish an endowment in Townsend's honor. They eagerly accepted and we reserved the Paramount for Saturday, April 9.

Before the concert, we wanted to brag on him at a black-tie dinner at the Bradford Hotel (the former Stephen F. Austin Hotel next to the Paramount), and we sold out our 100 accommodations for $25 a plate. Townsend was joined at the head table by his wife Rita, Mr. and Mrs. Davis Ford, Mr. and Mrs. Tom Pitts of *Performance*

Townsend Miller black-tie dinner at the Bradford Hotel (from left) Rita Miller, emcee Steven Fromholz, honoree Townsend Miller, Ranger Doug (Green), Floyd Tillman. April 9, 1983.

— Courtesy *Austin American-Statesman.*

Magazine, Mr. and Mrs. Doug Green, Floyd Tillman, and Nancylee and me, among others. Steven Fromholz was the master of ceremonies. The tributes came in all forms from all parts of the music business with flowers for Rita and gifts, plaques, and other honors generously bestowed on a smiling Townsend Miller, who said he did it only because he loved the music. The tribute dinner was so much fun it almost ran over into the concert time.

A few minutes after 8:00 P.M., however, with Rita and Townsend sitting in the guest box seats of honor, the show began. They were looking down at the sold-out downstairs, including the ten rows of $25 dress circle seats. Surprise guests on-stage included Fromholz, whose participation in the film *Outlaw Blues* had been heavily publicized in Townsend's columns; Leon Carter; Bobby Bridger (home briefly from the production of *Shakespeare and the Indians* in Omaha); Tim Henderson; Melissa Javors; Laura Lee McBryde, former Bob Wills vocalist; Robert Shaw; Kurt Van Sickle; Eliza Gilkyson; Floyd Tillman; Joe Ely; Nashville-based poet and lyricist Charles John Quarto (one of many in town from the Music City for the tribute); and many others.

The audience was also filled with music industry leaders, performers, and other personalities from recording, broadcasting, and publishing, as well as Townsend's compatriots from both the newspaper and his brokerage firm. Representative delegations were there from Kerrville, the Austin Folk Foundation, Austin Music Umbrella, Texas Music Association, Central Texas Bluegrass Association,

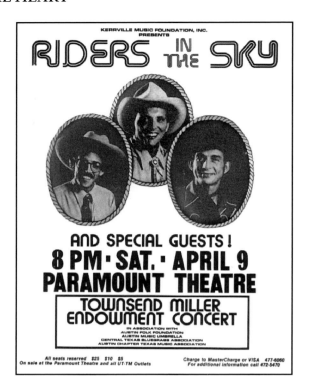

and most of the night clubs, music rooms, and dance halls in Central Texas.

The big finish was, of course, the harmonies and humor of Riders in the Sky. Townsend had first seen them at a taping for "Austin City Limits" and immediately called me to come see them. One show and I was hooked, and they started playing for huge audiences at the festivals right away.

The dinner and the Paramount concert were not only high-spirited and gala affairs but raised $2,000 clear after all the bills were paid. Then the Nashville office of ASCAP called and added another $1,000 to bring the new Townsend Miller Endowment Fund to $3,000!

The interest from the endowment would help pay New Folk award winner prizes for the next fifteen to twenty years. As the months passed, though, all of us realized more and more how much we missed Townsend's columns.

Two weeks after the Paramount show, our foundation co-sponsored another Austin street dance with the former Gaslight Theater, now renamed the Capitol City Playhouse, at 214 West 4th Street. For the modest $4 admission, we had an outstanding roster of bands from 3:00 to 10:00 P.M., starting with Tony Trishka and Skyline playing a danceable brand of "Progressive N.Y. Bluegrass." The seven- hour dance offered thirty- to forty-

minute sets by a trio featuring Jimmie Gilmore, David Halley, and Butch Hancock, by Bill and Bonnie Hearne's augmented Red River Band, some Austin kicker music by the Alvin Crow Band, and a final set of good-time Austin boogie by Ernie Sky and the K-Tels. A classic poster designed by Michael Priest had been recycled to draw large crowds to the warehouse district for the happening.

On April 30, as the culmination of a year's consulting with the Service League of Port Arthur to establish an annual festival there, I produced a pops concert in cooperation with Patty Oltremari and her committee. Co-sponsored by the city of Port Arthur, local business, and individual sponsors, we brought in David Amram to conduct a forty-three-member orchestra in an all-American concert at the Port Arthur Civic Center. The first portion offered a suite from *West Side Story*, three Scott Joplin rags, Amram's own "En Memorium de Chano Pozo," with Amram conducting from the piano, and selections from *The Sound of Music*.

The audience at the civic center was sizable, and at intermission they were told about the forthcoming Pleasure Island Music Festival planned for April, 1984, and of the League's plans to build a permanent multi-use structure on the island to be dedicated as part of Port Arthur's Texas Sesquicentennial celebration in 1986. You could feel the excitement in the hall as for years there had been a local clamor to see the island developed into a more useful park.

The remainder of the concert featured music of Gershwin, beginning with a suite from *Porgy and Bess* and closing with "Rhapsody in Blue" with special guest Thomas Wright at the piano. Wright had played "Rhapsody" ninety times in six weeks on a coast-to-coast tour with the Tommy Dorsey Orchestra. He'd also had the benefit of personal coaching by Paul Whiteman, whose orchestra had given the world premiere. Wright was also founder of the Gershwin Festival in Florida and had played "Rhapsody" with numerous symphony orchestras. He also had been, in former years, a staff pianist with the NBC Television Network featured on regular weekly network television and radio shows.

Amram made a hit with the league, the fans, and the orchestra members, and would be back to conduct the same orchestra in 1984.

Four days later we were in Mesquite, Texas, for the second Mesquite Folk Festival, May 5-8. It included most of the events of the first year plus a Thursday night full-fledged gospel concert by the Masters V, featuring top singers from famous quartets: Hovie Lister, who organized the Statesmen; J. D. Sumner, who was the acclaimed bass for the Stamps; legendary lead singer Jake Hess; James Blackwood, leader of the renowned Blackwood Brothers; plus Rosie Rozell, reputedly gospel music's greatest tenor. Presented as a free-will offering concert at the First Assembly of God Church, the event drew a house filled with appreciative followers.

Friday was "Bluegrass Night" at the Eastfield College Performance Hall, and fiddling Jana Jae, widely recognized for her regular appearances on TV's "Hee Haw," appeared as guest star with the popular Shady Grove Ramblers along with TVA, Grassfire, and the House Brothers. It was a good mix of hard-core, old-time bluegrass and some of today's more contemporary music, as exemplified by the original songs of Tom Uhr, and the traditional and pop variety offered by TVA from San Antonio. The bluegrass fans loved it.

A new event for the festival was Bob Gibson's songwriting school all three days. The school was limited to forty students and incorporated a new workbook devised by Bob.

Saturday was a busy day, not even counting the song school session. It began at noon with a huge crowd of kids and parents gathered at City Lake Park to hear the songs of Bill Oliver and enjoy magician Jules Caplan.

At 3:00 that afternoon at the Opry Hall, co-hosted by the Southwestern Bluegrass Club, the festival held its second band competition.

We named the Saturday night concert "Songfolk Night" and featured Allen Damron, Bob Gibson, Eliza Gilkyson, and Ray Wylie Hubbard before a cheering crowd.

Sunday's schedule began at 2:00 P.M. on Eastfield College's Upper Courtyard. Again, David Card coordinated the Rising Star Songwriters Competition that had a large audience of serious listeners and supporters for the finalists.

The festival closed on Sunday night with a rousing "Western Swing Night" showcasing the Light Crust Doughboys, Asleep at the Wheel, and Texas Playboys vocalist Leon Rausch. It was a straight-ahead three hours of genuine western swing music from the 1930s to the 1980s and had the whole audience moving, tapping their toes, and applauding every tune, many of which had been popularized by Bob Wills. Asleep at the Wheel was, by now, a nationally known Grammy Award-winning band, and their performance showed why.

From a logistical viewpoint, it was rewarding having Mary Jane Farmer along to work with Art Greenhaw and David Amidon from the college. She had the right answers for all their questions based on her extensive experience at Kerrville. We also had helpful support from Brunhilde Nystrom, who had been elected mayor of Mesquite since our last festival. The year before, she had operated a mini-cam for Warner Western, videotaping the festival for distribution on cable television.

Our next Miller Theatre concert in Houston would feature bluegrass and take place two weeks after our own bluegrass festival in September, leaving us three clear weeks now to concentrate on the festival arrangements. The 1983 folk festival was scheduled for a full eleven days, May 26-June 5. This twelfth edition would feature sixty songwriters from Texas, fifteen other states, and a two-day "Salute to Canada" featuring three outstanding Canadians I had chosen from the dozens I had seen at Winnipeg the previous year.

The 1982 folk festival had drawn 19,000 fans, and there was reason to believe that this year's turnout would be even bigger, if our work at the travel shows was successful. To prepare the ranch, there were two work weekends in advance to move more than 1,000 feet of seven-foot fencing to increase the size of the camping area.

There were to be eight evening concerts of seven artists each. We also wanted to continue the warm-up sets, Fromholz' new staff concert, and the

"Great Texas Harmonica Blow-Off," even though top competitors were becoming scarce. As we put the artists' roster together, we were pleased to realize that nine of this year's stars were former New Folk winners.

The middle three days between the two weekends was still in an experimental stage, but we continued the schools for songwriting, guitar, and the "Earth School." We also continued the faculty jams on Tuesday and Thursday nights and the Wednesday evening anniversary catfish fry with David Amram and Country Gazette splitting the dinner show, followed by a concert by Beto y los Fairlanes.

Country Gazette at the Kerrville Folk Festival. 1983.
— Courtesy Brian Kanof.

256

As the first big five-day weekend approached, some of the volunteers expressed concern that the larger audiences were going to ruin the ambiance and intimacy of the earlier festivals. While I had some concern about that possibility, too, I had been deliberately establishing our target audience, one that I felt compatible with our intimate format. Long ago I had deleted college fraternities and military bases from our mailings. We also had a large segment of our audience who had been here for many years who collectively set a massive example of what was expected.

Our notes in printed programs, distributed to the audience at the gate as they entered, explained every year that each member of the audience has a private experience listening to music. We know that in the festival setting, this private experience happens in public. While the private excitement of listening to music can make a fan want to whoop and holler with joy, or clap along, we hoped that everyone would respect the private listening excitement of the people around them. Being part of the experience together can be rewarding and even transforming, but should not invade or pollute the personal listening environment of the people around them. For the most part, the Kerrville audience continues to be respectful. *Texas Monthly's* Joe Nick Patoski described it as "almost reverent."

I assured my staff that we had worked diligently and thoughtfully to guarantee the quality of the experience and the kind of reward we wanted for both the performers and the audience, a reward not common in so many other performing situations. Larger audiences were needed to preserve our festival's stability, and if it became too crowded, we would add another weekend in the future to thin it out again.

The festival opened on Thursday, May 26, with Bob Livingston and Jimmie Gilmore co-hosting the first Ballad Tree and would close eleven days later with Ray Wylie Hubbard joined by dozens on-stage singing the anthem.

The first weekend held many highs for us, including the surprise appearance of Rosanne Cash with Rodney Crowell and Guy Clark, the workshop and evening performance of Bob Brozman with his wonderful collection of National guitars, the final farewell reunion of the Austin quintet Eaglebone Whistle, the reception given Chuck Pyle, a 1981 New Folk winner who was enjoying growing popularity, and the first festival appearance of Flaco's brother, accordionist Santiago Jimenez, Jr.

It was surprising to have met Santiago on-stage at Winnipeg when he lived just seventy-five miles down the road from me in Texas. That meeting in Canada the previous summer found us immediately bonded. I had also selected three remarkable Canadian players who exemplified to me the absolute best in Canadian music today. Their appearances in workshops, warm-ups, and main stage concerts made up the "Salute to Canada" created with the help of Judi Hanna, public affairs officer in the Canadian Consul General's office in Dallas. With the help of Air Canada and Western Airlines, we brought these three artists in from three separate regions of Canada. Connie Kaldor, Stan Rogers, and Al "One-Man Band" Simmons were immediate hits with our audiences. Besides their impressive main stage appearances, we also did a workshop with all three of them where they were asked to describe the festivals at Winnipeg, Edmonton, Owen Sound, Vancouver, and Mariposa, and to invite their American audiences to come to Canada. We displayed the Canadian flag on-stage and gave out Canadian flag pins. It was a warm, hospitable experience.

The children were drawn immediately to the clever antics and zany music of Al Simmons and his trunk-load of props. The cutting edge and spirit of Canadian songs by both Connie Kaldor and the Stan Rogers trio stole the hearts of the Americans, and there was an immediate kinship between the members of the audience and the performers. Connie Kaldor had the heart and the power of a Broadway star, and Stan Rogers' songs of the people, the lakes, and prairies of Canada brought tears of understanding to our eyes. In the campgrounds and backstage, Stan was the congenial goodwill ambassador.

Winnipeg's one-man band Al Simmons. 1983.
— Courtesy Brian Kanof.

Rodney Crowell at Kerrville. 1983.
— Courtesy Richard Orton.

Colorado's Chuck Pyle. 1983.
— Courtesy Brian Kanof.

Surprise guest Roseanne Cash. 1983.
— Courtesy Merri Lu Park.

Bob Brozman playing one of his National guitars. 1983.
— Courtesy Brian Kanof.

Santiago Jimenez, Jr., stretching his style. 1983.
— Courtesy Brian Kanof.

Connie Kaldor of Canada. 1983.
— Courtesy Brian Kanof.

Stan Rogers at Kerrville. 1983.
— Courtesy Brian Kanof.

We were also pleased when Bob Gibson brought with him fellow Chicagoan Anne Hills, and we enjoyed the night that the Banded Geckos and Nanci Griffith played on the same concert. There was a magic moment when Jon Ims closed the first Saturday night concert, and one more when Lyle Lovett joined Nanci Griffith to sing "Closing Time."

The Kerrville campfires had become legendary across the folk world. Dozens of them already were named by their participants and established as places to be if you wanted to hear heartfelt songs after the main stage concerts were over. Each campfire was surrounded by songwriters sharing their songs. Whether a couple or a dozen or hundreds gathered at each campfire, the experience was similar: the respectful quiet of those not performing, and the patient waiting for one's turn to play as the performance opportunity went around the circle in the flickering firelight. The songs could be by a main stage performer, an enthusiastic New Folk, a talent-

ed volunteer, or a musical member of the ticket buying public. The song was the thing and applause followed each offering at some fires while quiet was the rule at others. Many nights Stan Rogers' voice could be heard somewhere on the ranch soaring above the smoke singing "The Field Behind the Plow" or the saga of the "Mary Ellen Carter."

When the other Canadians left to return home, Stan stayed to extend his visit and enjoy another day here, just one more night at the campfires. We were all taken by the man and his music and happy that he had found a home here. He finally left for home, but a phone call from the CBC at 2:00 A.M. told me that Stan never made it back. He had perished in a fire aboard Air Canada Flight 797, along with twenty-two other passengers.

I don't know whether it was the abruptness of the call, the accumulated fatigue of a festival week without much sleep, or the affection and intense respect I had for Stan, or maybe it was a combination of all three, but I totally came apart on the phone and couldn't sleep afterward. I knew I had to share the news with those gathered at the ranch and go on with the festival in spite of my overwhelming grief. During the next few festival days remaining, I tried to keep it together, but often found myself

Bob Gibson brings Anne Hills to the festival. 1983.
— Courtesy Brian Kanof.

crying unashamed while trying to see that everyone did not let this mourning for Stan diminish the value of their time together.

It was a matter of months before I could put the grief in proper perspective. I had not been a close friend of Stan's. I had admired his work, but until our days and nights together, I had not known his great heart and patriotism. I finally rationalized that I might never have known him at all and that this mourning was the price of having had him in my life. I would have missed the whole flood of well-being that came from knowing him.

The festival went on, but I felt his loss every moment the Canadian flag flew at half-mast.

The 1983 New Folk concerts, with Nanci Griffith, Eliza Gilkyson, and Tim Henderson as judges, were a gold mine of outstanding new artists. Selected winners were Seattle's Michael Tomlinson, Austin's Buddy Sims and Robert Earl Keen, San Antonio's Alex Abravanel, Jan Marra of Minneapolis (who had been late in arriving from Minneapolis and almost missed the competition, arriving in tears), and Cris Plata of Sun Prairie, Wisconsin.

The final weekend began with a 10:00 A.M. Friday music business seminar that I hosted with Bob Gibson, Bob Light of ASCAP, and Mike Williams. Other experienced performers in the audience contributed and shared their experience with the large group of attendees. Gibson had just finished his three-day songwriters' school with faculty members Dick Goodwin, David Amram, and Jon Ims, and was full of useful suggestions.

The daytime events that weekend included a storyteller workshop on Chapel Hill, the staff concert hosted by Steven Fromholz, a harmonica jam with Philadelphia's Saul Broudy as special guest, the Folk Mass, the New Folk award winners concert, and the harmonica contest, plus Friday and Saturday Ballad Trees hosted by Melissa Javors and David Amram, Carolyn Hester, and Charles John Quarto.

Friday night's Outdoor Theater concert featured, among others, Ramblin' Jack Elliott, Utah Phillips, Rosalie Sorrels, Gamble Rogers, and Riders in the Sky, and reminded me of how the scope of the festival had grown to include so many out-of-state family members.

The Saturday night concert began with the country blues of Roy Book Binder, then saw Carolyn Hester on-stage with her two daughters, the popular team of Houston artists John Vandiver

Bruce a.k.a. "Utah" Phillips, master storyteller. 1983.
— Courtesy Brian Kanof.

and Shake Russell, Allen Damron, a reunion of Frummox, and Peter Yarrow closing in his own special way with everyone singing in harmony.

The final night paid tribute to Red River Dave's fifty years in country music as Vicki Bell surprised him on-stage when she portrayed Amelia Earhart as Dave sang his famous ballad about the lost aviatrix.

Carolyn Hester's children make their Kerrville debut. 1983.
— Courtesy Richard S. Orton.

Spirited veteran artist Rosalie Sorrels. 1983.
— Courtesy Brian Kanof.

Bill and Bonnie, Saul Broudy, Marcia Ball, Tim Henderson, and David Amram preceded the closing set by Ray Wylie Hubbard, and then all joined him for the finale with dozens of others coming out for the now universal chorus.

It had been a festival loaded with personal ups

Marcia Ball singing the blues. 1983.
— Courtesy Steven's Stills.

Roy Book Binder, one-of-a-kind acoustic blues artist. 1983.
— Courtesy Brian Kanof.

and downs, but the crowds came and we had, after all, a rewarding twelfth festival with business manager Paisley Robertson managing a big smile when she made her report.

With the exception of a three-day Discover Texas Association conference in mid-July and a trip to the Philadelphia Folk Festival in late August, we were able to stay on the ranch and work toward the success of the next three events: Kerrville Summer Music Festival, July 22-24; the tenth anniversary bluegrass festival on Labor Day weekend; and our new traditional music Good-time Music Festival, October 7-9. We were still looking for an additional event so that the folk festival income wouldn't have to support expenses year-round by itself.

The Summer Music Festival was to be a celebration of American music with three free one-hour concerts played by Austin pianist Kay Rivers Sparks at River Hills Mall at noon and 6:00 P.M. and at the Hummingbird Gallery at 3:00 P.M.

On Friday night, we offered as the first outdoor concert an all-Gershwin piano recital by Florida's Thomas Wright. He played major classical excerpts as well as moments from Gershwin's Broadway and film music. Mozart on Fifth was back from New York to play the 7:00 P.M. warm-up each night.

Saturday's early afternoon children's show at the auditorium was a dollar concert by the Bijuberti Puppet Players set to music of Ferde Grofe's "Grand Canyon Suite" and Copland's *Billy the Kid.*

At 3:30 P.M., with Amram back downtown following an orchestra rehearsal at the ranch, he joined composers Donald Grantham and Karl Korte, talking about and playing some of their music, assisted by the flute of Megan Meisenbach. Included were previews of the Amram works to be played at the ranch that night and portions of the world premiere Donald Grantham piece to be debuted Sunday afternoon, "The Diary of Adam and Eve."

The Saturday night concert by the Festival Orchestra under Amram's baton was a diverse evening of gems by American composers including Howard Hanson's Serenade for Flute (Harp) and String Orchestra with Megan Meisenbach as soloist. Amram conducted his own "Shakespeare Concerto" and his "Shakespeare Songs" sung by soprano Carmen Balthrop and bass-baritone Dorceal Duckins. Trumpet virtuoso Stacey Blair soloed in Copland's "Quiet City" and the Hovhaness "Prayer of St. Gregory." The concert also included Samuel Barber's popular "Adagio for Strings." The unusual closing offering for the night was Ray Tate's orchestration of Gibson-North's dramatic ballad "Let the Band Play Dixie" in its first orchestrated performance with Bob Gibson as baritone soloist assisted by Ray Tate, guitar, and Steve Kriechbaum, harmonica. It was an eminently successful conclusion to an acclaimed evening.

Sunday's 3:00 P.M. auditorium concert was a recital of American music by Houston Grand Opera stars Carmen Balthrop and Dorceal Duckins including excerpts from *Porgy and Bess*, Joplin's ragtime opera *Treemonisha*, and Grantham's premiere of excerpts from "The Diary of Adam and Eve" on a text by Mark Twain, commissioned for the festival. The recital closed with a number of spirituals and two popular songs, and the program was warmly received.

Ralph Emerson (Terry) Waldo played the festival's closing concert on the ranch at 8:30 Sunday night, an evening of classic rags, stride piano, jazz, blues, and novelty tunes from the turn of the century by Eubie Blake, Scott Joplin, Jelly Roll Morton, Irving Berlin, and others.

The festival was another artistic triumph and a stimulating survey of American music performed by an impressive array of accomplished artists.

The tenth anniversary Kerrville Bluegrass Festival was five days long with more than forty-eight hours of music on the main stage alone, including international appearances by the Lost City Mad Dogs of Kobe, Japan, and Transatlantic Bluegrass from Paris, France. The weekend included, as well, outstanding soloists Merle Travis (*guitar*), Bryan Bowers (*autoharp*), Mark O'Connor (*mandolin* and *fiddle*), Jana Jae (*fiddle*), Chris Hillman and Al Perkins, Peter Rowan, Joe Stuart (*fiddle* and *guitar*), and Paul Glasse (*mandolin*).

The roster of bands listed Buck White and the Down Home Folks, Hot Rize, McLain Family Band, the Lewis Family, Jim and Jesse and the Virginia Boys, Country Gazette, the Country Gentlemen, Tony Trishka and Skyline, with Lonzo and Oscar and Mac Wiseman as special guests. Eight regional bands, including two-time champions TVA helped create the appropriate anniversary excitement for the crowds.

Our concerts at Miller Theatre in Houston on September 23 and 24 were in celebration of ten years of bluegrass at Kerrville and offered the hillside crowds relaxing on blankets an opportunity to hear in person Peter Rowan and Jana Jae as headliners with Hickory Hill from East Texas, the Shady Grove Ramblers from Dallas, and TVA from San Antonio. The concerts were our first attempt at evenings of bluegrass in Houston, but were received by a crowd large enough to gain us an encore bluegrass appearance next season.

In place of the "8 Great Hours" or the "12 Great Hours" at the ranch in October, we thought we'd offer the "48 Great Hours" and rename it the "Kerrville Good-time Music Festival" with a focus on traditionally rooted music. We were not aware of a major traditional music festival anywhere else in Texas and believed we could fill that void by presenting a whole roster of nationally known traditional stars, many of whom had never made personal appearances in Texas.

Starting with North Carolina's ninety-year-old Elizabeth Cotton (who wrote "Freight Train") escorted by Mike Seeger (*fiddle, banjo, guitar, Jew's*

Rod Kennedy Presents
1st Annual
Kerrville GOODTIME MUSIC Festival

OCT. 7-8-9
COLUMBUS DAY WEEK-END

QUIET VALLEY RANCH
KERRVILLE, TEXAS
9 MILES SOUTH OF KERRVILLE
ON TEXAS HIGHWAY 16

Sylvester Rice, and Tommy Hancock), Austin's Sillocks and Tatties, Grimalkin, Lindsay Haisley, Turk Pipkin, Houston's Four Bricks out of Hadrian's Wall, Tinker's Dam and the House Brothers both from Dallas, and Alabama's bluegrass gospel band, the Sullivan Family. With five workshops by the Austin Friends of Traditional Music, we felt we had all the bases covered. The slogan for this Columbus Day weekend was "Rediscover America."

The event, while extremely refreshing and enjoyable, did not catch on as strongly as we hoped and did not break even. Money not withstanding, one of the most fun events was the wholesale square-dancing on the theater lawn with John McCutcheon, calling to music played by one of the biggest string bands ever seen with everyone who knew the tunes getting in on the action. We thought we'd try again next year!

During November, I worked on details for the coming season interrupted only by two trips to Mesquite on business and a three-day trip for a combination DTA and Festivals Association meeting. One of the events I worked on was a music foundation December 11 classical Christmas concert at the Kerrville Municipal Auditorium, where Amram would return to conduct the Bach *Magnificat* with the Kerrville community chorus.

Although I didn't realize it at the time, the *Magnificat* would be one of the last classical concerts our music foundation would do, as there was a growing difference between the goals of the foundation and those perceived by the board of directors, which had evolved from the original board.

My suggestion was that we go back to producing folk and bluegrass events and that I would turn all the classical music business over to the board. I also suggested that they form their own non-profit organization and call it the Kerrville Performing Arts Society (KPAS). They agreed, and we split up the areas of interest, with KPAS assuming the classical programs no longer to be held at the ranch, and we would appoint a new board and return to our original goals for which the foundation had been conceived.

I still hold as valuable and true many of the relationships that developed during that time and, thankfully, many of those friendships remain. Kerrville still has an annual season of classical events in town, locally sponsored and managed ever since.

harp, dulcimer, autoharp, pan pipes, and *harmonica*), we added John McCutcheon; Caryl P. Weiss; the Boys from the Lough with their music of Scotland, Ireland, Shetland, and Northumberland; Queen Ida and the Bon Temps Zydeco Band playing Cajun and Afro-American blues; Mike Cross (another North Carolina artist playing bottleneck blues, Irish jigs and reels and old-time fiddle tunes on fiddle and guitar); West Virginia's Trapezoid with its remarkable women's voices, fiddle, guitar, mandola, bass hammered dulcimer, bowed psaltery and cello; plus the self-accompanied singing of Debby McClatchy and Woodstock's Happy Traum.

Then we added Texas' own Fire-On-The-Mountain Cloggers from San Antonio, the Light Crust Doughboys from Ft. Worth, Flaco Jimenez and his *conjunto* from San Antonio, Lubbock's Flatlanders in reunion (Joe Ely, Jimmie Gilmore, Butch Hancock, Tony Pearson, Steve Wesson,

Nineteen-eighty-four was going to be one of the busiest years since we came to Kerrville with ten events tentatively on the calendar in Kerrville, Austin, Houston, Port Arthur, Mesquite, and Mexico.

While all the signs were good that our music had a bright future, I did note with some sadness the closing in 1983 of Austin's Soap Creek Saloon, where so much good music was fostered. They went out on a high note with a final night played by both Commander Cody and the Lost Planet Airmen and Asleep at the Wheel.

The new year began for me with my re-election as chairman of the Texas Festivals Association for a second term. We had nearly fifty members and had devised a marketing brochure to include all the member festivals for distribution in Texas and at selected shows nationally with the help of DTA.

My year also began with the realization that we had January and most of February and March free and clear to concentrate on our 1984 season. This time we would begin in earnest with a massive new festival in Austin, with Kerrville festivals being the general partner.

Even though the Kerrville Music Foundation and KPAS had gone their separate ways, I produced two more previously contracted events as they assumed the balance of the Kerrville Winter Music Festival.

The first of these was a February 26 traveling production of Puccini's tragic opera *Madame Butterfly*, the first full-length grand opera production ever staged in Kerrville. This was another Texas Opera Theatre offering in English with Nova Thomas as Cio Cio San and Richard Schuler as Lt. Pinkerton. Nine other artists filled out the cast of the lyric masterpiece produced with full costumes, sets, lights, and an orchestra conducted by Louis Salemno. The production was supported in part by grants from the Texas Commission on the Arts and the National Endowment for the Arts.

The KPAS board of twelve community leaders helped our publicity and promotion campaign immensely, and Mary Jane Farmer handled the patrons, mail orders, and box office. It was not only an artistic success, but the grants paid half the cost, and we came out of the KPAS/Foundation collaboration with the ledger looking much better than expected.

Our final season concert and my last event for KPAS was a charming Sunday, March 18, 3:00 P.M. concert by Megan Meisenbach, *flute*, and Mary

Golden, *harp*. They had performed together many times in recitals and concert tours and at James Dick's Round Top Festival. Miss Meisenbach had studied with Rampal and Galway and was considered one of Texas' most popular virtuosa performers. The music ranged from Bach to Debussy, covered a four-century span, and the appreciative audience begged them for several encores.

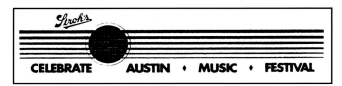

Recent press stories and criticisms about Austin losing its music community prominence prompted me to stage an Austin music celebration. In fact, I called it the Celebrate Austin Music Festival and scheduled it with the Austin Parks and Recreation Department for performances on Auditorium Shores, where the Austin skyline would provide the backdrop.

The festival, sponsored by the Stroh Brewing Company, would play from Friday, April 13, through Sunday, April 15, on Town Lake with pre-festival concerts at Symphony Square.

With Rusty Wier hosting, the Symphony Square concerts began on Tuesday, April 10, with

Bill Neeley, Michael Ballew, Lucinda Williams, Allen Damron, and Grassfire.

Steven Fromholz emceed the next night, introducing Courtney Campbell, CPR, Nanci Griffith, Grimalkin, and Kurt Van Sickle.

I hosted the final pre-festival concert, presenting Tim Henderson, David Halley, Robert Earl Keen and Some Other Guys, Christine Albert, Ponty Bone, and the Geezinslaw Brothers.

Back on Town Lake for the big Friday night show, we offered Beto y los Fairlanes, Joe "King" Carrasco and the Crowns, the LeRoi Brothers, and Little Joe y La Familia.

Saturday's 2:00 P.M. concert offered the Lotions, the Marcia Ball Band, Ernie Sky and the K-Tels, and Jesse Sublett's Secret Six.

That evening Eliza Gilkyson appeared with Passenger, followed by Asleep at the Wheel with Johnny Gimble, Gary P. Nunn, and Jerry Jeff Walker.

Sunday's 2:00 P.M. concert of jazz presented Paul Ostermayer and Sorcery, the Gene Ramey Sextet with Tina Marsh, the UT Jazz Ensemble led by Rick Lawn, Tomas Ramirez' Jazzmanian Devils, and the Bob Meyer Concept Orchestra.

The final night featured Robert Shaw at the piano, the W. C. Clark Blues Band, Townes Van Zandt Blues Band, Angela Strehli Band, and Stevie Ray Vaughan and Double Trouble.

It was a major undertaking, heavily publicized throughout the Southwest as an event showcasing both Austin's internationally known artists as well as its emerging new talent. Food and beverages and crafts booths lined the approach to the outdoor venue.

The festival did not make it financially, and most of the investors' money was needed to pay off the losses and put the event away until 1985. In spite of the losses, the festival ran smoothly in the capable hands of volunteers. While there were minor problems and logistical obstacles to overcome, every concert started and ended on time, and the audience received, without question, more than their money's worth with three-day tickets being priced at $15.

The following weekend we were at Miller Outdoor Theatre in Houston for a pair of folk concerts by the Banded Geckos, Steven Fromholz, Grimalkin, David Halley, Bill and Bonnie Hearne, John Vandiver, Townes Van Zandt, and Gary P. Nunn. The April 20-21 concerts drew a good-sized crowd, and we all had fun playing these low-key concerts. We would be back in August with bluegrass music.

The next week, starting on Wednesday, we were in Port Arthur for the first Pleasure Island Music Festival, opening on Friday, April 27, with a "Salute to the Big Bands" played by the Ed Gerlach Orchestra with Billie Castle.

Queen Ida and her Zydeco band played their Cajun blues concert at 1:00 P.M. to kick off Saturday's schedule and were followed at 4:00 by Gary P. Nunn and the Sons of the Bunkhouse Band in a concert called "Music from the Austin Scene." That night David Amram conducted the Festival Pops Orchestra with violinist Jana Jae as soloist.

The final day's major concerts were a Southern gospel concert at 1:00 P.M. by the Rex Nalon Singers, a 3:30 P.M. barrel house and jazz concert by pianists Robert Shaw and Teddy Wilson, and the festival closed with a western swing concert by the Light Crust Doughboys led by Smokey Montgomery.

Thousands of locals and visitors traveled across the 5,000-foot Gulfgate Bridge to and from the

Marcia Ball sits in at the piano with Leon McAuliffe (immediately behind her) and his band at Mesquite. 1984.

island for three days to hear the concerts and visit the dozens of arts and crafts booths, prompting chairperson Patty Oltremari to observe that more people had visited the island in three days than in the previous three years. The Golden Triangle had become more golden that weekend!

Next, we produced the second annual Mesquite Folk Festival, May 3-6, opening with the Singing Wills Family Gospel Concert at the First Baptist Church in Mesquite. The huge auditorium was almost filled.

The slogan of the festival this year was "Take It Away, Leon!," honoring the legendary steel guitar pioneer who had become a member of the Light Crust Doughboys until he left in 1935 to join Bob Wills' Texas Playboys. McAuliffe's "Steel Guitar Rag" had become a country music classic over the years, and Leon was popular and well loved both personally and professionally as he appeared on the first concert at the Eastfield College Performance Hall. A star-studded cast joined him, including his own band, Marcia Ball, Bill Staines, B. W. Stevenson, and Patsy Montana. A good turnout paid tribute to McAuliffe and enjoyed three hours of appealing music with multiple standing ovations awarded.

At the 11:30 A.M. children's concert at City Lake Park on Saturday, Don Sanders, Turk Pipkin, and David Amram kept the kids of all ages solidly entertained for the full hour.

Over at the Mesquite Opry at 2:00 P.M., Janet McBride coordinated Mesquite's own yodeling contest, an event they requested after hearing about the Kerrville competition. On hand to entertain and judge were Patsy Montana, champion Bill Staines, and Marcia Ball. The crowd roared approval of both the competition and the show.

Saturday night's concert staged Bob Gibson, Shake Russell and John Vandiver, Dee Moeller, David Amram, Berline Crary and Hickman, and Dallas singer-comedian Lu Mitchell.

The final event, following the afternoon's

Rising Star Competition, was Sunday night's concert of Irish music by Touchstone from Chapel Hill, NC, and four Texas bands: St. James Gate from San Antonio, Houston's Four Bricks Out of Hadrian's Wall, Grimalkin from Austin, and Tinker's Dam from Dallas.

After three years of getting the festival established to where it was earning fifty percent of its budget at seventy percent capacity, and the infrastructure established for its continuation, I returned from the project with many happy memories and experiences in my portfolio. The festival continued for many years as the Mesquite Music Festival.

With the 1984 World's Fair in New Orleans and the Olympic Games in Los Angeles, we were looking forward to the possibility that heavy tourist traffic going both ways on Interstate-10 would create a positive impact on our festival season. We had participated in three major travel shows in Houston, San Antonio, and Dallas in March and April, and anticipated some increased attendance from what we did at Austin, Port Arthur, and Mesquite. So, buoyed by extensive distribution of pre-festival brochures and posters, we approached our "Lucky 13th" Kerrville Folk Festival.

The dates were May 24-June 3, and the festival was again filled with popular regulars like Don Sanders, Rick Beresford, Bobby Bridger, Townes Van Zandt, Bill Staines, Odetta, Nanci Griffith, Carolyn Hester, Shake Russell, Ray Wylie Hubbard, Riders in the Sky, Charles John Quarto, and Peter Yarrow.

There were also fresh faces like Emily Aronson from Dallas who told me, "Kerrville is like a high octane filling station where we all come with our tanks empty to fill up for the coming year, and rationing it out until we can come back and fill up again." And there was young Lyle Lovett from College Station, a former New Folk, who had a two-hour Memorial Day afternoon spot joined by some musical friends.

The Ballad Tree had become an everyday event on both weekends with pairs of hosts from the main stage encouraging members of the audience who wanted to share their songs late each afternoon on Chapel Hill. Among those hosting were Fromholz and Courtney Campbell, Bob Gibson and Anne Hills, Jon Ims and Marcia Ball, Jimmie Gilmore and Butch Hancock, and Lindsay Haisley and Carolyn Hester.

The top of the class of 1984 New Folk winners

Bill and Bonnie Hearne at Kerrville. 1984.
— Courtesy Brian Kanof.

was a young man from Pennsylvania named John Gorka, one of six selected by judges Steve Gillette, Dee Moeller, and Shake Russell. Gorka made an

Nashville-based Texan Rick Beresford on stage.
— Courtesy Brenda Ladd.

Songwriter-bluesman Townes Van Zandt. 1984.
— Courtesy Brian Kanof.

The wry humor and songs of Ray Wylie Hubbard. 1984.
— Courtesy Brian Kanof.

Houston's popular Shake Russell. 1984.
— Courtesy Brian Kanof.

Bill Staines of New Hampshire first came to Kerrville as a contestant in the yodeling contest but has returned annually as a favorite songwriter. 1984.
— Courtesy Brian Kanof.

Jon Ims hosting the Ballad Tree. 1984.
— Courtesy Brenda Ladd.

Riders in the Sky bringing the Old West to life. 1984.
— Courtesy Brian Kanof.

impressive appearance at the Award Winners Concert on the second weekend of the festival and earned himself an immediate invitation for the main stage for 1985.

Peter Yarrow, Bill and Bonnie, Jimmie Gilmore, Butch Hancock, B. W. Stevenson, and John Vandiver were among the regulars on the second weekend, but we also had a chance to hear more recent additions to our roster like Gamble Rogers, Crow Johnson, Tinker's Dam, and Artie and Happy Traum, as well as Billy Joe Shaver, Riders in the Sky, and CPR (Calvert, Powell and Resnick) who played the 5:00 P.M. warm-up sets.

The thirteenth annual Kerrville Folk Festival turned out to be luckier than expected. We made a profit!

During the summer months, we continued daily preparations for the coming bluegrass concerts

Artie and Happy Traum from Woodstock, NY. 1984.
— Courtesy Brian Kanof.

Houston's blues specialist John Vandiver. 1983.
— Courtesy Richard Orton.

at Miller Theatre, the bluegrass festival Labor Day weekend and, perhaps, a little vacation south of the border before the Good-time Music Festival the first weekend in October. We also proceeded with our applications for certification as an official event of the 1986 Texas Sesquicentennial celebration. On the agenda as well was a Discover Texas Association meeting for three days in July and a number of committee meetings for the festivals association. All of these tourism meetings began to key on the 1986 150th birthday of Texas independence and the state-wide Sesquicentennial celebration. The Texas Highway Department's Ft. Worth "Tour-Con '84" tourism conference in September would also focus on 1986.

Our bluegrass concerts at Miller Theatre were on the calendar for Friday and Saturday, August 17 and 18, and we flew in our mandolin champion Mark O'Connor, who was also known nationally as a fiddling prodigy now grown to major artist status. We also imported Bryan Bowers of Seattle, generally considered America's greatest autoharp player. When he performs, he arrives on-stage with a whole stack of pre-tuned autoharps in a sort of Styrofoam sandwich — an impressive sight!

Joining these stars were mandolin champion Paul Glasse, whose popularity had grown like wildfire as he easily mastered lyric accompaniment, western swing, and many styles of bluegrass. To the pair of well-established bands TVA from San Antonio and Hickory Hill from East Texas (who had formed in the parking lot at Kerrville and won a band championship, deciding to stay together), we added Kerrville's own championship caliber String Factory Outlet with its classically trained leader David Dyer. The combination of star soloists and these bands created a broad spectrum of bluegrass that was a big hit with the large Houston crowds both nights.

The bluegrass festival started its second decade and had managed to break even every year of the first ten years. There is a saying in the music business to the effect that if you're still in business, you're successful. So with our optimism in neutral, we forged ahead, knowing that our odds for not losing any money were pretty good, and on top of that, we were going to share four days of good music! David Peters of Birmingham, Michigan, won the previous year's mandolin championship and would be on hand to join Paul Glasse and Mark O'Connor in performing and judging. Two other aspects of the festival would make this a particularly interesting year. First, we had two international bands on the program: Sergio Lara and the New Acoustic Unit from Mexico, and then, to provide a change of pace and a hint at the origins of bluegrass, I invited the Tannehill Weavers from Glasgow, Scotland. Most people thought we had these foreign bands because they would fit with our other "foreign" bands. This would be the first festival where

the Austin Lounge Lizards would play since their unexpected win of last year's band championships. No one challenged their musicianship, but most bluegrass fans wondered where their roots really were. I wasn't sure the Lizards were serious about anything, but their unique entertainment impact was impressive, and I wanted them on the festival.

Guaranteeing a full spectrum of music would be Buck White, whose Down Home Folks were beginning to be called The Whites, the innovative California trio Berline, Crary and Hickman, the Lewis Family, the McLain Family Band, the Doug Dillard Band, and Tony Trishka and Skyline.

The spectrum became even broader with the inclusion of the regional bands TVA, Hickory Hill, House Brothers, String Factory Outlet, Bluegrass Overdrive (a McLain offshoot), Special Edition, the Poverty Playboys, Powell Family, and mandolin craftsman Luke Thompson from Louisiana.

As expected, the music was diverse and the crowd loved it. There were some questions about the Tannehill Weavers, as the direct line between Celtic music and bluegrass was a little too blurred for some bluegrass fans. And then there were the Lounge Lizards. I decided that if they wanted to stay together another year, they had a standing invitation to play the 1985 Kerrville Folk Festival, where their innovative spirit would be amply rewarded by a guaranteed enthusiastic reception. They said, "Yes."

As expected, too, we broke even!

A week later, we helped stage the Jimmie Rodgers Jubilee at the Depot in Kerrville, and then headed south to an island off Mexico that Steven Fromholz had written a song about and that Paisley Robertson used as her annual Mexican retreat.

Coming into Isla Mujeres, Mexico. 1984.
— Courtesy Merrie Lu Park.

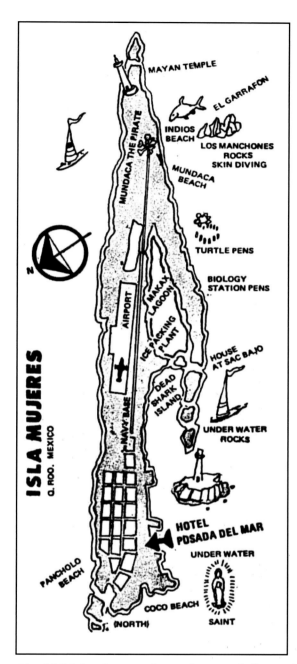

with swaying palms, and the climate seems to be pleasant all the time.

Mostly a fishing village, but also hospitable to tourists, we found the island to have a nice plaza, three or four good hotels, and a number of restaurants serving traditional Mexican food, international dishes, and seafood fresh from the sea. Everything seemed inviting and perfect for relaxation. We also found a few attractions, including a natural underwater park called El Garrafon, a small ruin of a Mayan observatory, the remains of the pirate Mundaca's ranch, built in honor of a beautiful girl who spurned his affection, and Coco Beach with its fine sand and crystal-clear, shallow waters. There were also two good places to dive — the Manchones Reef and Los Cuevones, the caves of the sleeping sharks. A boat ride away was Contoy Island, a natural bird sanctuary of about sixty species.

While there were a small disco or two and a few mopeds to rent, it was an otherwise unspoiled place to be amongst very hospitable natives and a few tourists. A good part of the population was of Mayan origin and their broad smiles extended a genuine, if not shy, welcome.

There was not much to do except sleep and rest, relax in a hammock, talk, swim, walk the beautiful beaches or the dirt streets of the town visiting a few shops, dining on delicious, fresh, and inexpensive seafood, and sipping tropical drinks or Mexican beer. It was truly an unspoiled paradise for hanging out and doing nothing.

The most intense person on the island, and perhaps the most hospitable as well, was our hotel manager at the Posada del Mar, Victor Zapata. He had the warmest smile of all and a naturally friendly way about him. Speaking perfect English, he let us know

David Richardson and Merri Lu Park flew with Nancylee and me to Cancun and we caught a launch for the forty-minute ride to Isla Mujeres. There we wanted to spend three or four days swimming, dancing, relaxing, and generally getting away from our busy day-to-day regimen.

The island was discovered in 1517 by Spanish navigators who, seeing the statues of Mayan goddesses guarding the coast, called it the "island of women." Located in the Caribbean's turquoise blue waters, Isla Mujeres is only five miles long and one mile wide. The beaches feature fine, white sand lined

The palapa by the pool at Posada del Mar. 1984.
— Courtesy Merri Lu Park.

that he was happy to have us as his guests. The Posada del Mar, by the lighthouse, with a couple of dozen spotless, comfortable rooms with tile showers and ceiling fans, seemed to be the largest hotel on the island except for the El Presidente at the northeast tip of the island.

Sitting under the palapa by the pool with Victor Zapata one day, I mentioned the reason we came to his island was that a good friend had written a romantic song about Isla Mujeres that was popular in Texas. He was immediately interested, and I suggested that he might like to hear the song. Perhaps, he'd even like to hear the song sung by the man who wrote it. Maybe we could bring some of our performers to meet some of the island officials and begin a little festival on the Plaza.

He immediately liked all these suggestions and wondered if we'd like to come back next month, in October, and he'd make all of his rooms and meals available for our group at half-price. In fact, he would introduce us to the mayor.

Victor made a phone call and the next day we joined the mayor for lunch. Mayor Gilberto Pastrana was a pharmacist, and while he spoke very little English and I spoke very little Spanish, the smile he shared and the warmth of his gentle eyes indicated that he was genuinely pleased to have us on his island. With Victor as translator, we told him that we would like to come back to Isla and bring a few performers to meet some of the officials and talk about having a small festival. I had asked what was the worst month for business on the island and Victor assured me it was October, so I responded, "Okay, we'll come back in October." Gilberto Pastrana was immediately agreeable, and we committed to a return visit in October.

The next day our brief vacation on Isla ended and we flew back to Texas to make final preparations for the October 5-7 Good-time Music Festival.

We had three weeks until the festival and three days after that before we were due back on Isla Mujeres. During pre-festival activities, I gathered participants to go to Mexico and arranged a deal with Aeromexico Airlines Houston office to fly my delegation to Cancun to arrange for a future festival. Fromholz called this my "ultimate scam." Suddenly, with a call from Victor, our meeting with Mexican officials in October turned into an instant festival. Gilberto Pastrana's people decided to have concerts to celebrate the island's joining the state of Quintana Roo, and leaving behind its status as a ter-

ritory. They would be building a platform for us to perform on in the Plaza if we would tell them what size we wanted!

I was excited about the Good-time Music Festival because both Pete Seeger and John Hartford had agreed to come close it. Also coming would be international artists Patrick Couton from France and the Battlefield Band from Scotland, as well as top artists from the U.S. like David Holt and Texas' legendary Lydia Mendoza.

Even though last year's Good-time Festival lost $17,500 due in part to the rains that fell horizontally at forty mph during the Light Crust Doughboys set, we had high hopes for this year's event. We expected huge crowds for the stellar artists already named, and we also had Cathy Barton and Dave Para from Missouri, Roy Book Binder, Bob Brozman, Mike Cross, the klezmer trio Eclectricity from Indiana, the Juggernaut String Band, Bonnie Phipps, Touchstone, Trapezoid, Robin

Pete Seeger at Kerrville's Good-time Music Festival. 1984.
— Courtesy Brenda Ladd.

John Hartford's "Gentle on my Mind" at Kerrville. 1984.
— Courtesy Brenda Ladd.

and Linda Williams, and Texas artists Allen Damron, Grimalkin, Lindsay Haisley, St. James Gate, and the Fire-On-The-Mountain Cloggers.

But on Columbus Day weekend, 1984, the only thing we discovered was that this slate of incredible performers would not draw for us in Texas!

Farewell Good-time!

By the time we mailed out a few letters, made a few phone calls, and visited with some performers, we had gathered quite a contingent to go to Isla Mujeres.

Performers going as our guests would include Nanci Griffith, Steven Fromholz, Allen Damron, David Holt, and Caryl P. Weiss. Also joining Nancylee and me was Texas Music Association

president Mike Tolleson, who had been my music attorney for the Celebrate Austin Music Festival. He had also been one of Eddie Wilson's compadres during the early Armadillo World Headquarters days. By this time, the goodwill delegation numbered forty people with more than thirty people taking us up on our $199 package. Oh yes, Fromholz talked me into two guests because he had written the song "Isla Mujeres" that had gotten us all involved in the first place.

Sure enough, when we arrived on the island, they were ready with a mariachi band and welcoming banners everywhere. As foretold, we did play on the Plaza's new platform every night from 6:00 to 9:00, more or less, alongside mariachi, marimba, and popular bands and a native folklorico company. It suddenly became the Isla Mujeres First International Music Festival! Huge crowds of natives and tourists were celebrating with us every night.

A relaxing time at Isla Mujeres. 1984.
— Courtesy Merri Lu Park.

Playing the first Isla Mujeres International Music Festival in the Caribbean. From left: Steven Fromholz, Allen Damron, Nanci Griffith, David Holt. 1981.
— Courtesy Merri Lu Park.

Not only that, our entire troupe of forty was entertained at four dinners and several luncheons at the island's leading hotels and restaurants. One dinner was hosted by Mayor Gilberto Pastrana and another by the Chamber of Commerce.

We had welcoming cocktails at the Posada del Mar, dinner at Ciro's Lobster House, lunch at Garrafon de Castilla, dinner at Chino Gomar's restaurant, lunch at the Palapa Bar at Posada del Mar as guests of Victor Zapata. The mayor's dinner was followed by a dance in honor of late President Aleman, and on Sunday, they took us on a cruise to Contoy Island featuring lunch caught fresh and cooked on the beach. Following the final show on the Plaza, we were treated to dinner at Buho's as guests of Enrique Lima, who was to become my most trusted friend on the island in coming years.

Everyone had Monday on their own for diving, moped riding, snorkeling, shopping, and other sunburned activities. We departed with much fanfare and considerable regret. We said we'd be back in 1985.

By the time we returned to Texas, our folk festival had been designated as the official Sesquicentennial Touring Festival for the Republic of Texas 150th anniversary. We were deep in the middle of arranging our national tour while also getting back in touch with Sam Jenkins at the Mexican Government Tourist Office in Houston about the 1985 festival on the island. I was requesting some type of executive credit for three or four flights to Cancun during the coming year to complete the festival arrangements. We intended to make Aeromexico Airlines the official airline of the international festival.

The work on the tour, the festival in Mexico, and the 1985 season continued for the next couple of months with trips to New York, Boston, Philadelphia, and numerous trips to Austin for "City Limits" tapings at KLRU studios. We also had a two-day camp-out at the ranch on November 3-4, Nancylee's birthday weekend.

During the time we were in Isla Mujeres, I talked with Nanci Griffith and Steven Fromholz about how long it seemed between being together at the festivals and how good it was to be together on tours and special events. The outcome of this conversation was an event at Waterloo Ice House at 906 Congress Avenue in Austin so we could get back together on December 21.

It would be a Christmas reunion of sorts with two 2-hour concerts for the foundation and proceeds going to the New Folk and the Townsend Miller Endowment Fund.

Townsend was our guest, and playing the two concerts were Nanci Griffith and Fromholz, Charles John Quarto, Butch Hancock, Jimmie Gilmore, David Halley, Kurt Van Sickle, Melissa Javors, Courtney Campbell, and classical flutist Megan Meisenbach accompanied by pianist Kathryn Mishell. Among our other special guests were Eliza Gilkyson, Turk Pipkin, Bill Oliver, and Gary P. Nunn.

The concerts played to standing-room crowds as I announced the tentative lineup for 1985 and introduced Kathy Hudson, who had joined us from Ft. Worth as development director for the foundation. The whole evening was special, raised some

money, and provided four hours of fantastic music. It was a great way to cap off the year and we told Waterloo's Steve Clark that we'd like to reserve a weekend to do it again next December.

The first three months of 1985 were filled with planning sessions, board meetings, a six-day trip to Isla, a three-day travel seminar at Texas A&M, a three-day visit to the Dallas Irish Festival, and the final countdown to the Celebrate Austin Music Festival.

After last year's losses and the restrictions placed upon us by being on city park land, we worked it out with Chesley Millikan to move the festival to Manor Downs just north of town where there had been numerous horse races, motorcycle races, and concerts.

It was a good facility for us, and we moved in with optimism for the 1985 three-day festival April 19-21.

This year's festival would celebrate the return to Texas after sixty-three years of the legendary Sippie Wallace, last of the Texas blues shouters. To back her up I brought in Jim Cullum's jazz band from San Antonio and Chicago's James Dapogney, a good jazz pianist who had worked with Sippie in

the past. Because of her affection and admiration for Sippie, I also brought in unannounced Bonnie Raitt as part of the tribute.

We began on Friday night with an "Austin Rock Evening" played by Joe Ely, the LeRoi Brothers, Lou Ann Barton, and Joe "King" Carrasco and the Crowns. It would have been a terrific event except for the foreboding rain on the horizon that kept the crowds down and had me hurriedly re-negotiating fees during the concert.

Saturday's 2:00 P.M. concert was a "Third World Celebration of Jazz and International Music" in memory of Gene Ramey played by Tomas Ramirez, Eloise Burrell, and Dan Del Santo and the World Beat Orchestra.

Saturday's big 8:00 P.M. concert, "The Ladies Sing The Blues," was another blockbuster with Marcia Ball, Angela Strehli, Karen Kraft, and our special guest Sippie Wallace, who was honored by Secretary of State Myra McDaniel, presentations from the mayor of Houston, House of Representatives, and others. Robert Shaw presented Sippie with a big bouquet of presentation roses, and then Bonnie Raitt began her thirty-minute set honoring Sippie. But Sippie could not sit still for this and jumped up and joined Bonnie, singing and playing at the keyboard. About that time, the rains that had been viewed coming closer and closer across the Austin skyline hit with a fury. Within moments Bonnie's road manager had unplugged her electric guitar to keep her from being electrocuted and water could be seen pouring out of Sippie's Baldwin grand piano. If Sippie had it her way, she would have kept on performing her songs like "Special Delivery," "Bedroom Blues," and "Mighty Tight Woman." At eighty-six, Sippie had recovered from a stroke in 1970 and had come back strong. But now, she retired gracefully in the chaos of the scramble to save equipment from the pouring rain, thunder, lightning, and whipping winds.

The final day was soggy at the site, and we were financially devastated but looking forward to the afternoon concert, "Austin Songwriters Sing Their Songs." Three hours of songs by Walter Hyatt, Nanci Griffith, Butch Hancock, Christine Albert, and Tim Henderson brought the morale of the staff up considerably, and the crowds were elated.

Sunday night's final event, "Austin Country Music," starred Alvin Crow and the Pleasant Valley Boys, Steven Fromholz and the KTXZ Orchestra with Courtney Campbell, Gary P. Nunn, and Jerry Jeff Walker.

The losses on this year's festival would be absorbed largely by my executive producer Steve Kelso, but the rest of them would be picked up by the general partner, Kerrville Festivals, Inc. The celebration was over!

A couple of bright spots were on the immediate horizon. For one thing, the Lone Star State's most popular, best-read magazine, *Texas Monthly*, published by Roger Tremblay, had signed on as our first corporate sponsor for the folk festival, providing us with a four-color, full-page advertisement priced on the rate card at $13,800. It would reach thousands of upper-middle and high-income families all over the Southwest beginning in late April when the magazine hit newsstands and subscriber homes. It was expected to have a considerable impact on the gate of the fourteenth festival. Many people had heard of the festival, but didn't know the particulars. *Texas Monthly* would fill them in.

In addition, Peter had notified me that Peter Paul and Mary would be coming to play the festival! We received this great news the same week that Jerry Jeff let me know he also could play this year!

We didn't have much time to lick our wounds anyway as we were due at Houston's Miller Theatre four days later, April 26 and 27. Lyle Lovett was headlining and Anne Hills was flying in from Chicago. Joining them each night were Fromholz, Jimmie Gilmore, David Halley, Ponty Bone and the Squeezetones, and Houston's Don Sanders. It was a real treat playing for large audiences, knowing that everything was paid for in advance. I was getting a little gun-shy. The Miller Theatre Advisory Council and the Parks and Recreation Department people were always hospitable, and by now we knew every member of the professional stage crew by their first names.

It was like coming home to play Houston.

The exciting news for the 1985 Kerrville Folk Festival that Paul and Mary would be joining Peter was not exciting just because they were famous and would sell out that night, but because this had been a dream of Peter's for many years. He not only wanted to treat me and all the festival to what PP&M could bring to us, but he felt down deep that the festival would also be a personal treat for them. Peter so believed in the festival that he had become our most fervent ambassador, and now he could show his musical partners what he had been talking about all these years. They were going to play for the festival scale, but money was not an important motivation for them. The real goal for Peter, and what Paul and Mary joined him in, was validating Peter's vision.

We also had excellent pre-festival coverage in *Southern Living Magazine*, word that Jerry Jeff Walker was going to return to the festival, and the donation of a $1,400 Ovation "Elite" guitar for our music foundation raffle.

We needed all this good news to offset the impact of the tragic murder of John Vandiver in Houston and my recent experience of being an honorary pall bearer at Robert Shaw's funeral service at the Ebenezer Baptist Church in Austin just five days before the festival. We had lost two dear friends and two great Texas blues artists within a month of each other, and they had cut a wide swath while they were here. Just as we had done for Stan Rogers and others before him, we planted memorial trees for them. With advance news of Vandiver's death, we had already devoted the first Sunday Folk Mass to a "Celebration of the Life of John Vandiver," with Chaplain Walter Lee presiding.

Every day of the festival was filled with reward-

ing highlights. The first night started at 6:00 P.M. when the previous year's most admired New Folk winner, John Gorka, opened the main stage, and at the end of the night Bugs Henderson was Ray Wylie's guest as Hubbard closed the concert.

The 1985 New Folk was split, as usual, between Saturday and Sunday. This year's edition had been underwritten by Billy Bob's of Texas in Ft. Worth, thanks to Kathy Hudson's tireless efforts. Judging were former New Folk Chuck Pyle and David Halley joining the much-admired Kate Wolf from

Jerry Jeff Walker at Kerrville. 1985.
— Courtesy Brian Kanof.

California. Together they selected as winners Darden Smith (Austin), Brent Mitchell (Denton, Texas), Andy Wilkinson (Lubbock), two Californians Kristina Olsen (Venice) and Ilze Platis (Santa Monica), and Bill Ede (Louisville, Kentucky). We also noted writers like Hal Ketchum from New Braunfels and David Roth from Brooklyn.

Our newest chaplain, Rev. Walter Lee hosted the first weekend's Folk Mass while Rev. Charlie Sumners presided over the mass on the final Sunday.

Saturday night opened with Jimmie Gilmore and closed with Jerry Jeff Walker before more than 5,000 ecstatic fans. Sunday night was one of those nights

Amram Jam. From left: Mark Moss, Paul Glasse, Ray Tate, Butch Hancock (playing the air tank), Pedro Gutierrez, David Amram, John Reed. 1985.
— Courtesy Brenda Ladd.

Dee Moeller trades in her piano for a banjo. 1985.
— Courtesy Brian Kanof.

277

Gary P. Nunn plays his own distinctive brand of country music. 1985.

— Courtesy Brian Kanof.

Kate Wolf, much beloved California songwriter.
— Publicity Photo.

when it seemed that we heard every kind of music imaginable, from the Texas songs of David Halley and Melissa Javors, to the Celtic music of Tinker's Dam, to the swing-flavored tunes of the trio CPR. Steve Gillette was also there with his melodic ballads, and so were Dee Moeller and Gary P. Nunn with their distinctive brands of country music. The Amram Jam had David surrounded by half a dozen main stage performers, recording engineer Pedro Gutierrez on percussion, and *Sing Out!*'s Mark Moss playing as well. It was now established as an annual event, testing just how many different ways Amram could improvise on his masterpieces "Alfred the Hog" and "Kerrville On My Mind."

Memorial Day Monday had an appealing 1:00 P.M. concert by Robert Earl Keen and his friends, and that night marked the first appearance on the festival of Kate Wolf, whose "Give Yourself To Love" could be our anthem. Beautiful Christine Albert, who had appeared first in one of those concerts in downtown Kerrville with Eliza Gilkyson,

made her first appearance on her own on the main stage and was an immediate hit.

The Wednesday night catfish fry presented our two former New Folk winners from Colorado, Chuck Pyle and Jon Ims, with the after-dinner concert by "Just Friends," a trio resulting from the frequent collaborations between Bob Gibson, Anne Hills and Tom Paxton.

The second weekend included a Charles John Quarto poetry workshop, a staff concert co-hosted by Walter Hyatt and Lindsay Haisley, the New Folk award winners' concert under the guidance of David Card of Poor David's Pub in Dallas, and two 5:00 P.M. warm-up shows by the Austin Lounge Lizards. They had found their audience and were really at home with the folk fans!

The dynamite Friday night concert was one of the biggest Fridays in history and the line-up was unbelievable: Lyle Lovett, Rick Beresford, Tish Hinojosa, Ponty Bone, Guy Clark, Gamble Rogers, and Riders in the Sky, with Turk Pipkin juggling his way through some of the set changes.

Walter Hyatt opened Saturday night, and following a refreshing set by Artie and Happy Traum, the evening closed with the much heralded appear-

Christine Albert brought beauty and style to her music.
1985.

— Courtesy Brian Kanof.

Fifteen-year stage manager Mack Partain with Peter
Yarrow.

— Courtesy Brian Kanof.

ance of Peter Paul and Mary. Playing before a capacity crowd of more than 6,000, the trio never had a more dedicated audience, and I don't know who was happier about the magic moment. Peter was overjoyed to have his partners finally with him at Kerrville, and Paul and Mary were exuberant knowing how much it meant to Peter for them to be there. They all knew how much this meant to us! With Nancylee by my side, I sat in my producer's chair at stage right, with tears running down my face. Every time one of the trio would have a break, they were over at my chair hugging me. It was an astounding evening for everyone and the festival's largest concert ever.

Most of the crowd stayed for Sunday's final concert where Josh White, Jr., appeared along with a bill that included the Troubadors of Paraguay playing Jerry Jeff's "Mr. Bo Jangles" on a harp, and concert-closing performances by Marcia Ball and Billy Joe Shaver.

The good vibrations and positive effects of the huge crowds would have a long-lasting effect on the morale of everyone connected with the festival, including a completely rejuvenated Peter Yarrow!

Over the past eight or ten years, the festival slowly had been generating a language all its own as folks from around the world interacted in the campgrounds. The language was all built around the root "Kerr" and Kerrwords were in. The Kerrword that raised the most eyebrows in town was "Kerrvert," defined as a person "who has seen the light" or has been "Kerrverted" or who has "come to believe, like the rest of us, that music is the way to

Poet and lyricist Charles John Quarto. 1985.
— Courtesy Brian Kanof.

Peter Paul and Mary at the 1985 Kerrville Folk Festival.

— Courtesy Brian Kanof.

spread love." Those not familiar with our scene likened the word to "pervert" and were concerned.

Some of the other key words were "Kerrvivor," those who lived through the eleven days of the festival, "Kerrick," the pain in your neck from sleeping on rocks, and I became the "Kerrchief." Then there were other obvious words like Kerrage, Kerrfew and Kerrmercials, referring to my plugs for T-shirt sales and raffle tickets between performers on-stage. So it was, that in 1985, someone published a Kerrictionary with more than 120 Kerrwords.

We produced a special edition of the "12 Great Hours" on July 20 to announce the 1986 tour of thirteen states as "the official goodwill tour of the Texas Sesquicentennial," and to announce the 1986 folk festival as an official event of the 150th birthday celebration for the Republic of Texas.

We were presented with an official Sesquicentennial flag to fly over the ranch. We announced tour performers Steven Fromholz and Bobby Bridger who were also on hand at the "12 Hours." Their fellow performers at this ranch event

were Emily Aronson, Courtney Campbell, Melissa Javors, Darden Smith, Lyle Lovett, Lindsay Haisley, David Halley, Don Sanders, Tim Henderson, and Kurt Van Sickle.

Mark McCord was introduced as the designer of our official tour logo, a pair of running horses.

Lyle Lovett, Roland Denny, Darden Smith at the "12 Great Hours." 1985.

— Courtesy Brenda Ladd.

CELEBRATE ☆ TEXAS

CONCERT TOUR

© KERRVILLE FESTIVALS 1985

To me, they symbolized the older and more experienced songwriters watching over and encouraging the younger emerging songwriters, though I doubt anyone else shared that interpretation. Nonetheless, the drawing was outstanding at denoting the Texas feeling we wanted.

We already had confirmed tour dates in Nashville, Boston, New York, and Chicago, and were working on a dozen more.

We were approached by the Miller Beer people in Kerrville to stage with them a concert at the ranch by Joe "King" Carrasco and the Crowns during August. Joe had played our 1984 and 1985 Celebrate Austin Music Festivals, and we enjoyed him thoroughly. With local people not being able to see rock n' roll stars up close without traveling more than a hundred miles to do it, we thought it would work. We invited Ponty Bone and the Squeezetones to open for him and set the date for August 17, a three-hour concert from 8:00 to 11:00 P.M. It turned out to be a good time for everyone, and Joe had fans there from as far away as Switzerland! We and the Miller people were happy.

For the third consecutive year, the Miller Outdoor Theatre in Houston invited us to produce a pair of bluegrass concerts. Our bluegrass concerts in 1984 had drawn 15,000 fans over the two nights, and we scheduled another stellar lineup for August 23 and 24, 1985. Norman Blake, the remarkable Nashville-based guitarist who had toured with Kris Kristofferson, Joan Baez, John Hartford, and others, was scheduled to play the Kerrville Bluegrass Festival and agreed to headline the Miller Theatre events as well. Blake was joined by three-time-

champions TVA, Hickory Hill from East Texas, and the unique all-female, five-piece Dixie Dewdrops from Ft. Worth.

On Saturday afternoon, between the two evening concerts, we took all the performers to Aswell's Cafe on Brazos for a picking party with members of the Houston Folklore Society and the West University Acoustic Music Society. The music, the food, the visiting, and especially the opportunity to pick with some new-found friends proved a most enjoyable diversion for our performers, since all they got to play at Miller Theatre were short sets.

The twelfth bluegrass festival had at the top of its roster, besides Norman Blake and the Rising Fawn String Ensemble, the Whites, Bryan Bowers, Vassar Clements Band, the Doug Dillard Band, and John Herald's band from New York, plus Trapezoid, Peter Rowan, Joe Stuart, Whetstone Run, and Bill Grant and Delia Bell. The mandolin championships continued, and we had as judges and performers former champions Mark O'Connor (1982), David Peters (1983), and Paul Kramer (1984). To this power-packed list we added the regional bands Dixie Dew Drops, Hickory Hill, String Factory Outlet, triple champs TVA, current champions Tex Sweeney and the Grazmatics from Austin, and the Poverty Playboys.

BUCK WHITE
International ☆ Mandolin ☆ Championship
Kerrville Tx

Just as at the folk festival, we could see the impact of *Texas Monthly's* corporate sponsorship of our season as we were drawing many newcomers whose mail orders and license plates indicated they were from towns not on our mailing list. The blue-grass festival again managed to creep a few dollars over break even.

We were now aiming for the Good-time Festival and the second Isla Mujeres Festival in October, but in the meantime, and all along those past several months, we had kept steadily working on next year's national tour for the Texas Sesquicentennial.

The third Good-time Music Festival of October 11-13 was on us quickly and again included music from the Appalachian Mountains to the western frontiers as we invited people to "Rediscover America Columbus Day weekend." Texas performers were joined by those from Tennessee, California, Connecticut, Ohio, North Carolina, Maine, Washington, and Indiana.

Bagpiper Patrick Reagan opened the festival on Friday night (what a wonderful sound through the hills!) and was followed by MacDonald Craig, Jane Voss and Hoyle Osborne, Lindsay Haisley, David Holt (who had been with us on Isla Mujeres), and Tinker's Dam to close.

Saturday started with late morning workshops by David Holt, Gayle Ross, Patrick Reagan, Bill Staines, John Pearse, and Stephen Cicchetti (who later changed his name to Steve James — "easier to remember," he said) and then the wild and woolly square dance workshop with everyone involved.

Then, following the eighth annual Worst Hat Contest (can you believe this?) the evening concert started at 6:00 P.M. with the cloggers Linda Lowe Thompson and Maria Terres Sangren, Allen Damron, Preston Reed, David Holt, Bill Staines, Ohio's Hot Foot Quartet, and St. James Gate. Then, on Chapel Hill at midnight, Gayle Ross told ghost stories.

Sunday began with a sparsely attended Chapel Hill singing service, and our final concert began at mid-day with Ed Miller, Steve James, John Pearse and Mary Faith Rhodes, TVA, and the klezmer music of Indiana's Eclectricity to bring the festival to a close.

The box office counted, this would be the final Good-time Festival.

Isla Mujeres was awaiting us. My several trips to the island during the year for meetings with Enrique Lima and Victor Zapata, and visits with Mayor Pastrana and some of his officials, made me feel comfortable about returning with an entire planeload of our customers looking for the music, the promised sun, surf, sand, scuba diving, and seafood.

With our letter of introduction from the Mexican Consul General, we sailed through customs and immigration and were quickly on our way to the ferry to the island. Aeromexico had been a big help at the airport, assisting in getting all our luggage and instruments together in one place.

The festival itself exceeded my expectations. Back with us were Nanci Griffith, Fromholz, and Damron, and then I added the seven-member Beto y los Fairlanes. We played all three nights of the festival, learning that 8:00 P.M. meant 9:00 P.M. or even a little bit later, but having nowhere else to go, we just relaxed. To our surprise, Mayor Gilberto Pastrana had created for us a full-sized stage called Teatro del Pueblo on the Plaza. Alongside our performers were Mexican singers, dancers, and musicians of all sorts.

We had rooms at the El Presidente, Roca Mar, Vistalmar, Roca del Caribe, and the Caribe Maya. Those who decide things on the island decided that we should rotate hotels from year to year so people wouldn't feel envious of the Posada del Mar, but we

Isla Mujeres Mayor Gilberto Pastrana with the ceremonial Kerrville poster at council chambers. 1985.

— Courtesy Merri Lu Park.

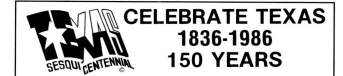

CELEBRATE TEXAS
1836-1986
150 YEARS

returned there several times during the five-day, October 17-21, weekend to swim, have lunch, and relax in their poolside palapa while visiting with Victor Zapata.

We had an exceedingly good time. The music was impressive, not only to the islanders, but to those of us who knew all the artists. Our hosts treated us like VIPs with the entire city council awarding every member of our party a special diploma in ceremonies at the imposing Municipal Building chambers overlooking the Plaza. I, in turn, presented Gilberto a framed 1984 folk festival art poster as a gift, along with a resolution of friendship from the Texas Legislature courtesy of Representatives Geistweidt and Colbert.

The year wound down nicely as we held our second Kerrville Christmas Reunion at Austin's Waterloo Ice House on December 7. Playing were Darden Smith, Tim Henderson, Jane Gillman, David Halley, Melissa Javors, Butch Hancock, Charles John Quarto, and Christine Albert. Showing up as a surprise guest was Shawn Phillips. We had a warm and cheerful two shows as we raised $950 for the foundation's "Music To Go" program in Kerrville. This fund provides festival performers with an honorarium to play for institutionalized patients in both the Veterans Hospital and the State Hospital. These patients, isolated from family and the outside world, really enjoyed the music even if sometimes their mental condition did not allow them to completely understand it. Nancylee had been running the program as a volunteer since Kathy Hudson left our foundation to become public relations director for Schreiner College.

The next day we enjoyed our annual visit to Austin's Armadillo Christmas Bazaar, where we enjoyed visiting with our crafts friends, shopping, running into people we knew, and listening to music. Then, as we headed back to the ranch, we were eagerly anticipating our 1986 fifteenth anniversary year coupled with the Texas Sesquicentennial celebration and our own extended tour as Texas ambassadors.

The Texas Sesquicentennial Commission had been very busy under executive director Randy Lee and his successor Lynn Neighbors, and there were going to be more than 1,000 official events of the celebration starting with the Cotton Bowl game on New Year's Day in Dallas. As far as we knew, however, we were the only official national tour

approved by the commission. So, besides our normal dedication to doing things right, we really wanted to do an exemplary job of representing Texas when we kicked off the tour from Houston's Miller Theatre in June.

The months of January and February were dedicated to weeks of paperwork, negotiations, renewing our sponsorship with *Texas Monthly*, and preparing schedules, news releases, and press kits for our fifteenth anniversary year.

We also began expansion of the campground theater that had begun with the small stage built for the Celebrate Austin Music Festival. Following my plans and guidelines, Lee Green and his crew were expanding the theater into a full-use, covered facility that would be used for all our children's concerts.

Volunteer carpenter Marcus Abrahams works on the expansion of the campground stage. 1986.
— Courtesy Ken Schmidt.

Also in the works was a "Portrait in Sound" project, an emotion-packed documentary LP recording being created by Roger Allen, who had spent the past five years recording and interviewing performers, staff, fans, and others. He would spend more than 100 hours that spring editing and producing the album.

During our fifteenth folk festival, we devoted our Wednesday evening fish fry to a preview of our national tour and a recognition party for area businesses and individuals who were making special contributions and purchasing display advertising. The funds thus generated would allow us to afford a professionally produced printed tour program to hand out across the U.S.

Also, during the past three years, Lindsay Haisley's father had made significant donations to our music foundation to allow us to build a record storage building, to provide scholarships for New Folk finalists to our songwriters schools, and to publish a Kerrville Song Book. By now the foundation building had been completed and was in use, and over the past several years more than two dozen New Folk had used the scholarships to reduce their tuition fee by fifty percent. The song book project was pretty involved and would take a number of years to complete, but it was about to get under way.

In March I made a three-day trip to meet with officials in Odessa, Texas, and with the Midland Chamber of Commerce, who wanted a summertime event to provide both an entertainment bright spot for local people and an attraction to draw positive attention and tourists to the area. Both Midland and Odessa had been through difficult economic times in recent years with the severe reversals in the oil business and could definitely use a celebration to boost everyone's morale. We were able to clear some dates in July, and I began to work on a festival format that would have popular appeal and would incorporate members of the symphony. My goal was to have the festival together and a brochure published in time to make significant distribution at our own folk festival in May. Luckily, preparations moved along rapidly with scheduling and budget approval coming quickly by the West Texans.

In the midst of all this frantic festival preparation, Mary Jane Farmer was released to go to Houston and help the Texas Parks and Wildlife Department plan and present their big April 21 "Texas 150 Celebration" at the San Jacinto Monument. April 21 was the anniversary of the victory over Santa Anna in 1836 at the battle of San Jacinto, where Texas won her independence from Mexico. The monument at the state park commemorated that victory and would be an excellent backdrop to all the anniversary activities. The giant party was to be an exciting celebration of Texas independence as well as recognition of our Spanish heritage and the 100-plus years of peace between Mexico and the U.S. Mary Jane would do for the celebration much of what she had done for us at Kerrville. She would coordinate the festival at the monument, working with the staging, transportation, housing, and scheduling of the Texas musicians performing there all weekend. I enjoyed my two-day visit to the

Mary Jane Farmer was a key member of the management and coordinating team at the Kerrville festivals during the 1980s.

— Courtesy Merri Lu Park.

festival, hearing Vice-President Bush make a commitment to future peace, and getting emotionally caught up in the event by the inspirational Barbara Jordan, whose address "Texans: Hearts of Compassion, Spirits Unbounded" was the most thrilling moment of the observance.

Over the next couple of days, the music was everywhere. Allen Damron sang on the deck of the Battleship *Texas* anchored nearby. The concerts continued day and night with stars like Jerry Jeff Walker, the Gatlin Brothers, Alex Harvey, and other celebrities from Texas.

The work continued pretty much on schedule as we made final preparations in May for the fifteenth anniversary Kerrville Folk Festival. In spite of the rains that began across the Hill Country and many other parts of Texas, the campground theater

Pat Alger, who wrote a number of Nanci Griffith's early hit songs. 1986.

— Courtesy Brian Kanof.

expansion would be completed on time, the final painting continuing up to the day before its first use. I also completed an agreement with Butch Hancock's Texas Music Network to try to have a Kerrville video ready before the end of the year.

Roger Allen's fifteen-year album was also ready in time for the opening of the festival. In fifty-three minutes, the "Portrait In Sound" LP recalled the early years and today's involvement by thousands of "Kerrverts." Recorded in six segments of eight to ten minutes each, the album surveyed the beginnings, the campfires, the Ballad Tree, the songwriters, on-stage performances, interviews, and comments. On the disc were Amram, Nanci Griffith, Guy Clark, Damron, Carolyn Hester, Bill and Bonnie, Bob Gibson, and others, plus music by more than a dozen Kerrville performers. It was extremely well done and more than 1,000 people took it home in 1986.

The festival began on May 22 and ran two weekends, through June 1, and we optimistically announced at the beginning that in 1987 we would be going to three weekends. We had reached the edge of the comfort zone on more than one occasion recently and felt it was time to begin to spread the crowds out over eighteen days. Attendance figures indicated that we could anticipate a ten to twenty percent growth annually.

We had a number of newcomers on the main stage for our anniversary year, including festival opener Darden Smith (a 1985 New Folk award winner), New York's Frank Christian (who had gone to Mexico with us as Nanci Griffith's guitar player), Nashville songwriter Pat Alger, Ft. Worth's Katy

Moffatt (now working out of Studio City, California, touring, recording, and making films), the legendary Shawn Phillips (our favorite concert performer at the Armadillo World Headquarters and an artist with sixteen albums to his credit), Tom Rush (one of the key figures at the Club 47, pioneering the early New England folk scene), and Angela Strehli and her blues band from Lubbock.

The opening Thursday night concert made it really worthwhile to get to the festival early. Following Darden Smith, who was already an impressive performer, the concert in order of appearance presented Richard Dobson, Lyle Lovett, Jon Ims, Marcia Ball, Gary P. Nunn, and Riders in the Sky. In spite of the news of rainy weather statewide, we had an impressive crowd on hand for opening night. John Gorka opened Friday night followed by Kurt Van Sickle, Jane Gillman, and Ray Wylie Hubbard, and a spellbinding but gentle Odetta followed by Shake Russell and the always moving Peter Yarrow. Fans hardly had a chance to sit down all evening before they were up again cheering. During the day Saturday and Sunday, we had our fifteenth New Folk competition with Pat Alger, Katy

285

Katy Moffatt, a Texas songwriter from Ft. Worth, took her music across the U.S. and to Europe and Scandanavia. 1986.

— Courtesy Brian Kanof.

Angela Strehli, Lubbock's acclaimed blues singer, songwriter, and band leader. 1986.

— Courtesy *Kerrville Daily Times*.

Tom Rush at Kerrville. A key figure in the Boston area folk movement of the 1960s, he is now a major artist who has assisted many new songwriters. 1986.

— Courtesy Brian Kanof.

Shawn Phillips, another Texan with his own unique sound. 1986.

— Courtesy Brian Kanof.

Kurt Van Sickle, a protege of Mance Lipscomb in the 1970s, developed his own style. Today he is a composer-producer of New Age music. 1986.
— Courtesy Jim Willis.

The legendary Odetta, a world-renowned artist, was impressive and at home at Kerrville. 1986.
— Courtesy Brian Kanof.

Moffatt, and Tom Russell selecting winners David Roth (New York), Suzanne Sherwin (California), Kevin "Bird" Connair (New Jersey), Lynnie Isaacs (San Antonio), and Hal Michael Ketchum and the Tolers (New Braunfels).

This often reprinted photo of Peter Yarrow was taken at Kerrville's fifteenth anniversary festival. 1986.
— Courtesy Brian Kanof.

Former New Folk, Kim Wallach has the attention of her audience at the expanded campground theater at Quiet Valley Ranch. 1986.
— Courtesy C. Moulton.

287

Peter Alsop plays to a crowded children's concert at the campground theater. 1986.

— Courtesy C. Moulton.

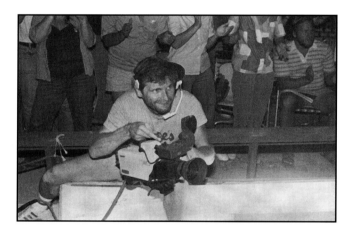

Butch Hancock was busy hosting, singing, and shooting footage for his Texas Music Network. 1986.

— Courtesy Brian Kanof.

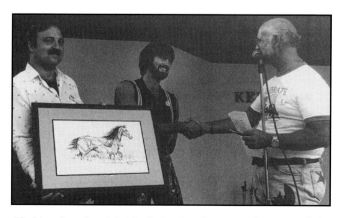

Shaking hands with Mark McCord, artist who created the Running Horses art work for Kerrville and presented me with the framed original. Judge Basquette holds the framed presentation. 1986.

— Courtesy Darron Spohn.

Nanci Griffith off-stage just before her sound check for the evening performance. 1986.

— Courtesy Ken Schmidt.

Winning songs and a winning smile from Nanci Griffith. 1986.

— Courtesy Brian Kanof.

Immediately following New Folk on both days, we established our children's festival at the newly expanded campground theater with Cherokee storyteller Gayle Ross and singer-songwriters Bob Gibson, Peter Alsop, and former New Folk Kim Wallach. The expanded theater was an immediate hit, and it was obvious that we'd have to extend the covered area, as there were as many people out in the sun as there were undercover.

As the weekend progressed, there were stellar appearances by Tom Russell, Dee Moeller, Robert Earl Keen, Pat Alger, Nanci Griffith, Katy Moffatt, Shawn Phillips, and Bridger, among others.

The seventh annual songwriters school had Rick Beresford joining Bob Gibson, Steven Fromholz, Nanci Griffith, and BMI's Del Bryant from Nashville. Ray Tate's guitar school classes were being taught with help from Steve Young and Dick Goodwin.

The Wednesday night fish fry was not only a fifteenth birthday party for the festival, but also a preview and press party for our national tour. Artist Mark McCord presented me with the framed original of his *Running Horses* pen-and-ink drawing that would become the official logo on our national tour, now called the "Celebrate Texas Concert Tour." Kerrville artist Bobby Rector, who had done so many of our other logos and posters, incorporated *Running Horses* on the tour posters for each city. We also used it as a t-shirt design and sold a signed and numbered limited edition suitable for framing.

While the fish fry concert didn't have everyone who was going on the tour, it did have Allen Damron, Butch Hancock, Santiago Jimenez, Jr., Bill and Bonnie Hearne, Steven Fromholz, and Bobby Bridger. We dedicated the concert to thirty institutions and individuals whose support had made the concert tour programs possible. It was a festive evening for the more than 1,000 gathered there. Many of them adjourned to the 10:00 P.M. anniversary ball at the Y.O. Hilton ballroom to dance to the music of Beto y los Fairlanes.

Butch Hancock not only appeared on the tour preview concert, he also co-hosted a Ballad Tree with Angela Strehli, performed on the main stage with Marce Lacouture, and was a camera man for the Texas Music Network's shoot of more than forty hours over eleven evening concerts. As vice-president of the small, independent video company, Butch knew what he wanted for his planned video release and for his statewide network programming.

As Mark McCord, our *Running Horses* artist,

Lubbock visual artist, pianist, singer-songwriter Terry Allen, out in the audience at Kerrville. 1986.
— Courtesy John Carrico.

was also a singer-songwriter, I'd asked him to play the second weekend warm-up sessions on Friday and Saturday, and he did so eagerly.

Second weekend concerts began with Jerry Jeff Walker and included Carolyn Hester, Chuck Pyle, Steve Young, Jimmie Gilmore, Terry Allen (also of Lubbock and a noted visual artist), Guy Clark, Tom Rush, the Austin Lounge Lizards' first main stage show, Santiago Jimenez, Jr., Bill Staines, and Eric Andersen. The festival closed with Angela Strehli's blues band well after 1:00 A.M.

The anniversary festival was a good celebration in spite of the four days of rain that cut our attendance by 5,000 from the previous year. I was grateful for the *Texas Monthly* corporate support, but we needed a stronger financial platform to furnish us with the kind of stability that would withstand losses from heavy rains. I would have especially liked to partner with a Texas-based national airline. This could cut our overhead and allow us to keep some cash from our travel budget in reserve for a rainy day.

The 1986 Celebrate Texas Concert Tour began with two concerts at Miller Outdoor Theatre in Houston on Tuesday and Wednesday, June 10 and 11. This kick-off concert had the national touring cast of Bobby Bridger, Steven Fromholz, Bill and Bonnie Hearne, David Halley, Santiago Jimenez, Jr., backed by his *conjunto* of Louis Gonzales and Ruben Contreras, Allen Damron, Butch Hancock, and Carolyn Hester, backed variously by Paul Glasse, *mandolin*, David Halley, *guitar*, Erik Hokkanen, *fiddle*, and from Bill and Bonnie's band, Steve Lindsay, *bass*. As we would in other cities on

Wednesday, June 25, *Penn's Landing*, Philadelphia, Pennsylvania.

Sunday, June 29, *Grant Park*, Chicago, with Bob Gibson and Ray Tate.

Monday, June 30, *Peony Park*, Omaha, Nebraska.

Tuesday, July 1, *Paramount Theatre*, Denver, Colorado, with Gary P. Nunn, Jon Ims, and Chuck Pyle.

Wednesday, July 2, *Poor David's Pub*, Dallas, Texas, "Homecoming Concert."

A relaxed closing to the Celebrate Texas Concert at Grant Park, Chicago. Carolyn Hester to my left, Butch Hancock setting his camera, Fromholz, Paul Glasse, Bob Gibson, David Halley. 1986.

— Courtesy Brian Kanof.

the tour, we had some special guests. For Houston, these were Gary P. Nunn and Shake Russell.

Austin's Paramount Theater concert followed on Thursday, June 12, with Gary P. Nunn as guest. The concert was sponsored by the Associated Republicans of Texas. Following the concert we had wine, food, and music a block up Congress Avenue at the Waterloo Ice House until 1:00 A.M.

We had a week's break before leaving for Arkansas and were all back in Austin for a Kerrville Folk Mass the night before our departure. Celebrated at St. David's Episcopal Church, the services were conducted by both festival chaplains, Rev. Charles Sumners, Jr., and Rev. Walter Lee, with a large number of Kerrverts there to see us off.

The next morning we had 477 miles to cover in our leased Greyhound bus to get to Little Rock where we played the SOB Club with Crow Johnson as our special guest. The balance of the itinerary with date, venue, city, and special guest(s) is listed below:

Friday, June 20, *Tennessee Performing Arts Center*, Nashville, with Guy Clark and Bob Gibson.

Sunday, June 22, *John F. Kennedy Center*, Washington, D. C., with Guy Clark, Bob Gibson, and Steve Gillette.

Monday, June 23, *Bottom Line*, New York City, with Bob Gibson and David Amram.

Tuesday, June 24, *Sumerville Theatre*, Cambridge, Mass., with Bob Gibson.

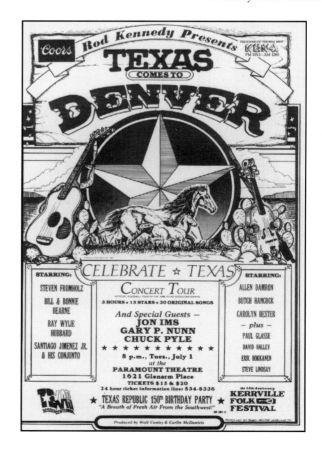

There were many memorable events, of course, such as Butch Hancock taking an estimated 1,000 photographs, at least 500 of them being of every overpass on our route, with no photos ever published; Erik Hokkanen, our boundless fiddle player on the tour, and Tex-Mex accordionist Santiago Jimenez, Jr., keeping all of us on the bus and everyone at almost every overnight hotel on the route wide awake with their newly discovered "Tex-Mex Bluegrass" jams; and Bill and Bonnie said they enjoyed "seeing" the rest of the country.

Seven days after our return, I was in Odessa for three days of meetings to make final arrangements for the July 25-27 Midland-Odessa Music Festival. Working with West Texans is a rewarding experience, and when I returned to Odessa a couple of days before the festival, everything was ready at Water Wonderland on Highway 80, the site they had chosen for the festival. The *Odessa American* and the *Midland Reporter Telegram* were joined by three TV stations, seven FM stations, and six AM stations in publicizing the festival.

The 8:00 P.M. Friday opening concert focused on western swing with the Light Crust Doughboys,

Rod Kennedy Presents

In cooperation with the Midland & Odessa Chambers of Commerce,

The First Midland-Odessa Music Festival
JULY 25 • 26 • 27

MIDLAND MUSIC FESTIVAL ODESSA

at Water Wonderland • Hwy. 80, Midland/Odessa

$1.00
SOUVENIR PROGRAM

Brought to you in part by BUD LIGHT

Alvin Crow and the Pleasant Valley Boys, and Asleep at the Wheel with guests Leon McAuliffe and Johnny Gimble.

Saturday's pair of bluegrass concerts at 2:00 and 8:00 P.M. began with an early afternoon West Texas Bluegrass Band Championship, and then full concerts by Hickory Hill, TVA, Country Gazette in reunion with Joe Carr, and Hot Rize with their alter ego Red Knuckles and the Trail Blazers.

The final concert, "Country Music: A Different Look" at 8:00 P.M. Sunday, starred fiddling Jana Jae and Riders in the Sky with a forty-five-member pops orchestra drawn from the Midland-Odessa Symphony and conducted by Dr. Thomas Hobstatt.

Back in Kerrville, we had a little over two weeks to catch up on paperwork and phone calls before we were due at a pair of bluegrass concerts at Miller Outdoor Theatre in Houston on August 15 and 16. Mandolin champion Dave Peters and his band, Third Coast, would headline on Friday night and Jana Jae "seen on 'Hee Haw'" would headline on Saturday. It truly is strange what the mass media needs to market individual artists. Jana was a really fine fiddle player, a two-time national champion who had thrilled audiences in Japan, Australia, and the Philippines. She had also starred at the Montreaux Jazz Festival in Switzerland, the Wemberly Festival in England, and closer to home at the New Orleans Jazz and Heritage Festival. She had recently played a concert with the Houston Pops, and yet the "Hee Haw" connection was important because of the show's millions of viewers.

The balance of the lineup both nights included Tex Sweeney and the Grazmatics, following their win of the 1984 Kerrville Bluegrass Band Championship. Returning by popular demand were Hickory Hill from East Texas, the House Brothers of Dallas, and three-time Southwestern Bluegrass Band Champions TVA from San Antonio.

Two nights of good music played before a responsive crowd, and we'd see all the musicians at Kerrville in two weeks for the August 29-31 Bluegrass Festival number 13. Also on the festival were Dry Branch Fire Squad, Bill Harrell and the Virginians, the John Herald Band, Jim and Jesse and the Virginia Boys, McLain Family Band, Warrior River Boys, the Weary Hearts, Paul Kramer, and the Poverty Playboys.

Number thirteen did it — one good day and two days of rain for a loss of $14,000. That, combined with the drop in attendance and income due to rain at the folk festival, gave us something extra to work for in the coming months!

The rest of September, once all the cars were out of the campgrounds and everything cleaned up, was spent on the October 10-12 Good-time Festival and the coming October 16-19 Isla Mujeres Festival.

As we were preparing for these two events, the video of the 1986 Kerrville Folk Festival concerts was already on the Texas Music Network with sixty half-hour slots weekly in fifteen cities on cable television. Viewers were able to see Riders in the Sky, Robert Earl Keen, David Amram, Odetta, Christine Albert, and others in homes in Austin, Dallas, Ft. Worth, and Corpus Christi. We were pleased for both our artists and for ourselves, and the live video looked great and gave a good insight into what the festival was really like.

Robert Earl Keen at Kerrville. 1986.
— Courtesy Darron Spohn

Mid-September found me at another Tour-Con meeting in Austin. Since watching Texas rise from twenty-third in the nation in tourism twenty-one years before to third that year, I believed in continuing to put time and energy into tourism through DTA, the festivals association, and the state-hosted tourism conferences. The Texas Tourist Development Agency was spending $18 million in support of the 150th birthday celebration and continued to be one of the few state agencies able to produce a profit for everyone involved.

The fourth Kerrville Good-time Music Festival on Columbus Day weekend was announced as "the last of four annual festivals devoted to traditional music" as we still had bills unpaid from previous years.

Friday night opened with three Austin-based Celtic artists back-to-back: Celtic Stone, Reynardine, and balladeer Ed Miller. Caryl P. Weiss, Steve James, and Debby McClatchy closed the evening.

Saturday afternoon's workshops included a Saul Broudy harmonica clinic, a workshop on songs of the Old West by Steve Cormier, and a collecting workshop by John Pearse and Mary Faith Rhodes, before the free-wheeling square-dancing workshop kicked up the dust, looking like organized chaos.

Later, accordionist Nada Lewis of California began the evening with Gypsy music at 6:00 P.M. followed in one-hour sets by Allen Damron, Rosalie Sorrels, Steve Cormier, John Pearse and Mary Faith, with San Antonio's award-winning Irish band, St. James Gate, winding things up.

Sunday's 1:00 P.M. closing concert featured the Tolers Family Band, Saul Broudy, *conjunto* music by Kerrville's Fritz Morcheso, western swing by the Light Crust Doughboys, Lindsay Haisley with his autoharp, Mariachi Campana de America, and finally Irish jigs, reels, and laments played by Tinker's Dam.

Even with a reduced budget, the festival failed to break even. The music was fantastic, but we retired the event as promised.

We were ready to return to the beautiful Isla Mujeres. Aeromexico had made some executive changes and did not honor our agreement, so I approached Continental Airlines, whose corporate headquarters was in Houston. They listened to my proposal and thought that the festival package would be good for them, and they joined us as our travel partners to Mexico.

We departed Houston for Mexico on Thursday, October 16, with nearly every seat filled by Isla-bound passengers. We had blocks of rooms at Posada del Mar, Roca Mar, and Roca del Caribe, and our welcoming poolside party was at Posada del Mar. Festival concerts were on the Plaza at the Teatro del Pueblo by Allen Damron, Nanci Griffith, Steven Fromholz, and the big band of Beto y los Fairlanes. We also brought Turk and Christy Pipkin, because if there is a universal language other than music, mime had to be it. We thought they'd entertain the children, and they did, but their biggest reception was from the adults. One of Mexico's best-loved entertainers worldwide was Cantiflas, one of history's great mimes, and the fans told Turk and Christy that they were "like Cantiflas' family"!

Again we enjoyed the island paradise with its hospitable people, the beauty of the pastel buildings with tile roofs, the romantic beauty of white sands, swaying palms, and emerald waters. Then there was the marvelous seafood caught fresh every day, the scuba diving, skin diving, swimming, and sailing in crystal-clear waters. This was a true paradise. After the Texas rains of May, July, and August, we were ready for paradise. As we left the island for home on the crowded ferry, our hearts were still with the island.

While it was unusual for us to have an event at the ranch in November, we responded to the urging of the state-sponsored Texas Meeting on the Outdoors to try to help reduce litter in Texas. We planned a camp-out weekend November 8-9 with early camping beginning on Friday night, November 7.

Our event was called the first "Great Texas Outdoors Celebration" with crafts, environmental and ecological booths, music, food, workshops, and a Chapel Hill service on Sunday. Our entertainers were David Amram, Shake Russell, Katy Moffatt, Kinky Friedman, Tim Henderson, Don Sanders, Bill Oliver, and Trash Gordon, who proclaimed "Texas litter is getting out of hand." Before our 3:00 P.M. show, there were some litter seminars at the Y.O. Ranch Hilton hotel with guest speakers including members of the Texas legislature. Tickets for our event were $10 in advance and $12 at the gate, and the income covered all the expenses. We couldn't tell how many fans came because it was the last chance to camp-out and listen to great music or because they wanted to help with the anti-litter campaign, but it didn't really matter because, ultimately, all of us were more litter conscious after the weekend. Another good thing that came out of the weekend was the fun poster conceived by our artist Bobby Rector, who had made up the logos for the Midland-Odessa Music Festival and for Isla Mujeres. Trash Gordon, a school teacher named Ronnie Blanton who had been known to be different when the occasion called for it, was one of our more imaginative volunteers.

The month of December, with our Christmas Reunion, visit to Wheatsville Co-op's street fair, and the annual visit to the Armadillo Christmas Bazaar, was an annual time of joy, but the passing of Kate Wolf from her lingering leukemia in California was a deeply felt loss. Austin's KUT-FM played Kate Wolf recordings most of the day, and we had a hard time dealing with her death. There had been something very special about her. It was fortuitous that we at least had recently seen her at the taping for "Austin City Limits" and that we had the CDs and videos of her warm and wonderful studio concert with Nina Gerber to help us remember her as we knew her.

The year came to a conclusion with our third annual Kerrville Christmas Reunion in Austin from 8:00 P.M. to 1:00 A.M., Saturday, December 6, at Waterloo Ice House, now located at Medical Parkway and 38th Street. The event brought back together Butch Hancock, David Halley, Jimmie Gilmore, Christine Albert, Allen Damron, Tim Henderson, Bobby Bridger, and Lindsay Haisley, plus the duo of Hudson and Franke. We played two shows and served complimentary Hill Country

Bakery apple-nut cake and Nancylee's hot apple cider. It was a close and warm evening with good friends and good music to bring our anniversary year to a cheerful close. We netted $656 for our foundation's "Music To Go."

Financially, 1986 had to be described as a year generally difficult with all three of our big festivals hit by rain. Regardless, we entered our sixteenth year with an optimistic outlook as *Texas Monthly* renewed their sponsorship and introduced us to GSD&M advertising executive Tina Williamson, who handled the Southwest Airlines account. Our proposal for Southwest Airlines to become our "official airline" dovetailed into their other marketing plans for Southwest and they joined us. We were proud to partner with Southwest, not only because it would help us to fly performers in from more distant points, but because Southwest was a corporation Texans were proud of, a very people-oriented company from the top down.

The ninety-minute Texas Music Network VHS color video cassette of highlights from the 1986 Kerrville Folk Festival was out in time for Christmas at the end of the year. It included Nanci Griffith, Riders in the Sky, Jerry Jeff Walker, Marcia Ball, and Shake Russell.

Working on the backlog of Kerrville audio cassettes, we began editing the 1983 folk festival album including the last recording by the late Stan Rogers.

Our first 1987 event was a small one. I had to go to Isla Mujeres on business for five days, January 20-25, and decided to announce the trip as available for twenty-five people. Don Sanders came along to entertain and provided twenty-five copies of his new album *Tourist* so each person on the trip with us would have one. Our package, worked out with the hotel, the airline, and a couple of restaurants, would provide round-trip air on Continental, the album, five nights at the Posada del Mar, a pool-side party with dinner and drinks, dinner three nights at Hacienda Gomar, and Ciro's Lobster House on the island plus a night on the town in Cancun on my birthday. Dinner, wine, and music at Club Salsa in Cancun, plus the ferry over and back was included. After dinner in Cancun, most of us agreed that the food and service were better on the island and a lot less expensive. Our twenty-five friends, however, had a good trip, and when my business was over, we returned to Texas with another open trip for twenty-five planned with Steve Gillette on September 14-19.

Don Sanders, "Dean of Houston Folk Music," sings selections from his new album, Tourist, *at Kerrville and then became a tourist to Mexico and Isla Mujeres. 1986.*
— Courtesy Brian Kanof.

The 1986 Kerrville video release party at Austin's Adventureland Video. From left: George Howard, president of Texas Music Network, George Lair of Adventureland Video, Rod Kennedy, Marcia Ball, Butch Hancock. 1986.
— Courtesy Accent Photography.

In early February I attended another Texas Festivals Association meeting at Texas A&M, but otherwise the early months were devoted to developing and distributing season and folk festival brochures and posters, shipping all over the U.S. We also sent out an emergency newsletter to raise money through early sponsorship renewals and also an invitation to buy lifetime tickets for two at $500, or, perhaps, advertising in the festival programs. The response was outstanding, as it always had been, and we proceeded with our plans for 1987.

We were finally able to work out the California dates for the Celebrate Texas Concert Tour that we had been unable to squeeze into our 1986 calendar. With just a few changes in our touring company, we set Friday, March 6, at the Palomino Club in Los Angeles, and Saturday, March 7, north of San Francisco at Luther Burbank Center in Santa Rosa.

Our touring company now consisted of Christine Albert with Ernie Gammage, Allen Damron, Jimmie Gilmore, Butch Hancock and Marce Lacouture, Carolyn Hester, Shake Russell, and Steve Gillette. We also took our three Kerrville All-Stars Paul Glasse, *mandolin*, Erik Hokkanen, *fiddle*, and singer-songwriter David Halley, *guitar*.

In Los Angeles the 9:00 P.M. concert was standing-room-only before we even began. I was surprised and pleased since the Palomino was pretty well-known as a kicker dance hall, and we had made a late move to that club after the original Venice Theatre deal didn't work out. Steve Gillette, Carolyn Hester, and a number of other Kerrverts in the Los Angeles area had helped with the advance publicity. The day of the concert, the *Los Angeles Herald* printed a three-column story by Todd Everett with a big picture of Butch and Marce. Both Steve and Carolyn had talked on the air about our concert with Roz and Howard Larman on KPFK's "Folk Scene" before we arrived in California. Anyway, it was a full house and an appreciative one. I only saw three people who discovered they were in the wrong place and left before it was over.

Thanks to Southwest Airlines' new deal, we could not only fly to Los Angeles from Texas, but from Los Angles to San Francisco for the concert at the Luther Burbank Center, arranged by Curtis Reinhardt, who had been part of the Rockefeller's team in Houston when we played our road show there. The center was in Santa Rosa, in the heart of Kate Wolf country, and quietly we invited Laurie Lewis and Nina Gerber to join us and help us pay a Texas tribute to Kate's memory. Kate's song "Give Yourself To Love" was led by Laurie and Nina and sung by everyone in the audience. It was a very moving and heartfelt tribute, followed only by a reverent rendition of our anthem, "Heal In The Wisdom" led by Allen Damron as the concert closed. We drove to San Francisco to fly home the next day, warmed by our California visit.

The weekend after we returned from California, March 15, Steve James had arranged a benefit for Kerrville at Leon Springs Cafe between

Kerrville and San Antonio, where he was opening for John Hammond. The event was a standing-room-only Sunday, and I had a good visit with Hammond. He said that places for acoustic blues musicians to play were becoming harder to find than nuns in a barber shop. He suggested during our conversation that it would be a great help if somehow the Kerrville Folk Festival could include some kind of an acoustic blues event each year. He pointed out that an acoustic event at a major festival like ours could draw considerable attention to some of the fine blues artists who were only known in their own regions. It sounded good to me and I told him I would see what I could do.

With all the rains of 1986, we had major repairs and work to do at the ranch, and so our volunteers planned a whole series of work weekends at the ranch, including March 21-22, April 11-12, May 9-10, and May 16-17.

In our office, the mailings, travel, and housing arrangements for folk festival performers and screening New Folk tapes were on the agenda.

On Thursday and Friday nights, May 7-8, we were back at Houston's Miller Theatre with the on-the-road concerts previewing our sixteenth festival. Houston's popular Shake Russell was joined by

Rod Kennedy Presents
KERRVILLE FOLK FESTIVAL
...on the road

Free!

CHRISTINE ALBERT
PONTY BONE
JIMMIE GILMORE
PAUL GLASSE
HICKORY HILL
ERIC HOKKANEN
TIM HENDERSON
SHAKE RUSSELL

IN A PAIR OF 3-HOUR PREVIEW CONCERTS OF THE 16TH ANNUAL KERRVILLE FOLK FESTIVAL AT QUIET VALLEY RANCH MAY 21 - JUNE 7 WITH MORE THAN 100 PERFORMERS

8 PM THURS & FRI, MAY 7 & 8
MILLER OUTDOOR THEATRE
HERMANN PARK — HOUSTON

SPONSORED IN PART BY THE CITY OF HOUSTON PARKS & RECREATION DEPT. THE MILLER THEATRE ADVISORY COUNCIL & THE CULTURAL ARTS COUNCIL OF HOUSTON

Christine Albert, Ponty Bone, Jimmie Gilmore, Paul Glasse, Jana Jae with Hickory Hill, Erik Hokkanen, and Tim Henderson.

We drove the five hours back to Kerrville on Saturday to catch the work weekend, where they were almost finished painting and repairing and were expanding the campground theater to provide more covered seating and also moving the big twenty-by-thirty-foot hospitality shed from the theater to backstage. That not only left more viewing area in the theater, but it also provided the staff with a covered area in which to eat.

In the meantime, as part of the fund-raising effort at our office, we were processing $25 Friends of the Kerrville Folk Festival memberships coming in response to our spring newsletter. While $25 seems a small amount in the face of $10,000 in rain losses, 100 memberships totaled $2,500 and 400 would pay off the $10,000 that was overdue. Support was coming in from everywhere, and many people were sending more than $25 to "protect their investment in the festival."

This was the year that we decided to go to an eighteen-day, three-weekend format. When the weather was good, the festival site was overcrowded, and we decided to take the chance on increasing our capacity while, hopefully, spreading the growing crowds over a three-weekend schedule. The third weekend really did not cost a third again as much to produce with many of the general ledger expenses like printing, ranch preparations, publicity, etc., already amortized.

So, while we were still hard-pressed for consistent cash flow and carrying a pretty significant debt, we launched into the expansion to maintain the ambiance of the festival, give us another weekend of vacation season travelers, and a chance to present more artists and more events for our growing waiting list of performers.

As part of the new festival schedule, May 21-June 7, the new weekdays, Monday through Friday of the added week, June 1-5, Hugh Sparks offered an eight-hour-a-day concert-lecture series covering the history of American popular music researched and produced by Hugh with staff musicians Kay Sparks, Saul Broudy, John Pearse, Mary Faith Rhodes, and others. Covering 100 years both chronologically and from an historical perspective, it was an incredibly informative and entertaining week!

At night at the campground theater, we did a series of four 2-hour country music concerts by the

Augie Meyers, big and gentle songwriter from San Antonio, a seasoned veteran of the Sir Douglas Quintet. 1987.
— Courtesy Ron McKowan.

Maines Brothers, Alvin Crow and the Pleasant Valley Boys, Beth Williams, and Clay Blaker and the Texas Honky Tonk Band. Then on Sunday afternoon of the last day, we did a fifth and final concert in the series with Al Dressen's Super Swing Revue, an all-star group, including Paul Glasse, Lynn Frazier, Al Gibson, Erik Hokkanen, Tana Cochran, Sherri Barr (from Grassfire), Dale Dennis, and Wes Star.

The eighteen-day festival, again sponsored by Southwest Airlines and *Texas Monthly*, began on Thursday, May 21, and the first weekend's five evening concerts listed thirty-five performers, including Guy Clark, Augie Meyers, Darden Smith, Rattlesnake Annie, former Newport talent coordinator and now Nashville record producer Jim Rooney, Shawn Phillips, Ian Tyson, and five warm-up sets by Paul Glasse and Brad Terry.

The 1987 New Folk concerts produced several

Jim Rooney, a Nashville record producer who never forget his folk roots. 1987.

— Courtesy Brian Kanof.

The O'Kanes from Nashville were refreshing, innovative, and extremely well received at Kerrville. 1987.

— Courtesy Al Messer.

Canada's Ian Tyson (right) with guitarist Andy Hardin. Tyson was once half of the hit duo Ian and Sylvia, and is now a quarterhorse raiser and rider, but also a major force in Canada's music world. 1987.

— Courtesy Darron Spohn.

winners who went on to earn national followings, including Buddy Mondlock from Chicago, Pierce Pettis of Marion, Ohio, Josh Joffen from Brooklyn, and James McMurtry of San Antonio. Judges were Jim Rooney, Suzanne Sherwin, and Ian Tyson.

While the mid-week activities of the added week have already been described, the first mid-week was also exciting. The two sundown concerts were by Jan Marra and the O'Kanes on Tuesday, and on Thursday by Bobby Bridger, who performed his complete *Aldebaran and the Falling Star*, narrated by Kathy Cronkite. The big Wednesday night fish fry was a special "Concert for Kate" by Caryl P. Weiss, Tish Hinojosa, Patricia Hardin, and California's Laurie Lewis with the Kerrville All-Stars. It was a heartwarming, if not somewhat tearful, remembrance of Kate Wolf, who had wanted to play the festival again.

Kate had written me from California:

"Here I sit surrounded by little pieces of Kerrville, luggage tags, t-shirt, button, coffee cup, and piles of letters from down your way. I really missed being able to come. The grapevine heart hangs in the skylight, turning in the sun with Kerrville rainbows shooting everywhere. Thanks so much to you and everyone for the gifts of the heart."

She went on about the hoped-for success of her coming bone marrow transplants and hopes of being back at Kerrville in 1987. She was with us. We could feel it.

The second weekend, with its staff concert hosted by Saul Broudy, and the New Folk award

Laurie Lewis was introduced to the Kerrville audience at the memorial "Concert for Kate" after guesting with the Kerrville tour at the Luther Burbank Center in Santa Anna, California. 1987.
— Courtesy Darron Spohn.

Lyle Lovett, a former New Folk, was quiet and almost shy offstage. His refreshing, quirky songs earned him an immediate family and rousing approval. 1987.
— Courtesy Brian Kanof.

winners concert hosted by David Card, had some really significant moments on its three 6-hour evening concerts, including a powerful reunion of Gibson and Camp, the Saturday night finale with Bobby Bridger, Lyle Lovett, and Nanci Griffith, and the Sunday night rock-a-billy closing by Ray Campi. The rains did not seem to dampen the spirits of those few thousand who really wanted to be there.

The third and final weekend had a one-hour Saturday afternoon concert by Hal Michael Ketchum and friends that seemed like a back porch pickin' party and was popular with the crowd. The evening concerts were highlighted by the Austin Lounge Lizards, Robert Earl Keen, Jim Post, Odetta, Tom Paxton, Peter Yarrow, the Angela Strehli Band, Michael Tomlinson, the trio of Butch Hancock, Jimmie Gilmore and David Halley, Country Gazette, Gamble Rogers, and the festival finale by Riders in the Sky.

It was a significant eighteen days in our lives, because for a moment it lifted us from the financial burden that had been weighing us down. The festival had always rejuvenated us for another year. Moreover, this one was filled with memorable moments like the renaming and dedication of the campground theater as the Kenneth Threadgill Memorial Theater. There was also the ball at the Y.O. Ranch Hilton on the Wednesday night of the fish fry when we had a chance to visit one-on-one with so many of our fans.

The problem with the 1987 folk festival was fourteen days of rain with a total of thirteen and a half inches, causing a thirty-five percent drop in attendance and a loss of $29,000!

I can remember standing on the stage as the constant rains continued. The concert was over, and the performers, crew, and sparse crowd had all left

Rock-a-billy favorite Ray Campi of Austin received a warm welcome at Kerrville. 1987.

— Courtesy Darron Spohn.

Gamble Rogers, virtuoso guitarist and storyteller, reminded us that "It's much easier to ask forgiveness than it is to get permission." 1987.

— Courtesy Brian Kanof.

Michael Tomlinson, an early New Folk from Austin, went on to sell 50,000 copies of his first album as an unsigned Seattle artist. 1987.

— Courtesy Darron Spohn.

the Outdoor Theater as I stood, depressed and alone, on the Kerrville Folk Festival stage.

It had been raining continuously for the first eleven days of the eighteen-day festival, and, as the producer, I didn't know how we'd make it through the final weekend.

We had been hit by rains many times in the past and were trying to continue under a severe deficit that had just increased. And, it was still raining. I began to have some serious doubts about my future and wondered how I ever got into the music business.

There was another week of the festival, and it finally stopped raining. With the outpouring of support from performers, staff, and the crowd, and the rejuvenation that came from just being a part of the magic that was Kerrville, I found myself sifting through all the offers of help, and knowing that to survive we'd have to organize the fund-raising energy and willingness that was becoming evident all across Texas and in many other parts of the country.

Willie Nelson had been producing major annual Farm Aid events to help the farmers, and I thought, "What we need is Folk Aid!" Others around me agreed, and I went to Bobby Rector and told him we needed a logo that would quickly dramatize our plight. He came up with a Folk Aid logo, and in the big "O" of the word "folk," he depicted a Kerrville Folk Festival logo slipping beneath the waves.

Taking the logo and running with it, Poor David's Pub in Dallas was the first Folk Aid fund raiser on July 20 with Emily Aronson, Allen Damron, Texas Shorty, Melissa Javors, Mike Williams, Ann Armstrong, and Steve Hughes, raising $2,046 and sending it to us in time to keep our phones and lights on!

In Austin at the Cactus Cafe, State Senator Ray Farabee of Corpus Christi was master of ceremonies with Cactus Pryor in a benefit performance by Nanci Griffith and Steven Fromholz heavily promoted by David Obermann and the staff at KUT-FM.

Then, before we knew it, Bill Seals helped organize a benefit dance in Abilene at Butterfield Junction by "Slim Chance and the Survivors." Their check in the amount of $450 made our payment to the bank on time, allowing us to keep our six ranch vehicles and our computer that were all securing the same note. Keeping faith with our banks was as important to us as keeping the tools we needed to do our job.

In Kerrville a Folk Aid Committee was established and it included ten local businessmen (including Tim Stoepel, Harry Parrish, Bill Dozier, Stroh's distributor Bill Crittenden, Jr., and NBC Bank's Ken Adams) along with three key performers (Jimmie Gilmore, Butch Hancock, and David Halley) who agreed to headline an August 17 dance at the Y.O. Hilton Hotel ballroom. The casual dance and modest buffet were quite successful, with lots of Kerrville-area people dropping by, and we began to feel as if we had a future.

Our Miller Theatre bluegrass concerts were staged Friday and Saturday, August 20-21 with Peter Rowan as the headliner, backed by TVA. The show also featured Paul Glasse, Tex Sweeny and the Grazmatics, and our 1986 Southwest Bluegrass Band Champions, Danger in the Air, from Dallas. There was plenty of bluegrass spiced with some of Peter Rowan's more adventurous musical detours, and the jazzy flavor of Danger in the Air.

The very next weekend was a music foundation event that had been planned long before the rains hit the festival, so in the midst of all the Folk Aid fund-raising for the festival, here came a Kerrville Music Foundation benefit street dance. Held at Rancher's Western Wear with two stages, the dance was a "battle of the bands," good time rock n' roll versus rock-a-billy starring the Hotcakes and veteran recording star Ray Campi, and the Rock-a-billy Review with Jon Emery. A western setting, Stroh's beer, barbecue, raffle, and crafts area all helped make for a successful evening.

The fourteenth annual Kerrville Bluegrass Festival, over the September 4-6 Labor Day weekend, was an attempt to trim the huge bluegrass budget and roster of previous years and still focus on the best musicians available, including some familiar names and some new ones.

The 1987 version introduced Eddie Adcock and Talk of the Town, new regional bands the Gore Brothers from West Texas and Wry Grass, with repeat appearances by the popular Hot Rize and Red Knuckles and the Trail Blazers, Peter Rowan, Jana Jae, and Doug Dillard, along with TVA, Hickory Hill, Texas Sweeney and the Grazmatics, String Factory Outlet, the Poverty Playboys, and hard-driving 1986 Southwestern Bluegrass Band Champions Danger in the Air.

While providing some cash flow and paying its own way, the bluegrass festival also provided a wonderful weekend of music, but did not change our cash position. We began to think seriously about looking for another event for Labor Day weekend.

On Sunday, September 20, Gruene Hall, just outside New Braunfels, hosted a Folk Aid benefit dance with Clay Blaker and the Texas Honky Tonk Band and Beth Williams Band. Among the surprise guests showing up was Hal Michael Ketchum.

Meanwhile, Andy Wilkinson scheduled a benefit in Lubbock on October 4, Steamboat Springs in

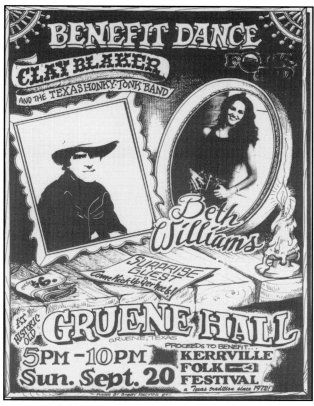

Austin staged their own benefit, and we received word of benefits being planned in Chicago and Winnipeg. It suddenly became evident that we could not attend every benefit and that people trying to help us would probably understand that.

The next Folk Aid event cleared through our own office was a big concert at the Outdoor Theater at Quiet Valley Ranch from 6:00 to 11:00 P.M. on Saturday, October 10, starring Jerry Jeff Walker, Christine Albert, and the Austin Lounge Lizards. It turned out to be a good concert and was a perfect event to brighten a three-day staff retreat for our volunteers, who were very concerned about the future of the festivals. We explained the deliberate aim and dedication with which we and hundreds of other people were pursuing support for the festivals. We were also looking for every possible way to trim expenses, and, hopefully, secure some appropriate additional corporate sponsorship. The support was forming all over the country, and we were keeping our heads up.

I felt that the staff returned to their homes encouraged and ready to help in any way they could. Many of them were already members of the Friends of Kerrville, festival sponsors, or even lifetime ticket holders.

The Austin Committee to Bail Out the Kerrville Folk Festival, which included, among others, Senator Farabee, Max Nofziger, Megan Meisenbach, Kathy Cronkite, and Hugh Sparks, was working on a major concert for November, and plans for others were coming in every week, so we were able to devote a little more time ourselves to running our business and keeping track of things.

We turned our immediate attention to the festival on Isla Mujeres scheduled for October 14-18. We had reserved the entire Posada del Mar and most of the Roca Mar with overflow rooms elsewhere. We had a large number of reservations for Continental flights on both the 14th and 15th. Our entertainers were Nanci Griffith, Allen Damron, Steve Gillette, Don Sanders, CPR, and Ponty Bone and the Squeezetones, who played the "all night dance."

We enjoyed the break from the hectic schedule at home by attending the poolside parties, swimming, dancing to reggae at Buho's, and, of course, playing the festival performance at Teatro del Pueblo on the Plaza. By now, even the Mexican fishermen were fans of Nanci Griffith, most called me by my first name, and, not infrequently, many offered to buy me a beer. It was the ultimate working vacation and home away from home.

We returned to join the Austin committee putting on the benefit at the Driskill Hotel and the Paramount Theater. The Austin committee of over forty supporters, including several media people, helped us host a Friday 6:00 P.M. celebrity dinner in the Crystal Ballroom of the Driskill with music by David Amram.

At 8:00 P.M., everyone from the dinner joined the crowd at the Paramount for a benefit concert co-hosted by Steven Fromholz and Cactus Pryor. The evening starred David Halley, Paul Glasse, Marcia Ball, Allen Damron, Chuck Pyle from Colorado, Carolyn Hester, Butch Hancock, B. W. Stevenson from Nashville, Kinky Friedman, just off the road promoting his second murder mystery, Jimmie Gilmore, just signed with Hightone Records, Shake Russell, Christine Albert, Shawn Phillips, David Amram, and Bobby Bridger. When the concert was over, Carolyn Hester and Allen Damron hosted an after-concert gala at the Driskill, where the entire nine-member Jamaican steel drum band, the Caribbean Steeltones, had driven in from Houston to provide the music.

The Caribbean Steeltones, shown here playing Kerrville, provided the music at the Driskill following the benefit concert at the Paramount. 1987.

— Courtesy Merri Lu Park.

Everyone was making a contribution in their own way, and there was a good feeling going around. It was revitalizing, and netted enough to retire the festival's past due tax obligations.

Nancylee and I drove to Houston the next day to attend the two benefit shows scheduled at Rockefeller's by B. W. Stevenson, Shake Russell, and Shawn Phillips, all three fresh from the Paramount benefit in Austin. Vicki Bell and the entire Houston

committee of twenty-five were there, and we had two full houses. Of course, the shows were rewarding musically while providing significant cash to continue our digging-out process.

Next up was our December 5 Kerrville Christmas Reunion at Waterloo Ice House on 38th Street. Allen Damron hosted the 8:00 P.M. show, and I hosted the one at 11:00. Playing both shows were Bobby Bridger, Tim Henderson, Butch Hancock, Christine Albert, Jimmie Gilmore, and Damron. As usual, it was a quiet, warm, and intimate evening with good friends. And there was some funding for "Music To Go."

Following our other events at the Driskill earlier in the year, we thought it might be rewarding to plan a New Year's weekend built around our performers, using the Driskill as the site. David Card at Poor David's planned a Folk Aid "Kerrville Holiday Party" for his club on Wednesday, December 30, with Butch Hancock, Kurt Van Sickle, Caryl P. Weiss, and Alex Abravanel (a staff volunteer and a former New Folk from Greece), with guests Ray Wylie Hubbard and Bugs Henderson.

So, we started our event on December 31, New

induced fatigue and decided we needed to assay the situation. In retrospect, we began to feel pretty good about our progress and about still being in business. We also felt good about the forty-three musicians who were playing benefits for us. We moved into the new year with a known schedule of seven more Folk Aid benefits coming up, including a major event in April with Peter Paul and Mary in concert in Ft. Worth at the Will Rogers Auditorium.

The first Folk Aid event of 1988 was on my birthday, January 22, in San Antonio at the 400-seat Sonova Beach Club on Wurzbach. This was the first of two benefits planned by the San Antonio committee and was planned as a fifty-eighth birthday party for me. Hosting the concert and singing six-song-sets were Alex Abravanel, Melissa Javors, and Steve James, who introduced the world champion Irish band St. James Gate, Santiago Jimenez, Jr., fresh from taping "Austin City Limits," and triple Southwest champions and now U.S. champions, TVA. Peter Rowan, just returning from France, Germany, and Spain, was the top of the bill. We were also joined by surprise guest Robert Earl Keen. As it was in other cities, the benefit concert was fun

Year's Eve, with Shake Russell and Christine Albert. Then, on New Year's night, we did a concert at Steamboat Springs with Jon Ims, Rick Beresford, Laurie Lewis, Darden Smith, and Ponty Bone and the Squeezetones.

The next day we had happy hour with the Austin Lounge Lizards, a three-hour nighttime concert starting at 8:00 with Chuck Pyle, Katy Moffatt, Butch Hancock, and Lyle Lovett, with an after-hours concert at Steamboat Springs by Marcia Ball.

While a great way to spend a New Year's weekend, it was probably overkill, and we realized only a marginal profit.

We began 1988 about sixty days behind in our preparations for the coming season. We were bogged down with the multiplicity of benefits and debt-

and filled with love and everyone feeling appreciated. Along with good ticket sales at the door, there were several donations and the Folk Aid t-shirts sold well too.

Sponsorships, crafts booth rentals, and program advertising began their normal early-in-the-year income cycle. As soon as we could get the pre-festival brochures and newsletters out, there would be mail order income.

In the meantime, Nashville songwriter Fred Koller had organized a Music City Folk Aid benefit at Studio 16 with Peter Rowan, the O'Kanes, Rick Beresford, Butch Hancock, Pete Kennedy, Shake Russell, Paul Glasse, and a whole gaggle of other tunesmiths.

Less than a week later, back in Texas, the Wednesday night, February 17 Folk Aid concert at Poor David's Pub was one of the most unusual evenings ever. With just a baby grand piano on-stage and no bands, Marcia Ball and Gary P. Nunn played their hits at two sold-out shows at 8:00 and 11:00 P.M. David Card grinned as he handed me thousands of dollars from admissions. Slowly, we were getting a handle on the debt while enjoying getting to know our performers better, one-on-one.

Driving straight to Houston, I had a chance to visit with numerous members of the Houston committee, including Vicki Bell before the 8:00 and 11:00 P.M., Saturday night Folk Aid concerts at Rockefeller's with Guy Clark, Townes Van Zandt, and David Halley. The committee had done their job as nearly 500 attended the concerts. Almost everyone wanted to know if there was going to be a folk festival in 1988 and wished us success with our fund raising. We told them we were working on it.

We finally completed the 1988 folk festival plans, did the brochure layouts, and with the rest of the season assured of happening, mailed out 10,000 newsletters and distributed our brochures and posters.

It was like bluegrass old-home-week at UT's Cactus Cafe on the UT campus on March 26, when the Austin committee presented a Bluegrass Jam for Kerrville with Erik Hokkanen, Paul Glasse, TVA, Danger in the Air, and the Grazmatics. The cafe was filled with shade tree pickers and fans from our bluegrass festivals making their contribution.

For the past sixty days, I had been talking with Peter Yarrow almost every night after midnight, as he directed the preparations for the big *Ft. Worth Star-Telegram* and KLUV-FM-sponsored Peter Paul

and Mary concert. Joining PP&M were Ronnie Gilbert, Tom Paxton, and Josh White, Jr. The concert date was April 6.

Peter coached me nightly, going over checklists to make certain that everything was done and nothing left to chance: higher priced VIP seats at the front, invitations with personal notes enclosed, keeping up with the progress of the statewide committee of twenty-four, the pre-concert cocktail party for big donors, after-concert reception for our sponsors and others, autographed PP&M albums, phone interviews with radio stations, special hosts for the concert including Speaker of the Texas House Gib Lewis, our Ft. Worth committee chair Cathy Hayes, and the Light Crust Doughboys. He also checked with me on the progress of our publicity and promotion being handled by Susan Jacobs' public relations firm. Not a stone was left unturned.

That effort, combined with the immense popularity of the trio and the incredible editorial and display advertising support provided us by the *Ft. Worth Star-Telegram*, resulted in a tremendous evening of marvelous music by all six performers, a love-filled event that provided us with our largest single chunk of cash to keep going.

By the time we were ready to return to Miller Outdoor Theatre for our folk concerts on May 12-13, we had paid off all of the high-pressure debts, attracted Coca-Cola and Budweiser as associate sponsors of the festival, and happily acknowledged hundreds of gifts ranging from $1 to $1,000. The reaffirmation of what we were doing at Kerrville had been terrific!

We felt positive as we greeted the audience from the stage of Miller Theatre. The Shake Russell Band was there as well as the Houston-based Caribbean Steeltones, Butch Hancock and Marce Lacouture, Allen Damron, Lindsay Haisley, and David Halley. It was always good to get back to the music, to the source of what we were about.

There were other things to be positive about. We were to celebrate Peter Yarrow's fiftieth birthday at the festival on May 31 and the taping of "Mountain Stage" radio show from the festival on June 10. Also, we would be honoring the memory of Kenneth Threadgill by dedicating the campground theater to him after further expansion. We would also be remembering B. W. Stevenson, who recently had died of heart failure in a Nashville hospital, by planting a memorial tree for him on Chapel Hill at

the Folk Mass. Further, while it wouldn't happen until August, I had been invited to bring a Kerrville Folk Festival road show to the Alaska State Fair. I was working on arrangements every week, and one of the pre-Alaska publicity stunts was to invite Alaska's Hobo Jim to Kerrville and to fly the Alaskan state flag during the week he was here.

I was also grateful for the presence of business manager Andrea LeBlanc, who had been on board since the folk festival of 1986, replacing Mary Jane Farmer. Because of her being here, I was free to travel, to be out of the office for extended business trips and an occasional vacation, and could know that everything back at the office was in good hands. In fact, for the first time, my business manager was actually running most of the business, taking care of all the accounting, payroll, taxes, and making some good executive decisions. Andrea had been a lifetime ticket holder working in Austin and responded to my newsletter request for someone to help us.

We had so much to look forward to now, especially since just a few months ago we didn't know whether or not there would even be a seventeenth festival.

For 1988 we had invited more than three dozen newcomers to our festival, including some widely heralded leaders in our field such as the Limeliters,

Festival business manager Andrea LeBlanc was a Lifetime Ticket Holder before she came to work for Kerrville Festivals, Inc., in 1986.
— Courtesy Merri Lu Park.

The Limeliters (from left) original members Lou Gottlieb and Alex Hasilev, tenor Red Grammer, and instrumentalist John David. 1988.
— Courtesy Brian Kanof.

Sonny Curtis, one of Buddy Holly's Crickets. 1988.
— Courtesy Brian Kanof.

Canadian award-winning writer-performer Murray McLaughlin. 1988.
— Courtesy Brian Kanof.

Red Clay Ramblers, John Stewart, and Casselberry-Dupree, whom I'd met at the Winnipeg Folk Festival along with award-winning Canadians Valdy and Murray McLaughlin. Connie Kaldor was returning, and we greatly looked forward to the appearance of Sonny Curtis, who had been one of Buddy Holly's Crickets and was writer of hits like "The Straight Life."

The other appearance all of us were celebrating, especially our volunteer staff, was the main stage appearance of Michelle Shocked, a former volunteer ticket taker who had been recorded in our campground two years earlier by English record producer Pete Lawrence for his independent label Cooking Vinyl. Recorded at night with the background sounds of crickets and passing trucks on Highway 16, the resulting *Campfire Tapes* album soared up the independent record charts in England and was re-released in this country on Mercury Records. Recorded on a professional Walkman recorder, the songs on the album thrust Michelle into the spotlight very quickly. When we met her, she was as shy as a fawn and was writing songs from her viewpoint at the very bottom of the social register looking up. As seen from a cardboard box, street-level home,

our institutions seemed seriously flawed and her candor was refreshingly stimulating. This time, when Michelle returned to the festival, she was already a Mercury/Polygram Records artist, and we all celebrated her good fortune.

This was the festival that was performed under the banner of "It's A Miracle!" and everyone was really up for it. Buddy Mondlock, one of 1987's New Folk award winners, was chosen to open the festival on Thursday night, May 26, and the early arriving press had plenty to write about when Shawn Phillips, Peter Rowan, and Billy Joe Shaver, in that order, brought the concert to a warmly received close near midnight.

The next night's six-hour evening concert included two other former New Folk winners, David Roth (1986) and Darden Smith (1985) along with Bill and Bonnie and Amram and his jam.

Michelle Shocked being interviewed backstage at Kerrville by San Antonio's Channel 5.
— Courtesy *Kerrville Daily Times.*

Veteran Texas songwriter Billy Joe Shaver. 1988.
— Courtesy Brian Kanof.

Saturday and Sunday's daytime events had Peter Alsop ("I Am a Pizza") and Kim Wallach joining Gayle Ross at the children's concerts at Threadgill Memorial Theater, and the 1988 New Folk concerts with judges Sonny Curtis, Buddy Mondlock, and Shake Russell choosing David Wilcox and Josh Joffen among the six winners. We were also aware of some other finalists among the forty, including Betty Elders of Austin, Rod MacDonald of New York, Hugh Blumenfeld from Connecticut, and Ann Armstrong of Dallas. Another New York finalist, Shawn Colvin, called to cancel because of her need to accept a well-paying date. It was always a hard choice to make for finalists to make the long trip to sing two songs, taking the chance on winning a token prize, or accept a sure thing close to home that would help make ends meet.

The two biggest nights of the weekend, Saturday and Sunday, were highlighted by Gamble Rogers, Robert Earl Keen, Sonny Curtis, Sabia from California, Shake Russell, the Caribbean Steeltones, Mike Cross, Red Clay Ramblers, Butch Hancock, and Marce Lacouture, and Hot Rize.

Colorado's popular bluegrass band Hot Rize. 1988.
— Courtesy Brian Kanof.

On Monday, Memorial Day, the Blues Project, hosted by Steve James, featured an outstanding roster — Marcia Ball, Spider John Koerner, Hans Theesink from Vienna, Rory Block, and Townes Van Zandt. That night's concert closed the first weekend with Chuck Pyle, Carolyn Hester, Santiago Jimenez, Jr., Josh White, Jr., and Bobby Bridger topping the bill.

The next night was a unique three-hour main stage celebration of Peter Yarrow's fiftieth birthday with a barbecue and concert. I had asked Lyle Lovett to co-host Peter's birthday celebration, but he had a conflict and sent me a personal note of apology with a $500 donation to the festival enclosed. The roster of fellow performers honoring Peter's birthday included Guy Clark, Bob Gibson, and former New Folk Jon Ims, Tish Hinojosa, Kurt Van Sickle, George Ensle, Emily Aronson, and Tim Henderson offering a tuneful salute. Peter responded with his own well-chosen set of classic Peter Paul and Mary songs, many having come directly from Peter's own pen. It was a special evening that not only celebrated Peter's birthday, but also his immense contribution and dedication to the festival, both financially and spiritually. He and seventy-five other performers had literally lifted the festival up out of the mud and were responsible, along with our loyal fans, for the miracle of its continuance.

Peter Yarrow in his birthday Kimono while I look on in disbelief. 1988.
— Courtesy *Kerrville Daily Times.*

As Bob Gibson's songwriters school, with Peter, Guy Clark, and Laurie Lewis teaching, filled the days for sixty students, the Wednesday night fish fry and concert provided royal entertainment by John Gorka, Christine Lavin, and Hans Theesink, followed by a ball at the Inn of the Hills by amazing fiddler Erik Hokkanen and his band, the Offbeats, plus Rusty Wier and his band.

Friday night of the second weekend was a huge turnout for Steve Gillette, Michelle Shocked, Nashville's Fred Koller, Valdy, Guy Clark, and Nanci Griffith.

As a 5:00 P.M. warm-up group that weekend, and contributing to the size of the crowd, was a duo from Houston called Trout Fishing in America, made up of two former members of St. Elmo's Fire, six-foot-nine Ezra Idlet, and five-foot-five-and-a-half bassist Keith Grimwood. With both doing vocals and harmonies and Ezra's hot guitar, the duo sounded like a full band and really created excitement for the early arriving crowds each night.

Saturday night was a contrasting line-up beginning with flat-picking notable Eddie Adcock and his wife Martha, then the highly regarded Oscar Brand, newcomer Mary Chapin Carpenter (her forty-minute tape sent to me from D.C. by Jane Gillman

became Chapin's first CBS album), who charmed us all with her melodic genuineness and down-to-earth lyrics, Nashville's SKB (Schuyler-Knoblich-Bickhardt), Jimmie Dale Gilmore, the Limeliters, and Gary P. Nunn.

Among those artists warmly greeted on Sunday night were Jim Rooney, Laurie Lewis and Grant Street, Peter Yarrow, and the strong female duo of Casselberry-Dupree from Jamaica Plains who had the crowd rocking.

Laurie Lewis and Grant Street. 1988.
— Courtesy Brian Kanof.

Music business workshops and the second songwriters school, plus four two-hour sundown concerts at Threadgill Theater, filled the midweek, and the third and final weekend began Friday at 1:00 P.M. with Larry Groce hosting the taping of "Mountain Stage" at Threadgill Theater with Bob Gibson, John Stewart, Tom Paxton, Eliza Gilkyson, and Cherokee storyteller Gayle Ross joining the Fabulous Twister Sisters and Eric Kitchen and the Mountain Stage Band. The Kerrville shows would be broadcast later on 100 stations across the U.S. The show had been on the air since 1981 from West Virginia Public Radio, and I had been fortunate to be on hand for their 100th broadcast in March in Charlotte, West Virginia. The second show was taped Saturday morning at 11:00 by Ray Wylie Hubbard, Michelle Shocked, the trio Uncle Bonsai, and David Halley.

The Friday night concert of this third weekend began with Native American performer Bill Miller and closed with Beto y los Fairlanes. In between

Oscar Brand at Kerrville. 1988.
— Courtesy Brian Kanof.

Eliza Gilkyson, daughter of Terry Gilkyson of the Easy Riders. 1988.

— Courtesy *Kerrville Daily Times.*

Beto y los Fairlanes. Robert "Beto" Skiles is far right at the keyboards. 1988.

— Courtesy Brian Kanof.

Canada's Hobo Jim played Kerrville in 1988 and 1989. He is the writer of the official song of the Ididerod dog sled race. 1988.

— Courtesy Brian Kanof.

were Eliza Gilkyson, Tom Paxton, Odetta, and John Stewart.

Saturday evening's concert offered such diverse artists as Steve Earle in his first appearance since New Folk so many years before, Peruvian artists Sukay, and Canada's Murray McLaughlin, whose song "Sweeping Up Dreams" about famed clown Emmitt Kelly is, in my book, an all-time classic. Sunday night opened with Hal Ketchum and closed with Lubbock's Terry Allen and the Maines Brothers. Connie Kaldor and Ponty Bone were also among those turning in crowd-pleasing performances that night. Alaska's Hobo Jim made one-song guest appearances all three nights on a stage decked out with the Alaskan flag. His presence reminded our audiences of our forthcoming visit to the Alaska State Fair by our on-the-road company in August.

We gratefully and joyously celebrated our seventeenth festival! One hundred-two performers and thirty-nine New Folk joined with thousands of re-energized fans to honor the donations, sponsorships, gifts, and benefit concerts that gave us the momentum to continue.

I should mention here that just prior to the *Ft. Worth Star-Telegram* benefit concert in early April, I received in the mail from England a thirty-two-page "transatlantic tribute to the Kerrville Folk Festival, Volume I" from Arthur Wood in Birmingham. Wood had visited the festival for the first time in 1986 and was, obviously, quite taken with it. His magazine contained interviews, comments, photos, record reviews, features, and, among other listings, a complete summary of all of the live documentary recordings to date from our festival. His unique inside look at our festival was being distributed not only in the United Kingdom, but also Finland, Norway, and many other countries on his list. This well-written publication has continued with its thorough coverage of the festival and its performers, and others compatible with our format, right up through 1996 and beyond with several dozen issues published more or less regularly throughout the first nine years. It often provided us with a major boost to our morale as we admired Wood's steadfast support of the festival and his belief in its future. His publication, much like our festival, was an obvious labor of love.

While we had most of June and July to prepare for our busy August schedule and to make both a twelve-day vacation trip and, seven weeks later, a three-day business trip with a visit to Winnipeg Folk Festival thrown in between, August was an intensely busy time for us.

I had made a July trip to California, at the request of Alan Arnapole of Napa, to explore the idea of beginning a festival similar to Kerrville in the heart of the Wine Country in 1989. As soon as I returned, somewhat encouraged about the feasibility of the project, we focused all of our resources on preparing for the August 19-20 Miller Theatre bluegrass concerts in Houston, the six-day tour to Alaska starting August 25, and the final bluegrass festival over the September 2-4 Labor Day weekend.

The Miller Theatre concerts were headlined by Dobro virtuoso Jerry Douglas and Tulsa's fiddling Jana Jae. We also featured some of our most popular Texas performers. Mandolin champion Paul Glasse lead the Grazmatics on this occasion and sat in with three-time champions TVA of San Antonio. Then, we added recent newcomers from Albuquerque, Weary Hearts. It was a fitting line-up

as all of these great players would also be on our final Kerrville Bluegrass Festival two weeks later. The weather held, attendance was in the thousands both nights, and, of course, there was plenty of spirited music.

On to Alaska!

We were taking nine performers whom we thought would give the audience at the state fair a pretty good slice of Kerrville while providing an appealing concert. Hobo Jim would be joining our line-up which included Marcia Ball, Butch Hancock, Allen Damron, and the Kerrville All-Stars, featuring Paul Glasse, *mandolin,* Erik Hokkanen, *fiddle,* David Halley, *guitar,* and Caryl P. Weiss, *bass.* Melissa Javors was also flying up to stage manage and to share the spotlight with us.

We played ten shows over the three days in various configurations and venues, including four major "Celebrate Texas" concerts with everyone appearing together.

The theme of the fair was a "Texas Salute" and Texas Agriculture Commissioner Jim Hightower was one of the honored guests. While we were hosted in high style by our presenters, our major concerts were probably more fun for us than they were for a luke-warm audience. For the first time in our history, we saw the crowds decrease in size once we began performing. It was my impression that the Alaska audiences were looking for something more raucous and less cerebral than our shows. The lumberjacks, Eskimos, and destruction derby all drew bigger crowds than we did, and my certificate of participation at the fair was left unsigned.

We did enjoy the massive and magnificent mountains and countryside surrounding Palmer, site of the fair just north of Anchorage. The wild game, plentiful fresh salmon, and lavish hospitality by our hosts made it a very worthwhile trip. I'd love to go back someday. I remember one bartender in particular who, upon learning that I was from Texas, set me up with seven complimentary shots of tequila as I listened to Tom Rigney's Sundogs in a packed tavern where Hobo Jim and I were guests. I upheld the legendary prowess of Texas when I walked out unassisted at the end of the evening.

We flew back to Texas two days before the bluegrass festival's three-day swan song. Joining the stars and bands that had been at Miller Theatre were Mark O'Connor, Peter Rowan, Tony Trishka, Dry Branch Fire Squad, Hickory Hill, Danger in the Air,

Gore Brothers, Warrior River Boys, and the Poverty Playboys.

We had enough rain for the greater part of the three days that we lost a thousand dollars for every year that we had broken even on the festival. Bluegrass could be expensive on the scale we attempted for the fifteen years.

With the bluegrass years behind us, we were excited about being back in Mexico for our fifth anniversary Isla Mujeres International Music Festival.

Our Isla Mujeres project was not about money. It was a working vacation and was about international good will. None of us were paid.

The performers joined us without fees, playing the concerts with the idea of sharing our culture with the Mexican people. We packaged the trips for our fans by acquiring the large number of rooms and airline tickets at reduced rates during off-season, requesting as many complimentary rooms and tickets as our suppliers deemed appropriate. Then, whatever tour expenses there were to be paid, such as transportation and rooms for performers and staff, ground transportation, shuttle boats to and from the island, phone calls, etc., we divided among the 80 or more fans who joined us, adding 1/80th to each fan's package that was still priced considerably below what they'd pay if they went by themselves without any entertainers, special receptions, parties, ceremonial meals, etc. It was good for everyone, especially the islanders. Eighty Americans spending vacation money for five days during the off-season was like a $15,000 to $20,000 gift to the island every time we had a festival. Then, on top of all that, we provided the American entertainment for a three-night festival

and attracted hundreds of other visitors to the island's otherwise vacant tourist facilities.

Being our fifth anniversary festival, we scheduled a ten-day event instead of the usual five and gave our fans the option of either one or both weekends, October 13-17 with Marcia Ball, Beto y los Fairlanes, and Allen Damron, or October 20-24 with Peter Rowan, Jana Jae, TVA, and the Hot Cakes playing their good-time rock n' roll.

When all of the arrangements were completed for the festival, we were about to send out our final instruction letters with airline tickets and the other documents to those who had confirmed their reservations, when Hurricane Gilbert tore a path across the Yucatan peninsula and hit Isla Mujeres, causing serious damage, throwing full-size boats up into the streets, knocking out power and water plants, and tearing up many buildings, both in the main part of town and in the colonius where many of the fishermen lived.

I scrambled around and caught a plane to Cancun on the first Continental flight authorized to land on the ravaged peninsula. It was September 27. I brought along medical supplies, children's clothing, and other items I thought would be helpful, and Continental cleared them through without charge.

When I reached the island, I discovered that, while there were no deaths on the island, many of the tall palm trees were uprooted and lying in the streets. There was damage everywhere and clean-up was under way. Many of the beach front palapas, huts, and service buildings were gone. Many fishing boats and the island's three big ferryboats were sunk. The bridge to the El Presidente Hotel was gone. Buho's was flattened and the seaward facing of our headquarters hotel, La Perla del Caribe, was gone and its swimming pool was folded in half like a hamburger in a bun. Many of the islanders lost everything they owned.

Still in place, however, were the plaza facilities where our concerts were to be staged and enough rooms at our hotel to accommodate us. The island officials had inspected the hotel and, finding it sound, barricaded off the damaged portion and started cleaning up the debris. They were grateful for the supplies and doubly grateful that I was still willing to bring the festival, once reassured that there would be sufficient clean water and electrical power in place to make it work. After a series of surveys of the island and several meetings with the island's officials, I flew back home to notify our participants of the situation so they could make a choice about continuing with us.

The letters asked each of the ninety people originally scheduled to go to reconfirm that they were still going with us. Only three people canceled ultimately, and many of the others sent cash donations so we could buy for the island necessary and immediately useful items, including new light bulbs for the stage fixtures in the Plaza. The Kerrville Wal-Mart store offered to sell us everything wholesale or two-for-the-price-of-one. They further gave us their Sam's credit card with $300 credit so we could buy whatever else we needed from Sam's in San Antonio. They also provided a truck from the San Antonio store to haul everything from San Antonio to Terminal C in Houston, where Continental would fly everything free to the truck waiting in Cancun. The *Austin Chronicle* donated two $285 quarter-page advertisements to publicize our April 9 benefit in Austin at Steamboat Springs.

The Steamboat benefit, from 2:00-10:00 P.M., had each performer playing two 30-minute sets. I emceed, and the performers included Caryl P. Weiss, Freddie Steadie's Wild Country, Allen Damron, Ponty Bone and the Squeezetones, Marcia Ball, Beto y los Fairlanes, and a one-hour set by Joe "King" Carrasco. Also making appearances were David Roth, Hudson and Franke, and others.

When it came time for departure, we had a full truckload of goods, including dried milk, some clothing, and several cartons of toys specifically requested for the fifty to one hundred children who had lost all their possessions.

There was some apprehension on the part of our fellow travelers, especially when we landed at Cancun and saw the downed power lines, damaged buildings, uprooted trees, and large boats of all sorts thrown onshore. We were all relieved to find a brand-new government ferry to carry us to the island, but were saddened as we landed to see Enrique Lima's beautiful yacht *Antares* sunk at the dock.

We were warmly greeted on arrival and handed cans of water from the thousands of cases shipped in by Budweiser. The hotel, the stage, and much of the plaza service area were all plugged into federal diesel generators that ran all night until they ran out of diesel and were hurriedly refueled and restarted. The festival was a welcomed bright spot for everyone on the island and, between the weekends of the festival, most of us worked to help clean up the beaches. It was quite an experience for everyone involved, and we heard later that we were the last

tourists to visit the island for nearly six months. The outpouring of appreciation from the islanders at all levels was heart warming.

It was a little strange to turn around and do benefits for Isla Mujeres after what we had been through in Texas, but we had another round of Folk Aid benefits coming up at Poor David's in Dallas, November 18, at Waterloo Ice House in Austin, December 3, at Rockefellers, in Houston, December 13, a New Year's weekend at the Driskill in Austin and others in San Antonio and elsewhere after the first of the year.

Poor David's Pub was fun on Friday night, November 18, when Rick Beresford flew in from Nashville to join Hudson and Franke fresh from their recording date with Nanci Griffith in Houston. Also on hand were former members of Tinker's Dam and Ann Armstrong, a New Folk winner who had played the 1988 Blues Project at Kerrville. I was able to bring the good news to the event that Southwest Airlines had increased their sponsorship of the festival by fifty percent for 1989.

The Dallas benefit was followed by a two-day staff retreat in Austin on Saturday and Sunday. Then, a few weeks later, we held the sixth annual Kerrville Christmas Reunion at Austin's Waterloo Ice House on Saturday, December 3. Allen Damron, Bobby Bridger, Tish Hinojosa, San Antonio's Melissa Javors, David Halley, and Lindsay Haisley were all on hand to do two shows at 8:00 and 11:00 P.M. Tish was leaving for Nashville right after her second set and couldn't get her car started. I went out and hooked up my battery cables and the car started right away. She was going to record her first Nashville album, and as she was leaving, I jokingly said to her, "Don't forget who jump-started your career!"

As I summarized 1988, I thought we had come a long way in a year from the seemingly terminal financial situation at the end of 1987.

With so much emphasis on the financial situation, it was easy to overlook the real joy of what we were trying to do and why we did it.

Amram, remembering the Kerrville campfires, described his vivid memories and how his life had changed for the better since his first Kerrville visit in 1976. He talked of feeling "totally connected" around the campfires at 3:00 A.M. "The smoke of the mesquite fires, the symphony of crickets, katy-dids . . . the extraordinary song-poems echoing through

Tish Hinojosa at Kerrville in the late 1980s.
— Courtesy Ken Schmidt.

the night create a magical feeling that suspends time and makes everyone . . . finally free at home on the range."

There were also memorable 1988 comments from people outside our family like Cynthia Heimel, writing in *Playboy*, who described our festival as "attended by the best songwriters in the world." Further, she advised her readers, "go to Texas to hear this amalgam of rock, country and folk music with the kind of lyrics that make you shiver. It's worth it!"

We also felt good about what Joe Nick Patoski wrote in *Texas Monthly* near the end of a twenty-page editorial section about Texas music:

> When it comes to hearing future stars under the great big Texas sky, there's no place like the Kerrville Folk Festival at Rod Kennedy's Quiet Valley Ranch. This folk and country extravaganza, spread over 18 days in May and early June, is a wholesome family affair that has replaced Newport as the best annual open air music fest in America.

Frank Dooly made us grin when his *Book of Texas Bests* described us as the "best folk festival (maybe destined to always be the best)" and then added, "After all it's the best in Texas, it's probably the best in the world."

Ron Young gave us another morale boost when, in an article in the *San Antonio Light* headlined "Kerrville Folk Festival Offers A Musical Feast," he wrote, "Almost two decades old, the event is a Texas treasure and holds the honor of being the longest folk festival in the United States."

It was cheering to look at our efforts from the outside in and to realize that all of our inside financial struggles were not dimming the outsiders' view of what we were trying to achieve. With strengthened determination and commitment to continuing excellence, we pledged to wrap it all up with a distinctive New Year's celebration and move optimistically into our eighteenth year.

Over the past several years, I had developed a close friendship with Valerie Farrell in Austin. She was a massage therapist and health enthusiast I had met through David and Merri Lu Park.

I stayed at Valerie's when I was in Austin, and we often traveled together. She gradually changed my eating habits, got me off coffee and sweets, and taught me yoga. Then she encouraged me to go bike riding. After borrowing her housemate Becky Smyth's bike two or three times, I bought my own, a used ten-speed Fuji. On my fifty-ninth birthday, January 22, 1989, I rode my first "long ride," nine miles from the ranch to Mr. Gatti's Pizza Parlor. After pizza and spaghetti, I had to call Nancylee to come get me. As I became better conditioned, however, bike riding felt good, and I worked out a schedule of regular weekly rides.

Southwest Airlines not only increased their sponsorship for 1989 but also offered us coupons for a discount on their already low fares. I used the coupons as an incentive in a campaign to increase advance sales from the present thirty percent. We also arranged with AT&T for a toll-free number to be used in conjunction with VISA or Mastercard. By calling toll free and using their credit cards before the festival started, advance discount ticket buyers also earned a Southwest Airline discount coupon. We would discover, when all the figures were in after the festival, that we had increased advance ticket sales to fifty percent of our total sales, the other half of the sales happening at the gate. This gave us a better early cash flow to work with, guaranteed a larger volume of ticket sales, regardless of the weather, and sped up ticket handling at the front gate where sometimes as many as 100 cars were lined up for tickets.

Benefit concerts, including an especially fun night at San Antonio's St. Mary's Grill, earlier payment of crafts booth rentals, program ads, and increased sponsorships gave us enough cash flow to operate more comfortably as we headed toward Peter Yarrow's second big *Fort Worth Star-Telegram*-sponsored benefit on March 29.

We were saddened by the death of Bob Claypool of the *Houston Post* on February 25. He had not only written hundreds of inches of positive reviews of our festivals over the past ten years, but he had become a good friend and counselor. The timing of Claypool's writing had been good for us. He wrote about Kerrville during the same years as Townsend Miller, so during our first decade we found ourselves in the enviable position of consistently having the personal and professional support of a major columnist in two major Texas dailies. Both of these writers helped introduce us to wider audiences during our start-up, and we valued those continuing endorsements.

While Townsend Miller was no longer writing his column, he did attend Allen Damron's fiftieth birthday party at the Austin Opera House that drew notables like Bob Gibson, Peter Yarrow, Alaska's Hobo Jim, Carolyn Hester, Steven Fromholz, David Ruthstrom, Segle Fry, and others.

**ALLEN DAMRON
50TH BIRTHDAY
ROAST & TOAST
8 PM WED MAR 1
AUSTIN OPERA HOUSE
A STAR-STUDDED
SPECIAL EVENT**

Following the previous year's successful date at the Palomino Club in L.A., we were invited back for a Saturday night pair of concerts on March 11.

New England's Patty Larkin, who had won two Boston Music Awards and had just released her newest LP, "I'm Fine," on Rounder Records, joined our show line-up of Texans: the Austin Lounge Lizards, Allen Damron, Eliza Gilkyson, Paul Glasse, David Halley, Butch Hancock, and Los Angeles-based Shawn Phillips and Carolyn Hester. We also added two other L.A.-based artists, Hamilton Camp (movie actor and former partner of Bob Gibson) and Lucinda Williams, a Kerrville regular since 1974 and now about to start a national tour in support of her new album for Rough Trade Records.

The night before the concerts, Shawn Phillips hosted a picking party at his Sherman Oaks home, and it was an especially delightful way to spend our first evening together in California.

The Palomino Club was sold out for both concerts, thanks in great part to advance work by a large committee that included movie publicist Sandy Goldfarb, Ed and Bernie Pearl of Ash Grove Productions, Hamilton Camp, Carolyn Hester and a dozen other Los Angeles supporters who set up interviews on three stations and assisted us in getting extended advance press in the *Los Angeles Times* and other publications. Broadcasters Roz and Howard Larman and Renee Engel were especially helpful.

With the air travel provided by Southwest Airlines and Ash Grove Productions help, the concerts were a tremendous success. We didn't even feel badly that Patty Larkin was the one who captured the best reviews of the evening!

Back in Texas on March 25, Alex Abravanel produced a Kerrville benefit at St. Mary's Cafe, headlined by Paul Glasse and the Lone Star Swing Billies, Robert Earl Keen, and TVA with surprise guests Jim Rooney from Nashville, G. Bob Siggins from California, formerly of the Jim Kweskin Jug Band and the Charles River Boys, plus Billy Ray Latham of the Kentucky Colonels.

Abravanel, a native of Greece and a former New Folk, did a good job of pulling a diverse package of people together who not only drew a good crowd but also found all the entertainers having fun playing for each other.

Peter Yarrow had again been my constant telephone companion during the first three months of 1989 as he checked almost daily on the preparations for the second *Fort Worth Star-Telegram* benefit for Kerrville set for March 29 at Will Rogers Auditorium. To assist me, we had a twenty-eight-member committee working in seven cities, including Vicki Bell in Houston, Bill Seals in Abilene, Emily Aronson, David Card, Paul Porter, and eight others in Dallas, Paul Colbert in Austin, and Cathy Hayes, John Hatley, Slim Richey, and many more in Fort Worth.

Peter had invited as performing guests, under the slogan "Peter Paul and Everybody," Noel Paul Stookey, Tom Chapin, Carolyn Hester, Tom Paxton, and Josh White, Jr. It was an impressive gathering of noteworthy performers, each of whom added a heartbeat and affectionate dimension to the evening.

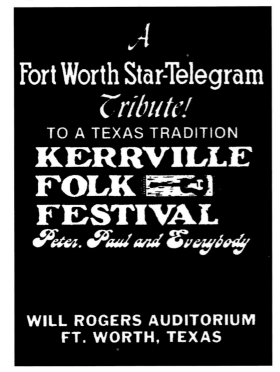

A Fort Worth Star-Telegram Tribute! TO A TEXAS TRADITION KERRVILLE FOLK FESTIVAL Peter, Paul and Everybody

WILL ROGERS AUDITORIUM FT. WORTH, TEXAS

From left: Josh White, Jr., and Tom Chapin at the Ft. Worth Star Telegram *benefit. 1989.*

— Courtesy John Hatley.

We went into the concert with sixty members of the audience in the first three rows paying for all the concert expenses at $60 to $200 a ticket. That meant that we were able to net $10,000 from the other 1,000 $10 ticket buyers.

The financial value from the benefit was matched in value by the outpouring of support and publicity for Kerrville. Peter opened the concert with "We Are One" and singing the praises of Kerrville. "Kerrville is sometimes difficult and precocious," he said. "It certainly doesn't like rain. But it is *our* festival and all of the performers here tonight are here to say 'Thank you' to Kerrville. And we will carry on at Kerrville!"

April 1 brought news of the death of Townsend Miller. I was grateful that we had let Townsend know how much he meant to us by honoring him at a banquet and establishing the Townsend Miller Endowment Fund for our foundation. We would miss Townsend and the business cards he always carried that said something like "how can anyone have a good day when it begins by getting up in the morning?"

Our 1989 Texas tour was one of those special events that came together beautifully and celebrated the creative powers and independence of some of the women on our festival. We had a five-day tour of four cities beginning with a tent show at Pedernales River Ranch at Johnson City on May 9.

The six featured artists were Mary Chapin Carpenter (Washington, D.C.), guitarist Nina Gerber (Richland, CA), Eliza Gilkyson (Los Angeles, CA), Anne Hills (Bethlehem, PA), Tish Hinojosa (Austin/San Antonio, TX), and Laurie Lewis (Berkeley, CA). All six women were also included on the eighteenth festival coming up May 25.

We played the Josephine Theatre on St. Mary's in San Antonio the next night and then moved on to the Austin Opera House on May 11. Our final two nights were at Miller Outdoor Theatre in Houston, May 12-13.

The attendance and audience response were outstanding, and we all had a good time together. It was like a traveling slumber party, and by the time we reached Miller Theatre all of them were singing harmony with each other, and the tour became a family of close-knit, euphoric sisters. The experience so struck Anne Hills with happiness that, when she learned she was pregnant, she named her first child Tamlyn by selecting the first letter from

Back row, from left: Nina Gerber, Tish Hinojosa, Eliza Gilkyson, Laurie Lewis. Front row, from left: Anne Hills and Mary Chapin Carpenter on the road for Kerrville. 1989.

— Courtesy Paul Glasse.

the first names of each of the six women on the tour. Eliza's "e" became a "y" somehow.

As an afterthought when the tour was over, I decided, after all these years, I had really learned how to put a rewarding tour together! I would probably do this again!

Back in Kerrville, we were all working on the final preparations for the eighteenth folk festival, but by now I had learned how to allocate thirty or forty minutes every day to go bike riding. I was feeling quite fit. I had lost twenty-five pounds over the past several years, and the combination of Valerie's frequent diet discipline, daily yoga, and riding at least 100 miles a week, found me healthier at fifty-nine than I'd been ten years before. I looked forward to getting up every day and getting after it!

I approached the May 25-June 11 festival with more energy and enthusiasm than I had in any year past. Part of it was my physical condition, and a good part of it was the kind of support I had been receiving to overcome our rain losses. We had been criticized by some for our numerous benefits and for choosing to stay on weekends "when it always rained," but Peter Yarrow and thousands of others continued to encourage us on a daily basis. Indeed, in offering us a little moral support, Peter mailed me this quote from Theodore Roosevelt:

It is not the critic who counts, not the man who points out how the strong man stumbled or where the doer of deeds could have done them better. The credit belongs to the man who is actually in the arena; whose face is marred by dust and sweat and blood; who strives valiantly, who errs and comes up short again and again; who knows great enthusiasm, the great devotions, and spends himself in a worthy cause, who at the best knows in the end the triumph of high achievement; and who at worst, if he fails, at least fails while daring greatly; so that his place shall never be with those cold and timid souls who know neither defeat nor victory.

Peter's attached note said, "Tack this on your wall! Remember to read it when times get rough. And count me as one person who respects you for daring to try to make the world a better place. Love, Peter."

This festival was going to be special for a number of reasons. We were dedicating the first part of the festival to Amy Kurland, whose Bluebird Cafe in Nashville was the focal point for original songwriters. She had dedicated her club to showcasing songwriters, who, in her best judgment, deserved a place to play. While there were many of Nashville's hit songwriters playing the club, she also made room for unknown writers by presenting them as opening artists. As they built a following, she gradually moved them to more prominent spots in her busy weekly schedule.

We had Amy as our guest for four days and presented her with a new bicycle on stage in front of the audience one night. She, too, needed the relief from stress that a bicycle had provided me.

Opening the festival, both as host of the Ballad Tree and as our first artist on opening night, was 1988 New Folk winner David Wilcox. The duo of Two Nice Girls also appeared that evening along with Tish Hinojosa and Steve Fromholz, among others. The second night included sets by Buddy Mondlock, Eliza Gilkyson, and Hugh Moffatt, while the Saturday combination bill of Jon Ims, Hans Theesink, Austin Lounge Lizards, Michelle Shocked, Peter Yarrow, and Nanci Griffith drew a capacity crowd of 6,000. No matter that Nanci had canceled the day before as she lost her voice while on her national tour. Only three customers out of our crowd requested refunds because of Nanci's cancellation!

The Saturday and Sunday afternoon New Folk concerts were judged by Shawn Phillips, Patty

Eager faces at the children's concert at Threadgill Theater. 1989.

— Courtesy Darron Spohn.

Michelle Shocked at Kerrville. 1989.
— Courtesy Brian Kanof.

Larkin, and David Wilcox, who chose among their winners L. J. Booth from Wisconsin and David Massengill of New York.

The children's concerts at Threadgill Theater the first weekend included Peter Alsop, Gayle Ross, Limeliters tenor Red Grammer, Peter Yarrow, and Kim Wallach. By now the children's concerts were regularly drawing overflow crowds to Threadgill Theater, and again, we were trying to figure out how we could expand the covered area.

The blues project on Memorial Day introduced to our audience Tom Ball and Kenny Sultan from California, Grey Ghost, Rory Block, and Sparky Rucker.

The Sunday and Monday night concerts included many sets popular with the crowds, among them Shawn Phillips with Van Wilks, Patty Larkin, Josh Joffen, David Halley with Syd Straw, Happy and Artie Traum with Russ Barenburg, and Gary P. Nunn closing the night "going home with the armadillo."

The midweek schedule included a three-day

Homespun Tapes guitar school conducted by the Traum brothers with Russ Barenburg and Rory Block. The Sundown Concerts were by Chuck Pyle and Anne Hills, and the fish fry was Wednesday night.

The second weekend included an event I had wanted to offer for a long time. Through my work with the American Indian Coalition in Austin to pass Indian burial rights legislation, I had become increasingly aware of the indelible stereotyping of Indian people through cartoons, sports teams, movies, television, and books. I thought, perhaps, I could begin to make a difference by bringing some outstanding Native American performers to our stage this year and then host a conference to plan a more dramatic Indian event for next year.

On Saturday afternoon at Threadgill Theater, we presented a two-hour "Native American Tribute" with Bobby Bridger, Carolyn Hester, and David Amram as the Anglo performers knowledgeable about contemporary Native American culture, and then our Cherokee storyteller Gayle Ross appeared with Indian poet Roxy Gordon, Bill Miller, and Floyd Westerman, who was best known because of his work in films and on television. Miller and Westerman also appeared on the main stage evening concerts. Then, on Monday we held our conference to talk about how we could proceed for a larger event next year.

The weekend evening concerts also included Pierce Pettis, Robert Earl Keen, Noel Paul Stookey and his band Bodyworks, Lyle Lovett, Ronnie Gilbert (formerly of the Weavers), Canada's Valdy,

Laurie Lewis, Shake Russell, David Amram, and others. Again we had good attendance and our redesigned facilities were working out fine for handling the larger crowds.

Four good sundown concerts by Bill and Bonnie, Don Sanders, Bob Gibson and Butch Hancock, and Marce Lacouture with Jesse Taylor connected the second and third weekends. Daytime events included the songwriters school led by Bob Gibson, Rick Beresford, and Dick Goodwin, with Peter Yarrow and Peter Rowan as additional faculty.

John Stewart's songwriters panel at Threadgill Theater. From left: David Rea, Steve Gillette, John Stewart, Jon Ims, and Tom Chapin. 1989.
— Courtesy Darron Spohn.

As an additional songwriters' event, John Stewart, formerly of the Kingston Trio, conducted a Friday afternoon alternative workshop based on the choices of "writing to be famous or writing from the heart." The panel included David Rae, Steve Gillette, Jon Ims, and Tom Chapin and drew a good crowd to Threadgill Theater as an open event.

Looking back for a moment, there were two well-attended weddings on Chapel Hill on June 4 as two of our most active, long-running Kerrverts married their sweethearts. First Bobby Bridger and Melissa were married, and then everyone's friend and volunteer maintenance leader Lee Green wed Sheryl. The weddings and the memorial services remembering Bob Claypool and Townsend Miller further sanctified the special space that Chapel Hill and its Ballad Tree had become in our lives.

Mary Chapin Carpenter closed the Friday night concert with her band on an evening that also included Rosie Flores. Hal Ketchum opened Saturday night's concert by Tom Russell, Katy

Moffatt, Tom Chapin, the Montreaux Band, John Stewart, and Darden Smith.

Steve Gillette hosted the Saturday afternoon staff concert at Threadgill Theater followed by the children's concert with Gayle Ross hosting Jim Valley (former lead guitarist with Paul Revere and the Raiders), Mark Ellinger, and the Twelve Moon Storytellers.

Jimmie Dale Gilmore closed the final night's concert that had featured David Rea (former Gordon Lightfoot guitarist), Rod MacDonald, Napa Valley mandolin virtuoso Evan Marshall, Crow Johnson, and Allen Damron.

It was a good festival all the way around, and this view of the experience by Boston's Patty Larkin was a delightful bonus. She wrote:

> Long before my first trip to Kerrville, I had heard the festival referred to as a "Mecca" for songwriters. I remember that as judge for the New Folk competition, I told the assembled writers that I expected my life to be changed somehow by the weekend of music ahead. It did. I learned how to listen — to all kinds of songs — anywhere — at campfires — on stages or off — beneath the shade of a tree — or a tower of lights — I learned again how to be quiet and wait for the story to unfold — the story that each songwriter brings. The kind of enthusiasm I found at Kerrville could be called "religious." I'd call it a celebration of all that we are as individuals and all that we have in common.

In July I had the chance to return to Winnipeg for their folk festival over the weekend of July 6-9. Rosalie Goldstein and her staff laid out their famous hospitality. At Winnipeg they have eight or ten stages where over 100 artists participate in daytime "workshops," most of which are mini-concerts. Then each night a selection of a dozen featured artists play short sets for 12,000-plus fans arrayed on blankets and lawn chairs in front of the huge stage. Getting sunburned in the daytime and chilled after dark is a normal pattern at Winnipeg. Every festival I have attended in Canada has been well staged and filled with the best American and Canadian performers, plus many overseas artists, including a good selection of Celtic pickers. Numerous visits to Canadian festivals have allowed me to become familiar with artists like Valdy and Connie Kaldor and even to discover American artists like Casselberry-Dupree and Santiago Jimenez, Jr.

On August 20 my mother died in Dallas, and Nancylee and I joined my two brothers and their wives for the service. I realized that her belief in me all my life combined with her encouragement and insistence on the "best schools" when she could afford them, gave me a real headstart in cultural and business growth. Although my older brother Jim sold off almost all of her possessions as executor of her estate, I came away with a favorite painting and a handmade Indian rug she gave us before her death and her 1973 Thunderbird which Nancylee bought when it became evident Mother could no longer drive. Jim returned to us a photo that we had given Mom of Nancylee and me with our horses. In spite of having only a few mementos, my mother's memory has been very much with me always. Many times when I produced something I knew she would have liked, I wished that I could share it with her. Now that both my parents were gone, I quickly developed a different viewpoint of my own mortality. It made me feel that I really must hurry to get debts paid and live up to the good faith that so many supporters have shown us, especially during the festival years. Somehow, when people close to me have died, it has had the effect of uncluttering my thinking and developing a closer understanding of the difference between dedication and obsession. I have learned and relearned repeatedly that everything is temporary and that every day is part of the future that so many people never get to enjoy. Part of the realization is that I have focused on being conscientious so that what we present is the best we can offer. I always try to know the difference between performers and artists.

For Labor Day weekend, in place of the bluegrass festival, I had decided to pursue more fully our investment in songwriters by staging a three-day Kerrville Folk Festival, Too!, or "little folk" as our volunteers called it. We had huge waiting lists of performers we'd screened and very few spots to repeat performers we'd already recognized. The Folk, Too! event gave me twenty-five more performer spots a year. Also, there were hundreds of bluegrass and traditional music festivals across the U.S. and very few devoted any significant time to original songwriters who were not stars. This event gave us another chance to expand on our original mission.

Ironically, the first two artists I booked were the songwriting bluegrass bands of Hickory Hill and TVA, two Texas groups who had become favorites. To these bands we added for opening

Listening in the rain at Folk, Too! 1990.
— Courtesy John Carrico.

night Lindsay Haisley, Melissa Javors, Robin and Linda Williams, and Robert Earl Keen.

On Saturday afternoon, Shake Russell and Jack Saunders played a two-hour concert at Threadgill Theater followed by a 6:00 P.M. main stage concert by Tim Henderson, Jane Gillman, Shawn Phillips, Ponty Bone, and Sara Hickman.

On Sunday, after the Folk Mass, we had a reunion of Grimalkin and a 6:00 P.M. concert to close the weekend by Emily Aronson, Ed Miller, Rich Brotherton, Pipo Hernandez, Hudson and Franke, Josh White, Jr., Christine Albert, Santiago Jimenez, Jr., and the Marcia Ball blues band.

While a number of our long-time bluegrass

fans were disappointed, many more who attended loved the new format in spite of the heavy rains that created a $15,000 loss. Maybe our critics were right!

A month later, after a full year of preparation, planning, publicity and promotion, I produced our first Napa Valley Folk Festival in association with Southwest Airlines and Domaine Chandon Winery. The festival site was the beautiful campus and outdoor theater of the Veterans Home of California at Yountville about a third of the way up the valley from Napa.

The first year's schedule called for three five-hour evening concerts at the festival site and two three-hour daytime events at Calistoga's Pioneer Park up the valley. The daytime events were abbreviated New Folk concerts we called "Emerging Songwriters" concerts at 1:00 P.M. on Saturday and Sunday.

What I wanted to create with this festival was an awareness of California songwriters and a chance for them to network with each other and other scattered facets of the folk community throughout the full length of California. Few California songwriters knew each other or even of the existence of a song-writing community except for the giant hit songwriter organizations. Most of the festivals in California at this time were either rock, pop, bluegrass, traditional, or Celtic. Events that included non-commercial songwriters were rare as sharks in the Guadalupe. I knew that this was the difficult route to success but the proper route if my hosts really wanted a "Kerrville" in California.

The California Zephyr band members, headed by Alan Arnapole, were the people who encouraged me to come out and produce the festival and each of them became primary chairmen of various facets of the festival. Steve Ewert and vocalist Suzanne Sherwin joined Alan as committee heads who worked the festival along with David Rea from Calistoga and Allegra Broughton and Sam Page, a

husband and wife duo from nearby. So, I had California Zephyr open the festival as the hosts and to free them to fulfill their festival management duties. We also had a good nucleus of volunteers who were trained by Andrea LeBlanc and some of our Kerrville volunteers whom we flew out to assist.

The all-California-based lineup for the first two nights had artists like Steve Seskin, Shawn Phillips, Phil Salazar, the Limeliters, Tom Ball and Kenny Sultan, Carolyn Hester, David Rea, Italian guitarist Peppino D'Agostino (now from San Francisco), and Laurie Lewis and the zany quartet from Berkeley called Celtic Elvis. On the final night Peter Yarrow was the only non-Californian on the concert. Additional artists were David Maloney, Kathy Kallick, Duck Baker, black blues artist E. C. Scott and her band, John Stewart, and Carol Denney.

With gold patron box-seat holders from leading Napa Valley businesses, we launched the first festival. Among those patrons were major wineries Louis M. Martini, Robert Mondavi, Silver Oak Cellars, Beringer Vineyards, Freemark Abbey, Sutter Home, and a small boutique winery called Casa Nuestra. While it was a good turnout for the first year, I found the California market a difficult one to break into and our losses were significant. Bailed out by a 1990 advance corporate sponsorship from Casa Nuestra, early renewals from many of the gold patrons, and by money from my mother's estate, we reviewed where we needed to work harder and began to plan the second festival.

A week later I was in Mexico with my crew and the Marcia Ball Band, Peter Rowan, Tish Hinojosa, and Allen Damron for the sixth Isla Mujeres festival. Our traditional welcoming gala party was on Thursday, October 12, with the evening concerts at Teatro del Pueblo on Friday, Saturday, and Sunday, October 13-15, and our farewell party at Nauti Beach the 16th and our Continental flight home on the 17th.

We offered our fans two packages including round-trip air fare, ground transportation, boat to and from the island, and hotel room for five nights at $398 and $498. The Continental flight was full and Tish Hinojosa was an immediate hit with the Mexican people. Coming from the States, many people brought used guitars and fiddles to donate to the Casa de Cultura to provide instruments for teaching youngsters. The cultural center had lost everything in Hurricane Gilbert.

Our eighteenth year came to a close with our seventh annual Kerrville Christmas Reunion at the 38th Street Waterloo Ice House on Saturday night, December 2.

The two concerts at 8:00 and 11:00 P.M. were played by reunion regulars Allen Damron, Lindsay Haisley, and Tim Henderson, plus Houston's Kimberly M'Carver who had just completed her first recording for Rounder Records, Don Sanders, Gayle Ross, Bobby Bridger, Christine Albert, and the Austin Lounge Lizards. Rosie Flores was a welcome surprise guest, and we shared our Hill Country Bakery "Nutcracker Cake" and the now traditional hot cinnamon apple cider with a standing-room-only audience. It was a heart-warming event to close out the year.

Our nineteenth year began with the traumatic declaration of bankruptcy by Kerrville Festivals, Inc. All of our banks had gone under in Kerrville along with hundreds of other Texas banks statewide when the boom came to a screeching halt due to problems in the oil industry and over-speculation in real estate and construction. Our attorney urged us to file a Chapter 11 petition immediately to allow us to restructure our debt retirement program and to avoid foreclosure by federal agencies taking over the assets and liabilities of the local banks.

The accumulation of heavy rain losses accruing huge interest payments, the loss of Southwest Airlines as our major sponsor (a decision by an advertising agency), and the cumulative slow down of the economy, made it easier for me to decide to file. While we were grateful for the Southwest Airlines support during the three years they were with us, the loss of that support in conjunction with the bank take-overs made it imperative to file unless we wanted the federal agencies selling off everything we owned for a few cents on the dollar just to close out our accounts with the troubled banks.

Kerrville fest is on despite debt troubles

I announced the bankruptcy on the road during my sixtieth birthday tour because I wanted to talk to as many of our fans face to face about it so they'd understand what it meant.

The tour played two shows at Poor David's Pub in Dallas on Friday, February 19, where the first announcement was made. Before departing for Dallas, we sent news releases to all major media with the intent that they would reach them on Saturday or Monday.

Considering the circumstances, the tour was a rewarding four days. Our traveling show included the Kerrville All-Stars opening and closing the show with each member featured in a solo spot — Paul Glasse (mandolin), Scott Neubert (guitar and Dobro), and Erik Hokkanen (fiddle). They also backed a number of the songwriters — Bobby Bridger, Christine Albert, Butch Hancock, Laurie Lewis (who flew in from California), Shake Russell and Jack Saunders, and Tish Hinojosa.

It was comforting to have these performers around me as I told the audience of our filing in Houston at Rockefeller's on Saturday, at the Cactus Cafe in Austin on Sunday, and at La Zona Rosa in Austin on Monday night. With two shows every night, we had a total of eight performances with guests sitting in on Monday night until 2:00 A.M. All the shows were standing-room-only except the one that ran until 2:00 a.m. The encouragement from everyone was reassuring, and by the time we arrived in Austin for the last dates, the story was on the Associated Press newswire.

Since few people understand the intricacies and tremendous expenses of producing a festival, I explained on the road that, given a period of relief by the courts, we could fully devote our financial efforts to preparing a three-part debt reduction plan allowing us to operate more efficiently and reduce our debt to a more manageable size. The festival had $70,000 to $80,000 in interest payments alone and last year's good weather and successful festival only netted $45,000. By the plan, we committed to paying all of our creditors under a mutually acceptable scheme.

We had indications from a number of well-known performers that they would like to join us in 1990 to guarantee a bigger gate. There was also an extended plan of major events that would increase the festival's cash flow into the twentieth anniversary year of 1991. Since we always were successful in good weather years, we had proven repeatedly that our format was valid and that the festival tradition at Kerrville should survive. Despite the estimated debt in excess of $400,000, we told each audience and the press that there would definitely be a festival in 1990 to be announced in the next sixty days.

Several days after the tour, I spent six days in Napa Valley working on the sponsorships and other business of the festival, and then spent three days in Spokane, Washington, consulting with people there who wanted a festival similar to the Napa Valley event. With these consulting trips, intense schedules of work on the bankruptcy and all the booking and publicity efforts to launch our 1990 season, I still maintained my exercise routines, bicycling, and yoga. This provided me with a resilience in the face of adversity that I have never experienced before.

Thanks to the efforts of State Representative Paul Colbert, we were able to renew Southwest Airlines participation directly through the executive offices of the airline. Then, we were overjoyed to have La Hacienda at Hunt, Texas, join us as a full corporate sponsor for a year. Founded in 1972 as a private facility to administer programs for alcohol and drug abuse, La Hacienda and the Kerrville Folk Festival would celebrate their nineteenth anniversaries together. For many years we had held meetings once or twice daily for the Friends of Bill W. (founder of Alcoholics Anonymous) so that recovering alcoholics could enjoy the festival and still have their twelve-step meetings to reinforce their resolve not to drink with the rest of the audience. Also, on the average, twenty-five percent of our volunteers were in twelve-step programs of recovery. The festival would become a part of La Hacienda's outreach program. When asked about their sponsoring an event where beer and wine were sold, they answered, "We really have to advertise where alcohol is present, or we're just preaching to the choir." They became a welcomed member of our festival family.

Our music foundation continued to host not only the Kerrville New Folk competition, but, with the help of *Sing Out!* magazine, the emerging songwriters competition in Napa Valley, and a new contest in the northwest as we worked out arrangements to co-produce a Columbia River Folk Festival at Spokane in July.

Although I had always said I would never file for bankruptcy, having been forced into it by the failure of all our banks, I found the requirements imposed by the bankruptcy court to be extremely helpful in learning how to better analyze and fully

understand how and where we were vulnerable to untimely losses.

The report requirements delineated by the courts mandated that we develop detailed records and learn more about where we could tighten budgets and how we could head off cash shortfalls. We asked Tom Frost III to be our financial advisor, and meetings with him were enlightening and extremely helpful.

We had already begun the process when we added the 800 phone number and credit card advance ticket purchasing. Now, by analyzing our AT&T monthly telephone reports of unanswered calls on our 800 line, we were able to quickly redesign our phone system, adding multiple 800 lines, two business lines, an unlisted call-out line, and lines for our FAX and computer. By the time the 1990 festival was over, we had increased advance ticket sales from thirty to fifty percent of our total ticket revenue and increased our ability to get information to the public more quickly so they could respond.

After all the angst involved in the bankruptcy, I became an enthusiastic believer in the legal system that allowed us to improve our operating acumen and to do twice as well as what we already thought we were doing well.

While concentrating daily on strengthening the business side of the festivals, the outpouring of support reminded us again that the Kerrville Folk Festival was not just a music festival. It had become an experience, a way of life, a state of mind, a time and place where once each year people could come and be renewed. It became a place where words like dignity, respect, originality, and humanity all had real meaning.

For those of us at the heart of it, not just the producers and performers, but the volunteers parking cars and handling all the other tasks required, it was not only a retreat from cluttered contemporary life, but a time and place where we could be decent to each other, even compassionate and joyful, and then carry that sense of well-being with us all year long.

In the middle of all this it became evident that Nancylee had become increasingly unable to get around due to extremely advanced arthritis in her hips and knees. Recent x-rays had shown serious deterioration and the required surgery for hip and knee replacements would cost somewhere in the $50,000 range with the first hip replacement required in April. Like many of us in the music business, we were without adequate hospitalization insurance. Immediately, many friends of Nancylee and the festivals organized to raise funds to supplement the insurance. Led by Sue Medley and Sheryl Green, the newly established Phoenix Fund raised thousands of dollars from across the country over the next several years. A significant boost to this fund-raising effort was the early matching challenge gift of $7,500 pledged and paid by our friend and travel agent John Miller. While I had been able to contribute several thousand dollars to the care she needed, the fund, with its garage sales, benefits, and other projects, allowed me to concentrate on getting the festival back on an even keel.

The spring of 1990 brought us good news almost every day. In quick succession we received folk festival appearance confirmations from Shawn Colvin, Brave Combo, Peter Rowan and his brothers, Poi Dog Pondering, Columbia Records award-winning country star Janie Fricke, two-time Grammy winner Janis Ian, and the acceptance for the Labor Day weekend's Folk, Too by Chris Smither, the Ann Arbor-based Chenille Sisters, Hal Ketchum, and Jimmie Dale Gilmore. These artists would provide additional visibility and drawing power for our first festival season following the bankruptcy filing.

We also had the fun of doing a concert in Johnson City on Sunday, May 13, at the Pedernales Hills Resort, again coordinated by Robin Henderson, publisher of the *Johnson City Record Courier*. Enjoying performing at the three-hour tent concert were Allen Damron, Melissa Javors, Lindsay Haisley, Tim Henderson, Don Sanders, and the three Kerrville All-Stars.

The Chamber of Commerce provided dinner after the concert of fried chicken, Hill Country peaches, and homemade cookies for dessert. It was one of those events that reminded all of us of the charm and hospitable warmth of small towns and the people who choose to live there. We also played San Antonio's Panama Red's later that evening to a full house and then returned to our pre-festival chores.

Our nineteenth Kerrville Folk Festival was receiving unprecedented advance publicity and ticket sales, and we felt pretty good going into the opening night on Thursday, May 24.

Butch Hancock hosted the Ballad Tree and also appeared on the 6:00 P.M. concert with former New Folk Hank Riddle, L. J. Booth, Rachel Polisher, and

Cheryl Wheeler on-stage at Kerrville's Outdoor Theater. 1990.

— Courtesy Ken Schmidt.

Bobby Bridger. On Friday David Wilcox hosted the Ballad Tree and played the big concert alongside first-timer Chuck Suchy, Melissa Javors, Damron, Red Grammer, and Jimmie Dale Gilmore.

Saturday night, May 26, was our tribute concert to the 40th anniversary of *Sing Out!* and saw a star-studded roster of New Englanders Cheryl Wheeler, Bob Franke, and Horse Flies, matched with Texas-based artists Robert Earl Keen, the Caribbean Steeltones, plus Shawn Colvin and Tom Rigney's Sundogs from Berkeley closing things down around 1:00 A.M. The crowds were huge!

Allen Damron and I hosted the afternoon New Folk competition with North Dakota's Chuck Suchy, Bob Franke, and 1989 New Folk winner Rachel Polisher as judges. They picked as award winners Mickey Cates (Antioch, TN), Sally Fingerette (Columbus, OH), Steve Fisher (Wellington, KS), Rob Lauren (San Francisco), and John Smith (Trempealeau, WI) to appear in the winners' concert June 3. We were also pleased to see as finalists T. R. Ritchie, Kat Eggleston, Karen Blaine, and Janis Carper — all from the state of Washington, where our first Spokane festival would be staged in July. Our presence in that market had stirred up interest in Kerrville and our bonus was four outstanding New Folk finalists from the northwest!

Sunday night was another good night on the main stage sparked by the return of Willis Alan Ramsey with Allison Rogers, Canada's Connie Kaldor, and the two closing artists, Steven Fromholz and the Marcia Ball Band.

Our Memorial Day Blues Project offered per-

Willis Alan Ramsey and Allison Rogers backstage at Kerrville. 1990.

— Courtesy John Carrico.

John Gorka at Kerrville. 1990.

— Courtesy Brian Kanof.

Celtic Elvis brings a little Berkeley culture to the Kerrville Folk Festival. 1990.

— Courtesy Ken Schmidt.

formers Kurt Van Sickle, Roy Book Binder, Spencer Bohren, Lillian Standfield, and Steve James, who hosted. The format of the event, now well established, was for the host to interview each of the blues performers before each of the three rounds of songs typifying their early, middle, and present-day careers followed by twenty-minute sets by each artist, and climaxed with a blues jam with all the artists playing and swapping licks. By now, the Blues Project was drawing a Memorial Day audience of 1,500-2,000 fans willing to sit in the hot Texas sun to soak up the rare three hours of acoustic blues.

Memorial Day night's concert included popular performers like Rosie Flores, Bob Gibson, Shake Russell, and Darden Smith.

Midweek was our songwriters school with Fred Koller and Bill Staines joining regulars Bob Gibson, Rick Beresford, and Dick Goodwin. Three sundown concerts by Sarah Elizabeth Campbell, Ponty Bone, and Valdy, led us to the second weekend when John Gorka hosted the Ballad Tree and played the Friday night concert with California-based guitarist Peppino D'Agostino, Two Nice Girls, Sparky Rucker, Sara Hickman, and others.

On Saturday, daytime events included a bluegrass concert at Threadgill Theater by Hickory Hill, the first of two children's concerts presenting Gayle Ross, Courtney Campbell, Valdy, mime-juggler Turk Pipkin, and Austin's national children's recording artist Joe Scruggs. Saturday night was another big one with crowds drawn to songs by Patty Larkin, Poi Dog, Country Gazette, Eliza

Gilkyson, and the zany antics of Celtic Elvis, whose show earned screams of laughter and standing ovations demanding encores.

Following Sunday's Folk Mass, the award winners concert hosted by David Card, and the second children's concert, the evening saw a swing in

325

moods from the ballads of Tommy Pierce, Courtney Campbell, and Fred Koller, to the jazz-rock songs of Houston's Tommy Lee Bradley, the rousing comedy and Latin tempos of Brave Combo from Denton, Texas, to the melodic political satire of Tom Paxton.

During the second midweek, we had tentatively scheduled but postponed until 1991 the Festival of the Eagle to celebrate American Indian history, spirit, and culture, but instead presented Floyd Westerman and Kevin Locke on one sundown concert and Joanne Shenandoah on another as a preview of what that proposed festival within a festival would offer next year.

With Peter Yarrow hosting the Friday Ballad Tree, the third weekend was under way and another winning combination of artists joined him for that night's concert, including Tish Hinojosa, Bill and Bonnie, the first Kerrville appearance of the Rowan Brothers (who were an immediate hit), Casselberry-Dupree, and David Amram to close.

Austin's Betty Elders backstage. 1990.
— Courtesy John Carrico.

Casselberry-Dupree created a lot of excitement. 1990.
— Courtesy Brian Kanof.

Peter Yarrow also hosted the staff concert on Saturday, followed by the two-hour children's concert at Threadgill by Gayle Ross, Peter Alsop, Tom Chapin, and Josh White, Jr.

Josh also appeared on the big Saturday night concert with Betty Elders, Bill Staines, and Danger in the Air and closing with the highly charged welcome given Texas country vocalist Janie Fricke.

Our final day exploded in the afternoon following the Folk Mass with a two-hour concert by Trout Fishing in America. That night's closing concert drew a large appreciative audience for seven

Country music's Janie Fricke back home in Texas. 1990.
— Courtesy Darron Spohn.

Janis Ian was a sensation, and we were glad to have her back! 1990.

— Courtesy Ken Schmidt.

New Folk t-shirt design by Bobby Rector. 1990.

performers topped by Tom Chapin, Janis Ian, and Gary P. Nunn.

The festival was very successful on all counts and allowed us to pay all the past due taxes and twenty percent of the other payments due under our four-year restructuring plan.

Several other things were accomplished during the 1990 festival. We created and sold a limited edition New Folk t-shirt, the first of its kind in the nineteen years New Folk had been staged. It was so well received in its sold-out introduction that we decided to make it an annual offering. The proceeds go to numerous foundation projects.

By 1990 I had over a full year of regular cycling and was beginning to get in pretty good shape. The Saturday morning twenty-six-mile bike rides at the folk festival were drawing up to three dozen riders each weekend. The Kerrville area was a beautiful place to ride and draws 1,200 riders each Easter

weekend for a big annual ride. Kerrville is also often the training area for Olympic team try-outs. The combination of highways and hills put Texas Highway 16 on the national cycling maps as one of *the* places to ride.

In February I had signed a letter of agreement to be the associate producer with Spokane's Bob Levigne of the first Columbia Folk Music Festival on July 20-22. Bob had attended the Kerrville Folk Festival in 1989, and we had numerous meetings over the winter months. My job was to provide guidance and planning service, including budgeting and scheduling, technical help, public relations and press kit preparation, recruiting and training of volunteers, packaging and marketing of sponsorship proposals, developing the festival philosophy and goals, designing an audience survey, recommending and obtaining artists, and administering the emerging songwriters' competition through the Kerrville Music Foundation.

The festival work was done mostly by local people in the Columbia Folk Association. We keyed the festival on Washington-area artists like Ranch Romance, Kat Eggleston, Bryan Bowers, David Maloney, and Ginney Reiley, all with a good history in Seattle. To this group we added some all-time greats like Utah Phillips and Rosalie Sorrels, California artists Tom Ball and Kenny Sultan, David Rea, Peter Rowan, the outrageous Celtic Elvis,

MUSIC FROM

Boston's Chris Smither originally came from New Orleans.
— Courtesy Tobey.

Texans Tish Hinojosa and Santiago Jimenez, Jr., Canada's seven-time Juno winner Valdy, and Chuck Pyle from Colorado. Bob Levigne also added Dan Maher, a performer and host of Spokane's "Inland Folk" radio show, pianist Mila, Wild Roses from Idaho, and Spokane's Planet Lounge Orchestra.

Bob had obtained sponsorship support from Rings n' Things in Riverpark Square as well as thirty-nine other companies and individuals, and scheduled the festival concerts in the Met, the 500-seat Metropolitan Arts Center in downtown Spokane. The arts and crafts booths and food venders were to be arranged along Sprague Avenue between Monroe and Lincoln in a street fair setting. Everything happened in the street fair except the three evening concerts and two matinees by Celtic Elvis and Utah Phillips. Songwriters circles, children's concerts, sets by local musicians, the songwriting competition, and Folk Song Service were all part of the street fair.

There were twenty finalists in the song competition, and the winners were Janis Carper of Seattle, Alisa Fineman of Pacific Grove, California, and Rob Lauren of San Francisco. Judges were Tish Hinojosa, David Maloney, and Chuck Pyle. In spite of the difficulty of drawing a crowd downtown in July, the festival was fairly successful. For its second year, it drew the endorsement of the 160-member Spokane Central Business District Association.

Back in Texas on Labor Day weekend, August 31-September 2, we staged our second Kerrville Folk Festival, Too! Friday's opening night included, among others, Jon Ims, Christine Albert, and Hal Ketchum. Saturday afternoon introduced our audience to the Chenille Sisters in a two-hour concert at Threadgill Theater, and at that night's concert we introduced New Orleans-raised Chris Smither, whom I had seen at Passim in Boston. Also playing were the cream of the crop from Lubbock — Jimmie Dale Gilmore, Butch Hancock, David Halley, the Maines Brothers, and Gary P. Nunn and the Sons of the Bunkhouse Band.

The Sunday night concert was also an impressive roster with Crow Johnson, Mike Williams, Chuck Pyle, and Anne Hills on a line-up that also starred Walter Hyatt and Champ Hood, Ray Wylie Hubbard, and Laurie Lewis with Tom Rosum.

It rained on and off, but the weekend was filled with enjoyable music and a number of magic moments. The crowds seemed to welcome eagerly an informal three-day weekend that was "like the early years of the folk festival." (P.S.: We made a profit!)

We zipped through the remainder of September, completing detailed arrangements for the back-to-back second Napa Valley Folk Festival October 5-7, and the seventh Isla Mujeres festival, October 18-23.

The Napa Valley Folk Festival was presented in association with Casa Nuestra Winery and Southwest Airlines at the Veterans Home of California with the emerging songwriters at Calistoga's Pioneer Park co-sponsored by *Sing Out!* and Calistoga Mineral Water company.

Peter Yarrow was back to close the weekend with Alan Arnapole's California Zephyr opening the festival on Friday night. In between were performances by Tom Ball and Kenny Sultan, Peppino D'Agostino, Hatsegana, Barbara Higbie, the Sundogs, Laurie Lewis, David Maloney, 1989 winner Sarah Elizabeth Campbell, and a reunion of

Bob Gibson and Hamilton Camp. Also returning from the previous year were Evan Marshall, Steve Seskin, and the duo of Allegra Broughton and Sam Page. Other headliners included the satirical quartet from Berkeley, Celtic Elvis (Jim Ocean, Marcy Straw, Randy Anger, and Rick Wescott) with their theatrical skits and new wave folk music.

With its second year, the festival edged nearer break-even, and the advanced press and attendance had increased dramatically. We aimed for break-even in 1992.

While the festival was a challenge to produce and break into the California consciousness, I really valued the new friendships with Mike Martini, Bill Knox, Bob Pusey at Calistoga Water Company, and so many more Napa Valley leaders who aligned themselves and their patronage with the festival. Aside from the fact that Napa Valley was probably the most beautiful agricultural valley in America, and the wines were among the best in the world, in the long run, it was the new friends we made in the valley who gave us our biggest return on our investment of time and energy to make the festival happen there.

Back home in Kerrville for ten days and then off to Mexico for the Isla Mujeres festival with Tish Hinojosa, Peter Yarrow, and Allen Damron for the five-day weekend, October 18-22. We were back on Aeromexico as there were major management changes at Continental and Aeromexico was ready to pick it up again. All of our people enjoyed their working vacation in Mexico and Tish was now the darling of the island. Peter spent a good amount of his time signing autographs and hugging folks . . . nothing new!

We completed our nineteenth year with our eighth annual Kerrville Christmas Reunion at Waterloo Ice House on 38th Street in Austin. Twelve twenty-five-minute sets began at 8:00 P.M. with the Austin Lounge Lizards, Kurt Van Sickle, Ann Feeney, and Bill Oliver, followed by Paul Glasse featured in a set with Scott Neubert. Then we heard Melissa Javors, Tim Henderson, Caryl P. Weiss, Allen Damron, and a set featuring Scott Neubert with Paul Glasse. Tish Hinojosa and Butch Hancock closed out the six-hour evening past 2:00 A.M. During the show we also enjoyed surprise appearances by Bobby Bridger, Michael Elwood and Beth Galiger, and Sarah Elizabeth Campbell. The reunion was always fun, and the glow of the season

was on all of us. Among the patrons to show up for the show was Becky Dozier of Kerrville.

As we looked back on 1990, we thought that on the whole, it had been a pretty good year. We knew last January that there was no way to go but up, and it seemed everything *was* up in a very productive first year of bankruptcy.

The year 1991 was our landmark twentieth anniversary, and we had been planning special anniversary events and trappings for months. We had Bobby Rector design us a twenty-year logo for use in promoting the festival and on special anniversary edition t-shirts. An anniversary on-the-road

tour was planned for March, and we were to release our first festival songbook. Author Larry Willoughby's new book, *Kerrville Folk Festival: A 20-Year Celebration* had been in preparation for six years and was to include more than 300 photos, history, comments, interviews, and narratives concerning the first two decades. We also planned to have Gamble Rogers entertain at our anniversary fish fry with our own label wines, followed by a memorial concert in remembrance of departed festival family members. The concert would be played by the Festival Orchestra conducted by David Amram with nine soloists. We would also unveil the Festival of the Eagle as part of our anniversary. Finally, for our Labor Day weekend Kerrville Folk Festival, Too!, I decided to schedule a full festival of former New Folk finalists and winners.

Our corporate sponsorship from La Hacienda

had expired, and Southwest Airlines had actually found themselves in a position where they had to cut back on their sponsorship due to the tripling of fuel costs, among other things, but we forged optimistically ahead.

The spring months were kept clear to prepare for the twentieth anniversary festival, and I took advantage of the flexible schedule to take off for a five-day bicycle tour of northern California. The ride wound its way from Sacramento, averaging fifty-five miles a day, through Davis and Winter, up Napa Valley to Calistoga, and over the mountains to picturesque wineries of Alexander Valley and Sonoma Valley, through the shaded backroads along the Russian River and the coastal foothills and the beautiful Marin coast. Once at Stinson Beach, it was up Mount Tamalpias and across the Golden Gate Bridge into San Francisco. The ride was sponsored by the *Sacramento Bee's* Environmental Fund and the American Lung Association, with the $125 registration including a donation for the organizations. The ride was such a kick that I rode it three or four more times over the years!

One of the things that I did on many of my cycling trips was to stay at American Youth Hostels. Offering low-cost accommodations, many of the hostels offered travel assistance and local activity programs. Most of these non-profit hostels have self-service kitchens, dining rooms, common areas, and dormitory sleeping accommodations. Some have private family rooms, laundry facilities, and bicycle storage. I've met interesting people from all over the world staying in hostels in Florida, California, Oregon, Washington, and Vancouver, as well as closer to home in Texas, Arizona, and New Mexico. Many of the hostels are located in national and state parks or in historic areas. I received so much from my hosteling experiencing that I served on the board of directors of the Austin International Hostel as a way of returning something to the system. It's strange, but most Americans buy the AYH membership to stay in English, European, and Scandinavian hostels without ever realizing that there are hundreds of hostels in the U.S.A. coast to coast.

Getting ready for the anniversary festival went along smoothly, but a phone call from writer Larry Willoughby told me that his project to publish the twenty-year book on Kerrville had come to a sudden end. The entire book layout, editorial text, and

photos were all stolen along with the back-up copy, computer, and cabinet in a robbery of the San Antonio printer who was contracted to produce the book. Larry was devastated and so was I!

He had done such a good job on his *Texas Rhythm, Texas Rhyme*, the most definitive book available on Texas music, including an overview of Kerrville and many photos of performers taken at the festival, that I knew his Kerrville book would have been an interesting and thorough publication. To start over was an impossible task for the disheartened writer. In annual visits with Pete Seeger at the Folk Alliance meetings, Pete would frequently inquire if anyone was doing a Kerrville book, and he'd encourage me to undertake the task year after year. His encouragement and the frustration of the sudden end of Willoughby's project began to generate the commitment to undertake *Music From the Heart* a few years later.

Our anniversary Kerrville Folk Festival on-the-road tour played the Waterloo Ice House in Austin on March 21, San Antonio on the 22nd, Rockefeller's in Houston on the 23rd, and Poor David's Pub in Dallas the 24th, and then rolled into Kerrville to play the Inn of the Hills Ballroom on March 25. Our performers were Allen Damron, to whom the tour was dedicated, Christine Albert, Bobby Bridger, Melissa Javors, Joanne Shenandoah of the Oneida Territory, Shake Russell and Jack Saunders, and the Kerrville All-Stars. We also introduced Michael Elwood on this trip. I had booked Elwood for the 1991 festival after hearing him at a campfire last year. At each city, we distributed prefestival brochures while also releasing the 1990 documentary recording and the new anniversary songbook. We had good publicity and good audiences in every city.

Following the anniversary performance tour and the cycling tour of California, the weeks before the May 23-June 9 folk festival moved rapidly by. We were caught up on all of our past documentary recordings and happy to see the eighty-six-minute, twenty-two-song 1990 recording out and available for the festival. We were also pleased and impressed with the finished Twentieth Anniversary Kerrville Songbook of ten songs. It included favorites like Shake Russell's "Deep In The West," Fromholz' "Isle Mujeres," Gary P.'s "London Homesick Blues," and had an attractive four-color cover plus photos and bios of all the songwriters. It also included songs by Carolyn Hester, Melissa Javors, Rick Beresford, Bob Gibson and Tom Paxton, Tim Henderson, Chuck Pyle, and, of course, Bobby Bridger, whose "Heal in the Wisdom" festival anthem became one of the most popular offerings. The songbook is still selling well as of this writing.

Newcomers to the 1991 festival were Canada's James Keelighan, Russia's Leonid Tikomirov, and the all-female Ranch Romance from Seattle. Other artists making their debut at Kerrville were Jonathan Edwards, the Chenille Sisters (who had played Folk, Too! the year before), Michael Smith, Claudia Schmidt, Austin's Timbuk 3, Steve Seskin, and Michael Elwood and Beth Galiger.

Top artists coming back to the festival were Patty Larkin, Willis Alan Ramsey, Gamble Rogers, Steve Earle, Trout Fishing in America, Cheryl Wheeler, and England's Rory McLeod.

With the roster of eighty-six main stage artists plus the eight Native American performers and the seven Anglo counterparts, we had an anniversary roster that the press found irresistible. There were so many stories that we received massive press coverage a month in advance, all during the festival, and for several weeks afterward. Besides the five television camera crews who frequented the festival, there were nearly 200 other press people coming and going during the event.

The anniversary t-shirts with Bobby Rector's design were a big hit and could be seen everywhere on the festival site. One of the most rewarding decisions I had made, after much soul searching, was the total ban on throw-a-way cups. We had been buying 50,000 beer cups per festival, and there were thousands of other cups also being distributed by beverage concessionaires and others. The previous year someone had handed me a petition with several hundred signatures, asking that I ban Styrofoam cups. I thought it was a good idea, but, remembering the "permanent" plastic cups at the Vancouver Folk Festival, I decided to do away with *all* throwaway cups! We purchased over 7,000 seventeenounce plastic cups with our anniversary logo on them and attached a Discovery Toys chainlink to each handle so the cups could be clipped to belt loops and conveniently carried that way. Then, we notified all of our concessions that throw-away cups would not be permitted and that their prices should be for sixteen-ounce servings from now on.

The idea caught on quickly with the fans who bought cups or brought their own without a complaint. We had hesitated to require performers to

buy cups, so we had rewashable stadium cups for them backstage, but most performers went out front and bought their own Kerrville cups. The net result was that we cut down on trash hauled to the dump ten miles away by a ton a day! We cut down on our trash to the landfill by eighteen tons over the duration of the festival and set an example for all of us. We sold every single cup in our inventory. Now, "permanent" cups are a standard part of the festival, and since 1991, we have saved the Kerrville landfill over 100 tons of Styrofoam and paper!

Poi Dog Pondering, originally from Hawaii, brought a younger audience to Kerrville. 1991.
— Courtesy Ken Schmidt.

The first weekend's concerts included Pete Kennedy, David Olney, Uncle Walt's Band, Poi Dog Pondering, Hugh and Katy Moffatt, Tim O' Brien, and our ragtime piano champion Terry Waldo, now one of the nation's most highly regarded ragtime concert artists. Our children's concerts that first weekend had the remarkable lineup of the Chenille Sisters, Trout Fishing in America, Australian *didjeridoo* player Paul Taylor, and Gayle Ross. The Monday Blues Project, hosted by Steve James, presented interviews and songs from Paul Geremia, Catfish Keith, and Paul Liniger. Also by now, the Saturday morning bike rides were printed in the program and sponsored by South Austin Bicycles.

The twentieth New Folk competition, judged by David Olney, John Herald, and Fred Small, selected as the six 1991 winners Steve Key (Washington, D.C.), Darcie Deauville (Scottsdale, AZ), Alisa Fineman (Pacific Grove, CA), Dick Siegel (Ann Arbor, MI), Barry Dow (LaCrescenta, CA), and Scott Freed (Campbell, CA). I was also favorably impressed with Carrie Newcomer from

Trout Fishing in America at the children's concert at Threadgill Theater. 1991.

— Courtesy Merri Lu Park.

The Dixie Chicks rehearsing backstage. 1990.

— Courtesy John Carrico.

Indiana and Michael McNevin from California, whom I'd met on the West Coast the previous year.

The twelfth Bob Gibson songwriting school included as faculty regulars Rick Beresford and Dick Goodwin, plus Steven Fromholz, Jon Ims, Tom Paxton, and Valdy. The class of sixty students received their money's worth with this dynamic crew of teachers.

The midweek sundown concerts pulled together a group of Seattle-area writers who all had been to Kerrville the year before as New Folk and had named their campsite Camp Coho. Adding the much-revered Seattle writer Heidi Muller, they performed as Camp Coho on Tuesday night. The event was so well received that I planned to put together other "camps" from other cities in future years to focus on the music scenes of these cities. There are often outstanding regional artists playing in local areas who have never received recognition outside their hometowns. A "camp" showcase at Kerrville could give them something to shoot for, and, for a moment, focus the spotlight on the local scene. I thought I'd try it over the next few years and see what happened. The other two nights were also rewarding with Brian Cutean and Friends on Wednesday and the Kerrville All-Stars playing a rousing two-hour concert Thursday to numerous ovations.

The second weekend opened with an impressive Friday night concert by, among others, Christine Albert, Valdy, and Tom Paxton, with Willis Alan Ramsey closing.

Following Saturday morning's bike ride, we staged a two-hour concert by cowboy song collector Steve Cormier and Tex Sweeney and the Grazmatics. The Saturday-Sunday children's concerts had big crowds listening to Jonathan Edwards, Sid Hausman, Josh White, Jr., and Gayle Ross.

Saturday night's concert was a big one, opened by Marley's Ghost from California. Leonid Tikomirov from Moscow charmed his audience with his music and his hesitant English explanations and greetings. The final five that night all hit home with the crowd — Anne Hills with her special guest Michael Smith ("The Dutchman"), Josh White, Jr., the beautiful Dixie Chicks, the all-time popular Shake Russell and Dana Cooper, and Timbuk 3 closing.

Sunday, following Rev. Joan McKee's Folk Song Service on Chapel Hill, David Card hosted the New Folk award winners concert of winners from four states and the District of Columbia.

The nighttime concert began with a hot blues set by Hans Theesink, and then rewardingly wended its way through sets by Steve Gillette and Cindy Mangsen, Bill Staines, Claudia Schmidt, Ponty Bone and his accordion and band, and a dynamic Jonathan

The twentieth anniversary festival site at Quiet Valley Ranch as seen from the air. The campgrounds are to the left and the Outdoor Theater is in the foreground. Texas Highway 16 is at the top of the photo. 1991.

— Courtesy Ken Schmidt.

Joanne Shenandoah, Bill Miller, David Amram, Larry Long, Paul Pearcy, and others at the Festival of the Eagle. 1991.

— Courtesy Colleen Pride.

Edwards. The Austin Lounge Lizards closed the night in true Lizards' style.

Our second midweek was dedicated to an anniversary celebration of American Indian history, culture, and spirit called Festival of the Eagle. This festival-within-a-festival began at Threadgill Theater with a purification, dedication, and welcome dance at 2:30 Monday afternoon. Thus began a powerfully moving event that saw, over four days, Floyd Westerman, Kevin Locke, Bill Miller, John Trudell, Roxy Gordon, Mitch Walking Elk, and Gayle Ross in concert, in stories, and in one-on-one conversations on Chapel Hill. We talked about American Indian contributions to our culture, Joanne Shenandoah taught everyone to sing an Iroquois song, John Trudell's tragic life and consummate spirit gave dramatic impact to his discussion of "The American Indian: Myths and Reality," and Floyd "Red Crow" Westerman, quickly recognized because of his film roles and TV appearances,

Claudia Schmidt can get intense. 1991.
— Courtesy Ken Schmidt.

Gayle Ross and Floyd Westerman take a break backstage at Threadgill Theater. 1991.
— Courtesy C. Moulton.

talked about opportunities to share with Indian people.

Westerman had been a principal advisor, among many others, who helped us develop some sensitive insights into the process of putting together an inter-tribal event. Our first goal was entertainment, but underlying our motivation was the idea of presenting the Native American in contemporary life in a way that would bring a better understanding to a fairly uninformed Texas population.

Besides the concerts and meetings with the performers, we included a Native-American crafts village, tee-pee and lodge area, ceremonial circles, and performances by Anglo artists compatible with the "old way" like Bobby Bridger, David Amram, Carolyn Hester, Peter Rowan, Larry Long, and others.

I had spent a number of years working alone and with the Austin- and San Antonio-based American Indian Coalition to get Indian burial

rights legislation passed in the Texas House and Senate. I was appalled by the lack of understanding of the Indian culture and value system. I hoped, through the Festival of the Eagle, to begin to undo the stereotypical view of our native peoples and to begin a larger dialogue that could better the lives of Indians everywhere, and still have a positive impact on our throw-away society.

The net result of our first Festival of the Eagle was a rewarding four days of sharing, building understanding, and being a witness to and a part of a deeply spiritual experience that altered many of our personal values and perceptions. The entertainment itself was unlike any other previous experience.

The final weekend saw California songwriter Steve Seskin hosting the Ballad Tree and opening Friday night's concert that offered not only Texas artists Don Sanders, the Gypsies of Houston, Tom

The Rowan Brothers. From left: Chris, Peter, and Lorin. 1991.
— Courtesy Merri Lu Park.

From left: Shug Maudlin, Carol Bender, Brian Young, and Maggie Montgomery at a Kerrville volunteer staff concert. 1989.

— Courtesy Darron Spohn.

Gamble Rogers backstage before the fish fry and memorial concert. 1991.

— Courtesy John Carrico.

Russell and Butch Hancock with Marce Lacouture, but also Robin and Linda Williams and the Rowan Brothers back for an encore appearance.

Chuck Pyle hosted the staff concert after the bike ride. All the children's concerts were packed to capacity again to hear Katherine Dines, Gayle Ross, Don Sanders, and Kim Wallach.

Rory McLeod hosted the Ballad Tree and opened the Saturday night concert. His energy-packed set was difficult to follow, but providing contrast was Sarah Elizabeth Campbell accompanied by Nina Gerber. Tom Ball and Kenny Sultan's blues set was followed by the western swing of Seattle's Ranch Romance, and then Jimmie Dale Gilmore put a Texas finish on the evening. Rev. Walter Lee conducted services on Chapel Hill during the Folk Mass, followed by a two-hour concert by the Hard Travelers. Our annual fish fry was moved from Wednesday to the final night of the festival, when the irrepressible Gamble Rogers entertained the huge dinner crowd non-stop for ninety minutes.

The concert for the evening was in memory of the dozens of performers, staff, and other friends of the festival who had died during the first twenty years. They were fondly remembered in a three-hour concert by our seventeen-member festival orchestra that included concert master Robert Rudié, Erik Hokkanen in the violin section, Dick Goodwin on string bass, Paul Pearcy as percussionist, and Nina Gerber's guitar, along with members of the Austin Symphony Orchestra conducted by David Amram.

David Amram conducting the Festival Orchestra with flute soloist Megan Meisenbach in the world premiere performance of Amram's "Theme and Variations on Red River Valley." 1991.

— Courtesy Ken Schmidt.

I had asked David to compose a Texas-flavored work that we could premiere at the concert, and he wrote his "Theme And Variations on Red River Valley for Flute and Strings" with Megan Meisenbach as flute soloist in the world premiere (June 9, 1991).

Then Amram introduced, one at a time, the festival soloists and conducted the orchestrations of their songs especially created by Dick Goodwin and

David Amram for the occasion. Bob Gibson performed "Let The Band Play Dixie," Bridger sang "Snow Goose," and Peter Yarrow sang "Weave Me The Sunshine." Amram performed an instrumental version of Jerry Jeff Walker's "Mr. Bo Jangles," conducting from the piano and adding a penny whistle solo. Marcia Ball at the piano sang "The Power of Love," and Nina Gerber, the late Kate Wolf's accompanist, played a moving guitar solo on Kate's "Give Yourself To Love." During the first half of the concert, Erik Hokkanen did an unaccompanied Lakota courting song, and during the second half Robert Rudié was violin soloist with Kathryn Mishell at the piano in a Gershwin medley.

The concert closed with the orchestra accompanying Gary P. Nunn in "London Homesick Blues" and Bobby Bridger, all the other soloists, and the entire audience in "Heal in the Wisdom."

The successful anniversary festival was an immensely satisfying experience for me and was a key event in my producing career. The festival played to 25,000 fans over the 18 days.

While there were many impressions of the Ballad Tree over the years, Merri Lu Park's poetic impression is one of the most enduring:

BALLAD TREE

Chapel hill and ballad tree
mean many different things to me

it's the center of the universe
it's an island in the sea

ballad tree is poetry
it's music in the shade

it's marriages, and baptisms
and where friend's ashes have been laid

it's a canopy above a choir
on sunday when we sing

where ministers and minstrels share
beneath its lovely, leafy wing

a place to sit, reflect and rest
and find out who we are

within the light of chapel hill
ballad tree's the star

Merri Lu Park

Sharing a song at the Ballad Tree in the 1980s.
— Courtesy Steven's Stills.

I had three festivals, a trip to Winnipeg, and a 1,000-mile bicycle ride ahead of me this year, and I looked forward to all of them.

I flew to Winnipeg for the folk festival, July 4-7, as a guest of artistic director Rosalie Goldstein and thoroughly enjoyed the cool weather, the Canadian hospitality, and seeing so many friends performing, including Valdy and Bourne and McLeod, formerly of the Tannehill Weavers.

There were countless Americans there also — Patty Larkin, Guy Clark, Townes Van Zandt, Timbuk 3, Ranch Romance, the Four Bitchin' Babes, and Cheryl Wheeler to start with.

I stopped by a workshop to see Steve Young, and on the panel of participants with him was the most amazing solo performer I'd ever seen! David Broza from Israel was an intensely focused and passionate guitar player and singer. He was the most popular performer in Israel's history, and his art reflected his background growing up in England and Spain. When I met him, we became instant brothers. I booked him on the spot for Kerrville in 1992.

I also spotted two impressive Canadian singer-songwriters. One was Wyckham Porteous, a fine songwriter with a dynamic presence. I also took note of Lynn Miles of Quebec, whose songs and voice moved me to include her on our festival list in the future.

I worked again with the Columbia Folk Association to produce the second, now renamed, Columbia Music Festival at Spokane's Met Theatre on July 19-21. They had booked a number of artists I didn't know, but also followed my recommendations on Eliza Gilkyson, Chuck Pyle, Ranch Romance, and Heidi Muller. The balance of the roster included last year's competition winner Janis Carper and noted fiddler Kevin Burke plus Scott Corsu, Electric Bonsai Band, Alice di Micele, Village Drum and Masquerade, Blue Road Rounders, Urban Coyote Bush Band, and Lendell Reason.

Sing Out! rejoined us as sponsors of the songwriters' competition, and there were song swaps, song circles, workshops, and the crafts and food booths at the street fair. Especially effective was the Sunday Folk Song Service with Native Americans participating and Kerrville New Folk winner Alisa Fineman.

While the festival was moderately successful, the thing we heard repeatedly from most customers was the wish that the festival would move out to the country. Bob Levigne said he would try to find a suitable site but hated to give up his downtown sponsors.

A week later I was in Seattle with my twenty-one-speed Specialized bicycle ready to work and ride the 1,000-mile, fifteen-day American Lung Association ride to San Francisco. As part of the volunteer crew, my job was to load everyone's tent, camping gear, and luggage into the truck each morning before I joined the ride. Sixty riders left Seattle in midday with a ferry ride across Puget Sound and a breathtaking view of Seattle and Mount Ranier. We rode over many mountain passes, through Redwood forests, and along the rocky coast line south through Oregon and northern California. There was plenty

On my way from Seattle to San Francisco. 1991.
— Courtesy Miles Photo.

of hearty food, and I joined the cooking team one night after riding ninety miles that day. We had a good and friendly support staff, including bike mechanics, and took a one-day break about halfway. It was a challenging and difficult ride, and while I enjoyed the trip and the outdoor life thoroughly, I was grateful to reach Josie Lenwell's San Francisco townhouse on August 11.

The next day I flew back to Texas to prepare for the Kerrville Folk Festival, Too!, August 30-September 1, with its twenty-year New Folk Reunion. Unlike last year's event, the weather held throughout the three-day festival. The New Folk Reunion was a good one, and the music was outstanding — no bands, just twenty-seven acoustic songwriters singing their original songs. The former New Folk were from many different years. Some had been finalists, some had been award winners.

The weekend was headlined by Tish Hinojosa (1979), Michael Tomlinson (1983), Darden Smith (1983), Jon Ims (1979), Chuck Pyle (1981), John Gorka (1984), David Wilcox (1988), Pierce Pettis (1986), and Jimmy LaFave (1987), but also included Buddy Mondlock, Alisa Fineman, L. J. Booth, Rick Beresford, Lucinda Williams, David Roth, and a dozen others. It was a true reunion and stimulated much storytelling around the campfires. It was such a good idea that we'll probably try it again on our thirtieth anniversary!

The third Napa Valley Folk Festival, October 11-13, was moved to the Napa Town and Country Fairgrounds. The three-day weekend scheduled five concerts with forty artists, including Peter Yarrow, Peter Rowan and the Rowan Brothers, Laurie Lewis and Grant Street, the Limeliters, and California Zephyr, now reinforced by smiling mandolin and fiddle virtuoso Evan Marshall.

Other notables on the roster included David Maloney, Alisa Fineman, David Roth, Marley's Ghost, Celtic Elvis, and first-time artists Penny Nichols, Carnahan and Petrie, Carol McComb, and John Kelly.

When the festival was over, it was pretty evident that it was time for me to turn the event over to the local organization. With the necessary paperwork coming to me in the mail to facilitate the changeover, I left for Texas to get on the Aeromexico flight for Cancun.

Our next event was south of the border, our "ultimate music lover's vacation" on the island of Isla Mujeres off the coast of Cancun. Mexican native singers, dancers, and musicians joined our stars on the Plaza October 18-20 for the eighth annual event. This time, we took our All-stars (Glasse-Hokkanen-Neubert) to perform their own show (rehearsed at Threadgill Theater before a live audience) and to back up Tish Hinojosa, Christine Albert, and Allen Damron. Damron and I co-hosted the gala opening night party, and everyone got to pick and sing a little. During the next few days we played music all over the island from night clubs and restaurants to beaches and then to the plaza in the middle of town. This year we brought over 100 fans with us, with a number of couples electing to stay over for another week.

The fall flew by as we caught up on the year's paperwork including the Napa Valley wrap-up. We actually got to put some things back where they go so we could find them in the spring. We were most grateful that there *would be* a next season. With all the challenges of the 1991 season filed away and a significant payment made on our reorganization plan, we began to enjoy some financial stability. Our creditors were pleased and often surprised to hear from us with the increasing good news and a check!

Our twentieth anniversary year's final event was the ninth annual Kerrville Christmas Reunion at the 38th Street Waterloo Ice House in Austin on Saturday, December 7.

For the first time, we asked that it be a non-smoking event, and it made the packed restaurant a much more pleasant place to be. Lucky for the smokers, there was a porch the length of the restaurant where they could smoke and still see and hear the performance. Since we had turned away over seventy people last year, there was a significant advance sale promising a full house again this year.

The Austin Lounge Lizards opened for us and then moved down to the other Waterloo at Sixth and Lamar for their own evening gig. They also had a full house. Allen Damron took the stage about 8:40 and then the performers in order of appearance were Lindsay Haisley, Don Sanders, Christine Albert, Bill Oliver, the Banded Geckos, and Bobby Bridger, with Ken Gaines and Doug Hudson sitting in for three-song sets.

During the evening, as people shared the complimentary "Nutcracker Cake" and the hot cinnamon apple cider, I announced the dates of the 1992 festivals and the names of several dozen performers who were already confirmed. A surprising number of fans gave us $200 sponsorship checks for the 1992 season, joining more than 100 others who had already renewed by mail!

As we looked toward the beginning of our third decade, I overlooked the difficulties of the past and instead valued the very meaningful experience in human relationships I had shared over the years because of being part of our annual events.

It provided us all with rich and significant memories and long-lasting satisfaction, and the highest and most genuine feelings. Music cuts across all boundaries, and our music would give us inclusive and lasting feelings of well-being. It was the feeling of accomplishment combined with a sense of relaxation, renewal, and togetherness. We were truly looking forward to our third decade!

KERRVILLE FOLK FESTIVAL: THE LATER YEARS

(1992–1996)

The early part of 1992 was devoted to paperwork and meetings. The paperwork was mostly the preparation of promotional materials, pre-festival brochures and posters, our annual newsletter, and music foundation materials for New Folk. It was stuff that we did every year about that time. We also finalized the plan for the songwriters school and put the final touches on the *Kerrville Directory*, edited by Steve Gillette and Cindy Mangsen. First published in the late 1980s and still in publication today, the directory is meant as a booking and touring aid for acoustic musicians.

The *Kerrville Directory* in 1993 was a 272-page catalogue of clubs, festivals, concert halls, coffee houses, radio stations and folk radio shows, entertainment editors and folk presses, newsletters, record companies, instrument dealers, performers, agents, managers and publicists, and a form for musicians to fill out for a free listing in the next edition. It's a major undertaking to update and correct each year.

The meetings were of all kinds — with Miller Theatre management about the coming season; the twice-monthly meetings of the American Indian Coalition in Austin; a January 22 session with Southwest Airlines in Dallas, renewing our sixth year of sponsorship; Austin International Hostel board and committee meetings; monthly wine tastings I staged for the membership of fifty wine enthusiasts in my chapter of Les Ami du Vin (The Friends of Wine); the South by Southwest (SXSW) four-day music conference in Austin; a two-day February trip to Isla Mujeres, planning our 1992 festival; regular organized bike rides all over Texas on various weekends; a March 7 staff retreat in Austin; a March 20-22 wine celebration I organized at the Kerrville Inn of the Hills, including a six-

course winemakers' dinner honoring Mike Martini and his wines from Napa Valley's Luis M. Martini Winery; and our annual Kerrville Folk Festival on-the-road show March 26-29.

Mike Martini (standing) talks about his wines at the vintner's dinner. 1992.

— Courtesy Ken Schmidt.

Our Miller Theatre concerts wouldn't happen in Houston until early May, so we decided to kick off our third decade with a Texas tour over the last weekend in March so we could be in touch with our fans well before the folk festival.

We opened the tour on Thursday, March 26, at the Waterloo Ice House at 6th and Lamar in Austin, went on to Poor David's Pub in Dallas the next night, played Mucky Duck in Houston on Saturday night, and finished up in San Antonio on Sunday, March 29, with a matinee 4:00 to 9:00 P.M. concert at Tim and Linda Holt's Cibolo Creek Country Club.

Helping us announce our 1992 season and the release of our 1991 twenty-two-performance festival album on the tour were Christine Albert, Bobby Bridger, Allen Damron, and Betty Elders, plus the Kerrville All-Stars. With the departure of Scott Neubert for Nashville, Paul Glasse recruited one of Austin's finest guitarists, Mitch Watkins, to temporarily fill that spot. Paul and Mitch had been playing jazz together, and Mitch fit right in. He was well-known and respected on both coasts and added a more virtuosic dimension to the All-Stars. Erik Hokkanen was our innovative fiddle star as always. The All-Stars backed our singer-songwriters and played some instrumentals, featuring each of the trio on solo leads. Betty Elders played the Austin date and was replaced in the other three cities by Houston's Banded Geckos acoustic quartet.

It was a good tour with full houses nearly every day and a positive audience response to the four shows as well as to the announced line-up for the twenty-first festival.

Between the Texas tour and the Miller Theatre dates, there were a growing number of wine events on my calendar. After having visited a number of Texas wineries and attended several annual meetings of the Texas Wine and Grape Growers Association, I decided to combine the Texas wines with our Folk, Too! weekend and change the cumbersome name of the Labor Day weekend event to the Kerrville Wine and Music Festival.

While most of the wine tastings and dinners I had been hosting featured California wines, I was encouraged by Susan Auler of Fall Creek Winery to make an extra effort to learn about and promote Texas wines. Following her persuasive lead, I visited a dozen wineries across Texas, familiarized myself with their wines, and became better acquainted with their winemakers, a number of whom had been winemakers in Napa Valley. My own Napa Valley wine experience over the last four years had given

me a working knowledge of wines, and by now I had read several dozen books on wine. One thing about wine is that you can never know all there is to know about it. What remained for me was to see where the Texas wine industry was in the scope of things, and I was really impressed! My winery travels gave me a good chance to try many different Texas wines and to compare them to their California counterparts. The best chance came at the April 2-5 Hill Country Wine and Food Festival in Austin. Following that festival, I included some Texas wines in my wine and pasta tasting at Mr. Gatti's on April 11 and had a good response to them. For me, wine was an accompaniment with food, so I tried to include food flavors at every tasting. For someone who didn't drink much, I spent a disproportionate amount of time learning about wine, while remaining quite moderate in my consumption.

For the first time, I was in good enough physical condition to participate in the big Easter weekend bicycle ride. Actually, it consisted of three selected rides out of Kerrville and Fredericksburg of about fifty to sixty miles a day, which drew over 1,200 cyclists to Kerrville annually. A number of my cycling friends from Austin came and camped at the ranch that weekend and rode from the ranch.

When the weekend was over, I turned to the enjoyable task of listening to New Folk tapes to select finalists. The bike ride with friends put me in a good frame of mind to listen to over 500 tapes over a solid three days.

On April 24 I flew out to California with my bike for the five-day ride of northern California, and right after I returned to Texas, I hosted my second three-day Hill Country Wine Ride, May 1-3. A wine tasting, dinner, and camping at Grape Creek Winery on Friday night, then an eighteen-mile ride to Oberhellmann's Bell Mountain Vineyards north of Fredericksburg for a tour and lunch was followed for some of my sixteen cycling guests by a ride on the popular Willow City Loop. We camped out that night, having some of Bob Oberhelman's wines with dinner, and then Brian Young from my office came over to sing some songs around a campfire before we turned in for the night. The next morning, we rode to Enchanted Rock and then made the twenty-eight miles back through Fredericksburg to the Pedernales Winery for a tasting and lunch before riding the eight miles back to our cars at Grape Creek, where we all said good-bye.

The folk concerts at Miller Theatre in Houston on Thursday and Friday, May 7-8, featured Anne Hills, who flew in for the dates. She would play Kerrville on Labor Day weekend. We also presented Houston's Shake Russell and Jack Saunders and Shake's former partner Dana Cooper. Jon Ims flew in from Nashville for the dates, still riding high as a result of Trisha Yearwood's taking Jon's "She's In Love With The Boy" to Number One on the country charts. We also invited Christine Albert, Michael Elwood and Beth Galiger, and the All-Stars. By now All-Stars regulars Paul Glasse and Erik Hokkanen had been joined by Champ Hood (*fiddle* and *guitar*), and young Jeff Haley, *bass*. Between the two evening concerts on Friday afternoon, our performers joined with Houston-area musicians for a jam at the Brazos Bottom Bar and Grill in Richland.

The 1992 Kerrville Folk Festival, May 21-June 7, definitely reflected the impact of my 1991 visit to Winnipeg, for in the first five days of the festival, our schedule included Canadians Valdy, Connie Kaldor, and newcomers Lucie Blue Tremblay from Montreal and Calgary's James Keelaghan, and the former Tannehill Weavers, Bourne and McLeod. Opening night also included Steve Young, with whom I had reconnected at Winnipeg. That same night also included the first main stage appearance by Washington's Steve Key and Austin's Jimmy LaFave, both former New Folk. Our Friday night concert found among its performers four other previous New Folk, among them Californian Alisa Fineman, who had been at both Spokane and Napa Valley in 1991. The participation by former New Folk as featured main stage performers was increasing every year, 1992 being typical as twenty-four former New Folk were on the schedule. In fact, the New Folk had become the most important source of regional artists who became Kerrville regulars.

We had been having Christian non-denominational Folk Mass and Folk Song Services (without Holy Communion) open to all since the beginning. This year, we hosted our first Saturday morning Shabbat service for the Jewish faith at Threadgill Theater. The well-attended, music-filled service was conducted by Rabbi Kerry Baker. Thinking back on the Chapel Hill services all these years, many of the most active participants were our Jewish performers. I hoped we wouldn't lose them!

Saturday and Sunday nights were both near-capacity with artists Trout Fishing in America, David Amram, Bob Gibson, Bill and Bonnie, Laurie

Alisa Fineman, a former New Folk award winner, playing the main stage. 1992.

— Courtesy Darron Spohn.

Lewis, and Peter Yarrow in the mix, drawing fans from all over the U.S. and overseas.

Allen Damron joined me in hosting the twenty-first New Folk concerts in the afternoon both days, with Steve Key, Christine Albert, and Rod MacDonald as judges, selecting as winners Cosy Sheridan (Portsmouth, NH), Michael McNevin (Berkeley, CA), Karen Taylor-Good (Nashville), Slaid Cleaves (Austin, TX), Trisha Walker (Nashville), and David Dodson (Camden, ME). We also noted T. R. Ritchie from the northwest and both Michael Camp and Jana Stanfield from the Nashville area. The six winners would be introduced again to our audience by David Card a week later at the May 31 award winners concert.

The Memorial Day's blues project, with Steve James at the helm, had an interesting and noteworthy trio of uncommonly fine acoustic blues artists, with Austin-based Antone Records artist Sue Foley, the veteran Nat Reese, and the remarkable restaurateur-pianist Johnny Nicholas, who owned one of

The blues project. From left: Steve James, Sue Foley, Nat Reese, unidentified drummer, and Johnny Nicholas. 1992.
— Courtesy Merri Lu Park.

Christine Albert at Kerrville. 1992.
— Courtesy Brian Kanof.

the Hill Country's most popular eating places, the legendary Hill Top Cafe. The combined variety of these performers provided one of the best received blues events in the series.

Joining regulars Bob Gibson, Dick Goodwin, and Rick Beresford on the songwriters school faculty were Nashville's Stephanie Davis, Boston's Bob Franke, and Canadian James Keelaghan. Again, the three-day session was filled to capacity with students and observers.

Monday night's main stage concert included the Doug Dillard Band and a reunion of Austin's long-disbanded Ain't Misbehavin', along with sets by Chris Smither, Christine Albert, and others.

Our midweek sundown concerts at Threadgill Theater began with a rousing two hours by The Billys from Ashville, NC. David Wilcox had introduced us to these hilarious songwriters who played all sorts of discarded containers for percussion. They also had a very funny answering machine routine between them, acting as roommates. The other two sundowns were unusual, too, bringing to the fore Ken Gaines and Friends from San Antonio and Michael Rex and Oasis from Houston.

The second weekend was highlighted by performances by Utah Phillips, Walter Hyatt and Champ Hood, former New Folk Kat Eggleston, Robert Earl Keen, Jonathan Edwards and the Sundogs, along with fourteen others, including Mitch Walking Elk from 1991's Festival of the Eagle, and Heidi Muller from 1991's Camp Coho. Sally Rogers, who had been my hospitable guide at

the Philadelphia Folk Festival, was also on hand from the northeast.

The three pairs of children's concerts of 1992 had quite an impressive roster coordinated by Gayle Ross: Trout Fishing in America, Don Sanders, juggling Turk Pipkin, Bob Gibson, Peter Alsop, Sally Rogers, Jonathan Edwards, Josh White, Jr., Tom Chapin, Sid Hausman, Tom Paxton, Bill Oliver, Paul Taylor from Australia, and Cathy Winter. Every children's concert every weekend and every festival was packed to capacity with a large number of kids, but we seemed to draw three times as many adults to these remarkable up-close two-hour events!

The second Festival of the Eagle, at Threadgill June 1-4, between the second and third weekends, starred Mitch Walking Elk and the Wolf River Band, poet Roxy Gordon, and Bill Miller and Joanne Shenandoah with Gayle Ross. Newcomers for the four days of concerts, dances, stories and one-on-one sessions were Ron Evans, Jack Gladstone, the Alabama-Coushatta tribal singers, Bird Family, Brian Crawford Akipa, and the Mountain Creek Singers. This year, Eliza Gilkyson, who produced the Rainbow Warrior Festival in Santa Fe, was the only non-Indian performer. Between the welcome dance and the closing ceremony, the crowds enjoyed performances, arts and crafts, and lengthy, wide-open discussions about celebrating the discovery of Columbus by the "Indians" 500 years ago, and a particularly moving session on Chapel Hill by Bill Miller and Joanne Shenandoah about trying to find their identity as native people in contemporary America.

Joanne Shenandoah and Bill Miller on Chapel Hill talk about trying to find their identity. 1992.
— Courtesy Merri Lu Park.

The third and final weekend starred, among more than a dozen other artists, the now nationally popular Austin Lounge Lizards, young audience hero David Garza, the spectacular and passionate David Broza of Israel, whom I'd met at Winnipeg, Tish Hinojosa, Eliza Gilkyson, Henry Sparks Bootfare (the five-member London rootsband on their first Texas visit), Dana Cooper, the Paul Glasse Sextet, and closing the festival, Timbuk 3. The day after the festival, most of the volunteers gathered, as they do each year, for a day of relaxation, storytelling, and songs at Luckenbach.

After their highly successful appearance at the festival, Bootfare did a week of sight-seeing, and then I hosted two nights of performances for them at the 6th and Lamar Waterloo Ice House in Austin.

Business manager Andrea LeBlanc reported another effective festival, allowing us to stay on schedule with our debt retirement.

With this success behind me, I took a four-day weekend to attend the Aspen Food and Wine Festival in Colorado, came home for a week, and then loaded my old Subaru wagon with tent, sleep-

Austin Lounge Lizards at home on the Kerrville stage. 1992.
— Courtesy Darron Spohn.

ing bag, a mountain bike and a touring bike, and took off for a thirty-five-day, 7,000-mile music, camping, and cycling trip to the northwest, visiting hostels and music friends along the way via El Paso, Reno, Napa Valley, Vancouver for a five-day ride of the Big Island, four days at the Vancouver Folk Festival, on to Spokane to help with the Columbia

The passionate David Broza perfoming at Kerrville. 1992.
— Courtesy Ken Schmidt.

Timbuk 3. From left: Barbara and Pat MacDonald, drummer Wally Ingram, and bassist Courtney Audan. 1992.
— Courtesy John Carrico.

A Kerrville regular, Eliza Gilkyson. 1992.
— Courtesy John Carrico.

Music Festival for three days, on through Yellowstone National Park, to Boulder to spend the night at Chuck Pyle's, through Santa Fe to Pecos, Texas, through Austin to the ranch, arriving home at noon on August 5. While the old Subaru had 150,000 miles on it and no air conditioning, I was amazed that the total gas and oil cost for the 7,000 miles was only $256! Even though it was a long drive, I felt good when I returned to the ranch.

At the Vancouver Festival back on July 13-15, I enjoyed visits with James Keelaghan and Oscar Lopez, Rosalie Sorrels, Bill Bourne, Holly Near, Rory McLeod, and Laurie Lewis, as well as with festival producer Gary Cristall and a large number of other Canadian music industry people.

At the Spokane festival, Bob Levigne told me that it would be the last one. His employer, the State of Washington, told him if he did the festival again, taking away from his job performance, they would have to let him go.

So we enjoyed the July 24-26 festival at Bob's new location, Green Bluff, ten miles north of Spokane. A good number of my favorite performers

were there — Alisa Fineman, Katy Moffatt, David Maloney, Chris Smither, the Sundogs, Sukay, and others. The first three of these artists were judges for the Kerrville Music Foundation/*Sing Out!* songwriters' competition.

When I returned to the ranch, it was back to paperwork, meetings, and a brief Santa Fe trip for the opera with Robert Rudié and Kathryn Mishell before our Labor Day weekend festival.

Our Labor Day weekend, publicized early in the year as our fourth Kerrville Folk Festival, Too!, had been converted to the first annual Kerrville Wine & Music Festival held September 4-6.

The festival's music schedule was intact — three 6-hour evening concerts, two 2-hour Ballad Trees, two 2-hour 1:00 P.M. concerts at Threadgill Theater, plus a Saturday morning bike ride and a Sunday morning Folk Song service. We simply added a dozen winery booths for wine tasting during the evening concerts, and after the 1:00 P.M. Saturday and Sunday concerts, we held wine seminars at Threadgill from 3:00 to 5:00 P.M. Ron Bechtol, wine and food editor of the *San Antonio Light*, hosted a Chardonnay seminar with four Texas winemakers on Saturday, and Susan Dunn, from the Texas Agriculture Department, hosted a wine and cheese seminar on Sunday with four more winemakers and cheeses from the Mozzarella Company of Dallas. This seminar earned the festival the nickname "wine and cheese festival" for some reason.

Wine had been a part of Texas history for more than 100 years. Having recovered from Prohibition, winemaking in Texas had once again taken root in the 1990s. Many of the wineries participating at the festival had earned medals and other recognition for their art both in America and overseas amongst the distinguished winemakers of France.

I thought that the parallel between the songwriters and the winemakers was so totally compatible, that they could easily be honored together. Both create a special, one-of-a-kind product that is original, or unique in character, and which appeals to a select group of enthusiasts whose lives are improved and graced by the quality and warmth of the craft. Another parallel could be drawn between fine varietal wines and our "folk" songs and jug wines and pop music. Both wine and a great song seem to become more important with age and both are a significant source of joy and enlightenment in our lives. The festival was to be a toast to all good things in moderation.

We had wine booths and winemakers from Bell Mountain Vineyards (Fredericksburg), Grape Creek Vineyards (Stonewall), Messina Hof Wine Cellars (Bryan), Ste. Genevieve Vineyards (Ft. Stockton), Sister Creek Vineyards (Sisterdale), Fall Creek Vineyards (Tow), Hill Country Cellars (Cedar Park), Moyer Winery (San Marcos), Schoppaul Hill Winery (Bonham), and Slaughter-Leftwich Winery (Austin).

The performers were from Texas and eight other states. Best known of the twenty-five artists were Austin's Betty Elders, Ed Miller, Erik Moll and Erik Hokkanen as a duo, Ponty Bone, Bill Oliver, Tim Henderson, Champ Hood and the Threadgill Troubadors, Nashville's Buddy Mondlock, Hugh and Katy Moffatt from Virginia and California respectively, Brave Combo from Texas, Fred Small, Anne Hills, and Michael Smith and Tom Russell. Three Texas bluegrass bands rounded out the schedule with one each night — the House Brothers, The Andy Owens Project, and Hickory Hill.

The concerts were outstanding, both the wineries and the public were impressed with the wine tasting and the booths, and the wine seminars were attended by more than 100 people each afternoon. Many wine lovers discovered our music and many music lovers discovered the wines. While we still prohibited throw-away cups and glass in the theater, we broke our own rule and sold over 500 festival wine glasses to tasters. The festival was successful and well-received.

On October 14, more than 100 of us departed Houston for the ninth annual October 15-20 Isla Mujeres festival on our Aeromexico flight. Peter Rowan and the Rowan Brothers were our headliners with bilingual Arleen Vance from California, Allen Damron, Paul Glasse, Michael Elwood, and Beth Galiger. Our headquarters hotels were Enrique Lima's Las Cabanas on Coco Beach, the twelve-unit Nabalam just down the beach, and the Roca Mar near the Plaza.

For some reason, many of our group became ill that year, especially Michael Elwood and Beth Galiger, who finally went to the hospital with dehydration. Also, over the years, the prices for our group had been increasing significantly and often the hotel arrangements were not honored or we were charged twice for rooms already paid. Also, the more recent island government officials were becoming inhospitable and jealous of our popularity on the island. Most of our guests had a lovely time, but behind the scenes I was being hassled by the politicians, and the unethical businessmen were becoming annoying.

And the island had changed over the past nine years. We wished for Gilberto Pastrana and his staff, who had worked so selflessly for the island and welcomed us so warmly. We were grateful that we could still turn to Enrique Lima, a former government tourism officer and friend, whose patience and insight were reassuring when things were going wrong. I must admit, however, that my feeling of good will was wearing thin.

Since the visit to Kerrville by Amy Kurland of the Bluebird Cafe in Nashville, she and I had talked about doing some Kerrville shows in Nashville. As the discussions progressed, we were invited to hold a Kerrville reunion at the Bluebird, just for the fun of it, during the 9:30 slot on Tuesday, November 10. I selected from former Nashville-area New Folk winners Jon Ims, who had just won BMI's Song of the Year, and added Mickey Cates, Jan Marra, Trisha Walker, Buddy Mondlock, Helen Hudson, and Karen Taylor-Good, plus ASCAP's Writer of the Year Pat Alger, David Olney, the Doug Dillard Band, David Ball from Uncle Walt's Band, Dana Cooper, and Stephanie Davis. Then I brought with me from Houston a new writer named Doug Clark Steiger.

The turnout was standing-room only with a club full of music industry people, publishers, songwriters and fans. Jim Rooney, producer of Nanci Griffith and John Prine albums, came and did a guest set, and Hal Ketchum was in the audience. The music was matchless and, at the end of the evening, we took our share of the cover charge money and went out for a midnight breakfast and picking party. It was great fun and good to see so many people whose friendships and regard we valued. We were also told that it was a good idea to have an annual performance in Nashville.

Our 1992 Kerrville Christmas Reunion on December 5 at the 38th Street Waterloo Ice House featured seven twenty-five-minute sets by 1992 New Folk award winner Slaid Cleaves, hot fiddler Erik Hokkanen, Sarah Elizabeth Campbell, Michael Elwood and Beth Galiger (now fully recovered from Isla Mujeres), Alisa Fineman, who flew in from California courtesy of Southwest Airlines, Butch Hancock, and Jane Gillman, who had moved back to Austin from Washington and was teamed with former New Folk winner Darcie Deauville. Hot cider, Christmas cake, and Bobby Bridger's closing set and anthem made for a rewarding tenth annual Christmas Reunion. The place was jam-packed from start to finish.

Here we were in 1993, and it looked as though every year we were getting closer and closer to an ideal work schedule. We were learning the difference between being devoted to our work and being obsessed by it. While nothing seems to happen in life without passion, life is more than work, and it should be a celebration! The closer we came to retiring our debt and to having some time to live outside of work, the better I felt. With seven events on the calendar for 1993, we were going to have some time again to get away. I was amazed with the return of my energy reserves now that I was in better condition and had some time to do some of the other things I enjoyed. I loved my work and the more flexible schedule, and I was also getting some positive feedback from many of our performers. Tish Hinojosa recalled:

> [Nineteen seventy-nine] was the year that saw my passion for music rekindled as it hadn't been since I was 14 (nine years prior, also known to my family as the year I picked up my guitar and almost missed high school). I was in my early 20's when I attended my first Kerrville Folk Festival, also braving two songs in the New Folk competition, I ended up being one of the winners and invited to perform on next year's festival (the other was Jon Ims). I hadn't written much yet, and earning the title might have leaned on my singing ability. However, this left me floating on clouds, high on encouragement, ready to pursue this "song writing" further. It

also found me scrambling to write enough more to fill a 20-minute New Folk Award Winner concert set. It was a while before the career could actually be called a *career*, but I did keep honing on both. Now, going back to Kerrville always feels like a real family reunion, especially with the addition of two young festival fanatics who feel right at home. My soul flutters whenever I remember the significance of 1979 and Rod Kennedy's willingness to listen.

Robert Earl Keen also had some good memories. In fact, he said:

> I have more good memories of the Kerrville Folk Festival than I have good songs.
> I started going there as a fan and a listener who couldn't tune a guitar and ended up years later playing the main stage Saturday night in front of thousands of people. Bringing us all to what Gamble Rogers used to call that "golden moment," a place where one is swept away in fascination of the performance.
> And the main stage magic of Kerrville is only a part of the experience. The Texas Hill Country, the people from all walks, the musicians, and the all-night campfire jams keep the place alive from the first stir till the last sunbaked picker turns onto Highway 16 and heads home.
> Some of the songs I sing today remind me of the festival every time I perform. My favorite cowboy song, "Sonora's Death Row," is a song I first heard John Gorka sing late one night at a campfire, and since then I bet I've sung that song a thousand times. It always takes me back to the Kerrville Folk Festival and the sound of a single clear voice echoing off the hills and climbing toward the star-lit night.

In January I was able to work at my own pace to get season promotional materials together. I was able to listen to some chamber music, to make a birthday trip to Isla Mujeres with friends, to attend hostel and Indian Coalition meetings, to hold an organizational meeting in Austin at Threadgill's on North Lamar for our First Kerrville Music Awards at the end of the year. Helping me were a dozen music and media people whose opinions I respected. In about two hours time, we had a workable format.

I was able to work at the ranch one whole weekend with an enthusiastic team of volunteers thinning cedar trees in the campgrounds. Four days later, I took off for Tucson, Arizona, for the February 18-22 national meeting of the North American Folk

Alliance. The alliance was becoming more and more important to the whole folk scene internationally as the organization evolved from a non-profit grant-seeking orientation to a full-scope, commercial, non-profit trade association of today's real folk world. Every year the membership of the young organization was growing, and every year the convention zeroed in more precisely on the strengths and weaknesses of our industry and how to improve the visibility, business, and financial well-being of our field while still retaining the non-commercial aspects that we all valued.

Now, at last, performers, agents, managers, club owners, festival producers, folk broadcasters, radio stations, and record labels could network among themselves and with everyone else in the fast-growing folk community coast-to-coast and across our northern border into Canada.

The dozens of formal and informal showcases of both traditional and contemporary folk music and dance gave performers a chance to play for new segments of the folk community and talent buyers, and other industry people could get a quick overview of how everyone was doing. The alliance and its annual meeting, moving to a different city each year, always fired me up.

When I returned to Texas I was able to attend the March 17-21 South by Southwest (SXSW) conference in Austin and then get away for another weekend to attend my first *Dallas Morning News* Wine Competition. Three weeks later I was on the road with the Kerrville Folk Festival, playing in Dallas at Poor David's Pub on Friday, March 26, Houston at the Brazos Bottom Bar and Grill concert barn on Saturday, and following a Sunday brunch with Houston supporters at the Marriott, we headed for Austin to play Waterloo Ice House at 6th and Lamar.

We were distributing the first 1993 brochures and posters in these cities, while back in Kerrville the post office was processing 15,000 newsletters with brochures enclosed being sent to all fifty states.

Bobby Bridger and Butch Hancock were the old hands, but new to our Texas tour in 1993 were the recently arrived in Texas duo of Jane Gillman and Darcie Deaville, Jimmy LaFave, and American Indian singer-songwriter Joanne Shenandoah, who had been touring Europe extensively from the Oneida Reservation in New York. Our All-Stars were with us in their most recent configuration with Paul Glasse, Erik Hokkanen, and Champ Hood being joined by bassist Dave Heath.

Remarkable young fiddler from Florida, who moved to Austin in the 1980s, Erik Hokkanen of the Kerrville All-Stars. 1993.

— Photographer unknown.

Joining the line-up in Dallas was Emily Aronson, joining in Houston was Nashville's Mickey Cates, and in Austin Dana Cooper.

While the turnout in Houston was a little sparse, both the Dallas and Austin dates were standing-room-only. On the tour, we brought our new New Folk t-shirt to sell with proceeds going toward the upcoming Kerrville Music Awards. We hoped the proposed awards would generate the same volume of publicity and the same validation for the experienced professional performers that our New Folk had generated for emerging songwriters over the past twenty-one years.

Working with our fourteen touring performers on these dates was a good experience and quite a morale booster for everyone involved, and it set the tone for the spring. We'd be back in Houston at Miller Theatre with different headliners and the All-Stars at the end of April.

April was a stimulating month of varied activities up to our April 29 Cactus Cafe date after the two nights in Houston. The first weekend was the four-day Hill Country Wine and Food Festival, the second weekend was the big Easter bicycle ride in Kerrville with a number of my cycling friends camping at the ranch, mid-month was New Folk tape-listening time, and then the five-day California Grand Tour North ride from Sacramento on April 22.

We played Miller Theatre with a pair of powerhouse concerts on April 29-30. Since we had already played Houston with our road show a little over thirty days before, I figured we'd better stack this one somewhat, and stack it we did. Israeli artist David Broza was on the bill with Trout Fishing in America, Austin Lounge Lizards, 1991 New Folk winner Alisa Fineman, and Bobby Bridger. We sweetened it with the All-Stars with David Heath, and added Mitch Watkins on guitar.

It was a high-energy show, drawing a large and lively crowd of loyal Kerrville fans. Then, apparently, because it was a free concert in the park, there was a huge group of folks who just came to the concert to see what was happening. Hundreds of them came backstage seeking folk festival brochures like they hadn't known this kind of music was available anywhere.

Broza's music had universal appeal, and it was easy to see why his albums in Israel had gone triple platinum while his tours there sold out, drawing up to 15,000 fans at an outdoor concert. With seven successful CBS albums, his first American album on EMI was named one of the year's top ten albums by *The New York Times*.

The next night, Saturday, May 1, we played to an overflow house in the Cactus Cafe before heading back to Kerrville to see how the first of the three pre-festival work weekends was progressing.

The last three weeks before each festival are always filled with telephone interviews, trips to radio stations for on-the-air talks, last minute travel and accommodations changes for 100 plus festival performers, proofing the festival program at Herring Printing, and working with volunteers to get the ranch and all of our old trucks and security vehicles up and running. It's a rewarding time, with many old friends returning to the ranch along with eager newcomers, some just for one or more of the work weekends, some who come and work daily for several weeks.

We also shore up our office staff. I always look forward to the time when Dalis Allen rejoins our office staff from about the middle of April to mid-

Dalis Allen accompanies me to a wine tasting at the Cowboy Steak House in Kerrville. 1993.
— Courtesy Dalis Allen Collection.

June. Dalis has been a close friend and traveling companion for about twenty-five years, and I enjoy our long-running friendship on many levels. She is also a calm, efficient worker in the midst of what can become high tension during the frequent crises before and during a festival working with more than 100 performers, 600 volunteers, 200 sponsors, and hundreds of press people. She quietly takes care of myriad problems every day, working alongside Andrea LeBlanc and Brian Young in the office. Just the seven phones ringing constantly and the hustle and bustle of office volunteers is enough to create a situation where everyone is looking for some calm. Dalis also doubles as troubleshooter, finder of everything I misplace, and at night, is a staff photographer.

The twenty-second Kerrville Folk Festival, May 27-June 13, was going to be especially fun for me as a producer, because I not only would welcome back old friends gone too long like Odetta, Mike Williams, and others, but I would also introduce four remarkably different groups of performers making their first appearances and each so unique that I could already visualize the crowds on their feet dancing in the isles.

The first two of these groups were West Coast all-female bands. One was the exciting Pele Juju from Santa Cruz, eight-member world beat band who took their name from the Hawaiian goddess of fire (*Pele*) and African magic (*juju*). I first heard them in 1992 at the High Sierra Music Festival in California. Their music was a combination of jazz, rock, and reggae. With blond keyboard player Dana

Dana Hutson at the front microphone is the exciting lead singer of Pele Juju of Santa Cruz. 1993.
— Courtesy Darron Spohn.

The crazy Russians, Limpopo, get into it! 1993.
— Courtesy John Carrico.

Hutson frequently in front of the band as an emotional, dancing lead singer who practically turns herself inside out, Pele Juju should really create some happy excitement at Kerrville!

Quite a different all-female group from the state of Washington was the four-member Righteous Mothers, together for eleven years and with three albums to their credit. Their sassy, irreverent, comedic, and often political folk rock combines tight vocal harmonies with zany theatrics to create a warm, wild, and engaging stage presence. Gary Cristall at Vancouver had tipped me off to them.

The other all-female group was Saffire: The Uppity Blues women from Virginia. It was a talented blues trio with an attitude that I felt would he particularly entertaining at the ranch after hearing them at a Folk Alliance showcase.

The fourth group was the crazy Russians, Limpopo, a quartet I first heard at SXSW Music Conference at Austin. They called themselves a "folk and roll" band, described by the *Fort Worth Star-Telegram's* Jeff Guinn as "four wild-eyed men hauling a trombone, an accordion, a normal sized but odd-looking balalaika and an odder looking mega-balalaika." Jeff also said that at their sound check they, "Broke into a howling, stomping Russian language rock anthem that disturbed livestock for miles in every direction." I felt they'd be a surprising concert closer as they were totally unknown to our audience. I was struck by them on-stage in that they are so physical, so funny, so mobile. They are all over the stage while they play and they're amazing athletes. They do Cossack kicks and all sorts of other things while continuing

to play flawlessly. They introduce themselves as Igor Igor, Oleg, and Yuri.

The other treat I looked forward to was the appearance of country star-turned producer, Gail Davies, playing her first folk festival ever. Originally from Oklahoma, she had her first single in 1978. On moving to Nashville, she was the first female to write, arrange, and produce her own albums. During

Gail Davies, country singer turned producer, returned to the stage and live performing at Kerrville. 1993.
— Publicity Photo.

the next twelve years she had nine albums on CBS, Warner Brothers, RCA, MCA, and Capitol Records, In 1986 Gail initiated the first female "Writers in the Round" on "Austin City Limits." Essentially, she became fatigued by the road and touring all over the world, so she turned her attention full-time to producing records. She hadn't really performed in public for years when Hugh Moffatt got Gail and I together. Gail was actually pretty nervous when she came to Kerrville.

With Southwest Airlines continuing as our sponsor, we were able to fly all of these various groups to the festival without devastating our limited budget.

On the first day of our festival, Mayor Joe Herring, Jr., proclaimed "Rod Kennedy Day" in Kerrville, citing how our festivals had enriched the quality of life in the Hill Country. It was a great way to start on Thursday, May 27, and our first concert ranged from David Garza's young pop-rock, to the grace and majesty of Odetta, the humorously off-kilter songs of the Austin Lounge Lizards, and the original country songs and western swing of Clay Blaker and the Texas Honky Tonk Band.

Friday night was a songwriters' party, including award winner Karen Taylor-Good, Jimmy LaFave, Gail Davies (who relaxed and was loved by our audience), the very dynamic Jon Ims, and an impressive Kevin Welch.

Michael Johnson ("Bluer Than Blue") was on Saturday night plus David Amram with his jazz trio, Cheryl Wheeler, Saffire, and Limpopo. I had guessed right. Limpopo tore the place up, and everyone was on their feet roaring approval.

Sunday was another blockbuster night that ranged from the Kerrville All-Stars, Mike Cross, and the triple-threat Shake Russell-Jack Saunders-Dana Cooper, to Pele Juju. Gary P. Nunn closed, and between Pele Juju and Gary P. the audience was on their feet for nearly two hours. There was dancing in the sandy area we prepared for dancing, dancing in the aisles, dancing backstage, dancing in the crafts booths — everything was in motion.

The 1993 New Folk concerts on Saturday and Sunday afternoons, which featured forty writers I had screened and chosen out of 628 entries from forty-two states, Canada, and Germany, were judged by Cheryl Wheeler, Charles John Quarto, and Michael Johnson. This was one of the best competitions in festival history, and the six winners were Tom Kimmel (Nashville), Tom Prasada-Rao (Takoma Park, MD), Michael Lille (Nashville), Kim

Michael Johnson on opening weekend. 1993.

Forehand (Blanchardville, WI), Michael Jerling (Saratoga Springs, NY), and Cully and Elliott (Antioch, TN).

The Monday blues project, hosted by Steve James, introduced Lightning Wells, Joan Fenton, and Robert Lucas, and, as always, produced an intriguing three hours of acoustic blues.

The Monday night concert was another wide-ranging cross-section of today's music by Anne Hills, Fred Koller, Bill and Bonnie, Montreal's Lucie Blue Tremblay, Steve Seskin, and others. The midweek songwriting school had been turned over to Rick Beresford with Bob Gibson's frequent illness, and Dick Goodwin was there to assist with faculty members Steve Gillette, Anne Hills, Fred Koller, Steve Seskin, and Lucie Blue Tremblay. In selecting the faculty, I was trying to balance those who wrote hit songs with those who wrote more folk-oriented material. In the case of this year's teachers, all of them were successful in both the creative and financial sides of the music business.

The sundown concerts were all quite impressive. I had invited Alisa Fineman to bring her Camp California for the Tuesday night concert, featuring Kristina Olsen, Rick Beresford and Friends (Michael Camp, Lisa Ashman, and Rex Foster), and Thursday was a taping for actual broadcast on Tom May's "River City Folk" show in cities all across the U.S. The two radio programs had as guests Allen Damron, Anne Hills, David Maloney, Chuck Pyle, Steve Seskin, and Lucie Blue Tremblay.

Chuck Pyle also kicked off the second weekend as host of the Ballad Tree from 3:00 to 5:00 P.M. on Friday, followed an hour later by the big evening concert, a diverse and entertaining six hours with the first appearance of Don Edwards, a great favorite at cowboy poetry gatherings, as well as Ireland's Tommy Sands, the duo of Erik and Erik (Hokkanen and Moll), and a finale by Seattle's Ranch Romance.

The Festival Big Band led by Dick Goodwin. Vocalist Mary Ann Price relaxes at right. 1993.
— Courtesy Darron Spohn.

The Saturday night concert climaxed with an appearance of the seventeen-member Festival Big Band, led by Dick Goodwin, with Mary Ann Price as vocalist. Many in our audience had never heard a live big band and to them this could be "folk music." Early in the evening David Wilcox, Utah Phillips, the Boston Latin band Flor de Caña, and Steve Gillette and Cindy Mangsen were the performers.

Bill Staines of New Hampshire, his Maine neighbors, the trio Deavonsquare, Native American Bill Miller, Patty Larkin, and Tom Paxton provided a rousing Sunday night concert to close the weekend.

The children's concerts from 3:00 to 5:00 P.M. Saturday and Sunday of the three weekends were loaded with first-rate performers who drew capacity-plus crowds to Threadgill Memorial Theater.

Patty Larkin from Boston earned a large following in Texas. 1993.
— Courtesy Darron Spohn.

Keith Grimwood of Trout Fishing in America at the Threadgill Theater children's concert. 1993.
— Courtesy Ken Schmidt.

With Gayle Ross in charge, audiences couldn't get enough of Limpopo, Sally Rogers, Sid Hausman, Kim Wallach, Larry Long, David Maloney, Utah Phillips, Tommy Sands, Cathy Winter, Marsha Webb, Paul Taylor, Don Sanders, and Trout Fishing in America.

The midweek between the second and third weekends was filled by the third Festival of the Eagle, involving performances, talks, ceremonies, and special appearances in the Native American crafts village by Joseph Bruchac, Bill Miller, Mitch Walking Elk, Gayle Ross, the Joseph Benally Family from Flagstaff, Ron Evans, Blackfoot Jack Gladstone, Douglas Spotted Eagle, Jackie Bird from South Dakota, and Canadians Elizabeth Hill and Laura Vinson.

While every attempt was made to attract an audience for this "festival within a festival," the unique and often stirring event kept falling short of coming anywhere near paying for itself. It averaged an annual loss of $18,000 at a time when we were trying, in Chapter 11 recovery, to pay our creditors. The event did have much positive impact, and for many years after we would be gracing our main stage with Native American performers from this festival.

We had also suffered stinging criticism that we were exploiting the Indians! The same year, several people from the coalition succeeded in sinking the burial rights bill in committee because they didn't think it went far enough. To this day, people are digging up graves for relics to sell at flea markets.

I resigned from the coalition, turned over all the files to one of the group's more stable members, and went back to trying to solve our own problems. I was disappointed, but there are certain limits to how far idealism can carry you.

The third and final weekend showcased two of the three reggae bands I had booked as a reggae salute, Root One from Austin, and Leroy Shakespeare and the Ship of Vibes from Dallas. The Houston reggae band found themselves in Colorado unable to get back to Texas in time.

The weekend was filled with outstanding song-writers — David Massengill, Dana Cooper, Kat Eggleston, Butch Hancock and Jimmie Dale Gilmore, Trout Fishing in America, Steven Fromholz, John Gorka, David Broza, the Righteous Mothers, who received two standing ovations, and Bootfare back in Texas from London for an encore appearance. To close the festival, Damron lead a rousing version of "Heal in the Wisdom" with nearly

Allen Damron leads a cast of thousands in the Kerrville anthem "Heal in the Wisdom." 1993.
— Courtesy Merri Lu Park.

fifty people on-stage, the entire audience locked arm in arm swaying to the anthem with shouts of "Long live Kerrville" at the end.

Four days after the festival, I flew to Colorado for the June 17-20 Telluride Bluegrass Festival, and a month later I was in Winnipeg, Canada, for their folk festival. I had found it helpful, in maintaining a balanced perspective, to attend three or four other major festivals each year. While we weren't deliberately looking for talent, since we had a long waiting list, it was rewarding to select an occasional contrasting artist or group for Kerrville. What I did get out of these trips, besides the pleasure of being with so many of my favorite performers, was either an insight into a new way to do things or a reconfirmation that the way we were doing it was right for us.

I was involved as a panelist at the Houston Music Expo the first weekend of August, as a wine taster at the national Les Ami du Vin tasting of over 900 wines by forty tasters over five days at Baltimore, Maryland, where I became an expert on Maryland crab cakes and visited the Smithsonian with Tom Prasada-Rao. Back in Texas, I attended an "Austin City Limits" taping of Joan Baez and then knuckled down to getting ready for the Kerrville Wine and Music Festival.

The second wine festival, September 3-5, included wine booths for a dozen Texas wineries, a seminar on "Discovering Texas Reds," and another on building a wine cellar. The music over the three days was by former Newport Convention member Iain Matthews from England, now residing in Austin,

Italian guitarist Peppino D'Agostino, the unique classical Gypsy jazz quintet Cafe Noir of Dallas, and two dozen others including Bill Morrisey, Tom Dundee, Michael Smith, Megan McDonough, Trout Fishing in America, Chuck Pyle, an unsteady Bob Gibson, David Roth, L. J. Booth, and the hit of the weekend, the energized and independent Ani DiFranco, who was wildly welcomed. I had first heard her at Vancouver and didn't know if she'd be well-received here by the more conservative Texas audience. But she was a smash, and my admiration for her, personally and professionally, prompted me to put in a bid for a return to Kerrville to play the folk festival in 1994. She was from my hometown of Buffalo, NY, was only in her early twenties, but already had two albums out on her own label. I knew Ani would rapidly earn national popularity over the next few years.

With a three-day visit to the annual Winefest at Grapevine, Texas, a quick trip to make deposits and final arrangements for the festival at Isla Mujeres,

Ani DiFranco, in her twenties, on her way to national recognition. 1993.

— Courtesy Ken Schmidt.

and a three-day trip to the state-sponsored Texas Travel Summit all in September, the month went quickly. I was deeply saddened by the death on October 1 and the ensuing funeral of my friend Ace Hindman, who had built or helped build everything on Quiet Valley Ranch. He had become a gunsmith in recent years when his failing health prevented him from working in construction. He was an opinionated, resourceful, and hard worker, and over the years he became a close friend, loyal supporter, advisor, and compadre. I would miss him always being there when I needed him.

On October 14 we headed to Mexico with 144 people for the last Isla Mujeres music festival, and if I doubted the wisdom of canceling the event, I was abruptly reminded of why. Three days before departure, I received a phone call from our headquarters hotel canceling our reservations for fifty rooms that I had paid the deposit on the previous month. It seems that they forgotten to put our reservations in the computer and had sold the rooms to someone else in Europe (for a higher price?). If I hadn't known the president of the hotel association on the island, who scrambled around and obtained fifty rooms spread over three other hotels, I don't know what I would have done. What I did, as people came ashore from the shuttle boat, was to tell them their new hotel assignments. It was a messy way to start.

On another trip to Isla, I'd had my confirmed price for rooms for my group denied by the desk clerk, who told me I have to see the manager. When I showed the letter confirming my rates to the owner, he took it and tore it up in my face and demanded the new price!

So, worn down by ineptness, deception, and behind-the-back political maneuvering, I was beginning to run out of international good will. My doctor giving me my annual physical said, "You're in good shape but something you are doing in October is causing a lot of stress." I agreed.

The farewell Isla festival, the tenth since 1984, found me in the company of Christine Albert, Allen Damron, Paul Glasse, Ponty Bone, and Erik Moll. Guitarist Marvin Dykhaus came along as accompanist for Tish Hinojosa and played with practically everyone. My good friend Slim Richey was along to run the sound as he had done for years. I enjoyed, as always, seeing Enrique Lima and Enriqueta De Avila, who had coordinated the Mexican side of the festival as a labor of love for many years.

We had a welcoming party at Rolande's Pizza

on Friday with music by Paul Glasse, Ponty Bone, and Marvin, and then to the Plaza, where Tish and Allen Damron played.

There was another reception the next night at La Peña Restaurant, where Damron and Erik Moll played. Then to the Plaza for a concert by all of our performers.

On Sunday there was a reception at Ciro's Lobster House with music by Christine Albert and Tish Hinojosa and then to the Plaza, where Erik Moll, Christine, Ponty Bone, and Paul Glasse performed. On Monday there was the final farewell party at Enrique Lima's Buho's on Norte Beach with everyone sitting in at an informal party. On our final night, with a day of leisure and last-minute shopping for everyone, we had a farewell dinner upstairs at Gomar's, and our customers provided the music.

Just to keep the record straight, we paid for all the receptions, meals, and drinks out of our "package" I'd put together.

While I remember fondly the heavenly tropical surroundings, the beautiful sunsets and refreshing evening breezes, and the broad smiling faces of my Mayan friends, plus the good feelings I shared with Gilberto Pastrana, Dr. Tony Salas, Michael and Greta, and the steadfast Juan Garza of Aero Mexico in Houston, there was a finality to this last festival. Like a typical American, I guess, I had lost patience with the lack of business ethics and loyalty, and the total lack of responsible infrastructure below management level in so many businesses in Mexico. I did not expect to return to Mexico to ever do any kind of business again, even if it was a non-profit goodwill undertaking. I'm told I should take solace in M. H. Anderson's admonition, "If at first you don't succeed, you're about average."

On October 23 I rode my bike the forty-plus miles from the ranch to the Fredericksburg Wine and Food Festival. It was always a good chance to see wine industry friends, taste the recent vintage and lots of good food, while also relaxing and catching some music under the fair's canopy in the historic square.

The 100-mile Kerrville Century bike ride was canceled because of rain, so I put my bike away and prepared to go to Nashville on November 1 for the second Nashville Kerrville Reunion at the Bluebird. While I was looking forward to it, I was a little concerned that last year's standing-room-only sell-out was a fluke.

But the Nashville papers were quoting BMI's Roger Sovine as saying Kerrville was "this country's greatest songwriting festival" and listing in order of appearance our entire November 2 line-up — Rick Beresford, Helen Hudson, Cully and Elliott, Mike Williams, Trisha Walker, Gail Davies, Tom Kimmel, Jon Ims, Christine Albert (in town co-writing), and Michael Johnson, while pointing out that surprise guests might also show up.

I went to the Bluebird early for dinner and enjoyed the early show, but there was only scattered attendance. By the time I went up on-stage to introduce Rick, the place was wall-to-wall people with no place to sit down for the overflow. The evening was rejuvenating and a reminder of why we do what we do. It was good to catch up on news with Gail Davies, with John Briggs at ASCAP, and to see so many friends. We capped a successful night with a picking party and breakfast in the back room at Perkins up the Pike.

From Nashville, I flew directly to Denver for a "Kerrville Campfire Weekend" at Swallow Hill Music Association, the non-profit organization that I had connected with through Meredith Carson, their concert director. She had arranged a weekend for songwriters with a Friday picking party at the Denver Folklore Center. On Saturday there was a 1:00 P.M. workshop at Swallow Hill with Debby Rose from ASCAP's New York office, Chuck Pyle, Stephen Allen Davis, Tim O'Brien, Dana Cooper, Denver's Bob Tyler, and me. The seven of us talked openly with members of the large audience on the panel's topic, "Is songwriting a viable career?"

At 4:00 P.M. I poured Texas wines at a reception sponsored by ASCAP. I had been honored by the Texas Wine and Grape Growers Association as a Texas Wine Ambassador, and I was taking my assignment seriously, pouring Texas wines whenever and wherever I could. People were still incredulous that Texas had a wine industry, but I had the pleasure of watching the faces when we poured the wines and they discovered their excellence.

That night, after a good dinner and visit with the participants, I was able to relax and enjoy with Debby Rose the concert by Dana, Chuck, Stephen Allen, and Bob Tyler. It was a good experience, and after a good dinner the next night with Meredith at Barolo's Grill on East Sixth, I flew home and back to work on Monday.

Beginning to book the 1994 season, I took a weekend in Austin for chamber music at one of Robert Rudié's Salon concerts. These events, held in pairs four times a season in magnificent private homes were, I am certain, the way string quartets and other small ensembles were meant to be heard. I was on the board of directors and my job, aside from giving an abundance of free advice, some of it useful, was to obtain the wines for the after-recital receptions. Four of my winemaking friends in California obliged and shipped excellent wines for each event for many years. This encouraged the board to listen to my advice on other matters.

Our Kerrville Christmas Reunion at the Waterloo Ice House this year became part of a three-day music foundation weekend beginning on Thursday, December 2, with the first Kerrville Music Awards, Friday with a New Folk Reunion hosted by David Wilcox, and Saturday with the Kerrville Christmas Reunion.

We produced the music awards as a black-tie affair with a champagne reception at 7:00 P.M. featuring music by guitarist Chuck Pennell, followed by the 8:00 P.M. awards dinner with music by Shake Russell and Jack Saunders. The awards show itself, sponsored by ASCAP, BMI, Southwest Airlines, and Hill Country Budweiser, was co-hosted by Sara Hickman and Gary P. Nunn.

There were fourteen categories of awards, plus the inductees into the Kerrville Hall of Fame. The evening sparkled with twenty performers, and the presenters included thirty-four artists and music industry leaders.

Kerrville Music Awards finale with Bobby Bridger leading the anthem finale. From left: Sara Hickman, Bridger, Butch Hancock, Christine Albert, Jimmy LaFave, Dana Cooper (partially hidden), and Shake Russell. 1994.
— Courtesy Darron Spohn.

Jimmy LaFave, who was nominated for seven awards, walked away with four of them, Robert Earl Keen was Songwriter of the Year, and Tish Hinojosa and Nanci Griffith won two awards each, with Crow Johnson receiving the Spirit of Kerrville Award.

It was an elegant evening with everyone cleaning up pretty well!

The next day the foundation hosted a luncheon for Art Menius to talk about the folk alliance and to invite new members from the Southwest.

That evening David Wilcox hosted and entertained at a 1993 New Folk Reunion concert by our six current winners.

The eleventh Kerrville Christmas Reunion was Saturday night at the larger 6th and Lamar Waterloo Ice House with Allen Damron, Christine Albert, Bobby Bridger, Lindsay Haisley, Melissa Javors, and some surprise guests.

All in all, it was a fine weekend to close out our twenty-second season. The next day we visited the Armadillo Christmas Bazaar, took visiting performers to airplanes, and then headed home to Kerrville.

We returned to Austin two more times in December for the "Austin City Limits" taping of Christine Albert and Paul Glasse, and for an Austin hostel Christmas party.

Back in Kerrville for a quiet New Year's Eve, I looked forward to 1994 and my tough assignment to look over a cruise ship for a week.

The year 1994 was starting out great! Not only had Southwest Airlines renewed their sponsorship for the eighth year, but they notified us that the folk festival would be featured in their "Best of Texas Events" in *Texas Monthly* in April. In addition to the airline joining us for the eighth year, Whole Foods Markets, Southwest Division, natural foods markets came on board as co-sponsors of the 1994 festival season. They had been supporting us in various ways for years, and they were now on our team on a par with Southwest Airlines.

On January 9 I boarded the cruise ship S. S. *Enchanted Seas* for a seven-day cruise of the western Caribbean to see if it was suitable for a 1995 folk cruise to replace the Isla Mujeres festival on our calendar. It was a small-class ship carrying only 715 passengers with American and European officers and an international crew of 350. When I returned to the office on January 17, I reserved fifty-two cabins for January 12-19, 1995. This ship would be perfect for us.

The Commodore cruise ship S.S. Enchanted Seas. *1994.*
— Publicity Photo.

I returned to a busy schedule of concerts, meetings, a Messina Hof wine tasting at the Cowboy Artists of America Museum for Les Ami du Vin, and the annual meeting of the Austin hostel where I was elected president of the board.

Our office turned the newsletter and brochure copy into the printers and then departed for a week in Boston at the American Folk Alliance. A week after returning from Boston, I was out on the ranch with a crew of volunteers thinning back the cedars in the campgrounds again.

The end of March, I took off on the road with a press tour to announce the 1995 festival season and our sponsorship by Whole Foods Markets. The press tour was in their stores in Austin, Houston, Dallas, and San Antonio. Near the end of the month, I spent a weekend at the Idlewild Lodge bed and breakfast in Comfort, Texas, on a retreat with volunteer staff coordinators Bobby Peele and his wife Sam, and with Vaughn Hafner and his wife Nancy. We studied all of the real and imagined logistical and business problems of the festival and came up with a series of solutions. The biggest problem was the excessive number of vehicles in the campgrounds that destroyed the ambiance, crowded out camping space, and prevented service and emergency vehicles adequate access. The decision was made to charge everyone with a vehicle in the campgrounds a daily rate of $5 while offering them free parking in our parking lot and an unloading pass to set up their campsite.

We also came up with a new system and a team to work to assure that the festival money was handled more efficiently on the ranch and accounted for properly when it hit the office. Running a festival is like running a small city, and we wanted to make certain that everything worked when we were under pressure with large crowds here.

The Easter tour bike rides, April 1-3, and the Texas Hill Country Wine and Food Festival in Austin, April 7-10, provided good breaks for me before I settled in to listen to 689 New Folk tapes. This year, we cut the number of finalists from forty to thirty-two to cut down the length of the competition that had been running into evening concert sound check time for the two biggest concerts of the weekend. The next weekend, April 21-26, I was back in California biking the five-day Tour North ride out of Sacramento.

The day after I returned to the ranch from California, I left for Poor David's Pub, where our Texas tour for the year would open. It truly was a rewarding and reinforcing four hours in front of 200 Kerrverts with both old friends and newcomers on our stage. Kerrville regulars playing the tour were Josh White, Jr., Chuck Pyle, Michael Smith, Katy Moffatt, Christine Albert, and the Kerrville All-Stars with Champ Hood playing guitar and fiddle. Then, for seasoning, we added the gentle lyrical writer from Maryland who was 1993 New Folk winner, Tom Prasada-Rao, to the group. At both Poor David's Pub and the next two nights at Miller Outdoor Theatre in Houston, Tom received unabated approval from the crowds in the company of some of the nation's best songwriters.

The month of May moved quickly toward the start date of the 1994 folk festival with office work, interviews, seven phones ringing all day, every day, interview trips to Austin and San Antonio, and a dozen telephone interviews crammed into the last few days before the staff meeting on Wednesday, May 25, before opening the gates to the public the next morning.

While there were a few complaints about the new $5-a-day charge for campground vehicle permits, once the festival was under way and into the usually overcrowded five-day weekend, the approval rating of the new ruling began to rise rapidly. It was again a pleasure to camp and road dust was cut to almost nothing.

The previous year's hit groups like Pele Juju and Limpopo were back, as well as Ani DiFranco and Gail Davies, James Keelaghan, and Ray Wylie Hubbard. Newcomers included the Chenille Sisters from Ann Arbor and the rocking Mumbo Gumbo from Sacramento, plus Cris Williamson and Tret

Fure. We were also introducing Sara Hickman's new trio, Domestic Science Club, and, for the first time in festival history, I had invited all six of last year's New Folk winners.

The public turn-out for the first weekend was again huge, but with the new rule in place, the campground was filled with tents as it should be and hundreds of cars were parked in the parking lot where they should be.

Among the most memorable moments of the first five days were evening concert performances by Jon Ims, the Austin rock-a-billy trio High Noon, sets by the Paul Glasse Sextet, Kevin Welch and Gail Davies, and the return of the Rowan Brothers, Laurie Lewis, Butch Hancock, Betty Elders, and Peter Yarrow. New Folk winners Tom Prasada-Rao and Tom Kimmel made a really good impression on their thousands of listeners as well.

This year's New Folk finalists, selected from entries from forty-five states and Canada, produced winners Ellis Paul (Wayland, MA), Michael Camp (Nashville), Les Sampou (Osterville, MA), Dan Colehour (Austin), Bob Cheevers (Franklin, TN),

and Steve Spurgin (McKinney, TX). The judges picking the winners were 1993's winner Tom Kimmel, plus Steve Gillette and Canadian James Keelaghan.

Steve James was again hosting the Memorial Day blues project with veteran Guitar Gabriel, Mary Flower, and the Jones Brothers of Eureka Springs sharing the three hours of acoustic blues ending in the four-way jam session that has become such an enjoyable finale. That night Shake Russell and Jack Saunders brought the first weekend to a close as the final performers on the evening concert.

The fifteenth annual songwriters school, now under Rick Beresford's direction and assisted by Dick Goodwin, saw as faculty members Christine Albert, Gail Davies, Jon Ims, Wyckham Porteous from Canada (whose writing so impressed me at Winnipeg), and Steve Seskin. The enrollment was full, and I noted that there were a number of repeat students back for more, and some New Folk who

Butch Hancock (center) at Kerrville with Jimmie Dale Gilmore (left) and Lindsay Haisley. 1994.
— Courtesy Ken Schmidt.

Shake Russell and Jack Saunders closing Memorial Day evening concert. 1994.
— Courtesy Ken Schmidt.

had taken advantage of the foundation scholarships to enroll.

Gail Davies really valued her Kerrville experience and looking back on her first two years here she remembered:

> The Kerrville Folk Festival was a catalyst for me to return to the stage after six years of not performing live. I'd grown weary of the concert stage and the distances between myself and the audiences.
>
> In 1991, Rod invited me to come to Texas and said I'd have the time of my life, and I did. The people were warm and friendly and for the first time in my career I was able to perform in front of my fellow songwriters and artists. It was an audience like none I'd ever known before. After the show, I strolled and listened to the campfire singers and realized the quality of people who had made up the audience. It was humbling and exhilarating!
>
> Afterwards, I was able to stay a weekend and participate in the songwriters' school. Once again, I saw the enthusiasm, the love, and the kindness towards everyone there and the general feeling of camaraderie. It was wonderful. It gave me the hope to continue writing and singing the kind of music I do and not what the music industry would have me do.

The Billys were back, too, playing the Wednesday sundown concert during the first midweek and the children's concerts on the following weekend with David Maloney, Josh White, Jr., and Gayle Ross. By now they had built a huge following at the festival.

The second weekend of the festival included Mike Lille, another of last year's winners with his quartet SGGL, and he received great response from the crowd. At Threadgill Theater on Saturday, after the bike ride, Bob Tyler hosted a Colorado Campfire sharing the two hours with Celeste Krenz and with former Nashville resident Stephen Allen Davis, who had a whole song bag full of great tunes, many of which had been major hits.

The Saturday night concert numbered among its seven artists Vienna's Hans Theesink, Christine Albert, Jimmy LaFave. And the eight energized and forceful, unrestrained women of Pele Juju had the crowds dancing in the aisles.

The Sunday evening concert followed a day filled with Walter Lee's Folk Mass, the New Folk winners concert, children's concert, and the Ballad

The Billys arouse the crowd at Threadgill Theater. 1994.
— Courtesy Ken Schmidt.

Tree hosted by Michael Elwood and Beth Galiger. Michael McNevin began and Gary P. Nunn closed and in between were the contrasting songs of

Steve James, Texas-based bluesman, hosted the Kerrville blues project during its formative years. 1994.
— Courtesy Ken Schmidt.

Blackfoot Indian performer Jack Gladstone became a Kerrville main stage performer after first appearing at the Festival of the Eagle. 1994.
— Courtesy Merri Lu Park.

Melanie reappeared at Kerrville and charmed the audience, many of whom had been loyal fans years before. 1994.
— Courtesy Ken Schmidt.

Carolyn Hester, Steve James, Michael Smith, and Flor de Caña.

Without the Festival of the Eagle, the four days between the second and third weekends were days of leisure — cooking out, singing around the camp-fires, relaxing, and, for some, a lazy trip for swimming, rafting, or shopping. The sundown concerts from 7:00 to 9:00 P.M. were loaded with popular pairs of artists — Joel Mabus and David Maloney, Alisa Fineman and Bill Staines, Don Sanders and David Roth, and on Thursday night, David Amram, and a dozen friends from the campgrounds and the main stage.

The third weekend, which was the first weekend of summer vacation for many families, was also a big one with great crowds drawn by artists like Katy Moffatt, Michael Johnson, David Broza, Tish Hinojosa, Jack Gladstone (who was so popular at the Festival of the Eagle), Valdy, the Austin Lounge Lizards, and the widely publicized appearance of Melanie to close Saturday night. Sunday's closing concert was highlighted by the appearance of, among others, Chuck Pyle, Ani DiFranco, Tom Paxton, and Limpopo, the crazy Russians. They had learned our anthem, and never before had "Heal In the Wisdom" sounded so much like the "Volga Boatman." It was a cheerful distraction from our dancing feet that everyone would have to go home tomorrow. Some thought eighteen days was not enough, so we jokingly began to talk about twenty-five days for our twenty-fifth festival. After all, Oscar Wilde told us that "nothing succeeds like excess!"

There was another change in the festival that I tried, which people liked. We offered, in a separate stand, vintage-dated varietal wines instead of the jug wines sold at most large outdoor events. This year's offering of thirteen-year-old Cabernet Sauvignon from Louis M. Martini of Napa Valley, and the Texas Chardonnay of Hill Country Cellars, as our "Folk Wine," completely sold out.

Four days after the festival, I was in the cool mountains of Colorado for four days at the Aspen Food and Wine Festival, and I returned refreshed and ready to ship our Wine and Music Festival brochures out nationally along with a major press release, before leaving for California and the High Sierra Music Festival where I had first heard Pele Juju and Mumbo Gumbo. It was another nice weekend in the mountains, but I was happy to get back to Texas to get work done before leaving for the August 5-7 Newport Folk Festival and a couple of days in New York with Peter Yarrow. At Newport I really valued the opportunity to catch up on twenty years of activity with producer George Wein and his wife Joyce. We talked over dinner on Saturday night. While at the festival I renewed my friendship with Iris Dement and enjoyed seeing Ellis Paul, Par Williams, and Richard Shindell. There were some outstanding moments on-stage when the Story and the Nields performed together informally. Producer Bob Jones, now a good friend from our many phone calls and frequent meetings and panels at Folk Alliance, extended me every courtesy.

I was fretful and disturbed to learn that George Wein had MS and that it was beginning to affect his daily life and no one could do anything about it. I was grateful for my own good health.

Incidentally, the view from the stage at Newport, out over the crowd of 10,000 to the harbor with its yachts and sail boats, rivaled that magnificent view from the Vancouver stage over the crowd, the boats, the skyline, the mountains, and the sunset.

I was back from New York for eight days when I was scheduled to fly to Denver, August 18, to go to the Rocky Mountain Folks Festival for the first time with Meredith Carson from Swallow Hill. The night I arrived we had a good bottle of wine and a gourmet dinner and then headed the next morning for the festival site by way of Meredith's radio show in Boulder. The festival at Lyons, a fifteen-minute drive from Boulder, was immediately appealing to me. For one thing, it was produced by the Telluride Festival people under the direction of Craig Ferguson, and they were doing everything right. The setting was gorgeous, set back against a rip-

pling stream at the base of a huge bluff. It couldn't be more picturesque. The roster of artists was similar to our festival, and I loved hanging out without any responsibilities and enjoying a festival that was up to my own standards. I wasn't nervous about sound problems or anything. Debby Rose was there from ASCAP, encouraging their early efforts at a songwriters' competition for young artists. I enjoyed, among other things, taking my shoes off and wading in the stream with Ani DiFranco and other performers. At Kerrville I had no time to hang out with my performers, so Lyons was paradise for me.

I was only glad that I hadn't brought my credit card, because the town of Lyons, which has a sports team called the Lions, has an antique shop filled with restored and original condition radios and super heterodynes, all vintages with polished cabinets, big megaphones, super dial controls — all sorts of interesting things to buy.

I was back ten days before our third Wine and Music Festival and settled into my bungalow, "Rod's Retreat," backstage, where I had moved a year before to make my own home. I left Nancylee for my own well-being and clear mind so I could focus on getting us out of bankruptcy. While Nancylee still supported my efforts as producer of the festivals, and we remained good friends, I couldn't live in our ranch house anymore. It was too emotionally and physically cluttered for me. We might have done better as a couple if we'd spent as much time on our marriage as we did on our festivals. Anyway, part of my new freedom was to enjoy watching the Dallas Cowboys on television when my schedule permitted it. And in 1994 the Dallas Cowboys were doing well!

Looking toward the bedroom from the living room of Rod's Retreat. 1996.

— Courtesy Ken Schmidt.

The Wine and Music Festival had the participation of a dozen wineries, and the songwriters came from Canada, Texas, Arkansas, Colorado, New York, Massachusetts, Illinois, California, New Hampshire, Tennessee, and Washington state.

Rick Beresford, Bob Franke, and Dana Cooper hosted the Ballad Tree, and the wine seminars featured Patrick Timponi and four winemakers in "Texas Wines and Pasta" on Saturday, while Sarah Jane English, author of the book *The Wines of Texas*, hosted the Sunday "Texas Sauvignon Blanc" seminar with four more winemakers and their wines.

The evening concerts were all well attended and offered music by Spider John Koerner, Hugh Moffatt, Bryan Bowers, Tom Russell and Andrew Hardin, the Bird Sisters from Ontario, Brave Combo, Walter Hyatt and Champ Hood, Peppino D'Agostino, Cosy Sheridan, Cafe Noir, Iain Matthews, Houston's Commercial Art (the house band for the club at Ruggles Grill), the three Ballad Tree hosts, and nine others.

Italian guitarist Peppino D'Agostino made his home in San Francisco and was a frequent Kerrville performer. He flew back to Italy regularly to tour and to compose film scores.
— Courtesy Darron Spohn.

With David Ball pursuing his Nashville career, Champ Hood (left) and Walter Hyatt, the other two-thirds of Uncle Walt's Band, often played Kerrville as a duo. 1993.
— Courtesy Darron Spohn.

The new festival format and interest in the wine aspect of it were catching on, and one indicator was that the seminars were up from 100 to 150 participants. The crowds were good every day, the wine sales had doubled with more people tasting, and we still retained the intimacy and sincerity that people valued so much in their visits to Quiet Valley Ranch.

I had heard a CD by a woman from Atlanta named Caroline Aiken, and I immediately wanted to hear her in person. I also knew that Atlanta was the home of the Indigo Girls, Don Conoscenti, Pierce

Pettis, and other good musicians, so I planned a five-day trip there the weekend after the festival, and while staying at Don's, we spent every night at Eddie's Attic. I had dinner with Caroline and took in her show at the Attic and the trip was worth it! She would make her Kerrville debut next year.

The balance of September was spent catching up on the ever-present overload of paperwork, a weekend hostel retreat, beginning the research for my book, a Saturday visit to Esther's Follies in Austin, a three-day Texas Travel Summit in San Antonio, and a reception in Austin at the Omni honoring Texas Wine Month.

The second weekend of October, I was in Los Angeles for six days for meetings, visits with old friends, planning for a future concert at UCLA, and to judge the Acoustic Artist of the Year competition for the National Academy of Songwriters at the Troubadour. As a guest of Brett Perkins, I took in the Westwood Street Fair and caught Caroline Aiken at Ghengis Cohen's on Fairfax, where unbe-

*Bryan Bowers of Seattle, generally considered American's
leading autoharp player. 1995.*

— Courtesy John Hatley.

*Carol Elliott from Atlanta moved to Nashville to pursue
her music career and become a full-time writer-performer.
She is seen here playing Kerrville. 1995.*

— Courtesy Ken Schmidt.

lievably I ran into my nephew, Colin Kennedy, Jr.,
and had a good visit.

On my return to Texas, between working on
the Nashville reunion and the music awards, there
was a three-day wine Harvest Festival in Austin at
the Omni and then the Fredericksburg one-day
Wine and Food Festival and lots of weekend
Cowboys games on TV.

For the third Kerrville Nashville reunion at the
Bluebird, I came to Nashville for a few days, staying
at Carol Elliott's home. She had been one of the
1994 New Folk finalists, who, while not one of the
six winners, impressed me as having a lot to offer,
and I included her in the Bluebird line-up, reaffirm-
ing my initial impression of her. Carol was dating
Buddy Mondlock and there was a chance to spend
some time with him.

The evening's songwriters at our 9:30 Bluebird
concert included, in addition to Carol, Michael
Camp, Alan Rhody, Bob Cheevers, Mike Lille, Jana
Stanfield, Mike Williams, the Cantrells from
Montana, Rick Beresford, Caroline Aiken who
came in from Atlanta, Tom Kimmel, and Dana
Cooper. Jana was joined on stage by Karen Taylor-
Good as a surprise guest.

It was, as before, a full house, and we all
enjoyed the music and each other thoroughly as we
adjourned to Perkins for our midnight breakfast.

One of our guests at the Bluebird was Lydia
Hutchinson, who was working days and nights and
weekends to make her new magazine, *Performing
Songwriter*, work. She is a good person who is thoroughly dedicated to her magazine that focused, for
the most part, on the kind of writers who might be
found at Kerrville. In fact, our festival and many of
our performers were already covered in the magazine from time to time. I felt that this magazine
with its attractive, well-organized, and easily read
format and interesting photos could be a major tool

in creating the kind of public acceptance that all of us had sought for our kind of music. Having Lydia as part of our family (she introduced the magazine at Kerrville) was a real treat for all of us.

Mid-November I was in Miami for four days for the national meeting of the American International Hostels, returning on the 7th to finalize our Kerrville Music Awards weekend. The awards this year would again be held in the lovely ballroom of the Texas Federation of Music Clubs, Floyd Domino played for the reception, Michael Elwood and Beth Galiger provided the music for the dinner, and Christine Albert and Jimmy LaFave cohosted the awards show.

Jimmy LaFave, Tish Hinojosa, and Butch Hancock were all double winners, with Butch Hancock winning Songwriter of the Year, and the Spirit of Kerrville Award going to Peter Yarrow. Peter was also inducted into our Hall of Fame along with Guy Clark and the late Gamble Rogers and Kenneth Threadgill.

The Austin Lounge Lizards at the 1994 Kerrville Music Awards.

— Courtesy Ken Schmidt.

Among the entertainers in 1994 were the Austin Lounge Lizards, Trout Fishing, Peter Rowan, and Caroline Aiken.

The next night, in place of the previous year's high-cost New Folk reunion, we scheduled a very successful songwriters' circle at Butch Hancock's Lubbock or Leave It Gallery on Brazos Street. The circle, hosted by Brett Perkins, included Caroline Aiken, Sarah Elizabeth Campbell, Dana Cooper, and Michael Fracasso.

The following night's Kerrville Christmas Reunion, Saturday, December 3, at the 6th and Lamar Waterloo Ice House, was, as always, a cheerful and appreciative crowd who went through our Nutcracker Cake and hot cinnamon apple cider well before midnight. Lindsay Haisley, Allen Damron, Tim Henderson, and Bobby Bridger were among the players.

The following week Dalis Allen and I made a quick five-day trip to New York to unwind and attend a benefit that Peter Yarrow was hosting at his home.

The year was over and we didn't look back. There was so much to look forward to in 1995, including our first Folk Cruise of the Caribbean.

I found it good luck to arrive in New Orleans on Friday, the 13th of January, as I was able to get dinner reservations at Susan Spicer's excellent restaurant, Bayona, for wine and a sumptuous dinner the night before embarking on the *Enchanted Seas* with Trout Fishing in America, Christine Albert, Paul Glasse, Mitch Watkins, and Ernie Gammage.

We had shipboard concerts the three days we were at sea, and our ports of call were Playa del Carmen, Cozumel, Grand Cayman, and Jamaica. We had outside state rooms for everyone, and the Commodore Cruise Line hosted a wine reception for us. Mitch Cox, our cruise broker from Orlando, accompanied us, and we really enjoyed the week of port hopping in the western Caribbean. Most of our group of eighty had never been on a cruise before and were already asking when the next cruise was before we returned to port at New Orleans. We did ask Mitch to reserve the same weekend for us on the Enchanted Seas next January. Cruising was a far cry from the year when we listened to most of our music at Folk Aid concerts!

With 1995 well under way, we dug into the business of our new season. With our annual financial review with Tom Frost III of San Antonio's Frost Bank behind us, sponsorship renewals by both Southwest Airlines and Whole Foods were approved and we approached our twenty-fourth season optimistically.

The regular meetings, chamber music concerts, and wine events that had become so much a part of my life, continued upon returning from the cruise along with the scheduled calender of step-by-step preparations for our new season.

In mid-February I headed for Mike Martini's home in Napa Valley for a short visit on my way up to Portland, Oregon, for the February 16-18 Folk Alliance meeting. Every year at these meetings Pete Seeger would ask me, "Where's that book about that fella down in Texas who keeps doing that folk festival when there's no money in it?"

I finally conceded to Pete that for the past two years I had been getting my files into chronological order so I could tell the story he wanted to hear. Many times during the throes of locating, hauling, and reorganizing files, I have thought of Pete and wondered if getting ready to write *his* book was this complicated.

A week after getting back from the enriching experience of being with so many people whose love of music matched mine and whose creativity drove me on, I was back on the road for a four-stop, three-day press tour.

We were announcing our season and our co-sponsorship while also distributing press kits. The U.S. Mail and UPS covered the rest of the nation for us.

We traveled with bassist Jeff Haley, Bobby Bridger, Buddy Mondlock, and Sarah Elizabeth Campbell, and were introducing newcomers Carol Elliott and the legendary Dave Mallet, whose seventeen-year career had produced nine albums. Now he was going to make his Kerrville debut in May, and I wanted some people to hear him in advance of that appearance.

We played a one-hour press party at noon in San Antonio at Whole Foods Market on Friday and then drove to Houston to play the Java Java coffeehouse on West 11th, where we ate a late dinner after the show. They really took good care of us! The next day we drove to Dallas for an 8:00 P.M. to midnight show at Poor David's Pub. Back to Austin on Sunday to wind up the press announcement concerts at the Cactus Cafe, where we played a three-hour 8:00 show. It was a real hoot being back with the music and the crowds.

After getting Carol, Buddy, and Dave Mallet to the airport on Monday for flights back to Nashville, I stayed in Austin for a hostel board meeting that night and then returned to the ranch the next day.

Among other things on my agenda was a Kerrleaders' retreat back in Austin on Saturday, March 11, with about twenty-five of our top volunteer staff so we could go through an extended list of considerations. It included a "yes" or "no" vote on whether to go to twenty-five days or not in 1996 for our twenty-fifth festival. They voted "yes!" We also talked about the new campground parking rules and

were pleased to learn from our traffic crew that the new policy had opened up 630 additional campsites last year and that with 30,000 attending the festival over the eighteen days, we never had to close the front gate to turn anyone away as we had in the past.

We also formalized the "land rush" that we began last year. People, including staff, had been moving onto the ranch earlier and earlier before the festival each year to set up camp. We couldn't mow, we couldn't work or spray for insect control, and customers arriving early on the first day were finding the campgrounds half-full with all the best spots taken. Also, our public liability coverage didn't start until the day before the festival began. So, we established the 12:00 noon "land rush" on the Sunday before the festival. With insurance in place and all of the campground preparations completed early, the official "land rush" was ready to roll. All approved staff and those holding at least a three-day ticket starting the first day were allowed early admission for a token daily fee. We had several hundred cars, trucks, bikes, and motorhomes lined up all over the parking lot waiting for the flag to drop, and, on cue, they were off to find their little bit of paradise!

We also established the "volunteer-of-the-year" award, talked about the internet, reset breakfast hours for the volunteers, discussed the continuing construction of a new staff kitchen, made plans to extend the official staff camping area backstage, announced the new gourmet coffee booth, and talked about first aid, insect control (fireants), and several dozen other areas that needed changing, improvement, or clarification. The amount of thought, planning, and energy put into the festival by the volunteers was phenomenal!

The next week, the 1995 edition of SXSW was back, and I managed to participate for a few days. Then, on the weekend, I met members of my staff back at the ranch for the annual cedar clearing. The remainder of the month included Austin hostel meetings, an annual physical, a chamber music Salon concert, and the Texas Hill Country Wine and Food Festival ending on April 2. That week, there was a Beringer wine dinner at Kerrville's Cowboy Steak House, and the next day began four days of New Folk listening. This year the entries were up to 764 from forty-four states and four Canadian provinces. I decided halfway through the screening that next year I was going to limit the number of accepted entries to the first 600, and return or refuse the rest. There is a factor of diminishing returns after listening four days, and my ears were becoming battle-fatigued. But I was especially pleased and impressed with the quality of what we received and looked forward to hearing the thirty-two finalists in person.

The last weekend of April we returned to Miller Outdoor Theatre in Houston with concerts that included Dave Mallet, Jimmy LaFave, Erik Hokkanen and the Snow Wolves, and Houston's Rounder Records artist Kimberly M'Carver. It gave me an opportunity to tell the large Houston audiences about our 24th festival a month away, give them brochures, and answer their questions while personally enjoying the evenings with the performers. With corporate sponsorships increased, we were now distributing almost 120,000 brochures in advance of the festival.

During this year, we were getting an increasing number of reports of the seriousness of Bob Gibson's illness. At first we were told that he had Parkinson's Disease, but a later and more thorough diagnosis revealed that he had Super Nuclear Palsy. Regardless of what they called it, he was now unable to play guitar and his ability to undertake normal daily tasks was deteriorating. While he was getting good home care, he still needed a powered wheel chair to get around. We talked with Peter Yarrow about the need, and he offered to do a tribute concert to Bob on May 31, Peter's birthday.

During April, I had a meeting with two of the administrators of libraries at The University of Texas where my career archives were on deposit. Many years before, I had been asked for my papers and had delivered many boxes dealing with theatrical events to the Hoblitzelle Collection and many more boxes of files on my music events to the Texas Music Collection of the Center for American History. Now, in preparing my own files for my book, I was running up against huge gaps in my records. All of the gaps could be filled by digging through files found and researched at these two collections plus the extensive microfilm files at the Travis Country Collection of the Austin Public Library.

Over the past several years I had telephone discussions with a former CBS Record executive who retired at thirty and was setting up his own small label. It seems he wanted to release CD compilations of earlier Kerrville LPs and cassettes. Murray Krugman had the production and marketing knowhow to get these past recordings out and also wanted to release our new documentary recordings on

his new Silverwolf label starting with 1995. He also wanted to upgrade the recording quality by going direct to DAT (digital audio tape). We worked out a partnership between Murray and the Kerrville Music Foundation where fifty percent of the profits, after production expenses, would go to the foundation, and we went right to work to get the first release out in time for the festival. It would be a ten-CD set of highlights from 1982 to 1991 called *The Ten Great Years of Kerrville*. The limited edition of 400 sets sold out immediately and provided cash flow for preparing the more expensive commercially distributed 1995 CDs. We were going to release, as soon as we could after the festival, a 1995 highlights CD and a favorite project of mine, what I hoped to be Volume One of "The Women of Kerrville." Murray was easy to work with, and we moved rapidly ahead to record about sixty artists' performances to select from at the 1995 festival.

The previous year, AT&T told us we answered over 3,900 calls on our 800 number during May, and in 1995 it appeared that we would exceed that number. Also in May this year, there were three more work weekends, following the one in April, plus all of the expected pre-festival chores and interviews. Even with this workload, however, I did manage to make use of one of my Houston business trips to attend an invitation-only special tasting of Italian wines hosted by the Italian Trade Commission at Houston's Hyatt Regency Hotel. It was an impressive array of excellent wines and tasty bites of good things to go with them. A week later, I was helping to conduct our volunteer meeting the night before the May 25 first concert of our festival.

As the twenty-fourth festival began, Anne Hills hosted the Ballad Tree and played that night's opening concert with Michael Camp, the first artist to perform. He was followed by John Smith, Jana Stanfield, Erik Hokkanen in his best fiddle form. Tom Russell and Andrew Hardin closed. The opening night crowd was larger than ever before, and we could feel a big festival coming on.

A nice touch in the theater this year was the new Cafe Aroma with its cafe latte, cappuccino, and other gourmet coffee drinks made from freshly ground imported beans. There was always a congenial line waiting for service in front of the booth. The purveyors, who were actually, in real life, wholesalers of imported coffees and cappuccino machines, were happily serving retail customers for the first time.

Tom Kimmel was back on our stage, after last year's warm reception, on the Friday night concert along with England's energetic Rory McLeod, the delightful Cheryl Wheeler, who made hilarious introductions to each of her songs, and Bill Morrisey, making his folk festival debut just before High Noon's rocking closing set.

The Saturday and Sunday New Folk concerts, now trimmed to thirty-two finalists, were an especially rewarding time for me each year, and again I was impressed by the songs the judges were concentrating on so intently. The three of them, Michael Camp, Anne Hills, and Atlanta's Pierce Pettis, chose as their winners Barbara Kessler (W. Roxbury, MA), Joel Rafael (Bonsall, CA), Susan Piper (Huntington Valley, PA), Tim Bays (Nashville), George Wurzbach (Brooklyn), and Dan Merrill (Portland, ME) I also liked Martin Sexton and Leslie Tucker among the other finalists.

The children's concerts were again standing-room only, with happy crowds enjoying Rory McLeod's harmonica antics, the award-winning performances of Trout Fishing in America, Katherine Dines of Nashville, and the jug band music of Sadie Green Sales.

Saturday and Sunday night's concerts, with near-capacity crowds both nights, were amazing! Receiving incredible response were newcomers Dar Williams, Ellis Paul, Kelly Willis, and Susan Werner. Denver's Stephen Allen Davis caught everyone's attention with songs like "Highway," and Tom Prasada-Rao was a big hit as well. Trout Fishing in America earned its normal riotous response, and closing sets by Jimmie Dale Gilmore on Saturday and Jimmy LaFave on Sunday substantially helped Austin's reputation for being a home to remarkable performers. Two huge nights, back-to-back, also proved again the wisdom of our campground policies and the extensive advance planning and forethought by our parking and traffic volunteers.

Shabbat services on Saturday and Chapel Hill Folk Mass services on Sunday had impressive turnouts as well.

The Monday blues project found me hosting in Steve James' absence and enjoying being up close with Dave McKenzie, California's Del Rey, and Cape Cod's Les Sampou, a 1994 New Folk winner.

Monday's concert with David Buskin, Cliff Eberhardt, the Cafe Noir quintet, and Bobby

Dar Williams making her Kerrville debut. 1995.
— Courtesy Ken Schmidt.

Tom Prasada-Rao of Takoma Park, MD, won New Folk and became a Kerrville main stage favorite. 1995.
— Courtesy Merri Lu Park.

Philadelphia's Susan Werner was studying opera when she first heard Nanci Griffith and thought, "I'd rather do that." 1995.

— Courtesy Ken Schmidt.

Bridger, was a nice way to taper off an immense weekend.

Our staff always enjoyed midweek, when attendance was down from the massive weekends. Of particular interest this year were the sundown concerts

Bob Gibson listens to his tribute concert from his wheelchair. 1995.

— Courtesy Mary Jane Farmer.

that included Bob Gibson's tribute concert on Wednesday night hosted by Peter Yarrow as his own birthday present to himself, and having Bob Gibson present in a wheelchair up close to the stage. The event, called the Legends of Folk, was performed by artists who had all had an association with Bob in the past — Josh White, Jr., Tom Paxton, Allen Damron, Anne Hills, Michael Smith, and, of course, Peter Yarrow. Between donations and the raffle of one item from every crafts vendor collected by Native American Nantiki Rose, who also sold most of the tickets, we were able to provide Bob with a demonstration of our regard for him, and a $2,500 motorized wheelchair. Nantiki Rose was just one of the many loving people who were such an important part of the festival. It is her beaded Indian bracelet I always wear on my right wrist.

Sometimes when I get carried away by how important the music is, the other facets of the festival are overlooked momentarily. For Nancylee, I think, some of the hallowed places on the ranch were what meant a lot to her. She actually wrote on one occasion,

> The Festival to me is Chapel Hill and the Ballad Tree, the Council Tree, Serenity Corner, and the staff circle where all may share. It's the sense of community among the songwriters as they collect and the way musicians resonate in each other's presence. It is the spontaneous rescue of tents in a storm and reaching out to an isolated woman on crutches. It's the memorial trees that carry the names of those they honor. And it is that special nurturing which inspired the song, "Tiny Piece of Paradise."

There were two songwriting schools in 1995 — the regular session during the three-day break with Anne Hills, Paul Reisler, Tom Paxton, and Michael Smith joining with Rick and Dick, and the second midweek's more advanced session, a one-on-one school with personal attention from Rick and Dick plus Eliza Gilkyson, Peter Rowan, Steve Seskin, Kevin Welch, and Mike Williams. I sometimes think that the opportunity to be closely working with these artists in a small group is almost as important as what they were teaching. How many people have this opportunity in their lives?

The second weekend's concerts also reflected my attempt to find more women for the festival's main stage as I introduced Catie Curtis, Iris Dement, Vicki Pratt Keating, and Caroline Aiken, all as new Kerrville artists joining some of the more famous regulars. Among the many popular returnees were Tom Paxton, Bill and Bonnie Hearne, and Eliza Gilkyson, and on the closing night, Peter Yarrow, Limpopo, and the Austin Lounge Lizards.

Another rousing moment on the weekend was the festival main stage performance by The Billys, who had worked their way up from guest spots, children's concerts, and a sundown concert, where I asked the audience if The Billys should go to the main stage this year. My ears rang for weeks afterward!

The Billys had also played the children's concerts again this year with Damron, Gayle Ross, and Limpopo.

Another pivotal moment was that of the Atlanta Campfire at Threadgill Theater hosted by Don Conoscenti (who attended his first Kerrville as a sideman for the Billys), where Caroline Aiken and Pierce Pettis made cameo appearances alongside a terrific group of performers from Eddie's Attic.

The Billys augmented on the Kerrville main stage. 1995.
— Courtesy Michael John Young.

The series of sundown concerts during the second midweek began with Mike Williams and his friends Tim Bays, Ellen Britten, and Shug Maudlin, followed by Tuesday's concert with Jabbering Trout of Boston, and finally on Wednesday night Stefan George hosted a Camp Cactus concert by such Tucson-area artists the Mollys, Ron Pandy and Common Folk, and national touring Jamie Anderson. I really felt these "campfire" concerts from various cities were a rewarding experiment. In fact, I asked Stefan George to become the host of the blues project and put Jamie on the future invitations list as a result of this one concert.

On Thursday we instituted a much-requested music business workshop from 10:00 A.M. to 4:00 P.M. by Steve Gillette, Fred Koller, and Jana Stanfield (all of whom had books published on their viewpoints), plus ASCAP's John Briggs from the

Don Conoscenti (left) with The Billys on-stage at Threadgill Theater for the children's concert.
— Courtesy Ken Schmidt.

Townes Van Zandt at Threadgill, his last Kerrville appearance.

— Courtesy Lela Perry.

From left: Chris Webster and Tracy Walton help make Mumbo Gumbo one of the West Coast's most exciting bands. 1995.

— Courtesy Ken Schmidt.

Nashville office. The $48 registration included signed copies of the three books for each student.

That night's final sundown concert, put together by Linda Lowe, a former New Folk and artistic director of Houston's Writers in the Round, placed her on-stage with the unlikely but surprisingly workable combination of David Broza, David Amram, and Townes Van Zandt. It would be the last time many would see Townes, as he died before he could come back to Kerrville.

The closing weekend of the festival was another near-capacity attendance and, again, I introduced new women, Carol Elliott, the two remarkable lead singers of Mumbo Gumbo, and Canadians Lynn Miles and Heather Bishop. The other first-time performers on the slate were Floyd Domino (who had actually appeared on our stage with Asleep at the Wheel in 1974), the Klezmatics from New York, L.A.'s incredible Freeway Philharmonic, and the recording duo of Lowan and Navarro from L.A., whom I had first heard live at the Rocky Mountain Folks Festival. Regulars, proving their staying

Former Chicago New Folk winner, Buddy Mondlock, now a songwriter in Nashville, whose song, "The Kid," was recorded by Peter Paul and Mary.

— Courtesy Darron Spohn.

power yet again, were David Amram, Buddy Mondlock, the Sundogs, and Butch Hancock.

After her set earlier in the festival, Susan Werner wrote from Philadelphia to say,

> there are days i'm just doing my job, and then there are the days when i wake up living out my most beautiful daydream — it was such a pleasure to be on stage at your festival. i enjoyed giving my show so much; your audience is extremely attentive and so ready to be entertained and moved, i'm still a little high from it all. it must be very satisfying for you to put together shows and to watch the music go out to people. thanks so much, for inviting me to be part of that.

I, too, savored the moments Susan recalled, but I also recalled the first time I heard her at a Folk Alliance showcase at the invitation of Philadelphia's Gene Shay. Susan is a rare gem, and I would never have known her and her enchanted music without Gene's thoughtfulness. In fact, one of the aspects I love most about our "non-commercial" folk world is the willingness of people at every level to be helpful. It brings out the best in us all!

My after-festival break was in cool Colorado at the Aspen Food and Wine Festival for five days with Mike and Jacque Martini and many other friends in the wine industry.

July held two significant dates for me. The first was on Saturday night, July 8, when I produced a Kerrville concert in Austin at Symphony Square. Symphony Square's totally remodeled office and complex used to be the old 11th Door club, where I first heard Damron. I've attended many concerts there over the years. The small stage sits behind a moat-like Waller Creek that provides a slight separation between stage and audience, but it works.

I'd been invited to participate by my old jazz friend Mike Mordecai, and for this summer concert series, I selected three artists from out of state who would be fresh to the Austin audience, plus two Texas artists who were very popular in Austin. The out-of-staters were Carol Elliott from Nashville, as well as Michael McNevin and Alisa Fineman, both from California, who were former New Folk, and whose performances comprised the first half of the concert. From Austin I chose Betty Elders, another former New Folk, to open the second half of the concert, and then Houston's Shake Russell and Jack Saunders, one of Texas' most popular duos, to close.

It was a golden opportunity to present five artists in an attractive smoke-free environment. The audience area was filled with hundreds of people in an almost festive picnic atmosphere. The weather was perfect, and with Southwest Airlines' help, we were able to present artists from distant cities to an audience over-exposed to the artists of their own region. It was golden — a golden moment in the middle of the summer with the kind of music that moved me. It was a perfect evening with a chance to see many friends from Austin I hadn't seen in a long time.

The other July happening that didn't turn out the way I expected it, but nonetheless a bright spot on my calendar, was the trip with Dalis Allen to Orlando to watch the launch of my astronaut friend Dave Walker's fifth and final space mission, which was canceled when high winds and driving rains caused NASA to move the space shuttle away from the gantry and put it back in its protective hanger until the weather subsided.

Since we were in Orlando, and I knew Disney's vice-president of entertainment, I called Ron Severini, and we met for lunch to catch up on the news and swap artist recommendations. At lunch he presented me with a pair of passes and an invitation for Dalis and me to visit all of the Disney properties as his guest. For the next three days, like a couple of kids, we stood in every line of every attraction, often dressed in our yellow Mickey Mouse ponchos to ward off the continuing rains, until we had seen everything we could at every Disney attraction. It was a totally different and fascinating experience to see how this entertainment giant really works. Thousands of people were loving it as they had for decades, in spite of the rains.

While we were in Orlando, we also spent an afternoon at the aviation museum, where they were restoring World War II aircraft, and I fell in love with a totally restored bright red 1934 Waco biplane. I have always wanted to fly one!

I managed to get home for a little over a week, and was then off on my scheduled flight to the Edmonton Folk Festival in Canada. It was another special experience of being with lovely people, enjoying exceptional hospitality, and having plenty of hanging out time with performer friends. I also reconnected with Wyckham Porteous, who had taught one of my songwriter schools. Christine Albert introduced him to Jimmy LaFave, who became Wyck's album producer and generated a hot new CD for him. On getting back together with

Wyck at Edmonton, I asked him to play the main stage at Kerrville and he accepted.

Back home for just four days, I quickly headed back up in the air again aiming toward Denver and the Rocky Mountain Folks Festival at Lyons with Meredith Carson.

During that festival, I had an especially long personal visit with Nanci Griffith catching up, talking about old times and mutual friends. Before it was over, she let me know that she would like to come to the twenty-fifth birthday Kerrville Folk Festival next year, and if possible, bring her Blue Moon Orchestra. Everything that happened at Lyons seemed to be good, and I've never regretted going up there — to relax, see old friends, and to listen to the kind of music I present as a festival producer.

The fourth annual Kerrville Wine and Music Festival, on September 1-3, was my first opportunity to have both Vance Gilbert and Martin Sexton on

Vance Gilbert from Boston, playing at Kerrville. 1996.
— Courtesy Merri Lu Park.

our main stage. I had admired both artists for a long time, but our long waiting list had delayed their engagement to perform with us. I'm glad I didn't wait any longer. Both have mastered their craft and are able to reveal themselves in stunningly artistic ways, drawing their audiences to them like magnets. They are each able to take us completely out of ourselves. And both received loving responses from the crowd who bought every CD the two had brought with them. I wondered why these guys were not on every major festival in the nation. Within a year, though, they would be. After their appearances, I immediately confirmed each of them for my anniversary festival and couldn't wait to spring them on an unsuspecting public.

There were many other rewarding moments at the festival — the afternoon with Emily Kaitz and the Therapy Sisters, the main stage appearance by Dave Moore from Iowa, Cafe Noir, Jon Ims, Carol Elliott, Betty Elders, Christine Albert, the fifteenth anniversary appearance of Hickory Hill bluegrass band (whose members had met at our ranch fifteen years ago that weekend), and Martin Simpson and the Band of Angels, including Alisa Fineman.

Dallas-based classical Gypsy jazz quintet, Cafe Noir. 1995.

Susan Dunn was back from the Texas Department of Agriculture to lead our panel on "Texas Wines and Mexican Food," and Sarah Jane English guided the seminar on "Texas Merlots and Morsels." Each seminar had four winemakers on their panel. Attendance this year at each seminar was 200! The limited seating (and supply of complimentary wines to be tasted) required that we now get advance reservations. We also required that everyone have a festival wine glass, as it is impossible to tell anything worth knowing about wine when it is consumed out of a plastic cup.

That year, the festival came solidly into its

Kerrville Festivals volunteer staff coordinators Bobby Peele (left) and Vaughn Hafner.

own. Every concert and event was well-attended by people who loved what they received.

September held for me four ground schools as I began to accrue some flying knowledge in the event I could ever get back to Orlando and grab hold of the joystick of that Waco biplane. There were also meetings of both the hostel and Salon concerts boards and a four-day meeting in Amarillo of the Texas Tourist Industry Association.

But I was really looking forward to the first week in October when Peppino D'Agostino and I flew to Rome for week. I loved Rome and Anzio, and especially Assisi, with its walled city and the simple Basilica of St. Francis. I loved the Italian people, the art, the lifestyles, the countryside, and Peppino's sold-out concert. I wanted to go back some day, especially after Peppino and I, on our last night in Rome, attended a concert by Pavarotti at the Academy of St. Cecilia.

When I returned to Texas, I made a scheduled trip to Lubbock to the Llano Estacado Winery to help evaluate their harvest festival, took in a Salon

Concert in Austin, returned to Austin for Jimmy LaFave's "Austin City Limits" taping on October 17, and worked out a renewal of Whole Foods' sponsorship for our 1996 season. Two weeks later, to the day, Schlotzsky's Deli, with 500 stores, confirmed that they'd like to join the sponsorship lineup at the corporate level, on par with Southwest Airlines and Whole Foods Markets, to celebrate the twenty-fifth birthday of their company, Southwest Airlines, and our festival — a triple birthday year. We thought that was a terrific idea and immediately added all their cities to our press list. Peter Yarrow and I really had something to celebrate when we met in San Antonio for dinner on November 1.

The next morning I flew out for Michigan and John Lamb's three-day songwriters retreat up the peninsula at Harbor Springs. These intimate seminars, in a beautiful, rural atmosphere, were always a rewarding experience and involved working with a group of aspiring songwriters and a handful of our own accomplished artists.

I flew directly from Detroit to Nashville for our reunion at the Bluebird, where I had the pleasure of presenting to a full house Tim Bays, Michael Lille, Jana Stanfield, Steve Key, Dana Cooper, Karen Taylor-Good, Michael Johnson, Tom Kimmel, Carol Elliott, Hugh Moffatt, Gail Davies, Rick Beresford, Michael Camp, and surprise guest Alan Rhody.

By now, our reunion party after the gig had grown to larger proportions with Texas wines shipped in for a reception, buffet, and picking party at Jule's Restaurant at Cummins Station. Our excuse was that we were actually celebrating our twenty-fifth birthday.

Although I had to miss Dave Walker's launch in Florida and his later completed mission, he was back on the ground for Thanksgiving, and I spent the day with him and his friends. Dave and his fiancé, Page, had been coming to the folk festival with the Mike Martinis for several years, and while we couldn't get Mike back to Texas for the November 30 Kerrville Music Awards, we did get Dave Walker back as a presenter and a guest at my table.

The 1995 Kerrville Music Awards had Lindsay Haisley playing the music for the reception where we unveiled Mary Doerr's watercolor of our *Outdoor Theater at Dusk*, commissioned for the Silver Anniversary poster. At the dinner, Bill and Bonnie Hearne provided the music, and the awards show was co-hosted by Tish Hinojosa and Kevin

Kate Wallace, myself, and Lucinda Williams at the Bluebird Cafe in Nashville. 1995.
— Courtesy Gail Davies.

Nashville songwriter Tom Kimmel at Kerrville. 1994.

Welch, with Jimmy LaFave winning Songwriter of the Year. Robert Earl Keen won three awards, including admission to the Hall of Fame. Three artists won their categories for the third consecutive year — Trout Fishing in America for Duo of the Year, Erik Hokkanen for Instrumentalist of the Year, and Tish Hinojosa for Community Service. Bill and Bonnie Hearne's winning the Spirit of Kerrville Award was a popular choice with the crowd that, in this third year of the awards, had filled the ballroom to capacity.

The next night we presented the second annual Song Writers Circle at Lubbock or Leave It with Christine Albert hosting. Her other writers were Tim Henderson, Iain Matthews, Don Conoscenti, and Paul Sanchez.

The Kerrville Music Foundation Awards weekend concluded with our thirteenth annual Kerrville Christmas Reunion at Waterloo with Allen Damron, Betty Elders, Emily Aronson, Lindsay Haisley, Kimberly M'Carver, Turk Pipkin, Don Conoscenti, and Emily Kaitz. This event always left us filled with good feelings.

Our early scheduling of the awards weekend left us four full weeks in December to get a good running start on our twenty-fifth anniversary season, and we had plenty to do to get ready for the twenty-five-day folk festival and all of the other special events for 1996.

We were grateful that the most time-consuming event of January was the second Folk Cruise of the Caribbean, January 13-20, out of New Orleans. Trout Fishing in America was our anchor (sorry) group, along with Michael Elwood and Beth Galiger, and The Billys. The cruise on the Enchanted Isle took eighty of us to Cozumel, Grand Cayman, and Montego Bay, Jamaica. Our concerts were on the three days at sea, and we had our group of eighty, plus a few people who wandered into the theater. The second concert had 160 people and the third one, when the word got around the ship, was overflowing. The food and the service were excellent, and the whole experience was revitalizing!

On January 30 Happy Shahan died. This was the passing of a man who helped me find the belief in myself that he had for me so that I could deal with some of the early financial pressures of keeping the festival together. Those problems don't seem so insurmountable now, but in that time I thought they were overwhelming. I will always remember Happy fondly and with continuing admiration.

Our 1996 press tour, February 7-11, allowed us an early start at promoting the four-week-long anniversary festival. The tour was by six original 1972 Kerrville performers — Allen Damron, Carolyn Hester, Bobby Bridger, Bill and Bonnie Hearne, and Ray Wylie Hubbard. Then I added one of the most exciting of the new artists, 1993 New Folk winner, Tom Prasada-Rao, as special guest.

The tour itself was actually a reunion. We had not all been together at the same time in the same place since 1972. Allen Damron was living in Austin, Bridger was in Houston, Carolyn Hester flew in from Los Angeles, Bill and Bonnie came down from Santa Fe, and Hubbard drove in from Poetry, Texas. Even our special guest had to fly in from Washington, D.C.

On the first day of the tour, Wednesday, we played the press party at Whole Foods in Austin at 1:00 P.M. and the Cactus Cafe at 8:00. The next day at 2:00 P.M, we were at San Antonio's Whole Foods and at 8:00 that night at Cibolo Creek Country Club. On Friday, we drove to Houston to play the Shepherd Whole Foods store at 1:00 P.M. and then went over to Rice University to set up at Hammond Hall for an 8:00 P.M. concert co-sponsored by Linda Lowe's Writers in the Round. Saturday saw us on the road to Dallas to play the Greenville Avenue Whole Foods Market at 3:00 P.M. and, after checking in at our hotel, played Poor David's Pub at 9:00 P.M. On Sunday we arose early enough to take Damron, Bridger, and Carolyn Hester to Kerrville to play a press party/concert at Inn of the Hills at 4:00 that afternoon.

We were joyfully announcing the triple-anniversary sponsorship by Southwest Airlines-Whole Foods Market-Schlotzsky's Deli, and the 150-performer, twenty-five-day anniversary folk festival.

One of the stories we were able to tell on the tour was of Radio ATL, Bree, Belgium, where broadcaster Raymond Swennen had a radio show called "Kerrverted Feeling," where he played Cosy Sheridan, Ray Wylie Hubbard, Jimmie Dale Gilmore, Hickory Hill, Kate Wolf, Chuck Pyle, Anne Hills, and other Kerrville artists to listeners in three countries.

Another letter we received was from David Broza written on the road:

I find myself playing some of the most fascinating remote locations in the world, yet I'll be selling the people on the festival where the music never stops.

So the show is over at 1:00 a.m., but that's when we all get charged up, and ready to roll around the seductive fires spread throughout the campgrounds. We musicians join accountants on guitars, chiropractors on bass and attorneys on banjo.

May another four generations enjoy and carry the song!

A week after the tour, with response already pouring in from all over the state, we had finished shipping 500 packets of 100 brochures to 500 locations and also a couple of hundred packets of 300 brochures to Texas clubs, record shops, music stores, tourist information bureaus, and other target locations, when it was time to leave for Folk Alliance in Washington, D.C. February 15-18. As usual, Pete Seeger approached me about the book, and I told him I'd already written the first chapter and would get him a copy in the mail. Again, the alliance was the best networking opportunity I've experienced with literally hundreds of people congratulating me on our forthcoming twenty-fifth anniversary, or asking me if I was serious doing a twenty-five-day folk festival. I thought at the time, "If I'm not serious about it now, I'd better *get* serious."

And I did get serious a week later after returning home, where I met Bobby Peele, Vaughn Hafner, and eighteen staff leaders in Ingram, just outside Kerrville, to head off any problems that we hadn't considered. The meeting was friendly, enthusiastic, and thorough, and we came away from it feeling ready for anything. I did continue to attend Salon Concerts but skipped SXSW and resigned from the board of the Austin International Hostel with regret, but something had to go. I needed time to deal with the combined work load of starting my book and dealing with the complexities of the anniversary year.

Aside from staying very busy, we didn't really have any problems, and even with the UCLA concert coming up the next week, I still made two days of the Hill Country Easter Ride, but because of the concert, I missed the Hill Country Wine and Food Festival.

The concert was on Saturday, April 13, at Veterans Wadsworth Theater. Our troupe was headlined by David Wilcox with Eliza Gilkyson,

Sara Hickman, and Tom Prasada-Rao. After the concert, which drew about half a house of solid fans, we had a brief party at Schlotzsky's nearby, and the next day headed for home.

Two weeks later, we were into the first of four work weekends to get the theater and all of the other ranch facilities fixed up and painted for our twenty-five-day birthday party. In the middle of our second weekend, we were devastated to learn that Walter Hyatt was aboard the Valujet that crashed into the Florida Everglades, killing all 110 on board. We didn't know what to do, and we were all numb. But with Champ Hood's help, we were able to schedule a memorial concert for Walter during the festival with a number of his friends playing.

The festival opened appropriately with our first director, Allen Damron, hosting the Ballad Tree. For that night's birthday party concert, we presented a reunion of 1972 original performers with several surprise guests. We had sent VIP invitations to several hundred officials, area suppliers, fans, and press, and during the course of the concert, Allen Damron cut our huge birthday cake and helped serve it to the crowds who gathered for a ceremonial bite.

The reunion concert itself opened with Allen Damron, Carolyn Hester, and Steven Fromholz. Then we took a break for the cake-cutting ceremony that was accompanied by an Indian flute solo by Sky Walkinstik man alone. The entire cake disappeared rapidly, and we returned our attention to the main stage and continued the music with Bill and Bonnie Hearne, Ray Wylie Hubbard, a surprise

Jerry Jeff Walker (left) visits with his old friend, Allen Damron, backstage before the opening concert of the anniversary festival. 1996.

— Courtesy Ken Schmidt.

Cutting of the twenty-fifth anniversary cake by Allen Damron on Thursday, May 23, 1996, during the reunion of 1972 original performers.

— Courtesy Ken Schmidt.

Michael Martin Murphey onstage for the anniversary reunion, seen here with his son Ryan. 1996

— Courtesy Ken Schmidt.

Oklahoman Kevin Welch, at home in Nashville since 1978, found another home at the Kerrville Folk Festival, playing there in 1993, 1994, and 1996.

—Courtesy Merri Lu Park.

Considered by many to be Europe's finest white exponent of country blues, Hans Theesink was born in the Netherlands and now resides in Vienna, Austria, with his wife Melica. 1996.

— Courtesy Merri Lu Park.

guest set by Jerry Jeff Walker backed by Bob Livingston and John Inmon. Bobby Bridger was next and then Michael Martin Murphey. It was a nostalgic concert in many ways, but in others it was very "today," as all of these artists were still full-time performers and still writing good songs, as it appeared they would continue to do for many years. The singing of the festival anthem at the end of the evening with Bobby Bridger leading everyone had deep sentimental and spiritual meaning for all of us.

I had deliberately produced a night-by-night line-up that, within each evening, would provide insight into what a single typical night at Kerrville should be. Writing here for you, I'll touch on a number of significant moments in the festival, but, obviously, it would be a major undertaking to touch on every one of the 150 sets.

The first five-night weekend schedule should be remembered for some of these moments — appearances by Tim Bays, RST, Joel Rafael, Barbara Kessler, Vance Gilbert and Celeste Krenz, the reunion of Ernie Sky and the K-Tels and the Mighty Big Horns, the return to Kerrville of Nanci Griffith and the Blue Moon Orchestra, the Monday night return of Robert Earl Keen, the much enjoyed

appearances by Lucinda Williams, Sara Hickman, Gail Davies, and Gary P. Nunn.

Highlights of the second weekend (May 31-June 2) included the first appearance of the Dick Goodwin Quintet, Wyckham Porteous of Victoria, B.C., and Richard Shindell — the return of Cheryl Wheeler, Artie and Happy Traum, Peter Rowan, Kevin Welch, Mumbo Gumbo and Dar Williams, Guy Clark, Peter Yarrow, and Brave Combo.

The third weekend (June 8-10) featured first-time appearances by Carrie Newcomer, Toronto's Cate Frieson, Lucy Kaplansky, The Nields and Ruben Ramos, and Texas Revolution — the return of Riders in the Sky, Jack Gladstone, Patty Larkin, Catie Curtis, Tom Chapin, Pele Juju, Hans Theesink, and Josh White, Jr.

And on the fourth weekend, we added the first appearances of Aztec Two Step, Joyce Woodson, jazz singer Kurt Elling, and the return of Chuck Pyle, Chris Smither, The Limeliters, Bob Franke, Jonathan Edwards, Odetta, the Austin Lounge Lizards, and so many, many more!

The final night, Sunday, was our anniversary fish fry played by Trout Fishing in America, followed by our memorial concert by the Festival Orchestra con-

Guy Clark, a Texas songwriting legend, is in the Kerrville Hall of Fame. 1996.

— Courtesy Ken Schmidt.

With Dar Williams, Razor and Tie recording artist, a tremendously exciting and winning live performer whose early popularity was attributable to the rapid word-of-mouth internet buzz. 1996.

— Courtesy Susan Roads.

ducted by David Amram with Megan Meisenbach, flute. The seventeen-member orchestra, playing Dick Goodwin arrangements, accompanied the following performers and their compositions:

- Jimmy LaFave — "Desperate Men Do Desperate Things"
- Christine Albert — "Who You Are"
- Paul Glasse — "Thang"
- A reprise of David Amram's "Theme and Variations on Red River Valley for Flute and Strings," given its world premiere here by this orchestra five years before and now played and recorded all over the world.
- Susan Werner — "Love Looks Like You"
- Trout Fishing in America — "Lullaby"
- David Amram — conducting from the piano and also playing penny whistle on Jerry Jeff Walker's "Mr. Bojangles"
- Christine Albert and Jimmy LaFave — "Come Away With Me"
- Tish Hinojosa — *"Orella de un Sonar"* ("Edge of a Dream")
- David Broza — "She Walks in Beauty"
- Bobby Bridger and company — "Heal in the Wisdom"

The concert was performed in memory of sixteen deceased performers (out of over 560 who have played Kerrville 1972-1996) and twenty-one other "family."

Obviously, there were many other significant moments in and among the eight children's concerts, the blues project, the Detroit Campfire, the staff concert, fourteen sundown concerts, the taping of two more radio shows for "River City Folk," the Dallas Campfire, and five other special concerts, the songwriters' schools (sold out before the program even went to press), the two Shabbat services, the Folk Masses on Chapel Hill, fourteen Ballad Trees, and more unaccountable hours of campfire singing than anyone could or would ever want to count.

There are those who remember fondly Sky Walkinstik man alone and his Indian flute workshop. One of the moments I remember with special warmth was the Threadgill Theater Sundown Concert by Adam and Kris from Los Angeles and the ensuing mayhem amid pleas for a main stage time slot next year (they got it!) — like The Billys'

Tish Hinojosa sings with the Festival Orchestra, conducted by David Amram at the twenty-fifth festival's closing memorial concert. 1996.

— Courtesy Ken Schmidt.

At the 1996 Kerrville Music Awards. From left: John Briggs of ASCAP Nashville, Carol Elliott, Buddy Mondlock, Dar Williams, Tom Paxton, Ray Wylie Hubbard, Casey Monahan of the Texas Music Office of the Governor, and Rod Kennedy.

— Courtesy Lela Perry.

rise to popularity at Kerrville, that was a moment of emotion-filled Kerrville magic.

As David Broza said, "The festival where the music never stops"; and Steve Given writing in *Acoustic Guitar Magazine*, wrote, "Going to Kerrville is a religious experience."

The twenty-fifth festival broke every record for a single day, week and total festival attendance and was a success that saw Tom Frost III and I burning the last of the bank notes on-stage in front of the audience on the last Saturday night of the festival!

In the total scheme of things, big and small, the

Kerrville Folk Festival probably makes an ounce of difference, but, "An ounce of difference is better than a pound of same."

By the end of 1996, with the Wine and Music Festival, Nashville reunion, music awards, and Kerrville Christmas Reunion all behind us, we could count on 1996 as Kerrville's most exciting and successful year.

Then within three weeks, for business reasons of their own, Schlotzsky's did not renew, Southwest Airlines did not renew as part of a fifty percent budget cut, and Whole Foods Market told me "No" for 1997, because the new president for the Southwest had other priorities.

It was like a bad inning in baseball — three up and three down!

I thought, "We've been through worse than this," when the phone rang. It was a nurse calling from the scene of an accident on Highway 16. A truck had swerved into oncoming traffic, and that traffic was Nancylee in her silver Subaru wagon on the way to the bank.

The head-on collision totaled the car, and Nancylee was rushed to intensive care, seriously injured.

On the fourth day of Nancylee's hospitalization, the ranch's water system went out when the pump died 500 feet down in the well.

I knew I should end my book here, and maybe re-title it *Hit or Myth*, the story that begins with a whimper and ends with a bang!

Nancylee's silver Subaru wagon after the December accident on Highway 16. 1996.

— Courtesy Ken Schmidt.

EPILOGUE

The resiliency of the human spirit is remarkable. Life goes on.

In February of 1997 John Spencer of the national marketing team for the new long-life Elixir Guitar Strings from Gore, at the suggestion of Joel Rafael and Cree Clover, selected the Kerrville Folk Festival to launch his company's miraculous product. At the Folk Alliance in Toronto, he signed a full corporate sponsorship for the twenty-sixth Kerrville Folk Festival with a two-year renewal option.

What could we do but continue to re-humanize America one song at a time?

P.S. — Nancylee is still healing in 1998.

P.P.S. — Elixir renewed for 1998, following one of the festival's best seasons, and plans for the twenty-seventh festival are under way.

Setbacks are inevitable, defeat is not.

P.P.P.S. — This Epilogue is actually Chapter 12. We did not want to end this book with a Chapter 11.

Peter Yarrow campfire singing at Camp Cuisine around 2:00 A.M. The PBS television crew was also there.

— Courtesy Alan Pogue.

APPENDIX A

Kerrville Folk Festival Main Stage Performers

(1972-1996)

Adam & Kris
6/5/96
Adcock, Eddie
6/4/88
Aguilar, Annette with Cas/Dupree
6/3/89
Aiken, Caroline
6/7/96 6/3/95
Ain't Misbehavin'
5/25/92
Albert, Christine
6/19/96 6/4/94 5/25/92 5/31/91
6/11/88 6/5/87 5/25/86 5/27/85
Alger, Pat
5/25/87 5/25/86
Allen, Terry
6/12/88 5/31/86 6/2/85
Alsop, Peter
6/11/94 5/26/89 5/29/88
Amram, David
6/16/96 6/9/95 6/9/94 5/29/93
5/23/92 6/9/91 6/8/90 6/4/89
5/27/88 5/21/87 5/26/86 5/26/85
5/27/84 6/5/83 5/31/82 5/30/81
5/23/80 5/26/79 5/28/78 5/30/76
5/28/96 Workshop
Amram, Lora Lee
6/16/96
Andersen, Eric
6/1/86
Armstrong, Ann
5/27/96
Armstrong, Ann with Steve Hughes
6/10/90 5/26/89
Aronson, Emily
6/4/93 5/31/88 5/21/87 5/30/86
6/1/85 5/24/84
Ash Family
5/28/82
Ashman, Lisa
6/2/93
Asleep at the Wheel
5/25/74
Austin Lounge Lizards
6/15/96 6/4/95 6/11/94 5/27/93
6/5/92 6/2/91 5/27/89 6/5/87
6/1/86
Aztec Two-Step
6/14/96
Ball, Marcia
6/9/91 5/27/90 5/24/87 5/22/86
6/2/85 5/28/84 6/5/83 5/27/79
5/27/77
Ball, Tom & Kenny Sultan
5/27/96 6/10/94 6/7/92 6/8/91
Ballew, Michael
6/3/84 5/29/83
Banded Geckos
5/30/92 5/31/87 5/24/86 5/23/85
5/24/84 5/30/83 6/5/82 6/4/82
Barenberg, Rus
5/29/89
Barr, Sherry
6/4/93

Barrett, Dick
5/27/73 6/2/72
Bays, Tim
5/24/96
Bensusan, Pierre
5/26/79
Beresford, Rick
5/28/96 6/4/95 6/2/93 5/22/92
5/26/91 5/28/90 6/4/89 6/9/88
5/30/87 5/30/86 5/31/85 6/3/84
5/30/83 5/29/82 5/21/81 5/26/78
Beto y los Fairlanes
6/10/88 6/3/87 5/28/86 5/31/82
Billys, The
6/2/95 6/1/94 6/12/93 5/26/92
Bird, Tony
6/2/90
Bishop, Heather
6/11/95
Blaker, Clay & the Texas Honky Tonk Band
6/9/96 5/27/93 6/5/88 6/4/87
Bluegrass Ramblers
5/30/76 5/24/74 5/25/73
Bluegrass Review
5/24/75
Bone, Ponty, & the Squeezetones
6/16/96 6/10/94 6/2/91 5/30/90
6/12/88 5/25/87 5/31/86 5/31/85
6/3/84
Book Binder, Roy
5/26/91 6/4/83
Bootfare
6/12/93 6/6/92
Booth, L. J.
6/9/95 5/24/92 5/24/90
Bourne & McLeod
5/25/92
Bowers, Byron
5/31/92 5/26/91 5/25/87
Bradley, Tommie Lee
6/3/90 5/25/89
Brand, Oscar
6/4/88
Brannon, Bow
5/31/91 6/10/90 5/31/89
Brave Combo
6/2/96 6/27/91 6/3/90
Bridger, Bobby
5/23/96 5/29/95 5/27/94 6/11/93
5/23/92 6/9/91 5/24/90 6/2/89
5/30/88 5/30/87 5/26/86 5/25/85
5/24/84 5/23/81 5/25/80 5/25/79
5/27/78 5/26/77 5/30/76 5/23/75
5/25/74 5/24/73
Brothers, Ken
5/24/79 5/25/78
Broudy, Saul
5/30/87 6/5/83
Brown, Gatemouth
5/30/82 5/21/81
Broza, David
6/16/96 6/10/94 6/13/93 6/6/92
Brozman, Bob
5/28/83

Brunelle, Joseph & Theresa
5/29/85 5/31/94 5/25/89
Buskin, David
5/29/95
Cactus Rose
5/24/79
Cafe Noir
5/29/95
Camp, Hamilton
5/28/89
Camp, Michael
5/28/96 5/25/95 6/2/93
Campbell, Courtney
6/3/90 5/25/85 5/25/84 5/26/83
Campbell, Sarah Elizabeth
6/11/95 6/11/93 6/8/91 5/29/90
Campi, Ray
5/31/87
Caribbean Steeltones
5/26/90 5/29/88 5/24/87
Carpenter, Mary Chapin
6/9/89 6/4/88
Carper, Janice
5/29/92
Carroll, Milton
6/2/89 5/25/80 5/25/79 5/26/78
5/28/77 5/27/76
Carter, Jr., Fred
5/27/82
Castleberry-Dupree
6/8/90 6/3/89 6/5/88
Cates, Mickey
5/22/92 5/23/91
Celtic Elvis
6/2/90
Chapin, Tom
6/8/96 5/30/92 6/10/90 6/10/89
6/8-9/96
Chenille Sisters
5/24/96 5/29/94 5/25/91
Christian, Frank
5/26/86
Cicchetti, Stephen (see also Steve James)
5/25/87
Cisneros, Carol
5/23/80 5/29/76 5/25/75
City Folk
6/3/94 6/6/93
Clark, Guy
6/2/96 6/3/88 5/21/87 5/31/86
5/31/85 5/28/84 5/27/83 5/31/81
5/24/80 5/24/79 5/26/78 5/29/77
5/30/76 5/25/75
Clayton, Lee
5/29/96 5/28/96 Workshop
Cleaves, Slaid
5/27/94 5/27/93
Colvin, Shawn
5/26/90
Conoscenti, Don
5/26/96
Cooper, Dana
5/29/96 5/27/95 6/11/93 6/7/92
Cormier, Steve
5/21/87

Country Gazette
6/7/92 6/2/90 6/7/87 5/29/83
CPR
5/26/88 6/7/87 5/26/85
Cross, Mike
5/30/93 5/29/88
Crow, Alvin
6/2/87 5/26/83 5/26/80 5/28/79
5/25/78 5/27/77
Crowell, Rodney with Guy Clark
5/27/83
Cully & Elliott
5/30/94
Curtis, Catie
6/8/96 6/2/95
Curtis, Sonny
5/28/88
Cutean, Brian
5/29/91
D'Agostino, Peppino
6/15/96 6/1/90
Dah-Veed
6/4/95
Dallas Campfire
6/15/96
Dallas County Jug Band
6/4/83
Damron, Allen
5/23/96 5/31/95 5/30/94 6/3/93
6/13/93 5/22/92 5/23/91 5/25/90
6/11/89 6/8/88 5/25/87 5/28/86
5/23/85 5/25/84 6/4/83 6/4/82
5/22/81 5/24/80 5/24/79 5/28/78
5/27/77 5/28/76 5/25/75 5/24/74
5/26/73 6/1-3/72
Danger in the Air
6/9/90 5/28/89
Davies, Gail
5/26/96 5/29/94 5/28/93
Davis, Guy
5/27/96
Davis, Stephanie
5/31/92
Davis, Stephen Allen
5/27/96 5/27/95
Dement, Iris
6/3/95
Denim
5/29/77 5/24/75
Detroit Campfires
6/1/96
Devonsquare
5/28/94 6/6/93
DiFranco, Ani
6/12/94
Dillard, Doug, (Band)
5/25/92
Dinsmore, Rick
5/30/76
Dixie Chicks
6/1/91
Dobson, Richard
5/22/86
Domestic Science Club
6/4/95
Domino, Floyd
6/9/95
Donohoe, Kitty
5/25/87
Dottsy
5/31/82
Driftwood, Jimmy
5/25/81 5/25/80 5/25/79 5/27/78
Durst, James
5/27/82
Eaglebone Whistle
5/28/83 5/25/81
Eaglebone Whistle Reunion
6/6/87
Earle, Steve
5/24/91 6/11/88
Eberhart, Cliff
5/25/95

Edwards, Don
6/4/93
Edwards, Jonathan
6/15/96 5/31/92 6/2/91
Eggleston, Kat
6/11/95 6/11/93 5/30/92
Elders, Betty
5/30/94 6/9/90
Elling, Kurt
6/15/96
Elliott, Carol
6/1/96 6/9/95
Elliott, Ramblin' Jack
6/3/83
Elskes, Tommy with Stephen Doster
5/26/94
Elwood, Michael & Beth Galiger
6/3/94 5/23/92 5/27/91
Ely, Joe
5/25/80 5/25/78
Emery, John & Leroy Preston
5/26/80
Ensle, George
5/29/83 5/27/82
Erik & Erik (Moll & Hokkanen)
6/4/93
Espinoza, Tom & Lorraine Duisit
5/28/89
Everitt, Danny
5/27/77
Ewing Street Times
5/26/74 5/24/73
Festival Big Band with Maryann Price
6/5/93
Fineman, Alisa
6/7/94 6/1/93 5/22/92
Fingerett, Sally
6/14/96
Finlay, Kent
5/31/82
Fisher, Steve
6/12/96
Flor de Cana
6/5/94 6/5/93
Flores, Rosie
5/28/90 6/9/89
Flower, Mary
5/30/94
Follet, Richard Ferrer
6/12/94
Fontenot, Allen
5/22/75
Forehand, Kim
6/3/94
Foster, Rex
6/2/93
Fowler, Vicki
5/31/82
Fracasso (Band), Michael
6/11/96
Franke, Bob
6/15/96 5/22/92 5/26/90 5/29/89
Freeway Philharmonic
6/10/95
Fricke, Janie
6/9/90
Friedman, Judith Kate
5/31/96
Frieson, Kate
6/8/96
Fromholz, Steven
5/23/96 6/13/93 5/27/91 5/27/90
5/25/89 6/7/87 5/24/86 5/28/85
5/24/84 6/5/82 5/21/81 5/22/80
5/27/79 5/27/78 5/29/77 5/28/76
5/23/75 5/25/74 5/24/73 6/3/72
Frummox (Fromholz & McCrimmen)
6/4/83
Frummox Reunion (Fromholz & McCrimmen)
6/5/82
Fry, Segle
5/29/81 5/25/75 6/3/72

Gaines, Ken
5/27/92
Garza (Dah-veed), David
5/27/93 6/6/92
Garza, John
5/29/77
Gerber, Nina
6/9/91
Gerber, Nina with Sarah E. Campbell
6/8/91
Gibson & Camp
5/29/87 5/26/79
Gibson, Bob
5/23/92 6/9/91 5/28/90 6/7/89
6/5/88 5/29/85 5/23/85 5/27/84
5/30/83 6/5/82 5/25/81 5/25/80
Gilbert, Ronnie
6/4/89
Gilbert, Vance
5/25/96
Gilkyson, Eliza
6/1/96 6/4/95 6/6/92 6/2/90
5/26/89 6/10/88 5/27/84 5/27/83
6/5/82 5/31/81
Gillette, Steve & Cindy Mangsen
5/26/94 6/5/93 6/2/91 6/1/90
Gillette, Steve
6/9/89 6/3/88 5/25/87 5/26/85
5/26/84
Gillman, Jane & Darvy Deauville
6/4/96
Gillman, Jane
5/23/91 6/2/88 5/23/87 5/23/86
5/23/85
Gilmore, Jimmie Dale
5/27/95 6/8/91 5/25/90 6/11/89
6/4/88 5/31/86 5/25/85 6/2/84
5/30/83 5/21/81
Gladstone, Jack
6/7/96 6/11/94
Glasse, Paul (sextet)
5/29/94 6/7/92 5/24/91
Glasse, Paul
6/16/96
Glosson, Lonnie
5/26/80
Goodwin, Dick
5/31/96 6/5/93 5/31/94 6/1/94
6/2/94
Gorka, John
6/13/93 6/1/90 6/1/88 5/23/86
5/23/85
Grammer, Red
5/25/90
Graves, Josh & Roanoke
5/29/77
Green, Wayne with Emilie Aronson
6/1/85 5/24/84
Griffith, Nanci
5/26/96 5/27/89 6/3/88 5/30/87
5/25/86 5/25/85 5/25/84 5/30/83
5/30/82 5/25/81 5/25/79
Grimalkin
5/26/84 5/26/83 5/28/82 5/29/82
5/30/82
Guitar Gabriel
5/30/94
Gypsies, The
6/7/91
Haisley, Lindsay
5/27/93 5/25/92 6/1/90 6/2/88
5/22/87 5/25/86 6/2/85 5/26/84
5/30/83 5/29/81 5/24/79
Halley, David
6/11/88 5/25/86 5/26/85 5/26/84
Halley, David w/ Syd Straw
5/29/81
Halley, Hancock, Gilmore &
6/7/87
Hancock, Butch
5/25/96 6/11/95 5/26/94 6/12/93
6/5/92 6/7/91 5/24/90 6/8/89
5/29/88 5/28/86 6/1/86 5/24/85

Mallett, Dave
6/8/96 6/3/95
Maloney, David
6/6/94 6/3/93 5/29/92 6/9/90
Marcoulier, Michael
5/25/80
Marley's Ghost
6/1/91
Marra, Jan
6/12/93 6/6/88 5/26/87 5/24/85
5/24/84
Marshall, Evan
5/31/91 6/11/89 5/28/88
Mason, Richard
5/26/77
Massengill, David
6/2/95 6/11/93 5/21/92
Masters Four
5/25/80 5/26/79
Matthews, Iain
6/7/96
McBride, Laura Lee
5/27/77
McCaslin, Mary
5/31/96
McCaslin, Mary and Jim Ringer
5/24/80
McClinton, Delbert
5/27/78 5/26/77
McColl and Tracey
5/31/89
McCrimmen, Dan
5/24/81 5/25/78 5/27/77 (also see Frummox)
McKinnon, Mark
5/30/76
McLauchlan, Murray
6/11/88
McLeod, Rory
5/26/95 6/8/91 6/5/82
McNevin, Michael
5/27/96 6/5/94 6/4/93
Meek, Charlotte
6/1/95
Meisenbach, Megan
6/16/96 6/9/91
Melanie
6/11/94
Meyers, Augie
5/22/87 5/25/75
Miles, Lynn
6/10/95
Miller, Bill
6/6/93 6/3/89 6/10/88
Miller, Ed
5/28/77
Minus, Rich
5/26/77
Moeller, Dee
5/26/85 5/28/94 5/27/83 6/4/82
5/26/77 5/29/76 5/24/75
Moffatt, Hugh
5/26/89
Moffatt, Hugh and Katy
5/26/91
Moffatt, Katy
6/10/94 6/10/89 5/24/87 5/26/86
Mondlock, Buddy
6/10/95 5/26/89 5/26/88
Montana Slim
5/23/75
Montana, Patsy
5/27/77 5/28/76
Montgomery, Monte and Maggie B.
5/31/82
Montreaux Band, The
6/10/89
Moore, Dave
5/30/94
Morrissey, Bill
5/26/95
Moss, Bill
5/23/81 5/27/76 5/26/74 5/27/73

Mother of Pearl
5/25/78 (see also Plum Nelly)
Muller, Chris
6/1/95
Muller, Heidi
5/31/92
Mumbo Gumbo
6/1/96 6/10/95 5/29/94
Murphey, Michael (Martin)
5/23/96 6/6/82 5/26/73 6/2/72
Murrell, Olin
6/1/95 5/31/94
Mustard's Retreat
5/27/94
Neely, Bill
5/26/86 5/25/84 5/31/81 5/27/76
Neely, Bill with Kenneth Threadgill
5/28/83 6/5/82
Neil and Leandra
6/14/96
Nelson, Tracy
5/28/78
Nelson, Willie
5/24/73
Newcomer, Carrie
6/7/96
Nields, The
6/9/96
Nunn, Gary P.
5/27/96 6/5/94 5/30/93 6/9/91
6/10/90 6/4/88 5/22/87 5/22/86
5/26/85 5/28/84 5/27/83 5/30/82
5/31/81 5/24/80 5/24/79 5/26/78
O'Brien, Tim
5/26/91
O'Kanes
5/26/87
Octave Doctors
5/28/82
Odetta
6/15/96 5/27/93 6/10/88 6/6/87
5/23/86 6/3/84 5/29/82 5/25/81
Oliver, Bill
6/7/90 5/27/85 5/27/84
Oliver, Bill and Glen Waldeck
5/23/91
Olney, David
5/24/91
Olsen, Kristina
5/31/96 6/1/93
Orta, Paul
6/10/96 6/5/82 Harmonica Reunion
Osborne, Riley
5/25/74
Owens, Andy
6/4/94
Paul, Ellis
5/25/96 5/28/95
Paxton, Tom
6/2/96 6/2/95 6/12/94 6/6/92
5/31/91 6/3/90 6/10/88 6/6/87
5/29/85 5/25/79 5/28/78 5/27/77
Pearse, John
5/31/87
Pele Juju
6/8/96 6/4/94 5/30/93
Peter Paul and Mary
6/1/85
Pettis, Pierce
6/1/96 6/3/95 5/27/90 6/2/89
Phelps, Kelly Joe
5/27/96
Phillips, Shawn
5/28/89 5/26/88 5/23/87 5/26/86
Phillips, Utah
5/29/92 6/3/83
Pierce, Tommy
6/3/90 5/31/89
Pipkin, Turk
5/23/92 5/31/85 5/31/82
Pipkin, Turk and Christy
6/5/87

Plum Nelly
5/25/75 5/23/74
Poi Dog Pondering
5/25/91 6/2/90
Polisher, Rachel
5/24/96
Porteous, Wyckham
5/31/96
Post, Jim
6/6/87
Prasada-Rao, Tom
5/26/96 5/28/95 5/28/94
Priest, Bill
5/29/77 5/24/74
Primich, Gary
5/27/96
Pyle, Chuck
6/14/96 6/12/94 6/3/93 6/6/92
5/30/89 5/30/88 5/31/87 5/30/86
5/29/85 6/2/84 5/26/83 6/6/82
Quarto, Charles John
6/3/83 5/28/76
Rafael, Joel
5/25/96
Ramos, Reuben and The Texas Revolution
6/9/96
Ramsey, Willis Alan
5/31/91 5/27/90 5/24/81 5/23/80
5/26/79 5/23/74
Ranch Romance
6/4/93 6/8/91
Rattlesnake Annie
5/22/87
Ray, Lou
5/23/75
Rea, David
6/8/90 6/11/89
Red Clay Ramblers
5/29/88
Red River Dave
6/5/83 5/24/81 5/29/76 5/22/75
Red, White and Blue (Grass)
5/29/76
Reed, Preston
5/29/87
Reilly and Maloney
6/9/89
Rex, Michael and Oasis
5/28/92
Rey, Del
5/29/95
Rhodes, Mary Faith and John Pearse
5/31/87
Rhody, Alan
6/13/96 5/26/95
Riddle, Hank
5/24/90
Riders in the Sky
6/9/96 6/7/87 5/22/86 5/31/85
6/3/83 5/28/82 5/24/81
Righteous Mothers, The
6/4/94 6/12/93
Ritchie, Jim and Bee Jay Fleming
5/24/81 5/27/79
Ritchie, T. R.
5/29/93
Ritchie, T. R. and Cosy Sheridan
6/3/96
Rodriguez, David
5/27/95
Rogers, Allison with Willis Alan Ramsey
5/27/90
Rogers, Gamble
6/9/91 5/28/88 6/7/87 5/31/85
6/2/84 6/3/83
Rogers, Sally
5/29/93 5/30/92
Rogers, Stan
5/29/83
Rooney, Jim
6/5/88 5/23/87
Root One
6/11/93

APPENDIX B

Kerrville Music Award Winners 1993-1996

SONG OF THE YEAR
1993 "Desperate Men Do Desperate Things" - Jimmy LaFave
1994 "Just a Wave" - Butch Hancock
1995 "Merry Christmas From the Family" - Robert Earl Keen
1996 "The Kid" - Buddy Mondlock

SONGWRITER OF THE YEAR
1993 Robert Earl Keen
1994 Butch Hancock
1995 Jimmy LaFave
1996 Dar Williams

TEXAS ALBUM OF THE YEAR
1993 *Austin Skyline* - Bohemia Beat - Jimmy LaFave
1994 *Destiny's Gate* - Warner Bros. - Tish Hinojosa
1995 *Gringo Honeymoon* - Sugar Hill - Robert Earl Keen
1996 *Erik Taylor* - Watermelon - Erik Taylor

NATIONAL ALBUM OF THE YEAR
1993 *Other Voices, Other Rooms* - Elektra - Nanci Griffith
1994 *Spinning Around the Sun* - Jimmie Dale Gilmore
1995 *Flyer* - MCA - Nanci Griffith
1996 *Life Down There on Earth* - Dead Reckoning - Kevin Welch

OUTSTANDING MALE VOCALIST
1993 Jimmy LaFave
1994 Jimmy LaFave
1995 Jimmie Dale Gilmore
1996 Kevin Welch

OUTSTANDING FEMALE VOCALIST
1993 Tish Hinojosa
1994 Tish Hinojosa
1995 Iris Dement
1996 Christine Albert

DUO OF THE YEAR
1993 Trout Fishing in America
1994 Trout Fishing in America
1995 Trout Fishing in America
1996 Jimmy LaFave and Christine Albert

GROUP OR BAND OF THE YEAR
1993 Jimmy LaFave and Night Tribe
1994 Austin Lounge Lizards
1995 Robert Earl Keen
1996 Austin Lounge Lizards

INSTRUMENTALIST OF THE YEAR
1993 Erik Hokkanen
1994 Erik Hokkanen
1995 Erik Hokkanen
1996 Paul Glasse

INDEPENDENT CD/CASSETTE OF THE YEAR
1993 *Austin Skyline* - Bohemia Beat - Jimmy LaFave
1994 *Highway Trance* - Bohemia Beat - Jimmy LaFave
1995 *Loco Gringo's Lament* - Dejadisc - Ray Wylie Hubbard
1996 *Reel Life* - Trout Records - Trout Fishing in America

YEAR'S GREATEST INDUSTRY CONTRIBUTION
1993 SXSW93
1994 SXSW94
1995 Lydia Hutchinson and *Performing Songwriter*
1996 The North American Folk Alliance

CHILDREN'S ENTERTAINER OF THE YEAR
1993 No Award
1994 Trout Fishing in America
1995 Trout Fishing in America
1996 Trout Fishing in America

COMMUNITY SERVICE AWARD
1993 Tish Hinojosa
1994 Tish Hinojosa
1995 Tish Hinojosa
1996 Sara Hickman

SPIRIT OF KERRVILLE AWARD
1993 Crow Johnson
1994 Peter Yarrow
1995 Bill and Bonnie Hearne
1996 Sara Hickman

PRODUCER'S AWARD - INDIVIDUAL
1993 Mac Partain
1994 Alfredo Flores
1995 Pedro Gutierrez
1996 Vaughn Hafner - Bobby Peele

PRODUCER'S AWARD - CORPORATE
1993 Southwest Airlines
1994 Whole Foods Market
1995 Silverwolf Records
1996 Schlotszky's Deli

KERRVILLE FOLK FESTIVAL HALL OF FAME - DECEASED
1993 B. W. Stevenson - Kate Wolf
1994 Gamble Rogers - Kenneth Threadgill
1995 John Vandiver - Stan Rogers
1996 Hondo Crouch - Walter Hyatt

KERRVILLE FOLK FESTIVAL HALL OF FAME - LIVING
1993 Nanci Griffith - Lyle Lovett
1994 Guy Clark - Peter Yarrow
1995 Robert Earl Keen - Townes Van Zandt
1996 Ray Wylie Hubbard - Tom Paxton

CO-HOSTS OF THE KERRVILLE MUSIC AWARDS
1993 Sara Hickman and Gary P. Nunn
1994 Christine Albert and Jimmy LaFave
1995 Tish Hinojosa and Kevin Welch
1996 Eliza Gilkyson and Peter Rowan
1997 Carolyn Hester and Ray Wylie Hubbard

INDEX

A

American Broadcasting
      Company (ABC), 27, 34,
      35
Abrahams, Marcus, 283
      Roger, 21, 37, 41
Abramsky, Simon, 114-115
Abrasevic Ensemble, 142
Abrasevic Orchestra, 142
Abravanel, Alex, 260, 302, 303,
      315
Acoustic Artist of the Year, 361
Acoustic Guitar Magazine, 378
Acree, Alan, 115, 116
Acuff, Roy, 86
Adair, Red, 40
Adam and Kris, 377
Adams, E. Z., 170
      Ken, 300
      Sharon Hudkins, 247
Adcock, Eddie, 300, 309
      Martha, 309
Adderly, Cannonball, 78, 105,
      107, 115, 124
      Nat, 107
Adventureland Video, 294
Aeromexico Airlines, 272, 274,
      282, 292, 329
Agnew, Spiro, 84, 88, 157
Aiken, Caroline, 361, 362, 363,
      368
Aikin, Harry, 19, 84
"Ain't Misbehavin'," 342
Akipa, Brian Crawford, 342
Akiyoshi, Toshiko (*see also*
      Toshiko Mariano), 71
Alabama-Coushatta, 342
Alamo, The, 199
Alamo City Jazz Band, 26, 31,
      39, 44, 58, 69, 144, 155,
      162, 169
Alamo Village, 200
Alaska State Fair, 305, 310, 311
Albert, Christine, 228, 265, 275,
      278, 279, 283, 292, 293,
      295, 296, 301, 302, 303,
      320, 322, 328, 330, 332,
      338, 340, 341, 342, 353,
      354, 355, 356, 357, 358,
      363, 370, 371, 373, 377
      Don, 50
Alcatraz, 96, 116
Alcoholics Anonymous, 323
Aldeburgh Festival, 21
Aldrin, Buzz, 84, 89, 111
Alexander, Scot, 177, 178
      Wiley, 206
      Willard, 118
Alford, Jim, 44
      John, 68
Algar Enterprises, 85, 98
Alger, Pat, 285, 289, 345
Allen, C. L., 43

Dalis, 163, 348, 363, 370
Henry "Red," 50
Paige, 130, 154
Rex, 187
Rod, 80
Roger, 283, 285
Terry, 289, 310
Allesandro, Victor, 104
Alley Cat Band, 177
Alley Theatre, 83
Alliance Wagon Yard, 207
Allison, Hugh, 11
Allman Brothers, 109
Almeida, Laurindo, 124
Alpine Lodge Restaurant, 162
Alsop, Peter, 288, 289, 308, 318,
      326, 342
Alta Loma Lodges, 149
Alvarez, Carmen, 248, 249
Amato, Dan, 117, 118
Amazing Grass, 199
American Bank, 125
American College Jazz Festival,
      125
American Folk Alliance (*see also*
      North American Folk
      Alliance), 356
American Folk Festival, 76, 88,
      106
American Indian Coalition, 318,
      334, 339, 352
American International Hostels,
      363
American Lancia Club, 81
American Lung Association,
      330, 337
American Raceways, 86
American Road Race of
      Champions, 96, 110
Amidon, David, 256
Amon, Chris, 94, 95, 96, 98, 105
Amram, David, 110, 185, 203,
      204, 205, 209, 220, 223,
      225, 228, 230, 233, 235-
      237, 240, 241, 244, 245,
      246, 247, 248-249, 250,
      251-252, 254-255, 256, 260,
      261, 262, 265, 266, 277,
      285, 290 , 292, 293, 302,
      307, 313, 318, 319, 326,
      329, 333, 334, 335-336,
      341, 350, 359, 369, 370,
      377, 378
Amram Jam, 185, 278, 307
An American in Paris, 11
Andersen, Eric, 289
Anderson Fair, 230
Anderson, Harry, 218, 221
      Jamie, 368
      Lynn, 86
      Maxwell, 52
      Skippy, 11
Andretti, Mario, 85, 87, 96, 103

Andrews, Julie, 18
Anger, Randy, 329
Anthony, Pat, 162
Antler Dave, 213
Antler Dave Memorial Run,
      213, 221
Apfel, Buddy, 169
Apollo program, 10, 11, 12, 13,
      57, 87, 89-90, 96, 103, 111
Applause, 137
Applejack, 215, 221
Appling, Kitty, 82, 168, 175
      Shane, 82, 168, 175
Arce, Joyce, 38, 50
Archy, Jimmy, 6, 7
Argir, Bernard & Hoberd, 99
Argir, Fred, 93, 99
Arhos, Bill, 56
ARKAY Vintage Racing, 20, 36-
      37, 64, 77
Armadillo Christmas Bazaar,
      283, 293
Armadillo World Headquarters,
      108-109, 111, 112, 147,
      207-208, 223
Armstrong, Ann, 300, 308, 313
      Bob Landis, 84, 104, 106, 112
      Louis, 6, 39, 50, 58, 171
      Major, 23
      Neil, 89, 90, 111
Armstrong Foundation Award
      for FM Broadcasting
      Excellence, 23
Arnapole, Alan, 311, 321, 328
Arnold, Eddy, 40, 47, 84, 85
Aronson, Emily, 245, 267, 280,
      300, 308, 316, 320, 347,
      373
Arthur Godfrey CBS show, 24
ASCAP, 260, 360
Ash, Jim, 231
Ashlock, Jesse, 194
Ashman, Lisa, 351
Asleep at the Wheel, 167, 177,
      194, 256, 264, 265, 291,
      369
Aspen Food and Wine Festival,
      343, 360, 370
*Associasion Deportiva
      Automovilistia Mexicana*
      (ADAM), 117
Associated Press, 21
Associated Republicans of
      Texas, 290
Aston Martin, 78
Astro Jazz Festival, 107
Astrodome Grand Prix, 84, 85
Aswell's Cafe, 281
AT&T, 314, 323, 365
Atamian, Dickran, 193, 217,
      224, 225, 226, 235-237,
      239, 241, 242-243, 247,
      249, 252

Sara, 235, 236
Atlanta Symphony Orchestra,
      63
Audan, Courtney, 344
Audioland, 18, 20, 26
Auler, Susan, 340
Austin Advertising Club, 21
Austin American-Statesman, 21,
      24, 32, 35, 142, 207, 209
Austin Aqua Festival, 25-26, 27,
      33, 36, 39-42, 47, 49, 51-
      54, 64-65, 79, 108, 118, 135
Austin Aqua Festival Vintage
      Race, 87, 90-92, 105
Austin Aqua Beauty, 26, 33, 40,
      41, 52, 54
Austin Aqua Festival
      Gymkhana, 37, 54, 108
Austin Aqua Festival SCCA
      National Championship
      Sports Car Races, 79
Austin Aqua Festival Texas
      Spokes Sports Car Club
      Gymkhana, 33
Austin Arts Council, 114
Austin Autocapades, 36
Austin Ballet Society, 21, 38
Austin Braves, 86
Austin Chamber of Commerce,
      25
Austin Choral Union, 237
Austin Chorale, 50, 62
Austin Chord Rangers, 26, 121
Austin Chronicle, 313
"Austin City Limits," 208, 243,
      355, 372
Austin Civic Ballet, 161, 179,
      224
Austin Civic Theater, 21, 24,
      105
Austin Committee to Bail Out
      the Kerrville Folk Festival,
      301, 302, 304
Austin Dragway Park, 86, 90,
      99, 105
Austin Federation of Musicians,
      194
Austin Fine Arts Society, 21
Austin Folk Foundation, 253
Austin Friends of Traditional
      Music, 263
Austin International Hostel,
      330, 339, 374
Austin Jaycees, 69-70, 122
Austin Jewish Community
      Center, 189
Austin Lounge Lizards, 270,
      278, 289, 298, 301, 303,
      315, 317, 322, 329, 333,
      338, 343, 348, 350, 359,
      363, 368, 376
Austin Municipal Auditorium,
      58, 171, 174, 192, 193